CROSSCURRENTS

DEBATES IN CANADIAN SOCIETY

EDITED BY

RONALD HINCH
THE UNIVERSITY OF GUELPH

CROSSCURRENTS

DEBATES IN
CANADIAN SOCIETY

Canadian Cataloguing in Publication Data

Main entry under title:
    Debates in Canadian Society

(Crosscurrents)
Includes bibliographical references.
ISBN 0-17-603525-7

1. Canada — Social conditions — 1971—   .*
I. Hinch, Ronald Owen. II. Series: Crosscurrents
(Scarborough, Ont.).

HN103.5.D43 1992   971.064   C91-095526-3

Acquisitions Editor: Dave Ward
Editor: Sarah Robertson
Cover Illustration: Simon Ng

Printed and bound in Canada

1 2 3 4   WC   95 94 93 92

Bound to stay open

Publisher's Note

Otabind (Ota-bind). This book has been bound using the patented Otabind process. You can open this book at any page, gently run your finger down the spine, and the pages will lie flat.

■ CONTENTS

■ INTRODUCTION

This book differs significantly from a standard introduction to sociology. As Goldenberg (1987) and Hinch (1988) have said, most introductory sociology texts tend to be encyclopedias. The typical standard text begins with brief summaries of three major theoretical perspectives: *functionalism, conflict theory*, and *interactionist theory*. Occasionally, other perspectives may also be included, and distinctions may be made between *macro* and *micro* theories. Most standard texts also include a chapter on research methods, as well as a number of chapters detailing what the authors regard as the most significant research in a variety of sociology's subdisciplines. In each case, readers of these texts are presented with a sea of facts, figures, diagrams, and charts that are presented as if they were beyond dispute. This Joe Friday approach ("Just the facts, ma'am") does not assist students in developing powers of critical thinking. As Goldenberg (1987) says, it does not encourage students to participate actively in their education, but rather to become unthinking consumers.

The intent of this book is to enable students to begin to develop their critical thinking skills. Through the debate format, they discover that sociological facts and analyses *can* be disputed. Students cannot be expected to become creative, critical thinkers simply by reading, memorizing, and regurgitating what they read. It is essential that they learn about sociological disputes. It is also essential that they learn that sociologists can sometimes be confusing. The debate style of presentation allows students to discover that differences in interpretation are the generating force that drives sociologists to ask questions and do research.

■ ORGANIZATION OF THE BOOK

This book also differs from those debate-style readers that settle for presenting two sides of an issue, an approach that leads to misleading and simplistic interpretations. While it is common practice among journalists to present only two sides of an issue, sociologists are aware that there are multiple viewpoints, and other ways to assess a debate than to take sides. This book introduces students to these other options in the various sections that are included in each debate. The Introduction provides a brief history of the issues leading up to each debate, including the variety of perspectives and orientations. The Postscript summarizes the main issues debated in the articles selected, but also refers to alternative perspectives and methods by which to study the issues. References to books and articles that support both sides of the debate, as well as books or articles offering alternative explanations, are included in Further Reading. A list of Questions is provided to focus understanding of the issues debated, and to encourage the examination of issues and perspectives beyond those presented in the articles. Students are frequently encouraged through these questions to reflect upon the ways in which their choices in the debate are influenced by their preconceptions of the issues.

The text has been organized into six sections. Part One presents a debate on the nature of sociological inquiry, dealing with the desirability of objective analysis (Is a Value-free Sociology Desirable?). Part Two deals with issues of stratification and inequality. It includes debates on social mobility (Does Class Limit Social Mobility?), ethnicity (Does Ethnicity Affect Social Mobility?), affirmative action (Is Affirmative Action Reverse Discrimination?), and pay equity (Is Pay Equity Justified?). Part Three focuses on politics and the economy. The issues debated here include free trade and Canadian sovereignty (Does Free Trade Threaten Canadian Economic Sovereignty?), environmental protection and economic development (Does Environmental Protection Threaten Economic Development?), and regional disparities (Can Market Forces Overcome Regional Disparities?). Part Four includes four debates assessing such social institutions as marriage (Does Premarital Cohabitation Increase the Risk of Divorce? Are Men the Main Victims of Spouse Abuse?), education (Does Streaming Allow Students to Develop Their Potential?), and unions (Is Support for Unions Declining in Canada?). Part Five deals with issues of deviance and social control, specifically focusing on pornography, gun control, and criminal justice. It asks the questions: Should Pornography be Illegal? Is Gun Control Effective? Should Retribution be the Objective of Criminal Sanctions? The final section, Part Six, is concerned with issues of human rights. It deals with the problem of defining human rights, as well as the ability of the law to protect human rights. It asks the questions: Is Mandatory Retirement Justified? Should Access to Abortions be Restricted? and Does Canadian Law Protect Human Rights?

Readers are cautioned that some debates may have relevance in more than one section. For example, the debates in Part Five on gun control and pornography have obvious relevance for Part Six on human rights. Similarly, the debates on affirmative action and pay equity are included in Part Two on stratification and inequality, but also have relevance for debates on the economy (Part Three), social control (Part Five), and human rights (Part Six).

Division of the book into these sections is intended to facilitate the use of the text as either a supplement to standard encyclopedic texts (if that is the instructor's wish), or as a companion to other less conventional texts such as Goldenberg's *Thinking Sociologically* (1987), Czerny and Swift's *Getting Started on Social Analysis in Canada* (1988), and others (Collins, 1985; Coulson and Riddell, 1980; Giddens, 1987).

■ HOW TO USE THIS BOOK

There is no best way to use this book. Individual instructors will adapt it to their teaching needs and styles. Nonetheless, some guidelines on how books of this type have been used in the past are in order. The most obvious way to use the book is to divide the class into two discussion groups. While by no means universal, many large introductory sociology classes devote at least one class lecture to seminars or tutorials. Where such a structure exists, these seminars/tutorials provide an ideal setting for use of the book.

Within each seminar group, groups of students (at least two students in each group) should be assigned to present the debates. Group One presents the "Yes" side of the debate, while Group Two presents the "No" side of the debate. In some instances, it may be necessary to alter the order. In a standard fifty-minute class, allow each group ten to fifteen minutes to present their main arguments, and an additional two minutes for rebuttal. (The rebuttal may be omitted if a longer time for main arguments is used.) Presenters should be encouraged to use handouts or other audio visual aids (including overheads, brief videos, etc.) to enhance their presentations. The remaining class time should be left open for questions and discussion with the rest of the class. Alternatives to the arguments presented by both sides of the debate may be introduced at this time, either at the initiative of the students or the instructor.

Students could also be required to submit written summaries of their side of the debate. In my experience, I have found it useful to require that these summaries be submitted either prior to the presentation or immediately after. Students who ask to submit the summary later are usually not as well prepared, and generally do not perform as well as those who are able to submit the summary on time. It is also advisable for the instructor or the teaching assistant (if any) to meet with presenters at least one week prior to the presentation. This reduces potential errors or confusion and allows students to have some feedback prior to making their presentations. Time permitting, some instructors may wish to meet with presenters more frequently.

Where classes are not divided into seminar groups, it is still possible to take advantage of the debate format. For example, the instructor might take the lead in summarizing the debate during the first half of a lecture period, then allow the class to offer critiques (negative or positive) of both sides. Since the idea is to allow as many participants as possible, the instructor's role at this point is to keep the focus sociological. While the students should be allowed to debate the issues, the instructor should intervene, either by asking questions or giving information, whenever the discussion strays from a sociological discussion of the issues. Instructors with the luxury of student seminars might wish to do this with their entire class before students make their seminar presentations.

There are other ways to use the book. These are merely the ways in which I have used this format with some success. The advantage of using a book of this type is that it allows for differences of interpretation to be discussed and assessed. To the extent that it encourages discussion and debate among students, it is preferable to the use of encyclopedic texts.

References

Collins, Randall (1985) *Three Sociological Traditions* (New York: Oxford University Press).

Coulson, Margaret and Carol Riddell (1980) *Approaching Sociology* (London: Routledge and Kegan Paul).

Czerny, Michael and Jamie Swift (1988) *Getting Started on Social Analysis in Canada* (Toronto: Between the Lines).

Giddens, Anthony (1987) *Sociology: A Brief but Critical Introduction*, 2nd ed. (New York: Harcourt Brace Jovanovich).

Goldenberg, Sheldon (1987) *Thinking Sociologically* (Belmont, Calif.: Wadsworth).

Hinch, Ron (1988) "Teaching Introductory Sociology," *Society/Société* 12, no. 1: 2-6.

Is a value-free sociology
desirable?

PART ONE

INTRODUCTION

As an enterprise devoted to the explanation of the way humans behave in groups, sociology has fought an unending battle to justify its existence as a separate discipline. Within that struggle, one issue has consistently surfaced. Should sociologists remain objective observers, or should they become active participants constructing the social world? This is the issue to be dealt with in this section.

IS A VALUE-FREE

SOCIOLOGY

DESIRABLE?

YES **Max Weber**, "The Meaning of 'Ethical Neutrality' in Sociology and Economics," in Max Weber, *The Methodology of the Social Sciences*, pp. 1-12

NO **Howard S. Becker**, "Whose Side Are We On?" *Social Problems* (Official Journal of the Society for the Study of Social Problems) 14, no. 3 (Winter 1967): 239-247

F rom its inception sociologists have debated the role to be played by sociology in society. The central issues in this debate have focused on the potential and the desirability for sociology to develop as a discipline capable of objective analyses of human societies. As Boguslaw and Vickers (1977) point out, there are three distinct approaches to the problem: a pure science approach, an applied science approach, and a critical approach. Boguslaw and Vickers' overview is summarized here.

The pure science approach begins with the assumption that the role of science is to understand the forces that make social order possible. To do that, it is necessary for sociologists to free themselves of their personal values and biases. This can be done by the use of the scientific method, that is, the use of standarized methods for collecting data so that others can verify the results. This means testing and retesting the relations between variables so that the causal effect one variable has on another can be understood. The objective is to discover general laws of human behaviour.

The applied science approach also seeks cause-effect explanations of human behaviour via application of the scientific method. However, rather than seeking explanations of the forces that make social order possible, applied scientists want to understand the forces that disrupt social order so that they might find solutions to social problems. The applied science approach requires that sociologists use values to select problems for investigation. Some would even allow their clients—the people for whom they are conducting the research—to define the problem to be investigated. Others insist on locating the client's problem within a more broadly defined sociological problem. Once the problem has been defined, however, applied sociologists say that the scientific method must be used. In other words, this approach calls for the use of objective research procedures to assist in a value-oriented task.

The critical science approach differs from the above approaches in several ways. Rather than seeking to understand how social order is made possible, or understanding the forces that disrupt social order, it seeks to understand the forces of social change. Unlike the previous approaches, which seek to establish cause-effect relations, critical sociologists explain social change as evolutionary. Societies are constantly changing, moving from what was to what is and what could be. Each stage of the process has within it the seeds of the next stage, existing as its negation or contradiction within it. Just as the oak tree exists within the acorn as the negation of the acorn, the next stage of societal development exists within the current stage as its negation. The task of the critical sociologist is to discover both the nature of these negations or contradictions and the direction in which they will take society. This is achieved via historical investigation, looking for both quantitative and qualitative changes, and by examination of the connections and interrelations between elements in the process of change as they are changing.

With regard to objectivity, critical sociologists make a distinction between value-neutrality and objectivity. Value-neutrality refers to the elimination of values from the mental processes of the researcher. Critical sociologists argue this is impossible. Research problems, theoretical perspectives, the choice of research method, and interpretation of the data are all dependent on personal and cultural influences. Objectivity "involves the process of using logic to convert phenomena and experience of social life into objects that can be studied by one or another set of procedures" (Boguslaw and Vickers, 1977: 80). Defined this way, objectivity is common to all three approaches. The difference is that critical sociologists argue that the objectivity in the sense of being value-neutral is impossible.

The differences between these approaches provides the basis for Debate One: Is a Value-free Sociology Desirable? The problems of objectivity and value-freedom have been hotly debated issues in sociology for a long time. They stirred the passions of Karl Marx, Max Weber, and Emile Durkheim, the founding fathers of sociology, as well as most sociologists ever since. Indeed, the selection arguing the "Yes" side of this debate is taken from Weber's book *The Methodology of the Social Sciences*. The "No" side of the debate is argued by Howard Becker, a prominent symbolic interactionist.

Reference
Boguslaw, Robert and George R. Vickers (1977) *Prologue to Sociology* (Santa Monica, Calif.: Goodyear Publishing).

THE MEANING OF "ETHICAL NEUTRALITY"

Max Weber

By "value-judgments" are to be understood, where nothing else is implied or expressly stated, practical evaluations of the unsatisfactory or satisfactory character of phenomena subject to our influence. The problem involved in the "freedom" of a given science from value-judgments of this kind, i.e., the validity and the meaning of this logical principle, is by no means identical with the question which is to be discussed shortly, namely, whether in teaching one should or should not declare one's acceptance of practical value-judgments, deduced from ethical principles, cultural ideals or a philosophical outlook. This question cannot be discussed scientifically. It is itself entirely a question of practical valuation, and cannot therefore be definitively settled. With reference to this issue, a wide variety of views are held, of which we shall only mention the two extremes. At one pole we find (a) the standpoint that the distinction between purely logically deducible and empirical factual assertions on the one hand, and practical, ethical or philosophical value-judgments on the other, is correct, but that, nevertheless (or perhaps, precisely because of this), both classes of problems properly belong within the area of instruction. At the other pole we encounter (b) the proposition that even when the distinction cannot be made in a logically complete manner, it is nevertheless desirable that the assertion of value-judgments should be held to a minimum.

The latter point of view seems to me to be untenable. Especially untenable is the distinction which is rather often made in our field between value-judgments of a partisan character and those which are non-partisan. This distinction only obscures the practical implications of the preferences which are suggested to the audience. Once the assertion of value-judgments from the academic platform is admitted, the contention that the university teacher should be entirely devoid of "passion" and that he should avoid all subjects which threaten to arouse over-heated controversies constitutes a narrow-minded, bureaucratic opinion which every independent teacher must reject. Of the scholars who believed that they should not renounce the assertion of practical value-judgments in empirical discussions, it was the most passionate of them . . . who were the most tolerable. As a result of their intensely emotional tone, their audiences were enabled to discount the influence of their evaluations in whatever distortion was introduced into their factual assertions. Thereby the audiences did for themselves what the lecturers were tempermentally prevented from doing. The effect on the minds of the students was thus guaranteed the same depth of moral

4

feeling which, in my opinion, the proponents of the assertion of practical value-judgments in teaching want to protect, without the audience's being confused as to the logical disjunction between the different spheres. This confusion must of necessity occur whenever the exposition of empirical facts and the exhortation to take an evaluative position on important issues are both done with the same cool dispassionateness.

The first point of view (a) is acceptable, and can indeed be acceptable from the standpoint of its own proponents, only when the teacher sets as his unconditional duty, in every single case, even to the point where it involves the danger of making his lecture less lively or attractive, to make relentlessly clear to his audience, and especially to himself, which of his statements are statements of logically deduced or empirically observed facts and which are statements of practical evaluations. Once one has acknowledged the logical disjunction between the two spheres, it seems to me that the assumption of this attitude is an imperative requirement of intellectual honesty; in this case it is the absolutely minimal requirement.

On the other hand, the question whether one should in general assert practical value-judgments in teaching (even with this reservation) is one of practical university policy. On that account it must, in the last analysis, be decided only with reference to those tasks which the individual, according to his own value-system, assigns to the universities. Those who on the basis of their qualifications as teachers assign to the universities and thereby to themselves the universal role of moulding human beings, of inculcating political, ethical, aesthetic, cultural or other attitudes, will take a different position than those who believe it necessary to affirm the fact (and its consequences) that the academic lecture hall achieves a really valuable influence only through specialized training by specially qualified persons. For the latter, therefore, "intellectual integrity" is the only specific virtue which it should seek to inculcate. The first point of view can be defended from as many different ultimate value-positions as the second. The second (which I personally accept) can be derived from a most enthusiastic as well as from a thoroughly modest estimate of the significance of specialized training (*Fachbildung*). In order to defend this view, one need not be of the opinion that everyone should become as specialized as possible. One may, on the contrary, hold the view in question because one does not wish to see the ultimate and highest personal decisions which a person must make regarding his life confounded with specialized training—however highly one may estimate the significance of specialized training not only for general intellectual training but indirectly also for the self-discipline and ethical attitude of the young person. One may hold the latter view because one does not wish to see the student so influenced by the teacher's suggestions that he is prevented from solving his problems on the basis of his own conscience. . . .

Like everyone else, the professor has other facilities for the diffusion of his ideals. When these facilities are lacking, he can easily create them in an appropriate form, as experience has shown in the case of every honest attempt. But the professor should not demand the right as a professor to carry the marshal's baton of the statesman or reformer in his knapsack. This is just what he does when he uses the unassailability of the academic chair for the expression of political (or cultural-political) evaluations. In the press, in public meetings, in associations, in essays, in every avenue which is open to every other citizen, he can and should do what his God or daemon demands. Today the student should obtain, from his teacher in the lecture hall, the capacity: (1) to fulfill a given task in a workmanlike fashion; (2) definitely to recognize facts, even those which may be personally uncomfortable, and to distinguish them from his own evaluations; (3) to subordinate himself to his task and to repress the impulse to exhibit his personal tastes or other sentiments unnecessarily. This is vastly more important today than it was forty years ago when the problem did not even exist in this form. It is not true—as many people have insisted—that the "personality" is and should be a "whole" in the sense that it is injured when it is not exhibited on every possible occasion.

Every professional task has its own "inherent norms" and should be fulfilled accordingly. In the execution of his professional responsibility, a man should confine himself to it alone and should exclude whatever is not strictly *proper to it*—particularly his own loves and hates. The powerful personality does not manifest itself by trying to give everything a "personal touch" at every possible opportunity. The generation which is now growing up should, above all, again become used to the thought that "being a personality" is something that cannot be deliberately striven for and that there is only one way by which it can (perhaps!) be achieved: namely, the whole-hearted devotion to a "task" whatever it (and its derivative "demands of the hour") may be. It is poor taste to mix personal questions with specialized factual analyses. We deprive the word "vocation" of the only meaning which still retains ethical significance if we fail to carry out that specific kind of self-restraint which it requires. But whether the fashionable "cult of the personality" seeks to dominate the throne, public office or the professorial chair—its impressiveness is superficial. Intrinsically, it is very petty and it always has prejudicial consequences. Now I hope that it is not necessary for me to emphasize that the proponents of the views against which the present essay is directed can accomplish very little by this sort of cult of the "personality" for the very reason that it is "personal." In part they see the responsibilities of the professorial chair in another light, in part they have other educational ideals which I respect but do not share. For this reason we must seriously consider not only what they strive to achieve but also how the views which they legitimate by their authority influence a generation with an already extremely pronounced predisposition to over-estimate its own importance.

Finally, it scarcely needs to be pointed out that many ostensible opponents of the assertion of political value-judgments from the academic chair are by no means justified when, in seeking to discredit cultural and social-political discussions which take place in public, they invoke the postulate of "ethical neutrality" which they often misunderstand so gravely. The indubitable existence of this spuriously "ethically neutral" tendentiousness, which (in our discipline) is manifested in the obstinate and deliberate partisanship of powerful interest groups, explains why a significant number of intellectually honest scholars still continue to assert their personal evaluations from their chair. They are too proud to identify themselves with this pseudo-ethical neutrality. Personally I believe that, in spite of this, what is right (in my opinion) should be done and that the influence of the value-judgments of a scholar who confines himself to championing them at appropriate occasions outside the classroom will increase when it becomes known that he does only his "task" inside the classroom. But these statements are in their turn all matters of evaluation, and hence scientifically undemonstrable.

In any case the fundamental principle which justifies the practice of asserting value-judgments in teaching can be consistently held only when its proponents demand that the spokesman for all party-preferences be granted the opportunity of demonstrating their validity on the academic platform.[1] . . .

But in no case should the unresolvable question — unresolvable because it is ultimately a question of evaluation — as to whether one may, must, or should champion certain practical values in teaching, be confused with the purely logical discussion of the relationship of value-judgments to empirical disciplines such as sociology and economics. Any confusion on this point will impede the thoroughness of the discussion of the actual logical problem. Its solution will, however, not give any directives for answering the other question beyond two purely logical requirements, namely: clarity and an explicit separation of the different types of problems.

Nor need I discuss further whether the distinction between empirical statements of fact and value-judgments is "difficult" to make. It is. All of us, those of us who take this position as well as others, encounter the subject time and again. But the exponents of the so-called "ethical economics" particularly should be aware that even though the moral law is perfectly unfulfillable, it is nonetheless "imposed" as a duty. The examination of one's conscience would perhaps show that the fulfillment of our postulate is especially difficult just because we reluctantly refuse to enter the very alluring area of values without a titillating "personal touch." Every teacher has observed that the faces of his students light up and they become more attentive when he begins to set forth his personal evaluations, and that the attendance at his lectures is greatly increased by the expectation that he will do so. Everyone knows furthermore that in the competition for students, universities in making recommendations for advancement will often give a prophet, however minor, who can fill the lecture halls the upper hand over a much superior scholar who does not present his own preferences. Of course, it is understood in those cases that the prophecy should leave sufficiently untouched the political or conventional preferences which are generally accepted at the time. The pseudo- "ethically-neutral" prophet who speaks for the dominant interests has, of course, better opportunities for ascent due to the influence which these have on the political powers-that-be. I regard all this as very undesirable, and I will also therefore not go into the proposition that the demand for the exclusion of value-judgments is "petty" and that it makes the lectures "boring." I will not touch upon the question as to whether lecturers on specialized empirical problems must seek above all to be "interesting." For my own part, in any case, I fear that a lecturer who makes his lectures stimulating by the insertion of personal evaluations will, in the long run, weaken the students' taste for sober empirical analysis.

I will acknowledge without further discussion that it is possible, under the semblance of eradicating all practical value-judgments, to suggest such preferences with especial force by simply "letting the facts speak for themselves." The better kind of our parliamentary and electoral speeches operate in this way—and quite legitimately, given their purposes. No words should be wasted in declaring that all such procedures on the university lecture platform, particularly from the standpoint of the demand for the separation of judgments of fact from judgments of value, are, of all abuses, the most abhorrent. The fact, however, that a dishonestly created illusion of the fulfillment of an ethical imperative can be passed off as the reality constitutes no criticism of the imperative itself. At any rate, even if the teacher does not believe that he should deny himself the right of asserting value-judgments, he should make them absolutely *explicit* to the students and to himself.

Finally, we must oppose to the utmost the widespread view that scientific "objectivity" is achieved by weighing the various evaluations against one another and making a "statesman-like" compromise among them. Not only is the "middle way" just as undemonstrable scientifically (with the means of the empirical sciences) as the "most extreme" evaluations; rather, in the sphere of evaluations, it is the least unequivocal. It does not belong in the university—but rather in political programs and in parliament. The sciences, both normative and empirical, are capable of rendering an inestimable service to persons engaged in political activity by telling them that (1) these and these "ultimate" positions are conceivable with reference to this practical problem; (2) such and such are the facts which you must take into account in making your choice between these positions. And with this we come to the real problem.

Endless misunderstanding and a great deal of terminological—and hence sterile—conflict have taken place about the term "value-judgment." Obviously neither of these have contributed anything to the solution of the problem. It is, as we said in the beginning, quite clear that in these discussions, we are concerned with *practical* evaluations regarding the desirability or undesirability of social facts from ethical, cultural or other points of view. In spite of all that I have said,[2] the following "objections" have been raised in all seriousness: science strives to attain "valuable" results, meaning thereby logically and factually correct results which are scientifically significant; and that further, the selection of the subject-matter already involves an "evaluation." Another almost inconceivable misunderstanding which constantly recurs is that the propositions which I propose imply that empirical science cannot treat "subjective" evaluations as the subject-matter of its analysis—(although sociology and the whole theory of marginal utility in economics depend on the contrary assumption).

What is really at issue is the intrinsically simple demand that the investigator and teacher should keep unconditionally separate the establishment of empirical facts (including the "value-oriented" conduct of the empirical individual whom he is investigating) and *his* own practical evaluations, i.e., his evaluation of these facts as satisfactory or unsatisfactory (including among these facts evaluations made by the empirical persons who are the objects of investigation). These two things are logically different and to deal with them as though they were the same represents a confusion of entirely heterogeneous problems. In an otherwise valuable treatise, an author states "an investigator can however take his own evaluation as a 'fact' and then draw conclusions from it." What is meant here is as indisputedly correct as the expression chosen is misleading. Naturally it can be agreed before a discussion that a certain practical measure: for instance, the covering of the costs of an increase in the size of the army from the pockets of the propertied class should be presupposed in the discussion and that what are to be discussed are means for its execution. This is often quite convenient. But such a commonly postulated practical goal should not be called a "fact" in the ordinary sense but an "a priori end." That this is also of two-fold significance will be shown very shortly in the discussion of "means" even if the end which is postulated as "indiscussible" were as concrete as the act of lighting a cigar. In such cases, of course, discussion of the means is seldom necessary. In almost every case of a generally formulated purpose, as in the illustration chosen above, it is found that in the discussion of means, each individual understood something quite different by the ostensibly unambiguous end. Furthermore, exactly the same end may be striven after for very divergent ultimate reasons, and these influence the discussion of means. Let us however disregard this. No one will dispute the idea that a certain end may be commonly agreed on, while only the means of attaining it are discussed. Nor will anyone deny that this procedure can result in a discussion which is resolved in a strictly empirical fashion. But actually the whole discussion centers about the choice of ends (and not of "means" for a given end); in other words, in what sense can the evaluation, which the individual asserts, be treated not as a fact but as the object of scientific criticism. If this question is not clearly perceived then all further discussion is futile. . . .

Notes

1. Hence we cannot be satisfied with the Dutch principle: i.e., emancipation of even theological faculties from confessional requirements, together with the freedom to found universities as long as the following conditions are observed: guarantee of finances, maintenance of standards as to qualifications of teachers and the private right to found chairs as a patron's gift to the university. This gives the advantage to those with large sums of money and to groups which are already in power. Only clerical circles have, as far as we know, made use of this privilege.

2. I must refer here to what I have said in other essays in this volume (the possible inadequacies of particular formulations on certain points do not affect any essential aspects of the issue) as to the "irreconcilability" of certain ultimate evaluations in a certain sphere of problems, cf. G. Radbruch's *Einfuhrung in die Rechtwissenschaft* (2d ed., 1913). I diverge from him on certain points but these are of no significance for the problem discussed here.

WHOSE SIDE ARE WE ON?*

NO

Howard S. Becker

To have values or not to have values: the question is always with us. When sociologists undertake to study problems that have relevance to the world we live in, they find themselves caught in a crossfire. Some urge them not to take sides, to be neutral and do research that is technically correct and value free. Others tell them their work is shallow and useless if it does not express a deep commitment to a value position.

This dilemma, which seens so painful to so many, actually does not exist, for one of its horns is imaginary. For it to exist, one would have to assume, as some apparently do, that it is indeed possible to do research that is uncontaminated by personal and political sympathies. I propose to argue that it is not possible and, therefore, that the question is not whether we should take sides, since we inevitably will, but rather whose side we are on.

I will begin by considering the problem of taking sides as it arises in the study of deviance. An inspection of this case will soon reveal to us features that appear in sociological research of all kinds. In the greatest variety of subject matter areas and in work done by all the different methods at our disposal, we cannot avoid taking sides, for reasons firmly based in social structure.

We may sometimes feel that studies of deviance exhibit too great a sympathy with the people studied, a sympathy reflected in the research carried out. This feeling, I suspect, is entertained off and on both by those of us who do such research and by those of us who, our work lying in other areas, only read the results. Will the research, we wonder, be distorted by that sympathy? Will it be of use in the construction of scientific theory or in the application of scientific knowledge to the practical problems of society? Or will the bias introduced by taking sides spoil it for those uses?

We seldom make the feeling explicit. Instead, it appears as a lingering worry for sociological readers, who would like to be sure they can trust what they read, and a troublesome area of self-doubt for those who do the research, who would like to be sure that whatever sympathies they feel are not professionally unseemly and will not, in any case, seriously flaw their work. That the worry affects both readers and researchers indicates that it lies deeper than the superficial differences that divide sociological schools of thought, and that its roots must be sought in characteristics of society that affect us all, whatever our methodological or theoretical persuasion.

If the feeling were made explicit, it would take the form of an accusation that the sympathies of the researcher have biased his work and distorted his findings. Before exploring its structural roots, let us consider what the manifest meaning of the charge might be.

It might mean that we have acquired some sympathy with the group we study sufficient to deter us from publishing those of our results which might prove damaging to them. One can imagine a liberal sociologist who set out to disprove some of the common stereotypes held about a minority group. To his dismay, his investigation reveals that some of the stereotypes are unfortunately true. In the interests of justice and liberalism, he might well be tempted, and might even succumb to the temptation, to suppress those findings, publishing with scientific candor the other results which confirmed his beliefs.

But this seems not really to be the heart of the charge, because sociologists who study deviance do not typically hide things about the people they study. They are mostly willing to grant that there is something going on that put the deviants in the position they are in, even if they are not willing to grant that it is what the people they studied were originally accused of.

A more likely meaning of the charge, I think, is this. In the course of our work and for who knows what private reasons, we fall into deep sympathy with the people we are studying, so that while the rest of the society views them as unfit in one or another respect for the deference ordinarily accorded a fellow citizen, we believe that they are at least as good as anyone else, more sinned against than sinning. Because of this, we do not give a balanced picture. We focus too much on questions whose answers show that the supposed deviant is morally in the right and the ordinary citizen morally in the wrong. We neglect to ask those questions whose answers would show that the deviant, after all, has done something pretty rotten and, indeed, pretty much deserves what he gets. In consequence, our overall assessment of the problem being studied is one-sided. What we produce is a whitewash of the deviant and a condemnation, if only by implication, of those respectable citizens who, we think, have made the deviant what he is.

It is to this version that I devote the rest of my remarks. I will look first, however, not at the truth or falsity of the charge, but rather at the circumstances in which it is typically made and felt. The sociology of knowledge cautions us to distinguish between the truth of a statement and an assessment of the circumstances under which that statement is made; though we trace an argument to its source in the interests of the person who made it, we have still not proved it false. Recognizing the point and promising to address it eventually, I shall turn to the typical situations in which the accusation of bias arises.

When do we accuse ourselves and our fellow sociologists of bias? I think an inspection of representative instances would show that the accusation arises, in one important class of cases, when the research gives credence, in any serious way, to the perspective of the subordinate group in some hierarchical relationship. In the case of deviance, the hierarchical relationship is a moral one. The superordinate parties in the relationship are those who represent the forces of approved and official morality; the subordinate parties are those who, it is alleged, have violated that morality.

Though deviance is a typical case, it is by no means the only one. Similar situations, and similar feelings that our work is biased, occur in the study of schools, hospitals, asylums and prisons, in the study of physical as well as mental illness, in the study of both "normal" and delinquent youth. In these situations, the superordinate parties are usually the official and professional authorities in charge of some important institution, while the subordinates are those who make use of the services of that institution. Thus, the police are the superordinates, drug addicts are the subordinates; professors and administrators, principals and teachers, are the superordinates while students and pupils are the subordinates; physicians are the superordinates, their patients the subordinates.

All of those cases represent one of the typical situations in which researchers accuse themselves and are accused of bias. It is a situation in which, while conflict and tension exist in the hierarchy, the conflict has not become openly political. The conflicting segments or ranks are not organized for conflict; no one attempts to alter the shape of the hierarchy. While subordinates may complain about the treatment they receive from those above them, they do not propose to move to a position of equality with them, or to reverse positions in the hierarchy. Thus, no one proposes that addicts should make and enforce laws for policemen, that patients should prescribe for doctors, or that adolescents should give orders to adults. We can call this the *apolitical* case.

In the second case, the accusation of bias is made in a situation that is frankly political. The parties to the hierarchical relationship engage in organized conflict, attempting either to maintain or change existing relations of power and authority. Whereas in the first case subordinates are typically unorganized and thus have, as we shall see, little to fear from a researcher, subordinate parties in a political situation may have much to lose. When the situation is political, the researcher may accuse himself or be accused of bias by someone else when he gives credence to the perspective of either party to the political conflict. I leave the political for later and turn now to the problem of bias in apolitical situations.[1]

We provoke the suspicion that we are biased in favor of the subordinate parties in an apolitical arrangement when we tell the story from their point of view. We may, for instance, investigate their complaints, even though they are subordinates, about the way things are run just as though one ought to give their complaints as much credence as the statements of responsible officials. We provoke the charge when we assume, for the purposes of our research, that subordinates have as much right to be heard as superordinates, that they are as likely to be telling the truth as they see it as superordinates, that what they say about the institution has a right to be investigated and have its truth or falsity established, even though responsible officials assure us that it is unnecessary because the charges are false.

We can use the notion of a *hierarchy of credibility* to understand this phenomenon. In any system of ranked groups, participants take it as given that members of the highest group have the right to define the way things really are. In any organization, no matter what the rest of the organization chart shows, the arrows indicating the flow of information point up, thus demonstrating (at least formally) that those at the top have access to a more complete picture of what is going on than anyone else. Members of lower groups will have incomplete information, and their view of reality will be partial and distorted in consequence. Therefore, from the point of view of a well socialized participant in the system, any tale told by those at the top intrinsically deserves to be regarded as the most credible account obtainable of the organizations' workings. And since, as Sumner pointed out, matters of rank and status are contained in the mores,[2] this belief has a moral quality. We are, if we are proper members of the group, morally bound to accept the definition imposed on reality by a superordinate group in preference to the definitions espoused by subordinates. (By analogy, the same argument holds for the social classes of a community.) Thus, credibility and the right to be heard are differentially distributed through the ranks of the system.

As sociologists, we provoke the charge of bias, in ourselves and others, by refusing to give credence and deference to an established status order, in which knowledge of truth and the right to be heard are not equally distributed. "Everyone knows" that responsible professionals know more about things than laymen, that police are more respectable and their words ought to be taken more seriously than those of the deviants and criminals with whom they deal. By refusing to accept the hierarchy of credibility, we express disrespect for the entire established order.

We compound our sin and further provoke charges of bias by not giving immediate attention and "equal time" to the apologies and explanations of official authority. If, for instance, we are concerned with studying the way of life inmates in a mental hospital build up for themselves, we will naturally be concerned with the constraints and conditions created by the actions of the administrators and physicians who run the hospital. But, unless we also make the administrators and physicians the object of our study (a possibility I will consider later), we will not inquire into why those conditions and constraints are present. We will not give responsible officials a chance to explain themselves and give their reasons for acting as they do, a chance to show why the complaints of inmates are not justified.

It is odd that, when we perceive bias, we usually see it in these circumstances. It is odd because it is easily ascertained that a great many more studies are biased in the direction of the interests of responsible officials than the other way around. We may accuse an occasional student of medical sociology of having given too much emphasis to the complaints of patients. But is it not obvious that most medical sociologists look at things from the point of view of the doctors? A few sociologists may be sufficiently biased in favor of youth to grant credibility to their account of how the adult world treats them. But why do we not accuse other sociologists who study youth of being biased in favor of adults? Most research on youth, after all, is clearly designed to find out why youth are so troublesome for adults, rather than asking the equally interesting sociological question: "Why do adults make so much trouble for youth?" Similarly, we accuse those who take the complaints of mental patients seriously of bias; what about those sociologists who only take seriously the complaints of physicians, families and others about mental patients?

Why this disproportion in the direction of accusations of bias? Why do we more often accuse those who are on the side of subordinates than those who are on the side of superordinates? Because, when we make the former accusation, we have, like the well socialized members of our society most of us are, accepted the hierarchy of credibility and taken over the accusation made by responsible officials.

The reason responsible officials make the accusation so frequently is precisely because they are responsible. They have been entrusted with the care and operation of one or another of our important institutions: schools, hospitals, law enforcement, or whatever. They are the ones who, by virtue of their official position and the authority that goes with it, are in a position to "do something" when things are not what they should be and, similarly, are the ones who will be held to account if they fail to "do something" or if what they do is, for whatever reason, inadequate.

Because they are responsible in this way, officials usually have to lie. That is a gross way of putting it, but not inacurrate. Officials must lie because things are seldom as they ought to be. For a great variety of reasons, well known to sociologists, institutions are refractory. They do not perform as society would like them to. Hospitals do not cure people; prisons do not rehabilitate prisoners; schools do not educate students. Since they are supposed to, officials develop ways both of denying the failure of the institution to perform as it should and explaining those failures which cannot be hidden. An account of an institution's operation from the point of view of subordinates therefore casts doubt on the official line and may possibly expose it as a lie.[3]

For reasons that are a mirror image of those of officials, subordinates in an apolitical hierarchical relationship have no reason to complain of the bias of sociological research oriented toward the interests of superordinates. Subordinates typically are not organized in such a fashion as to be responsible for the overall operation of an institution. What happens in a school is credited or debited to the faculty and administrators; they can be identified and held to account. Even though the failure of a school may be the fault of the pupils, they are not so organized that any one of them is responsible for any failure but his own. If he does well, while others all around him flounder, cheat and steal, that is none of his affair despite the attempt of honor codes to make it so. As long as the sociological report on his school says that every student there but one is a liar and a cheat, all the students will feel complacent, knowing they are the one exception. More likely, they will never hear of the report at all or, if they do, will reason that they will be gone before long, so what difference does it make? The lack of organization among subordinate members of an institutionalized relationship means that, having no responsibility for the group's welfare, they likewise have no complaints if someone maligns it. The sociologist who favors officialdom will be spared the accusation of bias.

And thus we see why we accuse ourselves of bias only when we take the side of the subordinate. It is because in a situation that is not openly political, with the major issues defined as arguable, we join responsible officials and the man in the street in an unthinking acceptance of the hierarchy of credibility. We assume with them that the man at the top knows best. We do not realize that there are sides to be taken and that we are taking one of them.

The same reasoning allows us to understand why the researcher has the same worry about the effect of his sympathies on his work as his uninvolved colleague. The hierarchy of credibility is a feature of society whose existence we cannot deny, even if we disagree with its injunction to believe the man at the top. When we acquire sufficient sympathy with subordinates to see things from their perspective, we know that we are flying in the face of what "everyone knows." The knowledge gives us pause and causes us to share, however briefly, the doubt of our colleagues.

When a situation has been defined politically, the second type of case I want to discuss, matters are quite different. Subordinates have some degree of organization and, with that, spokesmen, their equivalent of responsible officials. Spokesmen, while they cannot actually be held responsible for what members of their group do, make assertions on their behalf and are held responsible for the truth of those assertions. The group engages in political activity designed to change existing hierarchy relationships and the credibility of its spokesmen directly affects its political fortunes. Credibility is not the only influence, but the group can ill-afford having the definition or reality proposed by its spokemen discredited, for the immediate consequence will be some loss of political power.

Superordinate groups have their spokesmen too, and they are confronted with the same problem: to make statements about reality that are politically effective without being easily discredited. The political fortunes of the superordinate group—its ability to hold the status changes demanded by lower groups to a minimum—do not depend as much on credibility, for the group has other kinds of power available as well.

When we do research in a political situation we are in double jeopardy, for the spokesmen of both involved groups will be sensitive to the implications of our work. Since they propose openly conflicting definitions of reality, our statement of our problem is in itself likely to call into question and make problematic, at least for the purposes of our research, one or the other definition. And our results will do the same.

The hierarchy of credibility operates in a different way in the political situation than it does in the apolitical one. In the political situation, it is precisely one of the things at issue. Since the political struggle calls into question the legitimacy of the existing rank system, it necessarily calls into question at the same time the legitimacy of the associated judgments of credibility. Judgments of who has a right to define the nature of reality that are taken for granted in an apolitical situation become matters of argument.

Oddly enough, we are, I think, less likely to accuse ourselves and one another of bias in a political than in an apolitical situation, for at least two reasons. First, because the hierarchy of credibility has been openly called into question, we are aware that there are at least two sides to the story and so do not think it unseemly to investigate the situation from one or another of the contending points of view. We know, for instance, that we must grasp the perspectives of both the resident of Watts and of the Los Angeles policeman if we are to understand what went on in that outbreak.

Second, it is no secret that most sociologists are politically liberal to one degree or another. Our political preferences dictate the side we will be on and, since those preferences are shared by most of our colleagues, few are ready to throw the first stone or are even aware that stone-throwing is a possibility. We usually take the side of the underdog; we are for Negroes and against Fascists. We do not think anyone biased who does research designed to prove that the former are not as bad as people think or that the latter are worse. In fact, in these circumstances we are quite willing to regard the question of bias as a matter to be dealt with by the use of technical safeguards.

We are thus apt to take sides with equal innocence and lack of thought, though for different reasons, in both apolitical and political situations. In the first, we adopt the commonsense view which awards unquestioned credibility to the responsible official. (This is not to deny that a few of us, because something in our experience has alerted us to the possibility, may question the conventional hierarchy of credibility in the special area of our expertise.) In the second case, we take our politics so for granted that it supplants convention in dictating whose side we will be on. (I do not deny, either, that some few sociologists may deviate politically from their liberal colleagues, either to the right or the left, and thus be more liable to question that convention.)

In any event, even if our colleagues do not accuse us of bias in research in a political situation, the interested parties will. Whether they are foreign politicians who object to studies of how the stability of their government may be maintained in the interest of the United States (as in the *Camelot* affair)[4] or domestic civil rights leaders who object to an analysis of race problems that centers on the alleged deficiencies of the Negro family (as in the reception given to the Moynihan Report),[5] interested parties are quick to make accusations of bias and distortion. They base the accusation not on failures of technique or method, but on conceptual defects. They accuse the sociologist not of getting false data but of not getting all the data relevant to the problem. They accuse him, in other words, of seeing things from the perspective of only one party to the conflict. But the accusation is likely to be made by interested parties and not by sociologists themselves.

What I have said so far is all sociology of knowledge, suggesting by whom, in what situations and for what reasons sociologists will be accused of bias and distortion. I have not yet addressed the question of the truth of the accusations, of whether our findings are distorted by our sympathy for those we study. I have implied a partial answer, namely, that there is no position from which sociological research can be done that is not biased in one or another way.

We must always look at the matter from someone's point of view. The scientist who proposes to understand society must, as Mead long ago pointed out, get into the situation enough to have a perspective on it. And it is likely that his perspective will be greatly affected by whatever positions are taken by any or all of the other participants in that varied situation. Even if his participation is limited to reading in the field, he will necessarily read the arguments of partisans of one or another side to a relationship and will thus be affected, at least, by having suggested to him what the relevant arguments and issues are. A student of medical sociology may decide that he will take neither the perspective of the patient nor the perspective of the physician, but he will necessarily take a perspective that impinges on the many questions that arise between physicians and patients; no matter what perspective he takes, his work either will take into account the attitude of subordinates, or it will not. If he fails to consider the questions they raise, he will be working on the side of the officials. If he does raise those questions seriously and does find, as he may, that there is some merit in them, he will then expose himself to the outrage of the officials and of all those sociologists who award them the top spot in the hierarchy of credibility. Almost all the topics that sociologists study, at least those that have some relation to the real world around us, are seen by society as morality plays and we shall find ourselves, willy-nilly, taking part in those plays on one side or the other.

There is another possibility. We may, in some cases, take the point of view of some third party not directly implicated in the hierarchy we are investigating. Thus, a Marxist might feel that it is not worth distinguishing between Democrats and Republicans, or between big business and big labor, in each case both groups being equally inimical to the interests of the workers. This would indeed make us neutral with respect to the two groups at hand, but would only mean that we had enlarged the scope of the political conflict to include a party not ordinarily brought in whose view the sociologist was taking.

We can never avoid taking sides. So we are left with the question of whether taking sides means that some distortion is introduced into our work so great as to make it useless. Or, less drastically, whether some distortion is introduced that must be taken into account before the results of our work can be used. I do not refer here to feeling that the picture given by the research is not "balanced," the indignation aroused by having a conventionally discredited definition of reality given priority or equality with what "everyone knows," for it is clear that we cannot avoid that. That is the problem of officials, spokesmen and interested parties, not ours. Our problem is to make sure that, whatever point of view we take, our research meets the standards of good scientific work, that our unavoidable sympathies do not render our results invalid.

We might distort our findings, because of our sympathy with one of the parties in the relationship we are studying, by misusing the tools and techniques of our discipline. We might introduce loaded questions into a questionnaire, or act in some way in a field situation such that people would be constrained to tell us only the kind of thing we are already in sympathy with. All of our research techniques are hedged about with precautionary measures designed to guard against these errors. Similarly, though more abstractly, every one of our theories presumably contains a set of directives which exhaustively covers the field we are to study, specifying all the things we are to look at and take into account in our research. By using our theories and techniques impartially, we ought to be able to study all the things that need to be studied in such a way as to get all the facts we require, even though some of the questions that will be raised and some of the facts that will be produced run counter to our biases.

But the question may be precisely this. Given all our techniques of theoretical and technical control, how can we be sure that we will apply them impartially and across the board as they need to be applied? Our textbooks in methodology are no help here. They tell us how to guard against error, but they do not tell us how to make sure that we will use all the safeguards available to us. We can, for a start, try to avoid sentimentality. We are sentimental when we refuse, for whatever reason, to investigate some matter that should properly be regarded as problematic. We are sentimental, especially, when our reason is that we would prefer not to know what is going on, if to know would be to violate some sympathy whose existence we may not even be aware of. Whatever side we are on, we must use our techniques impartially enough that a belief to which we are especially sympathetic could be proved untrue. We must always inspect our work carefully enough to know whether our techniques and theories are open enough to allow that possibility.

Let us consider, finally, what might seem a simple solution to the problems posed. If the difficulty is that we gain sympathy with underdogs by studying them, is it not also true that the superordinates in a hierarchical relationship usually have their own superordinates with whom they must contend? Is it not true that we might study those superordinates, presenting their point of view on their relations with their superiors and thus gaining a deeper sympathy with them and avoiding the bias of one-sided identification with those below them? This is appealing, but deceptively so. For it only means that we will get into the same trouble with a new set of officials.

It is true, for instance, that the administrators of a prison are not free to do as they wish, not free to be responsive to the desires of inmates, for instance. If one talks to such an official, he will commonly tell us, in private, that of course the subordinates in the relationship have some right on their side, but that they fail to understand that his desire to do better is frustrated by his superiors or by the regulations they have established. Thus, if a prison administrator is angered because we take the complaints of his inmates seriously, we may feel that we can get around that and get a more balanced picture by interviewing him and his associates. If we do, we may then write a report which *his* superiors will respond to with cries of "bias." They, in their turn, will say that we have not presented a balanced picture, because we have not looked at *their* side of it. And we may worry that what they say is true.

The point is obvious. By pursuing this seemingly simple solution, we arrive at a problem of infinite regress. For everyone has someone standing above him who prevents him from doing things just as he likes. If we question the superiors of the prison administrator, a state department of corrections or prisons, they will complain of the governor and the legislature. And if we go to the governor and the legislature, they will complain of lobbyists, party machines, the public and the newspapers. There is no end to it and we can never have a "balanced picture" until we have studied all of society simultaneously. I do not propose to hold my breath until that happy day.

We can, I think, satisfy the demands of our science by always making clear the limits of what we have studied, marking the boundaries beyond which our findings cannot be safely applied. Not just the conventional disclaimer, in which we warn that we have only studied a prison in New York or California and the findings may not hold in the other forty-nine states—which is not a useful procedure anyway, since the findings may very well hold if the conditions are the same elsewhere. I refer to a mere sociological disclaimer in which we say, for instance, that we have studied the prison through the eyes of the inmates and not through the eyes of the guards or other involved parties. We warn people, thus, that our study tells us only how things look from that vantage point—what kinds of objects guards are in the prisoners' world—and does not attempt to explain why guards do what they do or to absolve the guards of what may seem, from the prisoners' side, morally unacceptable behavior. This will not protect us from accusations of bias, however, for the guards will still be outraged by the unbalanced picture. If we implicitly accept the conventional hierarchy of credibility, we will feel the sting in that accusation.

It is something of a solution to say that over the years each "one-sided" study will provoke further studies that gradually enlarge our grasp of all the relevant facets of an institution's operation. But that is a long-term solution, and not much help to the individual researcher who has to contend with the anger of officials who feel he has done them wrong, the criticism of those of his colleagues who think he is presenting a one-sided view, and his own worries.

What do we do in the meantime? I suppose the answers are more or less obvious. We take sides as our personal and political commitments dictate, use our theoretical and technical resources to avoid the distortions that might introduce into our work, limit our conclusions carefully, recognize the hierarchy of credibility for what is is, and field as best we can the accusations and doubts that will surely be our fate.

Notes

* Presidential address delivered at the annual meeting of the Society for the Study of Social Problems, Miami Beach, August 1966.

1. No situation is necessarily political or apolitical. An apolitical situation can be transformed into a political one by the open rebellion of subordinate ranks, and a political situation can subside into one in which an accommodation has been reached and a new hierarchy been accepted by the participants. The categories, while analytically useful, do not represent a fixed division existing in real life.

2. William Graham Sumner, "Status in the Folkways," *Folkways*, New York: New American Library, 1960, pp. 72-73.

3. I have stated a portion of this argument more briefly in "Problems of Publication of Field Studies," in Arthur Vidich, Joseph Bensman, and Maurice Stein (Eds.), *Reflections on Community Studies*. New York: John Wiley and Sons, 1964, pp. 267-284.

4. See Irving Louis Horowitz, "The Life and Death of Project Camelot," *Transaction*, 3 (Nov./Dec., 1965), pp. 3-7, 44-47.

5. See Lee Rainwater and William L. Yancey, "Black Families and the White House," *Ibid*, 3 (July/August, 1966), pp. 6-11, 48-53.

■ POSTSCRIPT

Weber's position is quite clear. Sociologists must not allow values to influence any aspect of their research. He is joined in making this statement by many prominent sociologists, past and present, including Emile Durkheim (1964), George Lundberg (1967), and Raymond Ries (1967). All would agree that allowing values to influence any aspect of the research process blocks the potential for understanding social facts. Allowing values to influence sociological research means seeing the world as the researcher would like it to be, not as it is.

Becker's thinking is obviously in stark contrast. Like many others before him, including C. Wright Mills (1959), Robert Lynd (1939), and Robert Redfield (1948), he argues that the task of eliminating personal and political values is impossible. He also adds that sociologists should actually choose sides, sometimes intentionally, sometimes unintentionally, "as our personal and political commitments dictate." While sociologists should use their theoretical and methodological knowledge to reduce the distortions of their personal and political biases, they should at the same time attempt to describe the social world from the vantage point of the people whose side is chosen. This implies using the scientific method to uncover and describe that social world, but it also means remaining faithful to that world, allowing it to explain itself through the efforts of the sociologist.

The analyses presented by both Weber and Becker have been criticized by sociologists like Alvin Gouldner (1970), Martin Nicolas (1970), and many others. These critics have suggested that neither side in this debate provides a full understanding of the issues. For example, Gouldner criticizes Becker for not being able to answer his own question: "Whose side are we on?" Gouldner says that, while Becker implies support of the underdog, he is unable or unwilling to answer his own question because it might prove harmful to further research plans. For example, would "overdogs" be willing to provide information and research grants to Becker if he openly stated that he was on the side of the underdog? Gouldner also says that Becker's analysis leaves him on the side of the overdog. By concentrating on explaining the behaviour of the underdog, Becker makes its easier for the overdog to control the underdog. Knowledge is double-edged. It can help make the underdog seem more human, but it can also be used to make the underdog easier to control. Gouldner is saying that Becker may have chosen sides, but it is not clear that Becker's actions in choosing sides helps the side he has chosen.

At the end of most of the debates in this book, you will be asked to assess how your personal beliefs and experiences influence your decisions with regard to the issues being debated. It might be useful to refer back to Debate One whenever you are confronted with this question.

■ QUESTIONS

1. Which side of this debate do you believe has presented the most convincing argument? Why is it the most convincing? Has your decision been influenced by your preconceptions of what sociology and/or science is?
2. In what ways are the arguments of Weber and Becker similar?
3. Are the critics of value-freedom correct in saying that value-neutrality is impossible?
4. Is the distinction between value-neutrality and objectivity useful? Why or why not?

■ FURTHER READING

In Support of Weber

Durkheim, Emile. *The Rules of Sociological Method.* New York: The Free Press, 1964.

Lundberg, George. *Can Science Save Us?* 2nd ed. New York: David McKay, 1967.

Ries, Raymond. "Social Science and Ideology." In *Readings in Introductory Sociology.* Edited by Dennis H. Wrong and Harry L. Gracey. New York: Macmillan, 1967.

In Support of Becker

Lynd, Robert. *Knowledge for What? The Place of Social Science in Literature.* Princeton, N.J.: Princeton University Press, 1939.

Mills, C. Wright. *The Sociological Imagination.* New York: Oxford University Press, 1959.

Redfield, Robert. "The Art of Social Science." *The American Journal of Sociology* 54 (1948): 181-190.

Other Voices

Berger, Peter I. *Invitation to Sociology: A Humanistic Perspective.* Garden City, New York: Anchor Books, Doubleday, 1963.

Giddens, Anthony. *Sociology: A Brief but Critical Introduction.* New York: Harcourt Brace Jovanovich, 1982.

Goldenberg, Sheldon. *Thinking Sociologically.* Belmont, Calif.: Wadsworth, 1987.

Gouldner, Alvin W. and S.M. Miller, eds. *Applied Sociology.* New York: The Free Press, 1965.

Gouldner, Alvin W. (1970) "The Sociologist as Partisan: Sociology and the Welfare State." In *The Sociology of Sociology.* Edited by Larry T. Reynolds and Janice M. Reynolds. New York: David McKay, 1970.

Nicholas, Martin. Text of a speech delivered at the A.S.A. Convention, August 26, 1970. In *The Sociology of Sociology.* Edited by L.T. Reynolds and J.M. Reynolds. New York: David McKay, 1970.

Does class limit social mobility?

Does ethnicity affect social mobility?

Is affirmative action reverse discrimination?

Is pay equity justified?

PART TWO

INTRODUCTION

The study of stratification is an integral part of sociological investigation. It is extremely difficult to engage in sociological inquiry without dealing in some way with the methods, processes, or consequences of human efforts to stratify the social world. Whether those investigations are done at the micro level, via symbolic interactionism, or at the macro level, via Marxism, functionalism, feminism, etc., sociologists have an unquenchable thirst for knowledge about human stratification and its consequences.

This section raises issues of class, race, ethnicity, and gender as they relate to the stratification of Canadian society. Sociologists have taken many different approaches to understanding these issues, and have often arrived at contradictory research findings, some of which result from differences in theoretical orientation. Others arise from varying interpretations of data. Whatever the explanation, Canadian sociologists have not yet reached a consensus about either the nature of the problem or about how to study the problem.

DOES CLASS

LIMIT SOCIAL

MOBILITY?

YES **A.W. Djao,** "The State and Social Welfare," in A.W. Djao, *Inequality and Social Policy: The Sociology of Welfare*, pp. 91-100

NO **R. Ogmundson,** "Good News and Canadian Sociology," *Canadian Journal of Sociology* 7, no. 1 (1982): 73-78

There is considerable debate within sociology about the extent of upward social mobility in Canadian society. A core issue in the debate is the degree to which class position determines educational, occupational, and economic opportunities in Canada. On the one hand, Marxists argue that class is the most significant factor affecting these opportunities. On the other hand, Weberians, functionalists, and feminists argue that class is only one of many factors limiting mobility. It is worth summarizing these viewpoints before proceeding with Debate Two.

It has been said that sociolgical debates on class are in fact debates with Marx's ghost (Zeitlin, 1987). In Marxian terms, class is first and foremost an economic category determined by people's relation to the means of production (land, machinery, equipment, etc.). There are three main classes: capitalists, petite bourgeoisie, and proletariat. Capitalists own the means of production, and buy the labour power of the proletariat. The petite bourgeoisie, which includes farmers, fishers, professionals (doctors, lawyers, etc.) and other independent producers, owns smaller-scale economic enterprises, and may also buy the labour power of the proletariat. Unlike capitalists, the petite bourgeoisie supplies its own labour power to produce commodities or provide direct service. The working class, or proletariat, sells its labour power to either the capitalists or the petite bourgeoisie. Some Marxists also speak of an underclass composed of people who either refuse to sell or are unable to sell their labour power. They survive by illegal means or by scavenging. Marx referred to them as the lumpenproletariat. Each class is also divided into smaller units, or fractions, with each fraction having a slightly different relation to the means of production. According to Marxists, there is limited upward mobility from one class to the other.

Marxists also distinguish between classes-in-themselves and classes-for-themselves. Classes-in-themselves are defined entirely by their relation to the means of production, as indicated in the previous paragraph. Classes-for-themselves arise when classes-in-themselves develop an awareness of their position in the class structure, become aware that their interests are opposed to the interests of other classes-in-themselves, and take steps to secure their interests and oppose other interests. Unless the proletariat becomes a class-for-itself, the transformation to a classless society will not occur.

Weberians argue that class is only one factor influencing life chances. They argue that class, status, and power interact to either limit or enhance opportunities. Weberians define class in terms of the amount of wealth, in the form of property and income, controlled by an individual. Status refers to the amount of prestige or honour accorded someone. Power is the ability to control the life chances of others. Each of these factors is distributed unevenly in society. Some social groups may have high-class positions, but may not have a great deal of power. Others may have power but lack either class or status. Weberians generally argue that there is more social mobility than Marxists are willing to admit, and that inequality is an inevitable, although undesirable, feature of human society.

The functionalist conception of stratification differs significantly from Weberian and Marxist conceptions. Functionalists argue that inequality between social groups is a necessary feature of human societies (Davis, 1949). Inequality, say functionalists, ensures that the most capable people occupy the most important positions in the social order. Those with the most desired skills receive the greatest rewards for performing the most important social tasks. According to functionalists, then, social mobility is dependent on merit and ability.

Finally, feminists argue that the most significant influence on life chances is gender, and that, regardless of other factors, women as a group are disadvantaged compared to men as a group. Feminists criticize theories of stratification that fail to recognize the importance of gender by arguing that the system of male domination (patriarchy) limits women's opportunities at every step in the social system. Even though women in higher-class positions may live materially more comfortable lives than women in lower-class positions, their opportunities for advancement in the social structure are limited compared to the opportunities open to men in the same class.

The articles selected for Debate Two are examples of Marxist and Weberian perspectives. Arguing for the "Yes" side of the debate, Djao concentrates on the role of the state in maintaining class divisions. Arguing for the "No" side of the debate, Ogmundson concentrates on the origins and composition of the bureaucratic elite.

References
Davis, Kingsley (1949) *Human Society* (New York: Macmillan).
Zeitlin, Irving M. (1987) *Ideology and the Development of Sociological Theory* (Englewood Cliffs, N.J.: Prentice-Hall).

THE STATE AND SOCIAL WELFARE

A.W. Djao

Social inequality in our society does not spring from differences between individuals in terms of height, weight, colour of skin or eye, ability, intelligence, or talent, although all these have been used at various times in human history to justify or rationalize social inequality. Social inequality is generated by social structures. In the discussion of social inequality in Canada in the previous two chapters, two trends have been made quite clear. First is the widening gap in income between the capitalist class and the working class. In the drive for capital accumulation, capitalists usually resort to labour-replacing technology that renders many workers redundant; this enlarges the pool of potential but unemployed workers and depresses wage rates. Accumulated capital is reinvested, while control of production is centralized in the hands of the capitalists. Moreover, in corporate capitalism the larger corporations, especially the multinationals, have a competitive edge over smaller companies. The small enterprises either go out of business or are bought out by the larger ones; capital becomes concentrated in the hands of a few giant corporations. The overall consequence has the small number of capitalists becoming enormously rich, with the large majority of workers becoming relatively poorer over time.

A second trend in Canada related to social inequality is the fragmentation of the working class. Cleavages in the working class appear along lines of occupation, education, ethnicity, race, sex, and age. There are also differences between the primary labour market and the secondary labour market, between the unionized and the nonunionized workers, and between the employed and the unemployed. These differences within the working class are often reflected in income differentials to the extent that those with higher salaries and wages and higher socio-economic status often regard themselves as the "middle class." The differences in the objective economic conditions and self-perceptions by members of the working class have resulted in the absence of unity within the class. In fact, there are often tensions and conflicts among the various fragments of the working class. Consequently, there is no concerted line of action by the working class toward the capitalist class.

These two trends—inequality between capital and labour, and inequality within the working class—stem from the very nature of the capitalist system, and are closely linked to the array of programs and services known as welfare activities. In the early years of small-scale, competitive industrial capitalism, which in Canada roughly covered the 30 years after Confederation, principles of *laissez-faire* were the dominant ideology. The free enterprise system allowed individuals to look after their own well-being, and no need was seen for the government to meddle in people's private affairs. While these notions lingered until the 1930s, in practice the Canadian state was never a *laissez-faire* state in the economic sense (Panitch, 1977). Furthermore, the state was involved in legislating social laws and in implementing social programs both before and after the First World War. During the Great Depression of the thirties, the pace of devising and carrying out social policies by the various levels of government accelerated. But it was not until after the Second World War that the welfare state came into its own in Canada and the principle of state responsibility for individual welfare was generally accepted.

In this chapter we shall discuss the role of the state in developing social welfare in the midst of continually generated social inequality. The functions of the state in capitalist society will be treated first, one function being the provision of social welfare. Then, the activities of the welfare state will be delineated. Here we should clarify that the state is the power structure of the government. But as Miliband (1969) has pointed out, the state is far more than just the government. The power structure consists of a complex of institutions: government (at central and sub-central levels), the bureaucracy (civil service, public corporations, regulatory agencies, central banks, and so on), the military, the judiciary, and the representative assemblies.

■ FUNCTIONS OF THE STATE

It must be stressed that discussion of state functions does not validate a functionalist explanation of the welfare state. As Gough (1979, p. 50) states, functionalism contains the implicit assumption that analysis will reveal the causes of state action and responses to the functional requirements of capital. But this assumption is quite unjustified: stating the requirements for the accumulation or reproduction of capital does not give any indication as to whether the state fulfills those requirements or how it meets them. Such issues call for an empirical study of the manner in which those requirements are translated into political demands and state responses are formulated into policies. Although it is useful to specify the functions of the welfare state, we do not use the logic inherent in the structural-functionalist theory of society. According to that logic, whatever exists is necessary to bring about some consequence. In place of the functionalist logic, we use a Marxist methodology which postulates (a) a hierarchy of social phenomena, and (b) the existence within any society of internal contraditions that counteract the tendency of the system to maintain itself as a going concern. These two conditions in Marxist theory explain why and how societies change and transform themselves (Hobsbawn, 1972).

As has been mentioned earlier, the state is not a neutral arbiter between different social classes, but acts to ensure the political domination by one class over other classes (Gough, 1979, p. 41). Acting in the interest of the capitalist class, the state tries

> to fulfill two basic and often mutually contradictory functions—accumulation and legitimization. The state must try to maintain and create the conditions in which profitable capital accumulation is possible. However, the state must also try to maintain or create the conditions for social harmony (O'Connor, 1973, p. 6).

Panitch lists four tasks that the state performs in its first function— that of facilitating the capitalist class to accumulate capital:

1. The state provides a favourable fiscal and monetary climate for economic growth by private enterprises. This is reflected, among other things, in the fiscal policies presented in the national budget and in other economic policies intended to provide capitalists with incentives to invest. The state also promotes foreign trade by sending trade delegations abroad.

2. The state underwrites the high production risk faced by some private enterprises. For example, the Canadian state finances some private developers in building inexpensive housing for low-income families, considered to be high risk projects that yield low profits. Thus, the developers are ensured a profit. Such financing in housing is done through the Crown corporation Canada Mortgage and Housing Corporation, or through finance institutions that are guaranteed by CMHC.

3. The state has provided for capitalist development such physical infrastructure as railroads, airports, and port facilities, that are too risky or costly for private capital to undertake on its own. State construction, ownership, and operation of these facilities "were never undertaken as ends in themselves with the aim of managing or controlling the economy, but always with a view to facilitating further capital accumulation in the private sphere to the end of economic growth" (Panitch, 1977, p. 14).

4. The state has played a key role in creating and maintaining a sizeable amount of the social cost of production of capitalist enterprise through such mechanisms as immigration, public education, health care, and unemployment insurance.

The state carries out these four tasks (within its capital accumulation function) through public security, economic, and social policies.

The second function of the state, legitimization, encompasses those social policies aimed at integrating the subordinate classes within the capitalist social order. Labour legislation protecting workers' and unions' rights, governmental consultation with labour leaders, grants and subsidies to citizen action or dissident minority groups, and social assistance programs are some examples of the legitimization function. The aim of this function is social control by promoting social harmony. This is done through the introduction of reforms, or through the co-operation with leaders of labour, welfare, or ethnic groups by offering them a semblance of power and participation (Panitch, 1977).

■ WELFARE ACTIVITIES OF THE STATE

The welfare activities of the state can best be broached by examining how the state spends its money. Corresponding to the capital accumulation and legitimization functions of the state, nearly all state expenditures have a twofold character: social capital and social expenses. Furthermore, social capital can be subdivided into two types of activities: social investment (constant social capital) and social consumption (variable social capital). Thus, there are altogether three categories of state expenditure[1]:

1. *Social investments*: services and projects that raise labour productivity (constant social capital).

2. *Social consumption*: services and projects that lower the costs of reproducing labour-power (variable social capital).

3. *Social expenses*: services and projects that maintain social stability and promote social harmony.

Social capital expenditures, that is, social investment and social consumption, are indirectly productive for the capitalists in that they contribute to economic growth in the private sector. Social expenses, on the other hand, consist of various programs designed to maintain social order so that production and capital accumulation can proceed unhindered. They encompass assistance to the nonworking population and various ideological or coercive activities of the state concerned with controlling groups within that population that threaten social stability. "This would include the activities of some social workers, community workers, and race-relations bodies as well as the more obvious work of police, prison, and probation staff" (Gough, 1979, p. 52). Social expenses are necessary but unproductive for capital.

Almost every state agency performs both functions—capital accumulation and social control. Also, elements of social investment, social consumption, and social expense are found in almost every state expenditure. For example, education can be seen as social investment in that it raises labour productivity. Yet much of public education consists of socializing the young in values and ideas that support the capitalist system. Thus, education falls within both capital accumulation and legitimization functions of the state.

Most of the activities associated with social welfare are similar to education in that they have a dual function. Welfare activities are a social expense insofar as they fulfill the legitimization function; for example, social assistance that defuses the discontent and frustration of the poor helps to maintain social order. But they can also be seen as part of the capital accumulation function. Insofar as welfare programs more often lower the cost of reproducing labour-power than raising labour productivity, they are items of social consumption rather than social investment.

Reproduction of Labour-Power

The twofold function of welfare programs can be better understood if we first probe the meaning of the welfare state. According to the Marxist theory of the welfare state, the state uses its power to modify the reproduction of labour-power and to maintain the nonworking population (Gough, 1979, pp. 44-45). As has been mentioned earlier, labour-power is defined as a person's capacity to work. It is, therefore, necessary in all human societies to reproduce this capacity continually, a process which takes two forms: the daily and the generational. In capitalist societies, the daily reproduction of labour-power takes place in two stages. First, workers sell their labour-power to earn a wage or salary, which provides the means to buy consumption goods and services, such as food, shelter, clothing, transport, and entertainment. These are the items workers need in order to replenish their capacity to work. The second stage of daily reproduction comprises the various tasks in planning and budgeting for the purchase of consumption goods and services; in actually buying these items; and in further processing and preparing these items. The tasks include planning, shopping, cooking, laundry, cleaning, and so forth. In working class families, tasks in the second stage are usually performed by the housewife, who is not paid.

The generational reproduction of labour-power refers to physical procreation, which provides a new generation of workers whose labour-power will be available for sale in the future. In addition, child care and socialization duties must be considered part of the generational reproduction of labour-power. Again, the tasks associated with them are performed by the housewife.

As mentioned earlier, the state undertakes social consumption expenditure in order to lower the cost of reproducing labour-power. It does this by providing certain goods and services either free of charge or at lower price, so that they are available to the working class. Low-cost housing, medicare, public education, retraining programs, and community services are examples of social consumption that help to lower the cost of reproducing labour-power. The state also intervenes in another way, that is, by directly providing the working class with amounts of money to spend on consumption goods and services through the income security system, such as family allowances and unemployment insurance benefits. Furthermore, the state also regulates the standard and quality of goods and services sold on the market. Particular goods and services are subsidized, such as certain kinds of housing, foods, and transport.

Finally, since children make up the future labour force, the state has increasingly expanded its role in modifying the generational reproduction of labour-power. "Almost all social policies have a direct bearing on the capacity of the family to bring up children" (Gough, 1979, p. 46). The entire field of child welfare seeks not only to protect the physical well-being of children, but also to ensure their proper rearing and socialization. The most extreme measure is to make the children temporary or permanent wards of the state because the parents are judged to be unable or unwilling to care for them. In addition to family allowances, refundable child tax credit, education, specific health services (such as Saskatchewan's free dental care for children), and housing policies are all aimed at providing special benefits to families bringing up children.

Maintaining the Nonworking Population

The second major activity of the welfare state is maintaining the nonworking population. All societies contain categories of people who are not economically productive and must depend on others for their living. They are the young, the old, the sick, the mentally disabled, and other unemployable people. In most nonindustrial, noncapitalist societies, the dependent members share in the fruits of labour (called social product) of the productive members through the mechanisms of the nuclear family and extended kinship. In other words, family and relatives usually assume the responsibility of providing for and looking after the dependent members. But in capitalist societies, family and kinship structures are increasingly replaced or regulated by a variety of state measures. Old age security, social assistance, and a variety of social welfare services provide different kinds of support or supplement to the elderly, the sick, the unemployable, and the casual labourer, "gradually usurping the role of kinship and community in the past, and of charitable and voluntary bodies in the more recent past" (Gough, 1979, p. 47). These programs comprise social expenses because the basic aim is to promote social harmony with the effect of controlling the nonworking population. The effect of social control is institutionalized: it stems from the very structures of providing assistance to the nonworking population. This effect is produced, regardless of any altruistic motives of social workers and others who provide the actual assistance.

Just as elements of social investment, social consumption, and social expenses exist in state expenditures, the boundaries between the working and the nonworking populations are not always distinguishable. For example, children are part of the nonworking population, but they form the future labour force. Hence, the cost of their maintenance at present cannot be separated entirely from that of reproducing future labour-power. Another example is that of social assistance. O'Connor (1973) assigns welfare assistance programs to the category of social expenses on the assumption that welfare clients exist outside the capitalist mode of production whose subsistence nevertheless must be provided for by the state in the interest of social order. While this may be true to a certain extent, as in the case of assistance to the underclass, it is also true that social assistance clients move through a "revolving door" between short periods of employment and short periods of assistance (Butler & Buckley, 1978). They are the job-seekers on the marginal labour market, usually in the competitive sector of the capitalist economy. In a sense, then, social assistance is the marginal worker's unemployment insurance (Adams, 1978). These groups—the young, the unskilled seasonal worker, the working-age sick but not chron-ically sick—constitute the reserve army of labour; their maintenance can therefore, be seen as a measure of reproducing labour-power. What these examples show is that the two activities of the welfare state, that is, reproducing labour-power and maintaining the nonworking population, cannot be distinguished clearly from one another.

■ CONTRADICTIONS WITHIN THE WELFARE STATE

We have shown that state expenditures, whether as social capital (in capital accumulation function) or as social expenses (in legitimization function), ensure the political domination of the working class and the underclass by the capitalist class. Social capital expenditures are indirectly productive for private capital: the state assumes the cost of preparing the appropriate and useful labour-power for the capitalists. Social expenses, on the other hand, provide the stable social environment required by the process of private capital accumulation. The capitalist class, therefore, stands to benefit the most from the activities of the welfare state.

These same activities also have the effect of manipulating and controlling the working class and the underclass. To end the analysis here would be to submit to the logic of structural-functionalism. This means, first of all, simply accepting the view that various societal institutions, including social welfare, exist for the survival and maintenance of the system; secondly, denying the existence of internal contradictions which counteract the self-maintaining tendency of the society; and, finally, denying the possibility of societal change. However, in the Marxist theoretical framework we use in this book, it is important to explain the internal contradic-tions within a society, which are the seeds of change. In dealing with the activities of the welfare state it is, therefore, also important to stress that their effect on the subordinate classes is not merely one of social control. To focus only on this "negative" aspect of the welfare state is to neglect the fact that the welfare state is a contradictory phenomenon and that years of class conflict have resulted in some real gains for the subordinate classes.

Many, though not all, of the welfare programs provide real benefits to workers and their dependents by improving their standard of living. This is to say that the development of welfare activities has two aspects. On the one hand, an increasing part of the social capital costs of production and the expenses of ensuring capitalist relations is met through the state. The function of social expenses of the state in maintaining harmony in the capitalist relations of production is particlarly important. The mechanisms for carrying out this function include the coercive apparatus (army and police), the judiciary, the state bureaucracies, and the ideological apparatus (the public school system and state controlled media). On the other hand, the wage system has also been increasingly socialized in the sense that the state has taken over from the private capital sector the responsibility of providing for the production and reproduction of labour-power. "Put differently, the worker's standard of living depends not only upon what he or she takes home in his or her paycheck, but also upon the goods and services provided by the state" (Adams, 1978, p. 47). These state-provided goods and services, which help to produce and reproduce labour-power, constitute the social wage. The social wage is, of course, distinct from both the wage paid by the employer (money income and employee benefits) and other types of state activities (for example, policing and nonlabour social capital expenditures). Moreover, the social wage is not synonymous with government social welfare expenditures. The latter include a variety of activities that may have a "social control" function (for instance, policing the existing social order) or a "social wage" function (for instance, health services), which improve the living standard of the working class. Social welfare expenditures may also be a combination of both functions.

The combination of both functions is especially noticeable in education and personal social services. These services may provide real benefits that enhance the recipients' standard of living; conversely, cutbacks in these areas would lead to a decrease in the standard of living. On the other hand, teachers and social workers who provide these benefits may act as policing agents vested with coercive power or as ideological agents for the socialization of clients with values and norms supportive of the capitalist relations of production (Adams, 1978).

What is delineated here are the contradictions within the welfare state. The roots of these contradictions lie within the capitalist mode of production. As we have seen above, the capitalist mode of production is a way of organizing production in which the capitalist class acts in pursuit of one goal; maximization of profits. In the process, it is compelled to accumulate capital. Such a way of organizing production "differs utterly from an economic system which serves to meet human needs, yet this is exactly where many orthodox studies of social policy begin and end" (Gough, 1979, p. 12). Parenthetically, many social welfare and social work textbooks prefer to point to meeting human needs as the primary goal of social welfare. They tend to ignore such harsh realities as the class structure and the profit-maximization motive of the capitalist class. Such a benign neglect of the facts is a grave disservice to social work and social welfare students, as they will encounter these realities again and again in their practice later.

As social control and social wage are two sides of the same coin, or in more technical terms, the two opposites of a dialectic, the distinction between them in specific welfare programs is difficult to draw. The differences between them should, nevertheless, be kept in mind for analytical purposes. If social services and income security programs have intrinsically only the social control function, then there would be no more reason for opposing cutbacks in social wage expenditures than for opposing cutbacks in military or intelligence expenditures. However, for those who are concerned with social inequality in class societies, there are reasonable grounds for opposing cutbacks in social wage expenditures. The reason is that these cutbacks are in fact a disguised wage cut. They are part of a strategy of the state to lower personal and social consumption, in order to facilitate capital accumulation. The concept of social wage highlights the fact that transfer payments, health programs, and various social services are as much part of the real income of working class families as the paycheque. "The income is disposed of by the capitalist state on behalf of those families who exercise neither individual nor collective control over it, but a cutback is a reduction in real income for all that" (Adams, 1978, p. 50).

The social wage has become such an important feature in advanced capitalist societies since the Second World War that there is a tendency for class conflicts to extend from the economic sphere to the political sphere. The working class, in safeguarding its standard of living, is not only engaged in the struggle with the employers over wages and working conditions, but it is also increasingly involved in a struggle over social policy, that is, "over what proportion of the social product should go to what purposes and who should decide" (Adams, 1978, p. 51). While the underclass is excluded from many forms of social wage that are employment-related, it nevertheless shares in some social benefits. For example, unemployment insurance is employment-related, while medicare in Canada is not. This kind of development potentially questions the basic social structures of the class society.

■ SUMMARY

The state in capitalist society has two major functions: capital accumulation and legitimization. In its capital accumulation function, the state socializes the cost of producing and reproducing labour-power, while in its legitimization function, it maintains the nonworking population. These tasks of the welfare state are translated into social policies. The contradictions in the welfare state have consequences for the subordinate classes. Welfare programs are often experienced by them as measures of social control, yet they do derive social benefit from some of these programs.

Note

1.   This section relies a great deal on Gough's (1979) analysis of the British welfare
     state.

References

Adams, P. Social control or social wage: On the political economy of the 'welfare
    state.' *Journal of Sociology and Social Welfare, 1978, 5* (1): 46-54.

Butler, P.M. and Buckley, P.C. *Living on work and welfare: A closer look at linkages
    between income security and the world of work.* Halifax: Institute of Public
    Affairs, Dalhousie University, 1978.

Gough, I. *The political economy of the welfare state.* London: Macmillan Press Ltd.,
    1979.

Hobsbawn, E. Karl Marx's contribution to historiography. In R. Blackburn (Ed.),
    Ideology in social science. Glasgow: Fontana Collins, 1972.

Miliband, R. *The state in capitalist society.* London: Weindenfeld and Nicolson,
    1969.

O'Connor, J. *The fiscal crisis of the state.* New York: St. Martin's Press, 1973.

Panitch, L. The role and nature of the Canadian state. In L. Panitch (Ed.), *The
    Canadian state.* Toronto: University of Toronto Press, 1977.

GOOD NEWS
AND CANADIAN
SOCIOLOGY

R. Ogmundson

It is always an interesting exercise in the sociology of knowledge to observe how different scholars have different perceptions of what is important about a single piece of work. The recent review of a book called *The Superbureaucrats* (1979) by C. Campbell and G. Szablowski in this journal by Lorna Marsden (1980) has provided an interesting case in point for me. Marsden was impressed by the findings of Campbell and Szablowski to the effect that this elite is minimally accountable to the Canadian public and her review quite naturally emphasized that point. However, she hardly mentioned what, to me, and I suspect many other Canadian sociologists, was an even more interesting finding. Given the fact that Campbell and Szablowski are political scientists, it is unlikely that this finding will become common knowledge in Canadian sociology unless it is brought to wider attention through some mechanism such as this note.

The significant finding to which I refer is that Campbell and Szablowski found that the social origins of their "superbureaucrats" (probably more powerful than Olsen's (1977) bureaucratic elite) were highly representative of the Canadian population. After considering comparative data, they are led to comment:

> We find that central agents' socio-economic backgrounds resemble those of the country's general populace much more closely than do the backgrounds of bureaucratic elites in other advanced liberal democracies for which we have comparable data. Moreover, in the past decade Canada has seen a remarkable influx of bureaucrats representing segments of the populace traditionally excluded from senior positions in the public service. (1979:105)

Furthermore, their data indicated that recruitment to this elite was remarkably open. Indeed, their interview data (superior in quality to the secondary source data usually used in elite studies) show that there has been a substantial amount of mobility into this elite from working class origins. They note, for example, that: ". . . our finding that 44 percent of their fathers never graduated from high school highlights how our respondents have experienced rapid upward mobility" (1979:121).

Given the importance attributed to elite social origins and recruitment in the powerfully influential Porter/Clement/Olsen tradition in Canadian sociology, these findings should be of interest to sociologists in Canada generally. They indicate that this part of our elite system is generally representative in origin and open in recruitment. Thus the impression of rigidity, exclusivity, and closure provided by Porter (1965) and Clement

(1975) would appear not to apply in this sphere. The findings are also of interest because the results from direct interviews indicate that a middle class social origin cannot be reliably inferred from a university education. Since Porter (1965), Clement (1975), and Olsen (1977) all made this mistaken inference, it follows that their entire tradition of study has systematically under-estimated the amount of upward mobility to Canadian elites. If results from one study of the civil service may be generalized to other institutions, it may well be that the rate of upward mobility into Canadian elites has been at least twice as great as previously thought.[1]

A significant theoretical implication of these findings is that the "instrumentalist" Marxist position of Miliband et al. (1969) fails to be supported by these data. Hence those wishing to theorize within a neo-Marxist framework will find themselves encouraged to retreat to a diluted "structuralist" Marxism of the Althusser/Poulantzas variety (see Olsen, 1977; Cuneo, 1979). Others might be tempted to risk ostracism and to interpret the data as providing support for some kind of modified pluralist position. More practically, the findings may indicate that there is no great need for "affirmative action" in the federal civil service.

More generally, it is interesting to note that the Campbell and Szablowski findings are similar to those of much recent research which indicates that the amount of social injustice in Canadian society may not be nearly as great as many of us have believed it to be. At the elite level, it can be plausibly argued that the trends are positive. It is true, of course, that Clement's (1975) work has recently told us that two of the seven elites Porter studied—business and mass media—are the preserve of a British upper class group. On the other hand, White's work (1979) has indicated that the boards of directors who compose these elites may have little power.[2] Furthermore, the data available on two of the other elites provide a very different picture than that provided by Clement's widely diffused findings. Studies of both the civil service elite and the legislative/judicial elite indicate that they are becoming much more representative in their social characteristics (see Olsen, 1977; Campbell and Szablowski, 1979; Ogmundson, 1977[3]). Unfortunately, nobody has done a replication of Porter's work on the labor, church, and intellectual elites. Consequently, we have trend data on only four of Porter's seven elites.[4] Nonetheless, the available research is encouraging. Grayson and Grayson (1978) have found that leading Canadian authors have relatively representative social characteristics. Cheal (1978) has provided evidence that religion may not legitimate established class and power structures in Canada, after all. Kelner (1970) found increasing "ethnic" penetration of the Toronto elite structure.

Similar "good news" is to be found in recent studies of the general population. We used to believe that ethnicity was a strong determinant of life chances in Canada (Porter, 1965: Ch. 3; Forcese, 1980:43-50). However, more recent research (e.g. Pineo, 1976; Darroch, 1979) indicates that this is simply not so. It has been shown that: ". . . no more than two percent of the current occupational status of the Canadian male labour force can be said to derive from ethnic origin" (Pineo, 1976:120). Similarly, we used to believe that income discrimination against females was getting worse. (See the well-known article by McDonald, 1975—the main points of which have been uncritically repeated by Himelfarb et al., 1979; Cuneo, 1980 and Ogmundson, 1981). Here again, more recent research has indicated that this is not true (Carroll, 1980). Furthermore, other research has indicated that much of the difference in the incomes of those with different ascribed statuses in Canada may be attributed to factors other than discrimination (Tepperman, 1975:Ch. 6). So far as income distribution is concerned, we used to believe that income distribution in Canada was relatively unjust (Porter, 1965:Ch. 4) and that it was rapidly becoming more unequal. (See the famous paper by Johnson, 1974, whose main argument has been uncritically repeated by people such as Marchak, 1975; Ogmundson, 1976 and Cuneo, 1980.) More recent research has indicated that our income distribution is about "normal," if not unusually equal for industrialized countries (Tyree et al., 1979; Stack, 1980), and that, if anything, the trend is toward greater equality (Hamilton and Pinard, 1977; Armstrong et al., 1977)! So far as mobility is concerned, we used to believe that opportunity in Canada was unusually unequal (Porter, 1965:Ch. 6). More recent mobility studies have indicated that there is very little status transmission over three generations in Canada (Goyder and Curtis, 1979) and that the amount of mobility in Canada may be unusually great (Tyree et al., 1979; Rich, 1976). Across a broad spectrum, then, an accumulating body of evidence indicates that we have not been doing so badly after all. In fact, many indicators suggest that we have been doing rather well. This is not to say, of course, that there does not remain great room for the improvement of Canadian society. It does suggest, however, that matters are not nearly so desparate as many of us have been teaching our students to believe.[5]

Indeed, all this "good news" might well lead us to further reconsider the "bad news" provided by Porter (1965) and by Clement's (1975) partial "replication" of his work. As noted earlier, the amount of upward mobility into elite positions was probably very substantially under-estimated in these studies. Furthermore, it is conceivable that much of the very substantial "missing data" in both studies concerned individuals of relatively humble origins.[6] It is also reasonable to bring attention to the critically important point that Clement failed to replicate Porter's method for selecting dominant corporations. Clement's new methodology may well have been an improvement over Porter's, but one cost of adopting the new approach was to make any inferences about trends questionable (see Hunter, 1976:147; Baldwin, 1977a:19). Hence, there has to be doubt about the validity of his claims about trends toward greater exclusivity. Even as it is, his findings clearly indicate an increase in the representation of non-British ethnic groups in the business elite (Hunter, 1976:127).

The naive reader might imagine that considerations such as these would be greeted with pleasure by Canadian sociologists and sociology students. However, such is not likely to be the case. Many of us have a vested interest in a previous conventional wisdom which lamented our many woes (see, for example, Ogmundson, 1976). Those of us who believe in revolution as a cure for all that ails us will be dismayed by this reversal. The temptation will presumably be to ignore or to minimize such findings. More fundamentally, we, as sociologists, have a fundamental material interest in the discovery, creation, maintenance, and widespread perception of "social problems." Student enrollment, publication opportunities, consulting fees, research money, and jobs for our students (to say nothing of ourselves!) very much depend on the success of a continuous effort to convince the public of the existence of a number of social problems requiring sociological expertise. Furthermore, our collective self-esteem is largely based on the belief that our primary motivation is to help others, not ourselves. We also like to believe that we have the knowledge to be successful in that regard. Consequently, our interests demand "bad news."[7] Even more fundamentally, we are part of what Gouldner (1979) has recently called the *New Class*. Sociologists are in the forefront of those seeking to legitimate the advancement of this class based on cultural capital at the expense of the "old class" based on material capital. It is unlikely that our commitment to scientific norms will be allowed to prevail over our need to provide evidence which coincides with our collective interests. Hence, one can be confident that sociologists in Canada will rebound from these temporary setbacks to discover more problems which only they can solve.

Notes

1. Using university education as an indicator, Rich (1976) found that 87 percent of an Ontario civil service elite was of upper middle class or higher social origin. Using more complete data from questionnaires, he found that only 36 percent of this elite belonged to this category.

2. Another of the interesting findings of Campbell and Szablowski indicates that civil servants perceive themselves to be powerful and are happy to admit to an interviewer that they are "where the action is." Contrast this to the interview findings of White (1979) in his important study of boards of directors in which directors of private corporations report that they perceive themselves as not being very influential. Such findings appear to indicate that White's findings are not an artifact of his measure.

3. Campbell and Szablowski (1979: 115) report that: ". . . Kornberg and Mishler found in 1971 that a considerable proportion of MPs belong to non-charter groups . . ." but do not provide a reference.

4. Perhaps no more fitting memorial to Porter's work could be imagined than a replication of his work on the labor, church, and intellectual elites. It would also be desirable to have studies of the elites of the defensive system (the military and the police) and to have studies of the educational elite (e.g., university presidents).

5. I recall with chagrin the vehemence with which I disagreed with students who insisted that Porter and Clement were mistaken and that: "maybe all this was true once, but ethnicity doesn't matter any more." Now it turns out that the students were right and I was wrong.

6. This point has also been made by Baldwin (1977a:10; 1977b: 216). One might wonder how much upward mobility by non-British groups has been obscured by changes of name (e.g., Cohen to Cole; Eymundsen to Emerson; Pajekowski to Patrick) or religion (e.g., Jewish to Anglican). Similarly, one might also wonder how much upward mobility through the female side has been missed. Campbell and Szablowski's data (1979: 259), however, would indicate that this has been minimal.

7. One might speculatively note that this also seems to be true of both the mass media and the state. Since "bad news" apparently attracts more attention than "good news," those in the media are motivated to search for problems. Similarly, those employed by the state are motivated to find problems so as to provide a rationale for further expansion (and personal promotion). For example, I know of cases in which demographers have been forced to "re-estimate" (i.e., "fudge") their data so as to make problems appear bad enough to warrant further support from other levels of government (e.g., a deaf person with one arm would be counted twice under two different disability categories so as to beef up the estimate of total handicapped in the population).

References

Armstrong, D. et al. 1977 "The measurement of income distribution in Canada: some problems and some tentative data." *Canadian Public Policy* 3:479-488.

Baldwin, E. 1977a "The mass media and the corporate elite." *Canadian Journal of Sociology* 2(1):1-27.

_____. 1977b "On methodological and theoretical 'muddles' in Clement's media study." *Canadian Journal of Sociology* 2(2):215-222.

Campbell, C. and G. Szablowski. 1979 *The Superbureaucrats: Structure and Behaviour in Central Agencies.* Toronto: Macmillan.

Carroll, M.P. 1980 "The gap between male and female income in Canada." *Canadian Journal of Sociology* 5(4):359-362.

Cheal, D. 1978 "Religion and the social order." *Canadian Journal of Sociology* 3(1):61-69.

Cuneo, C. 1979 "State, class and reserve labour: the case of the 1941 Canadian unemployment insurance act." *Canadian Review of Sociology and Anthropology* 16(2):147-170.

_____. 1980 "Class, stratification and mobility." In *Sociology*, edited by R. Hagedorn, Chapter 7. Toronto: Holt, Rinehart and Winston.

Darroch, A.G. 1979 "Another look at ethnicity, stratification and social mobility in Canada." *Canadian Journal of Sociology* 4(1):1-26.

Forcese, D. 1980 *The Canadian Class Structure.* Second edition. Toronto:McGraw-Hill Ryerson.

Gouldner, A. 1979 *The Future of Intellectuals and the Rise of the New Class.* New York: Seabury.

Goyder, J. and J. Curtis. 1979 "Occupational mobility in Canada over four generations." In *Social Stratification: Canada*, edited by J. Curtis and W. Scott. Second edition. Scarborough, Ontario: Prentice-Hall of Canada.

Grayson, J.P. et al. 1979 "The Canadian literary elite: a socio-historical perspective." *Canadian Journal of Sociology* 3(3):291-308.

Hamilton, R. and M. Pinard. 1977 "Poverty in Canada: illusion and reality." *Canadian Review of Sociology and Anthropology* 14(2):247-252.

Himelfarb, A. and C. James Richardson. 1979 *People, Power and Process: Sociology for Canadians.* Toronto: McGraw-Hill Ryerson.

Hunter, A. 1976 "Class and status in Canada." In *Introduction to Canadian Society,* edited by G.N. Ramu and S. Johnson, Chapter 4. Toronto: Macmillan.

Johnson, L. 1974 *Poverty in Wealth.* Revised edition. Toronto: New Hogtown Press.

Kelner, M. 1970 "Ethnic penetration into Toronto's elite structure." *Canadian Review of Sociology and Anthropology* 7:128-137.

Marsden, L. 1980 "Review of *The Superbureaucrats* by Campbell and Szablowski," *Canadian Journal of Sociology* 5(4):449-450.

McDonald, L. 1975 "Wages of work: a widening gap between women and men." *Canadian Forum* (April-May):4-7.

Miliband. R. 1969 *The State in Capitalist Society.* London: Wiedenfield and Nicholson.

Ogmundson, R. 1976 "The sociology of power and politics." In *Introduction to Canadian Society,* edited by G.N. Ramu and S. Johnson, Chapter 5. Toronto: Macmillan.

――――. 1977 "A social profile of members of the Manitoba legislature: 1950, 1960, 1970." *Journal of Canadian Studies* 12(4):79-84.

――――. 1981 "Social inequality." In *Essentials of Sociology,* edited by R. Hagedorn, Chapter 5. Toronto: Holt, Rinehart and Winston.

Olsen D. 1977 "The state elites." In *The Canadian State,* edited by L. Panitch, Chapter 7. Toronto: University of Toronto Press.

Pineo, P. 1976 "Social mobility in Canada: the current picture." *Sociological Focus* 9(2):109-123.

Porter, J. 1965 *The Vertical Mosaic.* Toronto: University of Toronto Press.

Rich, H. 1976 "*The Vertical Mosaic* revisited." *Journal of Canadian Studies* 11:14-31.

Stack, S. 1980 "The political economy of income inequality: a comparative analysis." *Canadian Journal of Political Science* 13:273-286.

Tepperman, Lorne. 1975 *Social Mobility in Canada.* Toronto: McGraw-Hill Ryerson.

Tyree, A. et al. 1979 "Gaps and glissandos: inequality, economic development and social mobility." *American Sociological Review* 44:410-424.

White, T. 1979 "Boards of directors: control and decision-making in Canadian corporations." *Canadian Review of Sociology and Anthropology* 16(1):77-95.

■ POSTSCRIPT

According to Djao, the state does not simply govern, it consists of a complex set of institutions that function to maintain class society. In this regard, the welfare system is intended as a means of maintaining control over people in the lowest socioeconomic strata: the working-class recipients of welfare programs, including unemployment insurance, welfare, etc. As a result, there is little mobility out of the lowest rung on the social ladder.

Ogmundson argues that there is a substantial amount of mobility into the bureaucratic elite, and that this elite is representative of the total population. He suggests that analysts who argue that there is a lack of movement into the economic elite have made some errors in the way they have gathered and interpreted their data, especially in the way they have defined and interpreted middle-class status. Canadian stratification, Ogmundson concludes, is less unjust than commonly assumed.

Both studies, however, may be criticized for either ignoring or paying scant attention to gender issues and the importance of patriarchy in determining social mobility. Both may also be criticized for rejecting data that fail to confirm their arguments.

■ QUESTIONS

1. Which argument do you find most convincing? Why? How have your preconceptions of the issues affected your answer?
2. How might you improve both Djao's and Ogmundson's examinations of the issues?
3. Is inequality necessary?
4. How might inequalities be reduced?

■ FURTHER READING

In Support of Djao

Clement, Wallace. *The Challenge of Class Analysis.* Ottawa: Carleton University Press, 1988.

Cuneo, Carl. "Class, Stratification and Mobility." In *Sociology.* Edited by R. Hagedorn. Toronto: Holt, Rinehart and Winston, 1980.

Djao, A.W. *Inequality and Social Policy.* Toronto: John Wiley and Sons, 1983.

Hunter, Alfred A. *Class Tells: On Social Inequality in Canada.* Toronto: Butterworths, 1981.

In Support of Ogmundson

Atkinson, A.B. *The Economics of Inequality*. London: Oxford University Press, 1975.

Lennards, J.L. "Education." In *Sociology*. Edited by R. Hagedorn. Toronto: Holt, Rinehart and Winston, 1980.

Stack, S. "The Political Economy of Income Inequality: A Comparative Analysis." *Canadian Journal of Political Science* 13 (1980): 273-286.

Other Voices

Armstrong, Pat and Hugh Armstrong. *The Double Ghetto: Canadian Women and their Segregated Work*. Toronto: McClelland and Stewart, 1978.

Burstyn, Varda and Dorothy Smith. *Women, Class, Family and the State*. Toronto: Garamond Press, 1985.

Davis, Kingsley. *Human Society*. New York: Macmillan, 1949.

Duffy, Ann, Nancy Mandell, and Norene Pupo. *Few Choices: Women, Work and Family*. Toronto: Garamond Press, 1989.

Grabb, Edward G. *Social Inequality: Classical and Contemporary Theorists*. Toronto: Holt, Rinehart and Winston, 1984.

DOES ETHNICITY AFFECT SOCIAL MOBILITY?

YES   E. **Hugh Lautard and Donald J. Loree,** "Ethnic Stratification in Canada, 1931-1971," *Canadian Journal of Sociology* 9, no. 3 (1984): 333-344

NO   **A. Gordon Darroch,** "Another Look at Ethnicity, Stratification and Social Mobility in Canada," *Canadian Journal of Sociology* 4, no. 1 (1979): 1-25

In Debate Two the issue was whether or not class affected social mobility. In Debate Three the issue is whether or not ethnicity influences social mobility. One of the most influential books on this topic was John Porter's *The Vertical Mosaic* (1965). Porter compared the statuses of the so-called charter groups, English and French Canadians, with later immigrants to Canada. He found that the British were overrepresented among the economic elite of Canadian society, while the French were underrepresented. He also noted that other ethnic groups had varying rates of success in adapting to Canada's social structure. Immigrants from Germany, Holland, and Scandinavia were more successful in rising in the structure than immigrants from Poland, Italy, and the Ukraine. Porter's research has been the subject of considerable debate ever since.

It has also sparked considerable discussion of the differences among patterns of immigration into Canada and the United States. In describing Canada as a vertical mosaic, Porter's analysis indicates that Canada has developed as a multicultural, multi-ethnic society. Immigrant groups have not been assimilated into the dominant group. In the United States, the pattern has been described as a melting pot. Within the melting pot, ethnic and racial characteristics are said to become less important over time. Whether or not the American pattern is really illustrative of a melting pot is arguable. It is also arguable that Canada can be defined in terms of a vertical mosaic.

It is important to remember that some ethnic groups are more easily recognized than others. These easily recognizable ethnic groups, such as

North America's native peoples, blacks, Chinese, etc., are called visible minorities. Consequently, some sociologists argue that racism—discrimination on the basis of race—must also be considered as an important factor influencing the placement of particular ethnic groups. Race refers to the apparent physical differences among members of the human species. Strictly speaking, there is no biological basis for the classification of races. The criteria are subjective and based upon superficial characteristics like skin colour, lip size, the shape of the eyes, and so forth. Ethnicity refers to the racial and cultural differences between groups. In some instances, members of the same race may be members of different ethnic groups. For example, the British and French are members of the same race but belong to different ethnic groups.

Whatever the measure of differences, several questions remain. Which social differences are the most important indicators of life chances in Canada? Is race more important than ethnicity? Is ethnicity more important than class? Is class more important than race?

The articles included here focus on the impact of ethnicity. Arguing for the "Yes" side of the debate, Lautard and Loree say that Porter's original description of Canada's ethnic structure as a vertical mosaic is as valid today as ever. Arguing for the "No" side of the debate, Darroch says that ethnic groups are less likely in contemporary Canadian society to be segregated occupationally.

Reference

Porter, John (1965) *The Vertical Mosaic* (Toronto: University of Toronto Press).

ETHNIC STRATIFICATION IN CANADA

YES

E. Hugh Lautard and Donald J. Loree

■ THE RESEARCH PROBLEM

The relationship between ethnicity and occupation in Canada has been under systematic investigation for over a quarter of a century, and patterns of considerable inequality have been described. For example, the first use to which Blishen's original socioeconomic index for occupations was put was to measure occupational inequality among the major ethnic groups, as of 1951 (Blishen, 1958: 523-524, 531). Porter (1965: 85-86) drew on Blishen's findings, regarding them as constituting some of the strongest evidence for "the vertical mosaic." Blishen (1970) went on to show the persistence of ethnic inequality among immigrants, as of 1961. Kalbach reported similar results and concluded that "the general concept of assimilation has limited value for an analysis of the occupational characteristics of the country's immigrants" (Kalbach, 1970: 283). Similarly, from their analysis of the 1971 Census data on birthplace and ethnicity, Richmond and Kalbach found little support for the "convergence model of occupational assimilation" (1980: 338).

The literature on time trends reports the same types of patterns, but often with a more optimistic tone because there is evidence of decreases in ethnic differences over time. For example, Darroch's (1979) calculation of dissimilarity indexes for Porter's main data series indicated that ethnic differentiation in the male labor force declined over the thirty-year period from 1931 to 1961, and his similar analysis of Forcese's (1975) data suggested that this trend continued to 1971. Also on the basis of a reanalysis of some of Porter's data, Reitz (1977: 184) called for a revision of "Porter's original hypothesis." In addition, Reitz (1980: 150-173) has reported on a decline in occupational inequality among ethnic groups during the 1970s. He found educational differences to be responsible for much of the inequality of occupational status among the ethnic groups covered by the five-city Non-official Languages Survey of 1973. Studies of social mobility have contained similar conclusions. For example, whereas DeJocas and Rocher (1957) and Dofny and Garon-Audy (1969) found that francophones in Quebec were handicapped in social mobility compared to their anglophone counterparts, in 1954 and 1964, respectively, McRoberts et al. (1976) reported that differences in mobility between francophones in Quebec and anglophones throughout Canada were much smaller among the younger cohorts by 1973 (cf. Pineo, 1976). In a similar view, Boyd et al. concluded

49

from the 1973 Canadian National Mobility Survey that in Canada currently, as in the United States and Israel, "ethnic differences in occupational status are largely attributable to, or are quite dramatically attenuated by adjustment for, respondents' social origin and background characteristics together with respondents' own education" (Boyd et al., 1980: 224).

Questions concerning the relation between ethnicity and occupation in Canada remain, however, particularly in light of some omissions and weaknesses in previous studies. One of the most serious omissions in the research has been the tendency to pay little if any attention to women, leaving conclusions based largely if not solely on data for men. For example, in his discussion of "Ethnicity and social class," Porter (1965: Chapter 3) devotes only a couple of paragraphs and one table, in passing, to women. Similarly, except for the work by Kalbach (1970) and Richmond and Kalbach (1980) all other studies cited above were based on data either for males only or for both sexes combined. In addition, the limited range and detail of ethnic distinctions employed in many of the previous studies make them less than ideal tests of the vertical mosaic thesis. Some are confined to comparisons of anglophones and francophones (DeJocas and Rocher, 1957; Dofny and Garon-Audy, 1969; McRoberts et al., 1976). Others use more detailed approaches, but these are still very crude. For example, Reitz (1980) excludes the British and French and classifies non-charter Europeans as North, East or South Europeans. The use of only a few broad categories of ethnicity, with the masking of ethnic group differences within categories, can mean underestimation of the extent to which inequality in occupations is a function of ethnicity.

In these circumstances, one of the most trenchant challenges to Porter's vertical mosaic thesis is Darroch's (1979) study which appeared in this *Journal*, based as it is on the reanalysis of Porter's own data. However, the use of Porter's data is a weakness as well as a strength. Darroch's findings show vividly that Porter did misinterpret *trends* in occupational differences among ethnic groups, that there was evidence of change in the direction of greater similarity which Porter did not perceive. However, Darroch's findings are less than definitive with regard to *how much* ethnic dissimilarity prevailed in 1931, 1951, and 1961. The six broad occupational categories used by Porter and adopted by Darroch were appropriate for a rough scanning of the occupational distributions of the ethnic groups in order to determine the direction of changes in these, if any. This occupational scheme, however, is not appropriate for precise summary measurement of differences among occupational distributions, i.e., for calculating dissimilarity indexes, the values of which, as Darroch (1979: 12) notes, are inversely proportional to the breadth of the categories used, other things being equal. By 1961, for example, over half the male labor force (58 percent) was contained in the residual "All Others" category. The crude classification probably masks many important differences in the attainment of more precisely defined occupations by the different ethnic groups. The levels of ethnic dissimilarity Darroch calculates with Forcese's (1975) data for 1971 must be viewed with caution for the same reason. Although the classification scheme used is more detailed than Porter's, its twenty-two categories are very broad relative to the nearly 500 occupational titles used in the 1971 Census.

In addition, Darroch's analyses are characterized by the two limitations described above for much of the literature. First, the differences, if any, between patterns for males and females are not studied. The 1971 data are for males and females combined, while the analyses for 1931-61 were for males only. Second, although Darroch's study includes the summary measurement of inequality as well as a measure of differentiation, the former is restricted to using some of Blishen's (1970) data on birthplaces to measure the occupational status of three categories of immigrants (British, American, European) relative to that of the Canadian-born, as of 1961 (Darroch, 1979: 13-15).

In sum, while Darroch's analyses provide an important corrective to Porter's conclusions on trends, they probably leave us with underestimates of ethnic occupational dissimilarity, and this for men only for 1931, 1951, and 1961 and for both sexes combined as of 1971. Also, there is no equivalent analysis of occupational inequality among the major ethnic groups. To address these limitations, the analysis reported below measures occupational dissimilarity and inequality among females as well as males, using the most detailed cross-classification of Census data on ethnicity and occupation published for 1931, 1951, 1961, and 1971, with a partial extension to 1981.

■ DATA AND METHODS

The *ethnic groups* included in the present study are the same as those upon which Porter's and Darroch's analyses focus, except that Polish and Ukrainian replace East European for 1951, 1961, and 1971, giving twelve groups (eleven for 1931): British, French, German, Italian, Jewish, Dutch, Scandinavian, Polish, Ukrainian, other European, Asian and Native Indian. The *occupations* used are the several hundred occupational titles identified in the Census. There are 388 occupations for 1931, 278 for 1951, 332 for 1961, and 496 for 1971. Given a direct relation between the magnitude of the dissimilarity index and the number of categories to which it is applied, the net increase in the number of occupations loads the evidence in favour of finding an increase in occupational dissimilarity among ethnic groups, the opposite of the trend found by Darroch. Since we are more concerned with estimating the level of occupational differentiation in the recent period, in 1971, than with time trends, there is little to be gained in matching occupational titles.[1]

Occupational differentiation and inequality among ethnic groups are analyzed with the measures used by Darroch. The *index of dissimilarity* is employed to measure occupational differentiation. It represents the percentage of a given ethnic group which would have to change jobs in order to have the same occupational distribution as the rest of the labor force. We use Duncan and Duncan's (1955: 494) adjustment factor to correct for the presence of each ethnic group in the total labor force. Otherwise the calculation and interpretation of our dissimilarity indexes are identical to Darroch's.

The *index of net difference* (ND) is used to measure the relative occupational status of each ethnic group in 1951, 1961, and 1971, the years for which occupational rankings are available (Blishen, 1958: 1967; Blishen and McRoberts, 1976). A negative ND value indicates the extent to which the probability of a given member of the ethnic group in question having a lower occupational rank than a given member of the total labor force exceeds the opposite probability assuming random pairing. A positive value represents the opposite relation, and zero would indicate that the two probabilities are the same (cf. Lieberson, 1975: 279-280). In the absence of an adjustment factor to correct ND for the presence of each ethnic group in the total labor force, our indexes necessarily underestimate somewhat the degree of ethnic inequality.

■ RESULTS

Table 1 contains the indexes of occupational dissimilarity for each ethnic group compared with the rest of the labor force. This shows the decline in ethnic occupational differentiation found by Darroch, but, as we expected, the levels of dissimilarity are considerably higher than those reported by Darroch. Our indexes for men in 1961, for example, include no values lower than 15 percent, and the mean (29) is more than double that yielded by Darroch's analysis (14). By 1971 there is one value for men lower than 15 percent (that for German Canadians at 14), and four more at 15 percent, but, again, the mean (24) is nearly double that calculated by Darroch (14) with Forcese's (1975) data for both sexes combined. After 1931, when the average dissimilarity for females is the same as that for males (37 percent), ethnic differentiation among women in the paid labor force is less than that among men, but even by 1971 only four groups (German, Dutch, Scandinavian, and Polish) have indexes of 15 percent less and all these are above 10 percent; the mean for women in 1971 is 21 percent. Thus, on average, a quarter of the male labor force, and a fifth of the female labor force would have to change jobs in order to eliminate ethnic dissimilarity. Dissimilarity between *pairs* of ethnic groups, moreover, is even greater, averaging 33 and 27 percent, respectively, among males and females in 1971.

Some of the indexes in Table 1 would be even higher were finer ethnic distinctions possible. In 1971, for example, "Asian" includes thousands of

TABLE 1 Occupational Dissimilarity between Selected Ethnic Groups and the Rest of the Labor Force, by Sex: 1931, 1951, 1961, and 1971

	MALE				FEMALE			
ETHNIC GROUP	1931	1951	1961	1971	1931	1951	1961	1971
British	22	20	19	15	27	23	22	16
French	15	17	16	14	26	23	17	17
German[1]	24	23	17	15	20	14	13	11
Italian	48	34	40	35	39	24	45	38
Jewish	65	63	59	51	51	40	34	32
Dutch	21	20	17	17	14	17	15	15
Scandinavian	29	23	18	17	25	13	10	12
Polish	34*	23	18	15	45*	21	17	14
Ukrainian		28	21	15		22	21	16
Other European[2]	43	21	19	21	49	18	20	23
Asian[3]	61	46	45	36	50	25	20	25
Native Indian[4]	49	57	57	41	59	53	48	31
Mean (X)	37	31	29	24	37	24	24	21
S.D.(s)	17	16	17	13	15	11	12	9
V (s/X)	.46	.52	.59	.54	.41	.46	.50	.43
Number of occupations	(388)	(278)	(332)	(496)	(265)	(226)	(277)	(412)

Sources: 1931 (Dominion Bureau of Statistics, 1936: Table 49)
1951 (Dominion Bureau of Statistics, 1953: Table 12)
1961 (Dominion Bureau of Statistics, 1964: Table 21)
1971 (Statistics Canada, 1975: Table 4)

* Eastern European (Polish and Ukrainian combined)
1. Includes Austrian in 1931
2. Other central European in 1931
3. Weighted average of Chinese and Japanese in 1931
4. Includes Eskimo in 1951

"East Indians" and "Syrian-Lebanese" (gross categorizations themselves), as well as Chinese, Japanese, and other Asian groups. Similarly, "Other European," with indexes of 21 for males and 23 for females in 1971, embraces nearly two dozen groups identified by the 1971 Census in published bulletins but with no cross-classifications of ethnicity with occupation. Dissimilarity indexes for two of the "Other European" groups, Greek and Yugoslav Canadians, calculated with unpublished 1971 Census data, are 48 and 33, respectively, for males, and 51 and 35 for females.

As Darroch has indicated, summary measurement fails to reveal "numerically small differences between specific groups which may have particular importance, such as ... professional groups" (1979: 8n). However, measures can be calculated to reflect such differences to the same degree as those in larger occupations. This can be done by assigning an equal number of persons to each occupation, maintaining the original within-occupation ethnic composition, to yield "standardized" indexes free of the effects of overall occupational structure (cf. Gibbs, 1965: 163). Standardized indexes of the occupational dissimilarity of ethnic groups tend to be higher than those in Table 1, averaging 28 and 35 percent, respectively, among men and women in 1971. Average standardized dissimilarity indexes for pairs of ethnic groups are 37 percent among males and 47 among females.

Returning to the dissimilarity shown in Table 1, it is evident that while the standard deviations decline between 1931 and 1971, relative variation (V) undergoes a net increase. The rankings of ethnic groups by degree of dissimilarity, however, remain remarkably stable. Table 1 shows that the Italian, Jewish, Asian and Native Indian groups tend to be more dissimilar than other groups. Spearman coefficients for the intercensus correlation of the rank order of ethnic groups by degree of dissimilarity range from .82 to .93, all significant at the .01 level.[2] Nor is this variation merely a function of another property of the dissimilarity index, namely its inverse relation to relative group size (see Cortese et al., 1976: 631-632). Although there is, indeed, a consistently negative (product-moment) correlation between measured dissimilarity and relative group size, none of the coefficients are significant, and the r^2 values show that relative group size would account for an average of only 12 percent of the variation in ethnic dissimilarity.

These results are for the country as a whole, and they reflect, or include, the effects of regional differences in ethnic composition and economic structure. A similar analysis of ethnic occupational differentiation within each of the country's five major regions (Lautard, 1983), however, indicates that occupational dissimilarity among ethnic groups at the regional level is greater than that observed at the national level. Average ethnic occupational differentiation was highest in the Atlantic region, followed by Quebec (perhaps in part because of the generally smaller size of the minority goups in these two regions); British Columbia occupied a middle position; and the lowest average levels of ethnic differentiation were found in Ontario and on the Prairies. Again, however, in all regions average ethnic occupational dissimilarity is greater than that observed in the national data, where the level of aggregation apparently obscured some of the ethnic differences. Finally, the occupational dissimilarity among ethnic groups is not simply the result of educational differences either. Identical analysis of special tabulations of 1971 Census data with a control for level of schooling yields average dissimilarity indexes for men with post-secondary education, eleven to thirteen, seven to ten, and less than seven years of schooling of 21, 21, 26 and 29 percent, respectively; the equivalent figures for women are 17, 15, 21 and 31 percent. Thus, among men with high school education or more, the relation between ethnicity and occupation is nearly as strong as that observed without the control for education (24), while for men with less than a high school education it is even stronger. Only among women with eleven to thirteen years of schooling is average ethnic occupational dissimilarity substantially lower than that observed without taking level of education into account (21). For women with a college education average ethnic dissimilarity is nearly as great as that found without the educational control, while for those with seven to ten years of schooling it is the same, and for those with less than seven years it is about 50 percent greater.[3] These findings indicate that the association between ethnicity and occupation cannot be dismissed as a spurious relationship explainable by regional or educational differences.

Occupational dissimilarity, of course, does not *ipso facto* imply occupational inequality, and trends in the two phenomena may not coincide. Table 2 presents ND values for the occupational status of each ethnic group relative to the total labor force, to check on patterns of occupational inequality. The few positive indexes document the occupational advantage of the British, Jewish and, by 1971, Asian groups, as well as a slight

---

TABLE 2 Net Difference in Occupational Status between Ethnic Groups and the Total Labor Force, by Sex: 1951, 1961, and 1971

ETHNIC GROUP	MALE			FEMALE		
	1951	1961	1971	1951	1961	1971
British	.09	.11	.07	.11	.12	.07
French	−.11	−.10	−.04	−.11	−.07	−.01
German	−.03	−.06	−.07	−.13	−.11	−.09
Italian	−.15	−.28	−.21	−.08	−.37	−.34
Jewish	.41	.42	.35	.20	.21	.24
Netherlands	−.10	−.09	−.09	−.15	−.12	−.10
Scandinavian	−.04	−.05	−.08	−.01	−.03	−.01
Polish	−.14	−.07	−.07	−.20	−.16	−.12
Ukrainian	−.11	−.10	−.09	−.20	−.19	−.12
Other European	−.12	−.11	−.11	−.17	−.19	−.20
Asian	−.14	−.03	−.10	−.06	−.05	−.01
Native Indian[1]	−.68	−.63	−.34	−.55	−.47	−.23
Mean (X)	.18	.17	.14	.16	.17	.13
S.D. (s)	.19	.18	.11	.14	.13	.10
V (s/X)	1.06	1.06	.79	.88	.76	.77
Number of occupational ranks[2]	(208)	(298)	(496)	(178)	(252)	(412)

Sources: 1951 (Dominion Bureau of Statistics, 1953: Table 12)
1961 (Dominion Bureau of Statistics, 1964: Table 21)
1971 (Statistics Canada, 1975: Table 4)
1. Includes Eskimo in 1951
2. May not equal the number of occupations in Table 1 because of ties

advantage in 1951 and 1961 for Scandinavian-Canadian women. The negative values indicate the relatively low status of the other groups. The largest negative indexes with one exception (women of Italian origin in 1971) are those for Native Indians, for whom even the 1971 indexes exceed $-.30$ for males and $-.20$ for females. Between 1951 and 1971 mean ethnic inequality declines, as do the standard deviations and the relative variation (V), but the latter remains very high for both sexes. Moreover, the British, Italians, and Scandinavians of both sexes, and German and Jewish males, as well as Other European females, all experience a net decline in relative occupational status over the two decades under consideration. Yet the ethnic ranking by relative occupational status is almost as stable as that by degree of segregation: all the Spearman coefficients are significant at the .05 level, and all but one at the .01 level.

It must be recognized, too, that the occupational ranking used here is essentially a prestige scale, which tends to yield lower (absolute) ND values than, for example, do income data. By way of comparison, the ND index for the relative occupational status of women vis-à-vis men in 1971 is $-.03$, while that calculated with income data from the same census is $-.48$, sixteen times larger. Comparisons with sex differences also help put into perspective the absolute magnitude of occupational inequality among the ethnic groups — for 1971, the inequality by ethnicity averages over four times greater than that by sex (cf. Darroch, 1979: 13).

Finally, it should be borne in mind that the levels of inequality indicated in Table 2 underestimate the disparities in relative occupational status among the ethnic groups. If the overall occupational structure were taken into account, if the ND indexes could be corrected for the presence of each ethnic group in the total labor force, if inequality were calculated between pairs of ethnic groups, or if the ethnic classification were more refined, the inequality levels would be even greater.

Data published by Statistics Canada (1984: Table 1) permit a partial extension of this analysis to 1981. Although the data are not entirely comparable and cannot be ranked to measure inequality, dissimilarity indexes may be obtained for the British, French, German, Italian, Dutch, Ukrainian, and Native peoples. The values for males are 11, 15, 15, 26, 17, 14, and 37, respectively; and 10, 14, 9, 25, 13, 10, and 29 for females. The averages are 19 for males and 16 for females, compared to 22 and 21 respectively for the corresponding groups in 1971. Thus, the decline probably continued at least for these seven groups. However, relative variation in the indexes for men decreased only slightly (from .50 to .47) and increased slightly for women (from .48 to .50), and the rank order of the groups according to degree of dissimilarity in 1981 is virtually identical to that in 1971 for both sexes. Moreover, standardized dissimilarity indexes, free of the structural effects of overall occupational composition, show less (relative) decline over the 1970s: from an average of 26 to 24 for males, and from 33 to 26 for females. These figures suggest that some of the apparent decline in ethnic differentiation may be the result of shifts in occupational structure, rather than a consequence of the decreasing significance of ethnicity per se. We must reserve judgement concerning the relation between ethnicity and occupation in 1981, however, until we have a more complete set of findings, including results for Asians, Jews, and other missing groups.

■ DISCUSSION

Despite declines since 1931, occupational dissimilarity among ethnic groups is much more pronounced than suggested by Darroch's analysis. This relation between ethnicity and occupation remains a durable feature of Canadian society. Moreover, average occupational inequality is still substantial enough to justify the use of the concept "vertical mosaic" to characterize this aspect of ethnic relations in Canada. The patterns by ethnicity do not seem to be explainable by the effects of differences in regions and differences in education. There was a tendency for the relation between ethnicity and occupation to be stronger at lower levels of education. However, this, and reports that ethnic differences in education help explain ethnic differences in occupational status attainment, can be interpreted as evidence that ethnicity affects occupation *through* education (cf. Cuneo and Curtis, 1975: 19).

There is a need for more research on a full explanation of the current differences in occupations by ethnicity. This should provide part of the explanation for the trend toward lesser ethnic differences as well. Hopefully the trend will continue, but this is probably more likely if we proceed to develop a clearer understanding of the dynamics of ethnic stratification. Our findings underscore the importance of using detailed occupational data in our further research on ethnic differentials, showing that patterns differ for males and females, and that separate analyses by gender are called for. There is also a need for future studies to employ more refined ethnic classifications. Finally, of course, it is important to complete the extension of the analysis to 1981.

Notes

1. Although matching for ten-year comparisons might include seemingly small proportions of occupational titles, it would exclude varying proportions of the ethnic groups both within and between years, putting into question any trends found.

2. For purposes of calculating these correlations, weighted averages of the Polish and Ukrainian indexes for 1951, 1961, and 1971 are used as "East European" indexes, to correspond to the index for 1931.

3. Introducing education as a test variable, of course, reduces the subclass frequencies. Accordingly, subgroups in which the average number of persons per occupation was less than 30 were not included in these averages. Because the

smaller groups tend to be most dissimilar with regard to occupational composition, the evidence is loaded in favor of finding lower levels of occupational differentiation.

References

Blishen, Bernard R. 1958 "The construction and use of an occupational class scale." *Canadian Journal of Economics and Political Science* 24: 519-531.

———. 1967 "A socio-economic index for occupations in Canada." *Canadian Review of Sociology and Anthropology* 4: 41-53.

———. 1970 "Social class and opportunity in Canada." *Canadian Review of Sociology and Anthropology* 7: 110-127.

Blishen, Bernard R. and Hugh A. McRoberts. 1976 "A revised socioeconomic index for occupations in Canada." *Canadian Review of Sociology and Anthropology* 13: 71-79.

Boyd, Monica, David L. Featherman, and Judah Matras. 1980 "Status attainment of immigrant and immigrant origin categories in the United States, Canada, and Israel." *Comparative Social Research* 3: 199-228.

Cortese, Charles F., R. Frank Falk, and Jack K. Cohen. 1976 "Further considerations on the methodological analysis of segregation indices." *American Sociological Review* 41: 630-637.

Cuneo, Carl J. and James E. Curtis. 1975 "Social ascription in the educational and occupational status attainment of urban Canadians." *Canadian Review of Sociology and Anthropology* 12: 6-24.

Darroch, A. Gordon. 1979 "Another look at ethnicity, stratification and social mobility in Canada." *Canadian Journal of Sociology* 4(1): 1-25.

DeJocas, Yves and Guy Rocher. 1957 "Inter-governmental occupational mobility in the province of Quebec." *Canadian Journal of Economics and Political Science* 23: 57-68.

Dofny, Jacques and Muriel Garon-Audy. 1969 "Mobilités professionelles au Québec." *Sociologie et Sociétés* 1: 277-301.

Dominion Bureau of Statistics. 1936 *Seventh Census of Canada, 1931.* Vol. VII, *Occupations and Industries.* Ottawa: King's Printer.

———. 1953 *Ninth Census of Canada, 1951.* Vol. IV, *Labour Force: Occupations and Industries.* Ottawa: Queen's Printer.

———. 1964 *1961 Census of Canada.* Vol. III, Part 1 (Bulletin 3.1-15). *Labour Force: Occupations by Sex, Showing Birthplace, Period of Immigration and Ethnic Group: Canada and Provinces.* (Cat. No. 94-515) Ottawa: Queen's Printer.

Duncan, Otis Dudley and Beverly Duncan. 1955 "Residential distribution and occupational stratification." *American Journal of Sociology* 60: 493-503.

Forcese, Dennis. 1975 *The Canadian Class Structure.* Toronto: McGraw-Hill Ryerson.

Gibbs, Jack P. 1965 "Occupational differentiation of Negroes and whites in the United States." *Social Forces* 44: 159-165.

Kalbach, Warren E. 1970 *The Impact of Immigration on Canada's Population.* (Cat. No. 99-546) Ottawa: Queen's Printer.

Lautard, E. Hugh. 1983 "Regional variation in Canada's cultural mosaic." *Canadian Issues* 5: 59-65.

Lieberson, Stanley. 1975 "Rank-sum comparisons between groups." In *Sociological Methodology 1976*, edited by David R. Heise, pp. 276-291. San Francisco: Jossey-Bass.

McRoberts, Hugh A., John Porter, Monica Boyd, John Goyder, Frank E. Jones, and Peter C. Pineo. 1976 "Différences dans la mobilité professionelle des francophones et des anglophones." *Sociologie et Sociétés* 8: 61-79.

Pineo, Peter C. 1976 "Social mobility in Canada: the current picture." *Sociological Focus* 9: 109-123.

Porter, John. 1965 *The Vertical Mosaic.* Toronto: University of Toronto Press.

Reitz, Jeffrey. 1977 "Analysis of changing group inequalities in a changing occupational structure." In *Mathematical Models in Sociology*, Sociological Review Monograph, no. 24, edited by P. Krishnan, pp. 167-191. Staffordshire: University of Keele.

──────. 1980 *The Survival of Ethnic Groups.* Toronto: McGraw-Hill Ryerson.

Richmond, Anthony H., and Warren E. Kalbach. 1980 *Factors in the Adjustment of Immigrants and their Descendents.* (Cat. No. 99-761) Ottawa: Ministry of Supply and Services.

Statistics Canada. 1975 *1971 Census of Canada.* Vol. III, Part 3 (Bulletin 3.3-7). *Occupations: Occupations by Sex, Showing Birthplace, Period of Immigration and Ethnic Group, for Canada and Regions.* (Cat. No. 94-734) Ottawa: Information Canada.

──────. 1984 *1981 Census of Canada.* Vol. 1, *Population: Labour force occupation by cultural characteristics: Canada, provinces.* (Cat. No. 92-918) Ottawa: Ministry of Supply and Services.

ANOTHER LOOK AT ETHNICITY, STRATIFICATION AND SOCIAL MOBILITY IN CANADA

NO

A. Gordon Darroch

INTRODUCTION

Discussions of Canadian stratification and mobility have had as a central theme the relationship between class and ethnicity. Clearly, this is partly so because of the unique bicultural nature of Canada. But the dominant thesis of Canadian stratification studies does not have as its central focus the deprivation of any one group, rather it focuses on a more general relationship between ethnic pluralism and socio-economic stratification. The focus is succinctly expressed in the title of Porter's pioneering work, *The Vertical Mosaic* (1965). Specifically, it has become a first premise in the analysis of Canadian stratification that ethnicity has been a principal component, and indeed a principal cause, of the class structure. "Immigration and ethnic affiliation (or membership in a cultural group) have been important factors in the formation of social classes in Canada" (Porter, 1965:73).

In this paper I reassess the main assumption of the thesis and re-examine the kind of evidence which has generally been cited in its support. A reanalysis of the main cross-sectional evidence in support of the conventional interpretation suggests that it may seriously exaggerate both the generality and the strength of the relationship between ethnic status and socio-economic status. Further, a review of currently available but limited social mobility data for Canada reinforces the argument that there is no sound evidence to sustain the quite common assumption that ethnic affiliations operate as a significant block to educational and occupational mobility in Canada.

WHY THE MOSAIC IS VERTICAL

Perhaps the most commonly reiterated view of stratification in Canada has as its main datum the apparently significant and persistent relationship between ethnic affiliations and occupational status. These data have often been interpreted in terms of the postulate that the persistence of ethnic identity directly restricts social mobility. Porter's pioneering work clearly set the terms of reference for what has become the dominant view. In fact, in addition to the analysis of census data which he provided, only Bernard Blishen's subsequent series of researches on immigration and occupational status has systematically attempted to assess empirical implications of the thesis of *The Vertical Mosaic* (Blishen, 1958; 1967; 1970). Moreover, as to the precise nature of the empirical relationship to be found between ethnicity (or immigrant status) and class, Porter's original text is actually rather tentative. There were at least three ways in which the relationship was thought to hold. First, there was the implication of ethnic affiliations for entrance into positions of power and command. On this, Porter's evidence, like that of the impressive recent work of Clement, is unequivocal. Almost no elite positions are held by members of minority ethnic groups (Clement 1974: 335). I will not consider this relationship further here.

Porter argued in a more general way that over time a reciprocal relationship between ethnicity and class may develop, beginning with the initial "entrance status" of immigrant groups. On the one hand, he suggested that there may be important ideological elements contributing to restricted mobility. "Speculatively, it might be said that the idea of an ethnic mosaic, as opposed to the idea of a melting pot, impedes the processes of social mobility. This difference in ideas is one of the principal distinguishing features of the United States and Canadian society at the level of social psychology as well as that of social structure" (1965:70). Whatever the merits of the original speculation, I suggest that it has not been the ideological implications of the mosaic idea which writing on stratification and mobility in Canada has taken most seriously, but the social structural implications. The latter may consist of a variety of processes which block the mobility opportunities of members of minority ethnic groups varying from the prejudice of "charter group" members to supposed low achievement aspirations of the minority group members (Blishen, 1970). In any case, the assumption that "ethnically blocked mobility" is especially characteristic of Canada, has served as one of the central propositions regarding the form of the Canadian class structure.

The argument that ethnic affiliations limit social mobility was given an explicit historical interpretation by Porter. In this perspective it is the lack of cultural assimilation which perpetuates initial "entrance status" differentials in the economic positions of immigrant groups. Recently, he has expressed the view in the following terms: "Over time this marked differentiation at the period of entry can either harden into a permanent class system, or can change in the direction of absorption, assimilation, integration, and acculturation as a result of which the relationship between ethnicity and class disappears" (1974: 6). The interpretation is persuasive partly because of the tautological element in the synonym between the broad notion of assimilation or integration employed and the disappearance of the relationship between ethnicity and class. By definition, the disappearance of this relationship is integration. However, we cannot take for granted what the relationship between ethnicity and socio-economic status actually is, or whether it is, in any important sense, a resultant of continued ethnic identities themselves.

Clearly, the conventional view implies first, that there is a demonstrably general and quite strong relationship between ethnicity and class. Secondly, the view implies that a reduction of the salience of ethnicity would directly increase social mobility and, in so doing, materially reduce levels of economic and political inequality in Canada (Porter, 1974: 13). It should be recalled that these are not the same processes, since it is entirely possible for mobility rates to alter over time without affecting the structure of inequality, depending on the source of the mobility. . . .

■ MOBILITY STUDIES AND ETHNICITY

. . . One conventional account of the effects of immigrant and ethnic statuses on stratification is couched in terms of limitations on individual social mobility. However, to date we have very few studies of mobility *per se* in Canada and even fewer relate ethnicity to occupational status changes. I review here some of the main findings of studies which attempt to measure the impact of ethnicity on mobility, including two which are unpublished.

Richmond (1964) compared the occupational mobility of postwar immigrants in a national study. He found the clear pattern of advantage of British immigrants over other immigrants which we have come to expect. He also reported that the initial advantage diminished over time and that differences in both career and intergenerational mobility were, in fact, comparatively slight between Great Britain and other European immigrant groups. Certainly the differences were not so great as to lend much support to a notion that language and national identity alone should be counted as crucial bottlenecks to mobility for European immigrant groups.[1]

On the other hand, focusing on French-English differences and not immigrant status, Rocher and DeJocas' study (1957) of intergenerational mobility in Quebec showed that in the 1950s French Canadians suffered more severe handicaps to social mobility than did English-speaking Canadians in the province. Dofny and Garon-Audy (1964) matched the procedures of the previous study and argued that the occupational status gains made by French Canadians between the mid-1950s and the mid-1960s were largely a result of the structural changes in labor force distributions, rather than a result of equalization of opportunity or of increased "exchange" mobility (but see Turrittin, 1974:173-174). To these have been added two recent and more detailed studies of occupational mobility of French and English Canadians. Cuneo and Curtis (1975) examined the differences between Anglophones and Francophones in relatively small samples of the population aged 25-34, living in Toronto and Montreal. They applied the basic Blau-Duncan model of status attainment processes and an extension of it, incorporating additional background variables. They compare the models for four subsamples, Francophone men and women and Anglophone men and women. They emphasize, in general, that their data as well as the American data actually give greater credence to a view that ascriptive factors, especially family background, play a very significant role in status attainment, in contrast to the more commonplace emphasis on the dominance of achievement, through education especially. More important here is the fact that they report measurable differences *between* Francophones and Anglophones especially with respect to the greater effect of family size on education among Anglophones and the greater effect of educational attainment on current occupation for Francophones than for Anglophones.

By far the most detailed and important study of the differences between Anglophones and Francophones in mobility and status attainment processes has recently been reported by McRoberts, Porter, Boyd and their colleagues, as part of a larger national study (1976). They compare the Francophone experience in Quebec with the Anglophone experience in Canada as a whole on the persuasive grounds that these are the principal respective occupational realms of the two populations. They carefully explore the sources of the differences between Anglophones and Francophones in intergenerational occupational achievement and they decompose the processes of status attainment through the application of the basic Blau-Duncan model. Like the previous studies they find that there are measurable differences between Anglophone and Francophone experiences. Applying loglinear analysis to control for differences in the marginals of mobility tables, they conclusively extend the analysis of Dofny and Garon-Audy. The differences in mobility are primarily the result of differential changes in labor force distributions affecting the two populations and the differences between the two groups have diminished in all respects. Moreover, their cohort analysis provides strong evidence of convergence in mobility patterns between the two groups especially for the youngest members of the labor force. With respect to processes of status attainment, the striking features are the similarities in form for the two linguistic groups (the relative size of the coefficients in the models are identical for each) at the same time that there are significant differences in the relative impact of specific variables, such as family size and father's education, and they are such as to disadvantage Francophones in comparison to Anglophones (1976:75). In sum, the authors find what they consider to be surprising evidence of convergence in the experiences of Anglophones and Francophones and thus, evidence of the diminishing salience of linguistic stratification (1976:78).

A review of studies serves to provide some perspective on the evolution of our knowledge regarding ethnic-linguistic differences in social mobility. In the light of these most recent specifications of the mobility process, it is well to recall that conventional interpretations of Canadian stratification have broadly implied: (1) more obvious differentials in mobility experiences between French- and English-speaking populations than those reported, (2) perhaps more persistent differentials and, (3) differentials which were thought to hinge at least as much on differences in aspirations and values as on differences in opportunity structures. It is again of contextual interest that in the subsample comparisons which Cuneo and Curtis undertook, the gender differences in status attainment models were often as striking, and occasionally more striking, than the differences between Anglophones and Francophones. For example, the direct effects of education on first and current jobs were much stronger for men than for women in both linguistic groups (1975:21, also see Figures 2 and 3), although the authors are sensitive to the difficulties of drawing strict comparisons of this sort from their data (1975: footnote 8:10-11).

Finally, the complexities of mobility processes revealed in recent work should remind us that the differences between Francophone and Anglophone experiences cannot be generalized to the way ethnic affiliations or immigrant status enter the mobility process. At the time of writing only two studies are known to me which assess the direct and indirect effects of ethnic origins and immigrant status on occupational attainment and income in competition with other variables, such as social origins and education. They are instructive, although both refer only to selective Ontario populations and neither are published. Unfortunately, the authors have indicated that publication of their studies is not forthcoming in the foreseeable future. I take advantage of the opportunity to report some important results here, though I take no credit for the research.[2]

Goldlust and Richmond (1973) provide mobility data on "ethno-linguistic" groups of immigrants for metropolitan Toronto. They show that there are, as expected, substantial differences among the immigrant groups in their average occupational statuses in their *former* countries, among their statuses after arrival and at two subsequent points in their occupational histories. But the pattern of occupational differences is also found to be a *direct* reflection of the occupational differences of their fathers' statuses, i.e., of their differences in socio-economic origins. For six of the eight "ethno-linguistic" groups there was a difference of *less than* three points on the Blishen occupational scale between the mean of the fathers' scores and the mean of the respondents' current occupational scores. Ethnic group differences correspond closely with the average differences in social class origins of the group members which were a result of selective immigration processes.

Taking the analysis a step toward the separation of effects, Goldlust and Richmond computed the contributions of several variables to *income*, including the effects of ethnicity which entered a regression analysis as a set of dummy variables. At the most, when the ethnic variables enter the regression first, they accounted for 7 percent of the variance in incomes among all respondents; the total variance in income explained was 35 percent, with education, current occupational status and father's occupational status accounting for almost all of the remainder. From the table given by the authors it appears that, when ethnicity is made to compete with the other variables in the regression, education, current occupation and father's occupation explain respectively 18 percent, 10 percent and 5 percent of the total variance, while the impact of ethnicity is entirely indirect, acting through these variables. In statistical terms, ethnicity appears to have *no* unique effects.[3]

A second unpublished work is a very extensive study by Ornstein (1974) based on a reanalysis of Porter and Blishen's data for Ontario high school students and their parents. One part of the study is a detailed analysis of the impact of ethnicity on occupational mobility undertaken by means of regression and analysis of variance techniques. Employing nine ethnic groups in the analysis, Ornstein first shows that ethnicity can account for a maximum of only 3.3 percent of the difference in occupational ranks (Blishen scores) of first jobs of this sample of the Ontario population and can account for 5.2 percent of the respondents' current job status differences. Ethnicity did account for slightly over 10 percent of the variation in education attainment of the sample.

The author notes that the *pattern* of benefits in occupational ranks accruing to ethnic group affiliation is much as we expect—the Scots and English benefit most, the West Europeans and East Europeans follow in order and the recently immigrated Italian population is at the bottom. But again, I emphasize, a distinct pattern of advantage must not be confused with the significance of the effect of ethnicity on the actual occupational attainment of individuals.[4] Ornstein shows that the average differences among the ethnic groups in occupational attainment are not, in fact, very great. Moreover, the differences *within* the ethnic groups in occupational status are very much greater than the differences between them. The implications of this important finding have never been seriously considered in the Canadian context and warrant further comment.

If variations within ethnic groups in individual mobility experience are generally large, and there are good *prima facie* reasons to think they might be, then it is quite conceivable that for some members of a given ethnic population there exist serious "mobility traps," while for other members ethnic identity may be of no consequence to mobility whatsoever. Still others may be able to translate their heritage into distinct occupational opportunities. Moreover, variations *within* ethnic groups in status achievement require explanations in terms of non-ethnic variables, that is, in terms of any number of factors which cannot themselves be broadly subsumed under the label ethnic identity or affiliation.

Consistent with my earlier discussion it should be noted that Ornstein is able to show that the results from his sample of Ontario residents are strikingly similar to the results found in examining the impact of ethnicity on mobility in an American national sample (Duncan and Duncan, 1968). It may also be added that in a longitudinal study of large metropolitan areas in the United States, for the decade 1957-1967, Featherman (1971) found only indirect effects of differences in "religio-ethnic" background (that is, acting through other variables) on occupational achievements. There was some significant, though not large, direct effect of the religio-ethnic variables on educational attainment, a finding also duplicated by Ornstein for Ontario. The impact of the ethnic mosaic again does not appear as unique to Canada as we have often thought it to be.

Despite the fact that these studies refer to limited segments of the Canadian population, the evidence they provide regarding the influence of ethnicity in the process of individual occupational mobility reinforces the conclusions derived from the re-examination of conventional cross-sectional data given above. Both kinds of evidence provide sufficient cause to be very skeptical of a thesis which argues that sustained attachments to ethnic communities force some sort of trade-off, in which opportunities for upward mobility must be foregone as a price of maintaining "primordial" sentiments (Porter, 1974), or, for that matter, as a consequence of restricted occupational aspirations or achievement motives.[5]

■ THE MOSAIC REVISITED

One basic emphasis regarding the effects of ethnicity on the Canadian class structure has centred on the notion that a release from ethnic identities (assimilation) will result in enhanced mobility opportunities and, subsequently, in relative status achievements. The thesis may be seen as a version of the theory of "modernization" which assumes that men and resources are increasingly freed from ascriptive ties in order to compete for achievement in the marketplaces of industrial or post-industrial society. In this respect, it is a functional theory of stratification.

With respect to ethnic community affiliations, at least, the argument no longer seems very convincing (but on ascriptive characteristics in general, see Cuneo and Curtis, 1975). Diminishing ethnic group attachments would have to affect one or more of the three conditions determining mobility rates, that is, to alter the opportunity structure, especially the occupational structure, or to affect differential rates of fertility between upper and lower status positions or to alter the rates of pure or exchange mobility between upper and lower strata. I have argued that recurrent emphasis has been given to a blocked mobility thesis in which ethnic assimilation is expected to increase exchange mobility, with some of those who occupy more privileged positions being replaced, or having their sons and daughters replaced, by those whose ethnic affiliations previously hampered their achievements. In any case, any argument about the effects of ethnic pluralism on stratification and mobility now requires this degree of specification.

It is generally known that the pure exchange portion of measured mobility rates for standard inflow-outflow tables is relatively limited in comparison to the mobility accounted for by structural changes in occupational distributions (see Turrittin, 1974: Table II for relevant Canadian data). Moreover, revisions of our view of the possible implications of ethnic affiliations for social mobility are necessitated by the most recent analyses of mobility opportunities in Canada and the United States. In attempting to overcome acknowledged limitations of standard mobility analyses by applying multivariate, contingency table analysis, Hauser and his associates have concluded forcefully that systematic variations in the relative intergenerational mobility chances of American men with different social origins are *entirely* accounted for by changes in occupational structure over time (1975a; 1975b). As the authors state, "Despite the many social changes in the United States in the last two decades, it is a more favorable occupational structure, *and only that*, which has sustained or improved the mobility opportunities of American men" (Hauser et al., 1975b:597: emphasis added).

McRoberts, Porter, Boyd et al. adopted the same methodology in their analysis of the differences in mobility between Francophones in Quebec and Anglophones in Canada as a whole. They conclude, no less forcefully, "La comparaison des matrices croisant le statut socio-économique du père avec le statut actuel du fils en contrôlant les marginales n'a révélé aucune différence significative dans l'association père-fils entre les deux groupes. Ce fut également le cas lorsque nous avons étudié les différences entre les deux groupes, tant dans le cas de ceux qui étaient mobiles que dans celui des non-mobiles (qui se trouvent sur la diagonale principale)" (1976:77).

Thus, structural changes in Canada will surely be found to be the key to alterations in the relative mobility opportunities of members of various ethnic and immigrant populations. Further, given the review of evidence above showing that measures of the simple association between ethnic affiliation and socio-economic status are generally quite moderate, we may expect to find that in analyses of the process of status attainment, ethnic affiliations will play the role of one ascriptive factor among many variables and one which has only a slight effect on occupational achievement and income in Canada.

■ CONCLUSION

The vertical mosaic thesis has served as a provocative hypothesis. However, I have argued that in Canada as a whole it is an exaggeration of any data available to date to suggest that ethnic affiliations can be counted as a primary factor sustaining structures of class or status. Recent studies separately have tended to moderate an earlier, stronger emphasis on the centrality of ethnicity in this respect. What is clear is that there has been a quite stable pattern of occupational status positions among large ethnic and immigrant populations, although there is strong evidence that occupational differences have systematically declined with time. The pattern has been revealed in several, detailed examinations of the occupational distributions of ethnic and immigration groups (Porter, 1965; Blishen, 1958; 1967; 1970) and less often, but no less convincingly, in terms of income and educational distributions (Royal Commission on Bilingualism and Biculturalism, 1969: vol. IV, 40-41; Kalbach and McVey, 1971:209). It is clearly important to recognize the implications of these patterns, for example, in terms of the ethnic bias in the recruitment and structure of elites in this country or, perhaps, in terms of ideology (Porter, 1965; Clement, 1974). But the tendency to conflate the existence of these patterns with an assessment of the degree to which ethnicity is a fundamental source of national structures of inequality has been unwarranted.

It bears noting that one of the most important results of the tendency to overestimate the magnitude of ethnic group differences and to focus on the putative central role of ethnicity in social mobility has been to divert attention from other, more consequential sources of the maintenance of the class structure in Canada. Drawing on a broad familiarity with Canadian social history, S.D. Clark made the argument clearly.

> If one were to quarrel with the Porter analysis of society as it was, it would be only on the score that by seeking to relate ethnic affiliation to the hierarchical structure he tended to obscure the underlying forces producing this hierarchical structure. Members of the British charter group were admittedly very much on top, but they were on the very bottom as well, occupying marginal farm lands in eastern Nova Scotia, northeastern New Brunswick, and eastern and central Ontario, or engaged in subsistence fishing industry in Newfoundland. The division of the country into French and English has led to viewing Canadian society too much from an ethnic standpoint. (1975:28)

The reassessment of evidence presented in this paper, I hope, adds weight to this conclusion for the present as for the past.

Notes

1. Most specifically, Richmond employed samples *matched* in terms of social class, background, education, length of residence and marital status to compare career mobility of British immigrants and other European immigrants. He concluded that British immigrants in Canada did have some advantage over non-British immigrants, when other things were equal, but that this advantage was a comparatively small one.

2. I thank the authors of these studies for generously permitting me to report some of their findings in the absence of full publication of their work. Goldlust and Richmond have briefly referred to their findings in one recent paper (1974:209).

3. The authors do not assess direct and indirect effects in the analysis, but they do report a separate analysis of interaction effects (AID) in which father's occupation is not entered as an independent variable. In this analysis ethnicity accounts again for a maximum of 7 percent of the total variance of income.

4. Ornstein summarizes his separate analyses in a regression with many variables, including ethnicity. Computing the variance explained in occupational

status so as to *maximize* the effects of ethnicity and social class background, he finds that the 5.2 percent contributed by ethnicity is only greater than the predictive power of the respondents' first job (3.8 percent). By comparison educational achievement contributed 32.9 percent and father's occupation, 11.2 percent, accounting for a total of 53.1 percent of the variance in occupational status. In an analysis of the determinants of household income, including first and subsequent occupations as independent variables, ethnicity and father's occupation were found to have *no* significant predictive power—a conclusion similar to that of Goldlust and Richmond cited above.

5.   Providing one conceivable reason for the differences in occupational status among immigrant groups, Blishen (1970) suggests that the differences in occupational status of the groups on entering Canada may be translated into persistent differentials because, "aspirations are relative to distance of a given position from the one presently occupied" (p. 121). He is here citing Breton and Roseborough's study (1968) in which the employees of one large corporation were surveyed to consider the validity of a reference group hypothesis for explaining differential mobility aspirations and, ultimately, achievements. The authors provide evidence that French Canadian employees were *satisfied* with lower level achievements. Their data do not in fact show that differences in *expressed satisfaction* between French- and English-speaking employees were related to the differences in reference group. I find the authors somewhat ambiguous on this point. They note, however, that their data do not allow them, in the end, to choose between an interpretation of ethnic differences in terms of differential opportunities or in terms of the postulated reference group effects on aspirations. In fact, the French Canadian employees may have tailored their sense of satisfaction—or their expressions of it—to felt circumstances of limited occupational mobility.

References

Blishen, Bernard R. 1958 "The construction and use of an occupational class scale." *Canadian Journal of Economics and Political Science* 24:519-531.

———. 1967 "A socio-economic index of occupations in Canada." *Canadian Review of Sociology and Anthropology* 4:41-53.

———. 1970 "Social class and opportunity in Canada." *Canadian Review of Sociology and Anthropology* 7:110-127.

Breton, Raymond and Howard E. Roseborough. 1968 "Ethnic differences in status." In *Canadian Society*, edited by B.R. Blishen et al., pp. 683-701. Toronto: Macmillan.

Clark, S.D. 1975 "The post Second World War Canadian society." *Canadian Review of Sociology and Anthropology* 12:25-32.

Clement, Wallace. 1974 *The Canadian Corporate Elite: An Analysis of Economic Power.* Ottawa: McClelland & Stewart.

Cuneo, Carl J. and James E. Curtis. 1975 "Social ascription in the educational and occupational status attainment of urban Canadians." *Canadian Review of Sociology and Anthropology* 12:6-24.

DeJocas, Yves and Guy Rocher. 1957 "Inter-generational occupational mobility in the province of Quebec." *Canadian Journal of Economics and Political Science* 23:58-66.

Dofny, Jacques and Muriel Garon-Audy. 1969 "Mobilités professionnelles au Quebec." *Sociologie et Sociétés* 1:277-301.

Duncan B., and O.D. Duncan. 1968 "Minorities and the process of stratification." *American Sociological Review* 33:356-364.

Featherman, David L. 1971 "The socio-economic achievement of white religio-ethnic subgroups: social and psychological explanations." *American Sociological Review* 36:207-222.

Goldlust, John and Anthony H. Richmond. 1973 *A Multivariate Analysis of the Economic Adaptation of Immigrants in Toronto*. Unpublished ms.

Hauser, Robert M., John N. Koffel, Harry P. Travis and Peter J. Dickinson. 1975a "Temporal change in occupational mobility: evidence for men in the United States." *American Sociological Review* 40:279-297.

_____. 1975b "Structural changes in occupational mobility among men in the United States." *American Sociological Review* 40:585-598.

McRoberts, Hugh A., John Porter, Monica Boyd, John Goyder, Frank E. Jones, and Peter C. Pineo. 1976 "Différences dans la mobilité professionnelle des francophones et des anglophones." *Sociologie et Sociétés* 8:61-79.

McVey, Wayne W., and Warren E. Kalbach. 1971 *The Demographic Basis of Canadian Society*. Toronto: McGraw-Hill.

Ornstein, Michael D. 1974 *Occupational Mobility in Ontario*. Unpublished ms.

Pineo, Peter. 1976 "Social mobility in Canada: the current picture." *Sociological Focus* 9:109-123.

Porter, John. 1965 *The Vertical Mosaic*. Toronto: University of Toronto Press.

_____. 1974 "Canada: dilemmas and contradictions of a multi-ethnic society." In *Sociology Canada: Readings*, edited by C. Beattie and S. Crysdale, pp. 3-15. Toronto: Butterworths.

Richmond, Anthony H. 1964 "The social mobility of immigrants in Canada." *Population Studies* 18:53-69.

_____. 1967 *Post-War Immigrants in Canada*. Toronto: University of Toronto Press.

Royal Commission on Bilingualism and Biculturalism. 1967 *The Cultural Contribution of the Other Ethnic Groups: Book IV*. Ottawa: Queen's Printer.

Turrittin, Anton H. 1974 "Social mobility in Canada: a comparison of three provincial studies and some methodological questions." *Canadian Review of Sociology and Anthropology* 11:163-186.

■ POSTSCRIPT

Lautard and Loree argue that at the national level ethnic differences remain a powerful indicator of the degree of assimilation among ethnic groups. They also indicate, via reference to an earlier study, that ethnic differences are stronger at the regional level. These differences remain even when the factors of education and gender are considered. Even though ethnicity is less important for women than men, it is still a powerful predictor of ethnic women's social standing.

Darroch, on the other hand, says that the importance of ethnic differences is declining, and that other factors, such as the changes in the occupational structure over time, are a more powerful predictor of social standing. He observes that, while some groups are overrepresented among the elite, they also have membership at the bottom. Within each ethnic group, there are mobility traps, located within the occupational structure, that limit upward mobility.

Neither Lautard and Loree nor Darroch directly assesses the impact of racism. Given that Lautard and Loree were able to confirm that ethnic status is an important predictor of status, a more specific analysis of the visible minority—racism—factor would have been helpful. The opportunity, however, has been missed in both studies.

This debate also has implications for relations between French and English Canadians. It has long been argued that French Canadians are at a disadvantage when it comes to ascending the Canadian social structure. It has even been argued that French Canadians are at a disadvantage in the National Hockey League (Lavoie et al., 1987). The feeling that they are at a disadvantage contributes to the demands of people in Quebec for greater control—sovereignty—over their affairs.

■ QUESTIONS

1. Which argument is most convincing? How have your preconceptions of the issues affected your decision?
2. Is Lautard and Loree's analysis of the importance of gender sufficient to satisfy the need for a thorough assessment of gender issues?
3. Do you believe that your own ethnic status is a benefit or a barrier to your opportunities for success?
4. How prevalent is racism in Canada?

■ FURTHER READING

In Support of Lautard and Loree

Lavoie, Marc, Giles Grenier, and Serge Coulombe. "Discrimination and Performance Differentials in the National Hockey League." *Canadian Public Policy* 12, no. 4 (1987): 407-422.

Porter, John. *The Vertical Mosaic.* Toronto: University of Toronto Press, 1965.

In Support of Darroch

Brym, R.J. "Anglo-Canadian Sociology." *Current Sociology* 34 (Spring 1986): 1-152.

Denis, A.B. "Adaptation to Multiple Subordination: Women in the Vertical Mosaic." *Canadian Ethnic Studies* 18 (1986): 16-74.

Wilson, William J. *The Declining Significance of Race.* Chicago: University of Chicago Press, 1979.

Other Voices

Calliste, Agnes. "Race, Class, Gender: Bonds and Barriers." *Socialist Studies* 5 (1989): 142-172.

Frideres, J.S. *Native Peoples in Canada.* 3rd ed. Scarborough: Prentice-Hall Canada, 1988.

Heap, James, ed. *Everybody's Canada: The Vertical Mosaic Revisited and Reexamined.* Toronto: Burns and MacEachern, 1974.

IS AFFIRMATIVE

ACTION REVERSE

DISCRIMINATION?

YES **Walter Block and Michael A. Walker,** "The Plight of the Minority," in W.E. Block and M.A. Walker, eds., *Discrimination, Affirmative Action and Equal Opportunity*, pp. 5-11

NO **Mona Kornberg,** "Employment Equity: The Quiet Revolution?" *Canadian Woman Studies* 6, no. 4 (1985): 17-19

In Debates Two and Three, the types and nature of inequality in Canada were documented. Debate Four focuses on how to deal with inequality. There is increasing pressure in Canada to adopt affirmative action policies — policies that require or encourage employers to hire racial or ethnic minorities or women. Advocates of affirmative action justify it on the grounds that it is an attempt to remedy the effects of long-term, systematic discrimination against the target groups. Opponents denounce it as reverse discrimination.

The mechanisms to deal with inequality have taken many forms over the years. In the nineteenth century, attempts to eliminate racial inequality centred on eliminating slavery. Slavery in Canada was abolished in a two-stage process by the British Parliament in the early 1800s. The first stage was a ban on the purchase or sale of slaves throughout the British Empire. The second stage was a ban on ownership of slaves.

In the United States, the abolition of slavery took a violent path. While it is arguable that the Civil War was not fought just to end slavery, that other economic and political issues caused the war, it is nonetheless true that the slave issue was a key factor used by both sides to justify the war. It is also worth noting that the states of Missouri, Kentucky, West Virginia, Maryland, and Delaware entered the war on the side of the North even though slavery was not abolished in these states until after the Civil War.

But elimination of slavery did not bring an end to racial inequality. The slave was free, but freedom did not guarantee a home or a job. The

Civil War decimated the economy of the South, and the Northern economy was unable to absorb all of the freed slaves. This left many former slaves homeless, unemployed, and, as Tannenbaum (1946) said, without moral standing in the community. A society that has morally, socially, and legally defined some people as slaves does not grant equality just because slavery has been abolished. The experience of freed slaves and their descendants in North America is sufficient proof that social, political, and economic equality does not come with the granting of legal equality. The civil rights movement in both Canada and the United States resulted from the failure of the abolition of slavery to bring about these other forms of equality.

Similarly, women's struggles to achieve equality have been marked by many ups and downs. The suffrage movement, the efforts by women like Emily Murphy to have Canadian women declared persons, and various provincial and federal statutes prohibiting discrimination on the basis of sex have been some of the high points. But despite these successes, social and economic equality for women has not been achieved. Most Canadian women still work in occupations that can be classified as female ghettos, and earn less than men (Parliament, 1990).

It is the failure of past efforts to prohibit racial, ethnic, and gender discrimination that has led to the demand for affirmative action. The articles presented here offer clearly contrasting viewpoints on what can or cannot be done to solve the equality problem. The issues are complex. Readers are encouraged to examine the list of Further Reading to become better acquainted with the issues. In arguing the "Yes" side of the debate, Block and Walker challenge many of the assumptions of affirmative action, including the assumption that discrimination in inherently wrong. In arguing the "No" side of the debate, Kornberg argues that resistance to affirmative action must be met with a two-pronged attack that deals with legislative action as well as the resistance of anti-affirmative action forces.

References

Parliament, Jo-Anne (1990) "Women Employed Outside the Home," in *Canadian Social Trends*, edited by Craig McKie and Keith Thompson (Toronto: Thompson Educational Publishing).

Tannenbaum, Frank (1946) *Slave and Citizen: The Negro in the Americas* (New York: Vintage Books).

THE PLIGHT OF THE MINORITY

Walter Block and Michael A. Walker

Nothing abuses a person's sense of natural justice more than unequal treatment of equals. In recent times, the existence of discrimination has increasingly concerned citizens and lawmakers. This concern has been expressed in the drive for "equal pay for equal work" legislation, in the demand for affirmative action programs, and by the feminist movement.

Legislators have responded by establishing civil rights tribunals, issuing equal pay for equal work directives, and by engaging in a widespread program of affirmative action. In some cases, the latter has involved the establishment of quotas to ensure that people of different sexes, races, and ethnic backgrounds are proportionately represented in employment and educational situations.

■ EVIDENCE ON DISCRIMINATION

The issues associated with discrimination and the legislative attempts to deal with it are highly emotional and, as a consequence, it is often difficult to discuss the subject dispassionately. However, there is mounting evidence, discussed elsewhere in this book, that the attempts to eradicate discrimination are producing unforeseen negative consequences. In some instances, the problems were inherently difficult to anticipate. In the vast majority of cases, however, they were perfectly predictable. The reason they were not foreseen is that analytical perspective was often lost in the haste to "right the wrongs" seemingly committed in the past.

This introduction will provide an analytical perspective on discrimination and the programs proposed to end it. As well, it serves as an overview of the results presented in the rest of the book.

■ WHAT'S WRONG WITH DISCRIMINATION?

What Is Discrimination?

In the 1980s the term "discrimination" has acquired an unambiguously negative meaning. It conjures up the image of racial and/or sexual prejudice. Strictly speaking, however, the term is neutral in application. Discriminatory behaviour may have consequences which are benign, malevolent, or innocuous.

While it may appear pedantic to draw fine distinctions of this sort, it is of the utmost importance to do so. First of all, it must be recognized that discrimination is a natural part of everyday behaviour. We all like some foods and dislike others; most are attracted to beauty and repelled by ugliness; everyone finds interaction with some people more or less comfortable. The act of preferring one thing, one person, or one situation over another is an act of discrimination against all the non-preferred things, person, or situations.

Discrimination Defines Individuality
Secondly, these acts of discrimination or preference are of more than superficial interest, since in a fundamental way, they define the limits of individuality. While we may speculate about "what makes some people tick," in the final analysis we assess people as individuals by the choices they make, or fail to make, and the actions which follow from those choices. Moreover, individuality and the right of human beings to make choices is a fundamental characteristic of free societies and, presumably, ought to be preserved to the greatest extent possible.

So, to answer the question posed at the outset, discrimination is nothing more than the expression of a preference. And in that neutral sense, without assessing the consequences of the behaviour, the right to discriminate is a desirable feature of free societies.

Majorities vs. Minorities
Individual acts of preference may sometimes result in a majority preference which by its existence excludes or inconveniences some minority. For example, the majority of people are right-handed and, hence, most languages are written from left to right—a convention which, while convenient for right-handers, means ink stained hands or cramped styles for those who are left-handed. Also school children are often observed to form a clique at the expense of some outcast children who differ in some physical or behavioural way from the rest of the group.

By the same token, the expression of preferences by a minority group may sometimes exclude the majority. Many segregated neighbourhoods, clubs, and societies are instances where a group of people conspire to express their individuality by blatantly rejecting the majority. This is particularly true of religious societies and associations which also typically have a strict internal hierarchy so as to discriminate new from long-standing members. Examples include the Masons, the Knights of Columbus, Hell's Angels, the Shriners, Rotarians, Black Panthers.

Discriminatory Enactments
Sometimes the majority may cause laws to be passed which institutionalize discrimination. Such enactments need not be limited to, or even purposefully aimed at, any particular racial, sexual, or ethnic categories. When

the majority votes for a military draft, for example, minorities who are opposed—specific racial, sexual, or ethnic characteristics notwithstanding—are forced to go along. Pacifists are perhaps singled out in this case, but the law is neutral with regard to other characteristics.

Other examples of majority rules suppressing minority interests abound. Most central Canadians support tariff and trade barriers which protect inefficient industrial jobs in Ontario and Quebec; but people in the less well-populated Atlantic and Prairie provinces are forced to purchase high-cost manufactured goods, and suffer as a result. A majority of citizens in North America have voted for building codes; but this interferes with the rights of owners to do with their property as they please (even if they adhere to the proscriptions against nuisance).

Majority Discrimination

The untoward aspects of discrimination that people are familiar with—and which give discrimination such a bad name—are usually of this majority rule variety.

There is no doubt that the majority can use the system of laws to exploit and disadvantage minorities. This is—or at least certainly has been—a problem. It was the law which restricted black minorities to separate and vastly inferior restroom facilities in the southern U.S. from the post Civil War period until midway in the twentieth century. Legislation prohibited minorities who wanted to engage in "intermarriage"—and these laws continued until about the same period. European Jews too have had a long history of being legally restricted from entering certain professions and even industries.

Does this mean that minorities are doomed to their fate at the hands of the majority? It does indeed, if the majority is able to harness the power of the political process in its quest to subjugate the minority. Given this disadvantage, the minority is in a singularly unenviable position—in jobs, in schools, in restaurants, and indeed, with regard to almost every aspect of existence that makes life worth living. For this reason, all societies which have some form of majority rule must be constantly vigilant to ensure that the inherent power of the majority is not used legislatively to limit the freedom of minorities.

Minorities Doomed?

But what about activities outside the sphere of legislation? A majority which is predisposed to discriminate will surely do so whether discriminatory treatment is codified in laws or not. Thus, whether inside the system of laws or outside it, minorities seem doomed to shabby treatment at the hands of the majority.

There is, however, a great difference between the forms of discrimination possible when the laws of the land conspire against minorities and when they do not. The difference is the coercive power of the state. If the law says blacks must ride in the back of the bus, or that minority group members may not intermarry, or that Jews must live in certain areas, the state has the power to ensure that these minorities comply.

On the other hand, discriminatory behaviour not enshrined in law cannot be physically enforced since the use of compulsion by private citizens is not normally condoned. This is not to say that individuals have not used or do not continue to use force against minorities—indeed there are daily instances of it. However, anti-racial or other minority violence not condoned by law is regarded as criminal behaviour.

Criminal activity aside, how much discrimination can or will exist if there is no law against such behaviour and no law reinforcing it? Basically, this will depend on how strongly people feel—that is, how strong are their preferences for discrimination.

■ THE ECONOMIC PERSPECTIVE

Discrimination—A Form of Choice
Except in rare instances, people's preferences are not absolute. Rather, they are malleable over a fairly wide range. Under different circumstances, different choices would be made. One of the circumstances that has a substantial effect on choices is the cost or benefit of making that choice. In general terms, the higher the cost (the lower the benefit), the less likely the choice will be made.

Individuals who prefer imported beer and would like to discriminate against the domestic variety may cease to do so when the price differential between the two products rises high enough. A rich aunt, whose maladroit social behaviour makes her unacceptable as a bridge partner, may be accepted by some nieces and nephews if the cost of excluding her were reciprocal exclusion from her will. Similarly, those inclined to discriminate among individuals according to race, sex, or colour may cease to do so if the cost is high. Conversely, if the cost is low or non-existent, then even people with only the slightest tendency to do so will be inclined to discriminate.

As we shall see below, sexual, racial, or ethnic discriminators must pay for their preference just like those who discriminate against domestic beer. Discrimination has a price. It will be demonstrated that the existence of this price tends to limit the amount of discrimination and to reduce the financial and other costs that minority groups would otherwise suffer.

In the Market, Discrimination Costs Money
How, and in what way, must discriminatory practice be paid for? Suppose employers were smitten with a sudden prejudice against redheads and either lowered their salaries or refused to hire them. The initial effect would be greater unemployment and lower wages for this newly created down-trodden group and, potentially, lower profits for the employers. Having rejected redheads as employees, the employer would have to hire more brunettes, blonds, and black-haired employees to take their place. In at

least some instances—perhaps many—the replacements would be less effective in their jobs than the redheads, with the consequence that employer profits would be reduced.

Since there is no reason to believe that the productivity of people with red hair is different from that of other folk, forces would soon be brought to bear which would move the situation for redheads back toward the one that prevailed before the sudden onset of discrimination. For with a pool of under-employed and underpaid redheads, there would be great profits to be made by employing them! Colourblind employers (those who have no preference for or against people with any particular hair colour) would begin to hire redheads, and so would employers for whom the foregone profits represent too high a cost for them to indulge their preference for discrimination.

These employers will not necessarily be motivated by benevolence. If all employees originally earned $400 per week and redhead wages were reduced to $300 by the onset of discrimination, the colourblind firm will not offer the redhead $400. Why should it? All it need do is offer $305 or any small increment above the lower salary to which the redhaired person has been reduced. The unfortunate redhead will have little choice but to accept, and the employer can garner huge benefits. (If it is worthwhile to hire the redhead at $400, it will be immensely profitable to employ an equally productive redheaded worker at $305.)

The Ceaseless Quest for Profits

In their turn, other employers will also seek to hire the low-paid redheaded employees. True, they will have to offer more than the prevailing $305. Their sense of propriety may be offended by offering high wages to people they see as despicable redheads. They will, nevertheless, be comforted by the thought that it is better for them to earn extra revenues from employing additional redheads (even at the unconscionably high wages of $310, for example) than to leave them to the tender mercies of their current employer, even if the latter is earning a larger profit by employing them for $305. (It is better, in other words, for "me" to take $90 than for "you" to receive $95 in pure profit.)

Such thoughts will strike all other potential and actual employers. It will set up a process of raiding and counter-raiding, which will bid up redhead wages at each step. Where will it end? There is only one ultimate destination: the $400 earned by other equally productive employees. Of course the wage and employment situation may not reach this theoretical configuration, but it will always tend toward it. Unwittingly, profit seekers will gradually reduce all gaps between the wages of redheads and others of equal profitability. (This is achieved, as we have seen, by "exploiting" these gaps; by hiring and offering higher wages to the undervalued redhead.) There is, therefore, a tendency for the self-interested action of profit seekers to ensure that persons who are subject to discrimination will not suffer financially from this affliction.

Prejudice Not Profitable

In the quest for profits, those employers who indulge their hair colour preferences will obviously pay for this choice. The price of their prejudice is the profit they must forego. Some employers may be willing to pay this price, and their discriminatory behaviour will thus not be eliminated. However, the existence of other employers more sensitive to the cost of discriminating means that redheads will not have to suffer the degree of unemployment or low wages that would otherwise be the consequence. The key to the redheads' escape from the full force of prejudice is their ability to offer other employers a profit possibility in the form of lower wages.

The Dollar Vote or the Political Vote?

Coercive discrimination imposed by law provides no such escape route. The majority doesn't have to bear the costs of its actions, as it would in the private sector. And this naturally short circuits the normal financial incentive escape path for the minority.

From the point of view of a disadvantaged minority, the cherished majority rule feature of democracy becomes a tyranny, making the law conspire against that minority. The marketplace, on the other hand, at least provides the minority group member with the possibility that the situation will improve or not worsen so radically in the first place. In the case of discriminatory laws, the minority must first seek to *become* the majority, or at least to convince the majority to vote appropriately. In the case of economic undertakings, only one or a few persons need to be convinced, and their own selfish financial interest gives them incentive to help the minority. . . .

EMPLOYMENT EQUITY: THE QUIET REVOLUTION?

NO

Mona Kornberg

The change in the sex composition of the workforce—in less than two decades the proportion of women in the workforce rose to 41%—has been referred to as "The Quiet Revolution."[1] The dramatic increase in women's workforce participation has been attributed to a variety of factors, including increased education, an increase in divorces, longer life expectancy, fewer years spent in child-bearing and rearing, and a rising standard of living necessitating two incomes per family.

But all this has meant up to now is that an increasing number of women are being segregated into low-paying, low-status, dead-end jobs. Attention is just beginning to focus on the prevalence and persistence of discriminatory practices in the workplace. Oblivious to this, Statistics Canada describes the phenomenon as "the revolution that has been sweeping the Canadian workplace:"[2]

- For the first time in the nation's history, more than one-half of women aged 15 and over were in the labour force in 1981, either in a job or actively seeking one.

- The participation of women in the labour force increased at a rate two and one-half times that for men, or 60 percent over 10 years to about 4.5 million.

- Although participation rates were highest for women in their early twenties (over 77% in 1981)—the largest increase of women workers came from married women.

Despite the increase in numbers, 77% of women are concentrated in only 5 major job categories: those five are the low-pay, low-status, dead-end jobs characteristic of clerical, sales and service occupations. To take one instance, the percentage of women in "pink-collar" jobs has increased from 71 to 74% over the last ten years with only some slight increases in managerial and non-traditional jobs. In addition, women constitute about 72% of all part-time workers (although one in four would prefer to be full-time) and their jobs are more vulnerable to obsolescence because of technological change. Equally dismal figures confirm that women continue to earn less than men—as of 1980—at every educational level. "In 1980 a woman with a university degree earned slightly more than half what a man with similar education earned, and about the same as a man with less than a grade 10 education. Similarly, a woman with less than grade 10 education earned half as much as a man with the same amount of education" (Statistics Canada).

As the numbers of women in the workforce swell, as better educated women find themselves earning less than their equally educated male counterparts, the quiet revolution is beginning to find its voice. Receiving impetus from the American Civil Rights movement of the 60s, efforts to remedy workplace discrimination have relied on two interrelated strategies for change: one has been directed toward passing anti-discrimination legislation, and the other toward promoting affirmative action programs.

■ A BRIEF SUMMARY OF A DECADE OF AFFIRMATIVE ACTION IN CANADA

Although affirmative action measures, now known as *employment equity* measures, aim to redress the workplace inequities of four target groups— the disabled, native people, visible minorities, and women—this paper will address itself to the situation of the last, and largest, group: women.

Starting with the Equal Employment Opportunity Program for women in the Federal Public Service in the 1970s, we have had over ten years to assess the accomplishments of voluntary affirmative action programs in Canada. With few exceptions, what does stand out, in the words of one authority, "is that measurable and observable results after 10 years must be classed as disappointing."[3] Part of the problem has been the difficulty of agreeing upon a definition of what constitutes an affirmative action program, and then applying that definition to measure progress. Accordingly, there has been tremendous variation in how affirmative action is applied and measured.

The experience of federal and provincial bodies points to some of the confusion and difficulties. In its 1982 employer survey the Ontario Women's Directorate found that out of 198 respondents, 65 employers reported having formal affirmative action programs, 35 had informal programs, and 98 had *no* affirmative action programs. (The formal/informal definitions of the Directorate itself covered a broad range.) Similarly, the response rate to federal initiatives has not been encouraging. Since 1979 The Canada Employment and Immigration Commission has had responsibility for providing consultative and technical services to assist the private sector and crown corporations in affirmative action planning. Between 1979 and 1983 CEIC contacted 900 companies and wound up with 34 official agreements. Of these 34 agreements, no trends or similarities were identified. Although there have been individual cases of public and private sector employers initiating and implementing affirmative action programs that resulted in measurable changes, *the overall situation for women in the workplace has not changed appreciably.*

Recent developments point to a step—albeit a modest one—in the direction of equity. In March 1985 Flora MacDonald, Minister of Employment and Immigration, announced the Federal Government's response to

Judge Rosalie Abella's Royal Commission Report on Equality in Employment, and cited the new federal measures as a "major step toward achieving genuine Employment Equity in Canada."[4] These measures include the requirement for crown corporations, federally-regulated businesses (with 100 or more employees), and firms contracting with the government (for goods and services of $200,000 or more) to implement employment equity and to report annually to Parliament on their plans and progress. *What these measures did not do was set up a separate standard-setting or enforcement agency; nor do they assign the responsibility uniformly to any existing agency.* Instead, the government chose to "draw on the energies and inventiveness of employers in removing barriers" and to rely on the public pressure that supposedly would follow the public reporting of company records. As it now stands, it is not clear what the outcome of the federal initiatives will be. There seems to exist an expectation that some of the problems will be resolved informally and that the private sector will voluntarily want to emulate any progress made by the federal sector.

■ REASONS FOR FAILURE

There are a number of important lessons to be drawn from both the Canadian and American experiences in affirmative action. *Voluntary affirmative action is ineffective.* Where demonstrable changes can be shown in the U.S., they are attributable to an emphasis on mandated affirmative action and enforceable contract compliance. The key instruments for implementing affirmative action measures within organizations are monitoring and accountability. Unless goals and timetables are incorporated into such programs, there is no way to evaluate progress and measure results. *Unless commitment for employment equity is made at the top and passed on to senior level staff through accountability, little change will occur.* Too often the task of overseeing and implementing affirmative action has been handed over to departments lacking enforcement powers. The clarity and force — not to mention the effectiveness — of commitment can become obscured when managers are not held accountable.

The problem of accountability is reflected in the 1982 employer survey of the Ontario Women's Directorate. Of 65 respondents who claimed to have formal goal-oriented programs, only 24 held managers accountable for promoting women. What is even more striking, is that 27 had not even informed employees that such a plan existed! *As a means of combatting systemic discrimination, the case-by-case approach adopted by human rights commissions is costly and cumbersome, and ultimately affects very small numbers.* Far more effective are class-action suits, like the AT & T case in the U.S. (1974) which changed the entire hiring, pay, and promotion structure of the country's then-largest employer of women.

A number of other overt and covert factors inhibit the momentum toward employment equity. Not least of these is that Canada is in the midst of an economic recession. At a time when companies are concerned about streamlining their operations, it is difficult to convince them of the benefits of establishing good data-collection bases, flexible work conditions, and opportunities for training and development. Equally important, and often more covert, is the threat of increased competition to the entrenched male workforce for the already scarce jobs. This threat is often expressed by charges of "reverse discrimination" and general feelings of increased hostility toward female workers. These feelings in turn add fuel to the persistent under-valuation of what women do. Not only is this message brought home by a wage system which devalues jobs performed by women in the paid (and unpaid) labour force, but by the accumulating research findings that both men and women tend to attribute women's successes to good luck and men's successes to ability.[5]

One of the greatest barriers to employment equity has been the almost universal under-estimation of resistance and the absence of measures to combat it. Resistance can take many forms—from half-hearted attempts to implement the minimal number of employment equity measures necessary to refusing to even consider that inequities may exist in a company. Resistance may be active or passive, overt or covert. In many cases resistance is a reaction to the possibility of change. Change is frightening at any time, especially frightening if one is not feeling too sure about one's own position (as in recessionary times). A great deal of the backlash appearing can be attributed to fear of anticipated change.

Most of the arguments raised by opponents have not been supported by any evidence. The charge that competence is being sacrificed in the name of equality is not backed by any data. Nowhere do advocates of employment equity suggest that unqualified employees should be hired or promoted; nobody would benefit from this situation—least of all the employee hired. The argument that business will suffer from mandated employment programs is also unsupported: even employers in the U.S. who initially resisted these programs have reported the positive impact affirmative action has had on their business practices.[6]

■ DEALING WITH RESISTANCE

These reactions, and the more subtle negative ones, have to be met on two different levels. On the content level: the arguments and concerns must be acknowledged and refuted. Resistance to proposed change (especially change directed at some of our most basic social premises) should be expected, acknowledged, and coping strategies developed ahead of time. Although it is crucial for the initial commitment to employment equity to come from the top, where the authority lies, it is also important to have a cross-section of employees involved in the early planning and implementation. If people are encouraged "to own" the ideas and the program, they will have an investment in making it work. It is usually uncertainty that fosters anxiety: knowing what to expect, whenever possible, reduces it.

Viewed systemically, a change in one part of the organization will affect other parts. Building support networks for all sides is essential. Good fortune can suddenly ostracize people. A consultant friend of mine recently described a situation in her company whereby a secretary, through hard work and initiative, was promoted to an administrative position. Not only did the other secretaries stop talking to her, but they banded together to condemn her "uppity" behaviour. It is a common scenario and one that should not be ignored; it is important to acknowledge what is happening and provide opportunities to deal with the mixed reactions when one "breaks rank."

Instituting employment equity procedures within a familiar framework, with familiar terminology, also makes for a more gradual, comfortable change. Employment equity can thereby be handled as any other problem-solving activity in the organization. As such, it should aim for short and long-term goals that are realistic and measurable. Achieving short-term goals provides reinforcement for the longer, more difficult organizational changes.

■ THE RATIONALE FOR EMPLOYMENT EQUITY

Employment equity is like motherhood: we are all committed to it *in principle.* The crucial question is, what are we going to do to promote and support it? Why should we do anything? There are two main arguments for implementing employment equity measures. The first is based on an economic rationale. "Affirmative action is good business."[7] The proportionate participation of women in the workforce continues to increase. As the Honourable Robert Welch has stated, "In Ontario, women now make up 43% of the total workforce and our projections see the participation rate of women in the workforce rise to 50% by the year 2000 . . ."[8] By 1990 women will account for two-thirds of labour force growth and will represent a sizeable underutilized resource. In recessionary times particularly, businesses recognize the need for efficient and effective utilization of *all* human resources. This message is increasingly brought home by business leaders, as George Vila, chairman and chief executive officer of Uniroyal Inc., attests: "In the decades ahead, any organization which ignores or underestimates the potential of women—or overlooks any source of talent, for that matter—will be making a fatal mistake."[9]

Women themselves are demonstrating their abilities in increasing numbers. Partly in response to their frustration in being denied admittance to the inner executive circles of the big companies, women are going into business for themselves. Not only are Canadian women starting businesses at a rate three times that of men (paralleling the rate of American women which is five times that of men) but they "are a major force in small business, are more successful than men and are responsible for a significant portion of job creation in Canada."[10] However, despite women's contributions to the economy as both employees and entrepreneurs, they have not yet benefitted accordingly. The argument from the economic rationale is a powerful lever of change: "In the future, there will be no room for the economic inefficiency of (these) wasted resources. Equity in the work place is not only just in a democratic society but is a key to economic growth."[11]

The second argument for promoting employment equity is based on another reality: we are not discussing a minority population. We are discussing a potentially powerful force. Revolutions—quiet or otherwise—cannot be ignored and cannot be turned back. It may well be "that women in the (under)paid labour force will not continue to suffer in silence."[12] As awareness of inequities increases, so do demands for effective organizational change.

What we need is a two-pronged approach to employment equity, one that includes legislated changes (enforced and implemented) and that at the same time effectively deals with the anticipated resistance. These changes must occur at all levels. "No matter how much the law changes, it is up to the individuals who make up society to struggle against the beliefs and assumptions that relegate all women to second-class status—to the detriment of our whole society."[13] The attainment of equity objectives is good business and everybody's business.

Notes

1. J. Farley, *Affirmative Action and The Woman Worker* (New York: Amacom, 1979), p. 6.

2. *Statistics Canada, Canadian Women in the Work Place* (Canada Update from the 1981 Census).

3. Leah Cohen, "Affirmative Action in Canada: Ten Years After," (Ottawa: Department of the Secretary of State Human Rights Directorate, March 1983), p. 4.

4. Statement to the House of Commons by the Honourable Flora MacDonald, Minister of Employment and Immigration, on the Federal Government's Response to the Royal Commission Report on Equality in Employment (March 8, 1985).

5. Nina Colwill, "Lucky Lucy and Able Adam: To What Do You Attribute Your Success?," in *Business Quarterly*, 49(1) (Spring 1984), 93-94.

6. Paul Scott, "The American Experience with Affirmative Action: Debunking the Myth," in *CEIC* (November 1982).

7. Peter Robertson, "Affirmative Action: What's It All About?," in *CEIC* (March 1980).

8. The Honourable Robert Welch, "Productivity and Affirmative Action," in *Productivity* (October 1984), p. 24.

9. Quoted in Paul Scott, p. 25.

10. Jerry White, "Businesswomen Meet Success," in *Ontario Business* (May 1985), p. 5.

11. *Employment Equity and Economic Growth, A Background Paper* (8 March 1985).

12. Dorothy Gillmeister, *The Equal Opportunity Fantasy: A Hard Look At Voluntary Affirmative Action*, p. 18.

13. Anne E. Thorkelson, "Women Under the Law: Has Equity Been Achieved?," in A. Sargent (ed.), *Beyond Sex Roles* (St. Paul, Minnesota: West Publishing, 1977), 493-4.

■ POSTSCRIPT

A key question to ask in reference to these articles is the same question asked in Debate One. Is it possible to discuss the subject objectively? Block and Walker imply that they have done so by speaking dispassionately against affirmative action. They argue that discrimination is unprofitable because it robs the employer of the best possible person for the job. An employer sensitive to the needs of finding the best possible employee disregards race, ethnicity, and gender and hires the best person. Similarly, they argue that affirmative action forces employers to hire employees who are less qualified, and that this results in inefficiency and higher costs to the employer.

But is this an objective analysis? Kornberg implies that it is not. She argues that the assumptions of those who reject affirmative action are faulty. She says that most of their arguments have not been supported by evidence, and that no data support the charge that competence is being sacrificed in the name of equality. But is Kornberg's analysis any more objective? Kornberg justifies affirmative action on the grounds that it is good business, and because women, who make up the majority of the population, are not going to suffer in silence.

Block and Walker's assumption that employers hire the best available worker regardless of race may also be questioned. Research suggests that some employers use racist and/or sexist criteria when hiring employees (see Debates Three and Seventeen). Some employers prefer to hire white males rather than blacks or women. To the extent that employers do this, it is possible that they are hiring less competent people and not, as Block and Walker argue, more competent people.

There are some critics, however, who argue that affirmative action programs are ineffective. For example, McMillan (1985) argues that affirmative action has not helped women in nontraditional occupations, and Balkan (1985) points out that many male-dominated unions have been resistant to affirmative action. Employer and employee resistance to affirmative action programs frequently undermines the success of even legislative changes.

■ QUESTIONS

1. Which side of this debate presents the most convincing argument? How have your own beliefs on this issue influenced your decision?
2. Is it possible to present a dispassionate argument for or against affirmative action?
3. Which social groups are likely to favour affirmative action? Why?

4. Which social groups are least likely to favour affirmative action? Why?

5. Are Block and Walker correct in saying that discrimination is a desirable feature of free societies?

■ **FURTHER READING**

In Support of Block and Walker

Block, W.E. and M.A. Walker, eds. *Discrimination, Affirmative Action, and Equal Opportunity.* Vancouver: The Fraser Institute, 1982.

Knopff, Rainer. *Human Rights and Social Technology: The New War on Discrimination.* Ottawa: Carleton University Press, 1989.

Winn, Conrad. "Affirmative Action and Visible Minorities: Eight Premises in Quest of Evidence." *Canadian Public Policy* 11, no. 4 (1985): 24-46.

In Support of Kornberg

Abella, Judge Rosalie. *Report of the Royal Commission on Equality in Employment.* Ottawa: Minister of Supplies and Services, 1984.

Bankier, Jennifer K. "Equality, Affirmative Action, and the Charter: Reconciling 'Inconsistent' Sections." *Canadian Journal of Women and the Law* 1, no. 1 (1985): 134-152.

Bruce, Mary. "Equal Opportunity, Affirmative Action: The Toronto Experience." *Affirmation* 4, no. 3 (1983).

Other Voices

Balkan, Donna. "Practising What We Preach: Women, Unions and Affirmative Action." *Canadian Woman Studies* 6, no. 4 (1985): 49-51.

Cohen, Marjorie. "Employment Equity is not Affirmative Action." *Canadian Woman Studies* 6, no. 4 (1985): 26-29.

Geller, Carole. "Critique of the Abella Report." *Canadian Woman Studies* 6, no. 4 (1985): 23-25.

Jennett, Christine and Randal G. Stewart, eds. *Three Worlds of Inequality: Race, Class and Gender.* Melbourne: MacMillan, 1987.

Sawyer, Marian, ed. *Program for Change: Affirmative Action in Australia.* Sydney: Allen and Unwin, 1985.

IS PAY

EQUITY

JUSTIFIED?

YES **Roberta Edgecombe Robb**, "Equal Pay for Work of Equal Value: Issues and Policies," *Canadian Public Policy* 13, no. 4 (1987): 445-461

NO **Thomas Flanagan**, "Equal Pay for Work of Equal Value: Some Theoretical Considerations," *Canadian Public Policy* 13, no. 4 (1987): 435-444

It is a fact of life in Canada that women earn less than men. Recent data indicate that women working full time are paid approximately two-thirds of what men working full time are paid (Parliament, 1990). Even among those with university degrees, women are still paid only 70 percent of what men are paid. However, the gap between men's and women's wages is decreasing. In 1971, women working full time were paid approximately 60 percent of what men were paid. But while the gap is decreasing, its continued presence is an indication to many that women and women's work are not as valued as men and men's work. The objective, therefore, in developing pay equity is to affirm that women and women's work are just as valuable and just as valued as men and men's work.

Pay equity may take several forms. In its most basic form, it means paying persons with the same qualifications occupying the same job the same wage. But men and women work in different occupations. Most women (73 percent in 1988) work in clerical or service occupations, as sales clerks, or health-care professions (nursing, etc.), which are dominated by women (Parliament, 1990). These occupations, especially the clerical and sales occupations, are generally lower paid than the occupations in which men work. Therefore, as a means of reducing the male/female wage gap, this basic form of pay equity will not work. That is why the concept of pay equity has been extended by inclusion of the concept of comparable worth.

The reformulated concept emphasizes equal pay for work of equal value. This formulation means that men and women working in jobs requiring similar training and skills, and which are performed under similar working conditions, should receive the same wage. Four governments in Canada, including the federal government (in 1978) and the provincial governments of Ontario (in 1987), Manitoba (in 1984), and Quebec (in 1976), have introduced pay equity legislation. While there are differences in each case, the general concept is the same.

While Debate Five is waged between two economists, sociological questions are posed, most importantly the social justification of pay equity, and the methods used to legitimate or reject it. The essentially economic arguments presented here have a profound effect on social policy formation. Roberta Edgecombe Robb, arguing the "Yes" side of the debate, says rejection of pay equity will condemn many women who are the sole supporters of their families to a life of poverty with all its associated negative consequences. Arguing the "No" side of the debate, Thomas Flanagan suggests that pay equity has serious theoretical flaws that render it ineffective as public policy. Implementation of pay equity, he claims, may have such adverse effects as increasing employment and rewarding relatively well-off groups, such as teachers, social workers, and technicians, more than less advantaged groups, such as waitresses, chambermaids, and telephone solicitors. In both cases, arguments are directed at the social consequences of economic planning.

Reference
Parliament, Jo-Anne (1990) "Women Employed Outside the Home," in *Canadian Social Trends*, edited by Craig McKie and Keith Thompson (Toronto: Thompson Educational Publishing).

EQUAL PAY FOR WORK OF EQUAL VALUE: ISSUES AND POLICIES

YES

Roberta Edgecombe Robb*

After months of debate and extensive public hearings, the Peterson govern-ment, in June 1987, passed Bill 154—an Act which will legislate equal pay for work of equal value in the Ontario public service, the broader public sector (hospitals, universities, school boards, etc.) and the private sector.

As a result of this legislation, a considerable amount of interest and concern has been generated about the rationale for an equal value policy and its implications for the labour market. In view of the controversial nature of such legislation, this concern is not surprising, particularly in the private business sector. What is a little surprising, perhaps, is that despite all the information that has been disseminated on this issue, there still appears to be considerable misunderstanding about the concept. This confusion seems to exist not only with respect to the substantive issues in the debate (e.g., what are the likely effects in the labour market from implementing this policy?) but also with respect to some of the more simple issues (e.g., why is this policy thought to be necessary in the first place?). In hopes of clarifying these issues, this paper addresses the follow-ing questions: firstly . . . what are the costs and benefits of equal pay for work of equal value and what particular form of legislation helps to minimize the costs and maximize the benefits of the policy? [Secondly], is affirmative action an alternative policy to equal pay for work of equal value, or should the two be used together to help close the portion of the wage gap that is attributable to occupational segregation? The final section of the paper presents a summary and some conclusions. . . .

■ EQUAL VALUE POLICY: THE POTENTIAL COSTS

From an economics point of view, the potential costs of implementing equal pay for work of equal value seem to fall naturally into three overlap-ping categories: (1) the potential allocative inefficiences in the labour market resulting from a move away from a system of market determined wages; (2) the administrative and wage adjustment costs for firms which implement equal pay for work of equal value; and (3) the adjustment costs for particular groups of employees. In this section, we consider each of these separately.

Potential Allocative Inefficiencies in the Labour Market
To an economist, the main concern about implementing equal value legislation is that such a policy requires wages to be determined by an

administrative system (job evaluation) as opposed to market forces. Apart from a basic worry that job evaluation may be very subjective and/or technically difficult in some cases (see discussion below), the crux of economists' objections to such a system can be easily understood by focusing on the following question: even in a sex neutral labour market (i.e., non-discriminatory), would jobs which might be determined to be "of equal value" by some job evaluation process necessarily be paid the same? The economist's answer to this question is a clear no. Two important cases where jobs with similar requirements and characteristics will not be paid equal wages are: (1) occupations in which there is a shortage (in the short run) of the particular skill required to perform the work;[1] and (2) occupations in which there is overcrowding (a large supply of workers relative to demand). The first case need not concern us because, as indicated above, wage differentials between jobs of equal value based on a temporary labour shortage are recognized and allowed for both in the federal and in the Ontario legislation.[2] The second case—the problem of overcrowding in occupations—does warrant attention, however.

Two likely causes of overcrowding are workers' preferences or tastes for, or against, certain types of jobs[3] or some form of pre-labour market or employment discrimination that restricts the range of occupations open to a particular group in the labour market.[4] With respect to workers' preferences, the theory of competitive equilibrium wage differentials that serve to "compensate" workers for some undesirable characteristics of the job is well-developed in economics.[5] Other things being equal, those occupations which have higher risk of injury, greater instability of employment, unpleasant working conditions, etc., often command wage premiums relative to other jobs with otherwise similar job requirements and characteristics. Preferences between jobs can also occur simply because of differing tastes for a particular line of work. In choosing between university options involving the same amount of investment time, for example, some individuals will choose to be economists, some to be classicists, etc.[6] As indicated earlier, moreover, some women might be expected to prefer jobs that are compatible with household responsibilities, especially the rearing of children. If such tastes result in a large supply (relative to demand) in some occupations then wage differentials between jobs of equal value will occur here as well.[7]

The existence of occupational preferences in labour markets creates an operational problem for the equal pay for work of equal value legislation in the sense that such differentials may be difficult to identify or may be difficult to capture adequately in job evaluation schemes. Such an identification problem may be more likely to arise if the occupational preferences are based on a taste for a particular line of work, as opposed to a preference for jobs that are less risky, have less employment stability, etc. In the latter case, it might be argued that the category "conditions under which the work is performed" would pick up any substantial differences of this sort so that the jobs being compared would not, in fact, be classified as being of equal value. Even allowing for this contingency, however, we note that such factors may be difficult to weight appropriately. It is clearly the case, for example, that when the wage premium in such jobs is determined in competitive markets, it is the preferences of the individuals at the margin that, in effect, determine the size of the premium. Many individuals in a risky occupation earn rents in the sense that they would be willing to work in the occupation for less than the prevailing wage because they do not place as much weight on the risk factor as do the individuals at the margin.

The important issue, therefore, is whether or not job evaluators will weight some factors (especially the category "conditions under which the work is performed") in the same way as the market. That there may indeed be some difficulty in doing this is suggested by some statistics presented in a recent paper by Ehrenberg and Smith (1984). Summarizing the results of three job evaluation studies done for state employees in Minnesota (1981), Washington (1976) and Connecticut (1979-80), the authors note that, in all three cases, the average point scores and the range of variation of point scores for the three compensable factors "knowledge and skill," "mental demands" and "accountability" far exceeded the comparable variables for the fourth compensable factor "working conditions." In particular, this latter category was characterized by a large number of observations (jobs) that had zero scores, very small maximum values in comparison to the other factors, and a small range of variation in the scores across jobs.[8] Such results suggest that, at the very least, the factor "working conditions" is measured with considerable error in the job evaluation plans.[9]

In view of the above discussion, it may be the case that the potential does exist for eliminating appropriate compensatory differentials through the application of equal value legislation. This is not meant to imply, however, that economists assume that all, or even the major proportion of wage differentials between the male and female jobs are compensating differentials. Rather, to the extent that such differentials do exist in some cases, and are eliminated, then allocative inefficiencies will occur in the sense that firms may face difficulties in terms of attracting a sufficient supply of workers to risky or otherwise unpleasant occupations.[10]

Overcrowding resulting from tastes for a particular line of work or some form of discrimination (pre-market or market) will also result in lower productivity (given the law of diminishing marginal productivity) and lower wages for workers in those occupations relative to workers in occupations with similar characteristics.[11] If such differentials are eliminated by the legislation (as they probably will be) then reduced employment opportunities for women may occur (see below).[12] We note in this case, however, that while the unemployment created in this way can be thought of as an allocative inefficiency in the economy, the existing allocation of labour may not be efficient either in view of the possible barriers to entry in some occupations. Hence, the implementation of an equal value policy would simply be moving the economy from one inefficient position to another, and it is not clear, a priori, whether such a move would be an improvement or not.[13]

Looking at the problem in a more general context, we note that underlying these potential difficulties of trying to discern what is or is not a discriminatory interoccupational differential is the basic and fundamental problem of trying to decide when two jobs are of equal value and when, in fact, they are not. Job evaluation is clearly not an exact science and the probability that bias in the wage determination process can manifest itself through this system (just as it can through the market) is certainly not zero.[14] It must also be recognized that job evaluation is likely to be technically very difficult in very small firms—those with fewer than 50 employees, for example.[15] Two problems seem particularly noteworthy in this regard. Firstly, there is not likely to be a wide range of occupations in the smaller firms so that comparisons may have to be made between dissimilar occupations. This raises the concern that while blatant abuses of job evaluation may be very easy to discern in comparisons between jobs that are reasonably similar in nature, they may not be at all easy to discern between jobs that are very different in nature. Secondly, in small firms, the smaller number of people in the various occupational groups may mean that wages are very person specific, i.e., there are insufficient numbers to provide a good idea of what the occupational wage of the individual with an average set of productive characteristics would be. In such a case, there is the danger (as noted above) that the cause of any observed differentials may be misinterpreted. For these reasons, therefore, I would argue that applying job evaluation in very small firms is an issue that merits some serious thought.[16]

Implementation Procedures to Minimize Allocation Inefficiencies

Given the arguments that a bureaucratically administered system of wages may result in allocative inefficiencies in the labour market, a relevant question to be addressed is whether or not there is any way that an equal value policy could be designed and/or administered so as to minimize these costs.[17] Several possibilities seem worth exploring.

Firstly, it is not at all clear that a move to an administered system of wages needs to be a permanent one. It is certainly the case that if employers have been systematically undervaluing women's jobs relative to comparable male jobs, then some process is required to make them change their expectations (and hence their behaviour) about the value of these jobs before the market is allowed to operate freely again. To the extent, moreover, that at least some portion of the current problem results from a form of socially and culturally-induced perceptions about the inferior value of women's work as opposed to hard-core discriminatory attitudes, forcing employers to confront these perceptions through across-the-board gender bias free job evaluations is perhaps the best way to effect this change.[18] It should be noted, however, that we have already had experience in this country with market interventionist policies designed to change expectations (and behaviour), and they have been of a temporary nature. The wage and price control policy of 1975-1978, for example, is claimed to have changed the way expectations were formed about price inflation. Bill 101 in Quebec, moreover, is believed to have changed some employer's perceptions of francophone workers as less qualified, and now (after nine years) appears to require a decreasing share of resources to administer. Perhaps one could hope, therefore, that a temporary shift to an administered system of wages might work to effect the changes necessary with respect to pay equity, although how temporary the program could be is not an easy question to answer.

Secondly, it should be noted that although the process of job evaluation is usually thought of as a system which will totally ignore the market, this has not generally been the case in practice. Many job evaluation schemes, in effect, capture the behaviour of the market—either by statistically analysing market wage data so as to determine the market weights for various compensable factors of jobs, or by analysing "benchmark" jobs (for which there is a well-defined external market) in order to determine the weights for the job evaluation plan.[19] It is clearly the case that because discrimination is present in the female labour market, job evaluation plans which utilize weights for various compensable factors based on existing wage relations in women's jobs would not be acceptable. It is not clear, however, given the assumption that male jobs are taken as a non-discriminatory norm, that statistical analysis of these jobs could not be used to provide the implicit value placed by firms on various compensable factors.[20] Although there are undoubtedly compensable factors unique to women's jobs (i.e., not commonly found in men's jobs), the sex-neutral market weights for a large number of compensable factors (present in both male and female jobs) could be identified. These could then be used to help evaluate the women's jobs.[21]

Thirdly, given the potential difficulties of using job evaluation in very small firms, perhaps an alternate method of achieving pay equity might be feasible in this sector.[22] For example, some form of modified equal value policy, such as that discussed by Killingsworth (1985), might be useful. In Killingsworth's plan, no job evaluation would take place, but there would be a policy requiring increases in wages for jobs in which women are over-represented. In practice, this would require identifying (probably using statistics for Ontario as a whole), (a) those occupations which are predominantly female, and (b) some idea of the average male/female interoccupational wage differential. To the extent that any particular small firm employed women in the designated female occupations, they could be required to adjust the base rates in these occupations by the average male/female differential.

Finally, to conclude this section, it is worthwhile to consider two additional points. First, although a widespread system of administered wages is a departure for the economy, the process of job evaluation is not a new phenomenon for many firms. A recent Labour Canada publication, for example, indicated that 67 per cent of large firms (1000-4999 employees), 70 per cent of medium size firms (200-999 employees) and 50 per cent of small firms (50-199 employees) use some form of job evaluation plan.[23] Of these, 71, 52 and 42 per cent respectively were the types of plans that would be suitable for equal value comparisons. Hence, the concerns that mistakes will be made (and inefficiencies created) because of inexperience with the technique of job evaluation may be a little exaggerated. Second, when it comes right down to it, the current problem may be one of choosing between two evils: the market which may be discriminatory (and hence inequitable) and the use of job evaluation to determine wages, which may be somewhat allocatively inefficient.[24] In the absence of any other alternatives, therefore, an administered system of wages, even if only on a temporary basis, may be justifiable on equity grounds.

Costs to Firms of Implementing Equal Pay for Work of Equal Value

The two broad categories of costs incurred by firms from implementing pay equity are: (1) the administrative costs of setting up and implementing the job evaluation procedure; and (2) the costs of any wage adjustments that have to be made.

With respect to the administrative costs, there seems to be little evidence on their likely size, although some estimates from the Canadian Federation of Independent Business indicate that they are in the order of $300-$500 per employee for small firms, and $200-$300 per employee for large firms.[25] This difference is not surprising in view of the facts that the use of job evaluation plans suitable for equal value comparisons is not widespread among small firms (50-199 employees), and most of the cost is likely to be fixed. Hence, the administrative costs, per employee, will be higher for small firms than for medium and large size firms which may already have job evaluation plans in place. For this reason (given the importance of covering all firms in the legislation), and perhaps because of the earlier discussed technical difficulties of using job evaluation in small firms, the Ontario legislation does not make the use of job evaluation plans mandatory for firms with fewer than 100 employees. These employers must review workers' jobs and salaries, however, in order to identify and correct any pay inequities.

The potential estimates of wage adjustment costs depend on a wide variety of factors. A recent study by Gunderson (1984), for example, attempts to derive a reasonable per employee estimate by looking at approximately 45 different estimates of the expected wage adjustment, based on a number of different sources.[26] From these different scenarios, Gunderson suggests that a reasonable estimate of the per employee cost of closing a 10 percentage point gap is probably in the order of $2,000-$3,000 (in 1983 dollars) or (approximately) $2,200-$3,300 in 1986 dollars.

Clearly, the underlying worry about costs for any given firm is how they will affect the firm's competitive position relative to other firms. It is argued, however, that there are three important features which, if included in legislation, would help to minimize the relative competitive disadvantage faced by any given firm. Firstly, in those firms where a wage adjustment may be very large, reasonable phase-in periods should be provided so that the firm does not bear large cost increases in the short run. Such phase-in periods have been used in the federal sector where, for example, a recent settlement involving home economists and physical therapists will be phased in over a six-year period. Also, in the Ontario proposals, firms in the broader public and private sector will have from two to six years (depending on firm size) before adjustments will have to be started, and adjustment costs (in any given year) will be limited to 1 per cent of the previous year's payroll. Secondly, the legislation should require (particularly in the private sector as it does in Ontario) a joint employer proactive-employee-complaints-initiated approach (which is monitored for compliance). If the legislation is activated only through complaints (as is currently the case in the federal sector) then firms will be hit selectively on a one-by-one basis which will certainly place them at a competitive disadvantage relative to firms which have not had to adjust their wages due to lack of employee complaints.[27] Thirdly, the legislation should have universal coverage. To the extent that there is competition in some product markets between some small and medium size firms, exempting the small business sector (as has sometimes been suggested) would give them a considerable cost advantage. In recognition of this problem, only firms with under ten employees are exempted from the Ontario pay equity legislation.

In the final analysis, however, while every precaution should be taken to minimize (by appropriate legislation) the potential effects of increased costs on the firm's competitive position, it is argued that the fact that such costs will be incurred is not a justification for refusing to implement an equal value policy. After all, it is not as if by implementing equal pay for work of equal value we are moving from a world in which there are zero costs (from discrimination) to a world in which there are positive costs (resulting from its removal). Although the administrative costs do represent a real, additional resource cost, the wage adjustment costs are simply a transfer of existing costs—away from women who currently incur costs in the form of foregone income—to employers and male employees.

Potential Costs to Workers Resulting from Equal Pay for Work of Equal Value

In cases where market intervention occurs to satisfy an equity criterion, it is often the case that some negative side effects will occur for the very individuals the policy is designed to help. In an earlier paper, Robb (1984) suggests that implementing equal pay for work of equal value may have three possible effects on some workers. First, to the extent that increased wages may make women's occupations more attractive to males, females may find that they face increased competition for these jobs; second, as a result of the increased cost incurred by firms, economic theory predicts possible employment effects for both male and female workers.[28] These employment effects result from two factors: (1) the possibility that the employers will substitute away from the now more costly females to either males or capital; (2) to the extent that the increased costs result in an overall decline in production in the firms, then unemployment of both females and males might occur.

It is important to emphasize, however, that the theory does not predict the size of any of these effects, although we know some of the likely determinants of their size. The structure of the product market, for example, should influence the size of the employment effects. To the extent that labour demand curves are less than perfectly elastic because firms have monopoly power in the product market (and hence can pass on increased wages in increased product prices), the employment effects should be smaller. If both labour and product markets are competitive, on the other hand, we might expect the effects to be larger.[29]

With respect to empirical evidence on the possible size of any employment effects, we note that although the data are very scarce in this area, two recent studies do provide some results. Using individual data from the 1980 Census of Population (US), Ehrenberg and Smith (1984) present simulations[30] which show that a comparable worth adjustment of 20 percentage points for all state and local female employees would lead to only a 2 to 3 per cent decline in female employment.[31] These results are for the public sector, however, and may not provide a good prediction for the effects in the private sector. The size of the wage gap is somewhat smaller in the public sector, for example, so that the resulting wage adjustments (and hence employment adjustments) may be smaller. Moreover, the demand for labour may be more inelastic in the public sector than in the private sector, such that a given wage increase would result in a smaller employment effect.

For direct evidence on the effects of such legislation in the private sector, it would appear that only the Australian experience provides any useful evidence. From the results of two recent papers,[32] the effects in Australia of a 30 per cent increase in female wages (over a five-year period) seem to be as follows: (1) the policy's cumulative impact on the female unemployment rate was approximately .5 percentage points; (2) the policy reduced the rate of growth of female employment (below the rate that otherwise would have prevailed) by about 1.3 per cent per year, relative to the rate of growth of men's employment. This represented approximately one-third the actual rate of growth of female employment (relative to that of men) during that period. In other words, the results suggest somewhat small effects on the actual unemployment rate, but somewhat more substantial effects on the employment growth of women as a result of introducing equal value legislation in Australia.

A final potential cost to workers arises in the case in which the policy is not implemented with universal coverage. To the extent that unemployment occurs in the covered sector, then some of these unemployed workers might move into the uncovered sector to look for jobs. This could have the effect of competing down the wages in that sector, particularly in the female-dominated occupations, thus exacerbating the low wage problem in that sector.

Overall, therefore, an equal pay policy is not likely to make everyone better off. Some females (and males) in the predominantly female jobs will benefit from the increased wages whereas some women (and men) may be made worse off (at least in the short run) if they become unemployed or if employment opportunities do not increase as quickly as they otherwise might. But it should be remembered, however, that very few market interventionist policies are without costs even for the group they are designed to help. Given the available evidence, moreover, and assuming that the policy will be introduced with features designed to minimize these costs, the size of the losses might well be small. Enforcing affirmative action as a complementary policy of equal value will also help to minimize any adverse employment effects.

■ POTENTIAL BENEFITS OF AN EQUAL VALUE POLICY

On the benefit side, the major effect of an equal value policy is that it will help to close a fairly substantial proportion (perhaps 10-15 percentage points) of the overall male-female earnings gap in Ontario. It is argued that this substantial loss is foregone income (particularly in view of the fact that 40 per cent of the Ontario female labour force is widowed, separated or divorced and hence may be solely responsible for their own support as well as other family members) constitutes a compelling case on equity grounds for implementing the legislation. It should be emphasized again, moreover, that to close as much of the gap as possible, complete coverage and a joint proactive-complaints-initiated approach is needed. Exempting sectors seriously weakens the effectiveness of the legislation.

A second argument in favour of the policy is the potential for increased productivity in the female-dominated jobs. To the extent that increased income (purchasing power) might lead to improved morale, and/or lower absenteeism and turnover (perhaps because of opportunities to purchase improved child care), then the potential for increased productivity in women's occupations should be recognized.[33]

Finally, as argued by Gunderson (1986), the actual process of evaluating jobs may generate information which, in turn, will generate interoccupational mobility. To the extent that females (males) learn, for example, which male (female) jobs require the same composite of skill, effort, responsibility and working conditions as their own jobs, they (and perhaps, more important, new entrants) may be willing to work in these occupations at some point. In other words, one direct effect of implementing equal value policy is that it might help to break down the occupational segregation of the labour force, as well as eliminate the earnings differentials.

As a final comment in this section, we note that employment equity/ affirmative action is often suggested as an alternative policy to equal value legislation for eliminating male-female interoccupational wage differentials. Such a policy is favoured by economists because it does not create the allocative inefficiencies inherent in an administered system of wages,[34] and by business, presumably because it is potentially much less costly than equal pay for work of equal value. It is argued in this paper, however, that while affirmative action is a necessary complementary policy to equal value, it should not be thought of as a substitute for several reasons. In the first place, while affirmative action might help new entrants obtain higher paying male jobs, it is not clear that this policy will benefit the group which historically, and currently, is suffering the foregone income losses from discrimination. Older cohorts of women, for example, may be unable, for various reasons, to move into traditionally male occupations. Even assuming that all women were willing and able to move, however, the process will be incredibly slow. US economists have estimated, for example, that it will take 75 to 100 years to achieve pay equity through the route of affirmative action.[35] In Canada, too, Boulet (1985) has demonstrated the slowness of occupational integration by estimating that *if every single woman* entering the labour force between now and the year 2000 were to go into a traditional male occupation, their representation in those jobs would still be only 35 per cent, whereas their overall representation in the labour force will be approximately 50 per cent. In view of the fact that considerably less than 100 per cent of female entrants can be expected to move into male jobs (only 44 per cent went into male-dominated jobs between 1971 and 1981, for example), occupational integration in Canada may not take place until well into the next century.

More importantly, however, it is not clear that an affirmative action program, as commonly perceived, addresses precisely the same issue as is addressed by an equal value policy. It is the case, of course, that part of the overall female-male wage differential is caused by the fact that some men and women are concentrated in jobs which in no sense can be thought of as equal value—secretaries versus executives—for example. Clearly, encouraging new female entrants to be executives instead of secretaries, and using affirmative action to open up such positions for females will help to close the wage gap. Equal pay for work of equal value, however, is not concerned with the differences in pay between secretaries and executives. This policy is premised on the fact that, relative to some comparable male occupation in the firm (salesmen, for example), discriminating employers have undervalued the secretaries' work. While one solution to this problem may be to use affirmative action and encourage new female entrants to be salemen instead of secretaries (in order to avoid discrimination), it is not clear why existing secretaries should have to bear the adjustment costs of occupational mobility in order to be paid equitably. In summary, while affirmative action may help new entrants, it will do little for the stock of women in the labour market who are suffering from discrimination. Equity considerations dictate that an equal value policy is necessary for this group.

■ SUMMARY AND CONCLUSIONS

Considering the empirical evidence, it would appear that approximately 10 to 15 percentage points of the overall 40 percentage point male-female earnings differential can be attributed to occupational segregation. An equal pay for work of equal value policy would help to eliminate at least some portion of this gap. It is not suggested that such a policy will be without cost; it is argued, however, that careful design and implementation of the legislation would help to minimize these costs. Affirmative action is also a useful policy for achieving pay equity, but it should be thought of as a complementary rather than as an alternative policy to equal value. Such a policy is likely to benefit new entrants, but will probably do little to help the stock of women currently in the labour market who are bearing the costs of discrimination.

Notes

* An earlier version of this paper was written while the author was on sabbatical at the Centre for Industrial Relations at the University of Toronto, and was given as a lecture in the Ryerson Lectures in Economics Series. I would like to thank Morley Gunderson, Frank Reid, Les Robb, the Associate Editor and two anonymous referees of this journal for invaluable discussions on this topic.

1. The concept of "shortage" used here is when the supply to an occupation, given the demand, is smaller than it will be in long-run equilibrium.

2. To argue that a wage differential is based on a shortage, the federal Human Rights Commission requires employers to demonstrate that they have been unable to fill their vacancies at lower wages. In a provincial context, for example, universities currently trying to hire male faculty with a PhD in Accounting at a premium would have to demonstrate why such a premium was necessary. Employers may also be required to demonstrate that this premium is paid relative to some other male occupation of equal value to guarantee that it is not a gender-based differential.

3. For an interesting discussion of this point in the context of job evaluation and an equal value policy see Killingsworth (1985).

4. Discrimination in the education sector, for example, might limit women's opportunities in the labour market. Also, of course, there are a number of models of employment discrimination that could give rise to segregation of a minority group into a few occupations (see Robb, 1984).

5. See, for example, Smith (1937).

6. Consider, for example, the case of a university that produces an educational product. To do this, the university hires professors in different disciplines to do jobs that are essentially identical — i.e., to teach and do research. However, if we compare the wages in, say, history and classics, on the one hand, with the wages paid in engineering or business, on the other, it is generally the case that earnings are substantially different (ceteris paribus) because of the differing supply conditions. Differentials between jobs of equal value for the same sex have also been found in the federal Public Service and are thought to be the result of differing bargaining unit strength as well as supply and demand factors (see Campbell, 1984).

7. As indicated by England (1984), however, the role of women's domestic responsibility as an explanation of their occupational distribution (and, consequently, their low wages because of a crowding differential) may be overemphasized. While interrupted work experience and domestic responsibilities may exclude women from jobs that require a lot of time input (management, professional occupations, etc.) or travelling, the majority of males do not work in such jobs either.

8. See Ehrenberg and Smith (1984: 14-21).

9. The two plans used were the Hay system and the Willis system. The measurement error problem arises, in part, because the Hay point scheme used in Minnesota assigns working conditions points only in certain jobs and *defines* most clerical jobs as having normal working conditions, and, therefore, zero working conditions points. In other words, a bias is built right into the plan.

10. Given that wage differentials based on a temporary skills shortage are allowed in the legislation, it could be argued that such a problem would not arise. On the other hand, it may be that the conditions under which the shortage argument would be accepted will not exist here. If the differential is a long-run equilibrium compensating differential, for example, then the firm will not be able to demonstrate that it has recently (and unsuccessfully) tried to fill its vacancies at lower wages. Clearly, the shortage argument could subsequently be used to validate the differential, but presumably only after the firm had incurred some real search costs. An additional concern expressed by economists in the context of compensating differentials is with the method of wage adjustment used in the federal sector. Essentially, a male and a female pay line are estimated by regressing wages on job point scores, and the wages in all the female jobs of a given point score are then raised to the male pay line. In effect, if any of the differentials between the female jobs (at a given point score) are compensating differentials, they will be eliminated by this adjustment. Note, moreover, that this type of adjustment will leave some male jobs (those that were beneath the male pay line to begin with) with wages lower than female jobs of comparable value. If under the new Charter of Rights, males in male-dominated occupations applied to have their earnings compared to the (now higher) earnings in some female or other male-dominated occupations, and this challenge were successful, the elimination of legitimate compensatory differentials and/or union/non-union wage premiums might well occur on a large scale. To avoid this problem, I would argue that the appropriate adjust-

ment would be to raise the female pay line to the male pay line, while leaving the male and female wage structures about that line as they are.

11. See, for example, Bergmann (1974; 1971).

12. For a theoretical discussion of this issue see Robb (1984).

13. For a discussion of this point see Lipsey and Lancaster (1956/57).

14. For a good discussion of these problems see Remick (1984: section II), and Schwab (1985).

15. In this paper we make the distinction between very small firms (less than 50 employees) and small firms (50-199 employees).

16. As will be argued below, however, this does not constitute an argument for exempting the small firms from the legislation. Rather it is meant to imply that pay equity might have to be achieved in this sector by methods other than the use of job evaluation.

17. We note at this point that, in view of the above arguments regarding efficiency, some economists would favour an affirmative action program for eliminating wage differentials, as opposed to an equal value policy. It is argued in this paper, however, that affirmative action, by itself, is not an appropriate policy in this case.

18. What is needed is a process which forces employers to examine their wage structures for various types of bias. For example, are similar factors weighted differently depending on whether they are found in male or female jobs?

19. For a detailed discussion of this point see Treiman and Hartmann (1981), Schwab (1985) and Weiler (1985).

20. See Treiman and Hartmann (1981) and Weiler (1985).

21. It is recognized, of course, that to the extent that some compensable factors are unique to women's jobs, non-market weights will have to be assigned. Also, there is still the problem of "equivalence" of compensable factors to be dealt with. For example, is the "dirt" encountered by a garage mechanic (and weighted heavily under "working conditions") equivalent to the "dirt" encountered by nurses and similarly evaluated?

22. Spokespersons for the small business sector in Ontario argued that these difficulties justified an exemption for them from the legislation. Since some 42 per cent of the female labour force in Ontario work in firms with under 50 employees, however, it was counterargued that an exemption would seriously limit the ability to achieve pay equity in Ontario in any meaningful fashion. In the end, some small firms (those with less than 10 employees) were totally exempted from the provisions of Bill 154, and job evaluation was not made mandatory for firms with between 10 and 99 employees.

23. See Labour Canada (1985). The sample consisted of 164 firms subject to the Canada Labour Code, and was randomly selected from all regions of Canada. Note that in Ontario, moreover, 43.8 per cent of all female employees work in either medium or large size firms.

24. This point was originally made by Gunderson (1986).

25. These estimates were obtained from the Ontario Provincial Director of the Canadian Federation of Independent Business.

26. The data sources used by Gunderson include court awards or implementation policies from Washington State, Minnesota, San-Jose, California and the federal and Quebec jurisdictions in Canada.

27. To the extent that employees vary in their level of sophistication and assertiveness, the incidence of complaints will probably differ across firms. Clearly, of course, it could be argued that discriminatory firms should be placed at a competitive disadvantage. However, to the extent that firms might be forced out of business because of this, female employees in such firms will be worse off. If all discriminating firms were forced to raise wages, however, then the relative disadvantage of any one firm will be lower, and the risk of going out of business smaller.

28. We note that such a prediction results from other wage fixing policies as well, e.g., minimum wages.

29. We note, however, that even in competitive markets, firms might be able to absorb or offset the increased labour costs—particularly if these costs are phased in over time. The possibility that the higher wages will allow the firm to attract higher-quality (more productive) workers, for example, might be one way of offsetting higher costs and mitigating the employment effects.

30. The simulations use estimated systems of demand curves for male and female employees to provide estimates of male/female substitution as relative wages change.

31. See Ehrenberg and Smith (1984:section V).

32. See Gregory and Duncan (1981) and Gregory and Ho (1985).

33. A similar argument has been used with respect to unions to partially explain the observed higher productivity of unionized versus non-unionized firms in certain industries. See Ehrenberg and Smith (1985:chap. 12).

34. See *Royal Commission on the Economic Union and Development Prospects for Canada* (1985), p. 642.

35. See McLean (1986).

References

Bergmann, Barbara (1971) "The Effect on White Incomes of Discrimination in Employment," *Journal of Political Economy* (March/April), pp. 249-313.

———— (1974) "Occupational Segregation, Wages and Profits When Employers Discriminate by Race and Sex," *Eastern Economic Journal* (April/July), pp. 103-10.

Campbell, John G. (1984) "Equal Pay for Work of Equal Value," a paper presented to the Canadian Industrial Relations Association Meetings in Guelph.

Ehrenberg, Ronald G. and Robert S. Smith (1984) *Comparable Worth in the Public Sector*, National Bureau of Economic Research Working Paper 1471 (Cambridge, Mass.).

———— (1985) *Modern Labour Economics: Theory and Public Policy*, 2nd ed. (Glenview, Illinois: Scott, Foresman and Company).

England, Paula (1984) "Socioeconomic Explanations of Job Segregation," in H. Remick (ed.), *Comparable Worth and Wage Discrimination* (Philadelphia: Temple University Press).

Gregory R.G. and R.G. Duncan (1981) "Segmented Labour Market Theories and the Australian Experience of Equal Pay for Women," *Journal of Post Keynesian Economics* (Spring), II:403-28.

Gregory R.G. and V. Ho (1985) "Equal Pay and Comparable Worth: What Can the U.S. Learn from the Australian Experience?" Discussion Paper No. 123, Center for Economic Policy Research, The Australian National University, Canberra, Australia.

Gunderson, M. (1984) *Costing Equal Value Legislation in Ontario* (Toronto: Ontario Ministry of Labour).

_____ (1986) *Equal Pay for Work of Equal Value* (Report to the Human Rights Commission), Unpublished Paper, Centre For Industrial Relations, University of Toronto, Toronto, Ontario.

Killingsworth, Mark (1985) "The Economics of Comparable Worth: Analytical, Empirical and Policy Questions," in Heidi Hartmann (ed.), *Comparable Worth: New Directions for Research* (Washington, DC: National Academy Press).

Labour Canada. Equal Pay Division (1985) *Job Evaluation Survey 1984, Report On A Survey of Job Evaluation Practices of Employers Subject to the Canada Labour Code and Relative to the Implementation of Equal Pay for Work of Equal Value* (Ottawa: Labour Canada).

Lipsey, R.G. and K. Lancaster (1956/7) "The General Theory of the Second Best," *Review of Economic Studies.*

McLean, Walter (1986) "Pay Equity Cost Need Not Be High," *The Financial Post*, March 15.

Remick, H. (1984) *Comparable Worth and Wage Discrimination* (Philadelphia: Temple University Press).

Robb, Roberta Edgecombe (1984) "Occupational Segregation and Equal Pay for Work of Equal Value," *Relations Industrielles/Industrial Relations*, 39:1.

Royal Commission on the Economic Union and Development Prospects for Canada (1985) Volume II (Toronto: University of Toronto Press).

Schwab, Donald P. (1985) "Job Evaluation Research and Research Needs," in H. Hartmann (ed.), *Comparable Worth: New Directions for Research* (Washington, DC: National Academy Press).

Smith, Adam (1937) *Wealth of Nations* (New York: Modern Library).

Treiman, D. and H. Hartmann (1981) *Women, Work and Wages* (Washington, DC: National Academy Press).

Weiler, Paul (1985) *The Uses and the Limits of Comparable Worth In The Pursuit of Pay Equity for Women*, Discussion Paper no. 15, Program in Law and Economics, Harvard Law School, Cambridge, Mass.

EQUAL PAY FOR WORK OF EQUAL VALUE: SOME THEORETICAL CRITICISMS

NO

Thomas Flanagan*

The concept of "equal pay for work of equal value" (EV) is currently a matter of controversy in Canada. There is also a large American literature on EV, or "comparable worth" as it is called in the United States. Much of the literature has been produced by economists and sociologists, who have tried to discover whether a "wage gap" can be measured between work performed by men and work performed by women. A good deal has also been written about formal job evaluation methods, and whether they can contribute to closing the wage gap. Finally, there is a legally oriented literature on the implications of various human rights and equal-pay statutes.

This paper, written by a political theorist, strikes out in a different direction by examining certain aspects of EV doctrine as a mode of thought. It will be shown that EV, as a way of looking at the world, is marked by three characteristics usually regarded as philosophical errors: animism, reification, and voluntarism. These intellectual difficulties make EV problematic as a public policy.

■ HISTORY AND MEANING OF EV

Although recently much debated, EV is not a new idea. Its first appearance seems to have been in the Peace of Versailles, 1919, which affirmed "the principle that men and women should receive equal remuneration for work of equal value" (article 427). The International Labour Organization, founded the same year, embraced EV from the beginning and embedded the phrase in its Equal Remuneration Convention of 1951. Canada abstained on the original vote but subsequently ratified the Convention in 1972 (Niemann, 1984).

Although EV terminology has existed for most of this century, it was for decades not clearly distinguished from the concept of "equal pay for equal work" (EW). International documents as well as domestic legislation often used both terms together or as synonyms for one another. Many jurisdictions seemed to think they could comply with ILO norms by enacting EW statutes, as happened in Canada at both federal and provincial levels during the 1950s and 1960s.

A clear distinction between EV and EW only began to emerge in the 1970s. In that decade, with encouragement from the Common Market, many European countries, including the major powers of Britain, France,

107

Germany, and Italy, enacted EV legislation, as did Australia and New Zealand. In practice, however, these laws are often enforced loosely or in such a way as to make them equivalent to an EW standard (Livernash, 1984:137-72; Goodwin, 1984).

The main development in the United States has been a trend for state and local governments to apply the concept of "comparable worth" to their civil service employees. Numerous state and local authorities have had or now have comparable worth projects (Stewart, 1985). Feminist attempts to use the courts to read EV into existing federal Civil Rights and Equal Pay legislation have not achieved a decisive result, although some interim victories have been achieved, such as *American Federation of State, Country and Municipal Employees v. Washington*, 378 F. Supp. 846 (1983). The Reagan administration remains unalterably opposed to the idea, and the presidentially appointed Chairman of the United States Commission on Civil Rights has called comparable worth "the looniest idea since Looney Tunes came on the screen" (New York *Times*, November 17, 1984). The Equal Employment Opportunity Commission also adjudicated against it in 1985 (Block & Walker, 1985:88).

Movement towards EV in Canada can conveniently be dated from the *Report of the Royal Commission on the Status of Women* (1970). That document criticized existing EW legislation as ineffectual and called for reforms in the direction of EV, without identifying the concept precisely (66-77). The first jurisdiction to respond was the province of Quebec, which used the term *travail équivalent* (equivalent work) in its Charter of Human Rights and Freedoms, 1975 (s. 19). Enforcement of this equivocal phrase has been weak, although at least a few cases could be considered to exemplify the EV principle (CDPQ, 1980). The next breakthrough was the inclusion of s. 11(1) in the *Canadian Human Rights Act*, proclaimed March 1, 1978: "It is a discriminatory practice for an employer to establish or maintain differences in wages between male and female employees employed in the same establishment who are performing work of equal value." The Act covers federal employees and federally regulated industries, about 11 per cent of the work force. The Canadian Human Rights Commission has enforced s. 11 by responding to complaints as they are made. As of summer 1985, the Commission had settled about 20 complaints; most of them were small but a few involved multi-million dollar backpayments to hundreds or thousands of workers (CHRC, 1984).

Although human rights advocates continued to press for enactment of EV legislation in other jurisdictions, nothing much happened until 1984, when the release of the Abella Report, *Equality in Employment*, coincided closely in time with the federal election. Feminist issues were prominent in the campaign, as symbolized by the special television debate. The leaders of the three major parties vied with one another in pledging commitment to EV, making it sound like a reform still to be achieved rather than a statute already on the books. The Treasury Board is now studying a pay equity project for the federal civil service, but details have not yet been made public.

In the wake of the federal election, EV has also made gains provincially. Manitoba passed *The Pay Equity Act*, 1985, for its public service, including hospitals and universities. EV was also a major issue in the Ontario provincial election of 1985. The Liberal government first released a Green Paper on Pay Equity and introduced legislation to apply the principle of EV to the public service. Before that was passed, the government also introduced Bill 154 to apply pay equity to employers in the private sector with more than 10 employees. Depending on the size of the firm, employers will have from three to six years to develop an EV plan. Annual costs of increased compensation for women will not be required to exceed 1 per cent of the previous year's payroll (*University Affairs*, March 1987, p. 40).

The subtle distinctions between "equal pay for work of equal value," "comparable worth," and "pay equity" need not concern us here. All three share a commitment to EV that differentiates it from EW. The difference is readily illustrated in statutory wording. The United States *Equal Pay Act*, based on EW, provides:

> No employer . . . shall discriminate . . . between employees on the basis of paying wages . . . less than the rate at which he pays wages to employees of the opposite sex . . . for equal work on jobs the performance of which requires equal skill, effort, and responsibility, and which are performed under similar working conditions (29 U.S.C. 206(d)(i)).

The wording of the Act implies that skill *and* effort *and* responsibility *and* working conditions must all be equal, or at least similar, before the pay of two jobs can be compared. This means in practice that the EW criterion can be invoked only for jobs that are completely or nearly identical. Two persons pumping gas at the same station would qualify; but if one fixed flat tires (or cleaned washrooms, or ran the cash register) and the other did not, a tribunal might well hold that EW did not apply.

In contrast, s. 11(2) of the *Canadian Human Rights Act* stipulates:

> In assessing the value of work performed by employees . . . the criterion to be applied is the composite of the skill, effort and responsibility required in the performance of the work and the conditions under which the work is performed.

Introduction of the term "composite" into the formula changes its meaning radically. Job evaluation now becomes a matter of adding skill, effort, responsibility and working conditions to each other to produce a single index of comparison rather than comparing jobs on four separate dimensions.

This interpretation is confirmed by the Canadian Human Rights Commission publication *Methodology and Principles for Applying Section 11 of the Canadian Human Rights Act*. It sets forth a model procedure in which point scores for skill, effort, responsibility and working conditions are awarded to jobs and then totalled additively. This approach maks EV far more sweeping than EW, for it allows comparison of the "value" or "worth" of jobs that, on the surface at least, seem to have little or nothing in common. As two Canadian management consultants have put it, "You *can* compare apples and oranges" (King and Vallee, 1982).

The final proposition in EV doctrine is that remuneration ought to be proportional to the point totals of jobs. Allowances can be made for seniority, productivity bonuses, and so forth, but there should be a trend line in which remuneration is proportional to arithmetically determined value. Illegal discrimination occurs if two equally scored jobs are compensated differently and if the incumbents are of different sex; there is no illegality, however, if the incumbents are of the same sex. Where prohibited discrimination exists, the remedy is to raise the wage of the lower-end job; EV (like EW) legislation always prohibits downward adjustments.

The above describes the simplest type of EV situation, where a woman complains on her own behalf and compares her job to one or more jobs of allegedly equal value held by men. Also possible are group complaints, in which a range of jobs dominated by women are compared to a range of jobs dominated by men. This requires an operational definition of gender dominance, which has been set at values from 50 to 70 per cent in different jurisdictions and under different circumstances. Finally, the current trend, as exemplified in the Manitoba and Ontario legislation, is not to wait for complaints but to revise the salary structure of the entire public service in proportion to the results of an EV job study.

A relatively simple example of a group complaint is furnished by the first major case settled by the Canadian Human Rights Commission, a comparison of federally employed librarians (female-dominated) and historical researchers (male-dominated). Median salaries were regressed upon job point scores for the two groups separately. The regression lines showed that, for any value of job except the very highest, the researchers tended to receive higher pay than the librarians. The remedy was to raise the pay of the librarians, most of whom were women, thus making their trend line coincide with that of the researchers, most of whom were men (Remick, 1984:179-81).

Real-life cases involve many fascinating questions. Should linear or curvilinear regression models be used? How should outlying data points be treated? How is justice to be achieved when more than two groups are involved? Should female-dominated groups be raised to the level of the worst-paid male group, the best-paid, or somewhere in-between (CHRC, 1985)? Should male groups be downwardly adjusted to female-group means (a valid theoretical question, even though it is never permitted by legislation)?

We can proceed from these complexities to focus on the main point of EV: the triumph of the job evaluation scheme over the market. An employer's instinctive response to charges of EV discrimination is to say that one pays whatever is necessary to attract and retain the needed work force. If it happens that one can get secretaries more cheaply than janitors, even though both jobs may have identical scores on a job-rating plan, that is not discrimination, that is supply and demand. EV proponents, however, regard the market as itself discriminatory. In the words of the Canadian Human Rights Commission:

> Since the demand for "male" qualifications has been greater than that for "female" ones, wages for so-called men's jobs have risen out of proportion to wages for so-called women's work. This has led to a shortage of male labour. The [Canadian Human Rights] Act, thus, challenges the economic principle of supply and demand . . . (CHRC, n.d.:4).

EW legislation is also an imposition of regulatory goals upon the market, but EV goes much further in this direction. EW lays down a simple, relatively clear rule in advance, whereas EV permits retroactive challenges to virtually any wage bargain.

■ THREE ASPECTS OF EV

Animism
Thomas Sowell has written:

> With unlimited time, either the processes of nature or the competition among men may lead to an intricate pattern of results unplanned by anybody . . . . Some events are in fact the result of purposeful activity toward the goal achieved, but the general presumption that this *must* be the case can be classified as "the animistic fallacy" (Sowell, 1980:97).

What Sowell calls *animism* is also often called "anthropomorphism," which originally meant the attribution of human characteristics to the Deity, but now also refers to any attribution of human traits to natural, impersonal, or social processes.

The literature of EV is permeated with the animistic fallacy. *The Ontario Green Paper on Wage Equity*, for example, claims there is a "wage gap" between men and women caused at least in part by "discrimination," "occupational segregation," and the "undervaluation" of women's work (p. ii). Each of these terms expresses the animistic fallacy.

The root meaning of "gap" is that of a space or opening between boundaries. In modern English, however, it is almost always used in phrases such as "the missile gap," "close the gap," or "the gap between expectation and performance," referring to situations where the space is at least potentially under human control. The phrase "wage gap" in context thus implies that something ought to and can be done to close it.

"Discrimination" originally referred to an act of judgment. In the late nineteenth century, it began to refer to differential treatment of groups based on unjustifiable preconceptions—still within the realm of conscious human decisions. More recently, "discrimination" is often used to refer to patterns of results that depart from some distribution expected on a priori grounds. Canadian theorists of such "systemic discrimination" cite the dictum of Justice McDonald that discrimination can exist "even in the absence of present or past intent to discriminate on the ground of sex. It is the discriminatory result which is prohibited and not a discriminatory intent" (*Re Attorney General for Alberta and Gares* (1976), 67 D.L.R. (3d) 635, at 695). But legislative and judicial approval does not mean that a phenomenon exists, as thousands of "witches" could testify. "Systemic discrimination" is an oxymoron, an animistic explanation for states of affairs that arise without being under anyone's conscious control or design.

"Occupational segregation" might better be called "occupational congregation," for it refers to the well-known fact that women predominate in certain jobs, such as waitress, nurse, schoolteacher, social worker, or secretary. One dictionary meaning of "segregation" is simply a factual state of separation, but that meaning is hardly what comes to mind in this connection. "Segregation" cannot escape the connotations of the legal system of racial separation that once prevailed in the American South. Analogous considerations would apply to the phrase "pink collar ghetto," often used in discussions of EV. To use the term "ghetto," which originally referred to legally defined places of Jewish residence, inevitably suggests that deliberate human agency has brought about job congregation.

This is not to deny that women have been adversely affected by deliberately constructed legal and administrative barriers to their career advancement. But even as such barriers have been gradually struck down by the enforcement of anti-discrimination legislation, occupational differentiation by sex has not disappeared. Indeed, that is precisely why proponents of EV deem it such an important measure, because they expect "men's work" and "women's work" to persist in the foreseeable future, even if all illegal discrimination is removed (Treiman and Hartmann, 1981:65).

"Undervaluation" of women's work logically implies that there is a standard in relation to which it can be shown that women's wages earned in the market are too low. But what is this standard? One objective standard is market value, which is objective in the limited sense that it emerges from the interaction of an unknown number of subjective decisions to buy or sell. It is not objective in a transcendental or absolute sense, and indeed no such standard of economic worth exists. To speak of "undervaluation" in this context is to imply animistically that an entity called the market performs an act of valuation that can be judged by some other standard. But in fact the only other standard is subjective opinion.

Naive advocates of EV speak as if employers can set wages arbitrarily at whatever levels they choose. More sophisticated proponents, being aware of supply and demand and the theory of wage determination by marginal productivity (i.e., that in the long run factors of production, including labour, are rewarded proportionally to their incremental contribution to production), have proposed accounts of why and how the market fails to recognize the true value of women's work. This is vital because, if market mechanisms work as they should, the existence of large numbers of "undervalued" workers is an invitation to other employers to hire them away. These employers should be able to pay something closer to the marginal productivity of these workers and still make attractive profits (Sowell, 1984:113). If such raiding does not take place, EV doctrine would seem to be falsified, unless market failure can be adduced.

The most plausible theory emphasizes rigidities in the labour market on both supply and demand sides. On the demand side, one factor alleged to be important is the existence of internal labour markets in large firms. Market forces do not act freely and directly upon employees who have spent years acquiring experience useful in a specific environment, who have (possibly nontransferable) pension rights, etc. Competition may exist at the initial recruiting level for "port of entry" jobs, but thereafter rigidities are said to grow in importance (USCCR, 1984:204-06).

On the supply side, we encounter the choices of women themselves. They may be socialized to prefer traditional women's work; or they may seek jobs which allow them time off for childbearing, childrearing, and other family obligations. Individually making choices, they may crowd into certain occupations, thus depressing the remuneration (Treiman and Hartmann, 1981:53).

There is undoubtedly some truth in both of these contentions. There are rigidities in labour markets, and men and women are not fungible modules of labour power. Society is more complex than the abstract model of perfect competition used by economists. As Hayek has written, "most of the markets in the existing world are undoubtedly very imperfect" (Hayek, 1973-79:III:67). But even if an imperfect market does not fully accord with an ideal model, imperfection is not non-existence. To the extent that it does exist, a market means that results arise through complex interaction and cannot be attributed to human intention.

The point at issue is the anthropomorphic turn of mind that leads proponents of EV to interpret the world's less-than-perfect conformity to an abstract model as evidence of "discrimination," albeit "systemic." In the end, this is an elaborate way of saying that someone must be at fault if the world is not what they would like—if workers cannot respond instantaneously to better opportunities; if women persist in marrying, having children, and spending time raising them, thus being cut off from some high-paying jobs; and if employers persist in paying men and women according to these "discriminatory" market signals.

Reification

Treating conceptual abstractions as if they were concrete things is one kind of reification. In this context, it refers to the treatment of job evaluation methods by proponents of EV.

Formal job evaluation methods were introduced in the United States during World War II to help rationalize the administration of controlled wages by the National War Labour Board. Subsequent to the War, job evaluation systems have been found useful by many large employers, in both private and public sectors. Some plans, such as the Hay and the Aiken, are well-known and widely used. It must be emphasized, however, that in this voluntary mode of application, job evaluation remains subordinate to the market in determining compensation. Employers use market data to determine baseline compensation rates for certain "key" jobs. They then use the results of the evaluation system to arrange other jobs in groups and hierarchies around the key jobs. Ideally the outcome is a system of compensation which is both externally responsive to the market and internally fair in relating jobs to one another (Livernash, 1984:88-93; 111-18).

The position of EV advocates is that, if the market and the evaluation system yield different pay levels for jobs, and if those jobs are predominantly held by different sexes, then the evaluation system must take priority over the market. To see whether job evaluation procedures will bear this weight, we must examine them more closely. The most sophisticated "point" systems involve, in highly simplified outline, the following steps:

1. analysis of jobs into a number of dimensions related to skill, effort, responsibility, and working conditions. There can be many subscales, e.g., physical effort, mental effort.

2. award of points for the value of difficulty of the job on each subscale. A variant of the Aiken Plan used by Treasury Board and the Canadian Human Rights Commission uses point ratings of 5 to 150 on each subscale (King and Vallee, 1982:56).

3. aggregation of the point totals for each job, most often by addition of the subscale scores.

4. ranking of jobs against each other and determination of compensation.

Like most measurement efforts in the social sciences, job evaluation is fraught with subjectivity. First, the choice of dimensions and subscales is open-ended. One plan may have several subscales reflecting the physical aspects of work, while another may be keyed to mental or emotional features. Large employers usually have to rely on more than one plan whose results are not necessarily comparable or compatible. Second, the award of points is subjective. The points are at best an ordinal indicator of rank, not an equal-interval type of measurement (Livernash, 1984:89). Third, the addition of such points is statistically dubious. "There is," writes Sowell, "no way to add apples and oranges to get a total of fruit. Giving so many points per strawberry, so many for mangoes, so many for pears, etc., does nothing more than put numbers on misconception"

(Sowell, 1984:107). Finally, even if the point totals for jobs were meaningful in themselves, there would be no a priori reason to think them related in linear or other simple fashion to pay rates, as long as pay is understood as a signal of demand for the product. Changes in taste and technology can render even highly skilled jobs, such as carriage-maker or cooper, unremunerative.

Similar criticisms could be made of most attitude scales and other measurement devices in the social sciences. This does not mean that all are worthless, simply that their validity is conjectural and that they should be considered no more than heuristic devices. On merit, it seems presumptuous for advocates of EV to tout them as means to be preferred over the market for setting wages. To attempt to elevate a consciously designed analytical tool, having a certain utility within a larger network of relationships, is to misunderstand the role of conceptual abstractions.

The proponents of EV usually devise job evaluation systems which show female-dominated jobs to be underpaid. They insist that the techniques of job evaluation be freed of possible male bias, that scales be inserted to measure nurturing skills like sympathy and encouragement, and so on (USCCR, 1984:105). There are, in contrast, approaches to job evaluation, known as "policy-capturing," which attempt to weight subscale point scores so as to reflect existing, market-driven pay scales; this circumvents, at least partially, the criticism that addition of point scores is arbitrary. But EV advocates object that "the weights will . . . necessarily reflect any biases that exist in market wages" (Treiman and Hartmann, 1981:76). EV advocates will, however, use a policy-capturing approach if it is applied in the first instance to male-dominated jobs, on the theory that no discrimination exists in that arena, and if the derived weights are then applied to female jobs (Remick, 1984:127-33). In the same vein is the proposal by the authors of the National Academy of Sciences study on comparable worth to include a term for "percent female" in the regression equation used to predict wages from weighted factors. If this term is demonstrated to have a statistically significant effect on wages, that is taken as evidence that the factor weights were discriminatory (Treiman and Hartmann, 1981:82-86).

No matter how sophisticated the methodology, the underlying reasoning is circular. Women's work is "known" to be undervalued by the market, so the only acceptable job evaluation schemes are those which will demonstrate the gap. The reifying trust in the consciously designed instrument is motivated by the animistic belief that the market is discriminatory.

Voluntarism

Voluntarism refers to the belief that future events can be moulded by human will; Lenin's theory of revolution is an often-cited example. Voluntarism is a logical consequence of animism and reification. If past events can be attributed to conscious human intention, and if intellectual constructs are elevated over the untidy flux of reality, it is consistent to believe that the future lies within human control, to be shaped according to a rational plan.

Voluntarism is, of course, not wholly false. Almost everyone, and certainly this author, believes that we can influence the future by understanding social processes and acting accordingly. Voluntarism in the sense criticized here is the direct attempt to attain preconceived goals for society. A more cautious view, advocated by authors such as Hayek, is that goals are best approached indirectly by the improvement of rules of conduct within which social processes take place (Hayek, 1973-79:II:24-7). Such improvements cannot be effective if they merely represent a "wish list"; they must be compatible with the whole complex of existing rules of conduct. Such theorists stress the likelihood that unintended and undesirable consequences will arise from incongruous rule changes.

An extreme example of voluntarism is this statement by Mao Zedong at the time of the Great Leap Forward (1958):

> Apart from their other characteristics, China's 600 million people have two remarkable peculiarities; they are, first of all, poor, and secondly, blank . . . A clean sheet of paper has no blotches, and so the newest and most beautiful picture can be painted on it (Schram, 1963:253).

Proponents of EV do not go nearly this far. They do not advocate the remodeling of society as a whole, but they do believe it is possible to refashion wage relationships to conform to their preferences about the "value" of work. Typical of voluntarism in a liberal-democratic polity, their approach tends to exalt legislation and formal statements of public policy while ignoring the unintended consequences of such policy. Yet such consequences are bound to arise because society is a complex system of interaction in which governmental initiatives evoke countless personal reactions. The consequences of EV, while perhaps unintended, need not be unforeseen. Economists have already used neo-classical theory to forecast the results of EV legislation (Livernash, 1984:105-6). Such predictions need to be checked by empirical studies, but they are plausible speculations to the extent that they accord with generally accepted principles of market behaviour.

EV is a particular type of minimum wage. Unlike the ordinary minimum wage, it applies only to women, and its value varies according to the situation and cannot be known in advance of an exhaustive job evaluation; but it has similar effects in other respects. It will raise the earnings of some women who are already employed, but in the long run it will tend to induce unemployment among women. Raising the remuneration of female-dominated jobs above market level sets up incentives for employers to economize on the use of such labour. Possible strategies include increased capital investment to make more expensive workers more productive, thereby requiring fewer of them; transfer of "women's work" to men to avoid the

EV hassle; and removal to jurisdictions in which EV has not been legis-lated. Such effects are already well-documented in the minimum-wage literature (West and McKee, 1980). Sophisticated proponents of EV admit both the analogy to minimum-wage laws and the possibility of "unantici-pated and unintended effects" (Treimann and Hartmann, 1981:67-8).

There are formidable obstacles to effective implementation of EV in the private sector, which comprises hundreds of thousands of employers, most them running small operations with no formal job evaluation plan. Large employers have such plans; indeed, they have them to excess, from a regulator's point of view. Employers may have multiple plans, and one employer's plans are generally not compatible with another's. It is hard to see how small employers can be touched at all. Large employers are more vulnerable, and some private-sector complaints have in fact been pro-cessed under Quebec and Canadian legislation. However, there appear to be inherent obstacles even for large private-sector firms. An EV settlement imposed on an employer with a large female work force could put that employer at a competitive disadvantage; to be workable, settlements would either have to be confined to small numbers of workers in restricted job categories or would have to be industry-wide so that the costs could be passed on to the consumer. An industry-wide approach might also be unstable, at least in sectors where international competition is intense or where product substitution is an easy possibility.

The initial problems of implementation are not nearly so great in the public sector. Federal and provincial governments are large employers, as are many Crown corporations, universities, hospitals, school boards, and police districts. Job evaluation plans are in common use already. Perhaps even more important, the unemployment-inducing effect of raising wages above market rates is not as direct as in the private sector. For many public services, government is a monopolist or near-monopolist; and in any case most public services are not priced to the consumer.

Induced unemployment, however, arises as an indirect consequence of government's attempts to pay for the increased labour costs. If it raises taxes, it draws the money out of the private sector, thereby reducing consumption and investment. If it borrows the money on the open market, it puts upward pressure on interest rates, again with a depressing effect on the private sector. If it creates the money, it produces inflation by increas-ing the money supply. This may have a temporary stimulating effect on the economy but in the long run tends to aggravate unemployment by distort-ing the information content of price signals in the market. However, since the unemployment is largely externalized onto the private sector, public sector enthusiasm for EV may be expected to continue undiminished.

One should also reflect about the equity of the income transfers involved in the implementation of EV in the public sector. Apart from part-time, temporary or casual workers, women in public-sector employ-ment do not rank among the poorest of the poor, or even among the poor.

Female teachers, nurses, librarians, social workers, and technicians in the public sector may be seen as underpaid in relation to an abstract standard of social justice, but they are well-off in comparison to waitresses, cleaning ladies, hotel chambermaids, seamstresses and telephone solicitors in private employment. It is the former categories who stand to profit from EV rather than the latter.

It is even questionable how much net transfer there will be from men to women. As has been recently pointed out regarding affirmative action, the family, not the individual, is still the focal point of living standards and economic equality (Winn, 1985:40). Women in public sector employment, having secure and reasonably well-paid jobs, may be more likely than average to be part of stable families. It is worth empirical investigation to see what sorts of redistribution among families would be entailed by EV in the public sector.

Voluntaristic attempts at social reform are rarely simple and direct in implementation. The action decreed by the reformer's will is the beginning rather than the end because other actors respond according to their own wills. The moral satisfaction produced by enunciating goals and passing them into law often obscures the long-range outcome of the reform.

■ CONCLUSION

Voluntarism interlocks with animism and reification to produce a mutually supporting triad. Animism tells the reformer that social processes can be understood on the model of personal decisions; reification implies that the conceptual abstractions of one's mind are superior to the concrete facts of social life; and voluntarism offers reassurance that determination can triumph.

Space does not allow a detailed study of existing and proposed Canadian legislation. Suffice it to say that, if the above analysis has any validity, the serious intellectual problems of EV make it suspect as public policy. An important contribution to the debate would be careful econometric studies of the effects of EV as implemented at the federal level and in Quebec, Manitoba, and Ontario. Such studies would help us to decide whether the theoretical criticisms of EV presented here are significant at the practical level of policy-making and implementation.

Note

*   The research reported in this article was financially supported by the Social Sciences and Humanities Research Council of Canada.

References

Abella, Rosalie Silberman (1984) *Equality in Employment* (Ottawa: Supply and Services Canada).

Block, Walter and Michael A. Walker (1985) *Focus on Employment Equity* (Vancouver: Fraser Institute).

Canadian Human Rights Commission (CHRC) (1984) *Equal pay casebook 1978-1984* (Ottawa).

———— (1985) *Background notes on proposed guidelines — equal pay for work of equal value* (Ottawa).

———— (n.d.) *Methodology and Principles for Applying Section 11 of the Canadian Human Rights Act* (Ottawa).

Commission des droits de la personne du Québec (CDPQ) (1980) *A travail équivalent salaire égal, sans discrimination* (Québec).

Goodwin, Cynthia (1984) *Equal Pay Legislation and Implementation: Selected Countries* (Ottawa: Labour Canada).

Hayek, F.A. (1973-79) *Law, Legislation and Liberty*, 3 vols. (Chicago: University of Chicago Press).

King, Donald L. and Pierre M. Vallee (1982) "Job Evaluation: You *Can* Compare Apples and Oranges," *Canadian Business Review*, 9:54-7.

Livernash, Robert E. (ed.) (1984) *Comparable Worth: Issues and Alternatives*, 2nd ed. (Washington, D.C.: Equal Employment Advisory Council).

Niemann, Lindsay (1984) *Wage Discrimination and Women Workers: The Move Towards Equal Pay for Work of Equal Value* (Ottawa: Labour Canada).

Remick, Helen (ed.) (1984) *Comparable Worth and Wage Discrimination: Technical Possibilities and Political Realities* (Philadelphia: Temple University Press).

Royal Commission on the Status of Women in Canada (1970) *Report* (Ottawa: Information Canada).

Schram, Stuart R. (1963) *The Political Thought of Mao Tse-tung* (New York: Praeger).

Scott, Ian, Minister Responsible for Women's Issues (1985) *Green Paper on Pay Equity* (Toronto).

Sowell, Thomas (1980) *Knowledge and Decisions* (New York: Basic Books).

———— (1984) *Civil Rights: Rhetoric or Reality* (New York: Willam Morrow).

Stewart, Debra A. (1985) "State Initiatives in the Federal System: The Politics and Policy of Comparable Worth in 1984," *Publius: The Journal of Federalism*, 15:81-95.

Treiman, Donald J. and Heidi I. Hartmann (1981) *Women, Work, and Wages: Equal Pay for Jobs of Equal Value* (Washington, DC: National Academy Press).

United States Commission on Civil Rights (USCCR) (1984) *Comparable Worth: Issue for the 80's* (Washington, DC: 1984).

West, Edwin G. and Michael McKee (1980) *Minimum Wages: The New Issues in Theory, Evidence, Policy and Politics* (Ottawa: Supply and Services Canada).

Winn, Conrad (1985) "Affirmative Action for Women: More Than a Case of Simple Justice," *Canadian Public Administration*, 28:24-46.

■ POSTSCRIPT

Flanagan objects to pay equity on several grounds. First, he suggests that the so-called wage gap between men and women is a product of market forces and not discrimination, and therefore pay equity aimed at eliminating this assumed gap is misguided. He also argues that advocates of pay equity incorrectly assume that the job evaluation measures used to remedy inequities in pay are objective when, in fact, they depend on subjective assessments of how many points should be awarded, or on subjective assessments of which values in the work—physical or mental—deserve more credit. Finally, he comments that pay equity plans will vary from one employer to another, and that small employers, who collectively employ large numbers of female workers, will not be affected at all.

Robb suggests that the costs involved in pay equity are offset by the benefits. She also says job evaluation does not necessarily mean that market forces are ignored in setting wage levels. Job evaluation schemes attempt to evaluate the market in one of two ways: statistical analysis of wage data, or establishing benchmarks for jobs. Robb also argues that the cost of implementation and its effect on business competitiveness can be minimized by phasing in pay equity over a number of years.

The policy implications for both sides in this debate are clear. In arguing that pay equity is a theoretically flawed concept, which may not provide the expected benefit to its recipients, Flanagan questions its implementation. However, given that pay equity is public policy, he concludes that detailed studies of existing pay equity schemes are needed to verify whether or not they provide the benefits claimed. Robb's analysis suggests that pay equity is the best mechanism for closing the wage gap between men and women. Pay equity, she says, would help increase productivity in female-dominated occupations, and may even contribute to breaking down the current pattern of men and women working in separate occupational categories. But she also argues that pay equity alone cannot solve all of the problems. Affirmative action programs are needed to work in conjunction with pay equity if longstanding inequities in the relative status of women vs. men are to be addressed.

Pay equity is a controversial public policy instrument for resolving a problem with both economic and social consequences. As an issue, pay equity straddles the apparently distinct academic disciplines of sociology and economics. Additional debates in which the concerns of sociology and economics overlap appear in Part Three.

■ QUESTIONS

1. Which side of the debate do you believe presented the most convincing argument? Why did you find it more convincing? Did your own beliefs about this issue influence your decision?

2. How would you attempt to verify the effectiveness of pay equity as a means of reducing the wage gap between men and women?

3. Would the requirement that all employers implement pay equity schemes result in diminished competitiveness for any business? Why or why not?

4. Do you believe there is general public support for pay equity? What is the basis of your belief? How would you attempt to verify your belief?

■ FURTHER READING

In Support of Flanagan

Block, W.E. and M.A. Walker. *Focus on Employment Equity: A Critique of the Abella Royal Commission.* Vancouver: The Fraser Institute, 1985.

O'Neill, June. "An Argument Against Comparable Worth." In *Social Issues: Conflicting Opinions.* Edited by N.I. Bateman and D.M. Petersen. Englewood Cliffs, N.J.: Prentice-Hall, 1990.

In Support of Robb

Grune, Joy Ann. "Pay Equity is a Necessary Remedy for Wage Discrimination." In *Social Issues: Conflicting Opinions.* Edited by N.I. Bateman and D.M. Petersen. Englewood Cliffs, N.J.: Prentice-Hall, 1990.

Hartmann, Heidi. *Comparable Worth: New Directions for Research.* Washington: National Academy Press, 1985.

Treiman, Donald J. and Heidi I. Hartmann. *Women, Work, and Wages: Equal Pay for Jobs of Equal Value.* Washington: National Academy Press, 1981.

Other Voices

Goodwin, Cynthia. *Equal Pay Legislation and Implementation.* Ottawa: Labour Canada, 1985.

Does free trade threaten Canadian economic sovereignty?

Does environmental protection threaten economic development?

Can market forces overcome regional disparities?

INTRODUCTION

The assumption that progress goes hand in hand with economic development or political reform has not gone unchallenged. The critics of the economic-development-equals-progress thesis argue that progress is frequently measured only in economic terms. The human and social costs are not always calculated (or calculable). Is it really progress if Canadians can no longer control their own economic decision-making? Is creating dependency on government subsidies progress? Does progress mean destroying the environment? Similarly, critics of the political-reform-equals-progress thesis argue that political reform can alter a society beyond recognition whether for better or worse. In this connection, some Canadians are asking if Canada will survive the constitutional struggle with Quebec.

DOES FREE TRADE

THREATEN CANADIAN

ECONOMIC SOVEREIGNTY?

YES   **R.A. Young,** "Political Scientists, Economists, and the Canada-US Free Trade Agreement," *Canadian Public Policy* 15, no. 1 (1989): 49-56

NO   **Michael R. Smith,** "A Sociological Appraisal of the Free Trade Agreement," *Canadian Public Policy* 15, no. 1 (1989): 57-71

The Canada-U.S. free trade agreement was hotly debated during the federal election of 1988. While much of the controversy in that debate centred on the economic impact of the agreement, the debate also focused on social issues. One of those issues was Canadian sovereignty. Some people argued that the agreement seriously eroded the ability of Canadians to make their own decisions about what type of social and cultural programs were in the best interest of Canadians. Others disagreed, saying that specific safeguards were built into the agreement to protect Canadian cultural industries, and thus Canadian sovereignty in cultural areas.

In general terms, those in favour of free trade argue that the agreement allows Canadian business access to the large U.S. market, and therefore the opportunity to expand and provide more jobs for Canadians. In a world economy that is increasingly dividing itself up into trading blocs, Canada needs to enter into a free trade deal with the United States or face the possibility of being isolated in the global marketplace. Advocates of free trade further argue that it will be impossible for Canada to maintain its welfare state policies (e.g., medicare) unless the economic benefits of free trade can be realized.

Opponents of free trade contend that the agreement will result in the transfer of jobs from Canada to the United States as U.S.-based firms consolidate operations there. One attraction is the lower wages paid to American workers in states that either lack minimum wage laws or set minimum wages at half or less the usual Canadian rates. Critics of the free trade agreement have even suggested that the recession of 1990-91 resulted, in part, from the transfer of jobs from Canada to the United States. The ongoing discussions concerning a possible free trade agreement with Mexico have accentuated the fears of the free trade critics, who predict that the job losses and increased welfare costs associated with high unemployment will result in increased social problems as formerly employed people slip from unemployment insurance into welfare and poverty.

The pro- and anti- free trade forces also disagree on another fundmental issue, which is the subject of the debate presented here: Does Free Trade Threaten Canadian Economic Sovereignty? Whatever the outcome on the debate over the effects of free trade on the rate of unemployment, or on access to markets, the debate over sovereignty has a powerful emotional appeal. Canadian nationalists have long feared and fought against U.S. domination of both the Canadian economy and Canadian culture. Although estimates of the extent of U.S. domination of the Canadian economy vary, it is generally accepted that 80 percent of Canadian exports go to the United States. Anti-free trade advocates argue that further reductions in trade barriers will make the Canadian economy even more dependent on trade with the United States, thereby strengthening U.S. control over the Canadian economy. This increased economic control will turn Canadian culture into even more of a mirror image of U.S. culture than it currently is.

Free trade advocates, in response, note that the Canadian economy until now has been constructed in such a way as to protect industrial development in certain sectors and regions (notably the manufacturing industries of Ontario and Quebec), while other sectors and regions (notably the natural resource economies of the West and East) have suffered under higher prices and, frequently, higher unemployment. In this context, free trade is seen as a means of addressing some historical wrongs beginning with the National Policy of the Macdonald government in the early years of Canadian Confederation.

The two articles which constitute Debate Six are by R.A. Young, who argues the "Yes" side of the debate, and Michael R. Smith, who argues the "No" side of the debate. Examine their arguments carefully. Pay particular attention to the reasons they give for their conclusions.

POLITICAL SCIENTISTS, ECONOMISTS, AND THE CANADA-US FREE TRADE AGREEMENT

YES

R.A. Young*

■ I INTRODUCTION

This paper was originally written for presentation at a meeting of economists, political scientists and sociologists. For a political scientist opposed
to the Canada-U.S. trade deal, it is a rare opportunity to address economists in a multi-disciplinary forum. Rather than debating the demerits of
the deal, or berating those who support it, I chose to share some reflections
about my own discipline. These were stimulated by the clear division on
the free-trade issue which exists between Politics and Economics, one
which has been apparent for some time. Although no systematic data have
been gathered, casual empiricism and informed opinion among those
familiar with the disciplines both suggest that while perhaps 70 percent of
economists in Canada support the proposed deal, the same proportion of
political scientists probably oppose it. Why is this so?

To approach this question from the political science side, it is essential
to discuss three topics which I take to be central to the discipline. These are
the state, ideology, and power. In contrasting "our" general views on these
matters with those characteristic of "mainstream economics," I hope that I
am not setting up the latter as a straw man. No one can long remain
unaware of the lively disagreements within economics, yet the political
scientist is most impressed by the extent to which they seem intra-paradig-
matic; that is, to take place within an accepted framework of assumptions
and theory. It is even more rash to lay out the "political science" view.
Although a preponderance of members of the discipline in Canada may
reject the current trade deal, I expect a large majority would deny that a
disciplinary perspective, even about those central topics mentioned above,
exists at all. This is one of the maddening charms of political science.

■ II THE STATE

The state is the main object of political scientists' work. Our research and
theories concern its institutions, its functions, how parties seek to capture it
and interest groups to nudge it, why citizens regard it as they do, what
policies it produces and how they are administered, and the ways it
interacts with other states. We also ask, consciously part of a long philosophical tradition which still informs our answers, what it should do.

In response to this last question, few political scientists in Canada say the state should shrink or disappear. Like economists with their central object of study, markets, we may share a disciplinary bias in favour of the state. It is ours to appreciate. In the mainstream, this favour may be limited to the modern liberal-democratic state, but there is certainly little support within the discipline for models in which individual self-interest drives all significant political actors, the necessary result is pernicious policy, and the only solution is to roll back Leviathan. Mainstream political scientists regard the Canadian state, with familiarity, as a pretty benign machine: most want to tinker with it a bit; some seek radical redesign; very few want to turn off the power.

There are several reasons for this. At the pedestrian level, we generally are rather close to governments. The great majority of political scientists know public servants personally, and politicians too. Our former class-mates, colleagues, and favoured students are among them, not as acquaintances or temporary co-workers but as friends. These people are an essential source of data for many political scientists. Not only friendship, but also the scientific need to understand their views in order to help explain what they do, drives us to empathize with them. We see, for the most part, honest people trying to improve things by making difficult choices under uncertainty. Few of us see systemic constraints on decision-makers, or a deep structure to their game, such that those choices are necessarily, or even generally, nefarious.

On the contrary, Canada appears to be a reasonably well functioning democracy, and political scientists overwhelmingly tend to be democrats. Regional policy or support for declining industries, for example, may be inefficient on narrow economic grounds, but if it commands popular support then in our eyes it acquires some legitimacy.[1] While there is room for educating the public about the costs of decisions, we have little doubt about where the locus of final choice should be. And, in general, we are interested in seeing those choices registered through the political process with some accuracy. Political scientists — who admittedly have some stake in the state — rarely think in terms of the opportunity costs of leaving decisions to those with duly constituted authority rather than to the private transactions of individuals in markets.

Were we to do so, most of us would still tend to favour collective alternatives. This is not so much because political scientists distrust the market (which they often do, out of a keen appreciation of power, in or out of markets), but because politics is essentially a collective, or joint, activity. Politics is about the choices communities make as communities. It is the "master science" because it establishes the framework within which members of the collectivity make all other choices. For most political scientists this represents far more than laying down and enforcing particular kinds of property rights. We see the process of politics — the condition of being part of a deciding community — as very significant for individuals (and as sometimes more important for them than the impact of any single decision on their welfare). It is a measure of the gulf between our disciplines that debate, discussion, argument, oratory, persuasion, and speech itself can be treated by economists as friction, as transaction costs, while being regarded by political scientists as an essential, indeed the highest, expression of man's nature as a social being.

Finally, members of my discipline in this country are involved primarily with the Canadian state(s). This is not a Canadian peculiarity. While there exist international networks in sub-disciplines ranging from area studies to voting behaviour to the Utilitarians, and while these are strengthening, the bulk of political scientists in the world concentrate on their own national system, either as a primary object of study or as a handy case. As a result, we are far less transnational a discipline than is economics.[2] In particular, we are less integrated across the Canada-US border. There is (shamefully in my personal view) only a handful of political scientists in Canada whose main research interest is American politics. Institutional links are weak. Relatively few students are sent south for graduate work. And, significantly, most young Canadian political scientists now are citizens educated in this country; in contrast, 70 per cent of the economics departments at Queen's, Western and UBC have doctorates from American universities (Hazledine, 1987:152).

What is the upshot of all of this for the Canada-US trade deal? On the side of mainstream economics, it seems to be enthusiastic acceptance of an agreement which undoubtedly constrains the inefficiently interventionist Canadian state, and exposes the economy to the free-market forces presumed to operate permanently and beneficially in the United States. But political scientists do not favour a deal which would limit the scope for political exchange in this country in order to liberate economic exchange (within a North American bloc dominated in reality by American policy). On the contrary, we see little virtue in choosing a course which will constrain the range of future collective choice, which expands the scope of the market, and which tightens links not only with the American economy but with the policies which prevail in it. Moreover, insofar as the trade deal is being sold on grounds like jobs and growth, rather than on its intrinsic deregulatory thrust, political scientists may be more concerned to unmask its content than to support it.

■ III IDEOLOGY

Ideology causes endless debate in political science, as do most of our core concepts. If ideology is the obverse of true knowledge, it is hard to imagine any agreement among my colleagues about its content. This reflects the indeterminancy of the discipline and of politics itself. Just as political arrangements can be constructed differently, so at any time can they be construed with considerable latitude. Under these conditions, it is difficult to cumulate knowledge, and most of us would admit that our discipline does not do so. Economics, on the other hand, stands at the interface of the material and the social worlds, with one foot securely set in the verities of technology, resources, and production constraints. It is this grounding which enables mainstream economists to speak so confidently about "good and bad economics," "fundamental truths," and, when people choose to be inefficient, about "shooting ourselves in the foot."

While political scientists may have a grudging admiration for disciplines which do appear to build over time, like the natural sciences, we distrust objective knowledge claims about major issues. (The other foot, for all of us, is moved by politics.) More concretely, one could easily make the case that in political science the rewards go to the critical thinkers, the masters of antithesis, rather than to the constructive builders. Instead of demanding that our brilliant students and young colleagues slog in the trenches for a decade or so, applying new statistical pyrotechnics to extend the scope of received stories, we are inclined, in the mainstream of political science, to encourage them to become demolition experts. In any case, to return to ideology, when ideas become successful in academic or public markets, political scientists instinctively tend to ask whose interests they serve.

When we look closely at economists' support for the proposed Canada-US deal, it appears ideological.[3] Of course mainstream economics is founded on the concept of mutually beneficial exchange, and trade theory is built upon the principle of comparative advantage, and the virtues of Free Trade are unquestioned for most members of the discipline (Block and Walker, 1988). But this does not entail that economists should support any document which is called a "Free Trade Agreement."[4] It is likely that even fewer economists than political scientists have closely studied the text of the Canada-US deal. Yet the most cursory acquaintance with the issue as it has evolved shows that Canada got both more and less than economists had first bargained for. On the one hand, the agreement goes far beyond goods, to embrace the movement of capital, of people (of a certain class), and of (dimly understood) traded services. On the other hand, there are elements of joint protection against the rest of the world, there is no subsidies code, there is no exemption from American trade remedy laws, and there are no guarantees against abrogation of the kind that early proponents had advocated on the grounds that the smaller partner, making relatively larger adjustments, had to be sure that its new access could not be suddenly terminated. Moreover, estimates of realizable Canadian economies of scale have shrunk considerably since the Harris-Cox era, and projections of GNP and job gains have been scaled down substantially. In his recent Innis lecture, at the same time as he called upon his fellow economists to write letters to newspaper editors explaining why free trade is "good economics," Richard Lipsey (1988) also urged them, because the projected GNP boost now seems rather low, to investigate and estimate all the other gains which must surely flow from the Free Trade Agreement (FTA) but which can't be caught by normal methodology.

Such faith seems just that to political scientists. It is doubly disturbing when the arguments advanced by those few economists who break ranks and carefully assess the weaknesses of the Mulroney-Reagan deal are not widely circulated and engaged within their discipline.[5]

In Canadian political science, only a small minority of practitioners subscribe to a full-blown Marxist notion of ideology according to which most academics are "organic intellectuals" whose work serves the interest of dominant classes. Far more of my colleagues are basically "thick journalists," with large stocks of knowledge about Canadian politics and reasonably good judgment. To the latter, the free trade deal can appear as the simple political initiative of a desparately unpopular government, and it does not take much effort to move through the agreement and to tot up the gains and losses for each side, relative to their objectives (Rotstein, 1987). We are also pretty good at estimating the political—as opposed to the economic—consequences of major institutional changes, and we regard these as negative under the FTA (Stairs, 1986; Clarkson, 1988). If the current government, for its own purposes, has made an agreement far less economically beneficial and far more politically threatening than that originally envisaged, why should economists automatically support it, even though it has "Free Trade" on the cover? Is there no choice?

■ IV POWER

Power may be the core concept of political science. If we conceive of political exchange as not being confined to elections and to coalitions among leaders but as no less widespread than economic exchange, then power moves through the polity like money. This last is not a mainstream fashion of thinking about power in political science, but every member of my discipline knows that power is significant. They understand it in subtle ways, too. Power is not just the demonstrated ability to realize one's objectives in the face of overt opposition; it also can be used to intimidate others from expressing preferences (just as market power is a barrier to the entry of new investment). Further, all political scientists are quite familiar with the notion that power can be exercised to change preferences, generally against the interests of the powerless, to realize more surely the objectives of the powerful.[6] We may disagree strongly about how much this occurs in liberal democracies or anywhere else, but few of us assume as a first principle that *homo politicus* is rational and autonomous. Indeed, some political scientists see the formation of citizens who are closer to this ideal as an important part of their work.[7]

Our appreciation of the nuances, dynamics, and verities of power certainly bears on how we assess the free trade deal or any other contract.

Political scientists are not satisfied with assurances based on the letter of the agreement (although we know how terribly important legal detail is). So it is not persuasive to argue that the text as written doesn't compel Canadians to change their social programs or to alter cultural policy or to abstain from demanding certain kinds of performance guarantees from foreign investors. There is a fundamental difference between legal rights and having the ability—and even the will—to exercise them. Many of us are concerned that the deal as proposed is conducive to political changes in Canada which over the long term will erode values and social norms and public policies we take to be desirable, not only in themselves but also because Canadians would continue to favour them had they the choice.[8]

Equally important are future Canada-US dynamics. Political scientists who study international relations probably have no more widely shared belief than that nations act in accordance with their own self-interest. We may not agree about whether the national interest is objectively determinable, but it is clear that it is defined domestically. (This is true even when policies must be framed in response to increasingly global economic forces.) States wield such power as they have in their own self-interest: that is the bottom line. There are few political scientists who believe in international altruism, and this is why we tend to favour systems of countervailing power or mutual constraint rather than to rely upon reason and self-restraint.[9]

In Canada, we have accordingly placed more trust in multilateralism than in bilateral interdependence. Most political scientists do not regard the United States as less self-interested, as more benevolent, than any other state. In the debate over the free trade deal, it seems that economists are far too optimistic that in cases of disagreement between the two countries, some sort of abstract reason will prevail over the exercise of power. If subsidies are inefficient, both sides will be able to reach mutually agreeable codes. If the International Trade Commission has been "politicized" in the past, the prospect of an appeal to a binational panel will discipline it. To a political scientist, this is quite unrealistic, and there also is a nice irony in the fact that such faith contradicts the very models of pathological politics which are so current in economics.[10]

The power-centred view, in contrast, recognizes that the USA has self-defined core interests, including the vital matter of Western security, which are non-negotiable. (Try having defence installations considered as regional development subsidies.) It also recognizes that depoliticization is impossible, if the term means insulation from domestic pressures. It presumes that in cases of direct negotiation about market access and the interpretation of bilateral agreements—and there is enormous room for further negotiation and for interpretation in the trade deal as it stands—the Americans will exercise power to further their interests.[11] Indeed, a succinct reading of the trade negotiations is that they were driven on the Canadian side by existing dependence—the fear that our large export flows would be diminished by American protectionism—and resulted in an agreement which would increase integration, dependence, and American leverage over Canadian policy in the future. Finally, a focus on relative power strongly suggests that Canada's influence over US domestic policy will not increase as a result of the deal; yet the effects of American policies certainly will be more substantial as economic integration proceeds. At this moment, economists may applaud how the proposed deal would force adaptation to the relatively free US market. But later they may have regrets should America's policy orientation change—and so would Canadians, for changes would not be made with our interests in mind, but as a result of American domestic politics.

There is always the counter-argument that *in extremis* Canada could abrogate the agreement. This is unrealistic: the costs of doing so in the future would be prohibitively high.[12] A second counter-argument is that Canada is doomed to dependence and adaptation to American power in any event, and that a comprehensive agreement at least extracts some concessions in return, and at worst merely codifies the existing state of affairs. But political scientists interested in the dynamics of power would argue against signing a permanent agreement which confers substantial rights upon the USA, and would favour instead retaining sufficient autonomy to make flexible, ad hoc responses to American initiatives, while bolstering the collective capacity to frame such responses.

■ V CONCLUSION

Canada-US trade is a great issue for social scientists. It has everything—cultural, social, political and economic implications. One big question for political scientists, for example, is whether governments can implement major policy changes successfully when public opinion is sharply divided. (Maybe it is only then that such changes can occur!) On the free trade issue, academic opinion is clearly divided in Canada between economists and political scientists, and if my analysis of the causes of this phenomenon is correct, then I must conclude that there is little prospect of a consensus emerging between the mainstreams of our disciplines. For those of us interested in political debate, this is true, but not sad. Whatever happens to the Mulroney trade deal, that debate will continue.

Notes

* These views were presented at a Canadian Economics Association panel, organized in collaboration with the Canadian Political Science Association, and the Canadian Sociology and Anthropology Association. As a diplomatic gesture, I have used the term "free trade agreement" here to refer to the document signed by Canada and the United States in January 1988, though I think it is more appropriately called the "economic integration agreement." For comments—not all of which could be incorporated—I am grateful to

Sylvia Bashevkin, André Blais, Stephen Clarkson, Tom Courchene, John McDougall, Andy Sancton, Abe Rotstein, John Whalley, and Ron Wintrobe.

1. On industrial policy, for instance, compare the phlegmatic assessment of Blais (1986) with the treatment by Watson (1983).

2. For a fuller discussion, see Macpherson (1974). It is true that the public choice approach claims to be transnational, but this school has made very little headway in Canadian political science. My own view is that it will have to be somewhat domesticated and applied from the left before it attains much standing here.

3. For a very systematic exegesis showing how free trade and anti-nationalism in Canadian economic thought can be read as ideology, see Clarkson (1978).

4. I remember, before the deal was struck, asking a prominent trade economist who had expounded upon the virtues of comparative advantage whether he could imagine any provisions of a real bilateral treaty which might nullify the operation of the principle. He did not understand the question.

5. See, especially, Wilkinson's careful work; e.g., 1987.

6. For a discussion of power not atypical of the complexities in which our graduate students immerse themselves, see Young (1978).

7. See, however, the comments of Paul Fox (1988:85): "The [political science] professors are, after all, research scientists, concerned more with intellectual matters such as amassing and testing data, creating parameters and paradigms, pursuing pure knowledge, publishing papers, and getting the next grant. They are no more interested in the political education of the general public than most medical researchers are in increasing the number of public washrooms." Note, however, that this comment applies to the general public, not to the thousands of students Paul Fox has taught.

8. See especially Stairs (1986). For a subtle appreciation of possible future dynamics in the energy field, see Plourde (1988).

9. For an economist's insightful application of this principle to the design of constitutions, see Scott Gordon (1986).

10. Here I refer to the view that politics can be modelled using the assumption that actors are motivated only by rational (material) self-interest, and to Olson's demonstration that small, highly interested groups will tend to organize better than associations representing broader interests. If these assumptions hold, then as much of the public-choice literature shows, the result is logrolling, rising deficits, and the general sacrifice of the broad public interest to a host of narrow ones. See Stanbury (1986:88-157). For a contrary view, and an exposition of the norms which such models themselves tend to erode, see Kelman (1987).

11. This is precisely where the heroic attempt of Harris (1985) to integrate free trade and industrial policy founders. In a Schumpeterian world, the small country has an interest in subsidizing competitive champions; the large country has no interest whatsoever in allowing the products of such firms access to its markets.

12. One is reminded of the conference at which a distinguished and tough former US trade negotiator was being berated at some length by a Canadian about how

his government had subsidized the R&D costs of the Boeing 747 through a Pentagon program. He cut in to say that if the Canadians were so upset about such subsidies they could countervail the _____ planes. Abrogation would have to be seen as a similar, but much larger calibre, shot in the foot.

References

Blais, André (with Claude Desranleau and Yves Vanier) (1986) *A Political Sociology of Public Aid to Industry*, Vol. 45, Royal Commission on the Economic Union and Development Prospects for Canada (Toronto: University of Toronto Press).

Block, W. and M. Walker (1988) "Entropy in the Canadian Economics Profession: Sampling Consensus on the Major Issues," *Canadian Public Policy—Analyse de Politiques*, XIV:2:137-50.

Clarkson, Stephen (1978) "Anti-Nationalism in Canada: The Ideology of Mainstream Economics," *Canadian Review of Studies in Nationalism*, 5:1:45-65.

_____ (1988) "The Canada-United States Trade Commission: The Institutional Implications for Canada of the FTA," mimeo, presented to the National Conference on the Free Trade Agreement, Osgoode Hall Law School, March 17-19.

Fox, Paul (1988) "Commentary: Political Science Education in the Universities." Pp. 85-86 in Jon H. Pammett and Jean-Luc Pepin (eds.), *Political Education in Canada* (Montreal: IRPP).

Gordon, Scott (1986) "Guarding the Guardians: An Essay on the History and Theory of Constitutionalism," unpub. MS.

Harris, Richard G. (1985) *Trade, Industrial Policy and International Competition*, Vol. 13, Royal Commission on the Economic Union and Development Prospects for Canada (Toronto: University of Toronto Press).

Hazledine, Tim (1987) "What Do Economists Know About Free Trade." Pp. 147-57 in A.R. Riggs and Tom Velk (eds.), *Canadian-American Free Trade: Historical, Political and Economic Dimensions* (Montreal: IRPP).

Kelman, Steven (1987) " 'Public Choice' and Public Spirit," *The Public Interest*, 87: 80-94.

Lipsey, Richard (1988) "Unsettled Economic Issues in the Great Free Trade Debate," Innis Lecture, Canadian Economics Association, Windsor, June 3.

Macpherson, C.B. (1974) "After Strange Gods: Canadian Political Science 1973." Pp. 52-76 in T.N. Guinsberg and G.L. Reuber (eds.), *Perspectives on the Social Sciences in Canada* (Toronto: University of Toronto Press).

Plourde, André (1988) "Oil Import Charges and the Canada-U.S. Free-Trade Agreement," mimeo, presented to the National Conference on the Free Trade Agreement, Osgoode Hall Law School, March 17-19.

Rotstein, Abraham (1987) "A Balance Sheet on the Free Trade Agreement." Pp. 243-7 in Murray G. Smith and Frank Stone (eds.), *Assessing the Canada-U.S. Free Trade Agreement* (Montreal: IRPP).

Stairs, Denis (1986) "Canada's Trade Relations with the United States: The Non-Economic Implications of an Economic Issue." Pp. 46-69 in Lee H. Radebaugh and Earl H. Fry (eds.), *Canada/U.S. Free Trade Agreement* (Provo, Utah: Brigham Young University).

Stanbury, W.T. (1986) *Business-Government Relations in Canada: Grappling with Leviathan* (Toronto: Methuen).

Watson, William G. (1983) *A Primer on the Economics of Industrial Policy* (Toronto: Ontario Economic Council).

Wilkinson, Bruce (1987) "The Canada-U.S. Free Trade Negotiations: An Assessment," mimeo, presented to the Conference on Canadian-American Economic Relations, Kent State University, October 5.

Young, R.A. (1978) "Steven Lukes's Radical View of Power," *Canadian Journal of Political Science*, XI:3:636-49.

A SOCIOLOGICAL APPRAISAL OF THE FREE TRADE AGREEMENT

Michael R. Smith*

Sociologists seem less willing or able than political scientists and economists (in particular) to generate prompt analysis of public policy initiatives. This is manifestly the case for the Canada-US free trade agreement. It is now more than a year since the agreement was signed but sociologists have not been prominent in the post-agreement public debate. Whatever the reasons for this, their writings make it quite clear that most sociologists interested in the economy would be against the agreement as a matter of course.[1] That is because the common presumption that runs through the bulk of the relevant sociological writing is that the functioning of markets produces unacceptable levels of inequality. *Within* countries markets depend on and create a large underclass of economically disadvantaged individuals (e.g., Johnson, 1974; Marchak, 1975, 1979; Cuneo, 1978; Rinehart, 1987); *between* countries international trade amplifies and reinforces initial inequalities between the trading partners involved (e.g., Marchak, 1983:379).[2] The free trade agreement involves one more, fairly substantial, step in the creation of a single North American market in goods, services, and capital. If markets produce unacceptable amounts of inequality within and between nations then their extension through the free trade agreement can only make things worse—or, at least, that is what the premises of most sociologists would lead them to conclude.

In this paper I will argue that such a reflexive opposition to the free trade agreement is inappropriate; that a closer scrutiny of its provisions and what they imply suggests that in terms of the central sociological concern with inequality (between individuals, classes, regions, and nations) the *net* effects of the agreement are not obviously harmful and in some instances and circumstances may be beneficial. That does not mean that there are no grounds for objections to the agreement. In fact, the implications of the agreement for future Canadian policy options probably provide sufficient grounds for most sociologists to object to it (whether convincingly or not is another matter). My most general point is, however, that the agreement deserves an altogether more nuanced appraisal than the simple hostility displayed by many of its critics, a hostility to which most sociologists can be expected to rally. . . .

I would note at the outset that I do not deal with one major preoccupation of many sociologists—the question of culture. It is an important enough issue to require a separate treatment.

■ THE FREE TRADE AGREEMENT AND INEQUALITY

The Poor

Along with the rest of the population, poor people can be expected to benefit from declines in the prices of some of the goods they consume. This effect does not feature prominently in critical discussions of the effects of the agreement on the poor. The two issues that are stressed are, first, the job losses likely to result from the elimination of tariffs and, second, its effects on spending on social programs to support the incomes and improve the quality of life of the poor. Consider these issues in turn.

The agreement provides for the elimination of all remaining tariffs and quantitative restrictions on trade between Canada and the United States. This will certainly require some "adjustment"; that is, some Canadian firms will be unable to compete without tariff protection and will lay off workers and in some cases close down. . . .

In appraising the free trade agreement, one ought to start out by acknowledging that some people will be hurt by it. The issue is, however, how many and to what extent? Three points are relevant here.

First, for those products for which significant tariff levels remain the cuts will be phased in over five or ten years (Article 401.2). Many of the older workers in the damaged industries will have retired or come close to retirement age in that period and the younger ones who are capable of mobility will have had the opportunity to find other jobs.

Second, the magnitude of the change is by no means unprecedented in the Canadian economy. Between 1961 and 1972 the Canadian dollar appreciated by almost 9 per cent and between 1976 and 1982 it depreciated by almost a quarter. These changes significantly affected the economic viability of the businesses and places of employment of many Canadians, to a degree that matches or exceeds the magnitudes involved in most of the tariff and quota changes provided for in the agreement. The national energy program (even in the modified version negotiated with Alberta) had a large and entirely negative effect on the Alberta economy. To the extent that the Foreign Investment Review Agency has deterred some investments it cost people jobs that they would have chosen to take. The point is that economies often change in ways that hurt *some* people, often in response to government policy. That is not, of course, any reason for celebration. But it is a reason for not dismissing the free trade agreement out of hand because it will hurt some people. One should make a judgment about it on the basis of its balance of advantages and disadvantages, in the same way that people have judged the Foreign Investment Review Agency or the National Energy Policy or, to the extent that they have determined the exchange rate of the dollar, the Bank of Canada's interest rate policies.

Third, there is a major ground for treating with some caution Cohen's judgment that the unemployment displacement effects of the agreement will be substantial. Many of her estimates of negative effects are derived from trade association briefs (see Cohen, 1987:22-34 and relevant footnotes). I do not believe that one should necessarily exclude such sources of informed opinion. But it is important to recognize that trade associations normally do not welcome increases in the amount of competition that the industries they represent have to confront and consequently are not likely to have erred on the side of caution in their estimates of the negative effects of the agreement.

I would argue, then, that although the agreement will certainly cost the jobs of some workers it is not clear that the numbers involved will be either particularly large (in absolute terms or relative to the effects of other policies) or that the degree of damage to *most* of those involved will be substantial.[3] . . .

Finally, consider the argument that some Canadian social programs constitute subsidies that are likely to be countervailable under new subsidy rules negotiated over the next five to seven years. This argument is weak for two reasons. First, it assumes that the federal government would negotiate away a set of programs that seem to be generally politically popular. But its past record of retreat in the face of opposition to attempts to partially deindex pensions, to tie the baby bonus to income, and to restrict substantially eligibility for unemployment insurance suggests the implausibility of that argument (Myles, 1988:78-79). Second, such a subsidy rule would fly in the face of postwar precedent. Subsidies are not countervailable if they are *generally* available. The final decision of the US Commerce Department to impose a countervail in the softwood lumber dispute turned on precisely this question (Wonnacott, 1987a:96-97).[4] The distinctive characteristics of most federal social programs is their general availability. (Regional development grants are another matter, to which I will return.)

All in all, I think that the claim that the free trade agreement will damage the poor is much exaggerated. There are grounds for doubt about the specifics of the claims to that effect. In addition, *if* the agreement produces significantly higher levels of income that can be taxed to provide more resources to the poor, its net effects are likely to be beneficial.

Unionized Labour

It is sometimes argued that by subjecting Canadian firms to greater competition from American firms, many of which are non-union, Canadian employers will be forced to resist the wage demands of their workers more aggressively and, in particular, to put pressure on government to legislate to weaken the bargaining power of workers and to lower labour costs by, for example, repealing equal rights legislation.[5] To appraise this assertion it is worth disaggregating the union movement into its component parts, for the agreement is likely to have different effects on different parts.

Five of the 15 largest unions in Canada and three of the four largest represent public sector workers.[6] Those five unions alone account for more than 20 per cent of the Canadian union movement and, of course, there are many more public sector employees scattered among other unions. The free trade agreement is unlikely to have any effect on them. Clearly, they do not produce goods subject to increased competition as a result of tariff reductions. Neither are the provisions on services likely to affect them. Services normally provided by the government are specifically not included in those covered by the provisions of Chapter 14 of the agreement (see Annex 1408).[7] Public sector unions are a powerful part of the Canadian labour movement and a major source of pressure for progressive legislation, including legislation on pay equity. They are largely sheltered from negative effects from the agreement. *If*, on the other hand, the agreement results in greater economic growth it is likely that the public sector unions will benefit from it as the provision of government services increases using the increased tax revenue generated by the growth.

Other industries with significantly unionized labour forces are exempted from the agreement. The construction unions are another major part of the Canadian labour movement. They, too, will not be negatively affected by the agreement. The agreement does allow American construction firms to bid on Canadian contracts (construction services are listed in Annex 1408) but does not allow them to bring their labour force with them. The communications, transportation and brewing industries are also both heavily unionized and excluded from the agreement (Chapter 14 and Article 1204). The unions built on workers in these industries cannot be weakened by the agreement but can be strengthened by whatever general economic growth *might* result from it.

One can make a pretty good case that autoworkers, the core of another powerful union, are not weakened by the agreement, although here the case is not straightforward. Chapter 10 changes the nature of the autopact in two, particularly relevant, ways. First it prevents the Canadian government from exchanging the remission of customs duties on imported vehicles manufactured outside North America (largely in Asia) for the establishment of parts plants that export the bulk of their output to the US. This closes off an area of significant potential growth in automotive employment and in CAW membership and influence. Yet a good case can be made that the "loophole" in the autopact that had made that source of employment growth possible was going to be closed anyway. Certainly, it was an important source of resentment in the United States and the political pressures to modify it (or to abrogate the autopact entirely) were substantial (Wonnacott, 1987a:79-82). Second, it provides for the elimination of tariffs on trade in automobiles between the two countries. This means that US companies can sell their automotive products in Canada, tariff-free, whether or not they meet the autopact's Canadian production safeguards. However, Wonnacott (1987b:75) has pointed out that this still leaves the big three auto producers with a substantial incentive to comply with the production safeguards; doing so will allow them to avoid tariffs on $3 billion of automotive products imported into Canada from overseas sources.

On balance, the most reasonable conclusion is probably that the automative provisions make the autoworkers and their union no worse off than they would have been anyway and probably better off since the alternative to the modifications to the autopact embodied in the free trade agreement would quite likely have been its abrogation.

Some industries are expected to do particularly well as a result of the agreement. Studies vary somewhat in their forecasts but tend to predict significant or moderate increases in production in forestry products, paper, nonferrous metals, machinery equipment, petroleum products, and transportation equipment, in each case with no decrease in employment (Wonnacott, 1987a:34-35).[8] These are all heavily unionized sectors. In general, unions are more powerful when their industries are prospering and there are profits to be negotiated away from employers and when growing production and employment produces new dues-paying members. The agreement is bound to increase the strength of some unions.

Some unions will, however, be weakened. Those representing workers in the clothing and footwear related industries will be weakened as production and employment are lost to lower cost US manufacturers. On balance, the rubber, steel, appliance, furniture, agricultural equipment, scientific equipment, and electrical equipment industries are also expected to experience declines in production as a specific result of bilateral free trade (Wonnacott, 1987a:34-35). But it should be recognized that *most* of the industries likely to be damaged by the agreement are already crippled, or threatened with being crippled, by competition from outside North America. The free trade agreement will only add a little to the process of decline or restructuring that is already underway in each industry and only adds a rather marginal additional threat to the unions drawing members from them.

All in all, examined on an industry by industry basis, I do not think that one can reasonably claim that the implementation of the free trade agreement is likely to devastate the Canadian union movement. It is likely to damage further some unions that are already under pressure from Third World competition; to strengthen some unions in industries where Canada has a significant cost advantage; and to leave the relative strength of a number of very important unions in sheltered industries unaffected, except insofar as the agreement has some effect on the overall rate of economic growth. The net effect is not clear but there is no a priori reason for judging it to be negative. . . .

Regional Inequality

Analysis of the agreement in terms of its effects on regional inequality is a bit tricky. One's conclusion depends on one's theory of the origins of regional inequality and on the aspects of the agreement emphasized. Consider first a case that can be made that the agreement will reduce regional inequality.

One of the hardy staples of Canadian political economy, widely accepted by sociologists (Matthews, 1983:100-2; Veltmeyer, 1978: note 20; Clement, 1983:63 ff.), is the assertion that the economic growth of eastern and western Canada was adversely affected by a set of government decisions that favoured central Canada. Thus, the tariffs imposed under the "National Policy" cut off the Maritimes from their natural markets and made it difficult for the West to develop its own, and the subsidized rail system and discriminatory freight rates concentrated communications in central Canada. The result of this was a Canadian economy in which central Canada exchanged manufactured goods with the east and west at terms of trade that were very much in central Canada's favour.

If this history is substantially correct, the effect of the free trade agreement, as the capstone of postwar trade liberalization, should be finally to put an end to the historical injustice that began with the national policy. Consumers in the West and East will no longer be obliged to buy high priced goods manufactured in Ontario and Quebec. Maritime entrepreneurs will exploit the opportunities provided by the relative cheapness of transportation by sea and the availability of the huge US eastern seaboard market to develop the kind of manufacturing strength that they would have had—had it not been for the national policy. A stronger manufacturing industry will develop in BC and the prairie provinces because it will be possible to ship goods to western US markets that are much closer than Southern Ontario.[9] Certainly, it has been asserted by one strong critic of the agreement that Ontario and Quebec will be the big losers from free trade with the United States (Gudmundson, 1986:15). . . .

However, the issue is not quite so straightforward. First of all, it is quite conceivable that the role of the national policy in the relative industrial decline of the Maritimes has been much exaggerated and that a variety of locational factors, including the larger market for industrial products in central Canada and the midwest of the United States were much more important. If that is so (and the fact that the Maritimes economy has failed to catch up in response to the sustained postwar decline in tariffs suggests that it is) then the agreement will be somewhat less of a force for regional equalization. At the same time, the fact that Ontario and Quebec already have the manufacturing industry to exploit the larger market that will become available may mean that they have the most to gain from the elimination of US tariffs (Whalley, 1987:211).

Second, it is widely thought (whether correctly or not is not at issue here) that the prosperity of the Maritimes in particular depends on regional development grants. Subsidy regulations have yet to be negotiated. So one cannot confidently predict the ultimate effect of the agreement on regional development programs. It is certainly possible (and in the spirit of the agreement), however, that the negotiations will culminate in restrictions on regional subsidies through industrial grants.[10] In fact existing grants might already be prohibited under GATT (as in the Michelin tire case: see Wonnacott, 1987a:101) and subject to countervail. But the agreement negotiated with the United States might produce more general and effective enforcement than is currently the case. If one accepts that regional inequality in Canada should be in part dealt with through industrial subsidies the free trade agreement may exacerbate regional inequality.

International Inequality

.... What about the more general issue of sovereignty? Clearly, the treaty restricts Canadian sovereignty in various ways, as treaties normally do. The federal government will no longer be able to regulate American direct investment as it could before. It has less discretion in its energy policies. The subsidy negotiations over the next five to seven years *may* produce additional limitations on the capacity of the federal government to allocate funds to firms in particular lines of business (for example, high technology) or in particular regions. The effect of the agreement will tend to be to further consolidate trade with the United States. All in all, there is no question but that the free trade agreement limits Canadian sovereignty.

However, I think that the loss of sovereignty is not nearly as considerable as the simple list above suggests. First, since the share of foreign investment in the Canadian economy is already in decline, and since the agreement is unlikely to change that, the *salience* of the issue, as a reason for government intervention, is also declining. The agreement prevents future Canadian governments from doing something that most would be less likely to want to do anyway. (Future NDP governments are another matter; I return to this point shortly).

A similar argument can be made for the energy provisions. The agreement prevents another national energy policy. But, even if another national energy policy were desirable, would it be politically feasible? Two things have changed since the previous one. First, everyone is now aware that both the supply and demand for energy, in the medium term, are quite elastic. When energy prices rose during the 1970s nobody (including the government of Alberta) thought that they would subsequently drop as dramatically as they did (Wood, 1985: 181). Since the collapse in oil prices during the 1980s, the *transience* of resource booms is now fixed in everyone's consciousness. Second, we have estimates, that have been incorporated into western political rhetoric, of the amounts of resources that were transferred out of the West as a result of the national energy program. They seem quite spectacular and are likely to stiffen the resistance of the provincial governments to any attempt to repeat it. So I think that the energy provisions of the agreement foreclose the possibility of a set of policies that, for domestic political reasons, would in any case be wildly improbable.

What about the limits that *might* be imposed on the government's capacity to subsidize industries for one or another reason, including to assist regional development? Since we do not know what will ultimately be negotiated, this is only a *potential* difficulty, to which I return. But it is worth underlining here that some of the industry specific subsidies provided by the federal government that might be at risk are probably already prohibited under GATT. The subsidy provisions of the agreement *may* end up simply reaffirming the limits on sovereignty that have already been conceded (but rather ineffectively enforced) under GATT.

Finally, consider the question of the further concentration of Canadian exports which is likely to follow from the agreement. As it stands, almost 80 per cent of Canadian exports go to the United States. If the agreement resulted in an increase to, say, 85 per cent in Canadian export concentration with the US, would that lead to a perceptible diminution in Canadian sovereignty? I would not have thought so. The US is already well equipped to retaliate devastatingly against any imagined or real political offence on the part of Canada, were it able to mobilize the political will to do so. I do not think that another five percentage points would make much difference. The only reasonable objection to the further concentration of trade would be that it makes even less likely any future shift to a less concentrated trade pattern. This is the problem of policy options.

■ THE POLICY OPTIONS PROBLEM

Even if one could persuade most sociologists that inequality between individuals and regions within Canada and between the United States and Canada is unlikely to be worsened and may even be improved a little, many would still oppose the agreement. This is because the bulk of sociological analyses of aspects of the economy start out with the assumption that the existing levels of inequality are wholly unacceptable and that only more intervention by governments can produce more acceptable levels. What form that intervention might take varies from, at the extreme, the notion that "Anti-imperialism, anti-capitalism and Canadian independence are an inseparable unity" (Drache, 1970:22) to a more moderate preference for some sort of industrial policy.

The free trade agreement, on the other hand, embodies a continentalist vision of Canada's future, a vision that consecrates the role of the United States as major trading partner *and* opts for market processes as the principal mechanism for allocating goods and services.[11] It accelerates the process of intensification of international competition that the GATT rounds involved; it limits the discretion of the federal government to set different prices for domestically consumed and exported energy; it prevents the government from using the Foreign Investment Review Agency to bargain with foreign investors to require particular levels of exports or R&D or world product mandates; it makes less possible subsidization through "buy Canadian" government procurement policies; and it *may* cause the government's ability to subsidize through tax credits or grants to be further circumscribed. Furthermore, after a decade or so within the agreement I take it that it will be very difficult for a future government with a more interventionist set of policy preferences to extricate the country from it. Socialists and/or people who think that some sort of *relatively ambitious* industrial strategy would be a better bet for Canada have good grounds for resisting the agreement.

This is not the place to discuss the relative merits of socialism or industrial policy oriented strategies versus continentalist market oriented strategies. I simply want to observe that the character of the agreement means that it would be perfectly consistent for sociologists to recognize that its effects on current inequality might be limited or rather beneficial and *still* oppose it because it would constitute an obstacle to the more interventionist policies that they believe to be warranted.

Suppose, however, that one was not in favour of the more ambitious forms of industrial policy involving, perhaps, an elaborate system of regional development grants and the regulation of energy prices and of foreign investment. Suppose, instead, that one had concluded that the centrality of technological innovation in modern economic performance required some system of subsidies to high technology industries (for the sorts of reasons given in Harris, 1985). What would be the implications of the agreement for such subsidies? Once again, since we do not yet know what form the subsidy regulations will take, it is impossible to say whether and to what degree such subsidies will be prohibited. But there are good grounds for arguing that, in this case, Canada is in a difficult negotiating position.

The United States provides what can reasonably be described as massive subsidies to industrial R&D through its defence budget. It is inconceivable that the United States would agree to limit subsidies for defence related R&D. It, of course, spends a very large amount of money on weapons development and procurement. Canada spends a great deal less. Consequently, the United States is likely to have a much more extensive *sheltered* set of subsidies to R&D than Canada. If the negotiations over subsidies over the next five to seven years produce a prohibition on grants or tax incentives for R&D then Canada, with its rather modest defence expenditures and defence industry, would be much more seriously hurt than the United States, which would be able to continue to subsidize its aircraft and electronics and nonferrous metals industries, in particular, with defence contracts. I wish I could be confident that future negotiations will not produce a lopsided outcome of this sort. But in the energy and foreign investment provisions Canada has already given away two major bargaining chips. There may be a serious problem here.

■ TOWARDS AN APPRAISAL

In this paper I have suggested two different sets of grounds on which sociologists might appraise the free trade agreement. First, there are its likely effects on the inequality which is one of the major preoccupations of the discipline. Second, there is the question of its effect on the feasibility of alternative future policy options.

With respect to the first set of grounds the case against the free trade agreement is weak. For the sake of argument, assume first of all that the agreement has no effect on the rate of economic growth in Canada. While some people will be hurt as tariffs come down, the net effect on the poor is unlikely to be substantial. In particular, despite (fervent) claims to the contrary, the agreement does not constitute a threat to the universally available social programs that are so important to the quality of life of the poor. Some unions will be hurt by the agreement, but for the most part they represent workers in industries that are already in trouble. Other unions will flourish and still others will be unaffected by it. After the agreement Canada is unlikely to be *significantly* more vulnerable to economic pressure from the United States and ought to be a bit less of a branch plant economy, and less subject to the distortions that that is thought to entail.

Now, assume that the agreement has positive effects on the rate of economic growth in Canada (just as the liberalization of trade during the postwar period seems to have done). Economic growth is usually good for the poor because it provides jobs and greater government revenues that can be used to support welfare programs, and for unions, because their bargaining power tends to increase as unemployment falls. On those aspects of inequality, at least, one's final appraisal of the effects of the agreement depends on one's forecast of its effect on economic growth. If the agreement produces an acceleration in aggregate economic growth its net effect on inequality will be beneficial. If it has no effect on aggregate economic growth it is unlikely to do any *net* harm to the poor and the unionized. Only if it produces a slower rate of economic growth could it be said that it would have a net negative effect on them. But that is surely the least likely outcome of the agreement; it is certainly not an argument that features prominently in the rhetorical arsenal of the agreement's critics.

The case against the agreement in terms of its effects on future policy options is somewhat stronger. Socialists and protagonists of rather ambitious industrial policies have good grounds for opposing it. Once entered into it will not be easy to extricate Canada from it and it will certainly prevent some interventionist policies. Indeed, the agreement may even produce some obstacles to a more limited form of intervention to encourage industrial R&D, and because of its much smaller defence budget do so to the relative disadvantage of Canada.

These considerations suggest three main conclusions. First, the distributive effects of the agreement cannot be finally appraised without taking a position on its effects on economic growth. But most of the critiques of the agreement fail to do that. Second, if limitations on the right of the federal government to subsidize are regarded as a disadvantage they are at present only a *potential* drawback of the agreement. Since the subsidy code that will ultimately be negotiated is not yet known one can only express broad concerns about what it might be; the subsidy provisions cannot yet be regarded as good grounds for rejecting the agreement. Third, the effect on broad policy options provides the one ground on which there is already sufficient information to allow a decision to reject the agreement.[12] Socialists and protagonists of interventionist policies, including ambitious industrial policies, should reject it. But my guess is that in trying to persuade the rest of us to go along with them they will have to provide better and more persuasive defences of the interventionist alternative policies they advocate than are at present available.[13]

Notes

* For their comments on an earlier version of this article I am very much indebted to Bill Watson, the editor of this journal, and three anonymous referees. But only I should be blamed for the final result.

1. In what follows, when I refer to sociologists I mean, specifically, those who have some academic interest in topics broadly related to the functioning of the economy.

2. Marchak writes "continentalism is a nationalist policy of a foreign government; it impoverishes the resource regions by extracting their surplus and directing it toward the enrichment of central institutions in the dominant country." A good review by a sociologist of the literature can be found in Evans (1979). Interestingly, most of the ideas developed in this literature originated with unconventional economists (e.g., Emmanuel, 1972; Amin, 1974) but were taken up enthusiastically by sociologists.

3. Cohen devotes some attention to job losses in the service sector (1987:70-79). Some of the issues she raises are dealt with in my discussion of social programs and of union power. In addition, she claims significant job losses in data processing. But, once again, her estimate is based on the claims of a trade association!

4. This is not, of course, to deny that political pressures led the Commerce Department to search around carefully for a reason to deny the general availability of the subsidy that they determined to be present in BC's stumpage policies.

5. For an extreme version of this argument see Gudmundson (1986).

6. They are as follows (with rank in parentheses): Canadian Union of Public Employees (1); National Union of Provincial Government Employees (3); Public Service Alliance of Canada (4); Centrale de l'enseignement du Québec (9); Fédération des affaires sociales (10). See Chaison (1982:153).

7. Cohen (1988:147) raises the possibility that some government services might be rendered vulnerable to competition from US firms by privatization. This is possible, but does not affect the point being made here. As in construction (discussed below), the provision of management services by US firms does not mean that they can bring their labour forces with them. They are still compelled to hire Canadian workers and to respect Canadian labour laws. This is not to deny that some Canadian governments have privatized or will privatize services and subject the workers in them to more competition than they

previously confronted. But that can happen with or without the free trade agreement.

8. I have constructed this list by taking from Wonnacott's summary of studies the industries forecasted to grow in one or more studies, with no studies predicting decline in production or decline in employment.

9. This is not to say, of course, that only in Ontario and Quebec can manufacturing firms be found that depend on tariff protection.

10. But almost certainly not in the prohibition of equalization payments to support social and educational programs which are, by definition, generally available.

11. The alternatives, and the debates over them, are laid out very clearly in Williams (1986; 1988).

12. It is worth noting that this particular ground is heavily stressed in Crean's (1988: especially 231-3) analysis of the implications of the agreement for Canadian culture. She particularly objects to the agreement because it will inhibit efforts to introduce relatively stringent limits on the access of American books, magazines, records, films, and television programs to the Canadian market.

13. With respect to sociological writing in particular, and the broad Canadian political economy tradition with which it is associated, what is striking is the abundance of attempts to document the inadequacies of contemporary Canadian society and the paucity of detailed policy alternatives. This is conceded in Panitch (1986). Patricia Marchak (1984) has attempted to go somewhat further in specifying policy alternatives. But I think it fair to describe the result as too general and unspecific to provide an *appraisable* option.

References

Amin, Samir (1974) *Accumulation on a World Scale.* 2 vols. (New York: Monthly Review Press).

Chaison, Gary N. (1982) "Unions: growth, structure and internal dynamics." Pp. 147-70 in John Anderson and Morley Gunderson, *Union-Management Relations in Canada* (Don Mills: Addison-Wesley).

Clement, Wallace (1983) *Class, Power and Property: Essays on Canadian Society* (Toronto: Methuen).

Cohen, Marjorie Griffin (1987) *Free Trade and the Future of Women's Work: Manufacturing and Services Industries* (Toronto and Ottawa: Garamond Press and the Canadian Centre for Policy Alternatives).

———— (1988) "Services: The vanishing opportunity." Pp. 140-55 in Duncan Cameron (ed.), *The Free Trade Deal* (Toronto: Lorimer).

Crean, Susan (1988) "Reading between the lies: Culture and the free-trade agreement." Pp. 223-37 in Duncan Cameron (ed.), *The Free Trade Deal* (Toronto: Lorimer).

Cuneo, Carl (1978) "A class perspective on regionalism." Pp. 132-56 in D. Glenday et al. (eds.), *Modernization and the Canadian State* (Toronto: Macmillan of Canada).

Drache, Daniel (1970) "The Canadian Bourgeoisie and its National Consciousness." Pp. 3-25 in Ian Lumsden (ed.), *Close the 49th Parallel, etc.: The Americanisation of Canada* (Toronto: University of Toronto Press).

Emmanuel, Arghiri (1972) *Unequal Exchange: A Study of the Imperialism of Trade* (New York: Monthly Review Press).

Evans, Peter B. (1979) *Dependent Development: The Alliance of Multinational, State, and Local Capital in Brazil* (Princeton, New Jersey: Princeton University Press).

Gudmundson, Fred (1986) "Free trade: The real agenda." *Canadian Dimension*, 20:5: Special insert:1-21.

Harris, Richard G. (1985) *Trade, Industrial Policy and International Competition* (Toronto: University of Toronto Press in cooperation with the Royal Commission on the Economic Union and Development Prospects for Canada).

Johnson, Leo A. (1974) *Poverty in Wealth* (Toronto: New Hogtown Press).

Marchak, Patricia (1975) *Ideological Perspectives on Canada* (Toronto: McGraw-Hill Ryerson).

_____ (1979) *In Whose Interests? An Essay on Multinational Corporations in a Canadian Context* (Toronto: McClelland and Stewart).

_____ (1983) *Green Gold: The forestry Industry in British Columbia* (Vancouver: University of British Columbia Press).

_____ (1984) "The ideology of restraint," *Canadian Dimension*, 18:6:3-7.

Matthews, Ralph (1983) *The Creation of Regional Dependency* (Toronto: University of Toronto Press).

Myles, John (1988) "Decline or impasse? The current state of the welfare state," *Studies in Political Economy*, 26:73-108.

Panitch, Leo (1986) "A socialist alternative to unemployment," *Canadian Dimension*, 20:1:40-41.

Veltmeyer, Henry (1978) "The underdevelopment of Atlantic Canada," *Review of Radical Political Economics*, 95-105.

Whalley, John (1987) "Economic Regional and Labour Market Adjustment Implications of Canada-U.S. Free Trade." Pp. 209-16 in Murray G. Smith and Frank Stone (eds.), *Assessing the Canada-U.S. Free Trade Agreement* (Halifax: Institute for Research on Public Policy).

Williams, Glen (1986) *Not for Export: Toward a Political Economy of Canada's Arrested Industrialization* (Toronto: McClelland and Stewart).

_____ (1988) "On determining Canada's location within the international political economy," *Studies in Political Economy*, 25:107-41.

Wonnacott, Paul (1987a) *The United States and Canada: The Quest for Free Trade* (Washington, DC: Institute for International Economics).

_____ (1987b) "The automotive sector in the U.S.-Canadian free trade agreement." Pp. 73-78 in Murray G. Smith and Frank Stone (eds.), *Assessing the Canada-U.S. Free Trade Agreement* (Halifax: Institute for Research on Public Policy).

Wood, David G. (1985) *The Lougheed Legacy* (Toronto: Key Porter Books).

■ POSTSCRIPT

Smith acknowledges that some Canadian businesses may suffer as a result of the transfer of jobs from Canada to the United States. However, on the primary issue in this debate, he says that anti-free traders have exaggerated the deal's threat to Canada's economic sovereignty, a sovereignty they believe would be best protected by the adoption of socialism and an interventionist governmental policy program. Smith also notes that much of the fear of free trade is based on the misconception that Canada has lost its right to regulate health care and other social programs. He says critics of the deal need to provide better arguments on these issues in order to gain support for the notion that the deal threatens Canadian sovereignty.

In contrast, Young argues that support for the deal is ideological and not supported by analysis of the nuances, dynamics, and verities of political decision-making. The agreement does not tell Canadians to alter their social programs, but the potential for political pressure from the United States is strong, and that pressure is undoubtedly going to be used to further U.S. objectives. According to Young, while U.S. influence on Canadian domestic policy has increased under the free trade agreement, Canadian influence on U.S. domestic policy has not.

Doubtless much of what is said about the effects of free trade on the Canadian economy will become outdated in time. The core debate, however, is not economic. Sovereignty is a political concern. The ultimate question concerns the ability of Canadians to control their economy the way they choose. Does the free trade agreement allow Canadians to make their own choices?

■ QUESTIONS

1. Which side of the debate do you believe presented the most convincing argument? Have your personal beliefs influenced your decision?
2. What kinds of evidence would convince you that the other side of the argument is stronger?
3. Is sovereignty the most important issue in the free trade debate?
4. Do the concerns of anti-free traders in some parts of Canada have any parallels in the movement for economic sovereignty in Quebec?

■ FURTHER READING

In Support of Young
Cameron, Duncan, ed. *The Free Trade Deal.* Toronto: James Lorimer, 1988.
Gudmundson, Fred. "Free Trade: The Real Agenda." *Canadian Dimension* 20, no. 5 (1985): 1-21 (Special Insert).

Levitt, Kari. *Silent Surrender: The Multinational Corporation in Canada.* Toronto: McClelland and Stewart, 1970.

In Support of Smith
Crispo, John, ed. *Free Trade: The Real Story.* Toronto: Gage Publications, 1988.
Wonnacott, Paul. "The United States and Canada: The Quest for Free Trade: An Examination of Selected Issues." *Policy Issues in International Economics.* Vol. 16. Washington, D.C.: Institute for International Economics, 1987.

Other Voices
Smith, G. and Frank Stone, eds. *Assessing the Canada-U.S. Free Trade Agreement.* Halifax: Institute for Research on Public Policy, 1987.

DOES ENVIRONMENTAL PROTECTION THREATEN ECONOMIC DEVELOPMENT?

YES **Tom Waterland,** "Integrated Land Use Key to Economic and Environmental Goals," *Canadian Speeches* 2, no. 8 (December 1988): 27-34

NO **Fazley K. Siddiq and M. Paul Brown,** "Economic Impact of Environmental Production," *Canadian Journal of Regional Science* 12, no. 3 (Autumn 1989): 355-365

Issues related to economic development and environmental protection have been debated for several decades. There are those who argue that the environment is actually improving, that the amount of pollution in the atmosphere is being reduced, and will continue to be reduced in the years ahead (see, for example, Simon, 1983). On the other hand, environmentalists argue that the greenhouse effect is real, and action must be taken now to either reduce or eliminate the threat of depletion of the ozone layer, as well as reliance on individual means of transportation, fossil fuels, and global destruction of wilderness areas.

The debate on the environment frequently focuses on two problems. First, it focuses on differing interpretations of scientific data regarding the rate of pollutants entering either the atmosphere or water supplies, and the ability of the air and water to absorb the pollutants before irreparable harm is done. Second, it focuses on the rate at which wilderness areas are being developed/destroyed to make way for either human habitation or food production. Neither of these issues is a typical problem for sociological investigation.

Sociologists are more likely to express interest in the social issues in the environmental debate. These issues include the impact on lifestyles, employment patterns, and problems of social control. For example, if throwaway packaging is replaced with reusable packaging, who will profit? Who will lose? Obviously, the consumer seeking convenience of product use may be less willing to buy reusable packaging (e.g., glass bottles instead of metal cans) that is perceived to be inconvenient. But the people who make or recycle the reusable packaging will profit from increased use of the product. The makers of the throwaway packaging, on the other hand, will face a decline in business opportunities and jobs.

It is this context that provides the focus for Debate Seven: Does Environmental Protection Threaten Economic Development? Tom Waterland, president of the Mining Association of British Columbia, and a former forestry minister in the provincial government of B.C., argues the "Yes" side of the debate. He says that environmental protection and wilderness preservation threaten to block economic development. Fazley Siddiq and M. Paul Brown, who argue the "No" side of the debate, say that the environmental industry is becoming an important source of economic development.

Reference
Simon, Julian (1983) "Life on Earth is Getting Better, Not Worse," *The Futurist* (August).

INTEGRATED LAND USE
KEY TO ECONOMIC AND
ENVIRONMENTAL GOALS

Tom Waterland

We in the mining industry more and more are finding that opportunities in our industry and for our industry are being foreclosed by uninformed decision makers who fail to recognize the contribution our industry has made and continues to make to the Province of British Columbia.

Even a cursory study of the history of B.C. will identify the fact that it was mining and the search for minerals that served as a catalyst for the development of the industrial and social infrastructure of western Canada. The miners, the geologists, the financiers—all of the mining risk takers of the past through their determination and entrepreneurial instincts—created untold opportunities for the people of B.C.

The miners of today and tomorrow can continue to create opportunities for our citizens and can continue to pioneer this Province if we can maintain the opportunities we have had for the discovery, and mining, of new ore deposits.

In recent years British Columbia has had some vigorous exploration and mine development activity in the precious metals area, and this has served to keep our exploration people very active and has seen the development of several new small gold mines.

The backbone of our industry though, our coal and base metal sectors, has slipped into the doldrums in terms of new developments and new opportunities.

Our coal industry has been barely breaking even in recent years but is in a good position to recover when the markets firm up and prices become more realistic. Our coal industry will be able to expand to fill the needs as markets expand.

Base metal mining on the other hand is approaching a state of decline. Most of our large metal producers are mature mines and many will exhaust their reserves during the next decade and will close. It the past as mines were closed other mines were developed to replace them and usually the new mines came on stream at a faster rate than old ones declined. Recently, however, there has been very little exploration directed at the discovery of base metal deposits. There have been a number of reasons for this including a prolonged period of low metal prices, a shortage of internally generated dollars for exploration, the glamor of and ease of raising speculative money for gold exploration, a deteriorating investment climate, and the increasing difficulty and cost of finding new deposits.

Bob Hallbauer, president and C.E.O. of Cominco, Norm Keevil, president and C.E.O. of Teck Corporation, and other prominent Canadian mining men have identified the major problem facing our metal mining industry as being the need for "more exploration and more effective exploration." These gentlemen believe that our resource endowment continues to be good and that with effective exploration we can replace our (dwindling) reserves.

I'm sure these gentlemen are right, and that we have or can develop the technology to discover new, high quality, base metal deposits in British Columbia. However, I think we have a larger and growing problem that will inhibit our future opportunities much more than will the difficulty of finding new ore deposits. It is a problem that will take our collective will and effort to overcome and one that we must address if our industry is to continue to be a part of the social and economic fabric of British Columbia. The means of overcoming this problem will require skills, knowledge, and tactics that are unfamiliar to us as engineers and scientists, and yet these are things that we must make the effort to learn if we are to continue to practice our professions here in B.C.

I am referring to the growing restrictions of our rights to enter public lands to explore for and develop mineral deposits, the tightening and sometimes unrealistic regulatory regime we work under, and the mounting pressure of special interest preservationist groups and the effect they are having on government decision makers and government policies.

I don't have all the answers to this mounting problem, but I do have some ideas as to actions we might take. But first, as any good engineer would do before trying to solve a problem, let me try to define in a little more detail what the problem is. I'll do this partly by presenting a few examples of recent happenings and then by talking to you about a current B.C. Government proposal to establish "Forest Wilderness" reserves over vast areas of British Columbia.

Before I begin, however, let me first emphatically state what my, and the Mining Association's, position is on a few related topics.

Firstly, even though all human activity has some impact on the environment, we in the mining industry believe in taking whatever practical means we can to minimize any negative environmental impact our mining activities may have.

Secondly, we fully subscribe to the mine approval guideline process that the Government of B.C. and the mining industry have co-operatively developed. It is a good process and if properly and practically administered serves well the interest of both the industry and the regulators.

Thirdly, mine sites when abandoned should be reclaimed to as usable a condition as existed prior to mining as is practical, keeping in mind that different is not necessarily worse and spending $50,000 to restore an acre of land to a value of $1000 doesn't make much sense.

Fourthly, when a mine site is abandoned there should be no ongoing maintenance cost left to the taxpayer.

And fifthly, we recognize the need for preserving examples of the various types of untouched wilderness in this great province and do not object to parks to accomplish this. We acknowledge that perhaps additional wilderness parks will come into being in the future. The vast majority of park lands, however, should be accessible to as many people as possible and as much of B.C. as possible should be managed in a wise, integrated manner.

And now let me try and define the problem for you. In the United States a few decades ago a group of preservationists began lobbying for a wilderness Act and their stated objective was for the creation of 15 million acres of roadless wilderness areas. They got their Wilderness Act passed and today they have removed from the natural resources base 85 million acres of land and had it placed in untouchable wilderness. They are still after more for they have an [unlimited] agenda, just as the preservationist movement in B.C. has an [unlimited] agenda.

Do you remember the battle over the Valhalla wilderness? (Why do all these areas have such sexy names—why can't they even try to save a place called Cactus Gulch?) A small but persistent group of preservationists lobbied year after year for a Valhalla wilderness and the answer from government was repeatedly No, we cannot affort to lock up valuable resources.

But no was not an acceptable answer and the lobbying continued until the answer eventually became yes. Of course the yes answer and resultant wilderness became inviolate. Before that it was the Purcell wilderness—the very creation of which eliminated access not only to the wilderness area itself but also to an adjacent resource area outside the wilderness area.

After the Valhallas, they moved (and literally moved for some of the same people were involved) to Moresby Island, and again the lobbying continued year after year after year. Ex U.S. President Jimmy Carter even lobbied, and of course David Suzuki was front stage centre. On one occasion David Suzuki's program showed a scene on Lyell Island (a part of the Moresby chain) of a bear beside a pristine stream—a heart warming sigh indeed—very effective until someone pointed out there were no bears on Lyell Island.

Well, as you know, the preservationists got their Wilderness Park on Moresby Island, and more natural resources were locked up.

Then we have the large stand of last old growth Sitka spruce in the world which must be preserved, even though it's adjacent to similar stands in the Nitinat triangle—which is part of the Pacific Rim Park.

Meares Island has to be protected, as does the Flathead Valley. The grizzly bears in the Kutzanateen Valley can't tolerate human beings or resource use, and of course every wild river in the province must not have miners or loggers anywhere in sight. The Stein Valley is sacred, etc. etc. etc.

We have wild river corridors, recreation corridors, wilderness areas, buffer areas around wilderness areas, ecological reserves, endless demands for new parks and thousands of "last untouched valleys" which must be protected.

The list goes on and the demand of the non-use preservationists continues. Each of these "special" areas has its own advocacy group and each group is as dogged and determined as was the "Save the Valhalla" or "Save the Moresby," or "Save the Cactus Gulch" bunch.

And what have we done as our resource base, our very work place, has been constantly whittled away?

Well, each time we make some half-hearted protest and gently stomp our feet. At times we may even write a letter to the editor of a paper. But when the preservationists finally win, and they always do, we meekly move over and half-heartedly fight the next battle.

Occasionally we think we win though. Occasionally they are only awarded half of "our" pie instead of the whole pie. But wait a minute—that whole pie belongs to all of us, and what right do they have to take half for themselves—some win!

I could go on and on, but I think you're getting the message as to what the problem is. We are losing the right to explore for and develop tomorrow's mines in British Columbia.

One of the most disturbing government initiatives to come forward under any government in British Columbia is the current proposal to establish Provincial Forest Wilderness Areas.

I was Minister of Forests when most of today's "provincial forests" were established. The term "provincial forest" was supposed to be synonymous with multi-use. The purpose of designating a provincial forest was to assure that areas so designated would be used in an integrated manner so as to make the best total use of all of the resources contained within the provincial forest. This was the purpose of the legislation which provided for the establishment of provincial forests and this was the reason given when the various land users were sold on the positive aspects of so designating large areas of land.

Last year the Forest Act was amended to provide for the establishment of wilderness areas within provincial forests. This one amendment to the Forest Act changes the very concept of provincial forests. It makes the means by which the original provincial forests were "sold" to the public fraudulent. The many land and resource users who were convinced that the establishment of provincial forests would assure them of continuous and unrestricted access to the "forests" were "double crossed" when the concept of provincial forest wilderness areas was passed by the Legislature.

And what makes it particularly disturbing to me is that I was the one who assured people that provincial forests simply meant that lands within them could not be alienated for single or "non-use."

If the trust of the land users is not to be breached what should be done now is to have all provincial forests "de-designated" and then to try to re-establish them with the provision for wilderness areas included. I can assure you that the Ministry of Forests would be fought every step of the way by many land users and there would be such an outcry by the land users (including we miners) that the government would dare not, for fear of their political lives, move ahead with such a concept. The forest industry, in particular, would never stand for it.

Let me explain to you why I don't like the provincial forest wilderness concept and why I think each of you, if you want to continue mining in B.C., should join me in my objections to the concept to government.

First of all, can you imagine what the "preservationists" (Greenpeace, the Sierra Club, and the save the everything crowd) will do the first time someone wants to move a diamond drill into a wilderness area? It doesn't matter that the provincial forest wilderness area may make provision for mineral exploration. The very fact that it's called a wilderness will invite confrontation from every preservationist kook in the country.

Let's look for a moment at some of the language in the Ministry of Forests' White Paper "Managing Wilderness in Provincial Forests." The first paragraph states:

"The Forest Act was amended recently giving us, the Ministry of Forests (and Lands), authority to recommend suitable areas be designated as wilderness and then to manage those areas for their wilderness values."

Well, there you have it—"manage for wilderness values." And what will the preservationist crowd or even Mr. John Q. Public in Vancouver think when some miner wants to pursue his interest in an area being managed for "wilderness values?"

Page two of the White Paper states:

"(2) A wilderness area shall be managed and used only for one or more of the following: (a) preservation of wilderness; (b) any use consistent with preservation of wilderness; (c) any purpose permitted for that wilderness area by or under the regulations.

"(3) No person shall carry on commercial logging in a wilderness area.

"(4) Unless permitted by the regulations and a permit, where a permit is required by the regulations, no person shall use or occupy land in a wilderness area in a manner that is inconsistent with preservation of wilderness."

It then goes on to say that "mineral and petroleum exploration . . . are specifically not prohibited. These activities, however, must . . . be in keeping with the wilderness designation."

It then states: "The proposed mission of the Forest Service's wilderness program is: To maintain the wilderness resource and provide the opportunity for a wilderness experience for British Columbians and visitors, now and in the future, through land allocation decisions and management plans, for specific areas, which protect the wilderness resource against incompatible uses."

The paper says that they'll do some wilderness research and the objectives of the research are "to assess the value and demand for wilder-

ness in order to assist in the overall planning of the wilderness resource";
and "to assess the impact of recreational and industrial uses on
wilderness."

Well, I guess they'll get enough letters "demanding" wilderness—
every preservationist in the country will "demand" the maximum wilderness. There's no mention of assessing the "demand" or need for "integrated" use areas.

The paper also states that a part of the "Designation Process" requires
that "resource values are identified and inventoried" and then "assessed
and compared."

Well, whoop de do—isn't that great? They're going to run into these
massive proposed wilderness areas and check to see if there are any
commercial mineral deposits. Whoever wrote that paper has no concept
whatsoever of the very basic fundamentals of mineral exploration or how
changing technology and material demands can dramatically alter mineral
resource values.

Can you imagine what would have happened if this dumb concept had
taken place 40 years ago and if a wilderness had been proposed for the
Highland Valley? Of course, no commercial ore would have been found—
even if they had carried out an exhaustive diamond drilling program. The
answer would have been, "no minerals" so this place is O.K. for a wilderness and by golly the miners aren't interested so we'll make this one
"taboo" for miners. Do you think these resource economists would have
identified any of B.C.'s mining areas through their "resource assessments?"

Of course if they can't identify the mineral resource how will we fare
when they "assess and compare" the mineral values to the other values?

Here's a neat line—and believe it or not it is from a supposedly serious
resource management paper: "Through the millennia, whatever was left
untouched by man was considered wild. The . . . wilderness was something
to be feared as it harbored beasts of prey and provided cover from which
enemies could strike. Our traditional relationship to wilderness was to
attack and subdue it."

Here are a couple more excerpts from the paper—just to give you some
food for thought:

"A wilderness area shall be managed only for the preservation of
wilderness, for any use that does not threaten that preservation, or for any
purpose permitted by the regulations . . . Under Section 5.2 of the Forest
Act, mineral and petroleum exploration and development in designated
wilderness areas are specifically not prohibited. These activities, however,
are required to follow all existing guidelines and to be in keeping with the
intent of wilderness designation."

The proposed mission of the MoFL [Ministry of Forests and Lands]
wilderness program is: "To maintain the wilderness resource and provide
the opportunity for a wilderness experience, now and in the future, through

land allocation decisions within Provincial forests and management plans for specific areas which protect the wilderness resource against incompatible uses."

And the objectives of wilderness research would be met by "working co-operatively with other agencies and groups, including provincial, national and international government and non-government groups."

So I guess where we'll be allowed to mine in B.C. will be determined in Ottawa or by the United Nations.

In fairness to the paper, it does attempt to explain that mining in the wilderness areas is O.K. and will still be regulated by the Ministry of Mines as long as we comply with the special wilderness regulations and as long as it is in keeping with the "wilderness experience."

The report states that "MoFL authority regarding mining in designated wilderness areas is limited to the question of 'how' rather than 'whether' mining activities may occur."

So you see it'll be O.K. to mine in these wilderness areas as long as you mine the way the Ministry of Forests wants you to.

Even if we can, as mining people, get through all the new hurdles required to mine "in a Wilderness area" do you think for a moment the public or "preservationist" will ever be convinced that a mine, or even mineral exploration, is in keeping with a wilderness experience?

Perhaps what we should do with the wilderness advocates is require them to live in the wilderness for just one year without benefit of any of the tools and conveniences provided by our minerals industry. Perhaps they might just think a little differently about both wilderness and us (providing one of those beasties doesn't get them).

Governments will respond to what they perceive the voters want. Right now they think the public wants B.C. made into a wilderness preserve.

We must inform the politicians and educate the public as to the land needs of our industry for exploration and mining. We must make them aware of the environmental care we exercise and the reclamation work we do. And we must make them understand the role we play in the economic and social fabric of B.C. and what part the products of our mines play in modern society.

There is a movement beginning in B.C. called the "Wise Use" movement. An initial meeting was held earlier this month in Vancouver, and it was attended by a very broad range of people who are interested in promoting the philosophy of wise integrated use of as much of B.C. as possible. The movement is the answer to the preservationists' on-going lobby and is designed to bring to the attention of government and the public the absolute need to make the best use possible of the land and resources in B.C. and to integrate the use of lands to the greatest extent possible.

You know some of we miners are a lot smarter than many people give us credit for. The "wise use" movement started in the United States, and is underway in several parts of Canada as a relatively new phenomenon. But let me read you a bit from the Vancouver Sun dated February 25, 1969 which really describes what it's all about. A well-known mining man of the day, Charles Campbell, defined conservation as "the wise use of the earth and its resources for the lasting good of men." In the article he went on to say: "The important thing as far as I am concerned is that the whole of our province must be developed in the public interest, having regard at all times for the citizen as an investor, as an employee and as a recreationist, and for the orderly development of our economy and civilization."

You'll be hearing more about the wise use movement in the months and years to come. I urge you to get involved.

Always remember that you as a citizen have a right and a responsibility to express your views on matters that will affect your future and the future of your children. No vociferous minority group has the right to deny you the opportunity of responsible use of your province in whatever manner is best for all of us. No government has the right to foreclose your children's options to do what they wish with the land they will be living in.

We all have a responsibility to make wise use and responsible integrated use of our land and to pass it on to future generations in a well-cared-for state.

Our common land will provide for our common future, and our children's future, only if we let our voices be heard today.

ECONOMIC IMPACT
OF ENVIRONMENTAL
PRODUCTION*

NO

Fazley K. Siddiq and M. Paul Brown

The contribution of the environmental industry to the economy of Nova Scotia will be revealed here by an analysis of industry size distribution, productivity levels, and growth potential. Few precedents exist for this kind of analysis. The characteristics of environmental firms in the European Economic Community (EEC) were assessed in a report to the Organisation for Economic Co-operation and Development (OECD 1985). And in a report to Environment Canada, William Glenn (1987) analyzed employment opportunities provided by the Canadian environmental protection industry. Such studies, however, focused on specific components of the environmental industry (such as pollution control firms) rather than the whole industry. This study is therefore the first to assess the output of a broadly defined environmental industry for a discrete region.[1]

For the purposes of this study, the *environmental industry* is defined as the aggregate of all the environmental goods and services produced by firms—that is, (1) the ongoing assessment of existing environmental conditions; (2) the development of conservation and protection objectives, standards, and procedures; (3) the application of resource management practices, alternative process options, waste management, and restoration measures; (4) the monitoring of compliance; and (5) research and development on future environmental management requirements.

Within this broad definition "environmental firms" are defined as firms that provide as their principal function (50 per cent or more) environmental information management, research, measurement, monitoring, planning, design, construction, installation, maintenance, and management services pertaining to the environmental management cycle, including conservation, protection, and enhancement of the natural environment.

Thus, the environmental industry as a whole includes the environmental part of so-called environmental firms (that is, those firms whose output is at least 50 per cent environmental in nature), as well as the environmental part of the output of all other firms whose production of environmental goods or services constitutes less than 50 per cent of their output. The focus of this paper therefore is essentially two-tiered. On the one hand, it analyzes the size distribution of all environmental output produced by the industry for sale; on the other hand, it focuses more specifically on the economic characteristics of environmental firms.

161

A broad-based approach was used in defining the extent and characteristics of the environmental industry in Nova Scotia because of the increasing interest in the growth potential of environmental firms and the pressing need to develop a data base that would allow identification of policy initiatives for support of the industry. Information was collected on such key dimensions as output, size of fixed capital, employment, and growth potential to determine the current contribution of and prospects for environmental production in Nova Scotia.

Because there was no agreed-upon definition or data base for firms engaged in the production of environmental goods and services, the first step in this study was compilation of an industry list. A number of directories, including the *Nova Scotia Directory of Manufacturers*, the "Yellow Pages," and *Scotts Industrial Directory*, as well as government files and listings, were used to compile a master list of firms potentially in the industry. These firms were then grouped according to eight categories of environmental activities: (1) waste recycling, (2) environmental consulting, (3) pollution control, (4) support services, (5) wastewater management, (6) solid-waste management, (7) water and exploration drilling, and (8) environment monitoring services. Each firm was assigned to only one category. This process produced a list of 459 firms potentially in the environmental industry.

To determine the structure and composition of the industry, a relatively simple 17-item questionnaire was developed. The survey sought information on size, relevant economic and financial data, and each firm's outlook toward future growth.

As indicated in Table 1, an overall response rate of 28 per cent, or 128 of the 459 firms initially identified, was obtained. Twenty firms or 15.6 per cent of those who responded indicated that they were not involved in environmentally related activities. Since 108 of the 128 firms responding to the survey indicated that they derive a percentage of their revenues from environmental production, it follows that approximately 387 firms in Nova Scotia have an environmental component. It is believed that the responding firms constitute a random sample of the overall listing since there is no apparent correlation between environmental category (or output) and the probability of response.[2]

Of the 128 firms that responded, 75 indicated that more than 50 per cent of their revenues were derived from the provision of environmental goods and services. By definition, these firms are classified in this study as environmental firms. Based on this response, it is estimated that 269 environmental firms exist in Nova Scotia.

■ ECONOMIC CHARACTERISTICS OF THE ENVIRONMENTAL INDUSTRY

The distribution of firms providing environmental goods and services indicates that environmental consultants, wastewater management firms,

TABLE 1   Summary of Survey Responses by Category

CATEGORY	No. of Firms Surveyed (1)	No. of Firms with Environ- mental Component (2)	No. of Firms Not in Environ- mental Industry (3)	Total No. of Responses[a] (4)	Estimated No. of Firms in Environ- mental Industry[b] (5)	Response Rate of Firms in Environ- mental Industry[c] (6)
Waste recycling	97	20	0	20	97	21%
Environmental consulting	112	32	5	37	97	32%
Pollution control	28	7	1	8	24	29%
Support services	65	11	7	18	40	28%
Wastewater management	99	23	3	26	88	26%
Solid-waste management	20	5	1	6	17	29%
Water and exploration drilling	35	8	3	11	25	32%
Environment monitoring services	3	2	0	2	3	67%
All	459	108	20	128	387	28%

[a] (4) = (2) + (3).
[b] Based on the assumption that the responses represent the surveyed population: (5) = (2)/(4) × (1).
[c] (6) = (2)/(5) × 100.

and waste recycling firms, in that order, constitute over 69 per cent of firms in the industry and almost 68 per cent of all environmental firms.

Our findings also indicate that environmental production in Nova Scotia is highly service-oriented. Nearly 73 per cent of environmental firms are engaged solely in the provision of environmental services. With respect to other activities, a greater proportion of environmental firms (13.3 per cent) indicated that they undertake both primary and service activities than do firms in the industry as a whole (9.4 per cent).

Table 2 presents the distribution of firms in the industry by proportion of environmental output. Over half of the firms have an environmental output in excess of 90 per cent. The average productivity of labour in these firms is also high; at $82,747, it is over 50 per cent more than for firms that have an environmental component of less than 50 per cent. As Table 2 indicates, the average value of fixed capital, employment, and the capital-labour ratio are also higher for the 90-100 per cent environmental compo-nent group than they are for other groups. Thus, on the whole, environ-mental firms appear to dominate the environmental industry since they do not constitute 70 per cent of all firms in the industry, but also have higher

TABLE 2 Economic Characteristics of Nova Scotia Firms in the Environmental Industry According to Their Proportion of Environmental Output

Proportion of Environmental Output of Firms	Proportion of all Firms (%)	Average Value of Fixed Capital[a] ($)	Average Annual Output ($)	Average No. of Employees[a]	Average Productivity of Labour[a] ($)	Capital-Labour Ratio[a] ($)
90-100%	51.5	645,401	1,067,438	12.9	82,747	50,031
50-89%	18.9	290,582	576,161	9.0	64,018	32,287
50% and Over	70.3	550,927	936,878	11.9	78,729	46,296
Less than 50%	30.7	296,073	488,097	8.9	54,842	33,267
All Firms	100.0	478,196	808,471	11.1	72,835	43,081

[a]All characteristics pertain only to the environmental component of firms.

average employment and higher productivity levels than other firms in the industry.

The environmental industry by its very nature consists of a wide array of heterogeneous activities (ranging, for example, from environmental consulting to waste recycling), and the kinds of environmental capital employed across firms reflect this characteristic. Thus, some activities (such as drilling) use heavy, durable equipment, and other activities (such as pollution control) use relatively less durable capital, leading to variations in the rate of investment required to sustain them. It therefore seems reasonable to confine the measurement of environmental capital to the financial value of a firm's capital stock. Any attempt to measure the relative durability of capital in such widely varying operations can be accomplished only by breaking the industry down into sectors. The differences in the kinds of capital employed also prevent any unambiguous conclusions about the impact of the capital stock employed by the industry on the environment relative to other kinds of capital.

The productivity of capital, moreover, does not represent a return to human investment in a particular type of skill. Indeed, the composition of the industry is such that the skilled workers required range from environmental engineers, some of whom work as consultants, to the various kinds of industrial workers and technicians engaged in the manufacture, installation, operation, and maintenance of environmental equipment. Given these variations in the characteristics of labour, it is not immediately clear what implications, if any, this would have on the regional labour force or on the development of the industry. Labour in the environmental industry is, however, generally highly skilled, which explains in large measure the relatively high average productivity of labour.

Tables 3 and 4 provide estimates of the output, employment, capital investment, average productivity of labour, and capital-labour ratios of Nova Scotia firms with an environmental component. Figures are given for both the environmental industry as a whole (Table 3) and so-called environmental firms (Table 4).[3] A notable feature that emerges from Tables 3 and 4 is the wide variation in output, employment, and central-labour ratios within the environmental component of firm activity. The

TABLE 3   Economic Characteristics by Quintiles According to Environmental Output of Nova Scotia Firms in the Environmental Industry

	Share of Total Output (%)	Average Annual Output ($)	Average Value of Fixed Capital ($)	Average No. of Employees	Average Productivity of Labour ($)	Capital-Labour Ratio ($)
Top Quintile	70.5	2,905,000	1,675,000	28.1	103,381	59,609
Fourth Quintile	17.2	710,000	460,300	9.7	73,196	47,454
Third Quintile	8.0	331,600	164,000	11.0	30,145	14,909
Second Quintile	3.4	139,900	69,000	5.2	26,904	13,269
Second Quintile	3.4	139,900	69,000	5.2	26,904	13,269
First Quintile	0.9	36,700	64,091	2.7	13,593	23,737
Mean		808,471	478,196	11.1	72,835	43,081
Median		300,000				

Note: All characteristics pertain only to the environmental component of firms.

TABLE 4   Economic Characteristics by Quintiles According to Environmental Output of Environmental Firms in Nova Scotia

	Share of Total Output (%)	Average Annual Output ($)	Average Value of Fixed Capital ($)	Average No. of Employees	Average Productivity of Labour ($)	Capital-Labour Ratio ($)
Top Quintile	69.9	3,356,250	2,068,750	33.8	99,297	61,206
Fourth Quintile	18.1	868,750	358,500	7.5	115,833	47,800
Third Quintile	7.8	373,875	233,125	12.0	31,156	19,427
Second Quintile	3.3	158,750	91,125	4.9	32,398	18,597
First Quintile	0.9	43,875	63,889	2.7	16,250	23,663
Mean		936,878	550,927	11.9	78,729	46,296
Median		340,000				

Note: All characteristics pertain only to the environmental component of firms.

value of output of environmental goods and services for all firms averages $0.81 million per annum; the top 20 per cent of firms, however, produce an average output of $2.91 million per annum, while the bottom 20 per cent produce only $0.04 million. This wide disparity in firm size is also reflected in the share of firms in total output: the top 20 per cent of firms control 70.5 per cent of the market and the bottom 60 per cent only 12.3 per cent. Similarly, firms overall have an average of 11.1 persons employed in their environmental component. The top 20 per cent of firms, however, average 28.1 persons, and the lowest 20 per cent only 2.7 persons. As well, firms in the top quintile average almost $1.68 million in their holdings of fixed capital; the corresponding figure for those in the lowest quintile is only $64,091. Average productivity of labour shows a similar variation: $72,835 overall but $103,381 for the top 20 per cent of firms and $13,593 for the bottom 20 per cent. Finally, the average capital-labour ratio for the environmental component of all firms is $43,081, but the ratio once again ranges from $59,609 for the top 20 per cent of firms down to only $13,269 for the second quintile of firms.

The statistics for environmental firms only (Table 4) again show that the top quintile clearly dominates the market. In particular, this group of firms commands some 70 per cent of the market with each firm employing almost 34 persons on average or 60 per cent of the total. As well, the top quintile of environmental firms has a significantly higher level of fixed capital—$2.07 million on average—which in turn translates into a high capital-labour ratio ($61,206).

One of the criteria traditionally used to assess the importance of an industry to the economy is its contribution to the gross domestic product (GDP). At $312.9 million, the value of the final output of firms in the environmental industry in Nova Scotia represents an estimated 2.5 per cent of the provincial GDP of $12.6 billion for 1986. A number of caveats are in order, however. First, the concept of an environmental industry is so recent that data on it have not been collected. As a result, the contribution of this industry is not considered separately in calculations of GDP, and some portions of the contribution of environmental production to the economy are already captured in figures for other industry groupings. What can be said is that the effect of crediting other industries with the provision of environmental goods and services, as defined in this study, is a slight downward bias in the relative (not absolute) contribution of the environmental industry to the GDP. This problem of data collection and accounting with respect to the provision of environmental goods and services is the subject of ongoing discussions between Statistics Canada, the Department of Industry, Science and Technology (DIST), and other interested departments in Ottawa. A second difficulty arises from the fact that the environmental industry uses some intermediate inputs. But because firms in this industry generally provide the kind of services that use very few intermediate inputs,[4] the resulting upward bias in the industry's contribution to GDP would not be great.[5] It must be acknowledged, nevertheless, that the above figure overstates, but not grossly, the industry's contribution to provincial GDP. By way of comparison, in 1985 OECD estimated that the contribution of the environmental industry to the GNP of the EEC countries ranged from 0.5 to 2.0 per cent. Thus, even if one used the value-added method to measure the actual contribution of the environmental industry (to remove the bias stemming from the presence of intermediate inputs), the contribution of the environmental industry to Nova Scotia's GDP would still compare favourably with that evident for the EEC countries.[6]

Environmental firms, on average, appear more vigorous than other firms in the environmental industry. Specifically, they account for over 80 per cent of total output, almost 75 per cent of total employment, and 80 per cent of fixed capital in the industry. Average productivity of labour increases from $72,835 for the industry to $78,729 for environmental firms and the capital-labour ratio from $43,081 to $46,296.

Our estimates indicate that some 4,300 persons are directly employed in the environmental industry in Nova Scotia. Nearly half of all firms expect the environment-related employment in their firms to grow by one to four jobs over the next five years. On the basis of the projected growth figures given by responding firms, it is estimated that employment will increase by over 1,600 over the next five years, or 37 per cent over the current level of employment. Environmental firms anticipate creating almost 1,300 new jobs, or 78 per cent of new employment, in the industry over the next five years, assuming no major changes in existing environmental regulations. Should current environmental practices and regulations be made more stringent, the growth rate of this industry could be higher.[7]

Most firms in the industry expect the growth rate of environmental output to rise rapidly. Over 13 per cent of firms project their environmental output to go up by at least 50 per cent over the next five years. Of environmental firms, 78 per cent expect their output to grow by 5 per cent or more over the next five years, while only 59 per cent of other firms in the industry expect this amount of growth.

This projected increase in the production of environmental goods and services stems partly from the continuing environmental damage caused by our high-consumption modern life-style. This damage, if not controlled, could cause productivity in all sectors of the economy to erode.[8] When supplies of petroleum were reduced in the 1970s, for example, opportunities were created in the petroleum industry, and those who could take advantage of those opportunities benefited. Nevertheless, the economy as a whole was affected adversely. It is conceivable that a scarcity of environmental goods and services could contribute to the same type of macroeconomic problems caused by a scarcity of energy.

Although the relative performance of the environmental industry in

Nova Scotia would be revealed by comparing it with those of other industries, estimates of output, employment, and capital are not available for other industries on a provincial basis. We thus had to rely on the less satisfactory national estimates (Table 5). The average productivity of labour and the capital-labour ratios are the most useful variables in Table 5. The data indicate that Nova Scotia firms in the environmental industry, and particularly environmental firms, have a significantly higher average labour productivity than Canadian firms in all selected industries, with the exception of mining, and have a capital-labour ratio that is significantly higher than those in forestry and fishing but lower than those in manufacturing, agriculture, and mining.

■ CONCLUSION

This study has shown that the environmental industry constitutes an important part of the Nova Scotia economy. Equally important is the impressive productivity level achieved by firms engaged in the production of environmental goods and services and that level's projected high growth rate. Within this general pattern of robust performance for the industry

TABLE 5 Economic Performance of Nova Scotia Firms in the Environmental Industry as Opposed to Canadian Firms in Selected Industries, 1986

	Total Output (Million $)	Total Value of Fixed Capital (Million $)	Total Employment (Thousands)	Average Productivity of Labour ($)	Capital-Labour Ratio ($)
Canadian firms in:					
Manufacturing	87,300.2	257,309.4	2,210.0	30,502	116,430
Agriculture	15,322.2	86,653.4	518.0	29,580	167,285
Forestry	3,132.6	2,366.0	91.0	34,424	26,000
Fishing	767.5	579.7	44.0	17,443	13,175
Mining	25,137.9	18,986.3	207.0	121,439	91,721
Nova Scotia firms in the environmental industry:					
All	312.9	185.1	4.3	72,835	43,081
Environmental firms	252.0	148.2	3.2	78,729	46,296

Sources for Canadian firms: Statistics Canada. *The Labour Force*, Cat. No. 17-001 (1984); *Fixed Capital Flows and Stocks*, Cat. No. 13-211 (1987); *Gross Domestic Product by Industry*, Cat. No. 15-001 (1988).
Note: All figures are expressed in constant 1986 dollars.

overall, environmental firms account for over four-fifths of output and three-quarters of employment. Current productivity levels and expected growth rates are also higher for environmental firms.

The performance of the environmental industry is all the more notable in that it has occurred at a very embryonic stage in our appreciation of the importance of the environment to the economy. But firms engaged in the production of environmental goods and services thus far have not fully appreciated their economic importance as an industry in these terms precisely because the environment-economy concept is only just gaining recognition. If the pattern of other industries is followed, the next logical step for the environmental industry would be the development of mechanisms to enhance its self-awareness, cohesion, and ability to make known its contribution to the economy.

Notes

* The authors wish to thank Alan V. Bell and two anonymous referees for their helpful comments. Thanks also are due to Environment Canada, the Department of Regional Industrial Expansion, the Atlantic Canada Opportunities Agency, and the Nova Scotia Department of Industry, Trade and Technology for their financial support of this study. Fazley Siddiq takes primary responsibility for this paper (and any errors remaining in it).

1. Nova Scotia is ideally suited as a study area because of the economic importance of its agricultural, forestry, fishery, and tourism industries, all of which depend on sustainable resource utilization and maintenance of environmental quality. Furthermore, Nova Scotia, like other Atlantic provinces, faces critical decisions about the rehabilitation and upgrading of an aging sewer infrastructure. Thus, it currently is addressing the increasingly complex issues of solid and hazardous waste disposal, using its developing capabilities in new technology, environmental analysis, and information applications.

2. The randomness of the sample is supported by the evidence in Table 1 which shows that the firms that responded to the survey are spread more or less evenly across the eight environmental categories identified. For example, the 28 per cent of all firms with an environmental component represented in the sample compares reasonably with the representation of the largest three categories in the sample: 21 per cent, waste recycling; 31 per cent, environmental consulting (not 33 per cent because two of the firms that responded declined to provide data and therefore had to be dropped from the sample); and 26 per cent for wastewater management.

3. Quintile shares of firm size and other variables were calculated after the firms were sorted in order of descending output per annum.

4. As mentioned earlier, this study shows that 73 per cent of firms provide only services, and an additional 18 per cent provide some combination of services and primary or secondary goods.

5. Environmental consultants, support services, and environment monitoring services, for example, use only negligible amounts of intermediate inputs since they mainly create, process, and disseminate information—all of which are

highly labour-intensive activities that largely contribute to the GDP in the final stages of production. Even activities that use more capital, such as waste recycling and water and exploration drilling, utilize relatively small amounts of intermediate inputs, such as fuel. This is not to imply that all service industries use very few intermediate inputs. Indeed, the airline industry probably uses a fairly large proportion of intermediate inputs, but their significance has not yet been studied.

6. It is important to remember, however, that because the definition of *environmental output* is not applied uniformly, such comparisons must be made with some caution. It is possible that environmental output as it is defined in this study covers a much broader range of goods and services than it does in the European studies.

7. In fact, Nova Scotia recently introduced new environmental legislation, imposing stiffer standards for environmental quality protection.

8. The growing public concern about environmental problems was evident in the 1987 recent report of the World Commission on Environment and Development (Bruntland 1987), which focused global attention on the inextricable linkage between the environment and the economy. It recognized that sustainable development can be achieved only if natural resources are managed efficiently. As well, the National Task Force on Environment and Economy of the Canadian Council of Resource and Environmental Ministers expressed a similar sentiment when it said, "The economy and its participants exist within the environment, not outside it; we cannot expect to maintain economic prosperity unless we protect the environment and our natural resource base, the building block of development" (CCREM 1987: 3). Indeed, as McConnell (1981: 3-17) cautioned, Canada's natural resource base is not as extensive as is generally believed, and, since "environmental neglect creates serious damage to human health and the quality of the resource base" (Economic Council of Canada 1986: 56), this concern over productivity and economic growth does not seem to be overstated.

References

Brundtland, G.H. 1987. *World Commission on Environment and Development Report: Our Common Future*. New York: Oxford University Press.

CCREM (Canadian Council of Resource and Environmental Ministers). 1987. *Report of the National Task Force on Environment and Economy*. Ottawa: CCREM.

Economic Council of Canada. 1986. *Changing Times: Twenty-Third Annual Review*. Ottawa: Minister of Supply and Services.

Glenn, W. 1987. "Jobs and the Environment: Some Preliminary Number Crunching." Corpus Information Services.

McConnell, J. 1981. "The Resource Based Industries," in R.C. Bellan and W.H. Pope (eds.), *The Canadian Economy: Problems and Options*. Toronto: McGraw-Hill Ryerson.

OECD (Organisation for Economic Co-operation and Development). 1985. *The Macro-Economic Impact of Environmental Expenditures*. Paris: OECD.

Statistics Canada. 1988. *Gross Domestic Product by Industry*, Cat. No. 15-001, Vol. 1, No. 12. Ottawa: Minister of Supply and Services.

_____. 1987. *Fixed Capital Flows and Stocks*, Cat. No. 13-211. Ottawa: Minister of Supply and Services.

_____. 1984. *The Labour Force*, Cat. No. 71-001, Vol. 39, No. 12. Ottawa: Minister of Supply and Services.

■ POSTSCRIPT

Some environmentalists agree with Waterland that the environmentalist lobby hinders economic development. For example, Trainer (1985) argues that protecting the environment will cost jobs, lead to factory closures, and so forth, but that this is acceptable because it is the only way to solve the environmental problem. Similarly, Howard (1980) implies that it is sometimes more important to protect the lives of people living near sources of industrial pollution than it is to protect the jobs of people working in the polluting industries. Obviously, Waterland's value position differs from Trainer and Howard, but all agree that environmental protection will hinder economic development in certain circumstances.

Similarly, while they may welcome attempts by business to market environmentally safer products, environmentalists sometimes question the motives behind the business world's current interest in environmental protection. They cite businesses that like to portray a public image of environmental consciousness while continuing to manufacture products that threaten the environment. Some disposable diapers, for example, although advertised as environment friendly because no bleaches are used to whiten the paper fibres, are not as safe as the advertising implies. Most of these diapers still end up in landfill sites, and some still contain liners or fasteners made of plastic. Nor are they as environmentally safe as reusable cloth diapers. Similarly, advertisements that claim styrofoam products are "CFC free" are misleading because CFC use in these products has been banned in Canada for several years. They may be CFC free but they still end up as landfill and are not biodegradable. Advertisements proclaiming environmental safety may be doing little more than attempting to gain consumer preference.

Whatever the case might be with regard to the discovery of the public relations value of environmentally safer products, Siddiq and Brown's analysis indicates that environmentally active firms have impressive productivity levels and high growth rate potential, which makes them an important part of the economic and social picture.

■ QUESTIONS

1. Which side of the debate offers the most convincing argument? Why do you find it the most convincing? Has your decision been affected by your own biases on this issue? What are your biases?
2. Should recycling be mandatory?
3. Would consumers accept trading convenience for recyclable and reusable packaging?

4. Would consumers pay higher prices for environmentally safer products?

5. Is it necessary to pay higher prices for environmentally safer products?

■ **FURTHER READING**

In Support of Waterland
Howard, Ross. *Poisons in Public.* Toronto: James Lorimer, 1980.
Trainer, E.F. *Abandon Affluence.* London: Zed Books, 1985.

In Support of Siddiq and Brown
Bradley, Jim. "Garbage is too Valuable to Waste." *Canadian Speeches* 2, no. 8 (December 1988): 19.
McMahon, S. "The New Forest in Nova Scotia." In *People, Resources, and Power.* Edited by G. Burrill and I. McKay. Fredericton: Acadienis Press, 1987.
Smyth, Ian R. "Assessing Costs and Benefits: The New Environmental Management Challenge." *Canadian Speeches* 2, no. 8 (December 1988): 13-19.
World Commission on the Environment and Development (The Brundtland Report). *Our Common Future.* London: Oxford University Press, 1985.

Other Voices
Burrill, G. and I. McKay, eds. *People, Resources, and Power.* Fredericton: Acadienis Press, 1987.
Leiss, William. *Ecology versus Politics in Canada.* Toronto: University of Toronto Press, 1979.

CAN MARKET FORCES OVERCOME REGIONAL DISPARITIES?

YES Thomas J. Courchene, "A Market Perspective on Regional Disparities," *Canadian Public Policy* 7, no. 4 (Autumn 1981): 506-518

NO Ralph Matthews, "Two Alternative Explanations of the Problem of Regional Dependency in Canada," *Canadian Public Policy* 7, no. 2 (Spring 1981): 268-283

While there is general agreement that Canada is a nation of regions, not everyone agrees on the definition of the regions. One conception splits the country into East and West using the Manitoba-Ontario border as the dividing line. But that division masks regional differences between the Atlantic provinces (Nova Scotia, New Brunswick, Prince Edward Island, and Newfoundland), and central Canada (Ontario and Quebec).

To solve this problem, Canada is sometimes divided into three regions: the West, central Canada (Ontario and Quebec), and the Atlantic provinces. This division, however, ignores differences between Quebec and Ontario, and between British Columbia and the Prairie provinces (Manitoba, Saskatchewan, and Alberta). Some analysts even suggest that Alberta should be classified as a separate region because its economy is much stronger than that of either Manitoba or Saskatchewan.

Each of these divisions, however, excludes the North (the Northwest Territories and the Yukon). Thus, taking all of the above factors into consideration, Canada can be divided into seven regions: the North, British Columbia, Alberta, the Prairie provinces (Manitoba and Saskatchewan), Ontario, Quebec, and the Atlantic provinces. Of course, even this division fails to take into account regional distinctions within these regions. There is considerable difference, for example, between the economies of Northern Ontario and Southern Ontario, between Halifax and

Cape Breton Island, between the Island of Newfoundland and Labrador, and between the northern and southern portions of the Prairie provinces, etc. Furthermore, some portions of a province may have more in common with a neighbouring province than with the rest of its own province.

Regardless of the definition used, the importance of understanding regional disparities cannot be understated. After more than one hundred years of government efforts to deal with regional disparities—first by attempting to develop the national economy, then by developing specific regional economic policies—regional disparities remain. Two of the most hotly debated theoretical models used to explain why these disparities exist are dependency theory and transfer dependency theory. Dependency theory was originally developed to explain the impoverishment of the Third World. The theory says that underdeveloped countries form hinterlands that provide low-cost resources, including labour and raw materials, to be used by advanced countries known as the metropolis. The metropolis dominates the economy of the hinterland, creating a state of dependency. The dependency model has been adapted and applied to the Canadian economy (Phillips, 1982; Veltmeyer, 1979). The "have-not" regions (either provinces or underdeveloped regions within provinces) of Canada provide low-cost raw materials and labour for the "have" regions.

Transfer dependency theory was developed by Courchene (1978, 1981) and others. It says that the current system of transfer payments, which were supposed to enhance economic development in the have-not regions, actually impedes development by interfering with market forces. The system of transfer payments encourages have-not regions to develop economic policies which take advantage of short-term gains inherent in the policy, but which leave the region at a disadvantage in the long term. Rather than develop their economies to meet the needs of the market, have-not regions develop policies which attract the transfer payments, but which do not allow them to develop strategies to meet current market conditions.

In Debate Eight, Thomas J. Courchene, arguing for the "Yes" side of the debate, advocates transfer dependency theory, while Ralph Matthews, arguing for the "No" side of the debate, supports dependency theory.

References

Courchene, Thomas J. (1978) "Avenues of Regional Adjustment: The Transfer System and Regional Disparities," edited by M. Walker. *Canadian Confederation at the Crossroads* (Vancouver: The Fraser Institute).

Courchene, Thomas J. (1981) "Regions, Transfers and Growth," *Canadian Business Review* 8, no. 1: 6-12.

Phillips, Paul (1982) *Regional Disparities*, updated ed. (Toronto: James Lorimer).

Veltmeyer, Henry (1979) "The Capitalist Underdevelopment of Atlantic Canada," in *Underdevelopment and Social Movements in Atlantic Canada*, edited by R.J. Brym and R.J. Sacouman (Toronto: New Hogtown Press).

A MARKET PERSPECTIVE ON REGIONAL DISPARITIES

Thomas J. Courchene*

■ INTRODUCTION

I have interpreted my role in this symposium on regional disparities to review and update my views on regional problems and issues in Canada. Since ideology and value judgment appear to play a much greater role in analysis of regional issues than is the case for most other policy areas, it is probably important to announce one's bias at the outset. I am in favour of allowing market forces to play a greater role in the allocation of resources across provinces and regions. Yet this cannot, in my view, imply a wholesale adoption of the tenets of the neoclassical paradigm to regional issues. This would be contrary to the very essence of a federal system. On the surface, the economic theory of federalism would appear to be very appealing to market-oriented economists. Provinces are viewed as providing alternative bundles of public services and citizens can choose their province according to their preferences for these various bundles. This "voting by foot" aspect of federalism introduces into the government sphere some of the flexibility and competition that characterizes the operation of decentralized markets. But because the provinces are autonomous in certain spheres, and indeed are backed up by constitutional guarantees, the concept of "national efficiency" loses some of its appeal since, pursued to the extreme, it would likely imply a unitary state. This does not imply that unitary states are likely to operate more efficiently than federal states. For example, I know of no policy measure in our federalism that does as much to impede labour mobility as do Great Britain's policies with respect to rent control and housing. What it does imply, however, is that for some policy areas the efficiency criteria must be constrained to take into account the division of powers within the federation. Nonetheless, the position I will take in the analysis below is that the failure over time to submit the provinces and regions to the discipline of the market has exacerbated regional disparities and has tended to rigidify our industrial structure. . . .

■ MARKET SECTOR DISPARITIES VS. PUBLIC SECTOR DISPARITIES

As a starting point, we can probably all agree on one issue. Regional disparities do exist. Unemployment rates differ across regions. So do incomes *per capita*, productivity levels, etc. Some of these economic differentials arise from the vagaries of nature, some are due to changes in relative prices and some no doubt are the result of government policies. The first point I wish to make is that at the present time, and certainly relative to what prevailed a few decades ago, regional disparities exist principally in the sphere of market sector incomes. Access to basic public sector goods and services does not differ nearly as much across provinces as access to private sector goods and services. To a large extent this is due to the system of intergovernmental transfers, including equalization payments, that has long been a hallmark of the Canadian federation. And if the Confederation debates last summer brought home any message at all it was surely that equalization payments are an essential part of the glue that binds us together as a nation. . . .

■ REGIONAL EQUILIBRIA AND TRANSFER DEPENDENCY

However, the fact that these regional disparities exist does not imply, as is frequently suggested, that there also exists a regional disequilibrium. Indeed, the opposite is true. Setting aside the recent energy-related transition period, *the on-going regional disparities reflect a regional equilibrium.* Now equilibrium merely describes a state that is self-reinforcing. We need not approve of the characteristics of the regional equilibrium, but we should not deny its existence. This is a critical issue and one I will come back to but first I want to spell out a few more closely related propositions.

In spite of the fact that the transfer system has some beneficial effects, it also has some deleterious ones. Basically, transfers impede the process of regional adjustment. Decades of interrupting the process of regional economic adjustment have led some provinces into a position where they are increasingly dependent upon government transfers for their economic well-being. This has now come to be known as "transfer dependency." . . .

There is no doubt that for any given year the impact of the transfer system is viewed by many to be "appropriate." It would be intolerable to force the required adjustment on these provinces immediately. Yet the long run is composed of a succession of short runs and very soon the behavior of all agents in these provinces will incorporate expectations of a growing system of transfers. Quebec's Finance Minister Jacques Parizeau made a comment in the context of the "battle of the balance sheets" that preceded the Quebec Referendum that, I think, illustrates this point most appropriately. He acknowledged that Quebec had benefitted, dollar-wise, from the federal transfers but questioned the longer-term impact of these monies on the Quebec economy. He noted that Quebec had been lulled into a false sense of security and, as a result, had delayed taking the needed action to restructure some of its industries. With the passage of time the problems magnified and Quebec soon found itself with an outmoded industrial structure in major parts of its economy. This is one effect of transfer dependency.

It is also the case that the incentives embedded in the transfer system are such that provincial governments are often encouraged to undertake initiatives on the policy front that are clearly not in their long-term economic interest. This too is part of "transfer dependency." One of the most obvious bits of evidence on this score is the fact that Quebec has had, until recently at least, the highest minimum wage on the continent, let alone in Canada. This does not make economic sense but it exists in large measure because Quebec does not bear the full financial and economic costs of such a policy decision. As unemployment rises, Ottawa comes to Quebec's aid with Unemployment Insurance (UI) transfers, increased equalization payments, and one half of any welfare costs. But even this is not the end of the story. Because of its high unemployment, Quebec can then lobby (successfully) for such things as quotas and tariffs on its beleaguered industries. The solution is, of course, to alter the incentives embodied in the transfer system so that one province cannot export, via Ottawa to the rest of Canada, the costs of its decisions on the economic front.

By way of summary to this general issue, I assert that the present regional disparities represent not only a regional equilibrium but to a large extent they reflect a *policy-induced* equilibrium. Once again, an example may be useful. The decision to allow UI benefits in the off-season for self-employed Newfoundland fishermen has led to the situation where today there are more fishermen and their operations are smaller in scale than the economics of the industry would dictate. The failure to grant the similar privilege (?) to self-employed farmers in Saskatchewan contributed to the massive capitalization in agriculture, to the emptying of countless hamlets and villages, and to a substantial loss of population for this prairie province. I think that Saskatchewan is lucky that it was not treated like Newfoundland. But one does not have to take a position as to which option was preferable. The essential point is that one cannot escape the fact that the equilibria in these two provinces are to some substantial degree policy induced.

It should be emphasized that this says nothing at all about the *motivation* of the inhabitants in these provinces. Put a Saskatchewan farmer in the shoes of a Newfoundland fisherman and he will behave as does any other fisherman. And within the context of the incentives he faces, this will be rational behavior. It may well be that the transfer system also serves to erode individual initiative which will in turn exacerbate the existing disparities, but this is quite a separate issue. Transfer dependency does not assume that people have different tastes and preferences, contrary to what Matthews asserts (1981).

There is another implication that follows from all this. One often hears that Ottawa must now pour more funds into the have-not provinces to combat their high unemployment rates. And perhaps Ottawa will, since, in the final analysis, such decisions are made in the political arena. However, the thrust of the above analysis is that the high unemployment rates in these provinces are part and parcel of the regional equilibrium that derives from the existing largesse on the transfer front. As a result of the existing level of transfers to persons and governments and the presence of such things as nationwide pay scales for federal employees, both wage rates and unemployment rates are higher than would otherwise be the case. On a *per capita* basis the Atlantic region has a greater-than-average share of government-source income and a less-than-average share of market-source income. This is a characteristic of the transfer-induced equilibrium. While all Canadians should be unhappy and concerned about these high unemployment rates it is also the case that they should recognize that increasing the magnitude of the transfer system may serve only to exacerbate the problem.

The conclusion drawn by many analysts is that I am in favour of scrapping or dismantling the transfer system. This is simply not the case. If we had our economic history to relive many of us, including no doubt some of the "beneficiary provinces," would argue for doing things quite differently on the transfer front. But we cannot relive history and now that the regional economies have adjusted to the existing transfer system it is unrealistic to argue for a dramatic retrenchment. Indeed, it would also be unfair in the sense that Quebec's problems with its economic structure, for example, are not entirely its own doing: in part they represented a calculated response (and over the short run possibly a rational response) to *federal* policy initiatives. Thus, the responsibility for regional disparities rests with all Canadians and not just with the particular provinces or regions. However, rationalization of the system to encourage initiative, efficiency and growth *is* a realistic goal, even if it is the case that from a political standpoint this rationalization will have to be implemented incrementally. . . .

■ THE NEW REGIONAL DISPARITIES

In the wake of the near twenty-fold increase in the price of energy, a new economic perspective has been forged both at the global and Canadian levels. This new perspective pits the industrialized countries against the resource-rich countries and within Canada it pits the centre against the peripheries of the country, particularly if one takes a positive view of the eastcoast resource potential. The new buzzword on the regional front should no longer be regional economic disparities but rather regional economic "adjustment" and just how much adjustment we ought to tolerate. . . .

In lieu of concluding comments on the general interaction between regional policy, intervention and protectionism, I find it instructive to quote at some length from a recent paper by US economist Lester Thurow:

> Within the category called industrial policies there are two broad choices.
> Policies can be built to help losers or winners. The correct solution is to have a

social safety net for helping individuals who are hurt when losers fail and an industrial policy for insuring that America has sunrise industries into which individuals can move when their old jobs disappear. . . .

Productivity and real standards of living rise by getting into new high productivity industries and getting out of old low productivity industries. If the latter are protected this stops labor and capital from leaving these industries. In addition, the bail-out funds must come from somewhere and they usually come out of funds that otherwise would be available for new industries. This leads to slower growth for the sunrise industries and a lower standard of living. (1981: 30-32) . . .

■ LABOUR MOBILITY: PEOPLE PROSPERITY OR PLACE PROSPERITY

One of the recurring criticisms of transfer dependency (or "market dependency," as I prefer to refer to it) is that it essentially boils down to a depopulation strategy for the poorer regions. To some extent the criticism rings true. Most policy initiatives embody implications for labour mobility. The granting of UI to self-employed fishermen in Newfoundland but not to self-employed farmers in Saskatchewan increased the population of the former and decreased the population of the latter. Likewise, the decision to keep the domestic energy price below world levels serves to increase the population of the non-energy producing provinces relative to the energy-producing provinces. And so it is with most policies. Market dependency may well mean that some of the provinces in the Atlantic region will suffer losses of population over the short term. But so what. To my mind the critical issues are (a) whether or not the migrants are better off in their new location and (b) whether the region will be more viable economically over the longer term. If these answers are in the affirmative, that to me is the end of the story.

It is interesting in this regard to focus on the position of Saskatchewan. In 1931 it had by far the largest population of the four western provinces. By 1979 it had the smallest population in the west. Over this roughly fifty year period the population of Canada increased by 127 per cent while the population of Saskatchewan increased by only 4 per cent. Comparable figures for the Atlantic provinces were: Nova Scotia (65%), New Brunswick (72%), Prince Edward Island (41%) and Newfoundland (59%).[1] I find it a bit ironical that on the one hand overall policy allowed (or encouraged) essentially zero population growth over a 50 year period for Saskatchewan while, on the other hand, the mere mention of submitting to a bit of market discipline for some of the present have-not provinces (and for the have provinces too!) is frequently met with claims that the policy is essentially a depopulation strategy. This is most evident in the recent article by Matthews (1981), but the concern is expressed in many quarters.

Let me admit at the outset that labour mobility is not a universal panacea. Not all migration will be in the best interests of the origin provinces or regions. Nor need it be consistent with overall efficiency (as we shall see later). From a political standpoint the concerns are even greater: no provincial premier wants to tolerate a population loss. Part of the concern is that the supposed or actual costs occur immediately whereas the benefits (including capital inflows) tend to arise in later periods. On the other hand, it is also important to recognize that there can be very substantial costs to inhibiting mobility. Some of them were covered in the above quotation from Thurow. To these I would add that one should take account of the fact that bribing workers to remain in a given area (whether by some form of labour or industry subsidy or by discriminatory actions on the part of potential recipient provinces) may well subject these individuals to low-productivity jobs and, depending on who receives the subsidy, lower income over their lifetime. This is especially true where younger workers are involved.

This is, in fact, the old "people prosperity" vs. "place prosperity" trade-off. My preference is and always has been to put more stress on the welfare of individual Canadians than on the welfare of geographical collectivities. . . . I have no illusions that governments will stand idly by and allow the unfettered market to call the adjustment tune. They will intervene. However, what concern over people rather than place implies is that this intervention be directed principally to accommodating the adjustment of individuals and families. Complicating this, of course, is the political reality that it is the "sunset" industries and not the "sunrise" industries and, perhaps more importantly, the potential losing constituencies (in the electoral sense of this term) that are able to mount the effective lobbies. . . .

Notes

*   I would like to thank my colleagues Peter Howitt and Ron Wirick for their comments on an earlier draft.

1.   The percentage for Newfoundland is the growth over the 1951-1979 period. The percentage population growth for the remaining provinces over the 1931-1979 period is as follows: Quebec (11%), Ontario (145%), Manitoba (47%), Alberta (175%), British Columbia (279%). It should be noted that if one were to focus on years prior to 1931 it is the case that for PEI one could obtain rates of growth similar to those for Saskatchewan. For example, compared to 1891 the population of PEI in 1979 had increased by only 3%. This does not hold for the other Atlantic provinces.

References

Matthews, Ralph (1981) "Two Alternative Explanations of the Problem of Regional Dependency in Canada," in *Canadian Public Policy—Analyse de Politiques*, VII:2:268-283.

Thurow, Lester C. (1981) "The Productivity Problem," in *Policies for Stagflation*, Vol. 2 (Toronto: Ontario Economic Council), pp. 11-34.

Ralph Matthews

This paper was written primarily because of my serious reservations about the assumptions and strategy for development contained in the *transfer dependency* approach. It is my belief that such an approach fails to clearly distinguish between economic and social welfare, and frequently advocates economic policies which would have deleterious social consequences. My discussion of *dependency theory* will show that I do not accept all of its assumptions and arguments, but the utility of this perspective in understanding regional dependency in Canada has been demonstrated (Matthews, 1977; 1978-79; 1980a; 1980b; 1981a; 1981b). The strength of the dependency theory position lies in this recognition of the linkage between economic and social aspects of regional dependency, and in the emphasis which it places on the role of external social structural factors in creating and sustaining regional dependency.

■ THE TRANSFER DEPENDENCY PERSPECTIVE

. . . . The assumptions of the neo-classical perspective are to be found in the works of many Canadian economists who deal with the problems of regional disparity. Rather than reviewing the Canadian economic literature in its entirety, we have selected for consideration the work of Canadian economist Thomas J. Courchene, who has written widely on the subject of regional disparity and whose work reflects the neo-classical assumptions. . . . I will focus particularly on one of his more recent works (Courchene, 1978a) which deals specifically with regional disparities and which brings together many of the themes developed in his earlier analyses.

Courchene's transfer dependency perspective has [two] major thrusts. The *first thrust* is his argument that transfer payments from Canada's federal government may actually serve to make poor provinces more dependent on federal assistance and less inclined to alter the conditions which create their underdevelopment. Courchene contends that one of the unanticipated consequences of cost-sharing agreements between the federal and provincial governments is that poorer provinces are enticed into expensive programs which may not be in their best interest, simply because this is the only way in which they are able to get federal assistance (Courchene, 1978a: 146). Courchene laments that "some of the provinces find themselves in such dire straights that they are literally forced into resorting to such measures" (Ibid: 163). As he sees it, provincial governments no longer have power to determine their own strategy of development, and he argues "that Canada is currently at a crossroad in its economic and political history where some decentralization of economic power from Ottawa to the provinces is inevitable" (Ibid.: 146).

I would argue that there are major problems with Courchene's position here. To demonstrate this, it is useful to compare his reasoning with that of the well-known "culture of poverty" perspective. The "culture of poverty" perspective contends that one of the dominant reasons for the persistence of poverty is the way in which poor people have adapted to the condition of being poor. . . . The culture of poverty perspective argues that some people in poverty psychologically adapt to it, and that welfare assistance can and frequently does create a change in role behaviour and social structure as many recipients exhaust their energies attempting to maximize their welfare receipts rather than searching for ways to alleviate their dependent condition. . . .

Is Courchene's work open to the same criticisms which have been levelled at the culture of poverty perspective? One general criticism is that the culture of poverty perspective misrepresents the outlook and motivations of the poor. Most empirical studies of the poor show that they are far from being the demoralized, present-time oriented automatons depicted by Lewis. Instead, most poor people and poor cultures display ingenuity and planning in their efforts to survive under conditions of extreme hardship (cf. Valantine, 1968). A further criticism of the culture of poverty perspective is that it tends to blame the victim for his own misfortune. . . .

One could argue that Courchene's work does not display these characteristic weaknesses. For example, he only indirectly deals with the psychological outlook associated with dependency while that is the major focus of the culture of poverty position. Also in fairness to Courchene, one should note that he does not depict the dependent provinces as demoralized welfare ghettos. On the other hand, there are strong similarities between his proposed *solutions* to regional poverty and those contained in the culture of poverty perspective. It is Courchene's contention that the problem of regional disparity in Canada can only be overcome when transfer payments to poor provinces are severely reduced, or when the monies currently paid through tranfer payments are turned over to the provinces so that they could spend them as they wish (1978a: 161). He argues that such a strategy would lead to a lowering of the real wage rates in such regions and that these changes, in combination, will likely lead to the out-migration of excess population from the region. However, if such changes did indeed reduce real wages and encourage migration, this would constitute a significant change in both the economic *and* the social structure of the dependent regions of Canada. In this sense at least, Courchene's proposals can certainly be seen as aimed at "changing the victim."

If the "victims," which in this case are the governments and people of Canada's poorest provinces, are indeed the authors of their misfortune,

Courchene's position may be valid. However, even then it is uncertain whether the measures he proposes will bring about the effects he desires. If, on the other hand, the poorest provinces and their residents are instead "victims" of far-reaching national and international forces over which they have no control, then attempting to rectify the situation primarily through changing the local situation may simply create unnecessary hardship. . . .

Furthermore, Courchene believes that the present system of transfer payments perpetuates an imbalance in trade and population, between the have and "have-not" regions of Canada. The drain of capital out of the developed regions results in a reduced ability on their part to stimulate their own economic growth. At the same time, such transfer payments allow the "have-not" provinces to maintain higher real wages than would be natural, and have lower levels of out-migration than would naturally occur. The result, as Courchene sees it, is that transfer payments actually exacerbate regional economic differences. . . .

Courchene's contention that transfer payments upset the adjustment between regional wage rates, migration, prices and trade is closely allied to the *[second] major thrust* of his dependency argument, which is that we must facilitate a return to a system of "natural adjustments" if regional disparity is ever to be overcome (Ibid.: 157 & 159). As many regional planners in Canada are trained in economics they are likely to find such proposals attractive. Many may already be predisposed to believe that the economic system contains a natural equilibrium and functions best when left to operate on its own. Furthermore, there is something rather comforting about the desire for a more "natural" state of affairs (presumably in contrast to an artificial one). Even the term "adjustment" which is commonly used by economists suggests that there will be no major disruption of the situation and that equilibrium is simply being re-established.

However, it is imperative to consider just what Courchene's "natural adjustments" would entail. If transfer payments are the root of the problem, one possible and seemingly obvious solution would be the immediate reduction or elimination of transfer payments. Wisely, Courchene rejects this alternative as "unthinkable at the present time." . . . His alternative proposal is to slowly phase out many of the unconditional transfer programs, while shifting to the provinces the responsibility for administering other programs that are now cost-shared between federal and provincial levels of government. This, he suggests, could be done by giving the provinces lump-sum payments equivalent to what they now receive more indirectly through cost-sharing arrangements for particular services. . . . It is Courchene's contention that such "adjustments" would lead to a possible lowering of both the real and minimum wage rates in the dependent provinces of Canada, the possibility of migration both within and out of such provinces, and a possible stimulus in labour demand as new industry is attracted to the region by the prospects of cheap labour. . . .

Without doubt, there is worldwide evidence that low real wages attract industry. Numerous Canadian resource industries have moved to third world countries largely because of the lower wage levels and low level of worker organization there. Nevertheless, we would argue that this is insufficient justification for the lowering of minimum wage rates in Canada's dependent provinces.

Minimum wage rates were introduced to protect those who are forced to sell their labour from the unfair exploitation of those who buy it. Without minimum wage legislation workers could be paid such low incomes that they would literally have difficulty surviving. This, we would argue, is an economic rationale for minimum wage legislation and it is incorrect to think of minimum wage legislation as simply a political expediency. In regions where unemployment is high and the level of unionization is low (such as one finds in the dependent regions of Canada) minimum wage legislation is particularly important. Without it, workers might be forced to compete for work at very low wages, just in order to have a job and some earned income.

However, while this justifies the retention of minimum wage legislation in the dependent regions of Canada, it still does not justify that these rates are occasionally as high or higher than those in richer regions. Despite Courchene's statement, there does appear to be some "economic rationale" for them. Though statistics vary, most studies show that approximately half of those who live below the poverty line in Canada are employed (e.g., Caskie, 1979: 40). Admittedly, some of these are in agricultural and other primary resource occupations which are not subject to minimum wage legislation. Still, a large number of them do have jobs which come under this legislation, and would likely see their incomes lowered if employers were permitted to pay them less. Thus, the lowering of minimum wage rates would bring even greater poverty to many of those who are least able to bear the burden. Considerations of economic and social welfare would therefore suggest that the lowering of minimum wage rates, unless accompanied by far-reaching changes in other aspects of the social and economic structure, is simply not possible. It is difficult to accept that the minimum wage rates are too high in poor regions, when they are still so low that the real wages of many fulltime workers are insufficient for them to rise out of poverty.

There would appear to be a further "economic rationale" for maintaining high minimum wage rates in the dependent provinces. Should these rates be lowered, those industries attracted by low minimum wage rates are likely to be those whose continued existence depends on their ability to pay lower wages for the same work than workers receive in other regions. *Such measures would not eliminate regional disparity, but rather they would institutionalize it.* It would become virtually impossible to close the wage gap between rich and poor areas of the country, and would lead to a further polarization of society into advanced and underdeveloped regions.

Furthermore, while it is likely that a lowering of the minimum wage rates might encourage some "low wage" industries to move into Canada's more dependent regions, their presence may not have the long-run consequences that Courchene anticipates. Within a short period it seems likely that workers in such enterprises would attempt to unionize (e.g., Michelin workers in Nova Scotia), both to protect themselves from arbitrary dismissal and replacement from the large pool of unemployed workers seeking their jobs, and to demand equal pay for equal work with their counterparts elsewhere in Canada. Past experience indicates that low wage paying firms would then approach the provincial government with requests for additional operating incentives and threats concerning their impending closure. As the government frequently has made political gain out of enticing such firms into the area, it often sees no choice but to bend to such economic blackmail and provide further assistance, often in the form of tax concessions, purchasing contracts and subsidized energy. As the people of the region usually must bear the brunt of these costs, they are now being futher victimized. Not only do they have lower wages than elsewhere, but they must also carry the costs of these concessions to corporate concerns.

Finally, the lowering of minimum wage rates may have yet another deleterious consequence. It is unlikely that workers who receive a level of remuneration essentially below the poverty line will have much of a personal investment in their jobs. The result is likely to be a high level of absenteeism, and a low level of productivity. Workers are likely to cling to the pattern of wage employment already prevalent in the marginal work world, whereby they work only long enough to earn the money necessary to buy the necessities that can't be produced at home, and to qualify for unemployment insurance. A number of economists have attributed the existence of this pattern to the high levels of unemployment insurance and transfer payments which the dependent regions already receive. However, it may be as much a product of the low wage levels and seasonal employment structure already existing in these regions. A lowering of minimum wage rates will likely exacerbate this situation.

However, the most contentious of the adjustments implied in Courchene's model are those related to migration. Courchene accepts the proposition that wage differentials encourage labour mobility. He also maintains that the inflow of federal funds into the "have-not" regions has permitted them to keep minimum wage rates high and still retain a sizable proportion of their populations. It would appear to follow that one consequence of reducing minimum wage rates is increased out-migration from dependent regions.

Several of Canada's previous regional development programs attempted to deal with the problem of regional dependency by encouraging the out-migration of "excess-population" and "excess labour force" from these regions. Such measures almost invariably met with opposition and resistance at both a local political and local community level (cf. Iverson and Matthews, 1968; Matthews, 1976). So widespread has this opposition become, that those who still openly advocate out-migration encounter much public hostility in many regions of Canada. Consequently, one of the ironies of Courchene's transfer dependency model is that it attracts interest and support at local planning levels, even though it implies a strategy of out-migration. A main reason for this is that Courchene rarely *explicitly* supports out-migration. Throughout his work he calls for a return to "natural adjustments" without making it obvious that migration is one of these potential adjustments. When Courchene (1978b) declared in a speech before a Newfoundland audience that "Too much of Canada's policies toward its regions has been directed towards preventing the economic adjustment of the area," his talk was favourably reported in the local newspaper (St. John's, *Evening Telegram*, Nov. 4, 1978). His audience apparently did not realize that one interpretation of this remark was that it was time for some of them to leave the region. . . .

When one takes into account these social, psychological and motivational factors, there are a number of other ways of interpreting Courchene's empirical finding that migration is associated with economic well-being after moving. It may indicate that those people who do move are economically motivated, while those who remain behind (i.e., the majority of the population) are motivated by more social considerations. Another possible interpretation of his findings is that, once people are forced to move, they certainly try to maximize the economic gains they get from doing so. However, this in no way suggests that economic considerations could be considered a primary motive. Indeed, people may so value their way of life that migration is simply a last resort when government policies have made life both socially and economically impossible in their present location. Under such circumstances, a reduction in transfer payments and the subsequent decline in minimum wage rates is not likely to produce the out-migration that Courchene's model anticipates. Rather, the first reaction may be for people to adjust to their way of life to a reduced standard of living. If so, their living conditions will have become worse rather than better. After all, if economic incentives were sufficient to make the residents of Canada's dependent regions move, the greater unemployment rates and lower average incomes in these regions should have already led them to do so. They have already demonstrated their desire to remain where they are despite the economic disadvantages involved in doing so.

There is yet a further obstacle to out-migration becoming a significant "adjustment" as appears to be assumed in the transfer dependency model. The model does not seem to fully take into account the fact that migration from any region is also a reflection of the opportunities available elsewhere. Lowering minimum wage rates in the dependent regions is not likely to produce out-migration unless there is somewhere for people to go. The historical evidence would appear to support this contention. For example, historically it would appear that, when unemployment rates in the Atlantic region of Canada have been high the rate of migration from that region has been comparatively low, while the migration rate from the region has been highest when the unemployment rates have been lowest (Matthews, 1982). On the other hand, there has frequently been a direct correlation between the rate of migration out of the Atlantic region, and employment rates in Ontario. As Ontario has been a favourite destination for many Atlantic province migrants, this may well be significant. It suggests that Atlantic province migration is not governed as much by forces pushing people out of the region, as by pull factors from the more developed regions. When conditions are bad and unemployment levels high in the Atlantic region, unemployment levels are also high in central Canada and *there is simply no place to go.* . . .

■ THE DEPENDENCY THEORY APPROACH

Most approaches to national or regional underdevelopment see underdevelopment as a consequence of some failure, deficiency or *lack* in the underdeveloped area. Such areas are claimed to lack resources, capital, education, infrastructure, achievement motivation, entrepreneurial initiative, or human capital. Such explanations of underdevelopment are generally referred to as modernization theories, as their usual conclusion is that development will occur only when these local lacks are overcome by the influx of modern industry, modern management, modern education or one of the other modernizations.

The sociological approach, known as *dependency theory*, was developed by Latin American economists as an alternative to these modernization theories in explaining underdevelopment in their home countries. In recent years it has also been used by sociologists in the developed societies to explain the persistence of regional pockets of underdevelopment in these more developed nations. Within Canada, there is no single proponent of dependency theory whose work exemplifies all of the approaches within it. Moreover, perhaps because of the youthfulness of the dependency theory paradigm, most Canadian work still leans heavily on work done elsewhere for its concepts and comparisons. Thus our discussion of Canadian dependency theory of necessity must include mention of the more general literature upon which the Canadian work is based.

From a dependency theory perspective, underdevelopment is not the result of some *lack* within the underdeveloped region, but it is caused by the continued *exploitation* of the dependent area by more powerful and wealthy ones. From the point of view of dependency theory, underdevelopment is not a condition, but a process—the process whereby a region is *made* dependent.

To those familiar with Marxian analysis it is obvious that the roots of dependency theory lie in the Marxist analysis of imperialism. This position contends that capitalism, by nature, is exploitive and must constantly subjugate other areas in order for it to survive. This, Marxists argue, is made necessary primarily because of the accumulation of capital into the hands of the few which threatens the viability of the system unless new sources of capital are constantly found.

As we have elsewhere examined dependency theory in some detail (Matthews, 1980a, 1980b), we will use our limited space here to provide only a brief overview designed to highlight those points on which dependency theory differs most clearly from the transfer dependency perspective as an interpretation of the nature and causes of regional dependency. *There are four basic stages to the dependency theory perspective*, and scholars in Canada and elsewhere have done empirical and analytical work at all four levels. The *first stage* involves the obvious analogy that the relationship of exploitation between nations has its counterpart at the regional level within nations. At this stage focus is primarily on the nature of exchange between regions. Within Canada this has led to a number of studies that have documented the process whereby the dependent regions have been historically drained of their resources and wealth by the developed ones (Acheson, 1972, 1977; Naylor, 1975).

The *second stage* of the dependency perspective also builds directly on Marxist analysis. This time the focus is on the supposed inherent necessity of capitalism to require a large "reserve army" of labour which it can exploit virtually at will. Mandel (1973), in particular, developed this into a theory of regionalism by noting that underdeveloped regions provide not only raw materials, wealth and a market for more developed regions, but also function as a reserve labour supply. Labourers can be drawn into the developed regions when industry is expanding, and simply laid off when economic conditions get bad. This regionalization of the reserve labour force is seen as particularly advantageous to the developed regions, as many unemployed workers return to their old homes. Thus the developed regions rarely have to pay the full economic or social costs of maintaining their reserve labour supply. Within Canada, Veltmeyer (1978) has shown that the migrant labour force of Atlantic Canada operates in much the same manner that Mandel's theory suggests.

However, to this point, dependency theory does not differ substantially from traditional Marxist analysis. It is the *third stage* of dependency analysis which marks the formation of a distinctive body of theory and empirical research. At this level attention shifts from a focus on wealth and population movement, to a direct consideration of the social structures which develop both to facilitate the process of regional dependency and as a consequence of it. In particular, the focus here is on the nature of social class, and on the way in which "bridgeheads" (Galtung, 1971) are formed between the dominant class of the developed area and the dominant class of the dependent area. In this way the elite of the dependent region becomes "compromised" (Don Santos, 1973) into supporting its own domination.

At the same time there is a conflict of interest between the elite groups and working class groups in both developed and dependent areas, and even a conflict of interest between the two working class groups. Though a number of Canadian sociologists, anthropologists and political scientists are engaged in this stage of dependency analysis, the best known work is by Clement who has empirically demonstrated that many of Canada's corporate elite are the coopted compradors of economic interests based in other countries (1975), and that the economic elite of Canada's dependent regions are also frequently the agents of economic interests based in Canada's more developed regions (1978). The focus of all this research is on the way in which the actions of such elite groups serve to increase the dependency of their home regions.

It is the *fourth stage* of dependency theory analysis that attention shifts from a consideration of the links between developed and dependent regions, to a direct consideration of the consequences of dependency for the social and economic structure of the dependent region itself. Much of the theoretical work here has dealt with the articulation between capitalist and non-capitalist modes of production (cf. LcClau, 1971; Amin, 1976) in the dependent society. It is argued that this produces economic polarization (Sunkel, 1973) which in turn creates two largely independent social structures. Cardoso (1972, 1973) and Cardoso & Faletto (1979) have also argued that the "dependent development" which occurs under conditions of dependency has characteristics which make it distinctive from that found in more developed regions. In Canada, Veltmeyer's (1978) work on class transformation in Halifax, Matthews' (1978) work on the development of underdevelopment in Newfoundland, and the essays in Brym and Sacouman's (1979) collection are all part of a growing body of literature which investigates the consequences of dependency on the social and economic structures of Canada's dependent regions. . . .

■ "TRANSFER DEPENDENCY" VERSUS "DEPENDENCY THEORY"

The "transfer dependency" approach and "dependency theory" constitute two quite different perspectives on the nature of regional dependency. Nowhere is this more obvious than in their conceptualization of the "cause" of regional dependency. The transfer dependency perspective sees regional dependency as the product of too much external money being poured into a region in the form of transfer payments. From a dependency theory perspective, dependency is caused by the systematic draining of capital and resources out of a region by other regions. In the case of Canada, there are data which can be used to support both positions. Dependency theorists rely heavily on the historical data documenting the movement of wealth from Canada's eastern provinces in the period from 1890 to 1920. In contrast the exponents of the transfer dependency approach point to the substantial inflow of money into that same region in recent years in the form of transfer payments. There is no simple resolution to this contradiction, though dependency theorists might legitimately argue that the eastern regions of Canada might not need today's transfer payments if they had not been drained of their wealth in an earlier era. It should also be stated that the existence of a substantial inflow of transfer payments into the Atlantic region is not, in itself, a justification for their reduction or elimination.

Both the transfer dependency perspective and the dependency theory perspective also incorporate theories of the nature and function of migration with respect to regional dependency. The transfer position on migration is the clearest—out-migration of excess labour from a dependent region is regarded as a desirable goal for it is seen as contributing to a natural balance in the region. The dependency theory position on migration is less clear-cut. Migrants are seen as victims of an exploitative economic system—and from this it appears that dependency theorists regard the programmed migration of those who would prefer to stay at home to be undesirable. It is less clear, however, how dependency theorists would overcome the existing conditions which require the seasonal migration of a large reserve army of the unemployed from one region to another. Presumably this would involve a more equitable distribution of economic power and industry in the country. It would also presumably require a reduction in the chains of dependency which tie local entrepreneurs to investment capital outside the region. It should also be noted that data on the existing pattern of out-migration from eastern Canada support the dependency theory interpretation that such migrants are indeed a reserve army whose movement is affected primarily by economic conditions in the developed regions.

A third difference between the transfer dependency and dependency theory approaches is in their implicit understanding of the power of local governments and local economic interests to change the conditions of their existence. It would appear that, from a transfer dependency perspective, provincial governments and local entrepreneurs do have this power. Thus it is argued that transfer payments should be reduced or eliminated in order to force provincial leaders to take the necessary steps which would ultimately move them out of their underdeveloped condition. However, dependency theorists argue that the conditions of the "world economic system" combined with the power of giant multinational corporations mitigate against the success of local initiatives. Indeed, they would suggest that the failure of many local initiatives has not been the result of a lower level of entrepreneurial ability, but a consequence of the inability of local leaders to control the major national and international economic forces which operate in such a way as to make them dependent.

Finally, some attention should be given to the difference in value orientation between the two dependency perspectives. It is clear that the dependency theory position is a value-oriented perspective and takes a normative stand against external exploitation. The dependency theory critique of the existing structure of capitalist economic organization in Canada is that it upholds the interest of certain groups within the central developed regions at the expense of many of those who live in the dependent peripheral regions of the country. It is not always realized that the transfer dependency position is likewise value-oriented and normatively biased. It is based on a capitalist model where maximization of economic welfare is the goal of the system and thus it tends to divorce considerations of economic well-being from broader social and cultural value orientations. The consequence of this focus is a fairly instrumental approach to development, and a tendency to treat the economic system as natural rather than man-made. Daniel Bell levels much of the same criticism at contemporary economists who, he contends, "make accumulation an end in itself." He further notes that "economic policy can be efficacious as a means; but it can only be as just as the cultural value system that shapes it" (Bell, 1978: xi). A major value bias of the transfer dependency position is its tendency to ignore the cultural values of many of those who wish to remain in Canada's dependent regions.

References

Acheson, T.W. (1972) "The National Policy and the Industrialization of the Maritimes, 1880-1910," *Acadiensis*, 1:2:3-28.

_____ (1977) "The Maritimes and Empire Canada" in D.J. Bercuson (ed.), *Canada and the Burden of Unity* (Toronto: Macmillan of Canada) 87-114.

Amin, Samir (1976) *Unequal Development: An Essay on the Social Foundations of Peripheral Capitalism* (New York: Modern Reader Paperbacks).

Bell, Daniel (1978) "Forward, 1978," in *The Cultural Contradictions of Capitalism* (New York: Basic Books).

Brym, Robert J. and R. James Sacouman (eds.) (1979) *Underdevelopment and Social Movements in Atlantic Canada* (Toronto: New Hogtown Press).

Cardoso, Fernando Henrique (1972) "Industrialization, Dependency and Power in Latin America," *Berkeley Journal of Sociology*, 17:79-95.

_____ (1973) "Associated-Dependent Development: Theoretical and Practical Implications" in Alfred Stefan (ed.), *Authorization Brazil* (New Haven: Yale University Press) 142-176.

Cardosa, Fernando Henrique and Enzo Faletto (1979) *Development and Dependency in Latin America* (Berkeley: University of California Press).

Caskie, Donald M. (1979) *Canadian Fact Book on Poverty* (Ottawa: Canadian Council on Social Development).

Clement, Wallace (1975) *The Canadian Corporate Elite* (Toronto: McClelland & Stewart).

_____ (1978) "A Political Economy of Regionalism in Canada," in D. Glenday *et al.* (eds.), *Modernization and the Canadian State* (Toronto: Macmillan of Canada) 89-110.

Courchene, Thomas J. (1978a) "Avenues of Adjustment: The Transfer System and Regional Disparities" in Michael Walker (ed.), *Canadian Confederation at the Crossroads: The Search for a Federal-Provincial Balance* (Vancouver: The Fraser Institute).

_____ (1978b) "Regional Disparities and National Unity," paper presented at Memorial University at Newfoundland, St. John's, Newfoundland.

Dos Santos, Theotonio (1970) "The Structure of Dependence," _American Economic Review: Papers and Proceedings of the 82nd Annual Meeting of the American Economics Association_, 60:2:231-236.

_____ (1973) "The Crisis of Development Theory and the Problem of Dependency in Latin America,' in Henry Bernstein (ed.), _Underdevelopment and Development_ (Middlesex: Penguin Books) 57-80.

Galtung, Johan (1971) "A Structural Theory of Imperialism," _Journal of Peace Research_, 8:81-114.

Iverson, Noel and Ralph Matthews (1968) _Communities in Decline: An Examination of Household Resettlement in Newfoundland_, Newfoundland Social and Economic Studies Number 6, Institute of Social and Economic Research, Memorial University of Newfoundland.

La Clau, Ernesto (1971) "Feudalism and Capitalism in Latin America," _New Left Review_, 76:19-38.

Mandel, Ernest (1973) _Capitalism and Regional Disparities_ (Toronto: New Hogtown Press).

Matthews, Ralph (1976) _There's No Better Place Than Here: Social Changes in Three Newfoundland Communities_ (Toronto: Peter Martin Associates Publishers Ltd.).

_____ (1977) "Canadian Regional Development Strategy: A Dependency Theory Perspective," _Plan Canada_, 17:2:131-143.

_____ (1978-79) "The Smallwood Legacy: The Development of Underdevelopment in Newfoundland, 1949-1972," _Journal of Canadian Studies_, 13:4:89-108.

_____ (1980a) "Class Interests and the Role of the State in the Development of Canada's East Coast Fishery," _Canadian Issues: Journal of the Association for Canadian Studies_, 3:1:115-124.

_____ (1980b) "The Significance and Explanation of Regional Differences in Canada: Towards a Canadian Sociology," _Journal of Canadian Studies_, 15:2:43-61.

_____ (1981a) _An Examination of Development and Dependency in Nova Scotia_ (Halifax: Institute of Public Affairs, Dalhousie University).

_____ (1981b) "Regional Differences in Canada: Social Versus Economic Interpretations" in D. Forcese & R. Richer (eds.), _Issues in Canadian Society_, 2nd ed. (Scarborough: Prentice Hall of Canada) forthcoming.

_____ (1982) _Atlantic Canada: A Sociological Profile_ (Toronto: Peter Martin Associates) forthcoming.

Naylor, Tom (1975) _The History of Canadian Business_, 1867-1914, 2 Volumes (Toronto: Lormier & Co.).

Sunkel, Osvaldo (1973) "Transnational Capitalism and National Disintegration in Latin America," _Social and Economic Studies_, 22:1:132-176.

Valantine, Charles A. (1968) _Culture and Poverty: Critique and Counter Proposals_ (Chicago: University of Chicago Press).

Veltmeyer, Henry (1978) "The Underdevelopment of Atlantic Canada," _The Review of Radical Political Economics_, 10:2:95-105.

■ POSTSCRIPT

Courchene argues that the practice of providing transfer payments from the federal government to the have-not provinces is the major reason for the persistence of regional disparities. Transfer payments have created transfer dependency as governments and economies in the have-not provinces have become dependent on transfer payments. According to Courchene, allowing off-season fishers in the Atlantic region to receive unemployment insurance benefits retards economic development by attracting people to an industry that is not economically feasible.

Matthews criticizes transfer dependency theory for misrepresenting the actions of governments in have-not regions. According to Matthews, the economies and governments of these regions are victims of forces beyond their control, and it is inappropriate for Courchene to imply that they are responsible for their own dependency. Courchene, however, argues that the responsibility for regional disparities rests with *all* Canadians, and that the have-not regions have responded in a calculated, rational way to federal policy initiatives.

According to dependency theory, however, the have-not regions have been drained of their resources, and are no longer able to respond to market forces in the way Courchene would have them respond. Further, dependency theorists like Clement (1975) argue that some of the native elite in the depressed regions serve the interests of the metropolis by working to maintain hinterland dependency on the metropolis. These people profit from their association with the metropolis, while the hinterland suffers economic decline.

But what should be the objective in reducing economic disparities? Simply to reduce the unemployment rates, or to increase per capita incomes to the levels found in Ontario? Savoie (1986) suggests that these are unrealistic goals because governments do not have sufficient control over the economy to achieve them. The objective should be to assess quality of life, raise educational levels, and develop policies that place emphasis on entrepreneurship. Ultimately, says Savoie, the economies of the have-not regions must be more effectively integrated into the national economy. To continue to develop the have-not economies as separate entities is a recipe for failure.

■ QUESTIONS

1. Which argument do you find most convincing? Why?
2. In what ways are the arguments of Courchene and Matthews similar?
3. Are regional disparities inevitable?

4. To what extent have regional disparities contributed to separatist movements in western Canada and Quebec? Why are there no separatist movements in the Atlantic provinces?

■ FURTHER READING

In Support of Courchene

Courchene, Thomas J. and Glen H. Copplestone. "Alternative Equalization Programs: Two Tier Systems." In *Fiscal Dimensions of Canadian Federalism.* Edited by Richard Bird. Toronto: Canadian Tax Foundation, 1981.

Thurow, Lester C. "The Productivity Problem." *Policies for Stagflation.* Vol. 2. Toronto: Ontario Economic Council, 1981.

In Support of Matthews

Clement, Wallace. *Canadian Corporate Elite.* Toronto: McClelland and Stewart, 1975.

Veltmeyer, Henry. "The Underdevelopment of Atlantic Canada." *The Review of Radical Political Economics,* 1978.

Other Voices

Canadian Journal of Regional Science. Contains articles in support of both Courchene and Matthews, as well as alternative explanations.

Savoie, Donald. *Regional Economic Development.* Toronto: University of Toronto Press, 1986.

Savoie, Donald, ed. *The Canadian Economy: A Regional Perspective.* Toronto: Methuen, 1986.

Does premarital cohabitation increase the risk of divorce?

Are men the main victims of spouse abuse?

Does streaming allow students to develop their potential?

Is support for unions declining in Canada?

PART FOUR

INTRODUCTION

Canadians spend much of their lives within the context of various social institutions. These institutions influence and regulate our existence within the family, at work, and at play. They regulate our religious beliefs and our morality. It is impossible to escape their influence. That is why it is important to understand how and why they work. It is also important to understand that they do not always work as we think they do, or as they should, or as we would like them to work. This section deals with current debates about the importance and/or effectiveness of three institutions: marriage, schools, and trade unions.

DOES PREMARITAL

COHABITATION INCREASE

THE RISK OF DIVORCE?

YES **T.R. Balakrishnan, K. Vaninadha Rao, Evelyne Lapierre-Adamcyk, and Karol J. Krotki,** "A Hazard Model Analysis of the Covariates of Marriage Dissolution in Canada," *Demography* 24, no. 3 (Autumn 1987): 395-406

NO **Jay D. Teachman and Karen A. Polonko,** "Cohabitation and Marital Stability in the United States," *Social Forces* 69, no. 1 (September 1990): 207-220

The divorce rate has been an area of public concern for many years. Prior to the Divorce Act of 1968, divorce was possible only on the grounds of adultery. The 1968 act added to this physical or mental cruelty, and marriage breakdown because of desertion or imprisonment. As a consequence, the divorce rate increased dramatically. In 1966, the divorce rate was 225 per 100,000 married women. It jumped to 557 per 100,000 in 1969 and 1,164 per 100,000 in 1982 (Adams, 1990).

In 1985, a new Divorce Act made marriage breakdown the only ground for divorce. Under the act, marriage breakdown occurs (1) after separation for one year, (2) when adultery has been committed, and (3) as a result of physical or mental cruelty. The revised Divorce Act had an immediate impact. Whereas the divorce rate had declined between 1982 to 1985, from 1,164 per 100,000 to 1,004 per 100,000, the divorce rate reached 1,255 per 100,000 in 1986 (Adams, 1990).

For many people, a rising divorce rate is an indication of a decline in the importance of family life, and an indication of social instability. To highlight their analysis, they point to evidence that shows fewer people are getting married, people are waiting longer to get married, marriages are not lasting as long, and the size of the average family is declining (for specific rates, see Adams and Nagur, 1990). Further erosion of family life is said to be signalled by the number of people living common-law, or cohabiting prior to marriage. Cohabiting couples increased by 37 percent from 1981 to

1986, while the number of married couples increased by only 2.7 percent in the same time period (Turcotte, 1990). From 1981 to 1986, common-law marriages increased from 6-8 percent of all marriages.

More importantly, some analysts have suggested that cohabiting couples have higher divorce rates than noncohabiting couples. Further evidence shows that couples entering common-law marriages are less committed to traditional family values, are more likely to cherish their individual freedom, and are more likely to view the relationship as a temporary arrangement than are noncohabitants (Clayton and Voss, 1977). Furthermore, research has shown that couples cohabiting prior to marriage divorce sooner after marriage than couples who do not cohabit before marriage (Bennett et al., 1988).

On the other hand, not everyone who enters a common-law marriage is seeking only a temporary partner. For some it is a trial marriage in which compatibility can be tested. Approximately 46 percent of men and 43 percent of women who enter common-law marriages eventually marry their partner (Turcotte, 1990). This suggests that, for some people at least, premarital cohabitation should produce a more stable marriage.

Balakrishnan et al. argue the "Yes" side of Debate Nine, saying that premarital cohabitation increases the probability of divorce. Teachman and Polonko argue the "No" side of the debate, saying that the divorce rate for cohabiting couples is no higher than that for noncohabiting couples.

References

Adams, Owen (1990) "Divorce Rates in Canada," in *Canadian Social Trends*, edited by Craig McKie and Keith Thompson (Toronto: Thompson Educational Publishing).

Adams, Owen and Dhruva Nagur (1990) "Marrying and Divorcing: A Status Report for Canada," in *Canadian Social Trends*, edited by Craig McKie and Keith Thompson (Toronto: Thompson Educational Publishing).

Bennett, Neil, Ann Blanc, and David Bloom (1988) "Commitment and the Modern Union: Assessing the Link Between Premarital Cohabitation and Subsequent Marital Stability," *American Sociological Review* 53: 127-138.

Clayton, Richard and Harwin Voss (1977) "Shacking Up: Cohabitation in the 1970s," *Journal of Marriage and the Family* 39: 273-283.

Turcotte, Pierre (1990) "Common Law Unions: Nearly Half a Million in 1986," in *Canadian Social Trends*, edited by Craig McKie and Keith Thompson (Toronto: Thompson Educational Publishing).

MARRIAGE DISSOLUTION IN CANADA

T.R. Balakrishnan
K. Vaninadha Rao
Evelyne Lapierre-Adamcyk
and Karol J. Krotki

YES

.... Research on the correlates of marriage dissolution in Canada has shown that certain factors have a strong relationship to the probability of divorce. Analyzing data from divorce statistics, McKie, Prentice, and Reed (1983) identified teenage at marriage, lack of education, poor employment, and premarital pregnancy as factors related to divorce. Greater differences between the ages of spouses also increased the chance of divorce. A clear relationship between educational attainment and proportion ever divorced was also reported by Burch (1985) in his analysis of the Family History Survey data of 1984. These Canadian findings fall in line with numerous studies done in the United States (Bumpass and Sweet, 1972; Carter and Glick, 1970; Gibson, 1974; McCarthy and Menken, 1979; Menken et al., 1981; Teachman, 1982; Thornton, 1978; Weed, 1974). The U.S. studies have found that young age at marriage, premarital birth or conception, race, religion, time period of marriage, educational attainment, religiosity, rural-urban residence, and husband-wife difference in age at marriage are some of the factors associated with marital dissolution.

The main objective of this paper is to analyze the data on marital histories collected in the first national fertility survey done in Canada to determine the correlates of marital dissolution by looking at duration-specific probabilities of dissolution for various subgroups and applying hazard models to estimate relative risks.

◼ DATA AND METHODS

The data come from the Canadian Fertility Survey conducted in April-June 1984, which used the telephone for both household selection and in-depth interviewing of the selected respondent—namely, a woman in the reproductive ages of 18-49, living in a private household that can be reached through the telephone. A total of 5,315 women of all marital statuses were interviewed. Of these, 3,884 were ever married; they are the group included in this study. Marital status is based on legal marriage. Therefore, single women cohabiting are not included, though they were of course covered in the survey. Detailed information on many standard topics—such as complete marriage, pregnancy, and work histories; contraceptive use; attitudes toward marriage and family; and socioeconomic characteristics of respondent and husband—were covered. The average interview lasted about 36 minutes, but with considerable variation. The response rate was 70 percent, including loss at the household contact (80 percent response) and the eligible respondent (87 percent response) levels, which is average or better than in similar telephone surveys. . . .

The hazard model, first introduced by Cox (1972), has been improved by others (Breslow, 1974; Holford, 1976; Kalbfleisch and Prentice, 1980). Excellent discussions with applications to demographic situations such as marriage dissolutions, infant mortality, and first birth abound at the present time and the development of programs in standard computer packages has made them readily available to all users (Menken et al., 1981; Teachman, 1982; Trussell and Hammerslough, 1983; Martin et al., 1983). In the analysis of marriage dissolution using data from U.S. fertility surveys, proportional hazard models have been effectively applied by Menken et al. (1981) and Teachman (1982). The core assumptions are that population heterogeneity is captured by the set of covariates included in the analysis, and relative risks remain constant over the duration of the marriage.

Since our prime interest is in the breakdown of the marriage rather than in its legal status, we have used data of separation as the date of dissolution rather than date of divorce. As pointed out by Menken et al., this may result in a slight overestimation of final dissolutions, since some of the separated women may reunite with their husbands. This bias, however, is expected to be small. Our analysis is confined to first marriages and their dissolutions only, and not to higher order marriages. Marriages ending because of death of the husband were not considered dissolutions and were removed from the analysis at the date of widowhood, in other words as censored observations. . . .

■ FINDINGS

Based on past research eight characteristics of the women are considered for analysis of their impact on marriage dissolution. These are age at first marriage, year of first marriage, cohabitation status before marriage, first-birth status (whether it was premarital or premaritally conceived but born after marriage), religion, religiosity as measured by church attendance, rural or urban place of residence, and educational attainment.

Many studies have shown that women who marry before the age of 20 have a much greater risk of experiencing divorce than those who marry later, say after the age of 25 (Menken et al., 1981; Teachman, 1982). One may suppose that teenagers are inadequately prepared to face the responsibilities of marriage or do not have the resources to make a marriage and family formation a success. Liberalization of divorce laws and the general acceptance of divorce as a way of ending an unhappy union may also mean that those who married in the last two decades are more likely to dissolve their marriage than those who married earlier, spent their early married life under more restrictive laws, and were socialized to have a relatively negative attitude toward divorce as a solution to marital problems. Of late, cohabitation before marriage, especially among the young, has been increasing significantly. The reasons for such cohabitation and its consequences for subsequent marital stability and childbearing are not yet understood. In our data we have found that cohabiting single women use contraception very extensively and have low fertility. They may be considering this cohabitation period a trial run for evaluating a possible permanent relationship. If this hypothesis is true, one would expect lower marital disruption among those who have cohabited before marriage. However, the opposite could also be argued. Those who do not have strong feelings against cohabiting before marriage may also find it easier to terminate a marriage that has gone sour.

That premarital birth or conception increases the chances of marital dissolution has been shown in some studies (Furstenberg, 1976; Menken et al., 1981; Teachman, 1982). It has been argued that many marriages following a premarital pregnancy may be forced and thus may miss the courtship process and lack the economic resources for a successful beginning of married life. A preliminary analysis of our data shows that childless women have a much higher probability of marriage dissolution than women with children born in their marriages, as has also been found in studies done in the United Kingdom (Chester, 1972; Gibson, 1980; Murphy, 1985). The presence and number of children in a marriage, however, are not considered here, because they depend on duration of marriage and hence violate some of the assumptions underlying proportional hazard models that we propose to use. The category "not conceived before marriage" includes the childless as well as women who had only legitimate children. Women who had a birth in the first 7 months of marriage were classified as premaritally conceiving.

Religion and religiosity have been found to be correlated with marital disruption. Catholics have lower probabilities of divorce, and those who are more religious, as indicated by going to church often, have lower rates of divorce (Menken et al., 1981; Teachman, 1982). Higher divorce rates in large urban areas compared with rural farm communities are more or less universal. Relationship of educational attainment to marital instability is not as clear cut and has varied, depending on controls used, indicating a greater interaction between educational attainment and other factors than exists for other variables mentioned.

Table 1 presents simple or "single-state" life table results calculated separately for each category shown. The values are estimates of marriage dissolution and indicate the proportions of first marriages terminating by various marital durations. For instance, 26 percent of the women who marry before age 20 will have their marriages terminated by 15 years; this

TABLE 1 Life Table Estimates of Probabilities of First Marriage Dissolution by Specific Durations by Selected Characteristics of Women

CHARACTERISTIC	N	YEARS SINCE FIRST MARRIAGE				
		5	10	15	20	25
Age at first marriage						
19 or less	1,235	0.11	0.21	0.26	0.32	0.37
20-21	1,108	0.07	0.15	0.20	0.25	0.29
22-24	987	0.06	0.11	0.15	0.22	0.24
25 or higher	539	0.05	0.07	0.14	0.15	—
Year of marriage						
Before 1965	1,046	0.03	0.08	0.13	0.19	0.24
1965-1974	1,509	0.08	0.16	0.22	—	—
1975-1984	1,313	0.13	—	—	—	—
First-birth status						
Premarital birth	276	0.23	0.30	0.37	0.47	—
Premarital conception	375	0.15	0.22	0.30	0.35	0.43
Not conceived before marriage	3,217	0.06	0.13	0.18	0.23	0.27
Cohabitation status						
Cohabited before marriage	666	0.17	0.31	0.35	0.40	0.48
Did not cohabit	3,202	0.08	0.14	0.19	0.25	0.30
Religion						
Catholic	1,790	0.08	0.12	0.17	0.24	0.26
Non-Catholic	2,074	0.11	0.18	0.24	0.30	0.35
Religiosity (church attendance)						
Weekly or more often	1,113	0.04	0.07	0.10	0.13	0.18
Sometimes	1,467	0.09	0.15	0.19	0.24	0.27
Rarely or never	1,284	0.16	0.25	0.33	0.42	0.47
Place of residence						
Large urban	2,346	0.11	0.18	0.24	0.31	0.36
Small urban	1,213	0.07	0.13	0.18	0.23	0.28
Farm	304	0.06	0.08	0.10	—	—
Educational attainment						
≤ grade 11	1,358	0.08	0.15	0.20	0.26	0.29
Grades 12-13	1,374	0.08	0.16	0.20	0.24	0.30
14 or more years	1,135	0.07	0.14	0.21	0.27	0.35

Note: Differences between dissolution probabilities for the categories are statistically significant at the 0.01 level (Mantel-Cox and Breslow tests) for all covariates except educational attainment.

proportion increases to 37 percent by the end of 25 years. For those who marry at ages 22-24, the proportion of marriages terminated by the end of 25 years is 24 percent. The slightly higher rate of dissolution for those who marry after age 25, found in some U.S. studies, is not found in the Canadian sample (Teachman, 1982). Premarital births, and to a lesser extent premarital conceptions, significantly increase the chances of marriage dissolution. Women with a premarital birth have a 37 percent chance of being separated after 15 years, compared with 30 percent for those with a premarital conception and only 18 percent for those who had neither. Since separate life tables for women cross-classified on both variables cannot be constructed because of small sample sizes, the proportional hazard model is used to look at the effects of these variables on marriage dissolution.

Of the marriages entered into before 1965, only 3 percent were dissolved by 5 years and 8 percent by 10 years of duration. For the 1965-74 marriage cohort, these proportions were estimated as 8 percent and 16 percent respectively. The proportion at 5 years' duration for those married after 1975 is even higher at 13 percent. One should realize, however, that all of these figures are affected to various degrees by age-at-marriage bias arising from truncation and should be interpreted with caution. For example, the cross-sectional nature of the survey means that those who married before 1965 have to have been married before age 30, and those who marry in 1975 or after could marry at any age between 18 and 49. In our sample, however, 98 percent of the ever-married women married before the age of 30. Therefore, this bias is not too serious. Subject to this limitation, we can clearly see that the marriage dissolution probabilities of recent marriage cohorts have substantially increased.

Most of the marriage history of our sample women refers to the period 1960-1984, a period of rapid increase in divorce rates. Though divorces have been increasing in Canada since the early '60s, the liberalization of the laws in 1968 resulted in a somewhat greater increase in the rates during the years 1970-1974 than in the '60s. The early duration dissolution rates for those in our sample who were married before 1965 may therefore be affected downward by the fact that divorces were relatively harder to get at that time. This period effect should have disappeared by 10 years' duration for early marriage cohorts and should not affect later marriage cohorts. It is, however, unlikely that marriage dissolution rates would have been much higher among the older women in our sample in the early 1960s given the long-term secular trends in divorce and the social mores existing at that time. In any case small numbers preclude any detailed analysis of this period effect in the early marriage dissolution probabilities among the older women.

Simple or single-state life tables in table 1 show that women who cohabited before their first marriage have much higher probabilities of dissolution. Thirty-five percent can be expected to have terminated their first marriage before 15 years, compared with only 19 percent among those who did not cohabit before marriage. Though not included here, we realize that duration of cohabitation could influence probabilities of dissolution. We believe, however, that to cohabit or not to cohabit is a factor worthy of consideration in itself in the analysis of subsequent marital stability. Religious affiliation seems to have a noticeable effect on dissolution probabilities, the higher probabilities for non-Catholics being statistically significant. Religiosity has a stronger influence on marriage dissolution than religious affiliation per se. Among those who went to church at least once a week, 18 percent can be expected to have terminated their marriage before 25 years, whereas this proportion is 47 percent among those who rarely or never go to church. One criticism of the religiosity variable is that it measures church attendance at the time of the survey and is only a surrogate for religiosity during the entire marriage period. Our assumption is that religiosity is acquired in early childhood socialization, and those who are religious at the time of the survey are likely to have been religious at the time of marriage and later. The strong relationship is an indication of the importance of religiosity to marital stability. As expected, women who reside in large urban areas have experienced much higher rates of marriage dissolution than those in smaller urban areas or in rural farm communities. Here again, place of residence is measured as at the time of the survey and does not necessarily mean that they have lived in such communities during the whole marriage duration, though the assumption is implicit in the models. Single life tables for education categories do not show much difference, and one would have to see whether hazard models may reveal any.

Tests of statistical significance of the differences in the dissolution probabilities among categories were performed separately for each covariate. Both Mantel-Cox and Breslow tests showed that the differences were significant at the 0.01 level except among the educational attainment categories, which were not significant even at the 0.05 level.

■ PROPORTIONAL HAZARD MODELS

The details of the application of proportional hazard models have been presented elsewhere in great detail, so they are not outlined here (see especially Menken et al., 1981, and Teachman, 1982, for a step-by-step exposition). Basically, the model allows the risk to depend not only on time, as in a simple life table, but on the personal characteristics of the individual. . . . The hazard function enables one to estimate the relative risks of other groups in relation to this baseline group. . . . Values greater than 1 indicate that the relative risk of marriage dissolution is greater for this group, compared with the reference group. Thus when the survivorship probabilities are known at various durations, the survivorship probabilities for the other groups can be found easily, subject to the assumption that the relative risks remain the same at all durations.

The hazard coefficients . . . are presented in table 2 for two different models. . . . The first model includes all eight variables. For example, in model 1 the figure of 1.394 for those who married on or before age 19 means that their risk for marriage dissolution is 0.394 times greater than the risk of

TABLE 2 Hazard Coefficients for Marital Dissolution ($N = 3,852$)

		MODEL	
VARIABLE	CATEGORY	1	2
Age at marriage	≤19	1.394*	1.376*
(20-21)	22-24	0.666*	0.674*
	25 or over	0.422*	0.435*
Year of marriage	Before 1965	0.470*	0.473*
(1965-1974)	1975 or after	1.622*	1.592*
Cohabitation	Cohabited	1.482*	1.495*
before marriage			
no cohabitation)			
First-birth status	Premarital birth	2.357*	2.349*
(not conceived	Premarital	1.489*	1.495*
before marriage)	conception		
Religion	Catholic	0.885	
(non-Catholic)			
Religiosity	Weekly	0.610*	0.610*
(church attendance	Rarely or	1.768*	1.836*
sometimes)	never		
Place of residence	Small urban	0.662*	0.665*
(large urban)	Farm	0.348*	0.355*
Education	≤ grade 11	1.126	
(grades 12-13)	14 or more	1.120	
	years		
Log likelihood		−5,239.9234	−5,243.2296
Model X^2		473.67*	468.20*
Degrees of freedom		15	12

Note: Reference categories are given in parentheses.
* $p < 0.05$.

those who married between 20 and 21, other characteristics being the same. The second model drops the two variables that have the lowest effect and were found to be not statistically significant. We can look on the second model as more efficient because it explains almost as much as model 1 but with two fewer variables. Likelihood ratio statistics show that both models are improvements on the model that assumes that covariates have no effect; in other words, the probability of dissolution is the same for all of the women at various durations. We will refer to model 2 in the subsequent discussions.

The coefficients in model 2 show that age at marriage is significantly related to marriage dissolution. The coefficient is only 0.435 for those married after the age of 25 but increases steadily to 1.376 for those who married before 20. In other words, other things being equal, the probability of dissolution is more than three times greater for those who marry before 20, compared with those who marry after 25. The same trend can be observed for the marriage cohorts. The coefficient is three times as large for those who married in 1975 or later as for those who married before 1965. Women who cohabited before marriage have about a 50 percent higher risk of marriage dissolution than those who did not cohabit before marriage. The coefficients show that premarital birth or conception significantly increases the chance of dissolution of the marriage, the relative risks being 2.349 and 1.495, respectively, compared with women who did not conceive before marriage. Religiosity has a strong relationship, as predicted. The coefficient for those who rarely or never attend church is about three times that for those who attend church at least once a week. Those residing in large urban areas at the time of the survey were much more likely to have had a divorce, compared with those living on a farm.

Though proportional hazard coefficients in table 2 help us determine the relative risks of marriage dissolution for a cohort of women with any particular combination of covariate categories, actual estimates of marriage dissolution by a certain duration first need the marriage survival probabilities for the reference group. . . . For example, the probabilities of dissolution at various durations for women who differ from the reference group in only one category are presented in table 3. Marrying before 1965, instead of during 1965-1974, decreases the relative risk by a factor of

TABLE 3 **Proportions of Marriage Dissolution for Reference Group (married during 1965-1974, legitimate first birth, no cohabitation, church attendance sometimes, large urban residence, and 20-21 at marriage) and Groups Differing by One Characteristic**

			DIFFERING CHARACTERISTIC				
YEARS SINCE MARRIAGE	REFERENCE GROUP (1.000)	MARRIED BEFORE 1965 (0.473)	PREMARITAL CONCEPTION OF FIRST BIRTH (1.495)	COHABITATION (1.495)	WEEKLY CHURCH ATTENDANCE (0.610)	SMALL URBAN RESIDENCE (0.665)	≤19 AT MARRIAGE (1.376)
5	0.06	0.03	0.09	0.09	0.04	0.04	0.08
10	0.13	0.06	0.19	0.19	0.08	0.09	0.18
15	0.20	0.10	0.28	0.28	0.12	0.14	0.26
20	0.28	0.14	0.39	0.39	0.18	0.20	0.36
25	0.36	0.19	0.48	0.48	0.24	0.25	0.45

Note: Proportions are calculated by the following formula: $1 - S_0{}^x$, where S_0 is the survivorship function for the reference group and x is the relative risk. Relative risk values are given within parentheses in column headings.

0.473. . . . The dissolution probability . . . of 0.20 at 15 years decreases to 0.10 for those who married before 1965. Similarly, having had a premarital conception increases the relative risk by a factor of 1.495 compared with the reference group, who did not have a conception before marriage. Correspondingly, the dissolution probability at 15 years for these women is only 0.28 at 15 years, higher than that for the reference group at 0.20. The effect of changes in the other variables can be noticed in the later columns in table 3. Since the relative risks are higher than those for the reference group, women who married before age 20, or cohabited before marriage, have higher dissolution probabilities than the reference group.

As another illustration, survival curves for six groups (including the reference group), highlighting the differences among them, are shown in figure 1. The relative risks for the six groups were calculated by multiplying the hazard coefficients. For example, the relative risk for the most recent marriage cohort who had a premarital birth, did not cohabit before marriage, rarely went to church, lived in a small urban area, and married before 20 years of age is the product $(1.592)(2.349)(1.000)(1.836)(0.665)$ $(1.376) = 6.28$. About 40 percent of these women can be expected to terminate their first marriages by 10 years. In comparison, women in the reference category have a chance of only 13 percent at this duration.

From figure 1 it can be seen that when the relative risks are very high, the dissolution probabilities can get higher than 0.5 after long durations. A comparison of the dissolution probabilities derived from the model and single-state life tables for a few selected subgroups showed that the dissolution probabilities of high-risk groups at 10-year durations may not be as unrealistic as may seem at first glance.

■ CONCLUSION

An examination of the marriage histories in the Canadian Fertility Survey confirms the fact that marriage dissolutions have been increasing rapidly in recent years. Cohort analyses by age and by year of marriage reveal that this is not just a timing effect and that the probabilities of dissolution in the first 10 years of marriage have indeed gone up, especially among the young and more recently married cohorts. Comparison of our results with those for the U.S. is difficult due to differences in the categories and the time the surveys were done. Subject to these limitations, we can still observe some apparent similarities. The relative risk for those who married before 1965 was 0.473, compared with those who married between 1965 and 1974, in the Canadian survey. This is similar to what Teachman found in his analysis of the 1973 U.S. National Survey of Family Growth. The relative risk was 0.51 for those who married in 1955-1959 and 0.69 for those married in 1960-1964, compared with those who married in 1965-1969, in the U.S. sample. Those who married at age 25 or over had a risk of 0.44, compared

FIGURE 1 Proportions of Marriages Dissolved by Marriage Duration for Reference and Comparison Groups

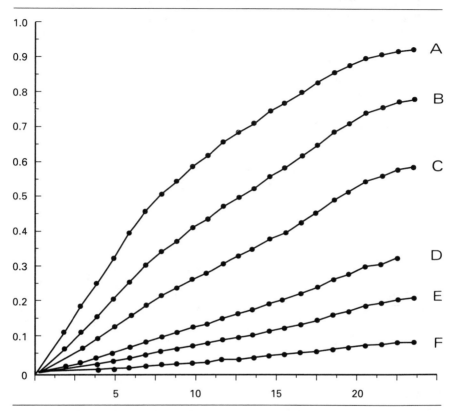

(A) Married 1975 or after, premarital birth, no cohabitation before marriage, rarely church, small urban residence, and ≤ 19 at marriage (relative risk: 6.28). (B) Married 1965-1974, premarital conception, cohabited before marriage, rarely church, small urban residence, and ≤ 19 at marriage (relative risk: 3.76). (C) Married 1975 or after, no preconception, no cohabitation before marriage, sometimes church, large urban residence, and ≤ 19 at marriage (relative risk: 2.19). (D) Married 1965-1974, no preconception, no cohabitation before marriage, sometimes church, large urban residence, and 20-21 at marriage (relative risk: 1.00). (E) Married before 1965, no preconception, no cohabitation before marriage, rarely church, large urban residence, and 22-24 at marriage (relative risk: 0.59). (F) Married before 1965, no preconception, no cohabitation before marriage, farm residence, and ≤ 19 at marriage (relative risk: 0.23).

with those who married at 20-21, in the Canadian sample, as opposed to 0.45 in the U.S. sample (Teachman, 1982).

This study was more concerned with the correlates of marriage dissolution than with trends that are better handled with vital statistics. There were very few surprises. Those who married early, were not religious, had a premarital birth, or lived in a large city had greater chances of a separation. Here again, where comparisons are possible, similarities can be observed with U.S. studies. In the Canadian sample the relative risk for those who had a premarital birth was 2.35 times that for those who had neither a premarital birth nor a premarital conception, whereas for the U.S. it was 2.03. The premarital conception group in the Canadian sample, however, had a relative risk of 1.50, whereas in the U.S. study it was 0.99 (Teachman, 1982).

Some obviously important correlates, such as income or occupation, were not included here mainly because of lack of adequate data and the time-dependent nature of these variables. The findings reveal that for marriage dissolution, the differences according to demographic or socioeconomic characteristics seem to be far more important than they are for such demographic events as childbearing or mortality, at least in the present social context in Canada. Conversely, it makes little sense to treat the population as homogeneous in analyzing survival probabilities of marriages, other than for cursory statistical analysis of global trends.

■ ACKNOWLEGMENTS

This is a revised version of a paper presented at the Annual Meetings of the Population Association of America, San Francisco, April 3-5, 1986. We gratefully acknowledge the financial support from the Social Sciences and Humanities Research Council of Canada for the Canadian Fertility Study on which this paper is based. We also wish to thank three anonymous reviewers for their helpful suggestions.

References

Breslow, N.E. 1974. Covariance analysis of censored survival data. *Biometrics* 30:89-99.

Bumpass, L.L., and J.A. Sweet. 1972. Differentials in marital instability. *American Sociological Review* 37:754-766.

Burch, T.K. 1985. *Family History Survey: Preliminary Findings.* Ottawa: Statistics Canada. (Catalogue No. 99-955)

Carter, H., and P.C. Glick. 1970. *Marriage and Divorce: A Social and Economic Study.* Cambridge, Mass.: Harvard University Press.

Chester, R. 1972. Is there a relationship between childlessness and marriage breakdown? *Journal of Biosocial Science* 4:443-454.

Cox, D.R. 1972. Regression models and life tables (with discussion). *Journal of the Royal Statistical Society*, Ser. B., 34:184-220.

Furstenberg, F. 1976. Premarital pregnancy and marital instability. *Journal of Social Issues* 32:67-86.

Gibson, C. 1974. The association between divorce and social class in England and Wales. *British Journal of Sociology* 25:79-93.

_____. 1980. Childlessness and marital instability: A re-examination. *Journal of Biosocial Science* 12:121-132.

Holford, T.R. 1976. Life tables with concomitant information. *Biometrics* 32:587-597.

Kalbfleisch, J., and R. Prentice. 1980. *The Statistical Analysis of Failure Time Data.* New York: Wiley.

Martin, L.G., Trussell, J., Salvail, F.R., and Shah, N.M. 1983. Co-variates of child mortality in the Philippines, Indonesia, and Pakistan: An analysis based on hazard models. *Population Studies* 37:417-432.

McCarthy, J., and J. Menken. 1979. Marriage, remarriage, marital disruption and age at first birth. *Family Planning Perspectives* 11:21-30.

McKie, D.C., B. Prentice, and P. Reed. 1983. *Divorce: Law and the Family in Canada.* Ottawa: Statistics Canada. (Catalogue No. 89-502E)

Menken, J., J. Trussell, D. Stempel, and O. Babakol. 1981. Proportional hazards life table models: An illustrative analysis of socio-demographic influences on marriage dissolution in the United States. *Demography* 18:181-200.

Murphy, M.J. 1985. Demographic and socio-economic influences on recent British marital breakdown patterns. *Population Studies* 39:441-460.

Teachman, J. 1982. Methodological issues in the analysis of family formation and dissolution. *Journal of Marriage and Family* 44:1037-1053.

Thornton, A. 1978. Marital dissolution, remarriage, and childbearing. *Demography* 15:361-380.

Trussell, J., and C. Hammerslough. 1983. A hazards model analysis of the covariates of infant and child mortality in Sri Lanka. *Demography* 20:1-26.

Weed, J.A. 1974. Age at marriage as a factor in state divorce rate differentials. *Demography* 11:361-375.

COHABITATION AND MARITAL STABILITY IN THE UNITED STATES

NO

Jay D. Teachman and Karen A. Polonko

The importance of cohabitation rests not only in its increased prevalence but also in its link to the process of family formation and dissolution. As the marital and fertility careers of young adults become more complex, it is important to understand the multiple determinants and consequences of variations in the timing and sequencing of important life-course events. In various theoretical and empirical reports, cohabitation has been linked to the rising proportion of out-of-wedlock births, delay in marriage, and increases in the divorce rate (see the review in Macklin 1987). In this article, we attempt to shed light on the debate surrounding the consequences of premarital cohabitation in the United States by examining data pertaining to subsequent marital stability.

◼ COHABITATION AND MARITAL STABILITY

Prior research and theory on the relationship between premarital cohabitation and subsequent marital stability has taken two basic positions. The first position argues that there is something about cohabitation, apart from the characteristics of cohabitants, that influences the success of marriage. As Bennett, Blanc, and Bloom (1988) indicate, marriage in the past was considered to be less of a personal bond between men and women than an economic arrangement designed for a gender-based division of labor as couples strove to meet the demands of community and economy. More recently, marriage has become less a social and economic exchange between spouses and more a source of personal gratification (Bellah et al. 1985; Blumstein & Schwartz 1983). There is now a more extended and well-defined period of courtship during which potential mates are sorted (Modell 1980).

In this context, it is possible to see premarital cohabitation as a form of "trial marriage" (Mead 1966; Rapoport 1965; Cherlin 1981). By cohabiting individuals are able to rehearse marital roles, strengthening the future marital bond. Strengthening may occur by developing a mutually satisfactory division of household and market labor, as well as enhancing sexual and interpersonal compatibility. At the same time, if appropriate and satisfactory role relationships cannot be developed, the partners are able to end the relationship before becoming subject to the additional constraints of the legal system. Following the logic of this position, one would hypothesize that cohabitation should lead to more stable marriages.

Available evidence on the nature of cohabiting relationships provides indirect support for this position. Recent evidence suggests that cohabiting unions are less stable than marriages (Bumpass & Sweet 1988; Hofferth & Upchurch 1988), consistent with the notion that only the most compatible unions survive to marriage. Other evidence indicates that most cohabitants organize their union much like married couples, although a gender-based division of labor is slightly less prominent (Macklin 1987). This suggests that individuals have the opportunity to practice and adapt to marital roles.

The second position is different from the first because it assumes that cohabitants are fundamentally different from noncohabitants. Specifically, it is asserted that cohabitants are a select group of individuals who are less committed to marriage than noncohabitants. It is not the experience of having cohabited itself that affects marital stability. Rather, it is a preexisting disposition toward lesser commitment on the part of cohabitants that influences subsequent marital stability. Thus, cohabitation is not viewed as a stage in the courtship process by which couples become more enmeshed. Instead, it is an alternative, albeit sometimes temporary, to marriage. Among cohabitants, the decision to marry is more likely to be the result of pressures from family and peers. Following the logic of this position, one would hypothesize that cohabitation leads to less stable marriages.

There exists indirect evidence supporting the thesis that cohabitants are less committed to relationships than noncohabitants. The data cited above concerning the higher dissolution rates of cohabiting versus marital unions may be construed as support for the thesis that cohabitants are less committed to stable relationships. Data from both abroad and from the United States also indicate that individuals who cohabit are less likely to hold traditional sex roles, are more likely to value individual freedom, and are less likely to desire children (Carlson 1987; Clayton & Voss 1977; Newcomb & Bentler 1980; Tanfer 1987). On the other hand, recent data from the United States do not indicate cohabitants are any less likely to desire marriage than noncohabitants (Tanfer 1987).

Cohabitants may also vary according to other characteristics that affect marital stability. For example, prior research suggests that cohabitants are more likely to have been married before and are more likely to have children at the beginning of marriage (Macklin 1987; Tanfer 1987), both characteristics that may lead to an increased risk of marital disruption. It is not the case, however, that all differences in characteristics would act to increase the likelihood of marital dissolution for cohabitants. For instance, cohabitants are likely to be older at marriage than noncohabitants, and an older age at marriage has been consistently linked to a reduced probability of divorce (Cherlin 1981).

Available empirical evidence linking cohabitation to marital dissolution is scarce. Only recently have appropriate data become available to test the competing hypotheses outlined above. Using data from the Canadian Fertility Survey conducted in 1984, Balakrishnan et al. (1987) find that cohabitation significantly increases the likelihood of subsequent marital disruption. Couples who cohabited before marriage had rates of marital dissolution 50% greater than noncohabitants. Using data from a 1981 Swedish study, Bennett, Blanc, and Bloom (1988) present similar findings. They report that cohabitation increases the rate of subsequent marital disruption by 80%.

Bennett, Blanc, and Bloom (1988:137) state that "the direction of effects found in Sweden in all likelihood holds true in the United States as well." Although the use of data from Sweden has been questioned with respect to its applicability to the United States (Cherlin 1981), similar results from Canada strengthen support for the hypothesis that premarital cohabitation impacts negatively on marital stability. We perform what we believe to be the first empirical test of the effect of premarital cohabitation on marital stability using representative data from the United States.

The proportion of men and women who have cohabited with their spouse prior to marriage is shown in Table 1. Men and women are about equally likely to report having cohabited (21-23%). The values observed for women are roughly congruent with those reported for Canadian women (Balakrishnan et al. 1987). However, the level of cohabitation is much lower than observed for Sweden. Bennett, Blanc, and Bloom (1988) report that almost two-thirds of the ever-married women in their Swedish sample had cohabited. The proportion of cohabitants who cohabited more than 6 months is about the same for both sexes (70-73%). In Sweden, although rates of premarital cohabitation are higher, about the same percent of women (76%) have cohabited for more than 6 months. Only a small fraction (2-3%) of ever-married respondents in the United States have cohabited more than once prior to first marriage.

We use a life table procedure to examine variation in marital disruption, because cohabitants and noncohabitants may have different periods

---

TABLE 1 Prevalence and Duration of Premarital Cohabitation in the NLS Sample by Sex

	WOMEN	MEN
Cohabited with spouse	20.7%	22.9%
Cohabited more than once	2.6%	2.4%
Duration of cohabitation with spouse:		
0-6 months	29.7%	26.5%
7-12 months	25.0%	23.2%
13-24 months	21.5%	26.5%
> 24 months	23.8%	23.8%

of risk to the event. Life tables yield estimates of the probability that a respondent has ended their marriage at each marital duration (which we calculate in terms of whole months). Individuals who end their marriages contribute exposure at each duration until the time of marital dissolution. Individuals who remain married contribute exposure at each duration until they are truncated by the survey.

The cumulative proportion of respondents ending their marriage, by sex and premarital cohabitation status, is presented in Table 2. The results are consistent with results from Sweden and Canada. Although the differences are small in the first few years following marriage, after 10 years cohabitants are more likely than noncohabitants to have dissolved their marriage. The level of marital dissolution registered for cohabiting women in the United States is only slightly higher than observed for Canadian women (10-year cumulative failure rate of .35 versus .31) but nearly twice that observed for Swedish women (10-year cumulative failure rate of .35 versus .18). The level of marital disruption experienced by non-cohabiting women in the United States is particularly high compared to Canada and Sweden (after 10 years the cumulative failure rates are .29 for the United States, .14 for Canada and .10 for Sweden). Our confidence in these results is strengthened by the fact that the same pattern appears for both men and women.

The life table results are consistent with the hypothesis that cohabitants are less committed to marriage. These results, however, do not control for variations between cohabitants and noncohabitants on varia-

TABLE 2 **Life Table Estimates of the Cumulative Proportion of Marriages Disrupted by Sex and Premarital Cohabitation Status**

MONTHS SINCE MARRIAGE	WOMEN		MEN	
	COHABIT	NOT COHABIT	COHABIT	NOT COHABIT
12	.028	.031	.041	.020
24	.067	.069	.073	.050
36	.103	.103	.105	.079
48	.139	.133	.149	.122
60	.166	.167	.173	.148
72	.198	.194	.222	.176
84	.262	.225	.258	.197
96	.289	.247	.295	.214
108	.320	.271	.326	.230
120	.351	.290	.379	.243
N[a]	(972)	(3,382)	(895)	(2,942)

[a] Values in parentheses are unweighted sample sizes

bles known to affect the risk of marital disruption (e.g., age at marriage, education). The values shown in Table 3 indicate that cohabitants possess characteristics that act to both increase and decrease the likelihood of marital dissolution. Several researchers have found that having a premarital birth (but not a legitimated birth) increases the likelihood of subsequent marital dissolution (Billy, Landale & McLaughlin 1986; Menken et al. 1981; Morgan & Rindfuss 1985; Teachman 1982, 1983). Cohabitants are more likely than noncohabitants to have a premarital birth, while there is little difference between the two groups with respect to legitimated births. Maritally conceived births have been linked consistently to a reduced likelihood of marital disruption (Billy, Landale & McLaughlin 1986; Morgan & Rindfuss 1985; Waite & Kanouse 1985). Cohabitants are less likely than noncohabitants to have a maritally conceived birth. The fertility careers of cohabitants therefore indicate greater risk of marital dissolution.

TABLE 3   Sample Means of Predictor Variables[a]

	WOMEN		MEN	
VARIABLE	COHABIT	NOT COHABIT	COHABIT	NOT COHABIT
Maritally conceived birth (%)	68	83	66	78
Premarital birth (%)	8	4	13	4
Legitimated birth (%)	10	11	10	9
Spouse married before (%)	29	12	26	7
Step-child in house (%)	5	2	14	4
Age at marriage	24.1	21.5	25.6	23.8
Education (%):				
Less than high school	4	4	2	2
High school	32	48	35	43
Some college	37	28	37	31
College degree	24	18	21	20
More than college	4	2	5	4
SES (%):				
Low	18	22	13	19
Medium	50	58	52	56
High	32	20	35	25

[a] Maritally conceived birth is measured as a time-dependent variable with 1=birth occurring after the first seven months of marriage, 0=otherwise; Premarital birth is measured as 1=birth occurring before marriage and living in the house, 0=otherwise; Legitimated birth is measured as 1=birth occurring in the first seven months of marriage, 0=otherwise; Spouse married before and step-child in the house are dummy variables where 1=spouse previously married, 0=otherwise, and 1=spouse has a child from another relationship living in the household, 0=otherwise; Age at marriage is measured in years; Education refers to level of education measured at the time of marriage where 1=less than high school, 2=high school, 3=some college, 4=college graduate, and 5=more than college; SES is a composite variable based on characteristics of the parental household (father's education, mother's education, father's occupation) and is divided into three approximately equal groups with 1=low, 2=medium, and 3=high.

The marital structures of cohabitants are more complex than those of noncohabitants in that: a) their spouses are more likely to have been married before (unfortunately, the NLS does not contain information on prior cohabitation for spouses), and b) they are more likely to have step-children living in the home (the greater percent in this category registered for men reflects the cultural bias toward giving women custody of children). Several authors have argued that more complex marital structures are more prone to marital instability, either because role performance is less institutionalized in such unions (Cherlin 1981) or because these unions are selective of individuals less committed to marriage in general (Halliday 1978). The empirical evidence shows that complex marital structures are associated with greater marital instability (McCarthy 1978; White and Booth 1985). As was the case for fertility careers, the marital structures of cohabitants indicate a greater risk of experiencing marital disruption.

The most consistent and strongest predictor of marital dissolution is age at marriage (Billy, Landale & McLaughlin 1986; Menken et al. 1981; Morgan & Rindfuss 1985; Teachman 1982, 1983). Individuals who marry early are much more likely to end their marriages than individuals who marry later. The data in Table 3 indicate that cohabitants marry later than noncohabitants. Cohabitants are also more highly educated than non-cohabitants and come from higher SES backgrounds. Both factors have been found to decrease the likelihood of marital dissolution (Billy, Landale & McLaughlin 1986; Menken et al. 1981; Morgan & Rindfuss 1985; Teachman 1982, 1983). Thus, variations on age at marriage, education, and SES, contrary to other characteristics distinguishing the two groups, indicate a reduced risk of marital instability for cohabitants versus noncohabitants. . . .

The results shown in Table 4 are consistent with the hypothesis that cohabitants are less committed to marriage than noncohabitants. To explore this proposition in greater depth, we follow Bennett, Blanc, and Bloom (1988) who suggest that long-term cohabitation indicates less commitment to marriage than short-term cohabitation. If this is true, then short-term cohabitants should be less likely to experience marital dissolution. To test this proposition, we reran the logistic-regression models including a control for length of premarital cohabitation (coded as a dichotomy—cohabitation of six months or less versus cohabitation of more than six months). The results are shown in Table 5 (since the coefficients for the control variables are virtually unchanged we do not show them).[1] We find that short-term cohabitants are less likely to experience marital dissolution than long-term cohabitants (the logistic regression coefficients imply that the odds of dissolving a marriage for those who cohabited 6 months or less are .65 and .75 times as great for women and men, respectively, in any given interval).

While the length of premarital cohabitation may indicate variation in commitment to marriage, it is also possible that this effect reflects some-

TABLE 4   Effects of the Predictor Variables on Marital Dissolution, Measured from Beginning of Marriage, by Sex[a]

	WOMEN	MEN
Cohabited	.187*	.139*
Cohabited more than once	.023	.366*
Maritally conceived birth	−.277*	−.298*
Premarital birth	.065	−.042
Legitimated birth	−.199*	−.203*
Age at marriage	−.208*	−.146*
Education at marriage	−.187*	−.298*
Spouse married before	.327*	.347*
Step-child in house	.119	.007
SES	.055*	.048
Intercept	−2.029*	−1.601*
Model X^2	26476	23184
df	14	14

* The coefficient is at least twice its standard error.

[a] Maximum likelihood logistic-regression coefficients, net of marital duration

TABLE 5   Effects of Premarital Cohabitation and Length of Premarital Cohabitation on Marital Dissolution, Measured from Beginning of Marriage, by Sex[a]

	WOMEN	MEN
Cohabited	.287*	.205*
Cohabited more than once	.036	.382*
Cohabited 6 months or less	−.427*	−.294*

* The coefficient is at least twice its standard error.

[a] Maximum likelihood logistic-regression coefficients, net of marital duration and control variables indicated in Table 4

thing very different. Specifically, couples who have been together longer, irrespective of marital status, may be more likely to dissolve their unions. For example, respondents who cohabited for two years prior to marriage and have been married for one year may have rates of marital dissolution similar to respondents who have been married for three years. Thus, the negative effect observed for short-term cohabitation may be due to the fact that these unions are still new at the time of marriage.

To test this alternative hypothesis, we estimate the hazard-rate models . . . using total duration in first union. Since premarital cohabitants in our sample cannot, by definition, end their unions before marriage, we censor their relationship histories before the time of marriage. For instance, a respondent who cohabited for 2 years prior to marriage is at risk of marital dissolution in the third year of union and beyond, but not before. The results from conducting this exercise are shown in Table 6. The coefficients indicate no effect of premarital cohabitation on the rate of marital dissolution, although having cohabited more than once is related to an increased likelihood of marital disruption for both men and women. In other words, the increased rate of marital dissolution associated with premarital cohabitation indicated in Tables 4 and 5 can be attributed to the amount of time cohabitants have already spent in union prior to marriage.[2] On the basis of these results, neither of the original hypotheses is supported.

TABLE 6   **Effects of Premarital Cohabitation on Marital Dissolution, Measured from Beginning of Union, by Sex**[a]

	WOMEN	MEN
Cohabited	.032	−.077
Cohabited more than once	.546*	.704*

* The coefficient is at least twice its standard error.

[a] Maximum likelihood logistic-regression coefficients, net of marital duration and control variables indicated in Table 4

■ DISCUSSION

American men and women are subject to considerable delay in marriage and high divorce rates. Age at first marriage is now higher than at any point since the turn of the century (Espenshade 1985), and estimates indicate that as many as 50% of recently contracted marriages will end in divorce (Weed 1980). In a typical American's life span, marriage has come to occupy an ever smaller proportion of adult years (Watkins, Menken & Bongaarts 1987; Schoen et al. 1985). In such a context, it is likely that cohabitation represents an advanced stage of courtship where marriage is desired but with less commitment to a lifetime partnership (Gwartney-Gibbs 1986; Tanfer 1987). While cohabitation, as a stage in the courtship process, may impact on the nature and timing of marital unions, our results indicate that cohabitation has no direct effect on the stability of marriage.

Our results show that net of important compositional controls, if consideration is given to the amount of time spent in marriage, premarital cohabitation in the United States increases the risk of marital dissolution. However, once allowance is made for the total amount of time spent in union, there is no difference in the rate of marital disruption by cohabitation status. While cohabiting unions remain less stable than marriages

(Bumpass & Sweet 1988; Hofferth & Upchurch 1988), the stability of marriages preceded by cohabitation, compared to marriages not preceded by cohabitation, does not indicate less commitment to marriage. Similarly, having cohabited does not confer advantage in terms of marital stability.

To increase confidence in our results, subsequent research should consider more broadly representative samples. As discussed above, we cannot be sure that our results apply to individuals with less than a high school education. Other research indicates that these individuals are more likely to cohabit than individuals with more education (Tanfer 1987) and to experience marital disruption (Morgan & Rindfuss 1985), making it important to determine the impact of cohabitation on their marital stability. It would also be informative to obtain information about the impact of cohabitation on marital stability in different historical contexts by considering earlier and later cohorts of individuals.

Notes

1. As one reader noted, the choice of six months as a cutoff between short- and long-term cohabitation is arbitrary. We chose six months because: a) about one-quarter to one-third of all cohabitations last six months or less, b) Bennett et al. (1988) use six months as a similar cutoff, and c) preliminary results indicated relatively similar results for various cutoffs up through a full year of cohabitation (beyond which we are hesitant to call cohabitation short-term). Moreover, this analysis is really a precursor to the more detailed analysis that follows.

2. Bennett, Blanc, and Bloom (1988) conduct the same exercise for their Swedish data but still find a significant effect of cohabitation on marital stability.

References

Balakrishnan, T.R., K.V. Rao, Evelyne Lapierre-Adamcyk, and Karol Krotki. 1987. "A Hazard Model Analysis of Marriage Dissolution in Canada." *Demography* 24:395-406.

Bellah, Robert, Richard Madsen, Ann Swidler, William Sullivan, and Stephen Tipton. 1985. *Habits of the Heart: Individualism and Commitment in American Life.* University of California Press.

Bennett, Neil, Ann Blanc, and David Bloom. 1988. "Commitment and the Modern Union: Assessing the Link between Premarital Cohabitation and Subsequent Marital Stability." *American Sociological Review* 53:127-38.

Billy, John, Nancy Landale, and Steven McLaughlin. 1986. "The Effect of Marital Status at First Birth on Marital Dissolution among Adolescent Mothers." *Demography* 23:329-50.

Blumstein, Philip, and Pepper Schwartz. 1983. *American Couples.* William Morrow.

Bumpass, Larry, and James Sweet. 1988. "Preliminary Evidence on Cohabitation from the 1987 National Survey of Families and Households." Paper presented at the annual meetings of the Population Association of America.

Carlson, Ellwood. 1985. "Couples without Children: Premarital Cohabitation in France." Pp. 113-30 in *Contemporary Marriage: Comparative Perspectives of a*

Changing Institution, edited by Kingsley Davis with A. Grossbard-Schechtman. Russell Sage Foundation.

Cherlin, Andrew. 1981. *Marriage, Divorce, Remarriage*. Harvard University Press.

Clayton, Richard, and Harwin Voss. 1977. "Shacking Up: Cohabitation in the 1970s." *Journal of Marriage and the Family* 39:273-83.

Espenshade, Thomas. 1985. "Marriage Trends in America: Estimates, Implications and Underlying Causes." *Population and Development Review* 11:193-245.

Gwartney-Gibbs, Patricia. 1986. "The Institutionalization of Premarital Cohabitation: Estimates from Marriage License Applications, 1970 and 1980." *Journal of Marriage and the Family* 48:423-34.

Halliday, Terence. 1978. "Remarriage: The More Complete Institution." *American Journal of Sociology* 86:630-35.

Hanushek, Eric, and John Jackson. 1977. *Statistical Methods for Social Scientists*. Academic Press.

Hofferth, Sandra, and Dawn Upchurch. 1988. "Breaking Up: Dissolving Nonmarital Unions." Paper presented at the annual meetings of the Population Association of America.

Macklin, Eleanor. 1987. "Nontraditional Family Forms." Pp. 237-63 in *Handbook of Marriage and the Family*, edited by Marvin Sussman and Susan Steinmetz. Plenum.

McCarthy, James. 1978. "A Comparison of the Probability of the Dissolution of First and Second Marriages." *Demography* 15:345-59.

Mead, Margaret. 1966. "Marriage in Two Steps." *Redbook* (July):48-49, 84-85.

Menken, Jane, James Trussell, Debra Stempel, and Ozer Babakol. 1981. "Proportional Hazards Life Table Models: An Illustrative Analysis of Sociodemographic Influences on Marriage Dissolution in the United States." *Demography* 18:181-200.

Modell, John. 1980. "Normative Aspects of American Marriage Timing Since World War II." *Journal of Family History* 5:210-34.

Morgan, S. Philip, and Ronald Rindfuss. 1985. "Marital Disruption: Structural and Temporal Dimensions." *American Journal of Sociology* 90:1055-77.

Newcomb, Michael, and Peter Bentler. 1980. "Cohabitation before Marriage: A Comparison of Married Couples Who Did and Did Not Cohabit." *Alternative Lifestyles* 3:65-83.

Rapoport, Rona. 1965. "The Transition from Engagement to Marriage." *Acta Sociologica* 8:36-55.

Schoen, Robert, William Utron, Karen Woodrow, and John Baj. 1985. "Marriage and Divorce in Twentieth Century American Cohorts." *Demography* 22:101-14.

Tanfer, Koray. 1987. "Patterns of Premarital Cohabitation among Never-married Women in the United States." *Journal of Marriage and the Family* 49:483-97.

Teachman, Jay. 1982. "Methodological Issues in the Analysis of Family Formation and Dissolution." *Journal of Marriage and the Family* 44:1037-53.

———. 1983. "Early Marriage, Premarital Fertility and Marital Dissolution." *Journal of Family Issues* 4:105-26.

Waite, Linda, Gus Haggstrom, and David Kanouse. 1985. "The Consequences of Parenthood for the Marital Stability of Young Adults." *American Sociological Review* 50:850-57.

Watkins, Susan, Jane Menken, and John Bongaarts. 1987. "Demographic Foundations of Family Change." *American Sociological Review* 52:346-58.

Weed, James. 1980. *National Estimates of Marriage Dissolution and Survivorship: United States.* Vital and Health Statistics, Series 3, No. 19. U.S. Government Printing Office.

White, Lynn, and Alan Booth. 1985. "The Quality and Stability of Remarriages: The Role of Stepchildren." *American Sociological Review* 50:689-98.

■ POSTSCRIPT

The Balakrishnan et al. study examines a number of factors that can lead to divorce. Age at marriage, year of marriage, first-birth status, religiosity, place of residence, and cohabitation prior to marriage all have an impact on the divorce rate. In this context, cohabitation is only one of several factors that influence the divorce rate, but it is clearly a factor. On the other hand, using data from the United States, Teachman and Polonko demonstrate that once the total time spent living together in both common-law and legal marriage is considered, cohabiting couples have approximately the same rate of marital dissolution.

The key factor in assessing this debate is methodology. While they acknowledge that time spent cohabiting prior to the legal marriage may increase the likelihood of divorce after marriage, Balakrishnan et al. consider only the length of time the couples spend together after a legal marriage. Teachman and Polonko's data indicates that cohabiting couples who later marry are at no greater risk of marital disruption than non-cohabiting couples. Further, both studies refer to marital dissolution rather than divorce,which is, of course, only form of marital breakup.

The implications of these studies are significant in terms of the expectations people have about marriage and cohabiting. Both studies indicate a low probability that cohabiting couples will survive legal marriage as long as their noncohabiting counterparts. Consequently, as a mechanism for testing compatibility, cohabitation offers little promise. On the other hand, if the total time spent living together is considered, cohabitation as a trial marriage is not detrimental to marital success.

■ QUESTIONS

1. Why are more people opting to cohabit before getting married?
2. Does marriage necessarily mean a loss of individual freedom?
3. What factors prompt cohabiting couples to get married?
4. Does marriage have the same social significance today that it had in the past?

■ FURTHER READING

In Support of Balakrishnan

Bennett, Neil, Ann Blanc, and David Bloom. "Commitment and the Modern Union: Assessing the Link Between Premarital Cohabitation and Subsequent Marital Stability." *American Sociological Review* 53 (1988): 127-138.

Newcomb, Michael and Peter Bentler. "Cohabitation before Marriage: A Comparison of Married Couples Who Did and Did Not Cohabit." *Alternative Lifestyles* (1980).

In Support of Teachman and Polonko
Cherlin, Andrew. *Marriage, Divorce, Remarriage.* Harvard University Press, 1981.

Other Voices
Macklin, E. "Nonmarital Heterosexual Cohabitation: An Overview." In *Contemporary Familes and Alternative Lifestyles.* Edited by E. Macklin and R. Rubin. Beverly Hills, Calif.: Sage Publications, 1983.

Tanfer, Koray. "Patterns of Premarital Cohabitation among Never-married Women in the United States." *Journal of Marriage and the Family* 49 (1987): 483-497.

ARE MEN THE

MAIN VICTIMS OF

SPOUSE ABUSE?

YES   **Merlin B. Brinkerhoff and Eugen Lupri**, "Interspousal Violence," *Canadian Journal of Sociology* 13, no. 4 (1988): 407-434

NO   **Walter S. DeKeseredy**, "In Defence of Self-Defence: Demystifying Female Violence Against Male Intimates," unpublished

In 1980, the House of Commons erupted in laughter when it was reported that a study commissioned by the Canadian Advisory Council on the Status of Women (see MacLeod, 1980) had found that one in ten Canadian women were the victims of spouse abuse. Until then, the issue of wife battering (i.e., husbands hitting, kicking, biting, or verbally and psychologically abusing their wives) had received some attention from academics (Gelles, 1974; Steinmetz, 1978) and social commentators (Walker, 1979) during the 1970s, but little significant public attention. As C. Wright Mills (1959) would say, wife battering was still a private trouble—a private concern between husband and wife.

Thus, the reaction in the House of Commons characterized Canadian attitudes toward wife battering at the time. Canadians were unwilling to acknowledge that the most idealized of social institutions—the family—was anything other than the epitome of tranquillity. Many people dismissed as unbelievable the mounting sociological evidence verifying the extent of wife abuse.

Much has changed since then. Some researchers have even suggested that the rate of violence within the family was much higher than the one-in-ten figure MacLeod reported. Using a telephone survey method, Smith (1988) found slightly less than 40 percent of the women he surveyed had been abused at least once by their male partners (husbands, boyfriends, dates, etc.), and that almost 15 percent had been abused during the previous year. Other researchers noted that women were not the only victims of family violence. Children were also frequent victims of abuse. For example, the report of the Committee on Sexual Offences Against Children and Youth (1984)—known as the Badgely Commission—reported that slightly more than 50 percent of Canadian females, and approximately one-third of Canadian males, are victimized by at least one act of sexual assault in their lifetimes. Even more startling was the Commission finding that nearly half of this abuse occurred before the victims were seventeen. A significant proportion of the perpetrators of such abuse were family members—fathers, uncles, brothers, etc. The image of the family as a refuge from the hardened world of wars, politics, and economic struggle crumbled under the increasing evidence of violence within it.

Not all of the attention focused on the victimization of women and children. Some researchers pointed out that men were also the victims of violent behaviour. Wives and children could be violent too. For example, Steinmetz (1978) and others (Straus, Gelles, and Steinmetz, 1980) drew attention to what they called the battered husband syndrome. Their studies indicated that wife-to-husband abuse was more frequent than husband-to-wife abuse.

This research has sparked a heated debate in social science research. Critics have charged that the research showing that husbands are more frequently victims of spousal violence than women overestimate the amount and severity of female violence toward men. The articles presented here are part of that debate. Brinkeroff and Lupri, arguing the "Yes" side of the debate, present data showing "wife-to-husband violence prevailed over husband-to-wife violence." DeKeseredy, arguing the "No" side of the debate, says that studies like the Brinkerhoff and Lupri study are misleading because they downplay the extent to which wife-to-husband violence is an act of self-defence in response to husband-to-wife violence.

References
Committee on Sexual Offences Against Children and Youth (1984) *Sexual Offences Against Children*, 2 vols. (Ottawa: Supply and Services).

Gelles, Richard J. (1974) *The Violent Home* (Beverly Hills, Calif.: Sage Publications).

MacLeod, Linda (1980) *Wife Battering in Canada: The Vicious Circle* (Ottawa: Canadian Advisory Council on the Status of Women).

Mills, C. Wright (1959) *The Sociological Imagination* (New York: Oxford University Press).

Smith, M.D. (1988) "The Incidence and Prevalence of Woman Abuse In Toronto," *Violence and Victims* 2: 173-187.

Steinmetz, S.K. (1978) "The Battered Husband Syndrome," *Victimology: An International Journal* 2: 499-509.

Straus, M.A., R.J. Gelles, and S.K. Steinmetz (1980) *Behind Closed Doors: Violence in the American Family* (New York: Anchor Books).

Walker, Lenore (1979) *The Battered Woman* (New York: Harper and Row).

INTERSPOUSAL VIOLENCE

YES

Merlin B. Brinkerhoff and Eugen Lupri

■ INTRODUCTION

Among the issues and questions relating to the study of the family, few have generated as much discussion and research as family violence. Two factors that contribute to this increasing interest are the rightful insistence by the women's movement on demystifying the family as a "haven in a heartless world" (Lasch, 1979) and the heightened public concern about various forms of domestic violence such as child abuse, elder abuse, wife battering, and family murder.

American family sociologists have conducted important research on family violence, but Canadian data are scarce.[1] According to Eichler (1983, 1985), no national representative study of wife battering has been conducted in Canada. There is also a lack of reliable information on wife-to-husband abuse, which has been de-emphasized, if not ignored completely, by most Canadian scholars. To gain a better understanding of domestic violence in a social context differentiated hierarchically by gender, we must give equal attention to the abuse committed by both sexes. In doing so we follow Eichler and Lapointe's plea for a "dualistic perspective" (1985: 19) in our study of interspousal violence. . . .

■ OBJECTIVES

Domestic violence is an ambiguous concept, difficult to operationalize for research. Generally, if not always, it occurs in a conflict situation in which two or more family members contest to settle an issue, in each of his or her favour. Violent conflict may be defined as an act which threatens or causes physical injury to another person. Research has identified several types of family violence such as "normal," "explosive," "abusive," and "verbal." Although verbal aggression is different from physical aggression, heated and angry verbal attacks can cause emotional damage to another person.

A 1981 Calgary study of 562 matched couples, married or living together, collected basic information on the extent of specific violent acts in the home. The aims of this paper, which uses data obtained in the Calgary study, are to explore 1) the incidence of conjugal violence in the home, 2) the extent of both wife abuse and husband abuse, 3) the extent to which interspousal violence arises according to several social and demographic factors, and 4) the relationship among conjugal violence, marital conflict, and physical as well as verbal aggression. Although we do not set ourselves the task of testing empirically a set of specific hypotheses, our analysis will be guided, more implicitly than explicitly, by assumptions derived primarily from conflict and social exchange theory.

The Conflict Model

We will assume that marriage is a dialectic relationship, governed by inherent contradictions. Following Sprey (1979) and particularly Straus and Gelles (1979), we may identify several structural characteristics that tend to make the family a conflict-prone social group.

First, many hours of the day are spent in face-to-face interaction with other family members, and this high frequency of interaction increases the "time risk" (Straus and Gelles, 1979) of conflict or violence. The frequency is greater between couples without children.

Second, family interaction covers a wide range of activities: daily routine tasks, leisure-time pursuits, conversations, the expression of intimate feelings. Because numerous events take place on any given day, greater likelihood exists for disagreement, tension, or dispute over these events.

Third, the marriage relationship demands intense interaction. Couples communicate often with openness and intimacy, which bring the opportunity for the development of affection, love, and deeply felt experiences. Yet intimacy also carries the risks of failure and emotional injury: openness can be one-sided. Intense involvement renders one partner vulnerable if the other remains uninvolved, distant, and aloof.

Fourth, dyadic relationships, such as couple interaction, contain built-in structural conflicts. As Simmel (1955) observed, either member can destroy the relationship by not participating, by not becoming involved, by withdrawing. By contrast, in larger groups the loss of one or more members does not cause the group to dissolve (Coser, 1956, 1968; Simmel, 1955, 1964). In addition, a couple has no chance for majority rule, to which a spouse can appeal for fairness or justice. To call in outside help is defined in our society as interference, and is legitimized only as a last resort "to save the marriage." The addition of children changes the structure of interaction in a dyad and creates the possibility of coalition formation.

Fifth, the family is hierarchial: interaction between members is influenced by relationships of power and dependence. Both age and sex shape family relations not only between parents and children but also between women and men. This situation makes the family an arena of cultural conflict (Straus and Gelles, 1979) because built-in control mechanisms and dependence relationships perpetuate age and gender inequality.

Finally, and most important, the family is a highly privatized social group and thus is shielded from public scrutiny. This fact is epitomized in such phrases as "My home is my castle" and in former Prime Minister

Trudeau's declaration, "The state has no business in the bedrooms of the nation." The norms of the nuclear family dictate that couples solve their own problems, regardless of their origin, nature, and extent. Unlike any other group, the family cannot rely on outside help to resolve its difficulties except in rare circumstances. Permanent reliance on outside help would undermine the very basis of the nuclear family. Furthermore, rational discourse is incompatible with the immense emotional investment that typifies family relationships. Family privacy is double-edged: it is needed to sustain emotional involvement and intimacy, but it renders the family vulnerable because it is ill-equipped to solve the problems that derive from emotional investment.

The family's built-in structural inability to solve its own problems makes it far more conflict-prone than other social groups. In light of the great propensity for conflict in today's marriage, it is astonishing not that so many marriages end in divorce but that so many endure. Because the family is governed by these inherent contradictions, conflict in marriage is inevitable. We define conflict as a struggle over values and goals or over claims to power and limited resources. Conflict can be constructive when the resolution of conflict through joint efforts strengthens the couple's relationship, but it is most destructive when violence is used as a nonlegitimate means of resolution. Thus the relationship between conflict and violence is important both empirically and theoretically.

The Social Exchange Model
Marriage also is an exchange relationship, in which each partner seeks to maximize his or her benefits (rewards) and to minimize his or her costs (punishments) (Blau, 1964; Gelles and Cornell, 1985; Nye, 1978, 1979; Safilios-Rothschild, 1976; Scanzoni, 1979). Norms of reciprocity dictate that partners have certain obligations toward one another, and it is expected that both partners will meet these obligations. Even though reciprocity is an important property of the marital exchange, reciprocal behaviour often is unequal; one partner may gain more from the exchange than the other. This imbalance frequently is caused by the unequal distribution of resources, which may lead to negative exchanges and injustice. Such a structured inequality is one of the major sources of marital strain and conflict. It is difficult to resolve because the need for basic realignments in the unequal exchange often is perceived only by one partner, the one who is being dominated. More important, structured inequality frequently is gender-based, generally in favour of the husband.

Not all marital conflicts are resolved successfully. If bargaining and negotiation do not succeed, separation or termination of the marital relationship is the most drastic outcome, although legitimate. Violence, however, is a *non*legitimate mechanism to resolve marital conflict, and a mode of exchange that is the theme of this paper.

■ STUDY DESIGN

Research Locale

A cross-section of couples was chosen from Calgary, a city of more than 600,000 which has experienced boom periods of extremely rapid economic and population growth since its founding a century ago. The city grew so rapidly in the 1970s that it showed evidence of great socio-economic activity, population mobility, familial instability, and consequent individual successes and failures. . . .

Sample

A systematic random sample was drawn from a current special reverse telephone directory by taking every *n*th residence, excluding businesses, after a random start. . . . A letter describing the nature of the research was followed by a personal visit from an interviewer who ascertained whether a heterosexual couple (either common-law or married) lived at that address.[2] . . . The sample of 562 couples is believed to be fairly representative of the 133,135 Calgary husband-wife families (including common-law unions) because the sample characteristics reflect the proportions reported for the total population of Calgary regarding family life-cycle profiles, age, employment characteristics, socioeconomic status, and educational level.

Data Collection

. . . . The data were collected by thirty trained interviewers of both sexes. After rapport was established with the couple and instructions were explained clearly, the interviewer selected one partner to be interviewed while the other was asked to complete a self-administered questionnaire in another part of the dwelling. This dual-faceted approach was employed because the questionnaire could deal more validly with potentially sensitive data such as marital power, family conflict, and violence, whereas the personal interview could maintain rapport while gathering background information such as age, employment status, and pertinent family characteristics. This procedure of simultaneous but physically separated data acquisition by two different methods minimized contaminating responses by each partner. . . .

Ethical problems also exist: to solicit verbal or nonverbal responses to intimate questions about physical and verbal abuse might bring back painful memories that should not be shared with another person. Obtaining such sensitive information from both partners compounds the ethical dilemma for both the respondent and the researchers. These and other ethical considerations led to the decision to refrain from eliciting data on victimization and perpetration. Consequently, for methodological, ethical, and substantive reasons, we solicited offender reports.

▮ FINDINGS

Specific Acts of Conjugal Violence

Table 1 contains the eight violent acts from the overall violence scale that respondents reported having committed against their respective partners in the previous year. The frequencies reported here may be substantial understatements of the actual violence that took place in the home for at least three basic reasons (see Straus, Gelles, and Steinmetz, 1980):

1. For some people a slap, push, or shove (and sometimes even more severe violence) is so much a normal part of family life that it is simply not a noteworthy or dramatic enough event to be remembered, particularly when the "previous year" is used as a time frame.

TABLE 1 Specific violent acts[1] by sex, for 562 Calgary couples[2]

... DURING THIS PAST YEAR OF MARRIAGE OR LIVING TOGETHER, I ...	WIFE-TO-HUSBAND VIOLENCE %	HUSBAND-TO-WIFE VIOLENCE %
1. Threatened to hit or throw something at the other		
– once the past year	8.9	10.5
– twice or more last year	10.8	6.8
2. Pushed, grabbed, or shoved the other		
– once the past year	7.8	9.8
– twice or more last year	6.2	5.2
3. Slapped the other		
– once the past year	5.2	4.1
– twice or more last year	2.6	1.8
4. Kicked, bit, or hit the other with a fist		
– once the past year	3.7	2.1
– twice or more last year	2.7	1.1
5. Hit or tried to hit the other		
– once the past year	7.5	5.7
– twice or more last year	6.5	3.1
6. Beat up the other one		
– at least once the past year	1.8	1.7
7. Threatened the other with a knife or gun		
– at least once the past year	1.3	0.6
8. Used a knife or gun on the other		
	1 case	None

1. Items 1-8 are those employed in the "Overall Violence Scale" and use Straus's "normal violence" indicators; the subset of items 4-8 constitutes the "Severe Violence Scale" and incorporates Straus's "abusive violence."
2. The percentages, by sex, indicate the proportion of persons who report to committing the violent act once or twice or more over the past year.

2. Another group of people may fail to admit or report such violent acts because of the shame involved if one is the victim, or the guilt if one is the attacker. Such violent acts as being hit with an object or a fist, kicked, bitten, beaten up, or attacked with a knife or a gun go beyond the "normal violence" of family life and are often unreported.

3. A third reason for thinking that these figures are underestimates lies in the nature of the Calgary sample: we included only matched couples *currently* living together. Thus separated or divorced women and men living alone were excluded deliberately from the study. Because severe and excessive violence often is a cause for divorce, the Calgary sample may omit the highly violent cases.

Several inferences can be drawn from our findings. First and foremost is the general observation that force and violence appear to be much more common among our sampled couples than is often assumed by experts and lay persons alike. Table 1 shows that almost one person in five had threatened to hit or throw something at his or her partner in the previous year. About one person in seven had pushed, grabbed, or shoved his or her partner. Almost 2 percent of each sex reported beating up the other. One wife admitted using a knife or gun on her partner. Although we do not know what precipitated the violence, we do know that these acts were reported.

A second pattern emerges in Table 1: interspousal violence includes abuse by both wives and husbands. Except for "pushing, grabbing, and shoving the other," the reported rates of violent acts by women against their partners exceed the rates reported by men. Although the differences are small, the direction is consistent. In fact, women's rates (6.4 percent) are fully double the men's rates (3.2 percent) for two acts: "kicked, bit, or hit the other with a fist" and "threatened the other with a knife or gun." Is this degree of violence toward husbands, as reported by our respondents, an anomaly? In a 1984 Edmonton survey of 1,620 residents, married or living together, significantly more women (22.6 percent) than men (14.6 percent) were also reported to have "hit or thrown things" at their partners (Bland and Orn, 1986).[3]

Because we do not know who initiated the violent acts, the context within which they occurred, or the consequence of these reported assaults, the comparative data on husband abuse and wife abuse must be interpreted cautiously. Although similar patterns of violence toward husbands have been reported by American researchers (Gelles, 1974; Gelles and Cornell, 1985; Steinmetz, 1978, 1987; Straus, Gelles, and Steinmetz, 1980; Szinovacz, 1983), the issue of wife-to-husband abuse has led to a heated debate over statistics whose origin and meaning often were ignored and interpreted out of context. Pagelow (1984), whose comprehensive and critical assessment of research on family violence has enjoyed high acclaim in the literature, comes to the conclusion that the number of men battered by their female partners is "miniscule." Others[4] dismiss these findings completely, a conclusion which prompted Steinmetz to state, "unfortunately, this conspiracy of silence fails to recognize that family violence is *never* inconsequential" (1987: 728).

Certainly, wife-to-husband abuse exists, but its nature and extent need careful scrutiny, particularly when it is compared with husband-to-wife abuse. The basic question is this: how can we interpret the finding that abuse of husbands occurs as frequently as wife abuse, or even more so? One possible explanation is that husbands are more likely than wives to under-report violent incidents initiated by them in the home. This tendency may be due to gender-based language differences in the perception of selected scale items. Szinovacz (1983), who also used the conflict tactics scales in a study of matched couples, found that husbands tended to report less use of violence on their own part than was indicated by their female partners. Furthermore, wives were "somewhat more likely than their husbands to acknowledge both their own victimization and the victimization of their spouses" (1983: 638).

Similar findings were reported by Browning and Dutton (1986), whose couple data showed also that husbands tended to perceive the context as mutually violent, whereas wives perceived it as husband-violent. Another possible explanation may be derived from research on aggression, which shows that although men, on average, are more likely to be aggressive than women, when women are provoked they are as capable as men of display-ing aggressive behaviour (Richardson et al., 1983). This idea suggests that women abuse their husbands in response to being abused by them. It also was supported by data from a recent study of fifty-two battered women, among whom the majority reported that self-defense was the most com-mon motive for both nonsevere and severe violence (Saunders, 1986). In contrast, only a few women reported that they had initiated an attack of nonsevere or severe violence.

Because respondents did not report what precipitated the violent incidents, we do not know the proportion of violent acts committed by wives in self-defense or in response to blows initiated by their husbands. We do argue, however, that men's superior strength results in far greater injury to women and that abuse by men causes more physical damage than abuse by women. Even though women also are violent, they are weaker and more vulnerable in regard to violence in the home: physically, psychologi-cally, and economically (Straus, Gelles, and Steinmetz, 1980).

A third trend in our data points toward the pervasiveness of violence in the home. Conjugal violence is rarely a one-time occurrence: once violent acts are committed by either partner or both they often are repeated (see Table 1, which illustrates this trend). Thus violence between partners who are married or living together becomes highly patterned; it persists.

The Annual Incidence of Interspousal Violence

Because the Calgary study obtained information from matched heterosex-ual couples, it is possible to determine the extent of mutual violence as well as the extent to which "only" one of the partners committed a violent act against the other. One way to calculate an annual incidence rate of violence is to use the percentage of the total sample who reported having committed at least *one* of the eight violent acts against their respective partners during the twelve months preceding the interview. We call such a measure an "Overall Violence Scale."

As suggested earlier, five of the eight acts in Table 1 include abusive violence: kicked, bit, or hit the other with a fist; hit or tried to hit the other with an object; beat up the other; threatened the other with a knife or gun; used a knife or gun on the other. These acts all carry a high risk of serious physical injury. If respondents in our survey reported having inflicted on their partners any *one* of these five serious physical acts, they were included in what we call the "Severe Violence Scale."

Estimates of interspousal violence based on reports of battered women from shelters show only the tip of the iceberg, as most cases are never reported. This finding is revealed clearly in Table 2, which presents data on the annual incidence of conjugal violence based on the overall violence scale and the severe violence scale. More than one couple in three (37.8 percent) indicated that at least one partner had engaged in some kind of violence toward the other in the previous year, and slightly more than one couple in five (21.5 percent) reported that at least one partner had committed a severe violent act against the other. These annual incidence rates of conjugal violence are considerably higher than we had expected and higher than family experts had estimated. Clearly, force and violence appear to be a fundamental part of family life in Canada.

The pervasiveness of interspousal violence is corroborated by other data not shown in Table 2. Of the 213 couples who experienced violence in their marriage, 61 couples (28.7 percent) reported that they were unable to

TABLE 2 Interspousal violence as measured by overall violence scale and severe violence scale and by type of spousal violence, Calgary sample

TYPE OF INTER-SPOUSAL VIOLENCE	VIOLENCE INDEXES			
	OVERALL[a]		SEVERE[b]	
	(%)	(N)	(%)	(N)
Wife-to-husband	13.2	(75)	10.7	(60)
Husband-to-wife	10.3	(58)	4.8	(27)
Mutual violence	14.3	(80)	6.0	(34)
Violent couples	37.8	(213)	21.5	(121)
Non-violent couples	62.2	(349)	78.5	(444)
Total	100.0	(562)	100.0	(562)

[a] Composed of Items 1 through 8 listed in Table 1.
[b] Composed of Items 4 through 8 listed in Table 1.

resolve the domestic disputes themselves; their interspousal violence was so severe that someone else had to be brought in to settle things. About half the couples did this once in 1980, 30 percent twice, and 20 percent reported that they had to call in someone else three times or more. Seeking outside help to resolve internal family problems indicates the seriousness of the marital conflict and the violent exchanges that had taken place between the couples. It appears that couples are drawn over and over again into a cycle of violence. Leonore Walker's (1979) well-known study of wife battering reveals a three-phase cycle: tension building, the explosion, and the "in love again" phase.

Mutual Violence

Conjugal violence is multifaceted and is a result of conflict exchanges between couples. It takes place in an interactive context that is governed by mutual dependence and reciprocity; thus we would expect mutual violence to be more prevalent than violence committed by only one partner. A test of this thesis can be made against the data, presented in Table 2, which show the extent of mutual violence, violence by women toward their male partners, and violence by men toward their female partners. Of those 213 couples reporting any violence (overall violence scale), 80 couples or 37.5 percent were mutual situations: both women and men reported having committed violent acts against their respective partners. The second most common type was violence by wives toward their husbands (75 cases or 35.2 percent of all violent couples), followed by husband violence (58 cases or 27.3 percent).

Use of the severe violence scale, however, causes a marked reduction in both mutual violence and husband violence but a sharp increase in wife violence: 60 (49.6 percent) of the 121 couples in that category represent couples in which only the female partners reported having committed severe violent acts against their male partners. The rate for violence by wives toward their husbands is more than double the rate for husband violence.

At least three interrelated sets of factors may account for the high rate of severe violence committed by wives against their husbands. As noted earlier, one reason is that husbands may be more likely than wives to underreport violent acts because violence and aggression are integral components of the male experience but not of the female experience. Thus men's perception of what is a violent act in the privacy of the home differs from women's.

A comparison of victim reports and offender reports from thirty matched couples revealed that "while wives almost universally saw the relationship as husband-violent, less than half (n=14) of the husbands had a similar perception" (Browning and Dutton, 1986: 377). Seven of the thirty assaultive husbands perceived the relationship as wife-violent, and nine saw it as mutually violent. Another reason is that women are more likely than men to act in self-defense and that wives abuse their husbands by "fighting back" (Saunders, 1986). Indeed, a woman may perceive that the only way to break the vicious cycle of violence is by retaliation, even though most women have no hope of prevailing in hand-to-hand combat with men. Among a sample of matched couples, Szinovacz (1983) found that wives reported more frequent use of violence by themselves than was perceived by their husbands.

Third, there is corroborative evidence to suggest that women also initiate violent acts in the home. Of a sample of eighty-two battered wives who had reported their violent experiences to various women's shelters in Michigan, 24 percent admitted to having abused their husbands physically at some time in their marriage (Roscoe and Benaske, 1985). Jealousy was cited as the most prominent precipitating factor leading to interspousal violence (62 percent), followed closely by alcohol (56 percent) and conflict over money (41 percent). More representative data are needed on what precipitates violence between all couples. . . .

Violent Couples: Who are They?

Who are the couples who report violence in their homes? Our findings and those of other researchers support one important generalization: they come from all segments of society. Interspousal violence is fairly widespread and, we suspect, is a source of unhappiness and pain for many women and men. . . . Our Calgary study found support for the following specific generalizations:

- Violent couples come from all socioeconomic groups. Correlations involving husbands' and wives' education (rs = .06 and −.02),[5] income (rs = −.10 and .04), and occupational status (rs = −.04 and −.08) are often nonsignificant and in opposite directions, indicating that domestic violence is *not* limited to the lower classes;

- Violent couples are of all ages; on average, however, younger couples (30 or below) had three times the rate of middle-aged or older couples. The prevalence of mutual violence is pronounced particularly among younger couples and among those married less than eight years (rs = −.30 and −.33)[6];

- Violence occurs among cohabiting couples more often than among those who are married. Perhaps this association is confounded with age, where cohabitants are younger, but it is clear that couples who lived together at the time of the survey had double the violence rate of those who were married (r = .15);

- Childless couples have higher incidence rates than couples with children, which are more a function of age and length of marriage than of being a parent (r = −.15);

- Women who were employed full-time were somewhat more likely to report violence against their husbands than women who worked for pay part-time and those who were homemakers (r = .07); further-more, women working full-time were also less likely to be victimized by their husbands than were wives who worked part-time or did not work for pay outside the home.

Being employed full-time makes women less dependent econom-ically, and renders wives less vulnerable to being abused physically by their male partners. These findings are consistent with exchange theory, which holds that a redistribution of resources lessens the traditional imbalance between the sexes and thus affects the rate of victimization. Propper (1984: 110-111) calls these imbalances "patterned power differentials between family members," a contest in which the strongest victimize the weakest.

Most appropriate in this context is the central tenet of feminist theory, which holds that wife beating must be seen within the historical cultural development of our patriarchial society in causing and maintaining the problem (Dobash and Dobash, 1979; Yllo, 1983). Our cultural prescription of male aggressiveness and male supremacy legitimate the use of violence as a means to enforce that dominance. When the achievement ability of the husband is less than or inconsistent with his prescribed superior status, however, physical violence is used to reaffirm that status (O'Brien, 1971; Goode, 1971; Allen and Straus, 1979).

Interactional Factors and Interspousal Violence

Conflict is a feature of any social group, including the family, which is governed by emotional and intimate relations. Such intimacy is inherently dialectic and has the potential for breeding both love *and* hatred (Simmel, 1955; Coser, 1956, 1968; Scanzoni, 1982); the latter is expressed often in verbal disputes, quarrels, outbursts, and attacks. . . .

Of special interest here are the effect of cumulative conflict and the question whether an escalation of *verbal* disputes is associated with the occurrence of physical violence. Previous research found a positive rela-tionship between verbal aggression and physical abuse: the more verbal expression of aggression, the more physical violence (Straus, 1974; Straus, Gelles, and Steinmetz, 1980). Thus the notion of catharsis (Bach, 1973; Bach and Wyden, 1968), which holds that verbal aggression functions as a substitute for physical violence, is not supported by these data. Although catharsis as a therapeutic approach to conflict resolution has become obsolete, it still enjoys considerable public support because of its deceptive face validity. . . .

Marital Conflict

Conflict in marriage derives from opposite interests, which are inherent in the structure of the family. It can be defined as a struggle over values or over claims to status, power, and scarce resources in which partners act as opponents; each seeks to achieve his or her goals, usually at the expense of the other (Coser, 1968; Scanzoni, 1982: 70-71). Thus conflict is an ubiquitous and inevitable element in marriage. Conflict also may be cumulative because not all couples are capable of resolving their conflict through bargaining and negotiation, but instead engage in violent behaviour. Thus we would expect to find a relationship between the topical content of conflict (what couples fight about) and the incidence of interspousal violence. . . . This is the case; couples who report a great deal of conflict (those above the mean) are much more likely than couples who experienced little or no interspousal conflict to report violent incidents in the home. Experiencing ongoing marital conflict is a major explanatory variable ($r = .45$, $\leq$ .001), accounting for 20 percent of the variance.

As in the previous analyses, data on couples in which each partner inflicted violence on the other are particularly noteworthy. Those mutually violent couples who report a great deal of conflict in their relationship have a violence incidence rate five times as high (25.2 percent) as couples who report little or no conflict in their marriage.

In summary, conflict and violence are correlated highly, as we would expect. These data corroborate American findings: the relationship between frequency of interspousal conflict and interspousal violence may suggest that conflict precedes violence (Gelles and Cornell, 1985; O'Brien, 1971; Straus, Gelles, and Steinmetz, 1980). Longitudinal data are needed to detail empirically the processual development of severe conflict and violence in marriage.

Marital Satisfaction

Marital satisfaction assesses the relationship between the perceived quality of the couple's marriage and the incidence of violence in the home. . . . Marital satisfaction is related inversely to marital violence ($r = .24$, $\leq .001$), confirming the exchange theory premise that abuse is less likely to occur when rewards surpass costs. We suspect that age and length of marriage may operate as suppressor variables. A close examination of the percentages reveals that even among those couples who reported a great deal of marital satisfaction, almost one couple in three (29.3 percent) reported violent incidents in the home.

Perceived Job Stress

Why is violence so widespread among our sampled couples? One major reason may be stress. Previous research shows that the incidence of violence is highest among groups most likely to feel stress, such as families with a jobless husband and those with four to six children (O'Brien, 1971; Straus, Gelles, and Steinmetz, 1980). We obtained a great deal of information from our respondents about work-related issues and how these possibly may interfere with family life. One question in our batteries read: "How much strain, irritability and worry results from these [work] problems?"

. . . The coefficients for both sexes reveal a statistically significant ($\leq.001$) association between perceived work strain and the incidence of domestic violence. The structural impact of work strain, however, is slightly stronger among women than among men in the labour force ($r = .25$ vs. $r = .18$), although the difference between these coefficients is not statistically significant.

Again, the cause-effect relationship must be addressed: does work strain lead to domestic violence or does domestic violence contribute to greater perceived work strain and irritability in job-related areas? In the absence of longitudinal data, a richer contextual analysis is needed. As we showed earlier, employed wives were somewhat more likely than homemakers to report committing violence and were less likely to be victimized, but again this relationship may be confounded by age. Nevertheless we feel strongly that women's experienced inequality at home and on the job (Armstrong and Armstrong, 1978, 1983; Lupri and Mills, 1987; Clark and Harvey, 1978; Meissner et al., 1975) is related significantly to the occurrence of violence in the home. Thus we concur with Gelles, who writes:

> An elimination of the concept of "women's work"; elimination of the taken-for-granted view that the husband is and must be head of the family; and an elimination of the sex-typed family roles are all prerequisites to the reduction of family violence. (1979: 18-19).

The next step is to detail in greater depth these complex links, as well as that between power and conjugal violence.[7]

■ SUMMARY AND CONCLUSION

A 1981 Calgary study of 562 couples attempted to uncover some of the hidden violence in the home. It used the conflict tactics scales that Straus and associates had developed in their endeavours to study family violence in the American home. As we have pointed out earlier, the scales contain two basic shortcomings: (1) The items deal with acts or incidents. Thus we do not know the context in which physical force or verbal aggression occurred or what precipitated specific acts of violence. (2) We have no information about the outcome of the specific violent acts that were committed. Because it was too difficult to measure accurately the consequences of the specific acts in a self-administered questionnaire, we do not know the severity of the injury, pain, and damage that men inflicted on their female partners and women on their male partners. We only know that these acts reportedly occurred.

Although our study corroborated many basic findings of previous American research in the area, several new and distinct patterns emerged in the Calgary data. Most important, we noted that conjugal violence in the Calgary home is much more prevalent than had been estimated by Canadian experts, particularly by women's groups, and reported for the United States (Straus and Gelles, 1986). To be sure, the findings can be generalized only to a limited degree, as they are derived from a city that in 1981 exhibited all the characteristics of a boom town: high divorce rates, high female labour-force participation, a high influx of foreign workers and migrants from eastern Canadian provinces, a highly transient, youngish population, and more. Some of these contextual factors point toward a social structure that is characterized by a low degree of social integration, and the community may have fewer effective social sanctions against both divorce andd domestic violence. Nevertheless, the annual violence incidence rate of one couple in three (overall violence scale) or one couple in five (severe violence scale) appears to be high by any standard.

Several previously undocumented facts about interspousal violence also emerged from this investigation. First, we observed that wife-to-husband violence prevailed over husband-to-wife violence, whether we measured interspousal violence by means of the overall violence scale or by the severe violence scale. Although this finding might be a function of the underreporting by male respondents, the consistency with which this pattern emerged in our data requires further empirical scrutiny. Preliminary analyses showed that wife-to-husband violence occurred most frequently among young, childless, and cohabiting couples; that is, among those couples in which the exchange relationship is characterized by a fairly equal distribution of resources, and in which partners are relatively independent.

In addition, interspousal violence is widespread: it was found among all segments of society. Even though the annual incidence of conjugal violence peaked among the younger couples, it was not absent among retired couples. In fact, there is some evidence that age and interspousal violence are curvilinear.

Aggression and violence are correlated highly. We suspect strongly that expressing aggression does not result in a decrease but in an increase in interspousal violence. To evaluate this suspicion an explicit analysis of longitudinal data is needed.

As we expected, marital conflict and interspousal violence are correlated (.45 overall scale). We suspect that couples who are unable to resolve their conflicts through bargaining and negotiation techniques are likely to use violence as a conflict-resolution strategy. Exchange theory suggests that violence is more likely to occur among couples in which one partner may gain or wants to gain more from the exchange than the other. High levels of perceived work strain might contribute to these negative exchanges between partners, with conflict, opposition, and retaliation as consequences.

The limitations of the present study and its regional sample require that the findings be interpreted cautiously. What we have labelled as "husband abuse" and "mutual violence" may at times have been acts initiated by women in self-defense and retaliation. Thus future surveys must include questions about the context of domestic violence, its motives and outcomes. Future research must also consider in greater depth the dialectic interplay of marital power imbalance, the unequal distribution of resources within and outside the family, and their combined influence on domestic violence. Such research might reveal further support for our suspicion that partners may use violence as an alternative to the lack of resources to obtain reward (dominance) or to avoid costs (equality).

Notes

1. For an excellent assessment of the Canadian situation, see MacLeod (1987, 1980); Propper (1984); and M. Smith (1988).

2. Because of the problem of language use, however, words and terms such as "marital," "spousal," "interspousal," "wife," and "husband" refer to couples, whether they are married or nonmarried cohabiting partners.

3. The Edmonton survey did not explore family violence but merely employed such items as correlates of mental illness, the major focus of the study.

4. See Pleck, Pleck, Grossman, and Bart (1978). "The battered data syndrome: A comment on Steinmetz's article." This ongoing debate originated from Steinmetz (1978). A recent survey of 150 Quaker families also found a higher frequency of wife-to-husband violence than of husband-to-wife violence. In fact, the incidence of severe wife-to-husband violence was three times the rate of husband-to-wife violence (Brutz and Ingoldby, 1984). In their 1985 follow-up study, Straus and Gelles found that the overall violence rate against husbands actually increased slightly from 1975 to 1985 while the rate for severe violence decreased slightly, but neither of these changes is statistically significant (Straus and Gelles, 1986: 470).

5. We follow the commonly employed approach of treating ordinal variables as interval (see Labovitz, 1970) and calculating the robust product moment correlation. Other measures of association more appropriate to ordinal-level variables, such as gamma, might be adopted, but they are not as clearly interpretable; that is, gamma is affected by ties, skewness, and other factors.

6. A separate analysis of older couples revealed, however, that couples in the retirement stage (men 65 years or older) had a considerably higher incidence rate than couples in the pre-retirement stage (men 55 to 64 years): 23 percent and 14 percent, respectively. Furthermore, in the retirement stage, husband-to-wife violence exceeded wife-to-husband violence by a two-to-one margin, an observation that points toward the strains experienced by men who may have been forced to retire. Because of the limited number of couples in the retirement stage (N = 40), a contextual analysis is needed to explore further this curvilinear relationship.

7. Throughout this paper we have concentrated on univariate and simple bivariate relationships while suggesting the need for multivariate analysis; for example, length of marriage may confound the relationship between age and violence. It should be clear that multivariate techniques, including stepwise regression and partialling, are required for further clarification of these complex relationships. Forthcoming papers will undertake such analyses.

References

Allen, Craig M. and Murray H. Straus. 1979 "Resources, power, and husband-wife violence." In M.A. Straus and G.T. Hotaling, eds., *The Social Causes of Husband-Wife Violence*. Minneapolis: University of Minnesota Press.

Armstrong, Pat and Hugh Armstrong. 1978 *The Double Ghetto: Canadian Women and Their Segregated Work*. Toronto: McClelland and Stewart.

———. 1983 *A Working Majority*. Ottawa: Minister of Supply and Services.

Bach, G.R. 1973 *Therapeutic Aggression*. Chicago: Human Development Institute.

Bach, George R. and Peter Wyden. 1968 *The Intimate Enemy*. New York: Avon Books.

Bland, Roger C. and Helene Om. 1986 "Psychiatric disorders, spouse abuse and child abuse." *Canadian Journal of Psychiatry* 31 (March): 129-137.

Blau, Peter. 1964 *Exchange and Power in Social Life*. New York: John Wiley and Sons.

Browning, James and Donald Dutton. 1986 "Assessment of wife abuse with the Conflict Tactics Scales: using couple data to quantify the differential reporting effect." *Journal of Marriage and the Family* 48 (May): 315-379.

Brutz, J. and B.B. Ingoldsby. 1984 "Conflict resolution in Quaker families." *Journal of Marriage and the Family* 46(13): 21-26.

Clark, Susan and Andrew S. Harvey. 1978 "The sexual division of labour: the use of time." *Atlantis* 2(1): 46-66.

Coser, Lewis A. 1956 *Continuities in the Study of Social Conflict*. New York: The Free Press.

———. 1968 *The Functions of Social Conflict*. New York: The Free Press.

Dobash, R. Emerson and Russell P. Dobash. 1979 *Violence Against Wives: A Case Against the Patriarchy*. New York: The Free Press.

Eichler, Margrit. 1983 "And the work never ends: feminist contributions to sociology." *Canadian Review of Sociology and Anthropology* 22(5): 619-644.

———. 1985 *Families in Canada Today*. Toronto: Gage.

Eichler, Margrit and Jeanne Lapointe. 1985 *On the Treatment of the Sexes in Research*. Ottawa: Social Sciences and Humanities Research Council of Canada.

Gelles, Richard J. 1974 *The Violent Home*. Beverly Hills, California: Sage Publications.

———. 1979 *Family Violence*. Beverly Hills: Sage.

Gelles, Richard J. and Claire P. Cornell. 1985 *Intimate Violence in Families*. Beverly Hills: Sage.

Goode, William J. 1971 "Force and violence in the family." *Journal of Marriage and the Family* 33: 624-636.

Labovitz, Sanford. 1970 "The assignment of numbers to rank order categories." *American Sociological Review* 35: 515-524.

Lasch, Christopher. 1979 *Haven in a Heartless World*. New York: Basic Books.

Lupri, Eugen and D.L. Mills. 1987 "The household division of labour in young dual-earner couples: the case of Canada." *International Review of Sociology*. New Series (No. 2): 33-54.

MacLeod, Linda and Andrée Cadieux. 1980 *Wife Battering in Canada: The Vicious Cycle*. Ottawa: Minister of Supply and Services.

MacLeod, Linda. 1987 *Battered But Not Beaten: Preventing Wife Battering in Canada*. Ottawa: National Council on the Status of Women.

Meissner, Martin, Elisabeth Humphreys, Scott Meiss, and William Scheu. 1975 "No exit for wives: sexual division of labour and the cumulation of household demands." *Canadian Review of Sociology and Anthropology* 12(4): 421-439.

Nye, Ivan R. 1978 "Is choice and exchange theory the key?" *Journal of Marriage and the Family* 40 (May): 219-233.

———. 1979 "Choice, exchange and the family." In W. Burr, et al., eds., *Contemporary Theories About the Family*, pp. 1-41. Vol. 2. New York: The Free Press.

O'Brien, John E. 1971 "Violence in divorce-prone families." *Journal of Marriage and the Family* 33(4): 692-698.

Pagelow, Mildred D. 1984 *Family Violence*. New York: Praeger.

Pleck, E., J. Pleck, M. Grossman, and P. Bart. 1978 "The battered data syndrome: a comment on Steinmetz's article." *Victimology* 2(3/4): 680-683.

Propper, Alice. 1984 "The invisible reality: patterns and power in family violence." In Maureen Baker, ed., *The Family: Changing Trends in Canada*, pp. 104-128. Toronto: McGraw-Hill Ryerson Limited.

Richardson, D.C., R.J. Vandenburg, and S.A. Humphries. 1983 "Gender versus power: a new approach to the study of sex differences in retaliative aggression." Unpublished manuscript, University of Georgia. Cited in Louis A. Penner (1986), *Social Psychology*. New York: West Publishing Company.

Safilios-Rothschild, Constantina. 1976 "A macro- and micro-examination of family power and love: an exchange model." *Journal of Marriage and the Family* 38: 355-362.

Saunders, Daniel G. 1986 "When battered women use violence: Husband-abuse or self-defense?" *Violence and Victims* 1(1): 47-60.

Scanzoni, John. 1979 "Social process and power in families." In W. Burr et al., eds., *Contemporary Theories About the Family*, pp. 295-316. 2 vols. New York: The Free Press.

———. 1982 *Sexual Bargaining: Power and Politics in American Marriage*. Chicago: University of Chicago Press.

Simmel, Georg. 1955 *Conflict and the Web of Group Affiliations*. Translated by Kurt H. Wolff and Reinhard Bendix. Chicago: Free Press.

———. 1964 *The Sociology of Georg Simmel*, edited by Kurt Wolff. New York: The Free Press.

Smith, K.W. 1974 "On estimating the reliability of composite indexes through factor analysis." *Sociological Methods and Research* 2(4): 485-510.

Smith, Michael D. 1988 "The incidence and prevalence of woman abuse in Toronto." *Violence and Victims*. In Press.

Sprey, Jetse. 1979 "Conflict theory and the study of marriage and the family." In W. Burr et al., eds., *Contemporary Theories About the Family*. Vol. 2. New York: The Free Press.

Steinmetz, Suzanne K. 1978 "The battered husband syndrome." *Victimology* 2: 499-509.

———. 1987 "Family violence." In Martin B. Sussman and Suzanne K. Steinmetz, eds., *Handbook of Marriage and the Family*, pp. 725-765. New York: Plenum Press.

Straus, Murray. 1974 "Leveling, civility and violence in the family." *Journal of Marriage and the Family* 36 (February): 13-29.

Straus, Murray and Richard J. Gelles. 1979 "Determinants of aggression in the family: toward a theoretical integration." In W. Burr et al., eds., *Contemporary Theories About the Family*, pp. 549-581. Vol. 1. New York: Free Press.

———. 1986 "Societal change and change in family violence from 1975 to 1985 as revealed by two national surveys." *Journal of Marriage and the Family* 48 (August): 465-479.

Straus, Murray, Richard J. Gelles, and Susan K. Steinmetz. 1980 *Behind Closed Doors: Violence in the American Family*. New York: Anchor/Doubleday.

Szinovacz, Maximiliane E. 1983 "Using couple data as a methodological tool: The case of marital violence." *Journal of Marriage and the Family* 45(3): 633-644.
Walker, Leonore. 1979 *The Battered Woman.* New York: Harper Colophon.
Yllo, K. 1983 "Sexual equality and violence against wives in American states." *Journal of Comparative Family Studies* 14(1): 67-86.

IN DEFENCE OF SELF-DEFENCE: DEMYSTIFYING FEMALE VIOLENCE AGAINST MALE INTIMATES

NO

Walter S. DeKeseredy

Abstract

This paper is a critical response to Murray Straus's attempt to negate the self-defence explanation for female violence against male intimates. The negative policy implications of his research are articulated. Moreover, this essay contends that "newsmaking criminology" can help radical scholars disseminate their feminist interpretations of female assaults through the mass media.

Male violence against female intimates has existed for centuries (Dobash and Dobash, 1979; Okun, 1986). Unfortunately, prior to the 1970s, this issue was ignored by sociologists. For example, the *Journal of Marriage and the Family*, from its beginning in 1939 through 1969, did not contain any articles on wife assault (O'Brien, 1971). Thanks to both the feminist and battered women's movements, however, sociologists are now paying a considerable amount of attention to the various types of abuse women experience in domestic relationships. Since the early 1970s, a large number of theoretical and empirical journal articles and books have been published which demonstrate that violence against women is a serious social problem in North America and other western societies (e.g., Brinkerhoff and Lupri, 1988; DeKeseredy, 1988a; Hamner and Maynard, 1989; Smith, 1987; Straus and Gelles, 1986; Straus, Gelles and Steinmetz, 1981). Moreover, this literature provides strong support for demands for better social support services for abused women.

Despite these two important contributions to the struggle against male hegemony, some prominent researchers write articles that include injurious myths about the nature of violence in male-female relationships. For example, in a paper presented at the 1989 annual meeting of the American Society of Criminology, Murray Straus declared that his research "casts doubt on the notion that assaults by women on their partners primarily are acts of self-defense or retaliation" (1989: 9). Since Straus's misleading study received widespread media attention,[1] it requires a critical response. Thus, the primary objective of this paper is twofold: (1) to challenge Straus's problematic assertion, and (2) to articulate the negative political implications of his research. The essay that follows will also describe briefly how "newsmaking criminology" (Barak, 1988) can enable critical researchers to present a more accurate image of female violence in domestic relationships.

■ ASSAULTS BY WOMEN: SELF-DEFENCE OR MUTUAL COMBAT?

Studies show that female violence, even with the intent to injure, is used primarily in self-defence (Berk et al., 1983; Browne, 1987; Dobash and Dobash, 1988; Makepeace, 1986; Saunders, 1986, 1988, 1989). Nevertheless, some scholars question the validity of this research (e.g., Stets and Straus, 1989). Moreover, some researchers maintain that male-female violence is a "two-way street" and that many men experience "husband abuse" (McNeely and Robinson-Simpson, 1987; Steinmetz, 1977-1978). Straus attempts to resolve this "debate" on female violence by presenting findings from a 1985 "National Family Violence Resurvey" (Straus and Gelles, 1986).[2]

Based on his analysis of female self-report data, Straus contends that:

> Regardless of whether the analysis is based on all assaults or is focused on dangerous assaults, about as many women as men, according to their own report, attack a spouse who does not hit back. This casts doubt on the "self-defence" explanation for the high rate of domestic assault by women (1989: 9).

Straus's findings do not support his interpretation because his data are gleaned from a controversial and much criticized measure, the Conflict Tactics Scale[3] (CTS) (Straus, 1979). The CTS was designed to measure only the incidence of both violent and psychological abusive acts. Thus, it ignores the context and motives of female violence. Without data on these two important factors, Straus's research does not negate the argument that women hit male intimates in self-defence.

In fairness to Straus, after presenting his flawed interpretation, he admits that his subjects may have acted in self-defence (1989: 9). Following this statement, he presents data derived from what he believes is a "more direct" measure of self-defence in intimate relationships. Subjects were asked, "Let's talk about the last time you and your partner got into a physical fight ... In that particular instance, who started the physical conflict, you or your partner?" (1989: 9).

Straus found that women initiate physical assaults about as often as men. Of the 428 women who responded to the above question, 52.7% reported that they hit first.[4] Straus (1989: 11) argues that "[t]hese results do not support the hypothesis that assaults by women on their partners primarily are acts of self-defense or retaliation."

Again, his findings do not cast doubt on the self-defence explanation for the following reasons. First, consistent with the CTS, Straus's initiation measure does not focus on the context and meaning of female violence against male partners. If Straus asked women about their motives for initiating attacks, they would have probably found that many women hit first because of a "well-founded fear" (Hamner and Saunders, 1984) of being beaten or raped by their husbands or cohabiting partners (Saunders,

1989). Male physical and sexual violence against women is often preceded by name-calling and other types of psychological abuse (Browne, 1987). Hence, these early warning signs prompt many women to hit first in order to deter their partners from hitting them (Saunders, 1989). Thus, most assaults initiated by women may actually be acts of self-defence.

Second, some respondents may have thought that the initiation measure asked who started the argument rather than who hit first (Saunders, 1989; Stets and Straus, 1989). Third, Straus's measure characterizes violence in domestic relationships as mutual combat (e.g., "Let's talk about the last time you and your partner got into a physical fight . . .") (Saunders, 1989). Hence, it obscures the fact that most violence in domestic relationships involves men beating or raping their partners (DeKeseredy, 1988b; Okun, 1986).

In summary, Straus's arguments are both incorrect and irresponsible because of the problematic nature of his measures. However, he is considered a "pioneer in his field" (Kittredge, 1989). Consequently, his paper received widespread media attention which can enhance the pain experienced by female victims of male abuse. Therefore, the implications of his arguments for social policy need to be carefully examined.

■ POLICY IMPLICATIONS

Social scientific research can influence state policies on female victimization (Dobash and Dobash, 1988; DeKeseredy, 1988b). For example, Steinmetz's (1977-78) incorrect assertion that husband beating is as prevalent as wife beating was used by Chicago state officials to block funding for a shelter for abused women and their children (Pleck et al., 1977-78). Similarly, Straus's arguments may legitimize the denial of state support services for both battered and sexually abused women. Evidence of a "battered husband syndrome" enables some patriarchal state officials to assert that since wives are as violent as husbands, new transition houses are not necessary and existing shelters do not need expansion or refurbishing (DeKeseredy, 1988b).

Straus's research also holds women partially responsible for their own victimization. He contends that women who physically defend themselves against unwanted touching or various types of sexual harassment precipitate violent attacks by men (1989: 11). This argument can legitimate victim-blaming in the judicial system. Some judges, for example, acquit rapists and wife beaters because they believe that the victims provoked their assailants (Elias, 1986; Karmen, 1984; Viano, 1983). Straus's research supports this sexist belief.

The influence of Straus's victim-blaming assertion moves well beyond the limited realm of the judiciary. Male members of the general population are also affected. Research shows that after abusing their partners, many men experience stress (Walker, 1983). Male peer support can prevent post-abuse stress (DeKeseredy, 1988a; Kanin, 1967). Similarly, Straus's study may "buffer" men from post-abuse stress by providing them with a "vocabulary of adjustment" (Kanin, 1967).

By arguing that a woman who uses violence as a defence against a sexual assault provides her abusive partner with "a precedent and moral justification for him to hit her" (1989: 10). Straus helps violent men to continue viewing their actions as normal and legitimate. In addition to acting as a buffering mechanism, Straus's discourse of legitimation may encourage men to continue asserting their authority through abusive means.

There are other dangers associated with Straus's research which need to be articulated. However, they will not be given consideration here. Instead, one strategy for conveying an alternative explanation of female violence in domestic relationships, "newsmaking criminology" (Barak, 1988), will be discussed briefly.

▐ PRESENTING A REALISTIC IMAGE OF FEMALE VIOLENCE: THE RELEVANCE OF NEWSMAKING CRIMINOLOGY

Since Straus's research has received a great deal of media coverage, his arguments are likely to be co-opted by apologists for male violence. Furthermore, media attention will make it easier for his message to be incorporated within the dominant patriarchal belief system (Dobash and Dobash, 1988). Thus, feminist researchers should not limit the presentation of their alternative messages to academic settings and community groups. They should also make strong attempts to disseminate their arguments through the mass media (Dobash and Dobash, 1988).

Although many critical scholars are aware of the media's misleading images of crime, social control and gender relations (e.g., Bohm, 1986; Box, 1983; Cohen and Young, 1973; Ericson et al., 1987, 1989; Fishman, 1978; Hall et al., 1978; Humphries, 1981), most of these researchers have not developed methods of using the media for the purpose of presenting more accurate portrayals (Barak, 1988). Strategies derived from newsmaking criminology, however, may enable radical academics to share their critiques of Straus's research with a large audience. Newsmaking criminology is defined as, "the conscious efforts of criminologists and others to participate in the presentation of 'newsworthy' items about crime and justice" (Barak, 1988: 565).

Some feminists (e.g., Dobash and Dobash, 1988) have struggled to convey their messages through the mass media. The news-producing community is, however, reluctant to articulate feminist arguments because it is oriented to presenting patriarchal ideologies about women. Moreover, many journalists tend to reduce the complex issue of woman abuse to an individual problem (Dobash and Dobash, 1988). Nevertheless, radical newsmaking criminologists can find contradictions within the news-producing industry that can benefit those with a feminist message.

For example, although many reporters support the values of patriarchal capitalism, some journalists are proponents of conflicting ideologies such as feminism and democratic socialism (Barak, 1988). Thus, people involved in the struggle against woman abuse should develop relationships with these reporters because they are likely to report radical interpretations of social problems. The presentation of a strong challenge to sexist research depends on the abilities of feminists to take advantage of these opportunities (Barak, 1988).

With the assistance of progressive journalists, radicals can be viewed as credible spokespersons. In fact, they may be eventually perceived by the larger newsmaking community as important professional sources of information (Barak, 1988). Furthermore, media exposure may facilitate radical academicians' participation in community activities and state-sponsored programs.

For example, because of his television appearances, and his many newspaper articles and editorials on wealth, poverty and black-on-black crime, an Alabama newspaper labelled Gregg Barak (a newsmaking, critical criminologist) as an "Alabama Voice." Barak's newsmaking experiences also helped him acquire two important government positions: (1) general advisor to the Alabama Attorney General's Task Force on Victims, and (2) advisory council member to the Alabama Department of Corrections. Barak is also a consultant to media-related productions in Alabama.

In a November 1989 interview (see Kittredge, 1989), Straus stated that he is trying to get publicity for his research. Similarly, feminists and others opposed to violence against women (and other forms of male domination), should attempt to get more popular attention. In addition to repairing the damage caused by Straus's research, newsmaking radicals will help "chip away" (Messerschmidt, 1986) at the wider social, political and economic forces that perpetuate and legitimate woman abuse.

■ SUMMARY AND CONCLUSION

Murray Straus does not cast doubt on the argument that women who hit male intimates are acting in self-defence. Instead, he presents incorrect assertions that hold women partially responsible for their own victimization. Straus's research can help state officials manufacture ideological support for sexist policies that focus on victims' characteristics rather than the patriarchal capitalist political economy which is a major source of woman abuse (Dobash and Dobash, 1988; Messerschmidt, 1986). His findings also provide abusive men with a discourse of legitimation. Thus, in order to provide an effective challenge to Straus's research, radical scholars must share their alternative knowledge with the general public. Strategies derived from newsmaking criminology can help progressive academics achieve this goal.

Notes

1. The Associated Press wrote an article on Straus's paper that was featured in many U.S. newspapers (e.g., November 9, 1989, *Cape Cod Times*).

2. For more detailed information on the methods used in this inquiry, see Gelles and Straus (1988), Stets and Straus (1989) and Straus and Gelles (1989).

3. For a detailed account of the limitations of this quantitative measure, see DeKeseredy (1988b, 1989) and Breines and Gordon (1983).

4. For more information on this finding, see Stets and Straus (1989).

References

Barak, G. 1988. "Newsmaking Criminology: Reflections on the Media, Intellectuals, and Crime." *Justice Quarterly*, 5, 565-588.

Berk, R.A., S.F. Berk, O.R. Loseke and D. Rauma. (1983). "Mutual Combat and Other Family Violence Myths." In D. Finkelhor, R.J. Gelles, G.T. Hotaling and M.A. Straus (Eds.). *The Dark Side of Families: Current Family Violence Research*. Beverly Hills: Sage, 197-212.

Bohm, R. (1986). "Crime, Criminal and Crime Control Policy Myths." *Justice Quarterly*, 3, 191-214.

Box, S. (1983). *Power, Crime and Mystification*. London: Tavistock.

Breines, W. and L. Gordon. (1983). "The New Scholarship on Family Violence." *Signs: Journal of Women in Culture and Society*, 8, 491-531.

Brinkerhoff, M.B. and E. Lupri. (1988). "Interspousal Violence." *Canadian Journal of Sociology*, 13, 407-434.

Browne, A. (1987). *When Battered Women Kill*. New York: Free Press.

Cohen, S. and J. Young (Eds.). (1973). *The Manufacture of News*. Beverly Hills: Sage.

DeKeseredy, W.S. (1988a). *Woman Abuse in Dating Relationships: The Role of Male Peer Support*. Toronto: Canadian Scholars' Press.

DeKeseredy, W.S. (1988b). "Woman Abuse in Dating Relationships: A Critical Evaluation of Research and Theory." *International Journal of Sociology and the Family*, 18, 79-96.

DeKeseredy, W.S. (1989). "Dating Violence: Toward New Directions in Empirical Research." *Sociological Viewpoints*, 5, 62-74.

Dobash, R.E. and R. Dobash. (1979). *Violence Against Wives: A Case Against the Patriarchy*. New York: Free Press.

Dobash, R.E. and R. Dobash. (1988). "Research as Social Action: The Struggle for Battered Women." In K. Yllo and M. Bograd (Eds.). *Feminist Perspectives on Wife Abuse*. Beverly Hills: Sage, 51-74.

Elias, R. (1986). *The Politics of Victimization: Victims, Victimology and Human Rights*. New York: Oxford University Press.

Ericson, R.V., P.M. Baranek and J.B.L. Chan. (1987). *Visualizing Deviance: A Study of News Organizations*. Toronto: University of Toronto Press.

Ericson, R.V., P.M. Baranek and J.B.L. Chan. (1989). *Negotiating Control: A Study of News Sources*. Toronto: University of Toronto Press.

Fishman, M. (1978). "Crime Waves and Ideology." *Social Problems*, 25, 531-543.

Gelles, R.J. and M.A. Straus. (1988). *Intimate Violence*. New York: Simon and Schuster.

Hall, S., C. Critcher, T. Jefferson, J. Clarke and B. Roberts. (1978). *Policing the Crisis: Mugging, the State and Law and Order*. New York: Holmes and Meiser.

Hamner, J. and M. Maynard (Eds.). (1989). *Women, Violence and Social Control*. Atlantic Highlands, New Jersey: Humanities Press International.

Hamner, J. and S. Saunders. (1984). *Well-Founded Fear: A Community Study of Violence to Women*. London: Hutchinson.

Humphries, D. (1981). "Serious Crime, News Coverage, and Ideology." *Crime and Delinquency*, 27, 191-205.

Kanin, E.J. (1967). "Reference Groups and Sex Conduct Norm Violation." *Sociological Quarterly*, 8, 1504-1695.

Karmen, A. (1984). *Crime Victims: An Introduction to Victimology*. Monterey, California: Brooks/Cole.

Kittredge, C. (1989). "Report on Family Violence Faulted: UNH Researcher says Women, too, Must Bear Some Blame." *Boston Globe*, November 26.

Makepeace, J.M. (1986). "Gender Differences in Courtship Violence Victimization." *Family Relations*, 35, 383-388.

McNeely, R.L. and G. Robinson-Simpson. (1987). "The Truth About Domestic Violence: A Falsely Framed Issue." *Social Work*, 32, 485-490.

Messerschmidt, J.W. (1986). *Capitalism, Patriarchy, and Crime*. Totowa, New Jersey: Roman and Littlefield.

O'Brien, J.E. (1971). "Violence in Divorce-Prone Families." *Journal of Marriage and Family*, 33, 692-698.

Okun, L. (1986). *Woman Abuse: Facts Replacing Myths*. Albany: SUNY Press.

Pleck, E., J.H. Pleck, M. Grossman and P. Bart. (1977-1978). "The Battered Data Syndrome: A Comment on Steinmetz's Article." *Victimology: An International Journal*, 3-4, 680-683.

Saunders, D.G. (1986). "When Battered Women Use Violence: Husband Abuse or Self-Defense?" *Victims and Violence*, 1, 47-60.

Saunders, D.G. (1988). "Wife Abuse, Husband Abuse, or Mutual Combat? A Feminist Perspective on the Empirical Findings." In K. Yllo and M. Bograd (Eds.). *Feminist Perspectives on Wife Abuse*. Beverly Hills: Sage, 90-113.

Saunders, D.G. (1989). "Who Hits First and Who Hurts Most? Evidence for the Greater Victimization of Women in Intimate Relationships." Paper presented at the annual meeting of the American Society of Criminology, Reno, Nevada.

Smith, M.D. (1987). "The Incidence and Prevalence of Woman Abuse in Toronto." *Violence and Victims*, 2, 173-187.

Steinmetz, S.K. (1977-1978). "The Battered Husband Syndrome." *Victimology: An International Journal*, 3-4, 499-509.

Stets, J.E. and M.A. Straus. (1989). "Gender Differences in Reporting Marital Violence and its Medical and Psychological Consequences." In M.A. Straus and R.J. Gelles (Eds.). *Physical Violence in American Families: Risk Factors and Adaptations to Violence in 8,145 Families*. New Brunswick, New Jersey: Transaction Press.

Straus, M.A. (1979). "Measuring Intrafamily Conflict and Violence: The Conflict Tactics (CT) Scales." *Journal of Marriage and the Family*, 41, 75-88.

Straus, M.A. (1989). "Gender Differences in Assault in Intimate Relationships:

Implications for Primary Prevention of Spousal Violence." Paper presented at the annual meeting of the American Society of Criminology, Reno, Nevada.

Straus, M.A. and R.J. Gelles. (1986). "Societal Change and Change in Family Violence Rates from 1975 to 1985 as Revealed by two National Surveys." *Journal of Marriage and the Family*, 48, 465-479.

Straus, M.A. and R.J. Gelles (Eds.). (1989). *Physical Violence in American Families: Risk Factors and Adaptations to Violence in 8,145 Families*. New Brunswick, New Jersey: Transaction Press.

Straus, M.A., R.J. Gelles and S.K. Steinmetz. (1980). *Behind Closed Doors: Violence in the American Family*. New York: Anchor.

Viano, E. (1983). "Violence, Victimization and Social Change." *Victimology: An International Journal*, 8.

Walker, L. (1983). "The Battered Woman Syndrome Study." In D. Finkelhor, R.J. Gelles, G.T. Hotaling and M.A. Straus (Eds.). *The Dark Side of Families: Current Family Violence Research*. Beverly Hills: Sage, 31-48.

■ POSTSCRIPT

The articles presented here raise some important theoretical and methodological issues that have significance for social policy formation. On the question of methodology, both articles acknowledge that survey methods might not be appropriate for measuring this type of violence. Both agree that the conflict tactics scale does not measure the context within which the violence takes place, and that future studies must ask more specific questions about the context. Brinkerhoff and Lupri nonetheless argue that violence is widespread. They also argue that the violence is mutual, meaning that both parties participate, and both parties are victims. DeKeseredy, on the other hand, argues that the notion of mutual violence masks the possibility that men's violence is more consequential, and that it is more frequently aimed at control and domination of the marital partner, whereas women's violence is a response to men's efforts to control and dominate.

These issues of methodology bear directly on the problem of explaining why husbands and wives use violence. Brinkerhoff and Lupri claim that violence is a method of conflict resolution, and that the conflict is produced by the stresses and strains of contemporary life. They say that the high rate of violence they uncovered may have been partially the product of rapid social change and the consequent decline in social integration in Calgary in the early 1980s. DeKeseredy argues that the violence is the product of a social system based on a patriarchal division of labour, and the ascription of dominant status within that division of labour to men. He argues, too, that the efforts of researchers attempting to demonstrate that husbands are more frequent victims than wives amounts to victim-blaming.

The social policy implications are clear. If Brinkerhoff and Lupri are correct, then social policy-makers, including those forming law enforcement policy, must begin to take violence perpetrated by women against men more seriously. Just as policy-makers during the past decade have developed policies to make it easier for women to make their victimization known (to report it to the police, to seek refuge in women's shelters, etc.), they must begin now to develop policies that will allow men to make their victimization known without being labelled "wimps." If DeKeseredy is correct, then renewed effort is needed to demonstrate the full context of violence within families. Policy-makers must also begin to take more seriously the need to develop programs and policies which will have the ability to protect women from violence, and which may help reduce the level of that violence.

■ QUESTIONS

1. Which article presents a more convincing argument? Why do you find this article more convincing?
2. On what issues do Brinkerhoff and Lupri agree with DeKeseredy?
3. What are the major points of disagreement between the two articles?
4. What issues, if any, have these authors not discussed?

■ FURTHER READING

In Support of Brinkerhoff and Lupri

Gelles, Richard J. *The Violent Home.* Beverly Hills, Calif.: Sage Publications, 1974.
Steinmetz, S.K. "The Battered Husband Syndrome." *Victimology: An International Journal* 2 (1978): 499-509.
Straus, M.A. and R.J. Gelles. "Societal Change and Change in Family Violence Rates from 1975 to 1985 as Revealed by two National Surveys." *Journal of Marriage and the Family* 48 (1986): 465-479.
Straus, M.A., R.J. Gelles, and S.K. Steinmetz. *Behind Closed Doors: Violence in the American Family.* New York: Anchor Books, 1980.

In Support of DeKeseredy

Berk, R.A. et al. "Mutual Combat and Other Family Violence Myths." In *The Dark Side of Families: Current Family Violence Research.* Edited by Finkelhor et al. Beverly Hills, Calif.: Sage Publications, pp. 197-212.
Breines, W. and L. Gordon. "The New Scholarship on Family Violence." *Signs: Journal of Women in Culture and Society* 8 (1983): 491-531.
Browne, A. *When Battered Women Kill.* New York: Free Press.
DeKeseredy, Walter and Ronald Hinch. *Woman Abuse: Sociological Perspectives.* Toronto: Thompson Educational Publishing, 1991.

Other Voices

Committee on Sexual Offences Against Children and Youth. *Sexual Offences Against Children.* 2 vols. Ottawa: Supply and Services, 1984.
Dobash, R.E. and R. Dobash. *Violence Against Wives: A Case Against Patriarchy.* New York: Free Press, 1979.
Finkelhor, D., R.J. Gelles, G.T. Hotaling, and M.A. Straus, eds. *The Dark Side of Families: Current Family Violence Research.* Beverly Hills, Calif.: Sage Publications, 1983.
MacLeod, Linda. *Battered But Not Beaten: Preventing Wife Battering in Canada.* Ottawa: Canadian Advisory Council on the Status of Women, 1987.

DOES STREAMING ALLOW STUDENTS TO DEVELOP THEIR POTENTIAL?

YES Gary Natriello, Aaron M. Pallas, and Karl Alexander, "On the Right Track?: Curriculum and Academic Achievement," *Sociology of Education* 62 (April 1989): 109-118

NO George Martell, "The Labelling, Streaming and Programming of Working Class Kids In School," *Our Schools/Our Selves: A Magazine for Canadian Education Activists* 1, no. 8 (1989): 19-30

The role of the education system in the development of Canadian society has been debated from the time public schools were created. A core issue in that debate concerns the role schools play in skills development. On the one hand, functionalists (Parson, 1959) say that schools perform the function of sorting children according to their abilities. Such categorization ensures that the most capable and meritorious rise to the top of the social structure, while those with lesser skills and capabilities are left to fill the less prestigious and important (but necessary) roles. On the other hand, critics of the education system argue that it does not differentiate on the basis of ability but on the basis of class or gender. Marxists (Bowles and Gintis, 1976) say that the school system serves the class interests of capitalism. It stunts development of skills among the lower classes, while allowing less able members of the middle and upper classes to advance in the structure. Similarly, feminists argue that schools perpetuate gender differences, thereby preventing females from developing to their full potential.

Streaming, also known as tracking or ability grouping, refers to the process of dividing students into groups or streams such as "gifted," "academic," "general," "vocational," and "basic." The gifted stream, which is the most recently developed stream, is designed primarily for students who score in the upper 2 percent on intelligence tests. The academic stream is designed as a university preparatory program. The general stream prepares students for entry into trade schools or community colleges. The vocational stream, sometimes combined with the general stream, prepares students for direct entry into the labour market. The basic stream is for the lowest level of achievers. It emphasizes basic reading, writing, and communication skills, while focusing on the employability of the basic student. The question is: Do the schools do the job as specified by the functionalists, or are the critics correct in saying that schools discriminate on the basis of class and/or gender?

The "Yes" side of this debate is argued by Natriello, Pallas, and Alexander, and the "No" side is argued by George Martell.

References

Bowles, S. and H. Gintis (1976) *Schooling in Capitalist America* (New York: Basic Books).

Parsons, Talcott (1959) "The School Class as a Social System: Some of its Functions in American Society," *Harvard Educational Review* 29, no. 4 (Fall): 297-318.

ON THE RIGHT TRACK?
CURRICULUM AND
ACADEMIC ACHIEVEMENT

YES

Gary Natriello
Aaron M. Pallas
and Karl Alexander

In an earlier study (Alexander, Natriello, and Pallas, 1985), we compared the gains in academic achievement of high school graduates against those of dropouts over a two-year period. Baseline data were procured during the sophomore year, when all were still in school. Two years later, these same youngsters were retested. About 14 percent of the retested youngsters had left school in the interval between testing sessions. The performance on the second test tended to increase for all youngsters, but those who stayed in school made larger advances than those who dropped out, and the margin of advantage could not be accounted for by other relevant characteristics, such as race/ethnicity and socioeconomic status (SES), that distinguished the composition of the two groups. Although the difference between groups was not large, neither was the comparison optimal, since it is likely that the development of most of the skills that are germane to standardized tests of the sort used as assessment devices in this exercise takes place much earlier. Nevertheless, comparisons of "schooled" versus "unschooled" persons over an extended period are impractical at earlier grade levels (although Heyn's [1978] comparison of learning patterns over the summer months against those while school is in session suggests that the effects of "schooling" would turn out to be impressive, indeed, if they could be studied in this way). Our study, then, demonstrated that schooling fosters academic achievement during the later years of high school, and this is likely to be an extremely conservative indication of the contribution that schooling makes to academic achievement overall.

The analysis reported here extended our earlier work by seeking to identify what it is about the experience of schooling that accounts for the benefits of staying in school. As a point of departure, we focused on curriculum tracking and entertained the hypothesis that the academic advantages of staying in school are most pronounced among youngsters who pursue an academically oriented high school program.

It surely is important to know that schooling accomplishes some good, but apart from possibly constituting a mandate for more schooling, knowledge at that level of generality is of little use in informing school reform; it provides few clues to how we might do better. To have any hope of improving practice, these benefits must be linked to specific, preferably alterable, features of the school environment. At least as far as gains in achievement over the latter years of high school are concerned, the differentiated curricula of the comprehensive school should be considered. Many studies (Alexander, Cook, and McDill 1978; Hauser, Sewell, and Alwin 1976; Jencks and Brown 1975; Rosenbaum 1976) have demonstrated that substantial academic advantages accrue to youths in the college-bound track (but see Alexander and Cook, 1982, for evidence that these advantages probably are overstated in studies that fail to adjust for various assets that distinguish youngsters who enroll in the college track from those who enroll in other programs).

The tracking issue has long attracted the interests of sociologists of education, perhaps because it joins basic interests in stratification processes to practical issues in the organization and management of schools. Longstanding concerns center on the advisability of dividing the school population into different groups to receive different curricula (Esposito 1973), the manner by which students are assigned to curricular tracks (Cicourel and Kitsuse 1963), the positive or pernicious effects of various curricular tracks (Oakes 1985), and the difficulty in moving students from one track to another (Rosenbaum 1976).

Such concerns are especially timely in light of the attention directed to curricular issues in the latest round of efforts to reform schools. The school-reform movement, which began with the release of the report of the National Commission on Excellence in Education (1983), has brought new attention to the tracking issue. That report called for the imposition of a curriculum rooted in the "New Basics," which included four years of English, three years of mathematics, three years of science, and three years of social studies, together with a half year of computer science. The curriculum of the New Basics resembled the course work that has been found in the academic or college preparatory track of many high schools throughout the United States. It departed markedly not only from the general curriculum that is the chosen path through high school of an increasing number of students, but from the vocational curriculum that has operated for most of the twentieth century as a mechanism for preparing students for work after high school and that was recognized as valuable in the previous round of discussions of high school reform (Coleman 1974).

Discussions of the value of the various curricular options has led to investigations of the effects of each curriculum for various types of students (Alexander and Pallas 1984). However, most such investigations have focused on the changes observed in students who participate in a given curriculum or with comparisons of students in one curriculum with those in another (often with extensive controls on the background characteristics of the students, which vary substantially). No studies have assessed the impact of different curricula in comparison with nonparticipation in any schooling. In the present study, we did just that.

Our basic approach was to compare the patterns of growth in achievement that are associated with participation in the three major curricula found in most U.S. high schools: the academic, the general, and the vocational. Using the spring of the sophomore year as a benchmark, we examined the gains in academic achievement of students in each track who continued through high school until graduation and compared these gains to those for students in each track who dropped out of school sometime between the spring of the sophomore year and high school graduation.

Although this focus on tracking has a long history in studies of school effects, it may not be entirely satisfactory for providing a full view of the experience of schooling. As Garet and DeLany (1988) and Gamoran and Berends (1987) observed, the traditional specification of curricular tracks that has been employed in most large-scale surveys is, no doubt, an over-simplified representation of the complexity and variety of curriculum patterns in U.S. high schools. Gamoran and Berends (1987, p. 424) noted that such survey research that fails to capture a significant portion of the variation in instruction may underestimate the effects of within-school stratification. However, Garet and DeLany (1988, p. 76) suggested that a more detailed measure of a student's position in the curriculum will not necessarily provide a better predictor of subsequent achievement and attainment. We view the tracking variable used in the present study as a useful simplification of the high school curriculum. However, we antici-pate that this analysis and others will indicate the direction for developing more refined variables to represent the experience of students with the program of the school.

The study used data from the sophomore cohort of the High School and Beyond (HSB) project. This nationally representative sample was first tested in 1980 as sophomores, and the same battery of tests was read-ministered two years later in spring 1982. The HSB fieldwork involved extensive efforts to obtain information from dropouts and transfers, as well as from youngsters who stayed in school; as a result, it is one of the few large-scale panels that can claim to be representative of an actual class cohort.

The HSB test battery includes assessments in the general skill areas of vocabulary, mathematics, and reading that together provide a general view of the growth in academic achievement of students in the three curricular tracks.[1] For the two-year interval covered by these data, our analysis estimated the "value added" in academic performance that can be at-tributed to persistence in each of the three curricular tracks. Our earlier analysis (Alexander, Natriello, and Pallas 1985) revealed that there is superior growth among youths who stay in school; the present study sought to determine which curricular options produce the greatest growth.

■ METHODS

The data for this analysis are from the HSB 1980 Sophomore Cohort Base Year and the 1982 First Follow-Up surveys (Jones et al. 1983). The HSB study originally surveyed roughly 30,000 sophomores in more than 1,000 high schools across the country in spring 1980. The base-year survey included a questionnaire and a battery of achievement tests (described more fully later). Eighty-four percent of the sampled students completed the sophomore questionnaire and 77 percent completed the test battery.

The first follow-up was fielded in spring 1982. Four groups of students from the 1980 base-year sophomore cohort were identified: students still enrolled in their base-year schools, dropouts, early graduates, and transfers. Students still enrolled in their base-year schools at the time of the first follow-up were sampled with a probability of 1.0. The other three groups were sampled with a probability designed to produce a present number of cases for the various school strata. The sample allocation consisted of 25,150 still-in-school seniors, 2,601 dropouts, 1,290 transfers to non-HSB schools, and 696 early high school graduates. Properly weighted, this sample projects to the population of roughly 3,800,000 high school sophomores of 1980.[2]

The response rate for the first follow-up was quite high for each of the four groups. The questionnaire-completion rate ranged from 88 percent for the dropout group to 95 percent for the still-in-school senior group. The response rate for completed tests ranged from 78 percent of the dropout sample to 90 percent of the still-in-school sample. The present analysis utilized data from 6,501 graduates and 302 dropouts in the academic track, 7,789 graduates and 1,376 dropouts in the general track, and 3,257 graduates and 670 dropouts in the vocational track.

HSB administered the same battery of tests to the 1980 sophomore cohort in the spring of the 1980 base year and the 1982 first follow-up phases of data collection. As reported by Jones et al. (1983), the tests used in the present analyses covered the following areas:

1. *Vocabulary* (21 items, 7 minutes). A brief test using a synonym format.

2. *Reading* (20 items, 15 minutes). A test based on short passages (100-200 words) with several related questions concerning a variety of reading skills (including analysis and interpretation) but focusing on straightforward comprehension.

3. *Mathematics I and II* (38 items, 21 minutes). Quantitative comparisons in which the student indicates which of two quantities is greater or asserts their equality or the lack of sufficient data to determine which quantity is greater. The mathematics score is constructed as the sum of the two mathematics subtests.

A test composite score was constructed as the sum of these three tests. For all tests, we used what are referred to as "formula" scores—raw scores (the number of items that are correct), adjusting for guessing. Further information on the HSB tests may be found in Heyns and Hilton (1982).

Throughout these analyses, all correlations involving the test scores were corrected for attenuation owing to random measurement error. Computationally, this involved adjusting the zero-order correlation matrix by dividing each correlation by the square root of the product of the reliabilities of the variables involved in the correlation (Nunnally 1978) and performing regression analyses on the adjusted correlation matrix. On the basis of KR-20 reliabilities for the sophomore tests, reported by Heyns and Hilton (1982), the estimated reliability for the composite is .92. Since correcting for attenuation in both the sophomore and senior tests results in correlations between the two tests of greater than 1 in some cases, we applied the reliability correction only for the sophomore tests. However, we did not use the same reliabilities for dropouts as for graduates, since achievement tests are often less reliable for low performers, and dropouts typically are low achievers (Bachman, Green, and Wirtanen 1971; Pallas 1986).

To determine any such differences in reliability, we turned to differences in the observed Time 1-Time 2 stability coefficients for the two groups. First, the test scores for the senior year were regressed on the sophomore-year scores separately for the dropouts and the graduates. The coefficients derived can be thought of as test-retest, or stability, measures. As expected, these coefficients were lower for the dropouts than for the nondropouts for every test. Although we recognize that these differences were not necessarily due to lower test reliabilities among the dropouts, they nevertheless are consistent with that possibility and, for the purposes of our study, that is what we took them to signify. Hence, our reliability correction for the dropout sample was derived as the ratio of the dropout-to-nondropout stability coefficients in each cognitive domain.[3] Procedurally, then, reliabilities for the dropout group were derived as the product of the overall reliability and its corresponding stability ratio. The overall reliabilities just reported were used "as is" for the still-in-school group. The reliability for the test composite was .92 for graduates and .84 for dropouts.[4]

The location of the curriculum is based on a self-report from the sophomore base-year questionnaire. The categories are General; Academic, or College Preparatory; and Vocational (Occupational Preparation), which includes seven more detailed categories. The remaining measures, which we used mainly as control variables, are either from the sophomore questionnaire or are composite measures derived from several sources. . . .

■ RESULTS

The performance of graduates and dropouts in the three curricular tracks is a useful starting point for examining the results of our analysis. The basic patterns of gains in academic achievement between 1980 and 1982 for dropouts and graduates in the three curricular tracks are presented in Table 1. Columns 2-6 of Table 1 present the means on the composite test for

TABLE 1   Scores on the Composite Achievement Test for Graduates and Dropouts in the Three Curriculum Tracks, 1980 and 1982

TEST	1980 TEST		1982		POOLED SDs FOR 1980 TEST	DIFFERENCES IN THE MEAN SCORES ON THE 1980 TESTS (GRADUATES VS. DROPOUTS)[a]	DIFFERENCES IN THE MEAN SCORES ON THE 1982 TESTS (GRADUATES VS. DROPOUTS)[a]	DIFFERENCES IN THE MEAN SCORES FOR DROPOUTS (1982 VS. 1980)[a]	DIFFERENCES IN THE MEAN SCORES FOR GRADUATES (1982 VS. 1980)[a]
	DROPOUT MEANS	GRADUATE MEANS	DROPOUT MEANS	GRADUATE MEANS					
Academic-track students	23.869	39.139	27.689	45.664	17.653	15.270 .865	17.975 1.018	3.820 .216	6.525 .370
General-track students	17.168	26.977	20.147	31.966	17.653	9.809 .556	11.819 .670	2.979 .169	4.989 .283
Vocational-track students	14.165	20.311	16.326	24.397	17.653	6.146 .348	8.071 .457	2.161 .122	4.086 .231

[a] In test points and SD units.

dropouts and graduates in the three curricular areas, as well as the pooled standards deviation for the 1980 test. Columns 7-10 are derived from Columns 2-6. They display patterns of change within the groups (Columns 9 and 10) and differences in the levels of performance among the groups (Columns 7 and 8) for each of the three curricular tracks.

The figures in Columns 2-5 reveal several things. First, students in all three tracks, whether they stayed to graduate or dropped out before graduation, improved their performance on the standardized tests over the two-year period between the first test and the second test. Thus, there is a general trend toward rising test scores among graduates and dropouts from all three curricular tracks.

Second, students in the academic track started out with the highest test scores in the tenth grade and maintained them through the two-year period. Third, students in the general track began with higher test scores than did those in the vocational track in the tenth grade and stayed ahead of them through the twelfth grade. These patterns held among graduates and among dropouts (that is, academic-track graduates scored higher than did general-track graduates and vocational-track graduates on both tests, and academic-track dropouts scored higher than did general-track dropouts and vocational-track dropouts on both tests).

Fourth, graduates from lower "adjacent" tracks scored higher than did dropouts from higher tracks. Specifically, students who graduated from the general track performed better than did those who dropped out of the academic track, and students from the vocational track performed better than did those who dropped out of the general track on the twelfth-grade tests. However, vocational-track graduates performed less well than did academic-track dropouts on the twelfth-grade tests. Clearly, as may be expected, these test scores reflect the effects both of the processes by which students are assigned to the three tracks and of the curricula themselves.

Columns 7 and 8 of Table 1 show that students who eventually graduated from each of the three tracks started with an academic advantage over those who eventually dropped out of high school before graduation and that this advantage increased by the time of the 1982 tests, when the dropouts had left school and the graduates were preparing for graduation. Columns 9 and 10 indicate that students who graduated from any of the three tracks experienced greater gains in achievement than did students who dropped out of any of the three tracks. They also clearly show that whether students stayed until graduation or left before graduation, those who were placed in the academic track in the tenth grade experienced greater gains than did those in either the general track or the vocational track and that those who were placed in the general track in the tenth grade experienced greater academic growth than did those in the vocational track.

That the gains were greater for those in the academic track who left school before graduation and thus discontinued their contact with the school curriculum than for students in the other two tracks suggests that selection effects play some role in producing these patterns of achievement. That the differences in gains among students in the three curricular tracks were greater for those students who remained until graduation than they were for those who dropped out suggests that curriculum effects also play a role. The figures in Table 1 provide no help in sorting out these effects and thus provide little guidance to policy-makers who are interested in developing recommendations for the reform of the high school curriculum.

Table 2 presents an analysis that isolates the portion of the test-score gains experienced by students in all six curriculum × dropout/graduate groups that can be attributed to exposure to the school curriculum. Columns 1 through 8 of Table 2 present the results of multiple regression analyses that relate the students' background characteristics and 1980 test scores to their performance on the 1982 tests, separately for dropouts and graduates in each of the curriculum tracks. Column 1 identifies the composite test as the dependent variable. Column 2 lists the predictor variables included in the analyses. Columns 3, 4, and 5 contain the means, the unstandardized regression coefficients, and the R^2s for the analyses conducted using the dropouts in each curriculum group. Columns 6, 7, and 8 contain the same data for the analyses conducted using the graduates in each curriculum group.

The profile of the dropouts in each of the three curriculum groups is much as might be expected from previous research.[5] As was already shown, the dropouts in each curriculum group were more likely to be low achievers than were the graduates. This likelihood is reflected both in their 1980 test scores and in their self-reported grade-point average. Dropouts also reported higher levels of absenteeism during the first semester of the sophomore year than did the graduates in each curricular track.

There were also substantial differences in the social backgrounds of the dropouts and graduates in each track. Dropouts in each track are more likely to be from lower SES households. Hispanics were overrepresented among dropouts in the academic and vocational tracks, where they constituted 24 percent and 20 percent of the dropouts, respectively; in the general track, Hispanics were 15 percent of the dropouts. Blacks were about 14 percent of the dropouts from the academic track (less than 10 percent of the graduates), 9 percent of the dropouts from the general track (about 9 percent of the graduates), and about 18 percent of the dropouts from the vocational track (less than 16 percent of the graduates).

The dropout patterns for boys and girls in the three curriculum tracks differed as well. Girls constituted about 51 percent of the dropouts and about 54 percent of the graduates in the academic track, about 50 percent of the dropouts and 49 percent of the graduates in the general track, and about 40 percent of the dropouts and 49 percent of the graduates in the vocational track. This pattern indicates that girls were more likely to be in the academic track and less likely to be in the general and vocational tracks than were boys and that boys in the academic and vocational tracks were more likely to drop out than were girls, while boys and girls in the general track were about equally likely to drop out.

These differences in the types of youngsters who made up the dropout and graduate samples in each of the curricular tracks reinforce our earlier argument that a proper consideration of the role of the different curricula in gains in achievement must take into account the differences that may be anticipated from other cognitively relevant factors. To make the appropriate comparisons, we used the technique of regression standardization (Althauser and Wigler 1972).

Columns 9 through 14 in Table 2 present the results of a partial decomposition of the regression results reported in Columns 4 and 7. Column 9 presents the predicted mean scores on the senior-year tests implied by the use of the mean scores of the dropout population on the predictor variables, together with the regression coefficients for the graduates. In other words, it indicates how the dropouts would score on the senior-year tests if they had continued in school as the graduates did (and realized the same cognitive "returns" on their various personal resources and characteristics as did the graduates and as reflected in their slope estimates). The comparison of the mean scores predicted in Column 9 with those actually observed for the dropouts and reported in Column 2 of Table 1 shows the improvement that would have been expected had the dropouts in the sample remained in school. This improvement is the goal of most programs designed to reduce the dropout rate.

The results of this comparison are presented in Column 11 as points on the achievement tests, and in Column 12 as standard deviation units. The differences in test scores ranged from a gain of 1.361 points for potential dropouts who might be held in school in the vocational track, to 1.154 points for potential dropouts who might be held in school in the general track, to 1.992 points for potential dropouts who might be held in school in the academic track. As shown in Column 12, these differences were .077, .065, and .113 standard deviation units for the three tracks, respectively.

Columns 10, 13, and 14 of Table 2 present the results of this same type of analysis using the mean scores of the graduate sample, together with the regression coefficients for the dropout sample for each curricular group. In other words, the figures in Column 13 show how those in the graduate sample would have fared on the senior-year test if they had left school when those in the dropout sample did. The figures in Columns 13 and 14 are computed in the opposite direction from those in Columns 11 and 12 so that a positive figure always indicates the advantages realized by graduates as a result of staying in school. In Column 13, the differences in test scores range from a gain of .151 points for vocational-track graduates over what they would have realized had they dropped out; to 2.012, for the general-

TABLE 2 Means, Regression Coefficients, and Difference Scores on the Composite Achievement Test for Graduates and Dropouts in Three Curriculum Tracks

DEPENDENT VARIABLES	PREDICTOR VARIABLES	DROPOUTS			GRADUATES			PREDICTED MEAN SCORES OF THE DROPOUTS IF THEY HAD GRADUATED[a]	PREDICTED MEAN SCORES OF THE GRADUATES IF THEY HAD DROPPED OUT[b]	ADVANTAGES FOR DROPOUTS OF STAYING IN SCHOOL		ADVANTAGES FOR GRADUATES OF STAYING IN SCHOOL	
		MEANS	REGRESSION COEFFICIENTS	R^2	MEANS	REGRESSION COEFFICIENTS	R^2			IN TEST POINTS[c]	IN SD UNITS[c]	IN TEST POINTS[c]	IN SD UNITS[c]
Academic-Track Students													
1982 Composite Test	1980 test	23.869	.945[d]	.886	39.139	.874[d]	.838	29.681	43.354	1.992	.113	2.310	.131
	Absence	2.909	-.214		1.896	-.138							
	Grades	4.247	.606[d]		2.791	-1.036[d]							
	SES	-.210	2.888[d]		.261	1.179[d]							
	Sex	.509	2.213[d]		.538	-1.244[d]							
	Black	.139	-1.011		.095	-.993[d]							
	Hispanic	.242	-.922		.077	-1.539[d]							
	NEAST	.176	1.621		.300	1.080[d]							
	NC	.151	3.272[d]		.262	.363							
	South	.376	1.862[d]		.220	-.050							
	Constant		1.552			14.785							
General-Track Students													
1982 Composite Test	1980 test	17.168	.864[d]	.741	26.977	.890[d]	.789	21.301	29.954	1.154	.065	2.012	.114
	Absence	3.337	-.189		2.197	-.250[d]							
	Grades	4.998	-.273[d]		3.731	-.908[d]							
	SES	-.427	1.988[d]		-.068	1.279[d]							
	Sex	.499	-2.850[d]		.494	-1.206[d]							
	Black	.090	.087		.092	-1.478[d]							
	Hispanic	.151	-2.623[d]		.124	-1.550[d]							
	NEAST	.153	.662		.155	1.455[d]							
	NC	.299	1.647[d]		.334	.354							
	South	.248	-.054[d]		.222	.193							
	Constant		10.620			12.531							

TABLE 2 (Continued)

DEPENDENT VARIABLES	PREDICTOR VARIABLES	DROPOUTS MEANS	DROPOUTS REGRESSION COEFFICIENTS	DROPOUTS R^2	GRADUATES MEANS	GRADUATES REGRESSION COEFFICIENTS	GRADUATES R^2	PREDICTED MEAN SCORES OF THE DROPOUTS IF THEY HAD GRADUATED[a]	PREDICTED MEAN SCORES OF THE GRADUATES IF THEY HAD DROPPED OUT[b]	ADVANTAGES FOR DROPOUTS OF STAYING IN SCHOOL IN TEST POINTS[c]	ADVANTAGES FOR DROPOUTS OF STAYING IN SCHOOL IN SD UNITS[c]	ADVANTAGES FOR GRADUATES OF STAYING IN SCHOOL IN TEST POINTS[c]	ADVANTAGES FOR GRADUATES OF STAYING IN SCHOOL IN SD UNITS[c]
Vocational-Track Students 1982 Composite Test	1980 test	14.165	−.815[d]	.691	20.311	.882[d]	.785	17.673	24.246	1.361	.077	.151	.009
	Absence	3.343	.033		2.209	−.240[d]							
	Grades	4.825	.361		3.888	−.916[d]							
	SES	−.473	−1.452[d]		−.287	.634[d]							
	Sex	.399	−1.356[d]		.492	−.772[d]							
	Black	.179	−4.111[d]		.156	−1.834[d]							
	Hispanic	.202	−8.112[d]		.177	−2.547[d]							
	NEAST	.182	−2.173[d]		.227	−.296							
	NC	.243	−.046		.286	.554							
	South	.262	−3.095[d]		.264	−.011							
	Constant		9.866			11.787							

[a] Predicted mean scores on the senior-year tests implied by the use of the mean scores of the dropouts[d] on the predictor variables, together with the regression coefficients for the graduates.

[b] Predicted mean scores on the senior-year tests using the mean scores of the graduates, together with the regression coefficients for the dropouts.[d]

[c] Observed dropout and graduate means and pooled standard deviations appear in Table 1.

[d] Coefficient greater than or equal to 1.96 its standard error.

track graduates; to 2.310 for the academic-track graduates. As Column 14 shows, these differences range from .009 to .114 to .131 standard deviation units for students in the three tracks, respectively.

■ DISCUSSION

The results of these analyses provide a more finely grained picture of the effects of schooling on academic achievement than did our earlier analysis (Alexander, Natriello, and Pallas 1985). Although students in all three curricular tracks in U.S. high schools appear to realize some gains in achievement by remaining in school as opposed to dropping out of school before graduation, students in the academic track realize the largest gains.[6]

Our results generally are consistent with Shavit and Featherman's (1988) study of the effect of schooling and tracking on the verbal aptitude of Israeli teenagers. Shavit and Featherman found that the effects of academic-track membership on the relative performance of Israeli youths were slightly larger for those who had completed 16 or more months of postprimary education than for those who completed 1 to 15 months and that these effects were statistically significant for the more-schooled group. General-track membership had negligible effects on the relative rankings of Israeli youths in both groups, regardless of the quantity of schooling.

We can contrast our results with those reported in Kerckhoff's (1986) study of the effects of tracking in Great Britain. Kerckhoff found strong evidence for what he termed the divergence hypothesis, showing that students in high-ability groups performed better than did comparable ungrouped students, while students in low-ability groups performed less well than if they had not been grouped at all. Our results also show divergence in that the gains in achievement that accrued to students who stayed in school were larger for those in the academic track than for those in the general or vocational tracks. An important difference, however, is that even among the "lower" (nonacademic) tracks, young people gained more by staying in school than they would have done had they dropped out. In contrast to Kerckhoff's pattern of winners and losers, students in the three tracks in our study were "winners" if they stayed in school, but students in the academic track won more than did the others. This finding accords well with Gamoran's (1987) analysis that pitted the effects of tracking against the effects of schooling. Gamoran's analysis, which also used data from HSB, showed that differences in test-score gains between academic- and nonacademic-track students exceeded differences between dropouts and similar students who stayed in school.

Such evidence would seem to lend support to calls for reform of the curriculum that would make the entire high school curriculum more like the curriculum of the academic track. However, a number of other factors make us cautious about drawing this interpretation from the present analysis. First, there is great variability in the specifications of different curricula. Although the New Basics prescribed by the National Commission on Excellence in Education have received a great deal of attention, efforts to reform curricula in various states have departed in different ways from the specific recommendations made by the commission. Moreover, the curriculum represented in our analysis by the category "academic track" varies from school to school and does not conform precisely to the pattern described as the New Basics. Thus, our analysis suggests that the academic track has greater effects in promoting cognitive skills, but we cannot use it as a basis for endorsing either the New Basics or the host of state-level variations in the current round of curricular reform.

Second, the intention of the nonacademic tracks, particularly the vocational track, may not be to develop the kind of cognitive skills that are captured in tests of vocabulary, reading, and mathematics. These tests are more likely to correspond to the materials that form the basis of the academic track and may thus place students from the other tracks at a disadvantage. Perhaps the students in the general and vocational tracks experience cognitive growth along dimensions that are not captured by these tests or derive other noncognitive benefits from remaining in school.

Third, we do not know the extent to which curricular placement influences students' decisions to drop out or remain in school. If the vocational track functions more effectively than does the academic track to retain students until graduation, then the superior gains of academic-track students may be vitiated by the higher dropout rates that would occur if students were denied vocational-track classes and were forced into the academic track.

Even with these factors in mind, the results of our study indicate that the different school curricula, as constituted and under present conditions of selection/allocation, do make a difference in the academic achievement of students. Thus, curricular reform is a topic that is worthy of further consideration by researchers and policymakers alike. In relation to our more general interest in the issue of the effectiveness of schools, we again conclude that persistence in school through graduation enhances academic achievement and we now know that these benefits are more pronounced for youngsters whose program of study presumably is more concerned with fostering such skills. Schooling, therefore, does make a difference, and in ways that are consonant with organizational goals. Critics of curricular tracking have been especially troubled by the procedures that are used to assign youngsters to the different curricula and the limitations on opportunities to transfer from one track to another once the initial assignments have been made. The results presented here do not speak directly to such concerns, but evidence of the "effectiveness" of this organizational form is relevant to a proper assessment of its merits and demerits. We find that the academic track is more effective in furthering gains in achievement than are the other curricula, and this fact probably is consistent with the intentions of planners. Hence, at least in this one respect, differentiation of curricula does appear to work, and this fact makes it all the more important that the practices of assigning and moving students be both pedagogically sound and fair.

Notes

1. Note that in our earlier paper (Alexander, Natriello, and Pallas 1985), we conducted analyses using each of the six HSB tests and the test composite and arrived at essentially similar patterns of results for each test. Thus, in the present analyses, only the results for the test composite are presented.

2. The present analyses used the HSB weighting factor for cases with panel-testing data.

3. On the chance that background controls might have partially proxied the very differences in which we were interested, we also tested whether these different stability coefficients became more similar when other background controls were included in the equations. They did not. Hence, we retained the zero-order stabilities as the basis for the differential reliability estimates.

4. We should note that our use of a differential correction factor in estimating the reliability of tests for dropouts provides conservative estimates of the differences in dropouts' and graduates' performance on tests. We believe that the figures used in our analyses are the most appropriate available, but if they are in error, it seems likely that they underestimate rather than overestimate the effects of the three curricular tracks in comparison with dropping out of school.

5. In these data overall, about 14 percent of the cohort was identified as having dropped out of high school sometime between the spring of the sophomore year and the spring of the senior year. This percentage is a bit lower than national figures would have led us to expect, but the HSB design missed those youngsters who dropped out at the first opportunity to do so (at the end of compulsory school attendance or at the beginning of tenth grade in many states), as well as those who did not withdraw until just before graduation. We do not know what fraction of the actual dropout population would fall in each category, but the latter group probably consists largely of youngsters who realize that they are not going to graduate and decide to leave early.

6. A rule of thumb that we have used here and elsewhere is that a 0.1 difference in the standard deviation of the performance for two groups is a minimum threshold for substantive significance. By this standard, none of the effects of staying in school can be said to be large, but, at least for the academic track, the estimated effect consistently exceeds the minimum threshold, as it does for the general-track students in one of the two possible instances.

References

Alexander, K.L., and M.A. Cook. 1982. "Curricula and Coursework: A Surprising Ending to a Familiar Story." *American Sociological Review* 47:626-640.

Alexander, K.L., M. Cook, and E.L. McDill. 1978. "Curriculum Tracking and Educational Stratification: Some Further Evidence." *American Sociological Review* 43:47-66.

Alexander, K.L., G. Natriello, and A.M. Pallas. 1985. "For Whom the Bell Tolls: The Impact of Dropping Out on Cognitive Performance." *American Sociological Review* 50:409-420.

Alexander, K.L., and A.M. Pallas. 1984. "Curriculum Reform and School Performance: An Evaluation of the 'New Basics.' " *American Journal of Education* 92:391-420.

Althauser, R.P., and M. Wigler. 1972. "Standardization and Component Analysis." *Sociological Methods and Research* 1:97-135.

Bachman, J.G., III, S. Green, and I.D. Wirtanen. 1971. *Youth in Transition*, vol. 3. *Dropping Out—Problem or Symptom?* Ann Arbor, MI: Institute for Social Research.

Cicourel, A.V., and J.I. Kitsuse. 1963. *The Educational Decisionmakers*. Indianapolis, IN: Bobbs-Merrill Co.

Coleman, J.S. 1974. *Youth: Transition to Adulthood: Report of the Panel on Youth of the President's Science Advisory Committee*. Chicago: University of Chicago Press.

Esposito, D. 1973. "Homogeneous and Heterogeneous Ability Grouping: Principal Findings and Implications for Designing More Effective Educational Environments." *Review of Educational Research* 43:163-179.

Gamoran, A. 1987. "The Stratification of High School Learning Opportunities." *Sociology of Education* 60:137-155.

Gamoran, A., and M. Berends. 1987. "The Effects of Stratification in Secondary Schools: Synthesis of Survey and Ethnographic Research." *Review of Educational Research* 57:415-435.

Garet, M.S., and B. DeLany. 1988. "Students, Courses, and Stratification." *Sociology of Education* 61:61-77.

Hauser, R.M., W.H. Sewell, and D.F. Alwin. 1976. "High School Effects on Achievement." In *Schooling and Achievement in American Society*, edited by W.H. Sewell, R.M. Hauser, and D. Featherman. New York: Academic Press.

Heyns, B. 1978. *Summer Learning and the Effects of Schooling*. New York: Academic Press.

Heyns, B., and T.L. Hilton. 1982. "The Cognitive Test for High School and Beyond: An Assessment." *Sociology of Education* 55:89-102.

Jencks, C.S., and M.D. Brown. 1975. "Effects of High Schools on Their Students." *Harvard Educational Review* 46:273-324.

Jones, C., M. Clarke, G. Mooney, H. McWilliams, I. Crawford, B. Stephenson, and R. Tourangeau. 1983. *High School and Beyond 1980 Sophomore Cohort First Follow-Up (1982) Data File User's Manual*. Washington, DC: National Centre for Education Statistics.

Kerckhoff, Alan C. 1986. "Effects of Ability Grouping in British Secondary Schools." *American Sociological Review* 51:842-858.

National Commission on Excellence in Education. 1983. *A Nation at Risk: The Imperative for Educational Reform*. Washington, DC: U.S. Government Printing Office.

Nunnally, J. 1978. *Psychometric Theory* (2nd ed.). New York: McGraw-Hill Book Co.

Oakes, J. 1985. *Keeping Track: How Schools Structure Inequality*. New Haven, CT: Yale University Press.

Pallas, A.M. 1986. *The Determinants of High School Dropouts.* Report No. 364. Baltimore, MD: Center for the Social Organization of Schools, Johns Hopkins University.

Rosenbaum, J.E. 1976. *Making Inequality: The Hidden Curriculum of High School Tracking.* New York: John Wiley & Sons.

Shavit, Y., and D.L. Featherman. 1988. "Schooling, Tracking, and Teenage Intelligence." *Sociology of Education* 61:42-51.

THE LABELLING, STREAMING AND PROGRAMMING OF WORKING CLASS KIDS IN SCHOOL

George Martell

How Gord Wilson approached his own experience of schooling, it seems to me, is how Labour generally ought to deal with the question of what happens to working class kids in school: an approach that is tough, unsentimental, and from the heart.

Looking out at the faces in this room it is clear that we all know that Gord got to the important truth about our schooling. It is a truth that has cut deeply into our lives, and we are very grateful to hear it spoken aloud, in public, for everyone to hear.

We also know, if Gord is right about what happened to most of us in school, much the same thing is going to happen or is already happening to our kids. The people who run our schools haven't stopped being hostile, not by any means, though their community P.R. may have become smoother over the years. We know now we can no longer hope, as we may have in the past, that our current school system will do well by our kids. Either we fight for a decent educational system, or they'll be hurt as much as we were. Maybe more.

My job this morning is to open up a broader discussion of this situation—the ways in which our elementary and secondary schools keep workers' kids in their place—and then consider what Labour's response ought to be.

■ KEEPING WORKERS' KIDS AT THE BOTTOM

What are the means by which schools insure that our kids stay at the bottom of the educational system in preparation, it turns out, for their living and working at the bottom of the society when they leave school?

What we want to get at, in other words, is the institutional process Gord Wilson had to fight so hard against when he was a student some 30 years ago. And against which all of you have had to struggle.

Everyone here knows how hard it was to stand up for your dignity in school. You know especially how hard it was to keep faith with your intelligence, with your knowledge that you were as smart and as able as anyone else. This knowledge should be obvious when we look at this room full of union leaders who have proved their competence and their smarts in the real world. But to those who wield power in this society and who control its education and its media, working class intelligence is not one bit

273

obvious—at least as it's portrayed to the public. The recognition of this intelligence is something you have had to fight for ever since you were kids.

For all of your lives you have had to go against the grain of what the society—and especially its school system—has told you about your capacity to understand and act upon the world. This judgement was not always on the surface, of course, but it was almost always there working against you as you grew up: "You don't have what it takes to make it in the world," it said, "you deserve to be in the bottom ranks of the society."

The basics of the process of keeping working class kids on the bottom, which Gord experienced, remain solidly entrenched in today's school. Only now the process is slipperier and sleazier. It's not so crude as it used to be. In some ways that makes it even harder for working people and their kids to get hold of and to fight. It is also a process that has become more all-encompassing, filling up the nooks and crannies of the system, making it seem increasingly "natural."

Now, more than ever, what happens to working class kids in school is all being done "for their own good," as our educational administrators never cease pointing out to us. And in the last couple of decades the process is increasingly laid on by an army of test experts and psychometricians, social workers and psychologists, who come at workers and their kids with obscure scientific jargon about diagnosis and treatment and a lot of heavy rhetoric about a student's personal fulfillment in life. "We care about your kid," they say. "Don't you care?" they ask. "Don't you want what's best for your children, what will help them in the future?"

What do they say?

For a caring parent it is a bewildering situation. You want to do right by your kid, but every intuition you have tells you something is terribly wrong here.

What I want to say this morning, is that we have to trust our intuitions here. We have to start saying "NO" to this process and at the same time get down to the very difficult task of trying to figure out, much more precisely, what really is wrong here.

■ LABELS, STREAMS, PROGRAMS

There are, it seems to me, three main ways in which those who run our schools try to keep workers' kids at the bottom and which we, in turn, have to resist.

(These administrative and political initiatives are resisted, I want to add here, by lots of good teachers; the worst thing we can do is to scapegoat teachers for a system largely outside their control.)

The first thrust is the labelling—at different levels or degrees—of more and more working class kids as dumber and crazier than middle class and rich kids. "Dumb"/"smart," "crazy"/"sane" are the two big category systems used to define kids, which are often linked together into one package when dealing with a kid. "Educationally retarded, with behavioural problems" to take a simple example. Usually there's a lot of fancy pseudo-scientific language in these definitions. Someone once figured out there were 52 euphemisms for "stupid."

Then there is the placement—or streaming—of these kids (defined as dumb and crazy in varying degrees) according to how dumb and crazy they are judged to be.

Finally, there is the programming that is laid on according to the labels.

These three system initiatives—labelling, streaming and programming—cover a lot of territory. I want to focus on two important elements within this territory, which connect directly with the issue of skills training, which you will be considering tomorrow and which are at the core of working class oppression in our schools.

(1) The process by which so many working class kids get to be labelled as not as smart as middle class and rich kids.

(2) The curriculum or program thrust that goes along with this understanding of who's intelligent and who's not.

■ INTELLIGENCE LABELLING

The intelligence label is the big label. It's the one that counts the most against our kids. The one that school officials tell us we can't do anything about. They shake their heads; they're sorry, of course. But "If your kid's stupid, he's stupid; if she's smart, she's smart. Nothing the school can do about that, is there? Don't blame us for poor marks."

So how do they decide if your kid's stupid or smart? There's an objective measure, you'll be pleased to know. It has to do with how well your kid does on certain tasks, like IQ tests, reading tests, and the repetition of various forms of mindless rote learning.

What these tasks are primarily about is your children's ability to hold unrelated facts or images in their heads and then carry out, as fast as they can, a very shallow kind of formal logic. They can be asked to do this in a whole range of activities: putting shapes to shapes (as in the Raven IQ test), putting words to words (which I'll explain in a second), or completing fill-in-the-blanks/multiple-choice/true-and-false tests (like the tests in the Senior High School Chemistry and Physics Review that came down last week from the Ontario Ministry of Education, which are part of the big push for standardized tests we're seeing right across the country.)

Let me give you an example of putting words to words. It's in the form of a little kid's I.Q. test:

Imagine four boxed pictures: a butcher, a baker, a candlestick maker and a police officer. What, the kids are asked, do these figures have in common?

The right answer, for 2 points, is that they are all "men" or "people."

What the kids who got it right have done it to put words like butcher, baker, candlestick maker and police officer under the broader category of "men" or "people." They have, in this context, put words to a word. It is a narrow skill, learned quite explicitly in most middle class homes.

What many working class kids do in a test like this, unless they have been coached to do otherwise, is to express a social relationship between the people in the boxes. For example: "The policeman is chasing the other three men," or "The butcher got robbed, and the others are helping him." If you tip them off on the right answer, many will look at you as if you're crazy. "What kind of an answer is that?" you can hear them thinking. "We know they're men, or people. What's that got to do with anything?"

At the most fundamental level these kids are right. But they still get 0 out of 2.

What these kids are, in fact, doing is a much more significant kind of thinking than they have been asked to do by those who are testing them. They are—if you don't mind me being a little pretentious here—thinking in the great tradition of western thought. Plato, Augustine, Aquinas, Kant, Hegel, Marx, Freud would all agree with their priorities. This tradition says that logic (or reason) is never to be separated from what goes on in the real world and what should go on there, whether among human beings or in nature; our thinking is part of the process by which we help rationalize the potential of our world. Understanding reality and changing it always go hand in hand. Thinking always leads to action of one kind or another, even if it's a decision to do nothing. And action, in its turn, leads to more thought.

This tradition of thinking says, for example, that there are "concepts" in the world which are real things and through which we live our lives. These "concepts" hold our world together: capturing the contradictory particulars of nature and society (which we experience directly) and at the same time holding out the promise of their fuller development. "Concepts" express the tension between what's actual and what's potential. What is and what could be.

Such "concepts" are denied by our IQ testers and those who make up our fill-in-the-blanks exams.

Little kids, however, know what they are about. Take the concept of "mommy." Kids know very early that there are good mommies and bad mommies and that all mommies have good and bad qualities. This knowledge scares them. That's why stepmothers are such popular figures in fairy tales; a stepmother keeps the contradictory reality of mommy at a distance so that kids can deal with it more easily. Their own short histories also bring them a sense of the potential in mommy—what they can hope for in the future. Thus they develop a concept of "mommy" or "momminess"— that holds together their growing experience of "good" and "bad" mommies, through which they understand and act upon the world. What I want to stress here is that this involves tough thinking about what really goes on in their small but very intense society. Kids know their lives depend on it. They take it very seriously.

It is the same kind of thinking we saw with many of the kids who flunked our earlier IQ test. What they were being offered wasn't much of a challenge, but they did their best to make the questions real.

Let me say it again: Serious thinking involves figuring out our relations with nature and with each other.

When we deny the importance of this kind of thinking, which our ministries of education are now busily doing, we are stripping our kids of their deepest human heritage.

Nobody understands this better than working men and women, even if they don't have the words to describe it. This understanding explains why workers have such disdain for what they call "ivory tower" thinking. They know that good thinking has to make a difference in the world, that it is deeply practical. "Really useful knowledge."

What workers and their kids rarely have—outside the field of union and political action—is the opportunity to move back and forth from thought and action, to think actively over a long period of time. This is, of course, never permitted on the job. But in politics and in the union movement, where this is possible, that's where workers develop sophisticated thinking. That's where they become "smart." The potential is there; it just has to be used.

To put this another way, intelligence is not something fixed. It's fluid. It can be crushed; it can be created. There isn't a person in this room who hasn't experienced this in their own lives and in watching newcomers enter the union or some political battle. What an extraordinary thing it is to watch someone get smart or experience getting smart ourselves—in battling the boss or Brian Mulroney. And it happens every day in the labour movement and wherever resistance to oppression takes place. What we have to make certain is that it happens every day in school.

■ THE FORMAL PROGRAM THAT GOES WITH INTELLIGENCE LABELLING

There is a whole informal or hidden curriculum in our schools, which I don't have time to discuss, but it's important to remember it's there. This is the social order of the school, which kids are expected to take as a "normal" social order: authority structures, how time is managed, how people speak to each other—that sort of thing. Kids resist it, but it cuts a lot of ice as the "norm" and undercuts thinking about an alternative social order.

The formal program, which I want to touch on here and which is the major public thrust of our ministries of education, fits hand and glove with the testing that I've been talking about.

It denies, for example, that we try to build "concepts" in our lives. It guts the social and scientific content of what kids learn in school. It focuses on such things as "thinking skills" in which content is irrelevant. It re-presses thought and language which have depth and strength of feeling. For our ministries of education anything goes by way of content—don't let the guidelines fool you—so long as the real world (its oppression and its joys) is avoided and the kids are kept in line.

There is nothing of "excellence" or "quality" here, the two major buzz words of the far right in education which our ministries now run with and which they have turned into the most complete public lies imaginable.

We have to be very clear about this: there are no serious purposes on our education ministries' agendas, other than the production of a docile workforce. For the different levels of the system they propose different levels of "Trivial Pursuit." It is what Frank Smith calls "programmed learning." Elementary "skills" for the bottom. Narrow high-tech "skills" for the top. No real learning for anyone. And everywhere the same process of putting words to words, filling in the blanks. What changes between the streams is the complexity of the classroom games, which in the end, of course, are deadly games, since they waste so much of our children's lives and determine so much of their future.

■ A WORKING CLASS RESPONSE

I want to conclude with three points:

The first point is that working class kids resist the labelling, streaming and programming that comes down on them.

That's hardly news to the people in this room. But it's important to keep in mind.

Most working class kids resist the hidden curriculum of their schools in one way or another. As much as they can they cut out their own time and space within the school order—cutting up, cutting classes, avoiding work, dropping out.

And they resist the formal curriculum of the school—its thought and its language. They know this formal curriculum doesn't really get them anywhere. Its "qualifications" are largely irrelevant for most of the jobs seriously open to them. Its capacity to help them understand the world about them is nothing short of grotesque.

The problem with this resistance is that kids being kids, they throw out the intellectual and creative baby with the bath water of what passes for intellectual and creative work in school. If school work is what using your mind is all about, they say, we don't want to have anything to do with it. It is only when they get to be adults do they learn that what power and happiness they can hope for in life depends on their being able to use their minds.

In the course of this experience, most working class kids come to separate mental and manual labour, in one way or another, and end up "choosing" to do manual labour as the honourable and realistic choice. This fits perfectly with an identical split made in the capitalist workplace, where bosses do the thinking and workers carry it out. Workers may resist this split later on in their lives, but as school children they take it into their hearts.

The second point I want to make is that teachers resist this government/corporate thrust in education as well.

Most of this resistance is inarticulate, especially in public. It sounds strange to be saying this about teachers, who spend their days talking, but they—and here I'm thinking especially of their organizations—don't have many words to describe what they know is wrong about how our schools work and what should be done about it. Mostly teacher unions are focused on salaries and job security, like a lot of unions you know.

Individual teachers don't have a way of collectively dealing with their classroom concerns, of talking honestly about daily work problems with their fellow teachers or with parents in a safe environment. Their bosses do most of the public talking about what goes on and should go on within the school. As a result most teachers end up closing their classroom doors and working hard on their own to keep some order and program alive among their students. But in doing so they have little sense that things could really be different: that they don't have to be at war with their working class students and afraid of their communities; that they could have much more power than they do now over what happens to them at work; that their curriculum could be a lot more meaningful to both themselves and their students.

The recent government thrust in education, however, is labelling, streaming and programming, which I touched on earlier, and which does more than hurt kids. It also hurts teachers, and much more obviously than in the past. Increasingly teachers are being treated more and more like workers. More and more they are being asked to take orders, not to think for themselves, to subject their classroom work to "teacher proof" programs and materials. Closing their doors doesn't work so well anymore.

Labour has to be there for teachers when they finally turn and fight over what should happen to kids in their classrooms, which they are now starting to do in places like British Columbia. In the end, kids' happiness and purpose in school are the teachers' happiness and purpose. Their interests are not opposed. This idea is hard to hold on to in the everyday practice of school politics and in the business unionism of so many of our teacher organizations. But it's true, and it's also true that most of the kids our teachers teach are working class kids. With enough good organizing we can all be on the same side.

My final point is that as Labour puts itself alongside student and teacher resistance in our schools, the key issue is what happens to kids in classrooms: the labelling, the streaming and the programming. It's all one package, part of one system. And that's how we have to deal with it.

We have to say what's wrong on all these fronts and we must also say what should take their place as part of a whole system.

We have to say "NO" to labelling working class kids—any kids at all—on the dumb/smart, crazy/sane spectrum. Don't tolerate it all. Sue the system for slander in the courts. And, more importantly, fight politically on every front there is to put a stop to it. None of these labels are necessary, even in today's bureaucratically controlled schools. There is a catholic school board in this province which hasn't given an IQ test since 1975.

We have to fight, instead, for classrooms where kids are defined as full citizens—members of a classroom community, capable of powerful and purposeful work. We do this not for any sentimental reason, but because that's the truth of the matter; the potential is there.

There are, of course, a very small number of kids who are honestly retarded or emotionally disturbed. They should be taken compassionately into the community of students and teachers; the last thing these kids need is to be thrown into lonely and humiliating ghettos, whether in special classes or special schools.

Of course, we need smaller classes to help make this kind of integration work and to give teachers the opportunity to make a deeper connection with all of their students. It's costly. But plugging a couple of corporate tax loopholes would do the trick. Seriously. There are billions of dollars available to the social sector even within our present tax structure.

We also have to say "NO" to any kind of streaming or placement that has a class, gender or racist bias—that is, a stream in which the people in it are somehow judged to be less than others: dumber or crazier. Not so able. Not so on top of their lives.

We have to fight, instead, for placement that insures a solid education for all our kids. Secretaries and plumbers, steelworkers and retail workers, mechanics and clerks must also be historians and economists, poets, intellectuals and artists. It is only through these activities that they can be full citizens. Many workers, of course, take on these tasks, but they are running deeply against the grain of what the society expects of them. We have to fight for placement which gives our kids access to all these activities.

In the end a serious curriculum means linking the work kids do in school with the larger fight to make a better world. It means telling the whole truth about the way things are and acting on that truth.

It will be a long and hard struggle. Mostly it will be kids of future generations who will benefit.

For the people in this room that comes as no surprise. The labour movement has had a proud history of lending a helping hand to the future—for freedom, for justice, for a life with love in it. We expect to continue doing this work. And if this conference is any indication, we know that nowhere is the future more at stake than in our kids' education.

The OFL has taken on a strong new mandate in looking out for working class kids in school. In so doing it has significantly changed the nature of the long battle this province's working people have had with their educational system. With union educators and activists like yourselves at the forefront of this battle, real victories on behalf of our kids are now possible. For all of those people—kids and adults—who have fought the good fight for working class kids in our schools, this is an important moment and one we should all be proud of.

■ POSTSCRIPT

The arguments made by Natriello, Pallas, and Alexander are similar to other recent analyses of streaming (see Jones et al., 1990) that generally cite two reasons in its defence. First, students achieve more when divided into streams according to their abilities. Second, teachers and students find it more rewarding and satisfying, teachers because it enables them to teach at one level rather than several levels in each class, and students because they believe it allows them to learn at their own level, according to their abilities.

On the other hand, Martell's view that streaming hinders achievement recalls that of Corrigan et al. (1987), who argue that streaming is designed to preserve class structures. Students are placed into streams on the basis of class backgrounds. Similarly, Hanrahan (1987) argues that gender is more important than class in determining stream placement. She says that schools perpetuate gender relations by emphasizing gender stereotypes. Boys are encouraged to be competitive and aggressive, and to enter the streams that will provide them with the math skills needed for industrial and science careers. Girls are discouraged from learning these skills, and from entering streams that provide them. Instead they are encouraged to learn stereotypical female skills such as dependence and sociability (hiding competence in order to enhance popularity).

The arguments presented in these articles have very different implications for social policy. Those of Natriello et al. suggest a need to improve skills testing to ensure even better linkages between skill level and stream placement. From Martell's perspective, however, it would make sense to redesign the school curriculum, and to train teachers to become aware of and eliminate class stereotyping in the classroom.

■ QUESTIONS

1. Which of these articles do you believe is the most convincing? How have your personal experiences in the education system influenced your decision?

2. What other policy implications result from accepting one of these arguments as the most convincing?

3. What other factors not considered by Natriello et al. could have influenced their findings?

4. What other factors not considered by Martell could be more important than class?

■ FURTHER READING

In Support of Natriello, Pallas, and Alexander

Cross, David. "Selection, Setting and Streaming in Language Teaching." *System* 16, no. 1 (1988): 13-22.

Jones, John, Anthony Harris, and Graeme Putt. "Streaming in First Year University Classes." *Studies in Higher Education* 15, no. 1 (1990): 21-30.

Sharit, Yossi and David L. Featherman. "Schooling, Tracking, and Teenage Intelligence." *Sociology of Education* 61, no. 1 (January 1988): 42-51.

In Support of Martell

Baily, Charles and David Bridges. *Mixed Ability Grouping: A Philosophical Perspective*. London: Allen and Unwin, 1983.

Corrigan, Philip, Bruce Curtis and Robert Lanning. "The Political Sphere of Schooling." In *The Political Economy of Canadian Schooling*. Edited by Terry Wotherspoon. Toronto: Methuen, 1987.

Hanrahan, Maura. "Producing the Female Reserve Labour Force: Women and Schooling." In *The Political Economy of Canadian Schooling*. Edited by Terry Wotherspoon. Toronto: Methuen, 1987.

Radwanski, George. *Ontario Study of the Relevance of Education, and the Issue of Dropouts*. Ontario: Ministry of Education, 1987.

Other Voices

Frideres, James S. "Native People and Canadian Education." In *The Political Economy of Canadian Schooling*. Edited by Terry Wotherspoon. Toronto: Methuen, 1987.

Garet, Michael S. and Brian Delany. "Students, Courses and Stratification." *Sociology of Education* 61, no. 2 (April 1988): 61-77.

Lee, Valerie E. and Anthony S. Bryk. "Curriculum Tracking as Mediating the Social Distribution of High School Achievement." *Journal of Education* 61, no. 2 (April 1988): 78-94.

IS SUPPORT FOR

UNIONS DECLINING

IN CANADA?

YES **Yonatan Reshef**, "Union Decline: A View from Canada," *Journal of Labor Research* 11, no. 1 (Winter 1990): 25-39

NO **Graham S. Lowe and Harvey Krahn**, "Recent Trends in Public Support for Unions in Canada," *Journal of Labor Research* 10, no. 4 (Fall 1989): 391-410

From their inception in the nineteenth century, unions have been both praised and vilified. There is no denying that their presence in the workplace has had a profound impact on relations between workers and employers. Unions have been seen to influence employer-employee relations even in companies that have no union (Rinehart, 1987). They have also been said to have had an impact on the quality of life in the home. It has been argued, for example, that improved working conditions (shorter work days/weeks, better wages, and improved safety on the job) brought about by union negotiations have given workers more leisure time to spend with their families and fellow workers.

Many people, however, reject the need for labour unions, accusing them of being narrowly focused on issues of wages, and unable (or unwilling) to respond to the needs of the whole community. The legitimacy of unions in the context of contemporary industrial relations is frequently questioned. Union leaderships are charged with having too much influence over their memberships, and of being undemocratic.

There is no doubt that support for unions is declining in the United States, but is it also declining in Canada? It has been argued that the Canadian movement is stronger than its U.S. counterpart and, therefore, in a less vulnerable position. But observers have also pointed out that Canadian economic trends away from the highly unionized resource extraction and manufacturing industries to the poorly organized service sector industries have left the labour movement in Canada in a weakened position.

These issues provide the background for Debate Twelve. Arguing for the "Yes" side of the debate, Reshef says that structural and institutional weaknesses have led to a decline in union membership. Arguing for the "No" side of the debate, Lowe and Krahn indicate that support for unions, as measured in public opinion polls, has either remained constant or increased slightly.

Reference

Rinehart, James W. (1987) *The Tyranny of Work: Alienation and the Labour Process* (Toronto: Harcourt Brace Jovanovich).

UNION DECLINE: A VIEW FROM CANADA

*Yonatan Reshef**

■ I. INTRODUCTION

The trade union movement in the United States is in dramatic decline. In 1987, only 17 percent of the labour force was unionized (Bureau of National Affairs, 1988), compared to one-third just after World War II. During the past decade, the number of successful certification elections has been declining (Goldfield, 1984); concession bargaining has been the order of the day; and, on several occasions, unions have granted concessions to employers, even though the need for them was not always great (Reisman and Compa, 1985). Meanwhile, Canadian unions have been standing tall. Unionization levels have been stable, at about 38 percent, the number of union certifications has not changed, and concession bargaining exists to a lesser degree than in the United States (Meltz, 1985; Kumar, 1986; Riddell, 1986). But this "comfortable stability" may not last. In addition to evidence that unions are facing growing difficulties in the establishment of new collective bargaining relationships (Walker, 1987), here it is argued that unions also can be facing a decline in membership density in the near future.

Important changes are occurring in the political and economic environments of Canadian unions. Such changes may be detrimental to Canadian trade unions, given their structural and institutional situation. To support this argument, this paper discriminates between private-sector union and nonunion firms in Alberta and uses the results together with information on trends in the discriminating variables to speculate on the prospects for union decline. This analysis uncovers some structural (union members' employment patterns and union firm characteristics) and institutional (union services) attributes of unions. In themselves, these attributes can induce long-term union decline. Combined with the politico-economic environments that Alberta unions have been facing since the early 1980s, these attributes have precipitated union decline. Because these attributes are shared by many other Canadian unions that might face similar environmental challenges in the near future, they may soon confront the same hardships currently plaguing their counterparts in the U.S. and in Alberta.

■ II. CHANGING UNION ENVIRONMENTS IN CANADA

A common theme in the research on Canadian industrial relations is that the divergence in union density between the United States and Canada cannot be accounted for by either sectoral demographic or market changes, but rather by the differences in labor laws and the public policies governing their administration (Riddell, 1986; Meltz, 1985; Rose and Chaison, 1985; Gunderson and Meltz, 1986). There are signs that this relative advantage is waning.

Panitch and Swartz (1988) pointed out that a new era in state policy toward unions is emerging. This era is marked by "a shift away from the generalized rule-of-law form of coercion (whereby an overall legal framework both establishes and constrains the rights and powers of all unions), towards a form of selective *ad hoc*, discretionary state coercion (whereby the state removes for a specific purpose and period the rights contained in labour legislation)" (p. 31). Recent events support this notion and suggest that the courts and some governments are increasingly using their authority to weaken unions at large.

Until 1984, for example, the federal and nine provincial jurisdictions relied on signed membership cards rather than on certification elections to determine union representation. In 1984, British Columbia amended its labor code to require a secret ballot in every certification if the union has the required 45 percent support to make an application (Craig, 1986, p. 130). Perhaps this requirement contributed to the decrease in the percentage of new certifications granted in British Columbia from 74.6 percent, between 1971 and 1983, to 60 percent in 1984-5 (Kumar et al., 1987, p. 380).

Recently, a new Labor Relations Code (Bill 22) in Alberta has introduced a similar amendment. In order for union membership to be eligible to carry out a secret representation vote, Bill 22 requires unions to have signed up at least 40 percent of a bargaining unit's members. Unions have to win a representation vote by 50 percent plus another vote to obtain certification. Given that "new organizing represents an important, if not the most important [unionization] process" (Rose and Chaison, 1985, p. 102), Bill 22 may improve employers' ability to thwart union organizing campaigns and thereby to hasten union stagnation and decline.

Further, in July 1986, a college teacher forced the Ontario Public Service Employees Union to stop using compulsory union dues to support political and social activities. The judge in the case ruled that it was legitimate to compel payment of union dues as long as the money was used for collective bargaining or union administration. The case has been granted leave for appeal and is currently awaiting hearing with the Supreme Court of Canada. In April 1987, the Supreme Court of Canada ruled that the Charter of Rights and Freedoms does not guarantee the right to strike or to bargain collectively. In June 1987, the government of British Columbia passed a new labor law (Bill 19) that, among other things, allows unionized firms to established nonunion subsidiaries to bid on jobs. And in July and October 1987, for the first time in its history, Canada Post hired replacement workers to substitute for striking letter carriers and inside workers.[1] In the case of the inside workers, the federal government, supporting Canada Post's business plan to privatize services involving 4,200 union jobs, legislated the inside workers back to work after being on the picket line for only eight days. This legislation provided for fines of up to $100,000 a day if the union's leaders or members violated the law. It also barred any violators from holding any union office or job for five years.

Moreover, a recent study has shown that the courts are being more sympathetic to employers in wrongful dismissal cases. Companies are allowed more room in changing employees' working conditions and in firing them. This trend reverses what was the rule during the late 1970s and early 1980s, when "it was very much a plaintiff's world" (Gibb-Clark, 1987).

In addition to changes in their legal and political environments, Canadian unions could soon face significant changes in their economic environment. Growing competitive pressures might result from current developments, such as deregulation, federal and provincial privatization plans,[2] and the October 1987 U.S.-Canada "free-trade agreement."

If these events herald the beginning of an era of less supportive labor legislation and public policies, can it be concluded that Canadian unions are about to face declines similar to those experienced by their U.S. counterparts? To answer this question we have to understand the state of the unions from a micro-level perspective. That is, in addition to understanding changes in the macro-level factors that affect the union movement, micro-level factors directly related to the likelihood that a firm will be unionized must be understood before predictions can be drawn about union decline.

■ III. POLITICO-ECONOMIC ENVIRONMENTS OF ALBERTA UNIONS

The experience of unions in Alberta provides a unique opportunity to test the above question. Private-sector unions in Alberta are not significantly different from many other Canadian unions regarding their "bread-and-butter" service agenda (Craig, 1986, pp. 75-77; Williams, 1971) and members' employment patterns (see Table 1). But unlike some of their more thriving counterparts—such as unions in Ontario, Quebec, and British Columbia—Alberta unions have faced a unique blend of a hostile polity and a severe economic recession since the early 1980s. A comparison of private-sector union and nonunion firms in Alberta highlights union structural and institutional weaknesses that have been exposed by economic downturn and the erosion of protective public policies and labor legislation during the 1980s.

Since the early 1980s, Alberta has faced a severe economic recession. Plummeting demand for products of its two major industries, oil and agriculture, has almost tripled the level of unemployment from 3.9 percent in 1979, to 9.8 percent in 1986. Conservative governments and courts have made unionization difficult.[3] For example, Alberta labor law contains

TABLE 1 Percentage of Workers Organized by Industry

INDUSTRY GROUP	WORKERS ORGANIZED IN CANADA		WORKERS ORGANIZED IN ALBERTA[c]		
	(1983)[a]	(1985)[b]	(1984)	(1985)	(1986)
Goods-Producing Industries	39.7	38.9	39.0	34.3	26.8
Manufacturing	39.1	37.7	25.0	32.0	29.0
Construction	47.5	47.8	81.0	78.0	51.0
Mining	26.4	26.3	6.0	6.0	6.0
Service Industries	28.5	27.9	24.8	24.3	24.2
Transportation, Communications, & Utilities	56.4	53.1	43.3	45.0	47.0
Trade	9.8	9.9	9.5	9.0	8.0
Finance	2.7	2.7	0.0	0.0	0.0
Service	36.9	36.2	32.4	32.0	32.0

[a] Statistics Canada, 1987, p. 75.
[b] Statistics Canada, 1988, p. 43.
[c] Alberta Labour, 1985-1987, p. 2.

neither a provision for settling a first collective agreement nor a provision regarding dues check-offs or technological change. A 1985 court decision granted employers the right to void expired collective agreements by locking out their employees for 25 hours. And in 1986, the Alberta Labour Relations Board, interpreting the duty to bargain "in good faith," ruled that an employer must make an offer "in good faith" but is not bound to reach an agreement.

Together, these factors help explain why Alberta is the least unionized province in Canada (Kumar, 1986, p. 99); why the percentage of granted certifications has plunged from 71.8 percent between 1971 and 1981 to 59.1 percent in 1982-3 to 45.0 percent in 1984-5 (Kumar et al., 1987, p. 380); why unionization levels have been declining, from 32.3 percent in 1983, to 31.9 percent in 1984, to 30.9 percent in 1985, to 29.4 percent in 1986, to 28.4 percent in 1987,[4] well below the national level of about 38 percent in each of those years; and why unions could not deliver high wage increases in 1986. During that year, when the local inflation rate was 5 percent, Alberta workers received the lowest pay raises of all Canadians. The average increase for Alberta workers was 3.8 percent while the average Canadian worker got 5.1 percent more. Interestingly, nonunion employees fared better, with an average wage increase of 5 percent, than union employees did, who received only 3.3 percent.[5]

Given such a blend of macro-level politico-economic conditions, some micro-level structural and institutional union characteristics—

which in themselves may cause long-term union decline—may catalyze such a process.

■ IV. CONCEPTUAL FRAMEWORK AND HYPOTHESES

The following is a list of firm characteristics that are expected to discriminate between union and nonunion firms.

Joint Labor-Management Committee (JLMC). There are two generic types of JLMCs: committees created to administer employee-involvement programs (e.g., quality circle programs, quality-of-work-life programs, gainsharing programs), and committees established to administer contract rights or procedures (e.g., job evaluation committees, safety committees, technological change committees). Different types of committees may result from different business strategies.

In the nonunion sector, employee-involvement JLMCs might be implemented to increase employee participation in how the firm is run, thereby diminishing workers' incentives to unionize (Kochan, Katz, and McKersie, 1986, pp. 99-100). In the union sector, such JLMCs might be implemented as a *quid pro quo* for union concessions, as in the automobile industry (Katz, 1985; Katz and Sabel, 1985). Alternatively, JLMCs could be created, independently of any *quid pro quo* for union concessions, to help discuss and administer issues of mutual concern to labor and management that fall outside the scope of a collective agreement (Kochan, Katz and McKersie, 1986, pp. 183-87).

Given the foregone possibilities and the lack of data on the distribution of the different JLMCs between the union and nonunion sectors, no hypothesis can be formulated about the likelihood of firms with JLMCs to be unionized or nonunionized compared to firms without JLMCs.

Personnel. "[A] firm will invest more in specialized personnel as the importance of a functional area (such as labor relations) increases" (Kochan, 1980, p. 193). Apparently, union presence in a company's environment increases the level of uncertainty in the particular area of labor relations. To successfully buffer the organization's core technology from possible union-induced disruptions, a company should establish a specialized, boundary-spanning unit (Thompson, 1967, pp. 66-67), in this case, a personnel unit. Hence, firms with personnel units are more likely to be unionized relative to firms without personnel units. Also, having to negotiate and administer a collective agreement, personnel people in firms will carry out more functions relative to nonunion firms, other things equal.

Industry. Table 1 presents union members' patterns of employment in both Canada and Alberta. It shows much lower unionization levels in Alberta for 1984 and 1985, which is consistent with the former discussion.[6] For both Canada and Alberta for either year, however, union members are concentrated in the goods-producing industries, even though these industries are declining (Kumar, 1986, pp. 140-41). Thus, the likelihood that service-producing firms will be unionized is low relative to goods-producing firms, other things equal.

Pension and Savings Plans. "A prime example of the difference between union and nonunion fringe benefits programs is in the pension program" (Freeman and Medoff, 1984, p. 68). While there is only a small difference between union and nonunion firms in the proportion of compensation spent on legally required fringes (e.g., social security, unemployment compensation), "there are sizeable differences in the proportion going to voluntary fringes," such as pension and saving plans (Freeman and Medoff, 1984, p. 62). Surveying 2,699 union and 4,633 nonunion plants between 1974 and 1977, Freeman and Medoff (1984) found that 91 percent of the former and only 47 percent of the latter had pension plans. Thus, the likelihood that firms with pension and savings plans will be unionized is high relative to firms without such plans, other things equal.

Size. Kochan (1980, pp. 141, 148) has shown that (1) union decertification elections tend to be concentrated in small bargaining units, because unions give inadequate attention to small units where union servicing costs are high; and (2) workers in very small (fewer than 11 employees) or very large (more than 1,000 employees) plants are less willing to unionize than workers in intermediate-size plants. In small plants, workers can solve problems by communicating face-to-face with employers. In large plants, management tends to provide workers with union-like benefits, thereby decreasing workers' incentives to join unions. Freeman and Medoff (1984, p. 32) demonstrated that highly unionized industries are also industries with "larger-than-average companies and work sites." In addition, as part of their union-avoidance activities, unionized companies created small nonunionized subsidiaries that specialize in one product (Cappelli and Chalykoff, 1985; Kochan, McKersie, and Chalykoff, 1986). Because my sample includes only 12 (4.6 percent) firms with more than 1,000 employees, it is assumed that, other things equal, the likelihood that larger firms will be unionized is high relative to smaller firms.

Age. Both Kochan, McKersie, and Chalykoff (1986) and Kochan, Katz, and McKersie (1986, p. 100) suggested that unionized firms tend to be older. Apparently, in their search for competitiveness, employers more and more create nonunionized establishments where they can experiment with new, cost-reducing technologies, flexible job rules, and quality of work life (QWL) programs free of union constraints. Therefore, other things equal, the likelihood that older firms will be unionized is high relative to younger firms.

Growing Firms. The evidence suggests that unions are concentrated in declining industries (Kochan, Katz, and McKersie, 1986, pp. 48-50). It appears that unions face great difficulties organizing growing firms, most of which are concentrated in the service-producing industries that historically have had a comparatively low proportion of union members. Therefore, other things equal, growing firms are less unionized than stable or declining firms.

To recapitulate, these variables are expected to discriminate between unionized and nonunionized firms. It is hypothesized that firms that are more likely to be unionized (1) are older; (2) are not growing; (3) are larger; (4) are in goods-producing industries; (5) have personnel units; and (6) have pension and savings plans.

■ V. METHODS

Sources of Data. Data for this study were secured by the Human Resources Management Research Center at the University of Alberta. Between September 1985 and February 1986, the Center carried out a two-stage questionnaire survey of 339 firms in Alberta's private sector. At the first stage, 163 questionnaires were sent to firms in goods-producing industries; 128 usable ones were returned, with a response rate of 78.5 percent. At the second stage, 176 questionnaires were sent to firms in service-producing industries; 131 usable questionnaires were returned, with a response rate of 74.4 percent. Table 2 presents the firms in the sample by industry.

TABLE 2   Firms in the Sample by Industry

INDUSTRY GROUP	NUMBER OF FIRMS ($n = 259$)	PERCENT
Goods-Producing		
Industries	128	49.4
Manufacturing	73	28.2
Construction	42	16.2
Mining	13	5.0
Service-Producing		
Industries	131	50.6
Transportation		
Communications, & Utilities	25	9.7
Trade	35	13.5
Finance	20	7.7
Service	51	19.7

Variables and Measurement. The dependent variable is whether or not a firm is unionized. There are 101 union firms (39 percent) and 158 nonunion firms (61 percent). There are seven independent variables. JLMC is a dichotomous variable measuring whether or not a firm has any committees for joint consultation between management and employees.

PERSONNEL is a scale comprising eight personnel/human resources activities. It ranges from zero (no personnel unit exists) to eight (all eight activities are carried out). The scale items and reliability are presented in Table 4. Each item is a dichotomous variable measuring whether or not a specific activity is carried out.

TABLE 3   Means, Standard Deviations, and Intercorrelations for All Variables[a]

VARIABLES	MEAN	SD	2	3	4	5	6	7	8
Dependent Variable									
1. Union Firms	.40	.49	.23	.40	−.34	.24	.25	−.20	.22
Independent Variables									
2. Age	37.48	26.92		.17	.07	.30	.34	−.18	.17
3. JLMC	.49	.50			−.04	.29	.36	−.05	.19
4. Service Industries	.50	.50				.01	−.04	.02	−.01
5. Personnel Unit	3.32	3.03					.45	−.07	.01
6. Pension & Savings	1.12	.81						−.08	.17
7. Growing Firms	.33	.47							−.09
8. Size	251.85	489.83							

[a] $N = 242$

$p < .01$ for correlations higher than − / + .17 (2-tailed test).

The omitted categories are: nonunion firms, no JLMC, goods-producing industries, stable/declining firms.

INDUSTRY is a dichotomous variable measuring whether a firm belongs in the service- or the goods-producing industries.

PENSION & SAVINGS is a scale comprising two items. It ranges from zero (no plan is available) to two (both savings and pension plan is available). Each item is a dichotomous variable measuring whether or not a plan is available. The scale items and reliability are presented in Table 3.

SIZE is a continuous variable measured in years from year of founding to 1986.

GROWING FIRMS is a dichotomous variable measuring whether or not a firm had grown over the three years prior to the survey.

Data Analysis. The aim of this paper is to gain understanding of structural and institutional problems facing unions in Alberta by distinguishing between union and nonunion firms. To gain this understanding, discriminating variables associated with a firm being unionized or nonunionized are identified and their power to discriminate between those firms is estimated. To maximize the information obtained, the set of discriminating variables comprises both determinants of unionization (INDUSTRY, SIZE, GROWING FIRMS, and AGE) and its effects (PER-

SONNEL, PENSION & SAVINGS, and *JLMC*). The most appropriate method for estimating the discriminatory power of such a set of variables is discriminant analysis (Klecka, 1982, p. 11). This procedure identifies the linear combinations of variables that best discriminate between the studied groups (Borgen and Seling, 1978). These combinations, in turn, highlight the relative discriminatory power of each variable in terms of structure correlations or loadings. Once the degree of discriminatory power is understood, it should be possible to look at trends in the discriminating variables and predict the future of unionization in Alberta. It may even be possible to generalize these predictions to a broader context.

■ RESULTS AND DISCUSSION

Descriptive statistics and intercorrelations for all variables used in the discriminant analysis are given in Table 3. The variables that discriminate

TABLE 4 Structure Correlations For Union-Nonunion Group Contrast

NUMBER OF UNION FIRMS — 96
NUMBER OF NONUNION FIRMS[a] — 146

VARIABLE	RELIABILITY[b]	STRUCTURE CORRELATION[c]
JLMC		.60
Service Industries		−.50
Pension & Savings	.66	.36
— pension plans		
— savings plans		
Age		.35
Personnel	.90	.34
— recruitment & selection		
— training		
— management development		
— wage & salary adminis.		
— industrial relations		
— job evaluation		
— manpower planning		
— employee communication		
Size		.32
Growing Firms		−.30

[a] 81 percent of the cases were correctly classified.
[b] All scale items are dichotomous — 0 = no; 1 = yes.
[c] Structure correlations were computed on a pooled-within-group basis between the discriminant function and discrimination variables.

between union and nonunion firms are presented in Table 4. Generally, variables with loadings of less than .30 are omitted.

A discriminant function was identified that significantly discriminates between the two groups at the .0001 level. The structure correlations are presented in Table 4 with higher scores related to union firms. The correlations indicate that the variables effectively discriminate between union and nonunion firms in the expected directions, with JLMC being the most powerful discriminating variable. It appears that the likelihood that firms with JLMCs are unionized is high relative to firms without JLMCs, other things equal.

Union firms are concentrated in the goods-producing industries. As expected, to cope with uncertainties introduced into its environment by a union and contract negotiation and administration, union firms are more likely than nonunion firms to create a personnel unit. Moreover, it appears that the personnel units in unionized firms carry out a higher number of functions relative to nonunion firms with similar units. This might be the result of a higher number of industrial relations activities, such as grievance and pension administration, which are more frequently carried out by personnel staff in unionized firms.

As predicted, growing, younger, and smaller firms tend to be nonunion. Note that growing firms are also smaller and younger than stable and declining firms. These firms could be nonunion subsidiaries of bigger firms trying to avoid unions, as in the construction industry in Alberta, or they may represent newly created firms that are still growing. Alternatively, they may indicate a growing sector of firms that have learned to avoid unions and cut labor costs by remaining or keeping their plants small. For example, Magna International, an automotive parts company, keeps its work force at 100 persons per plant to facilitate communication and to increase employee-management trust, thereby increasing its chances of avoiding unions and some of the personnel activities that accompany them.

JLMC is the most powerful discriminating variable found in this study. Firms with JLMCs are more likely to be union firms. In Canada, over the last decade, as the scope of collective agreements broadened to cover areas such as safety and health and pension administration, many functions of earlier JLMCs were gradually taken over by collective bargaining (Riddell, 1986, p. 11). But unions have been able to force management to include a JLMC provision in collective agreements on very few issues (Adams, 1986).

In 1986, out of 249 collective agreements (20.5 percent of a total 1,217 agreements) that were sampled by Alberta Labour (1986, pp. 58-59), 102 (41 percent) had a provision for a JLMC, with only a general statement of its purpose (e.g., improving service to customers). Fifteen agreements (6.0 percent) had a provision for a JLMC but restricted it to discussing a specific list of items (e.g., seniority, time studies, job evaluation, insurance programs). No agreement contained a provision expanding the jurisdictions of

JLMCs beyond the immediate workplace and contract administration to include strategic decisions (e.g., technological changes, shutdowns, subcontracting).[7] Given the nature of Alberta's political and economic environments that militate against trade unionism and the traditional, narrow agenda that falls under the JLMCs' jurisdictions, it is assumed that JLMCs have been created to assist the parties to administer collective agreements independent of any *quid pro quo* for union concessions. Hence, in Alberta, JLMC is probably not a mechanism that helps balance labor-management power.

■ VII. CONCLUSIONS

These data from Alberta highlight structural and institutional union weaknesses that can become all the more detrimental to unions when combined with political hostility and increased competitive pressures. More longitudinal studies are needed to reveal whether or not Canadian unions are facing long-term environmental changes and if they are to determine the effects these changes might have on the state of the unions. But because Alberta unions are not significantly different from Canadian unions as a whole, a few general speculations can be made based on the results of this study.

Structurally, over the past decade, while the service-producing sector has been growing and the goods-producing sector has been shrinking (Craig, 1986, p. 29) and while a growing number of small-size firms have been entering the market,[8] unions have not changed their organizing pattern. Although Canadian unions are better entrenched within the service-producing industries—mainly among schoolteachers and nurses and technical staff in hospitals (Kumar, 1986, p. 142)—than U.S. unions (Meltz, 1985), they are still concentrated in old union bastions, the goods-producing sector dominated by old and large firms. But this sector is losing ground[9] to newly created service-producing firms—such as paralegal, physical therapy, computer programming, retail sales, foods, and systems analysis—which increasingly employ more women, part-timers, retirees, immigrants, and highly educated and mobile workers (Bernstein, 1987). Hence, if unions are to retain their position as a countervailing power in society, they will have to make headway in the nonunion segment of the service work force.

Institutionally, unions may soon be facing a dual challenge: first, traditional union institutions, such as collective bargaining, cannot adequately deal with macro-level developments, such as deregulation, privatization, and changing legislation; and second, customary services, such as pension plans and JLMCs, may not cater to the needs of many of the aforementioned workers. If unions are to thrive under changing political and economic environments, they should adapt their traditional service agenda, organizing strategy, and institutions to the new circumstances. For example, new union services may be offered that will transcend the traditional "bread and butter" items that emphasize stability and certainty. The new services should be geared toward worker mobility and constantly changing industrial relations systems. Moreover, a new organizing strategy may be adopted that will involve higher union efforts to penetrate nonunion firms "from without" rather than adhering to traditional "from within" strategies. Instead of concentrating solely on on-site election campaigns and collective bargaining, more union resources should be allocated to public relations and political campaigns.

Although unions have recognized the importance of acting at the macro- (politico-legal) and micro- (firm) levels to arrest their current organizational decline, they have had very limited success at both. In the 1986 election in Alberta, the Conservative government lost 16 seats in the 83-seat legislature to the labor-oriented New Democratic Party (NDP). Although the NDP is now the official opposition, it has not yet been able to pressure the government to make legislative changes favorable to trade unions. A good opportunity to achieve such a legal reform arose in August 1986. In the wake of the violent, six-month strike at Gainers meatpackers, the government set up a commission to examine labor legislation. Major issues on the commission's agenda were the 25-hour lockout and the legislative provision that allows employers who have been struck to hire replacement workers. In February 1987, the commission tabled its recommendations for new legislation (Bill 60). Strong pressures by labor leaders notwithstanding, Bill 60 was not significantly different from the current legislation. Worse, Bill 22, Bill 60's successor, may even precipitate an organizational atrophy in Alberta unions. It still allows employers to employ the 25-hour lockout and to hire replacement workers, and it may hinder unionization.

Between January 24 and February 11, 1988, the 11,500-member United Nurses of Alberta (UNA) illegally struck the 104-member Alberta Hospital Association (AHA). In addition to improved wages and working conditions, UNA sought to repeal the 1983 legislation (Bill 44) that bans strikes by nurses. After ten days on the picket line, UNA has been taken to court and fined $400,000. In addition, AHA laid charges (civil contempt of court) against more than 100 individual nurses. During the strike, the government announced that it would neither review Bill 44 nor help finance the nurses' economic demands, thereby setting a model for private-sector employers to follow. Upon settlement, the nurses failed to win their economic demands, and Bill 44 remains the law.

At the micro-level, Canadian labor leaders have been trying to organize the trade and finance sectors since the mid-1970s. The drive to organize insurance and bank employees has had very limited success. A number of stores of the retail chains of Eaton's and Simpson's were organized during the mid-1980s, but all but one of the Eaton's stores have been decertified. It is noteworthy that these sectors employ a growing number of part-timers. During the last decade, part-time employment in Canada grew by 52 percent; full-time employment grew by 18 percent. But only a minority of part-timers are organized (Zeytinoglu, 1986).

To conclude, there has been a slight decline in union density in Canada, from a peak of 39 percent in the early 1980s to the present 37.2 percent. This study suggests, however, that it is not unreasonable to expect that percentage to drop even further, unless there are some major breakthroughs in union strategic responses to environmental challenges.

Notes

*   I am indebted to Brian Bemmels, Alan Murray, and John G. Fricke for helpful comments on an earlier version of this paper, and to Mike Jones for his research assistance.

1. In Canada, some public-sector employees are allowed to strike in the federal jurisdictions as well as in Quebec, Saskatchewan, British Columbia, Newfoundland, and New Brunswick.

2. *Financial Post*, October 26, 1987, p. 6.

3. A national survey of "labor climate" conducted by the Canadian Federation of Independent Business found the Alberta labor law the least pro-labor in Canada (Languedoc, 1986).

4. Alberta Labour, 1986, p. 1. These figures cannot be compared with previous years, because some of the increase in membership between 1979 (24 percent) and 1983 (32.3 percent) is due to improved survey techniques.

5. A national survey's findings reported in *The Edmonton Journal*, November 20, 1987, p. A1.

6. The only exception is the construction industry. In Alberta, however, in the construction industry in recent years, union membership figures greatly exceed those actually employed (the criterion used by Statistics Canada in its annual survey). A similar caution applies to the service industry. Union membership, particularly in education, included members who are retired or for other reasons are not included in the employed labor force. This industry includes, and union membership is primarily composed of, those employed in the education and health care fields. Apart from these two sectors, where membership is high, union membership in the service industry is very low.

7. In 1987, preliminary evidence suggested that this situation had changed somewhat. Between January 1 and May 31, 1987, 1,093 collective agreements were filed with Alberta Labour. Three hundred and thirty-five (30.6 percent) agreements had a JLMC provision, out of which 60.3 percent had only a general statement of its purpose and only 4.5 percent dealt with technological change. Only 17.6 percent of the JLMCs had executive power but no information is available on the issues they covered (Alberta Labour, December, 1987).

8. Between 1981 and 1984, the number of small businesses (with less than $2 million of gross annual revenue) has grown by 119 percent while the number of big businesses has grown by 11 percent (Statistics Canada, 1985-1987).

9. It is noteworthy that in 1984, the service-producing industries in Canada employed 65.2 percent and the goods-producing industries employed 26.3

percent of the nonagricultural labor force (Statistics Canada, 1987, p. 75). The respective figures for 1980 are 63.1 percent and 29 percent (Meltz, 1985, p. 321).

References

Adams, Roy J. "Two Policy Approaches to Labour-Management Decision Making at the Level of the Enterprise." In *Labour-Management Cooperation in Canada*, pp. 87-110. Edited by W. Craig Riddell. Ottawa, ONT: Minister of Supply and Services, 1986.

Alberta Labour. *An Examination of Labour-Management Communication Provisions in Collective Agreements and Third Party Investigations (Phase 1)*. Edmonton, AB: Planning and Research Branch, December 1987.

——. *Membership in Labor Organizations in Alberta, 1984, 1985 & 1986*. Edmonton, AB: Planning and Research Branch, 1985-1987. 3 issues.

——. *Negotiated Working Conditions in Alberta: Collective Agreements 1986*. Edmonton, AB: Planning and Research Branch, 1986.

Bernstein, Aaron. "Help Wanted." *Business Week*, August 10, 1987, pp. 48-53.

Borgen, Fred H. and Mark J. Seling. "Uses of Discriminant Analysis Following MANOVA: Multivariate Statistics for Multivariate Purposes." *Journal of Applied Psychology* 63 (1978): 689-97.

Bureau of National Affairs, February 11, 1988.

Cappelli, Peter and John Chalykoff. "The Effects of Management Industrial Relations Strategy: Results of a Recent Survey." *Proceedings* of the 38th Annual Meeting, Industrial Relations Research Association. Madison, WI: IRRA, 1985, pp. 171-78.

Craig, Alton W.J. *The System of Industrial Relations in Canada*. 2d ed. Scarborough, ONT: Prentice-Hall, 1986.

Financial Post, October 26, 1987, p. 6.

Freeman, Richard B. and James L. Medoff. *What Do Unions Do?* New York: Basic Books, 1984.

Gibb-Clark, M. "Courts Viewing Bosses More Favorably in Dismissal Suits." *The Globe and Mail*, November 30, 1987, p. B11.

Gunderson, Morley and Noah M. Meltz. "Canadian Unions Achieve Strong Gains in Membership." *Monthly Labour Review* 109 (April 1986): 48-49.

Katz, Harry C. *Shifting Gears: Changing Relations in the U.S. Automobile Industry*. Cambridge, MA: MIT Press, 1985.

—— and Charles F. Sabel. "Industrial Relations and Industrial Adjustments in the Car Industry." *Industrial Relations* 24 (Fall 1985): 295-315.

Klecka, William R. *Discriminant Analysis*. Beverly Hills, CA: Sage, 1982.

Kochan, Thomas A. *Collective Bargaining and Industrial Relations*. Homewood, IL: Irwin, 1980.

——, Robert B. McKersie, and John Chalykoff. "The Effects of Corporate Strategy and Workplace Innovations on Union Representation." *Industrial and Labor Relations Review* 39 (July 1986): 487-501.

Kochan, Thomas A., Harry C. Katz, and Robert B. McKersie. *The Transformation of American Industrial Relations*. New York, NY: Basic Books, 1986.

Kumar, Pradeep. "Union Growth in Canada: Retrospect and Prospect." In *Canadian Labour Relations*, pp. 95-160. Edited by W. Craig Riddell. Ottawa, ONT: Minister of Supply and Services, 1986.

_____, Mary Lou Coates, and David Arrowsmith. *The Current Industrial Relations Scene in Canada, 1987.* Kingston, ONT: Industrial Relations Centre, Queen's University, 1987.

Languedoc, Colin. "Entrepreneurs Pick Labor Headaches." *The Financial Post*, December 1, 1986, p. 21.

Meltz, Noah. "Labor Movements in Canada and the United States." In *Challenges and Choices Facing American Labor*, pp. 315-34. Edited by Thomas A. Kochan. Cambridge, MA: MIT Press, 1985.

Panitch, Leo V. and Donald Swartz. *The Assault on Trade Union Freedom.* Toronto, ONT: Garamond, 1988.

Reisman, Barbara and Compa Lance. "The Case for Adversarial Unions." *Harvard Business Review* 63 (May-June 1985): 22-36.

Riddell, W. Craig. "Labour-Management Cooperation in Canada: An Overview." In *Labour-Management Cooperation in Canada*, pp. 1-56. Edited by W. Craig Riddell. Ottawa, ONT: Minister of Supply and Services, 1986.

Rose, Joseph B. and Gary N. Chaison. "The State of the Unions: United States and Canada." *Journal of Labor Research* 6 (Fall 1985): 97-111.

Statistics Canada. *Corporations and Labour Unions Returns Act.* Part 2. Ottawa, ONT: Minister of Supply and Services, 1987-1988. 2 issues.

Statistics Canada. *Small Business in Canada: A Statistical Profile.* Ottawa, ONT: Minister of Supply and Services, 1985-1987. 3 issues.

The Edmonton Journal, November 20, 1987, p. A1.

Thompson, James D. *Organizations in Action.* New York, NY: McGraw Hill, 1967.

Walker, Julian. *First Agreement Disputes and Public Policy in Canada.* Research Essay Series No. 12, Kingston, ONT: Industrial Relations Centre, Queen's University.

Williams, C. Brian. "Trade Union Structure and Philosophy: Need for Reappraisal." In *Canadian Labour in Transition*, pp. 145-72. Edited by R.U. Miller and F. Isbester. Scarborough, ONT: Prentice-Hall, 1971.

Zeytinoglu, Isik U. "Part-Time Workers: Unionization and Collective Bargaining in Canada." *Proceedings* of the 39th Annual Meeting, Industrial Relations Research Association. Madison, WI: IRRA, 1986, pp. 487-95.

RECENT TRENDS IN PUBLIC SUPPORT FOR UNIONS IN CANADA

Graham S. Lowe and Harvey Krahn

I. INTRODUCTION

The 1980s have been a time of dramatic social, economic, and political change in Canada. High unemployment and widespread job instability characterized the first years of the decade, and those conditions still affect some regions of the country. Competition in the labor market increased, and employers in both the private and public sectors laid off workers. In addition, collective bargaining suffered a number of setbacks. These developments must be viewed against a changing political landscape that is characterized by a movement to the right in the 1984 federal election and in several recent provincial elections.

Of central interest to industrial relations is how these changes have been reflected in public opinion about unions. Unions are the major institutions championing the interests of employees, so we might expect growing support for organized labor as workers' economic circumstances deteriorate. Alternatively, government-imposed curbs on industrial relations, concession bargaining, two-tiered wage agreements, and employers' tactics to avoid unionization during the 1980s threaten to erode union power (see, e.g., Panitch and Swartz, 1988; Milton, 1986; Kochan et al., 1986). A more hostile climate for unions might also diminish their perceived usefulness as a means for improving wages and working conditions, especially within the context of relatively high unemployment.

These issues frame the analyses of public opinion toward unions presented in this article. The authors' previous research on union attitudes (Krahn and Lowe, 1984a, 1984b), which was based on 1981 survey data from the western Canadian cities of Edmonton and Winnipeg, is replicated and extended with 1987 data. The original study went beyond individual explanations of attitudes toward unions by documenting the effect of community on those attitudes. The study demonstrated that pro-union sentiments vary depending on the attitudinal dimension being studied. Public opinion in this regard is rather contradictory. Instrumental beliefs about unions are prominent, as are views that unions are overly powerful and contribute to economic problems. Analysis of the 1981 data also found a relatively high degree of latent unionism, with 40 percent of sample members indicating that they would join a union if one existed in their workplace.

This article addresses three general questions: First, have the social economic changes associated with the recession of the early 1980s, and the industrial and labor market restructuring it precipitated, affected how people perceive the role of unions in society? Second, given that we found significant inter-city differences in union attitudes in 1981 (Krahn and Lowe, 1984a), has the differential effect of subsequent economic events in Edmonton and Winnipeg brought further divergence or has it produced a convergence in union attitudes? Third, have "hard times" increased or decreased the propensity of nonunion employees to consider joining a union? . . .

■ II. RESEARCH QUESTIONS AND HYPOTHESES

A number of research questions and hypotheses are suggested. . . . First, has pro-union sentiment changed in the two cities since 1981? Results from recent public opinion polls in Canada suggest that support for unions is waning. The academic literature, while not based on recent data, also leads us to predict a growing endorsement of the negative "big labor" image of unions, but little change in the perceived economic benefits of unions for their members.

Second, evidence from the United States indicates that the level of support among nonunion employees for joining unions has remained fairly constant between 1977 and 1985 (Lipset, 1986, pp. 302-303). How might "latent unionism" in Canada have been affected by deteriorating labor market conditions and a changing political climate?

Our third question looks more closely at the local economic and political environment in order to detect different patterns of change in union attitudes in Edmonton and Winnipeg. Edmonton's continuing high unemployment rate, its economic decline, the success in Edmonton of the left-wing New Democratic party in the 1986 provincial election, and several high-profile labor disputes point toward greater union support in 1987. The absence of similar changes in Winnipeg would suggest more stable public opinion over time in that city. In short, the primary explanation we presented for relatively weaker support for the "business unionism" image (recognition of the instrumental role of unions) in Edmonton in 1981—a buoyant local economy—has disappeared. Because Edmonton has experienced more changes that are likely to bolster union support than has Winnipeg, is there a convergence in opinions and in a willingness to join unions in the two cities?

The fourth question focuses on strikebreaking, raising the issue of workers' collective rights (Johnston and Ornstein, 1985, p. 375). Employers' use of strikebreakers remains a highly contentious point in Canada (Krahn and Lowe, 1988, ch. 7). Only one Canadian province, Quebec, has reasonably effective anti-strikebreaking laws. Against the backdrop of the 1986 Gainers strike in Edmonton, residents in that city may have become more supportive of anti-strikebreaking legislation than they were in 1981, and in comparison with Winnipeg residents who were not exposed to the intense media coverage of the Gainers dispute. Alternatively, media coverage of union members being arrested by police could have convinced some Edmontonians that unions should be further controlled by government. In short, then, has there been any change over time and between cities in public opinion about legislation limiting the use of strikebreakers?

■ III. RESEARCH METHODS AND MEASUREMENT

The Edmonton data are from the eleventh annual Edmonton Area study conducted in 1987 by the Population Research Laboratory (PRL) at the University of Alberta. The sample was randomly selected from the population of households listed in the 1986 municipal census. A total of 620 addresses were chosen, introductory letters explaining the study were mailed to those households, and an interviewer was sent to the address to obtain an interview. A modified quota sampling technique[1] was used to select a respondent in the designated household. The completed sample was made up of 454 respondents, reflecting a response rate of 76.3 percent. Refusals accounted for 18.3 percent of the original sample, 4.4 percent of the households could not be contacted, and a few interviews could not be completed because of language problems (Kinzel, 1987).

Winnipeg data was collected as part of the fifth annual Winnipeg Area Study (WAS) carried out by the Department of Sociology at the University of Manitoba. A random sample of 742 addresses was selected from Winnipeg's 1986 tax assessment file, and reverse directories were used to obtain telephone numbers for those households. Telephone interviews were conducted if the household had a listed telephone; if not, an interviewer attempted to obtain an in-person interview (83 pecent of the interviews were completed by telephone). Interviewers were instructed in advance as to whether they should choose a female or a male respondent in a specific household. A final response rate of 78 percent produced a sample of 581. Refusals accounted for an additional 19 percent of the original sample (Currie, 1987).

In most cases, the questions addressed in the WAS did not replicate the questions asked in the EAS. Several equivalent measures of union attitudes and willingness to join a union, however, were included in each location. In addition, the EAS and WAS have tried to include standard measures of a considerable range of demographic and socio-economic variables. Hence, with a few exceptions, similarly worded independent variables were available in both studies. The Edmonton and Winnipeg data were merged into one file ($N = 1,035$) for this analysis.

Five of the attitudinal measures used in our 1981 study (Krahn and Lowe, 1984a, 1984b) were replicated in the 1987 studies: (1) "We need more laws to limit the power of unions"; (2) "Unions impose too many restrictions on employers"; (3) "During a strike, management should be prohibited from hiring workers to take the place of strikers"; (4) "Employees in an organization have better working conditions when all of them belong to a union"; and (5) "The selfishness of employers can only be fought by strong unions." As in 1981, responses in Edmonton were recorded on a 7-point "strongly agree – strongly disagree" Likert scale; Winnipeg used a 5-point scale in 1987.[2]

Four of the items — "big labor" (items 1 and 2) and "busness unionism" (items 4 and 5) — were chosen for replication because they represent the two major dimensions of union attitudes identified in previous research, including our own (Krahn and Lowe, 1984a, 1984b).[3] These dimensions reflect opinions about the negative effects of union power and about the economic benefits derived from union membership. Other research (McShane, 1986) also indicates that individuals can hold different, even contradictory, images of unions depending on which goals, strategies, and effects are being addressed.[4] The strikebreaking issue is more specific than the two general attitudes just noted. Our measure of support for anti-strikebreaking legislation taps possible changes in attitudes precipitated by the 1986 Gainers strike in Edmonton.

A binary variable was used to distinguish sample members in Edmonton and Winnipeg. Because differences in public opinion between the two cities could be a function of differences in the characteristics of sample members rather than because of changes in the economic and political climate, a variety of individual-level control variables were used in our multivariate analyses of union attitudes and workers' willingness to join unions. Age, gender, educational level, total individual and household income in 1986 (both coded as low, medium, and high), and a binary measure for home ownership constituted a set of demographic and socioeconomic status measures. Binary variables for current labor force participation, unemployment, and union membership, along with similar measures of managerial/professional occupations and clerical/sales/service occupations identified work-related statuses. Political orientations were indexed with three binary measures of current (provincial) preference for the Progressive Conservative, New Democratic, and Liberal parties. A pair of questions about current financial status compared to a year earlier and to a year in the future was used to measure respondents' feelings of economic security and optimism.

■ IV. RESULTS

Table 1 displays the percentage of the Winnipeg and Edmonton samples that agree with each of the five union attitude measures in 1981 and 1987. In both cities, support for laws limiting the power of unions declined somewhat, although a slight majority continued to agree with this sentiment.[5] Roughly half of the 1987 sample members in each city also agreed that "unions impose too many restrictions on employers." Winnipeg results

TABLE 1 Union Attitudes in Edmonton and Winnipeg, 1981 and 1987[a]

| | PERCENTAGE WHO AGREE[b] | | | |
| | EDMONTON | | WINNIPEG | |
	1981	1987	1981	1987
We need more laws to limit the power of unions.	57.9 *	52.2	56.3	50.8
Unions impose too many restrictions on employers.	50.7	55.5	49.8	49.4 #
During a strike, management should be prohibited from hiring workers to take the place of strikers.	50.9	45.8	47.3	41.8
Employees of an organization have better wages and working conditions when all of them belong to a union.	50.9 *	56.8	61.0 * #	53.2
The selfishness of employers can only be fought by strong unions.	40.0 *	37.4	51.3 * #	31.2 #
[N]	[400]	[454]	[336]	[581]

a 1987 interviews in Winnipeg were done by telephone; all other data were collected through in-person interviews.
b Percentages calculated with total sample (non-response included) as the base. In 1981, respondents answered on a scale of (1) Strongly disagree - Strongly Agree (7); responses of 5, 6, and 7 are included in "percentage who agree." The same applies to the 1987 Edmonton results, whereas 1987 Winnipeg respondents answered on a 5-point scale (scores of 4 and 5 are included in "percentage who agree").
* Differences over time are statistically significant ($p < .05$; one-tailed test).
# Differences between cities (in 1981 or 1987) are statistically significant ($p < .05$; one-tailed test).

from 1981 and 1987 were almost identical, and the relatively small increase over time in Edmonton (from 50.7 percent to 55.5 percent) was not statistically significant. In short, despite pronouncements that public support for unions is declining, we find little evidence of a substantial increase in the belief that unions are too powerful. While there is a small (nonsignificant) increase in agreement with the "unions restricting employers" belief in Edmonton, both cities registered a decline in the percentage calling for more governmental controls on unions.[6]

These comparisons over time and between communities also force us to reject the hypothesis that intense media attention on picket-line violence precipitated by the use of strikebreakers led to increased support for anti-strikebreaking legislation in Edmonton. Although there is somewhat more agreement in Edmonton than in Winnipeg in 1987, both cities experienced a small nonsignificant decline in support for such legislation. Less than one-half of the sample members in each community seem to favor the type of legislation now in place in the province of Quebec.

Edmonton residents in 1987 were significantly more likely than their counterparts in 1981 to agree that unions provide better wages and working conditions for their members. Alternatively, a smaller percentage of Winnipeg residents in 1987 (53.2 percent) compared to 1981 (61 percent) agreed with this statement. This interesting finding shows Edmonton respondents more—not less—inclined than Winnipeg respondents to agree with this "business unionism" sentiment. The second measure of business unionism does not show the same pattern of change. In both cities, support declined for the view that the selfishness of employers can only be fought by strong unions. The drop in Winnipeg was much larger, however, leaving Edmonton residents in 1987 significantly more likely to agree with this opinion. Thus, at least at this bivariate level of analysis, the changing economic and political climate in Edmonton may have led to a convergence in "business unionism" beliefs. In fact, these beliefs are more pronounced in Edmonton than in Winnipeg in 1987, a reversal of the situation six years earlier.

In sum, although "big labor" sentiments and support for anti-strikebreaking legislation have not changed very much, we can detect shifts in "business unionism" beliefs in Winnipeg and Edmonton. This lends support to our argument that economic decline, political realignment, and highly publicized labor-management disputes have fostered greater pro-union sentiments among Edmontonians. Table 2 examines to what extent

TABLE 2 Willingness to Join a Union in Edmonton and Winnipeg, 1981 and 1987[a]

	EDMONTON		WINNIPEG	
WILLING TO JOIN?	1981	1987	1981	1987
Yes	35.0%	38.0%	45.0%	35.7%
Yes, if compulsory[b]	—	18.0	—	12.4
Total Yes	35.0	56.0	45.0	48.1
No	65.0	44.0	55.0	51.9
TOTAL	100.0%	100.0%	100.0%	100.0%
[N]	[147]	[166]	[95]	[185]

a Labor force members (full-time and part-time workers, and the unemployed) not currently a member of a union or a professional association.
b Answer was volunteered by respondent (not suggested by the interviewer); in 1981 such answers were coded as "yes."

this growing pro-unionism has been accompanied by a parallel increase in workers' willingness to join a union.

In 1981, 35 percent of Edmonton respondents who did not belong to a union or a professional association said that they would be willing to join a union, compared to 45 percent of the Winnipeg sample. In the 1981 study, the minority who answered "yes, if I had to" were counted among the positive responses; in 1987, they were kept as a separate category. We find slightly more of the Edmonton sample (38 percent) than the Winnipeg sample (35.7 percent) answering "yes" in 1987. To obtain comparability between 1981 and 1987, we combined the "yes, if I had to" group with the unqualified "yes" responses in the 1987 data. Consequently, 56 percent of the nonunion Edmonton labor force participants in 1987 would be willing to join, compared to 48.1 percent of the equivalent Winnipeg population. Again, we find evidence of a reversal in union receptivity in these two cities.[7] Because our earlier analysis showed relatively little change in "big labor" beliefs, we can speculate that a growing commitment to "business unionism" sentiments in Edmonton may be associated with the rise in latent unionism.

In order to examine the impact of other variables on the several types of union attitudes discussed above, a "big labor" index was formed by averaging responses to the first two statements in Table 1. Similarly, responses to the last two statements in Table 1 were averaged to create a "business unionism" index. Table 3 contains the results of a series of multiple regression analyses used to identify the main predictors of these indices as well as of the "anti-strikebreaking legislation" measure. All of the independent variables discussed above were used in initial multiple regression equations for each of the three dependent variables. Nonsignificant predictors were dropped from these equations one or two at a time, until only variables with statistically significant net effects remained in the trimmed equations. The only exception to this procedure was the retention of the binary city variable in each equation to test for a community effect.

These multivariate results confirm our earlier bivariate findings with respect to city differences in union attitudes. Only in the "business unionism" equation do we observe a significant city effect after controlling for other variables in the equation (beta = .127); Edmonton respondents are more in agreement. Interestingly, our 1981 study found that Winnipeg residents were significantly more likely than Edmonton residents (controlling for other individual-level variables in the equation) to agree with statements about unions improving the wages and working conditions of their members.

Other multivariate results shown in Table 3, however, parallel our earlier study. In particular, we are unable to account for large amounts of variance in these union attitudes with the independent variables at our disposal. As expected, union members are more likely to agree with the other two types of union attitudes. An equally systematic pattern is that of

TABLE 3 Union Attitudes: Trimmed Multiple Regression Equations[a] for "Big Labor" and "Business Unionism" Indices, and "Prohibit Strike-Breakers" Measure; Edmonton and Winnipeg Combined

A. Dependent variable: Big Labor Index

Independent variable	Beta	b	st. error	T	r[b]
Edmonton resident (yes = 1)	.025	.050	.067	0.76*	.058
Union member	−.180	−.502	.091	−5.49	−.190
Age	.079	.005	.002	2.36	.119
Education (more than high school = 1)	−.102	−.208	.068	3.03	−.098
Respondent's 1986 income	.106	.163	.051	3.18	.086
Vote NDP provincially	−.204	−.472	.081	−5.86	−.241
Vote PC provincially	.089	.208	.082	2.53	.189
[Constant]		3.102			

$N = 839$ Adjusted $R^2 = .124$

B. Dependent variable: Business Unionism Index

	Beta	b	st. error	T	r[b]
Edmonton resident (yes = 1)	.127	.249	.065	3.86	.082
Union member	.187	.499	.088	5.71	.189
Respondent's 1986 income	−.147	−.216	.049	−4.40	−.133
Vote NDP provincially	.146	.325	.078	4.16	.186
Vote PC provincially	−.091	−.203	.080	−2.54	−.149
[Constant]		3.227			

$N = 845$ Adjusted $R^2 = .103$

C. Dependent variable: "During a strike, management should be prohibited from hiring replacement workers to take the place of strikers."

	Beta	b	st. error	T	r[b]
Edmonton resident (yes = 1)	.050	.136	.085	1.60*	.018
Union member	.188	.720	.117	6.14	.204
Vote NDP provincially	.087	.275	.102	2.69	.152
Vote PC provincially	−.148	−.468	.104	−4.52	−.180
[Constant]		2.944			

$N = 999$ Adjusted $R^2 = .075$

[a] Other independent variables used in regression analyses, and then dropped from the equations because of nonsignificant net effects, are discussed in the text.
[b] Zero-order correlation; pair-wise deletion of missing cases (unlike regression results where list-wise deletion was used).
* Partial regression coefficient is NOT statistically significant ($p > .01$); all other effects are significant at the .01 level.

New Democratic party (left-wing) supporters also being more pro-union, with those respondents favoring the Progressive Conservative party (right-wing) being less supportive of unions or of legislation that restricts strike-breaking. Although age and education have small effects on the "big labor" index (older and less-educated respondents are more likely to agree), demographic predictors are of little consequence in these analyses. Personal income is positively associated with beliefs about overly powerful unions and negatively associated with "business unionism" opinions. In short, the affluent are somewhat less supportive of unions. All other independent variables tested in these analyses failed to show a significant net effect on any of the three dependent variables.

Finally, the first part of Table 4 reports the results of a similar multiple regression analysis of the determinants of willingness to join a union

TABLE 4 Willingness to Join a Union[a]: Effects of Union Attitudes and Other Variables[b]

Dependent variable: "Would you join a union if one existed in your workplace or in your profession?" [Yes = 3; Yes, if compulsory = 2; No = 1]

Independent variable	Beta	b	st. error	T	r[c]
Edmonton resident (yes = 1)	.061	.112	.097	1.15*	.056
Age	−.183	−.015	.004	−3.45	−.221
Educational level	.144	.057	.022	2.61	.098
Managerial/professional occupation (yes = 1)	−.151	−.316	.114	−2.78	−.160
Unemployed (yes = 1)	.150	.405	.143	2.84	.159
Vote PC provincially	−.146	−.306	.110	−2.77	−.159
[Constant]		2.040			
$N = 342$ Adjusted $R^2 = .111$					
"Business unionism" index	.419	.392	.049	8.01	.530
"Big labor" index	−.256	−.247	.051	−4.82	−.437
"Management should be prohibited from hiring strike-breakers . . ."	−.080	−.054	−.035	−1.57*	.216
Edmonton resident (yes = 1)	.008	.014	.087	0.17*	.056
Age	−.125	−.011	.004	−2.64	−.221
Educational level	.026	.011	.020	0.52*	.098
Managerial/professional occupation (yes = 1)	−.075	−.154	.100	−1.54*	−.160
Unemployed (yes = 1)	.109	.290	.125	2.33	.159
Vote PC provincially	−.054	−.112	.100	−1.13*	−.159
[Constant]		2.087			
$N = 310$ Adjusted $R^2 = .372$					

[a] Labor force members (full-time and part-time workers, and the unemployed) not currently a member of a union or professional association.
[b] Other independent variables used in regression analyses, and then dropped from the equations because of nonsignificant net effects, are discussed in the text.
[c] Zero-order correlation; pair-wise deletion of missing cases (unlike regression results where list-wise deletion was used).
* Partial regression coefficient is NOT statistically significant ($p > .01$); all other effects are significant at the .01 level (except effect of unemployment in the second equation where $p = .02$).

among labor force participants who do not already belong to a union or professional association. Age has a small, but significant, negative net effect on workers' willingness to join unions. The more educated sample members and those currently unemployed are more likely to say they would join a union, while Progressive Conservative supporters and those in managerial/professional occupations are less likely to admit to this. City of residence does not have a significant effect. Overall, this equation accounts for a relatively small amount of the variation in willingness to join (11 percent).

While not exactly repeating the pattern observed in Table 3, these predictors of latent unionism resemble the variables that were of some importance in the analysis of the various types of union attitudes. This suggests, of course, that if these union attitudes were added to this multiple regression equation, their effects on the self-reported measure of willingness to join would overwhelm the effects of the demographic, work-related, and political preference variables already in the equation. The second half of Table 4 contains the results of such an analysis.

The combination of union attitudes and other (previously significant) independent variables accounts for 37 percent of the variation in willingness to join a union. Both the "big labor" and the "business unionism" indices have significant net effects, although the impact of the former (beta = −.256) is relatively less than that of the latter (beta = .419). This is in line with our earlier observation—based on changes in support for each of these types of union attitudes in the two cities—that sentiments about business unionism were more important for explaining the willingness to join a union. Controlling for these two predictors, the anti-strikebreaking measure has little effect on workers' willingness to join a union. Furthermore, the effects of age (less likely to join) and current unemployment (more likely to join) remain statistically significant after adding these three attitudinal measures to the equation. The other variables which had accounted for a significant amount of the variation in latent unionism, however, are now of little consequence.

■ V. DISCUSSION

There is little evidence of growing support for negative "big labor" opinions about unions in Winnipeg and Edmonton. Our analysis of 1987 attitudes about "business unionism," however, does reveal an interesting reversal. In 1981, Winnipeg residents were significantly more likely to agree that unions looked after the wage and job security concerns of their members. In 1987, Edmonton residents were significantly more likely to agree with such sentiments. This community difference remains even after introducing into the regression analysis a series of individual-level control variables. The reversal in opinion is supported by a noticeable change in latent unionism. In 1981, a higher proportion of eligible labor force members in Winnipeg stated that they would join a union if one were available. By 1987, Edmonton showed a higher degree of latent unionism.

We interpret these community differences as a reflection of the economic downturn and continued high levels of unemployment in Edmonton. A larger proportion of 1987 Edmonton residents (compared to 1981 Edmonton residents or 1987 Winnipeg residents) may have personally experienced financial difficulties as a result of the recession, or they may have known others who did. Such experiences could have a positive influence on opinions about the monetary or job security benefits of union membership. But given what we already know about the complexity and potential contradictory nature of beliefs about unions, it should not surprise us that economic hard times have less effect on "big labor" beliefs or on opinions about the need for anti-strikebreaking legislation. Thus, many union supporters and many potential members might consciously extol the economic benefits of membership while at the same time believing that unions are too powerful. Views that may seem contradictory to the industrial relations scholar may be fairly consistent in the minds of the public.

Factors other than the economic recession may have influenced the changes in public opinion observed in Winnipeg and Edmonton. As noted earlier, Edmonton has experienced a number of high-profile industrial disputes, and 11 of the 16 provincial electoral constituencies in the city have been represented by the New Democratic party in the provincial legislature since 1986. In contrast, industrial relations and politics in Winnipeg have been marked by relative stability over this six-year period.[8] Although it is clear that the economic recession precipitated some of the labor disputes (and possibly the left-ward shift in voting patterns), this study cannot conclusively untangle the effects of economic, political, and industrial relations factors on public opinion about the unions. For that matter, some of the change in Edmonton may also be a result of selective out-migration over the past few years. If the most entrepreneurial (and least collectively oriented) residents of the city left because of the recession, pro-union attitudes could become more common. Even here, however, the evidence points back to changing economic climate as the key causal agent.

The Gainers strike is perhaps the best symbol of what we perceive as a changing industrial relations climate in Edmonton that did not have a parallel in Winnipeg. But our results do not support the hypothesis that the well-publicized violence associated with the use of replacement workers in the Gainers dispute led to more support for anti-strikebreaking legislation in Edmonton in 1987 compared to 1981. Yet, media research suggests that the content of news about unions and industrial relations can reinforce or change the views of certain segments of the public (see, e.g., Curran et al., 1987; Kiecolt and Sayles, 1988; Cohen and Young, 1981). Probing this issue further, we discovered some evidence of a media effect in our Edmonton data. We found a weak but statistically significant positive association between time spent watching television and agreement with the statement that management should be prohibited from hiring strikebreakers.[9] This minor finding raises more questions than it answers, but it is clear that the issue of media influences on public attitudes about unions constitutes an important research agenda.

On a more general note, this study underscores the contribution that community studies can make to our understanding of attitudes toward unions. Compared to studies of individual workplaces, community surveys provide a means of assessing opinions and preferences of the larger population. Public opinion, for example, can have an influence on labor legislation. Moreover, research into support of unionism within communities can provide union organizers with valuable information for planning future organizing drives. Finally, community studies provide a clear advantage over national public opinion polls when it comes to interpreting trends. Only with knowledge of the local economic, political, and industrial relations contexts—past and present—can we begin to understand why shifts in union attitudes might occur and why some beliefs are more pervasive than others.

Our multivariate findings document more conclusively the community effect on "business unionism" beliefs and show that voting preferences are consistently associated with union attitudes. Future research could fruitfully explore this link between political orientations and union attitudes, as Johnston and Ornstein (1985) and others have begun to do. Although those voting "left" are more supportive of unions, the relatively small effects of voting preference on union attitudes suggest a more complex process. Recognizing that the causal direction might be reversed, this weak relationship also explains why union support has failed to materialize at the ballot box in many Canadian elections.

The multivariate analyses show a small effect of age, education, and income on specific types of union attitudes, but they show few other important net effects. The low explained variance is consistent with research on political values, beliefs about inequality and welfare, and related topics (see, e.g., Kluegel, 1987). This state of affairs might reflect basic difficulties in measuring political and social values or attitudes. Alternatively, it could mean that surveys have not directly measured the underlying factors that influence such beliefs. In other words, our theoretical model of the sources of variation in union attitudes should be broadened to include the personal experience that individuals have had with unions; their socialization regarding collective bargaining through family or friends who are union members; and the political ideologies expressed in their families, schools, workplaces, and communities. These are important shaping influences that, if carefully studied, could advance our understanding of union-related attitudes and behaviors.

Notes

1. When confronted with the choice of either a female or a male respondent in a household, interviewers were instructed to request an interview with a male. If he refused, the woman would be asked to participate in the survey. This strategy resulted in a relatively equal female-male ration in the final sample.

2. By combining values of 1 and 2 and the values of 6 and 7, the Edmonton data were recoded into a 5-point scale when the data sets were merged.

3. The correlation between the two "big labor" items in the 1987 Edmonton sample was 0.55 compared to 0.42 in the Winnipeg sample. Correlations of 0.42 and 0.37 reflected the relationship between the two "business unionism" measures in the 1987 Edmonton and Winnipeg samples, respectively.

4. See Fiorito (1987, pp. 277-79) for further discussion of the "big labor" attitudinal dimension.

5. Although both cities show a drop of about five percentage points, the slightly larger change in Edmonton translates into a statistically significant difference ($p < .05$) while the Winnipeg change over time does not.

6. Rather than taking this decline as evidence of growing support for unions, following Johnston (1986, p. 67), one could interpret it as a loss of public confidence in governments' ability to legislate effectively. The 1987 Edmonton study included an additional item (omitted in Winnipeg) that stated: "We need more laws to limit the power of employers in dealing with unions." Only 37.6 percent of the Edmonton respondents agreed, suggesting that support for laws limiting unions is still stronger than support for laws limiting employers.

7. It could be argued that "yes, if I had to" might as easily signify an anti-union sentiment. Assuming this to be the case, we still observe more people answering with an unqualified "yes" in Edmonton than in Winnipeg, whereas the situation was reversed in the earlier study. And because at least some of the "yes" answers in Edmonton in 1981 were also qualified, we still would observe an increase in willingness to join in that city.

8. The Manitoba provincial election in the spring of 1988 saw the New Democratic government replaced by a minority Conservative government. Thus, the trend in the province and in Winnipeg appears to be to the political right, whereas the 1986 Alberta provincial election was the first left-ward swing in voting in that province, particularly in Edmonton.

9. Controlling for age and education (because older individuals and the less educated tend to watch more television), the partial correlation between the amount of television watched and support for prohibitions against strike-breaking was .155 ($N = 436$). Partial correlations between television viewing and the other four union attitude items were much smaller and *were* nonsignificant, with one exception. Responses to the statement about "the selfishness of employers can only be fought by strong unions" were significantly associated with TV viewing (partial correlation = .112; $N = 431$). The television-viewing question was not asked in the Winnipeg survey, so across-city comparisons are not possible.

References

Cohen, Stanley and Jock Young, eds. *The Manufacturing of News: Social Problems and the Mass Media*, revised edition. Beverly Hills: Sage, 1981.

Curran, James, Anthony Smith, and Pauline Wingate, eds. *Impacts and Influences: Essays on Media Power in the Twentieth Century*. London: Methuen, 1987.

Currie, Raymond F. "Selected Findings from the 1987 Winnipeg Area Study." Department of Sociology, University of Manitoba, Winnipeg Area Study Report No. 16, 1987.

Fiorito, Jack. "Political Instrumentality Perceptions and Desires for Union Representation." *Journal of Labour Research* 8 (Summer 1987): 271-89.

Johnston, William and Michael Ornstein. "Social Class and Political Ideology in Canada." *Canadian Review of Sociology and Anthropology* 22 (August 1985): 369-93.

Kiecolt, K. Jill and Marnie Sayles. "Television and the Cultivation of Attitudes Toward Subordinate Groups." *Sociological Spectrum* 8 (1988): 19-33.

Kinzel, Cliff. "Sampling Report: 1987 All-Alberta Study (Including the Edmonton Area Study)." Population Research Laboratory, Department of Sociology, University of Alberta, Edmonton Area Series Report No. 51, 1987.

Kluegel, James R. "Macro-economic Problems, Beliefs About the Poor and Attitudes Toward Welfare Spending." *Social Problems* 34 (February 1987): 82-99.

Kochan, Thomas A., Robert B. McKersie, and John Chalykoff. "The Effects of Corporate Strategy and Workplace Innovations on Union Representation." *Industrial and Labour Relations Review* 39 (July 1986): 487-501.

Krahn, Harvey and Graham S. Lowe. "Community Influences on Attitudes Towards Unions." *Relations Industrielles/Industrial Relations* 39 (1984a): 93-112.

_____. "Public Attitudes Towards Unions: Some Canadian Evidence." *Journal of Labor Research* 5 (Spring 1984b): 149-64.

_____. *Work, Industry and Canadian Society*. Scarborough, Ontario: Nelson Canada, 1988.

Lipset, Seymour Martin. "Labor Unions in the Public Mind." In *Unions in Transition: Entering the Second Century*. Edited by S.M. Lipset. San Francisco: ICS Press, 1986.

McShane, Steven L. "General Union Attitude: A Construct Validation." *Journal of Labor Research* 7 (Fall 1986): 403-17.

Milton, David. "Late Capitalism and the Decline of Trade Union Power in the United States." *Economic and Industrial Democracy* 7 (August 1986): 319-49.

Panitch, Leo and Donald Swartz. *The Assault on Trade Union Freedoms: From Consent to Coercion Revisited*. Toronto: Garamond Press, 1988.

■ POSTSCRIPT

The authors of these articles have used different indicators of union support. Reshef uses a survey of businesses in Alberta to measure the extent of unionization. Lowe and Krahn measure support via a public opinion survey. There are good reasons for using, or not using, either method.

A survey of businesses in various economic sectors allows the reseacher to determine the extent of unionization in that sector. It does not, however, measure the number of actual union members. It is possible that the percentage of workers belonging to unions in each of the sectors may be lower or higher than the percentage of unionized businesses. For example, although 30 percent of the firms in a given sector may be unionized, the number of unionized workers in that sector as a whole may be more or less than 30 percent. The size of particular businesses is a key variable not examined by Reshef.

A public opinion survey, using a random selection of the general public, allows the researcher to gage public support via examination of a cross section of the general population, both union and nonunion. This allows the researcher to determine if people join unions willingly or out of necessity in order to hold their jobs. It also allows the researcher to determine how many nonmembers would join a union if they could. One problem with this kind of research is that respondents who say "yes" or "no" to joining a union when responding to a questionnaire may make the opposite choice when faced with a real-life choice.

It is interesting to note that both debates observe that the Canadian labour movement may be headed for difficult times if it is unable to organize the service sector, a rapidly growing sector in Canada in which the labour movement has been unable to gain a strong foothold.

■ QUESTIONS

1. Which article do you believe has presented the most convincing case? Why do you believe it is the most convincing? How have your own thoughts on the value of unions affected your decision?

2. Which methodology for assessing union support do you prefer? Why do you prefer this method?

3. Could you suggest any other method by which support for unions might be measured?

4. How important is it to the future of the union movement that it organize the service sector?

■ FURTHER READING

In Support of Reshef

Gilson, C. and I. Spencer. "Trade Union Growth: A Marketing Model." *Industrial Relations/Relations Industrielles* 42 (1987): 756-773.

Riddell, W. Craig. "Canadian Labour Relations: An Overview." In *Canadian Labour Relations*. Edited by W.C. Riddell. Toronto: University of Toronto Press, 1986.

Troy, Leo. "Is the U.S. Unique in the Decline of Private Sector Unionism?" *Journal of Labor Research* 11, no. 2 (Spring 1990).

In Support of Lowe and Krahn

Freeman, Richard B. "Contraction and Expansion: Divergence of Private and Public Sector Unionism in the United States." *Journal of Economic Perspectives* 2 (Spring 1988): 63-88.

Johnson, Richard. *Public Opinion and Public Policy in Canada: Questions of Confidence.* Toronto: University of Toronto Press, 1986.

Other Voices

Lipset, Seymour Martin, ed. *Unions in Transition.* San Francisco: ICS Press, 1988.

Should pornography be illegal?

Is gun control effective?

Should retribution be the objective of criminal sanctions?

PART FIVE

INTRODUCTION

Issues of deviance and social control are of interest to many Canadians. This section deals with issues of pornography, spouse abuse, gun control, and prisons. The overlapping concern in each case is the potential for methods of social control to cause more harm than good. Are advocates of restrictive measures on pornography correct in saying that more harm is done if pornography is allowed to continue without restriction? Are anti-censorship advocates correct in saying that restricting pornography causes more harm by restricting individual rights? Is gun control legislation effective in either reducing the amount of crime committed with the use of a gun, or the availability of guns? Is gun control justified if it does not reduce criminal use of guns? Is the use of prisons justified if it cannot be shown to reduce crime, or if it can be shown that alternative measures have as much, or greater, potential to reduce crime? The debates in this section attempt to deal with these and other important issues of social control.

SHOULD

PORNOGRAPHY

BE ILLEGAL?

YES **Neil Boyd**, "Sexuality, Gender Relations and the Law: The Limits of Free Expression," in J. Lowman et al., eds., *Regulating Sex: An Anthology of Commentaries on the Findings of the Badgely and Fraser Reports*, pp. 127-141

NO **Jane Rhodes**, "Silencing Ourselves?: Pornography, Censorship and Feminism in Canada," *Resources for Feminist Research* 17, no. 3 (1988): 133-135

The debate over the legal status of pornography is part of the larger debate on censorship. Censorship is usually demanded on the grounds that the material in question will cause some form of social harm. For example, advocates of censorship argue that pornography harms women by promoting male sexual violence against women as well as hatred of women. Opponents of censorship, on the other hand, argue that a ban on pornography would result in more harm because it would restrict the presentation of material that does not cause harm.

One of the major issues in the pornography debate concerns its link to other forms of sexual deviance. Research suggests that exposure to pornographic materials in laboratory settings increases male sexual aggression (Donnerstein and Berkowitz, 1981; Malamuth and Check, 1981). For example, Donnerstein and Berkowitz found that males exposed to pornographic films, showing degrading, violent sex, were more likely than men shown erotic films, showing nondegrading, nonviolent sex, to display aggressive behaviour toward women after viewing the films.

Other researchers argue that laboratory findings are invalid because they do not deal with the real world (Fisher, 1986; Goldstein, 1973). For example, Fisher argues that the laboratory situation usually distorts or ignores the real-life potential for punishment of sexual aggression by implying or stating that sexually aggressive behaviour will receive either minimal or no punishment. Fisher also notes that these studies are based on nonrepresentative samples of university students; because of the assumed potential for less violent behaviour in this group, studies based on university students may underestimate the effect of pornography on male sexual aggression. Finally, Fisher says that the pornographic materials used in these studies are not representative of the type of pornography found in real life. The sexually explicit materials available to the general public are generally less violent than those used in studies.

The debate on whether or not laws protecting the right to free speech should apply to pornography depends, in part, on the conclusions reached in response to the debate on the effects of pornography on male sexual aggression. Those who perceive a link between pornography and sexual aggression cite this as a valid reason to prohibit pornography (Dworkin, 1985), while those who see no connection between the two not only reject laws banning pornography, but argue that banning pornography may cause more harm than allowing it to continue (Fisher, 1986; Diamond, 1986).

In the two articles presented here, Boyd, arguing for the "Yes" side, says that a legal ban on pornography is justified under certain conditions, while Rhodes, arguing on the "No" side, says that a ban on pornography initiated by a male-dominated society will lead only to more sophisticated forms of male domination.

References

Diamond, Sara (1986) "Childhood's End: Some Comments on Pornography and the Fraser Committee," in *Regulating Sex: An Anthology of Commentaries on the Findings and Recommendations of the Badgely and Fraser Reports*, edited by J. Lowman, M.A. Jackson, T.S. Palys, and S. Gavigan (Burnaby, B.C.: School of Criminology, Simon Fraser University).

Donnerstein, E. and L. Berkowitz (1981) "Victim Reactions in Aggressive Erotic Films as a Factor in Violence Against Women," *Journal of Personality and Social Psychology* 41, no. 4: 710-724.

Dworkin, Andrea (1985) "Against the Male Food: Censorship, Pornography and Equality," *Harvard Women's Law Journal* 8: 1-29.

Fisher, William A. (1986) "The Emperor has no Clothes: On the Fraser and Badgely Committees' Rejection of Social Science Research," in *Regulating Sex: An Anthology of Commentaries on the Findings and Recommendations of the Badgely and Fraser Reports*, edited by J. Lowman, M.A. Jackson, T.S. Palys, and S. Gavigan (Burnaby, B.C.: School of Criminology, Simon Fraser University).

Goldstein, M.M. (1973) "Exposure to Erotic Stimuli and Sexual Deviance," *Journal of Social Issues* 29, no. 3: 197-219.

Malamuth, N.M. and J. Check (1981) "The Effects of Mass Media Exposure on Acceptance of Violence against Women: A Filed Experiment," *Journal of Research in Personality* 15: 436-446.

SEXUALITY, GENDER RELATIONS AND THE LAW: THE LIMITS OF FREE EXPRESSION

Neil Boyd

Two recent federal initiatives, the Fraser and Badgley Committees, have once again focussed attention on the legal control of "inappropriate" forms of sexuality. In the realm of pornography—the topic under discussion in this article—we see a relatively new preoccupation with sexual violence, as distinct from sexuality itself. Images of sexual violence are viewed as deserving of state control; erotica—consenting adult sexuality—is seen as beyond the pale of the apparatus of criminalization.

This new emphasis, apparently inspired by the work of certain Anglo-American feminists, presents new questions. Are images of sexual violence problematic in themselves? Is it the message of the depiction of sexual violence that is at issue? And most important, how is this form of control—a criminal definition of pornography—conceptually separate from the hate propaganda provisions of the *Criminal Code*? . . .

Well, what are we supposed to do about all of this? We have no shortage of solutions—from criminal prohibition of sexually explicit film[1] (see Boyd, 1985, p. 23), to civil suits for violations of women's rights (Burstyn, 1985, pp. 206-208), to pornography as political speech, properly protected by the emancipatory rhetoric of Canada's *Charter of Rights and Freedoms* (Arbour, 1985). . . .

■ NEW DIRECTIONS FOR PORNOGRAPHY CONTROL?

The Special Committee on Pornography and Prostitution (the Fraser Committee), created by the Trudeau government, submitted its report to Parliament in April of 1985. The Committee was established to respond to public concerns about prostitution and pornography. The phenomenon of street prostitution and the skilful advocacy of many "anti-pornography" women's groups prodded the government into taking some form of action. The Fraser Report suggests a significant shift in focus for the legal control of pornography, urging that sexual violence can be differentiated from explicit sexuality. The Report makes a substantial number of thoughtful recommendations, but its basic tone is clear enough—images of consenting sexuality are not properly the concern of the criminal law. I want to concentrate on two recommendations—the proposed definition of pornography and the role set out for the community standards test of criminal status.

The Committee would rewrite the existing obscenity section of the *Criminal Code*, criminalizing first, pornography in which real physical harm takes place, and second, pornography that depicts sexual violence. Two defences are created in the instances of sexually violent material— neither depictions of sexual violence with genuine educational or scientific purpose, nor depictions of violence with artistic merit would be prosecuted.

The difficulty here comes in accepting the notion that "depictions or descriptions" of sexually violent behavior should be considered criminal in nature, unless justified by artistic merit, or educational or scientific purpose. The variable of social class can too easily enter this formula for restricting expression. Depictions of sexual violence could be tasteless and banal, without actually promoting violence or gender-based hatred. Perhaps more important, the force of the image must always contend with the highly variable imagination of the given viewer (Rich, 1983). The cost incurred in prohibiting depictions of sexual violence is the creation of an over-inclusive system of criminalization.

Although the Fraser Committee proposal substantially improves upon section 159(8) of the present Code, it is not clear that tinkering with the legal definition of sexually violent pornography gets directly at the point of criminal control—is the impugned material hate literature, the advocacy or condonation of violence on the basis of gender?

Perhaps the most important contribution of the Fraser Committee's discussion on the law of obscenity relates to the issue of community standards—the notion that Canadian judges should be guided by community opinion in assigning criminal status to a publication or film imagery. The Committee writes persuasively:

> Simply because a majority of Canadians are said to tolerate or not tolerate something tells us nothing about their reasons for doing so and hence gives us no opportunity to decide whether they are indeed valid. It is our view that decisions in respect to criminal charges should be made on the basis of clearly articulated principles and not on the basis of majoritarian impulses. (p. 269)

The Canadian judiciary have had similar difficulties with the notion of community tolerance in the federal sphere of criminal definition. In *R. v. Prairie Schooner News*, Justice Dickson (as he then was) wrote, "the 'community' whose standards are being considered is all of Canada. The universe from which the 'sample' is to be selected must be representative of Canada and not be drawn from a single city."[2] In *R. v. Pink Triangle Press*, the Ontario Court of Appeal rules that there is no requirement that public opinion surveys on the subject of community standards form a part of the evidence led by the Crown, that it is ultimately the duty of the Court to determine the legal question of community tolerance.[3] While the Canadian community's standard of tolerance is amenable to empirical test, both Crown and defence have been reluctant to enter the fray, in any kind of systematic manner. The judiciary's construction of strict methodological requirements and the consequent costs of empirical study have tended to work against any routine introduction of opinion survey evidence. Implicit in such judicial analysis is the notion that research susceptible to any methodological criticism cannot be of any assistance to the court; the judiciary has often declined the role of evaluating social science data. Given the availability of both Crown and defence counsel to call expert testimony to assist the court, this seems an unnecessary reluctance.

And yet, as the Fraser Committee suggests, the community standards test remains inherently problematic, notwithstanding the practical difficulties involved in meaningful application. While community tolerance is crucial in circumscribing and enabling legitimate speech, it ought not to be determinative of a criminal sanction. The criminal powers of the state should be invoked for something more than mere intolerance.

The Fraser Committee writes of the community standards test of obscenity:

> Many people at the hearings criticized the community standards test referred to above as unworkable. We think that this component tells us more about the viewer, or hypothetical viewer, of the material than about the material itself. Although we are concerned that persons not be forced to look at or consume material which they find offensive, we think that provisions aimed at that problem are a better solution than a definition of pornography which contains as a key element this subjective approach. (p. 268)

The Fraser Committee is urging a definition of pornography that is also subjective—the criminalization of "sexually violent and degrading pornography." But as the Committee has noted, the problem posed by community tolerance lies less with its opaque subjectivity, and more with its potentially objective accounting of intolerance, an inappropriate target for criminal prohibition. In summary, then, the general direction of the Fraser Report reveals a sensitivity to the community standard benchmark, the problematics of the Committee's legal definition of pornography notwithstanding.

It is more difficult to send similar plaudits in the direction of the Badgley Committee. The Committee on Sexual Offenses Against Children and Youth submitted its report to the short-lived Turner government in August 1984, drawing some overly definitive lines on the subject of adolescent sexuality. The Badgley Committee was concerned with the potential sexual abuse of children in a variety of contexts, and its recommendations have received significant criticism from civil libertarians and others. In relation to pornography, the Committee urged that explicit sex films with participants under the age of 18 should be criminalized, and that pictures of explicit sex should not be seen by those under 16, criminal conviction the consequence of a known viewing.

These proposals seem problematic, particularly when coupled with the Badgley Committee's perception of the age of sexual responsibility. They argue for a minimum age of 18, and in a commentary that seems more than a trifle homophobic, they write (1984):

There is considerable medical opinion that sexual orientation is settled by age 16. There is also opinion to the contrary. The Committee is concerned that legal protection be retained where it may be useful to young persons. The Badgley Committee would therefore not reduce the age of sexual autonomy to 16 in the absence of persuasive evidence that such a reduction would pose no risk to developing sexual behavior. (p. 19)

This kind of analysis teeters on the brink of silliness; sexual orientation is not properly *enforced* by a process of criminalization. There is no doubt that the relationship between age and informed consent is a key to policy development. But do we want to get involved in punishing adolescent sexuality simply because we are afraid that heterosexual preference might be jeopardized by early sexual explorations? The moral logic of the criminal law requires at least some representation of social harm.

▮ THE LANGUAGE OF LEGAL CONTROL: ALTERNATIVES

Now, having acknowledged that pornography may facilitate social harm, and that the ideal targets of legal control seem elusive, we are faced with a number of competing strategies—the *Criminal Code*, the possibility of civil damages for loss of rights, taxation, provincial jurisdiction, and protection of pornography as free speech.

It is with this last strategy, the notion of limiting free expression, that the legal control of pornography faces perhaps its greatest challenge. Louise Arbour (1985) has argued that pornography is best conceptualized as political speech, and as such, qualifies for constitutional protection. She discusses the argument that pornography causes social harm and concludes that no cause-effect relationships can be sustained, that pornography is not political speech which creates "a clear and present danger" to women.

The claim is both fair and reasonable. But I am not sure of Arbour's contention, "There must, therefore, be something about pornography, apart from its advocacy and promotion of subordination of women, that makes it suitable for democratic limits" (Arbour, 1985).[4] I am inclined to find a rather thin line between the advocacy of subordination and the advocacy of hatred or violence.

And I cannot take what would seem to be Professor Arbour's further step here, i.e., defending non-prosecution of the advocacy and promotion of violence or hatred by gender. The subordination of women is a pervasive feature of social life, and is regrettable, but the promotion of violence or hatred that is gender specific is intolerable.

What Arbour's work does do, my own reservations notwithstanding, is, first, usefully place options of social control in context, and, second, classify pornography as political speech. In discussion of civil remedies, she expresses concerns about giving provinces and municipalities powers of prohibition. She writes (1985):

Previous legislative efforts on the part of a province to suppress the communication of ideas have not survived the encroachment on the federal criminal law power that was inherent in the types of remedies they adopted ... Anything beyond compensation in the form of damages may be found to amount to an attempt to legislate with respect to criminal law by using remedies more suited to the protection of a public interest than to the vindication of a private right. (p. 18)

This wariness of extending the power of prohibition seems warranted. As Arbour suggests, there is little hope or solace to be found "In mustering legal resources and public funds to 'silence the enemy.' " But unlike Arbour I do see value in using the criminal courtroom as a forum for debate about the boundaries of free expression. Arbour concludes her paper by arguing that, "Banning more things, more often, can only contribute to this deplorable legalization of morality and worse, in feminists' terms, to the legalization of politics."

I do not agree that the legalization of morality is an inherently deplorable matter, and do not perceive that law and politics are fairly separated. All law reflects morality, albeit in complex form, and law is simply a construction of power relations (i.e., politics). When we define categories of assault we are making moral judgements, prohibiting forms of social expression. Further, Arbour's reservations about the role of censorship in the admittedly political discourse of pornography do not seem to be entirely pivotal here. We must first acknowledge that the law already structures political speech through ever changing, if highly inequitable, allocations of resources; I cannot easily express concern over the "legalization of politics."

This is a separation of subject matter that is difficult to appreciate; one can agree with the notion that the law should not be the site of all political struggle, particularly given its historic and continuing role of buttressing patriarchal relations. But women have also seen their resistance enshrined in legal reforms; the law is not simply a vehicle that upholds male privilege. There are some difficulties, then, with the epistemology that underlies "the legalization of politics." The law can often be a valued site of social change; to argue otherwise is to argue for a jurisprudence that is morally sterile (Thompson, 1975).

With the criminal law itself, our first possibility, that of retaining the status quo, is problematic. The prohibition of the "undue exploitation of sex" is difficult to justify; the pleasures of sexuality between consenting adults cannot be unduly exploited. Perhaps more important, the combined weight of recent judicial pronouncements and the Fraser Report suggest that a new criminal definition of pornography is already upon us. It seems fair to say that the state is becoming at least somewhat less inclined to limit adult expression in the sexual sphere (although Bill C-114, which was introduced in June 1986 and defined all explicit sexual imagery as pornographic, certainly reverses this trend).

The language of the Fraser Committee takes us down a new road, placing an onus upon those who distribute sexually violent images to justify those images on the basis of artistic merit, educational or scientific purpose. There is certainly some value to this proposal; gratuitous sexual violence does not seem to be a commodity worth protecting under the veil of free expression. The criticism that the Fraser Committee definition is vague, and hence unlikely to be useful, is also not compelling. Obscenity is defined by the individual case; the common law gives life to a very general statement of principle.

And yet, as suggested earlier, sexual violence itself is not really a coherent category of behavior, easily capable of definition. There can be consenting involvement in bondage, a ritualized performance of sex with images of dominance, but without a dominance inherent in gender; there is a sense in which bondage can be a parody of power relations between consenting adults. And yet there are those who suggest that such a form of sexual expression is a form of sexual violence; so much must hinge on the imaginations of the participants and the issue of informed consent.

My point is that depictions or descriptions of sexual violence become problematic when they either urge or condone such behavior; the control of pornography is properly the control of a kind of hate propaganda by gender. Further, though, to the extent that the criminal definition of obscenity is reformed as "sexually violent," or more pointedly, simply as "violent," the opportunities for a theoretically relevant body of case law accelerate appreciably. It is a small step from sexually violent behavior to the dissemination of hatred by gender.

Perhaps the most novel method of pornography control is that popularized in Minneapolis by Catherine McKinnon and Andrea Dworkin. The city ordinance gives power to women (and men) to collect civil damages for pornography's presumed harms. The ordinance defines pornography as the "sexually explicit subordination of women, graphically depicted, whether in pictures or in words." Women who "are presented as dehumanized sexual objects, things, or commodities" can gain compensation from those who have produced such images. While the interest here is that of limiting sexist content, it is not clear that this is a form of legal control that can be easily focussed.

Varda Burstyn (1985, p. 161) and others have dismissed such civil remedies as "dangerous," but Dworkin is undaunted, writing (1985):

> The civil rights law puts a flood of light on the pornography, what it is, how it is used, what it does, those who are hurt by it. The civil rights law changes the power relationship between pornographers and women: it stops the pornographers from producing discrimination with the total impunity they now enjoy, and gives women a legal standing resembling equality from which to repudiate the subordination itself. (p. 23)

This is certainly a bold approach, calling men (and in some few cases, women) into court for the actionable private wrong of objectification. But where do we end this crusade? The pages of *Cosmopolitan* and the like are replete with potential clients, and a significant amount of all advertising depends upon a "dehumanized sexual commodity" to sell its product. Dworkin and MacKinnon are arguing for a revolution in the form of law; the target of social wrath here seems at times to be as much male or female lust as male or female subordination. There is certainly some point in an attraction to a body part that yields pleasure: objectification, like promiscuity, has its time and place. To put the matter bluntly, penises, vaginas and breasts are all fairly cast as "objects" of pleasure; they are quite understandably valued for the enjoyment that they give. Dworkin and MacKinnon have simply cut too wide a swath in their creation of the Minneapolis ordinance. Civil remedies for gender-based discrimination are sound state policy, but answers do not lie in law that casts too wide a net.

One state strategy for pornography control that is seldom considered is that of increased taxation, treating the material like alcohol or tobacco, a potentially dangerous product for which all customers should pay a surcharge; the taxes collected could fund organizations of victimized women. There is considerable appeal in this argument; pornography is like a drug that can easily be abused. Consumers are buying the promise and ultimately the lie of infinite attractiveness. Nonetheless, the utility of a taxation scheme is also problematic. Taxation would simply give access to pornography based on income; taxation also has a focus that may not go to the heart of the issue in dispute; the legitimacy of existing industry might be ensured, with the state dependent on anticipated revenue.

To conclude this discussion of legal alternatives, I develop a theme that has been neglected to this point—the relation of the criminal power of prohibition to the provincial power of censorship. In Bill C-19 the Trudeau government suggested the following amendment to the *Criminal Code*, ultimately rejected by the Fraser Committee:

> Where any film or videotape is presented, published or shown in accordance with a classification or rating established for films or videotapes pursuant to the law of the province in which the film or videotape is presented, published or shown, no proceeding shall be instituted under section 159 or 163 in respect of such presentation, publication or showing or in respect of the possession of the film or videotape for any such purpose without the personal consent of the Attorney General.

The section highlights the value of Censor Board decision-making in the sphere of film censorship and classification. While the criminal process may still be invoked against a provincially classified film, it is set out here as an extraordinary circumstance, requiring "the personal consent of the Attorney General." The section raises the profile of any public conflict that may develop between law enforcement perceptions of the boundaries of free expression, and Censor Board perceptions of properly prohibited material. Insofar as provincial powers of censorship diffuse responsibility for determining the limits of free expression, and honor regional variations divorced from a mythical national standard of tolerance, they can be seen as desirable. In this formulation, municipal control of expression can be viewed as a further progressive step. Decision-making is made more accessible to a greater number of individuals through a decentralization of political authority, and regional variations are increasingly reflected by relatively autonomous networks of control.

And yet there is another side to this tension. The Fraser Committee does not support the delegation of a power of prohibition to the provinces or municipalities. They write of the discretionary power given provincial attorneys general in C-19:

> We recognize that whether they have explicit power to ban films or not, an authority will inevitably make a preliminary determination of whether, in its view, a film offends the Criminal Code. Yet, even though this determination about criminality is going to be made, we do not think that it is desirable to elevate the board's judgement to the status of a defence or a discretionary bar to prosecution. If the board's decision were to constitute a full defence, then we would have, in effect, a delegation to provincial authorities of administration of the criminal law sanction. Where the decision of the board is a discretionary bar to prosecution, as in Bill C-19, the delegation is not complete, but the concern remains the same. (p. 335)

The Committee appears unwilling to allow individual provinces to make these modest contributions to the definition of prohibited expression in the spheres of gender relations and sexuality, giving jurisdictional purity as a justification for restricting the provincial role. There is some merit in their approach; an entirely local or even provincial definition of prohibited expression undermines the federal criminal law power—there is a tension between Canada's definitions of deviance and local or regional definitions, not an inevitable or desirable separability.

It may not be the case, however, that the greater provincial role suggested in Bill C-19 unfairly challenges federal supremacy. The provinces may produce competing definitions of properly prohibited expression, but the Supreme Court looms as a national forum of last resort (as does the House of Commons).

And yet the ideal structure of criminal control remains elusive, with criminalization, taxation, civil remedies, jurisdictional decentralization, and free speech all cast as potentially viable options. The argument that I have tried to set out here is one that looks beyond the sexual violence debate currently occupying the attention of many policy makers and academics. The arguments in favor of more restricted control of pornography are compelling; images of sexual violence are only fairly impugned if they advocate hatred by gender.

But this debate and these arguments are not really at the heart of the social storm that whirls about pornography. Pornography is most specifically and typically the advocacy of a sexual lie—the naked females of *Playboy* and the like are cast as eager and willing to serve the desires of the male and his formidable penis. This fantasy is fairly cast as illusion and deceit, and though it only deserves the scrutiny of the criminal process in the event that it advocates gender-based hatred, its pervasiveness remains a less than thrilling commentary on sexual relations in contemporary social life.

Notes

1. This was proposed in legislation (Bill C-114) tabled by the Conservative government in June 1986.
2. *R. v. Prairie Schooner News Ltd. and Powers*, (1970) 1 C.C.C. (2d) 251, 75 W.W.R. 585.
3. *R. v. Pink Triangle Press*, (1980) 45 C.C.C. (2d) (Ontario County Court).
4. Much of what follows here is edited from a presentation given at the Canadian Law and Society Meeting, held in Montreal, May 1985.

References

Arbour, L. "The Politics of Pornography: Towards an Expansive Theory of Constitutionally Protected Expression." Paper presented to the Pacific Institute of Law and Public Policy, Vancouver. March 1985.

Burstyn, V. (ed.). *Women Against Censorship*. Toronto: Douglas and McIntyre. 1985.

Committee on Sexual Offenses Against Children and Youth (the Badgley Committee). *Sexual Offences Against Children*. Ottawa: Department of Supply and Services. 1984.

Dworkin, A. "Against the Male Flood: Censorship, Pornography and Equality." *Harvard Women's Law Journal*, Vol. 8, pp. 1-29. 1985.

Rich, R. "Anti-Porn: Soft Issue, Hard World." *Feminist Review*, Vol. 13, Spring, pp. 56-76. 1983.

Special Committee on Pornography and Prostitution (the Fraser Committee). *Report of the Special Committee on Pornography and Prostitution*. 2 Vols. Ottawa: Department of Supply and Services. 1985.

Thompson, E.P. *Whigs and Hunters: The Origins of the Black Act*. New York: Pantheon. 1975.

SILENCING OURSELVES? PORNOGRAPHY, CENSORSHIP AND FEMINISM IN CANADA

NO

Jane Rhodes

The anti-pornography legislation (Bill C-54) recently proposed by the federal government has been criticized by numerous groups in Canada representing a range of interests. Artists, writers, librarians and a growing contingent of feminists are among those who oppose censorship laws. Historicially, feminists have been more closely allied with the position that violent pornography begets sexual violence and that there is a correlation between the availability of pornography and the incidence of sexual assault. For this reason many feminists have, in the past, advocated censorship as a means to prohibit images which incite violence or are degrading to women. Despite numerous studies, however, it has never been conclusively shown whether pornography creates abusive men or abusive men create a market for pornography. What is more certain, though, is that censorship will encompass much more than abusive pictures in men's magazines and films. Many of the words and images which sustain and invigorate the feminist movement could be restricted or prohibited, according to the definitions given in the recent anti-pornography bill. Women are beginning to consider the far-reaching effects of government-controlled censorship and to examine whether the possible benefits of censorship outweigh the negative results.

In this paper I address the concern that anti-pornography legislation will enable the courts to censor the broad range of words and images which could, in fact, jeopardize the progress of the women's movement.

An historical examination of censorship legislation in Canada reveals that there has been a shift in the definition of pornography, from something which causes moral corruption to something which causes physical and emotional damage to women and children. It is encouraging that legislators have finally acknowledged that the issue is not whether men have been corrupted by pornography but rather that women and children have been victimized by it. However, the interpretation of what is pornographic remains a subjective exercise and it is therefore not possible to provide an exhaustive inventory of pornographic images. Although anti-pornography legislation and the proposed amendments have become increasingly explicit, they necessarily leave much to the judgment of the courts.

The pornography debate in Canada, as elsewhere, has been burdened with semantic problems. In this country, anti-pornography legislation has hinged on a number of subjective and emotionally-charged terms such as obscenity, depravity and moral corruption. Until 1959, obscenity was defined in the courts by the *Hicklin* test:

329

Whether the tendency of the matter charged as obscene is to deprave and corrupt those whose minds are open to such immoral influences, and into whose hands a publication of this sort must fall.[1]

Depending on the prevailing political or religious attitudes of the court, the interpretation of what is "corrupt" could have a profound effect on freedom of expression.

The Criminal Code of Canada is the current source of anti-pornography legislation in Canada. Section 159 was most recently amended in 1959 in order to provide a more explicit definition of obscenity. According to it,

... any publication a dominant characteristic of which is the undue exploitation of sex, or of sex and any one or more of the following subjects, namely, crime, horror, cruelty and violence, shall be deemed to be obscene (section 159.8).

Although more explicit, the meaning of the legislation remains vague. What exactly is "undue exploitation of sex"? Case law has established that "undueness" is measured in accordance with community standards, that the "community" means the aggregation of all Canadians and that "standards" may change over time.[2] Currently, community standards in Canada are still very much defined within a patriarchal framework in which traditional family and religious values prevail. It is clearly undesirable to have a system of state censorship which incorporates the values that feminists have been trying to dismantle. The legislation effectively reinforces the patriarchal system by giving the male-dominated courts the power to censor certain images which do not conform to community standards in a patriarchal society.

An example of this is the obscenity charges laid in 1985 against Pages Bookstore in Toronto. Owner Marc Glassman had encouraged local artists to use the store window to display their art. A group of feminist artists known collectively as The Woomers installed an exhibit which focused on a variety of objects common to female experience, including plaster penises and sanitary napkins which had been stained with red paint. Throughout the case there remained the perception that it was the sanitary napkins that had inspired the police to lay the charge, not the display of sex toys. One of Glassman's lawyers, Lynn King, commented, "They have the right to lay the charge, of course. But, I can't help wondering—if men had periods, would they find this sort of thing disgusting?"[3]

For 14 months, anxieties and expenses amounted for the bookstore's owner and manager who faced a maximum of two years in jail and/or a $5000 fine. The charges were finally dismissed in July 1986 when the court found that Section 159 of the Criminal Code was an unreasonable infringement on freedom of expression guaranteed by the Charter of Rights and Freedoms. The installation, however, had long since been dismantled and confiscated by the police. Despite the dismissal of the charges, the artists had been silenced.

The police can lay criminal charges against anyone who makes, prints, publishes, distributes or sells anything which depicts the "undue exploitation of sex" or, from a feminist standpoint, anything which does not conform to the standards of a patriarchal society. The subjective determination of what constitutes undue exploitation to the police and the courts has resulted in an uneven application of the law in Canada. Depictions of gay male sex, for example, have routinely been censored (*The Body Politic*, a now defunct Canadian gay journal, and Glad Day Books in Toronto have been targets of harassment) while depictions of similar activities performed by heterosexuals are available at the corner store. This would suggest that the "community" has determined that depictions of men abusing women are more acceptable than even non-abusive depictions of men with men.

The Criminal Code provisions on obscenity are also linked with the Customs Tariff Act regulating the importation of obscene materials. Community standards, and degrees of tolerance, vary from province to province, resulting in an inconsistent definition of obscenity along Canadian borders. As well, film censorship is provincially regulated and intended to reflect local community standards. The Ontario Film Review Board, for example, is regarded as one of the most restrictive censor boards in the country.

Throughout the 1980s there has been growing dissatisfaction with the vague and subjective nature of anti-pornography legislation in Canada. In response to this, the Special Committee on Pornography and Prostitution (the "Fraser Committee") was formed by the federal Liberal government in order to gauge the public's attitude towards pornography and censorship legislation. In the winter of 1983-84 the Fraser Committee travelled throughout Canada, listening to various points of view and recording the conflicting evidence.

The immediate mobilization of women's groups which favoured stronger censorship laws was a credit to the organizing abilities of feminists throughout Canada, and it caught the anti-censorship feminists unprepared.[4] Most of the submissions provided an emotional purge for all women who are sickened by the extent of violent and degrading pornography, but few attempted to address the specifics of law reform. Since the Fraser Committee Report, the Conservative government has made repeated efforts to introduce amendments to the Criminal Code which would eliminate the vagueness of the current wording and explicitly define the types of activities which, if depicted, could be censored. In the history of anti-pornography legislation in Canada there has been a marked tendency towards increasingly specific language. There is a corollary to this. As the net is flung further to encompass more and more specific acts deemed to be pornographic, it also entangles an increasingly wide range of things which are acceptable to all but the most prudish. For example, Bill C-54 would make it unlawful for children visiting art galleries or libraries to view paintings or illustrations of nudes.

If the anti-censorship feminists were unprepared for the Fraser Committee hearings, the explicit wording of the proposed amendments to the Criminal Code has galvanized them—and other civil libertarians—for battle. At stake is the freedom of creative expression, whether in the service of art or political and social dissent. Librarians, artists, writers, curators, teachers, booksellers, publishers and others have actively begun to organize against an amendment which would force them to curtail the production, display or distribution of certain words and images.

In 1986 Justice Minister John Crosbie introduced an anti-pornography bill (Bill C-114) to amend the Criminal Code. It replaced the word "obscenity" with "pornography" and provided a more detailed definition of what is meant by pornography. It identifies pornography as:

> ... any visual matter showing vaginal, anal or oral intercourse, ejaculation, sexually violent behavior, bestiality, incest, necrophilia, masturbation or other sexual activity.

Although the wording is no longer as subjective, it encompasses a disturbingly wide range of behaviour. The inclusion of "other sexual activity" could, for example, refer to something as innocuous as kissing. Not surprisingly, the bill incurred extensive criticism and died shortly after being introduced.

Justice Minister Ramon Hnatyshyn, Crosbie's successor, introduced a new anti-pornography bill in May 1987. Taking the tendency towards more specific wording one step further, Bill C-54 replaced the phrase "other sexual activity" with an explicit and far-reaching list of sexual activities. Critics who had disparaged the vague wording of Section 159 of the Criminal Code and its earlier proposed amendments were now stunned by the sweeping range of images that would be expressly prohibited under the new bill. Pornography would not only encompass physical degradation, violence and the sexual exploitation of women and children, but it would also include any visual matter depicting bestiality, incest, necrophilia, masturbation or ejaculation, as well as anal, oral or vaginal intercourse. The bill makes no attempt to distinguish between depictions of consensual sexual activity and images of overt domination and coercion of women.

Bill C-54 also introduces the concept of "erotica" as something distinct from pornography. Erotica is defined as the visual depiction of "a human sexual organ, a female breast or the human anal region" in a sexual context. It is doubtful that the courts could conclusively determine what constitutes a "sexual context" because any image of a naked body or its constituent parts is potentially stimulating to some people. Thus the wording could be interpreted to mean that nudity could be defined as erotica. Unlike pornography, erotica is not illegal unless it is displayed, sold or rented to persons under 18 years of age or unless it depicts the body of a person who is, or appears to be, under 18 years of age. The bill stipulates that if erotica materials are not hidden by a barrier or wrapper then a prominent warning notice must be posted to advise viewers that erotica is on display. In other words, it would be unlawful for art galleries or libraries to display images of nudes, either as art or illustrations in books, to persons under 18 years of age, and it would be necessary to isolate such images from the larger collection in order to restrict public access.

The Art Gallery of Ontario's Reference Library recently estimated that 55 percent of its collection contained pornographic or erotic images. According to the proposed law, art books containing erotic images would have to be restricted to adult use. Books containing pornographic images would have to be removed from the shelves. Having to distinguish what is erotic and what is pornographic from what is morally acceptable would be a daunting task for librarians, curators, booksellers and others, and would force them to practice self-censorship.

Further, if an image on display is considered pornographic or erotic by the police, then the persons responsible for displaying that image are guilty of a criminal offence until they prove their innocence, based on the permitted defences of artistic merit or educational, scientific or medical purpose. This shifting of the burden of proof runs counter to the general principles of the Criminal Code which assumes innocence until proven guilty. The difficulty of proving the artistic merit or the educational, scientific or medical purpose of an image could be a time-consuming and expensive legal procedure, prone to endless speculation and subjective interpretations. For artists and writers who could not afford legal proceedings, harmful precedents could be established by default.

Feminists who have sought to curb violent and degrading pornography through legislative controls have found themselves in an uncomfortable alliance with religious fundamentalists and other groups representing the New Right. Although both groups advocate state regulation of sexual imagery, their agendas and objectives are very different. To reinforce the traditional moral values which uphold patriarchal structures, the New Right persistently attacks the central tenets of feminism, including sex education in schools, access to birth control and abortion, and gay and lesbian rights. Their opposition to pornography has more to do with maintaining sexual repression than with concerns about the violence and degradation of women.

Feminists, on the other hand, are opposed to sexual repression because, in part, it carries with it the negative connotation that sexuality—especially female sexuality—is offensive. Women have begun to criticize the dominating nature of male sexual power and to investigate our own erotic empowerment. Depictions of consensual sexual activity, at the very least, encourage healthier sexual attitudes and serve to offset the negative values embedded in exploitive pornography. However, the recently proposed amendments to the Criminal Code define depictions of consensual sex as pornographic and would empower the courts to censor any visual celebration of female sexuality and any critique of the inequitable nature of sexual power. The result of anti-pornography legislation could, ironically, be the creation of an increasingly repressive environment for women, where freedom of expression would be subject to interpretation by male-dominated courts.

Much of the opposition to censorship has come from artists and writers who regard freedom of expression as an essential condition for the creation of their art. Art is a process of revelation, bound to explore truthfully all areas of human experience and to reflect the social conditions which have informed its creation. Censorship of art has frequently been invoked in history in order to quell dissent and buttress unjust regimes. Michelangelo's *Last Judgment*, for example, was very nearly destroyed by Pope Clement VIII because the depiction of nude bodies did not conform to Catholic doctrine established in the Council of Trent. Despite Michelangelo's objections, draperies were painted over many of the nudes. From the repressive puritanism of Girolamo Savonarola in 15th century Florence, to the zealous iconoclasm of the Reformation and, more recently, to the proscriptive cultural policies of Stalin and Hitler, art has often been forced to pay homage to political and religious tyrants.

Comparing anti-pornography legislation in Canada with the restrictive censorship policies of the Stalinists and Nazis may seem to be a hysterical response, but there is, in fact, no reason to suppose that Canadian courts would not impose a rigid interpretation of the law. Though Justice Minister Hnatyshyn assured the Toronto Public Library that it was not the intention of the proposed amendment to prosecute librarians for having sexually-explicit materials on their shelves, his successors are not legally bound to share his opinion. And if his successors do not share Hnatyshyn's attitude, countless librarians, artists, booksellers, filmmakers, and so on, could lawfully be fined and imprisoned for producing and distributing pornography.

Much of the art produced by feminists falls within the definition of pornography or erotica given in the recently proposed amendment to Section 159 of the Criminal Code. Political artists such as Sue Coe provide unflinching images of man's inhumanity to other men and women. Coe forces the viewer to confront uncomfortable truths, from images of sexual assault to the oppressive atmosphere of apartheid, thus providing an enraged response to the depicted injustice. The work of feminist artists such as Joyce Wieland, Elvira Bach and Judy Chicago would fall within the definition of erotica in the proposed amendment and could therefore only be viewed in areas restricted to adults. Prohibiting children under the age of 18 years from viewing nudity in art introduces a repressive element to their sexual awareness and discourages healthy attitudes and open discussion about sexuality. At the same time, the legislation would not restrict most of the advertising images which depict women as sexual commodities. Children would be left with the message that sexuality is bad and, by extension, that women are bad because they are popularly identified as sex objects.

The problem that must be confronted with regard to anti-pornography legislation is not whether pornography encourages violence against women but whether censorship could actually silence the women's movement. Although violent and degrading pornography, marketed for the sexual stimulation of men, is abhorrent in all of its manifestations, the introduction of censorship could deprive women of the means to expose and criticize the underlying reasons for the existence of pornography. Making pornography illegal will not make it go away, it will only drive it underground and into the more expert domain of organized crime. Attitudes towards pornography can only be altered through progressive education programs and unrestricted debate. Freedom of expression is a fundamental condition of the development of a more equitable social structure, one that could redress oppressive depictions of female sexuality and encourage more open-minded attitudes towards sex. Censorship imposed by a patriarchal system would only impede our progress towards those goals.

Notes

1. *The Queen v. Hicklin* (1968) L.R. # Q.B. 360, 37 L.J.M.C. 89, 11 Cox C.C. 19, 18 L.T.R. (n.s.) 395.

2. Ridington, Jillian. *Freedom from Harm or Freedom of Speech?: A Feminist Perspective on the Regulation of Pornography* (Ottawa: National Association of Women and the Law, 1983), p. 3.

3. Quoted in Smith, Kathleen M. "Object Lesson," *T.O.* Winter 1985-86.

4. Burstyn, Varda. "Porn Again: Feeling the Heat of Censorship," *FUSE* vol. 10, no. 6 (Spring 1987), p. 12.

References

A Space Exhibition Committee. *Issues of Censorship.* Toronto: A Space, 1985.

Burstyn, Varda, ed. *Women Against Censorship.* Vancouver: Douglas and McIntyre, 1985.

Carmilly-Weinberger, Moshe. *Fear of Art: Censorship and Freedom of Expression in Art.* New York: R.R. Bowker, 1986.

Donnerstein, Edward, Daniel Linz, and Steven Penrod. *The Question of Pornography: Research Findings and Policy Implications.* New York: The Free Press, 1987.

Hovan, George. "Bill C-54: An Issue of Censorship." *ArtAction* 12, no. 3 (September 1987), pp. 7-10.

Lederer, Laura, ed. *Take Back the Night: Women on Pornography.* New York: William Morrow, 1980.

Ontario Film and Video Appreciation Society and Its Advisory Board. *A Brief to the Special Committee on Pornography and Prostitution from O.F.A.V.A.S.* Toronto: CARO, 1984.

Ridington, Jillian. *Freedom From Harm or Freedom of Speech?: A Feminist Perspective on the Regulation of Pornography.* Ottawa: National Association of Women and the Law, 1983.

Sex, Politics and Censorship: A Public Discussion. Papers by panelists Anna
   Gronau, Gary Kinsman, Varda Burstyn. Toronto: Canadian Artists' Repre-
   sentation Ontario, 1984.
Valverde, Mariana. *Sex, Power and Pleasure.* Toronto: The Women's Press, 1985.

■ POSTSCRIPT

In arguing for legal restrictions on pornography, Boyd does not confine legal sanctions to the Criminal Code. Although he says that use of the criminal law is justified in banning pornographic materials that promote gender-based hatred, he also cites additional legal remedies. The most promising of these is the extension of provincial censorship regulations. Boyd argues that extension of the authority of film censor boards to the community level would allow more people to become involved in determining the type of print and film material available in their communities.

In arguing against legal bans of pornography, Rhodes says that allowing the courts to continue to make judgments on pornography amounts to allowing continuance of subjective decision-making. The issue of what is obscene under the law is enmeshed in value judgments, which are subject to political and religious attitudes. Furthermore, Rhodes argues, continuing to ban all sexually explicit material interferes with legitimate rights of artists to engage in social commentary through their art. Artists demand that viewers and readers confront the problems of sexual assault. This demand helps to promote what Rhodes describes as healthy discussion of the issues.

It is also worth noting that while some feminists have argued in favour of legal restrictions on pornography (Dworkin, 1985), others have argued against censorship (Burstyn, 1985). Pro- and anti-censorship feminists agree that pornography degrades and dehumanizes women. They disagree on how to deal with it.

In essence, sociological work has been used to support both sides of the argument. Each side accuses the other of making fundamental errors in research, or of offering inconsistent results. For example, those who reject censorship claim a failure on the part of their opponents to do research in the real world, the world of everyday experience, using more representative samples. Similarly, advocates of censorship argue that the research disproving any relationship between pornography and violence against women is unreliable and often contradictory, sometimes showing a connection, sometimes not (see Special Committee on Pornography and Prostitution, 1985). Readers are asked to read the literature to assess the different claims.

In this ongoing debate, sociological work, as well as other social science investigations, will continue to be at the forefront. Social scientists will continue to be asked to provide evidence to validate or invalidate one side of the argument or the other. This will serve to keep the issue of the need for scientific objectivity front and centre.

■ QUESTIONS

1. Which of these articles presents the best argument? Is your answer to this question affected by your personal beliefs in this issue?
2. Can you identify the theoretical perspectives of both authors?
3. What research method would you use to either discredit or support a connection between pornography and sexual violence?
4. Is the distinction between erotica and pornography a useful one?

■ FURTHER READING

In Support of Boyd

Law Reform Commission of Canada. *The Limits of Criminal Law: Obscenity. A Test Case.* Ottawa: Supply and Services, 1979.

Special Committee on Pornography and Prostitution. *Report of the Special Committee on Pornography and Prostitution.* 2 vols. Ottawa: Supply and Services, 1985.

In Support of Rhodes

Burstyn, Varda, ed. *Women Against Censorship.* Toronto: Douglas and McIntyre, 1985.

Diamond, Sara. "Childhood's End: Some Comments on Pornography and the Fraser Committee," in *Regulating Sex: An Anthology of Commentaries on the Findings and Recommendations of the Badgely and Fraser Reports.* Edited by J. Lowman, M.A. Jackson, T.S. Palys, and S. Gavigan. Burnaby, B.C.: School of Criminology, Simon Fraser University, 1986.

Fisher, William A. "The Emperor has no Clothes: On the Fraser and Badgely Committees' Rejection of Social Science Research," in *Regulating Sex: An Anthology of Commentaries on the Findings and Recommendations of the Badgely and Fraser Reports.* Edited by J. Lowman, M.A. Jackson, T.S. Palys, and S. Gavigan. Burnaby, B.C.: School of Criminology, Simon Fraser University, 1986.

Other Voices

Lacombe, Dany. *Ideology and Public Policy: The Case Against Pornography.* Toronto: Garamond Press, 1988.

McCormack, T. "Machismo in Media Research: A Critical Review of Research and Pornography." *Social Problems* 25, no. 4 (1978): 544-555.

IS GUN

CONTROL

EFFECTIVE?

YES **Catherine F. Sproule and Deborah J. Kennett**, "Killing with Guns in the USA and Canada 1977-1983: Further Evidence for the Effectiveness of Gun Control," *Canadian Journal of Criminology* 31, no. 3 (July 1989): 245-251

NO **Robert J. Mundt**, "Gun Control and Rates of Firearms Violence in Canada and the United States," *Canadian Journal of Criminology* 32, no. 1 (January 1990): 137-154

The demand for more effective gun control often surfaces after highly publicized criminal events involving guns. The spectacles of gunmen killing three people during an assault on the Quebec legislature in 1984 and fourteen women students at the University of Montreal in 1989 intensified fears of violent crime and increased demands for tighter gun control. This raises a number of issues, ranging from civil rights to concerns over crime control.

As in the pornography debate (Debate Thirteen), the issue is whether or not controlling guns produces more harm than good. Gun control advocates say that gun control reduces the number of crimes committed using guns, as well as the number of deaths caused by guns. Therefore, gun control produces more good than harm. Opponents say gun control infringes on individual rights without producing significant benefits by either reducing the criminal use of guns or reducing the number of deaths caused by guns. Each side of this debate holds firmly to its beliefs.

Those who favour stricter gun control point to the number of people killed each year by guns. For example, Sugarman (1987) notes that handguns in the United States are used more frequently than any other weapons to commit murder and suicide. Use of handguns in the United States leads to approximately 22,000 deaths each year: 9,000 murders, 12,000 suicides, and 1,000 accidental deaths. Deaths from use of rifles and shotguns add to the total. Almost 60 percent of all murders in the United States are committed with guns, including rifles and shotguns. Dramatic figures like these are used by gun control advocates in both Canada and the United States to justify demands for limiting gun ownership. The argument is based on simple arithmetic. If the number of handguns is reduced, the risk of death from guns is reduced.

The death rate from shootings in Canada is much lower than it is in the United States. Canadian data indicate that only 34 percent of murders are caused by shootings. Gun control advocates argue that this is the result of strict Canadian gun control laws, which make it more difficult to purchase handguns in Canada than in the United States. Canadians own more rifles and shotguns than they do handguns, and the total number of deaths from all guns in Canada is significantly lower than in the United States. In Canada, approximately 1,400 deaths each year are caused by use of all types of guns. This total includes 180 murders and 1,100 suicides.

Thus, in contrast to the situation in the United States, much of the concern over gun control in Canada has focused on the control of rifles and shotguns. Gun control advocates argue that, since most murders are committed by persons known to the victim (e.g., family members, lovers, or friends involved in heated arguments), removal of all guns from the household would reduce the probability of guns being used to settle disputes. But not all gun control advocates say that gun ownership must be banned. Some argue that if guns are to be available they and/or the ammunition must be stored in some place other than the family home, such as a gun club or public armory.

On the other hand, opponents of gun control argue that there is little evidence to substantiate the claim that gun controls reduce criminal access to guns. They argue that if guns cannot be purchased legally criminals and noncriminals will seek out illegal sources (Wright, 1988), resulting in a decline in respect for law and order. Kaplan (1987) also argues that enforcing gun control legislation is not only difficult by costly. In order to regulate what people do in private, the police would have to use expensive enforcement strategies such as informants, undercover agents, and a number of other cloak-and-dagger methods that may be illegal. In the absence of strong public support for gun control laws and methods by which to enforce them, respect for both the law and the police would erode. According to Kaplan, this may be too high a price to pay for the control of guns.

Some of the above arguments are repeated in the articles chosen for this debate. Sproule and Kennett, arguing for the "Yes" side, say that Canadian gun control laws have led to lower murder rates in Canada than in the United States. Arguing for the "No" side, Mundt says that Canadian gun control laws have not reduced the number of guns available in Canada, and that the number of murders, suicides, and accidental deaths has been affected by Canadian gun control legislation.

References

Kaplan, John (1987) "The Wisdom of Gun Prohibition," in *Exploring Crime: Readings in Criminology and Criminal Justice*, edited by Joseph F. Sheley (Belmont, Calif.: Wadsworth).

Sugarman, Josh (1987) "The NRA is Right, but We Still Need to Ban Handguns," *Washington Monthly* (June).

Wright, James D. (1988) "Second Thoughts about Gun Control," *The Public Interest*, no. 91 (Spring): 23-29.

THE EFFECTIVENESS OF
GUN CONTROL IN CANADA
AND THE UNITED STATES

YES

Catherine F. Sproule and Deborah J. Kennett

Several studies have not yielded clear or unequivocal evidence for the effectiveness of gun control in the United States (e.g., [7, 8, 10, 11]). On the other hand, Sproule and Kennett[13] demonstrated a significant decrease in shooting homicide rates in Canada after the introduction of stringent gun control legislation in 1976. We propose that the discrepant findings regarding the benefits of gun control between Canada and the USA are likely the result of differences in the rigour and pervasiveness of gun control.

In comparison to Canada, gun control in the United States, particularly pertaining to handguns, is remarkably lax. There are an estimated 70 million handguns in the USA,[14] but in Canada, handguns are restricted weapons. Permits for ownership of handguns in Canada may be obtained only by a) police and others, such as security personnel, who demonstrate a need for handguns in their work, b) members of bonafide gun clubs, c) bonafide gun collectors, and d) persons who demonstrate a need for handguns for protection.[5] As far as we can ascertain, permits for handgun ownership have actually been granted only under the first three criteria. Further, infractions of the gun control provisions are indictable offences under the Criminal Code of Canada.[5] In contrast, gun control provisions and criminal law in the United States are not federal but reside in each state or jurisdiction. In the USA, then, avoidance of local gun control regulations may be accomplished simply by crossing jurisdictional boundaries. Thus, not only are provisions for gun control much looser in most, if not all, of the American jurisdictions than in Canada, but also these less stringent regulations cannot be as well enforced as in Canada with its stricter federal gun control legislation.

The purpose of the present study is to examine the incidence of killings with guns in the two countries. Given the demonstrated effectiveness of Canadian gun control,[13] it is expected that the rate of killing by guns will be lower in Canada than in the USA. Further, since the most rigorous regulations of firearms in Canada are for restricted weapons: i.e., handguns, the difference between the two countries' killing rates is predicted to be greater for handgun killings than for those committed by other firearms.

■ METHOD

Canadian data for the rate at which victims of homicide were killed by handguns, by firearms other than handguns, or by methods not involving

342

firearms, for the years 1977 to 1983 inclusive, were derived from Statistics Canada's annual publication on homicide.[1, 2, 6] American data for the same years for victims dying by the same methods were derived from the 107th Edition of the Statistical Abstracts of the United States 1987.[15]

It is important to note that the American data are murder rates whereas the Canada data are for the more inclusive category of homicide (i.e, first and second degree murder, manslaughter and infanticide). Comparisons of this more inclusive category of homicide to that of the more restricted category of murder should mitigate finding support for the hypotheses.

Equally important to observe is that standardized rates adjusted for age could not be calculated because the age of the victim was unknown. Although changes in age sructure have been demonstrated to affect crude rates,[4, 9] a comparison of killing rates by different methods between two nations with similar demographics is unlikely to be affected by the use of crude rates.

■ RESULTS

The crude killing rates per 100,000, averaged over the years 1977 to 1983, are shown in Table 1 for killings by handguns, firearms other than handguns, and nonshooting methods for both Canada and the United States.

TABLE 1 **Average Crude Killing Rates per 100,000 and (Standard Deviations)—1977 to 1983 for killings by handguns, firearms other than handguns, and nonshooting methods— Canada and the United States**

	HANDGUNS	FIREARMS OTHER THAN HANDGUNS	NONSHOOTING METHODS
Canada	0.276 (.0443)	0.666 (.1190)	1.790 (.0935)
USA	4.047 (.4108)	1.321 (.1716)	3.309 (.2070)

A 2×3 analysis of variance was performed on killing rates per 100,000 for the independent variables nation (USA vs Canada) and method of killing (handguns, firearms other than handguns, and nonshooting methods) over the years 1977-1983. Both main effects were significant. For all methods, the average American murder rate was significantly higher than the average Canadian homicide rate [$F(1,36) = 564.67$, $p<.0001$]. As well,

Scheffe's post hoc multiple comparison test for the significant main effect of method of killing [$F(2,36) = 170.22$, $p<.0001$] revealed that the mean killing rate for the two nations combined was significantly greater for nonshooting methods (2.55) than for handguns (2.16) [$t(36,3) = 4.90$, $p<.05$] and for firearms other than handguns (0.99) [$t(36,3) = 19.60$, $p<.001$]. In addition, the mean rate of killing by handguns (2.16) was significantly greater than the mean rate of killing by firearms other than handguns (0.99) [$t(36,3) = 14.70$, $p<.001$].

The significant main effect of method of killing, however, becomes less important in light of the significant interaction between nation X method of killing [$F(2,36) = 423.39$, $p<.0001$]. Employing Scheffe's post hoc multiple comparison test, all simple mean comparisons were significant except that no significant difference was found between the average Canadian homicide rate for handguns (0.28) and the average Canadian homicide rate for firearms other than handguns (0.67) [$t(36,6) = 3.46$, $p>.05$].

In addition, our prediction that the difference between the two countries' average killing rates over the years 1977 to 1983 would be greater for handgun killings than for those committed by other firearms was supported [$t(12) = 15.98$, $p<.0001$]. The mean difference in rates between the two countries for the years 1977-1983 for killings by handguns and for killings by firearms excluding handguns was observed to be 3.77 and 0.66, respectively.

Equally important are the following significant comparisons. First, the average USA murder rate for handguns (4.05) was found to be significantly greater than the average Canadian homicide rate for all methods of killing (2.73) [$t(12) = 7.81$, $p<.001$]. Second, even though the average American nonshooting rate of 3.31 is significantly higher than the average Canadian nonshooting rate of 1.79 [$t(36,6) = 13.43$, $p<.001$], significantly more Canadians were killed by nonshooting methods (1.79) than by shooting methods (0.94) [$t(12) = 14.61$, $p<.001$]. Third, the American shooting rate of 5.37 was observed to be significantly higher than the Canadian shooting rate of 0.94 [$t(12) = 23.26$, $p<.001$].

■ DISCUSSION

In strong support of our hypotheses and in a clear demonstration of the benefits of Canadian gun control, we found that Canadians kill less with firearms than Americans and that the difference between the two countries is larger for handgun killings (which are restricted weapons in Canada) than for those committed by other firearms. As well, American murder rates are higher for handgun killings than for killings by other firearms and for killings by nonshooting methods. Indeed, American murder rates for handguns are higher than the total Canadian homicide rate. The present findings combined with our earlier demonstration of a decrease in the Canadian shooting homicide rate after the introduction of gun control in Canada[13] emphatically show that Canadian gun control, especially the provisions pertaining to handguns, does have the beneficial effect of saving lives.

In addition, these findings undermine the apparent claim of gun control opponents in their slogan "people kill, guns don't," which appears to mean that gun control does not affect the likelihood of killing but rather only the means by which death is accomplished. Also, the present findings allay a concern we raised regarding a finding in our comparison of methods of killing in Canada before and after gun control. Our results reported in a previous study[13] indicated that there was a marginal tendency for non-shooting homicides to increase subsequent to gun control implementation, suggesting that gun control may encourage murderers to use other methods than firearms to kill. The findings we present here, however, do not support the claim that gun control operates simply to induce killers to find alternate means to kill. More specifically, in Canada, the definition of handguns as restricted weapons is not associated with higher rates of killing with other more accessible firearms: the Canadian homicide rates for killing with handguns and with other firearms did not differ significantly. As well, the Canadian rate for other firearms was lower than the American rate for firearms other than handguns. Similarly, evidence against the claim that gun control facilitates the use of other methods was found for nonshooting killings. Although Canadians kill more with nonshooting than shooting methods, the Canadian nonshooting rate is significantly lower than the American nonshooting rate. Finally, in our earlier study[13] we demonstrated that Canadian killers using firearms killed more victims than Canadian killers using nonshooting methods: a killer with a gun is more likely to have multiple victims than a killer without a gun. The high American murder rate for shooting methods may be attributable, in part, to the multiple victims of a killer with a gun.

Additional support for the effectiveness of Canadian gun control comes from Sloan and his colleagues'[12] comparison of crime, assault and homicide rates in Seattle, Washington, and Vancouver, British Columbia, from 1980 through 1986. Although crime rates were similar in the two cities, assaults involving firearms were seven times higher in Seattle than in Vancouver and differences in homicide rates in the two cities were virtually all accounted for by the 4.8-fold greater risk of being murdered by a handgun in Seattle than in Vancouver.

Because Canadian gun control is clearly beneficial, we are concerned about recent reports of a proliferation of gun clubs and gun club membership whose apparent aim is to obtain handgun permits and also of an increase in the number of handguns confiscated by Canadian customs at the border.[3] Because Canada's favourable situation regarding murder relative to the United States is to a large measure the result of Canadian gun control, Canadians must be vigilant against any erosion of our gun control provisions. Further, because gun ownership (at least in Detroit) is inversely related to individuals' confidence in collective institutions to protect their security of person and property,[16] maintenance of Canadians' confidence in the police and justice system to protect our collective security is an important means by which to deter gun acquisition. Above all, the important role played by gun control in Canadians' collective security must be stressed and more widely recognized.

References

1. Canadian Centre for Justice Statistics, Law Enforcement Statistics Section. *Homicide in Canada 1983: A Statistical Perspective*. Ottawa: Statistics Canada. Catalogue 85-209.
2. Canadian Centre for Justice Statistics, Law Enforcement Statistics Section. *Homicide in Canada 1982: A Statistical Perspective*. Ottawa: Statistics Canada. Catalogue 85-209.
3. Canadian Press. "More Americans having handguns seized at border, statistics show." *Toronto Star*. Toronto, February 1, 1988.
4. Conklin, G.H. and M.E. Simpson, "A demographic approach to the cross-sectional study of homicide." *Comparative Social Research*. 1985, *8* 171-185.
5. Criminal Law Amendment Act, 1977.
6. Justice Statistics Division. *Homicide Statistics, 1977*. Ottawa: Statistics Canada. Catalogue 85-209.
7. Kleck, Gary. "Capital punishment, gun ownership and homicide." *American Journal of Sociology*. 1979, *84*, 882-910.
8. Kleck, Gary. "Evidence that 'Saturday Night Specials' are not very important for crime." *Sociology and Social Research*. 1986, 70, 303-307.
9. Lee, G. Won. "Are crime rates increasing? A study of the impact of demographic shifts on crime rates in Canada." *Canadian Journal of Criminology*. 1984, *26*, 29-41.
10. Lester, D. "The murder of police officers in American cities." *Criminal Justice and Behavior*. 1984, *11*, 101-113.
11. Lester, D. and M.E. Murrell. "The influence of gun control laws on personal violence." *Journal of Community Psychology*. 1986, *14*, 315-318.
12. Sloan, J.H., A.L. Kellermann, D.I. Reay, J.A. Fenis, T. Koepsell, F.P. Rivara, C. Rice, L. Gray, and J. Logerfo. "Handgun regulations, crime, assaults, and homicide: A tale of two cities." *New England Journal of Medicine*. 1988, *319*, 1256-1262.
13. Sproule, C.F. and D.J. Kennett. "The use of firearms in Canadian homicides 1972-1982: The need for gun control." *Canadian Journal of Criminology*. 1988, *30*, 31-37.
14. Tenszen, Michael. "Keep handgun ban, U.S. police official warns Canadians." *Globe and Mail*. Toronto, August 27, 1986.
15. United States Department of Commerce. *Statistical Abstract of the United States 1987*. 107th Edition.
16. Young, R.L., D. McDowall, and D. Loftin. "Collective Security and the ownership of firearms for protection." *Criminology*. 1987, *25*, 47-62.

GUN CONTROL AND VIOLENCE IN CANADA AND THE UNITED STATES

Robert J. Mundt

Canada and the United States provide a laboratory for "natural experiments" that has not been sufficiently exploited. Differences in government structure are well known, and cultural differences have been much discussed, though with less consensus (see, most recently, Hagan 1984 and Lenton 1989). This is a preliminary attempt to examine, in light of these background characteristics, the effect of Bill C-51 as it amended the Canadian *Criminal Code* regulating the acquisition and bearing of firearms in Canada. Long-term trends in firearms acquisition and violent crime before and after the implementation of that legislation are examined and compared with trends in the United States.

■ VIOLENT CRIME AND GUN CONTROL IN CANADA AND THE UNITED STATES

> Crime in America is popularly perceived [in Canada] as something to be expected in a society which has less respect for the rule of law than does Canadian society. Canadians have long viewed Americans as more lawless than themselves.
>
> (Mercer and Goldbert 1986: 350)

Overall crime rates do not strongly support this Canadian view, but violent crime rates by themselves lend it credence. Figure 1 presents the well-known contrast in violent death rates between the two countries (recently dramatized in *Time* magazine's cover story of February 6, 1989). The specific "rule-of-law" explanation most often attached to these figures is manifested by the more restrictive (and more strictly enforced) regulations on firearms in Canada.

Kennett and Anderson (1975) have demonstrated the parallel development of legislative proposals on firearms in Canada and the United States. Although early initiatives of this sort in Canada were often stimulated by proposals raised (but rarely enacted) south of the border, the Canadian government took the initiative on its own in 1977 with passage of the *Criminal Law Amendment Act*. Among other provisions, that legislation mandated a Firearms Acquisition Certificate for the purchase of any firearm, strengthened the registration requirements for handguns and other "restricted" weapons already imposed in 1968, and placed automatic weapons, sawed-off shotguns, and rifles in a prohibited category. The amendment also provided for mandatory prohibitions, relating to the

347

acquisition of firearms for those convicted of serious crime, and required stiffer penalties for those convicted of firearms-related crime (Solicitor General 1983).

The next year, the Canadian Solicitor General commissioned a study of the law's effectiveness. Elisabeth Scarff (1983), writing for Decision Dynamics Corporation, responded with an evaluation report describing an increase in the murder rate by firearms from 1961 to 1975, and a consistent decline from 1975 to 1981. The use of firearms in rape, assault, and wounding showed no substantial change; the total number of robberies with firearms increased, although "the increase in firearm robberies was less than for total robberies" and "the percentage of robberies involving firearms decreased" (Scarff 1983: xvi).

The overall conclusions of the Decision Dynamics study concerning firearm crime were that "a moderate decrease [occurred] in the post-legislation period in the proportionate use of firearms in the criminal incidents examined," along with "a corresponding increase in the proportion committed by other means . . . knives in particular." (Scarff 1983: xvii). When firearms were used, "there was an increasing tendency for the firearm to be a handgun. These findings indicate that the greatest impact of the legislation has been on unrestricted firearms, such as rifles and shotguns," even though handguns are most often used in robberies. While the proportion of crime suspects using firearms remained stable at just over 50 percent, the proportion of these with five or more charges had increased from 1978 to 1981 (Scarff 1983: xvii).

It was, of course, not to be expected that major effects could be attributed to the 1977 *Criminal Code* amendments in a study conducted in 1981, especially when the law took effect only in 1978, with some of the major provisions not effective until 1979. Most provisions were of such nature that they could only have a long-term effect on gun-related crime by slowly restricting the access of "dangerous or irresponsible people" to firearms (Solicitor General, 1983). Further analysis of this legislation's effect on homicide by Sproule and Kennett (1988), in which the authors claim to have found a significant effect of gun control in terms of reducing the number of homicide victims per suspect, must also be viewed with some skepticism, since they used the years 1977-1982 for their "post-test" measure. Blackman's (1984) paper critiquing the Amendment also was limited to data from no later than 1982.

On the other hand, the preliminary crime statistics for 1988 have prompted a Canadian Centre for Justice Statistics memorandum to the effect that "A trend away from the use of firearms in robberies has been noticeable ever since the passage of the gun control provisions of the 1977 Bill C-51 (*Criminal Law Amendment Act*). For example, in 1988 only one quarter of all robberies involved the use of a firearm, down from the 36.6% reported in 1978" (Statistics Canada, Memorandum, February 17, 1989). The CCJS analysis, although it does not apply any control cases or control

FIGURE 1   Homicide Trends, U.S. and Canada

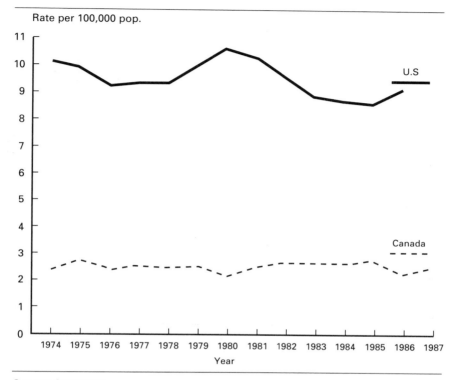

Rate per 100,000 pop.

Sources: Scarff 1983
Statistics Canada 1988
Statistical Abstract of the U.S.

variables, is based on a trend of such duration that it may now be possible to ascertain the independent effects of firearms regulation. Comparative research in Canada and the United States, employing adequate ecological controls, will give policy-makers of both countries information of value in assessing the effectiveness of firearms regulations in reducing rates of violent crime.

Simple visual analysis of the trends illustrated in Figure 1 allows the following summary description: Overall Canadian homicide victim rates, except for a dip in 1980, were essentially level from 1978 to 1985. Rates for 1986 and 1987 were lower, but that for 1987 is exactly at the mean for the years 1974-1987. During the same period, American homicide victim rates fluctuated between 9.1 and 10.2 from 1974 to 1979, rose to a recent high of 10.7 in 1980, and declined from 1980 to 1985. The 1986 rate of 9.0 was up .7 from the previous year, but was still below the 1974-1986 mean of 9.4— about 3.75 times the Canadian rate. Rates based on incidents known to the police show the same general trends as for victim-based rates in both

FIGURE 2 Rates of Homicide by Firearms, U.S. and Canada

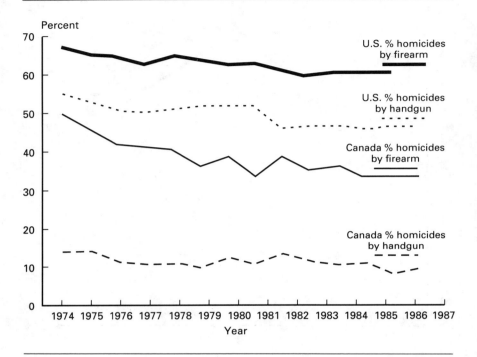

Sources: Scarff 1983: 29-31
Canadian Centre for Justice Statistics
U.S. Justice Department, BJS. 1986

countries. We have a figure of 2.2 homicides known to the police in Canada for 1988, identified by Statistics Canada as the "lowest . . . since 1969." The mean rate for Canada from 1974 to 1978 was 2.7, compared to a post-1978 rate (through 1988) of 2.6. One could admit the possibility that this decline resulted from the 1977 legislation, except that the mean rates for the United States in the same periods dropped from 9.2 to 8.9, an almost identical drop.

Canadian homicide by firearms as a proportion of all homicides dropped rapidly between 1974 and 1976 (Figure 2). It then stabilized through 1978 before declining more gradually to 1981. Except for a one-time upswing in 1982, it has stabilized through 1987 at about 31 percent. The American rate experienced a gradual drop of seven total points over the same period, to a proportion about twice the Canadian rate.

A report on city jurisdictions in Canada showed that the most frequent type of firearm incident was robbery (Canada, Solicitor General 1983: 29). As with homicides, armed robberies peaked in 1975 in both countries, then

FIGURE 3 Armed Robbery Trends, U.S. and Canada

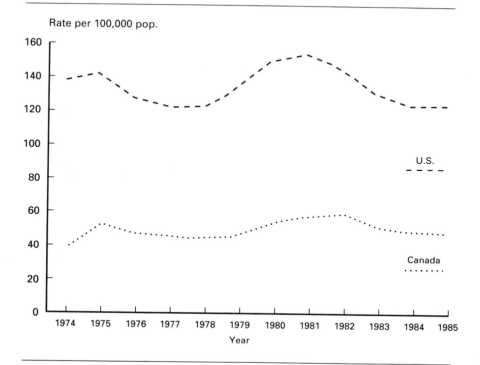

Rate per 100,000 pop.

U.S. – – – –

Canada ·······

Year

Sources: Scarff 1983
Canadian Centre for Justice Statistics
U.S. Justice Dept. Bur. of Just. Stats.

declined over the new few years (Figure 3). Each country then experienced a four-year increase, from 1978 to 1982 in Canada, and from 1977 to 1981 in the United States. Canada's rate then experienced a strong decline in 1983, followed by smaller declines in the next two years. However, the 1985 rate is still higher than the five-year mean for 1974-1978; the U.S. rate for 1985 is significantly *lower* than its 1974-1978 mean (see the discussion in Gabor *et al* 1987: 4-7).

The proportion of robberies involving firearms in Canada has dropped over the period examined, from 38 percent in 1977 to 34 percent in 1981 to 25 percent in 1988 (Figure 4); firearms have largely been displaced by other weapons, principally knives, in the totals (Solicitor General 1983: 29-31). The proportion of firearms in robberies in the United States has always been higher than in Canada, but has shown a remarkably constant secular decline since 1974 (from 45 to 33 percent). Still, the drop has been greater in Canada, so that the gap in percentage points is now eight, up from just three in 1979. Because we do not have comparable data prior to 1977 in

FIGURE 4   Percent of Robberies by Firearm, U.S. and Canada

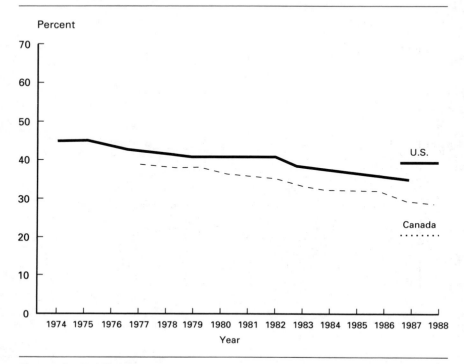

Sources: Scarff 1983: 29-31
Canadian Centre for Justice Statistics
U.S. Justice Dept. Bur. of Just. Stats.

Canada, we cannot say whether the decline in firearms robberies since then coincides with the adoption of the 1977 legislation, or is part of a secular trend as in the United States. Comparable national statistics relevant to firearm use in rape and assault are not available over the extended time period.

■ SUICIDE

From 1970-75, there were 5679 suicides with firearms in Canada which accounted for 71 percent of all firearm deaths. Suicide by firearm accounted for 35 percent of all suicides, and 44 percent of male suicides (Stenning and Moyer 1981: 174). This is clearly the area in which there is the greatest potential for intervention in firearms deaths in Canada (and perhaps even greater potential in the United States, where 57 percent of all suicides are gun-related).

FIGURE 5 Suicide Rates

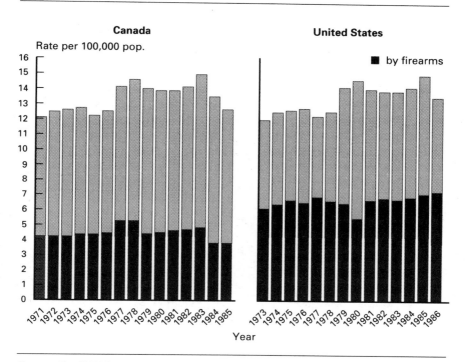

Canada

Rate per 100,000 pop.

United States

■ by firearms

Year

Sources: Scarff 1983
Statistics Canada: Vital Statistics

Sources: Statistical Abstract of the U.S.
National Center for Health
Stats. 1986

The report by Scarff (1983) on the Canadian legislation of 1977 notes that the Canadian firearm suicide rate "gradually increased from 1971 to 1978, followed by a decrease in 1979 and 1980," and that "the relative use of firearms in suicides was lower in 1979 and 1980 than it had been in any of the previous years for which data were available." However, evaluation of firearms regulation for its deterrent effect on suicide deaths must take into account whether a scarcity of guns reduces the *total* suicide death rate. Otherwise, it can be (and is) argued that the person who wants to take his or her own life will find a way to do it. The special problem with firearm suicide, of course, is that "guns add a dimension of harsh finality to suicide attempts" (*Time* July 17, 1989). According to this line of reasoning, since many of those who attempt suicide do not really want to die, less rapid methods would allow for some of these to be rescued. If rescue is possible in a significant number of cases, the unavailability of firearms should result in lower rates of suicide death overall.

FIGURE 6   **Accidental Deaths from Firearms, Canada and the United States**

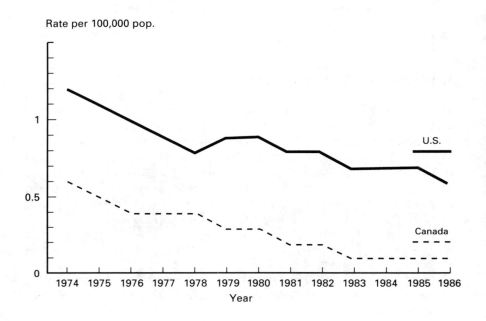

Sources: Scarff 1983
          Statistics Canada: Vital Statistics
          Statistical Abstract of the U.S.

The suicide/gun availability relationship was briefly examined by Lester (1987), who found a significant positive relationship between each of three measures of gun availability and the suicide rate by gun among the American states. The relationship was somewhat weaker between *total* suicide rates and gun availability, and inverse with the rate of suicides by other methods. These findings suggest some substitution of other means when guns are not available. A later note by Lester (1988) found no consistent effect of changes in handgun control on rates of suicide by guns in American states. In a review of pre-1977 suicide statistics in Canada, Stenning and Moyer (1981: 177) found no evidence of a relationship between gun availability and the firearms suicide rate.

The trend presented in Figure 5 shows a slight increase in suicide death rates in Canada. The mean annual rate increased from 12.8 over the years 1970-1977 to 14.1 during 1978-1985. The suicide rate by firearms has gone down from the 1978-79 peak, but just to the averages of the early and mid-1970s. The Canadian suicide rate has consistently remained slightly higher than that in the United States for both sexes and all age groups up to 65 in men and 75 in women. There has been a convergence in the past few years, perhaps explained by the relative decline in Canadian rates and a slight upward shift in the United States through the 1980s, parallel to an upward shift in firearms suicides. That trend has not been of sufficient duration to base firm conclusions on it, but bears watching as a possibly important shift.

ACCIDENTAL DEATH FROM FIREARMS

Death rates from firearms accidents are infrequent relative to homicides and suicides in both Canada and the United States, and have been in long-term decline in both countries (Figure 6), with the American rate remaining from two to three times greater. There is no statistical evidence of an independent effect from the Canadian legislation, given the parallel trends, although the constant gap between American and Canadian accident rates is more easily related to general availability of guns in the respective populations than is the case for violent crimes and suicides.

AVAILABILITY OF FIREARMS

The purpose of the 1977 legislation, of course, was to reduce the availability of firearms, on the assumption that there is a positive relationship between availability and use. Cook (1982: 264) has described the difficulty in measuring the effect of firearm regulation on violent crime without an independent measure of availability, in that if there is no effect evident, the cause may be either (a) that the regulation effort did not affect availability or (b) that lower availability did not reduce the crime rate.[1] Kleck (1984) argues that the possibility of reverse causality in the relationship between availability and violence is often overlooked: that is, that the rate of gun ownership increases *defensively*, as a *response* to increased violence. Whatever the pattern of causality, however, we can only test the effect of the Canadian legislation on its own premise, that there is a correlation between availability and use, so that reducing the former will reduce the latter. An important prior question is whether the 1977 amendment was successful in reducing the stock of firearms in Canada.

While we do not have accurate measures of the total stock of firearms, the provisions of the 1977 Act allow us to conclude that the total number and the rate per 100,000 of both handguns and long guns have increased. In 1976, the Solicitor General estimated that there were at least 10,230,000 firearms in Canada, about 60 percent of which were rifles, 34 percent shotguns, and six percent handguns (Stenning and Moyer, 1981). This translated into 44,500 weapons per 100,000 population. There were 1,727,635 Firearms Acquistions Certificates issued from 1979 through 1988. These do not provide an accurate measure of the number of firearms purchased, because the person possessing an FAC can purchase an un-limited number of firearms during its five-year validity. However, it seems conservative to assume that each FAC was used to purchase at least one weapon on the average. On that basis, there are now 1,275,000 more firearms in private ownership in Canada than when the Act was passed — about 11,960,000, or 46,000 per 100,000 population.

The stock of restricted weapons (almost all handguns) increased from an estimated 651,000 in 1976 to 923,000 in 1988 (based on the total number of restricted weapons registered with and reported by the RCMP, the number of registration certificates issued for the first-time acquisition of restricted weapons, minus the number of certificates withdrawn from registry. Although not all restricted weapons are handguns, it is likely that all but a very small proportion are handguns). This represents an increase from 2970 per 100,000 population in 1976 to 3560 in 1988. While the problems with these data are substantial, it is hard to interpret them in any fashion that would suggest a decrease in weapons availability in Canada since 1977.

To get comparable figures for the United States, Kleck's (1984) calcu-lations through 1978 are extrapolated through 1988 at the rate he used in the 1970s; an annual increase of total firearms of 3.6 percent per year and of handguns at 4.4 percent. Kleck's 1978 figures are considerably higher than those reported from survey data by Wright (1981), and remain higher than Zimring and Hawkins' (1987) estimate of 130 million guns in the late 1980s; however, the projection is consistent with the estimate of 60 million handguns reported for 1984 in the *Christian Science Monitor*, and with Wright, Rossi, and Daly's (1983) suggestion that 65 million new firearms were added between 1969 and 1978. Thus, the figures used here are Kleck's through 1978, while those for later years are the author's straight-percent-age projections from Kleck's. The result for 1988 is somewhat greater than the estimation of 180-200 million firearms and 55 to 60 million handguns quoted by the AMA Council on Scientific Affairs (1989).

Given the softness of these data, comparison is hazardous. But it is likely that, although the stock of firearms in Canada is growing, the growth is less rapid than in the United States. The data in Figure 7 allow estima-tions of a 26 percent growth rate in the number of firearms in the United States since 1979 (or 17 percent, using the more conservative AMA esti-mate), compared to four percent in Canada, and a 35 percent increase in U.S. handguns in the short time (26 percent using the AMA 1988 figures), compared to a 12 percent increase in Canada. On the other hand, the number of guns may not be as important as the number and proportion of *gunowners* in the population (Cook 1982: 267). Unfortunately, there are no data beyond occasional surveys as a basis for estimating the proportion of populations or households owning guns.

FIGURE 7   **Rate of Firearm Possession, Canada and the United States**

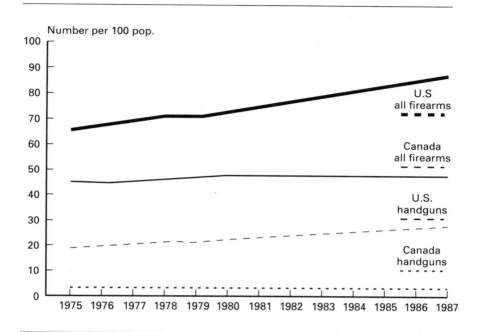

Sources: RCMP 1979-1988
Statistics Canada 1987
Kleck 1984: 112

■ CONCLUSIONS

When compared with the United States, trends in Canada over the past ten years in various types of violent crime, suicide, and accidental death show no dramatic results, and few suggestions of perceptible effects of the 1977 Canadian gun control legislation. This is scarcely surprising, except that expectations were high among the policy formulators, and some evaluations perhaps tried too hard to give them satisfaction. The decrease in the use of firearms in robbery appears to be the only change that stands out over time or in comparison with parallel trends in the United States.

This focus on explaining change in firearm-related violence has not shown dramatic results, but also suggests that the stock of firearms in general and handguns in particular has *grown* somewhat since implementation of the 1977 amendments. If there has been a significant effect of those measures, it may have been to slow the rise in firearms violence that might otherwise have occurred. The striking contrast, of course, is the evident effectiveness of the border in keeping violence rates relatively low in Canada. That long-term difference has been the subject of much speculation, but relatively little serious empirical analysis.

Such analysis must examine, at the local level, the demographic and cultural correlates of firearm violence. It must also explore possibly different combinations of premeditated crimes and "crimes of passion" in overall rates. Informed law enforcement officers in Canada readily concede that, as in the United States, the professional criminal who wants a weapon can obtain one. The impact of restricting the availability of firearms, then, is more likely to impact on those violent incidents that would not have happened had a weapon not been at hand.[2]

Notes

1. Based on studies using American data, Cook concludes (1982: 273) that, although it has been determined that the choice of a gun as a weapon used in a violent act is related to the density of gun ownership, the relationship between gun availability and overall rates of violent crime "has not received a definitive answer, though the answer appears to be no for robbery and yes for robbery murders."

2. This is a point not fully addressed by Wright and Rossi (1986), whose policy recommendations on gun crimes are based on interviews with prison felons, a population that surely underrepresents those who cause unpremeditated injury or death to relatives or acquaintances.

References

American Medical Association, Council on Scientific Affairs. 1989 Firearms injuries and deaths: A critical public health issue. Public Health Reports: 104: 111-120.

Blackman, Paul H. 1984 The Canadian Gun Law, Bill C-51: Its Effectiveness and Lessons for Research on the 'Gun Control' Issue. Paper presented at the annual meeting of the American Society of Criminology, Cincinnati, Ohio, November 7-11.

Canada—Royal Canadian Mounted Police. 1979-1988 Annual Firearms Report to the Solicitor General of Canada by the Commissioner of the R.C.M.P. (Section 117 Criminal Code).

Canada—Solicitor General. 1983 Firearms Control in Canada: An Evaluation. Ottawa: Minister of Supply and Services.

Cook, Philip J. 1982 "The role of firearms in violent crime: An interpretive review of the literature." In Marvin E. Wolfgang and Neil Alan Weiner (eds.), Criminal Violence. Beverly Hills: Sage.

Gabor, Thomas, Micheline Baril, Maurice Cusson, Daniel Elie, Marc LeBlanc and André Normandeau. 1987 Armed Robbery: Cops, Robbers, and Victims. Springfield, IL: Chas. C. Thomas.

Hagan, John. 1984 Disreputable Pleasures: Crime and Deviance in Canada (2nd Edition). Toronto: McGraw-Hill Ryerson.

Kennett, Lee and James LaVerne Anderson. 1975 The Gun in America: The Origins of a National Dilemma. Westport, CT: Greenwood Press.

Kleck, Gary. 1984 The relationship between gun ownership levels and rates of violence in the United States." In Don B. Kates, Jr. (ed.), Firearms and Violence: Issues of Public Policy. Cambridge, MA: Ballinger.

Lenton, Rhonda L. 1989 "Homicide in Canada and the U.S.A.: A critique of the Hagan thesis." Canadian Journal of Sociology 14: 163-178.

Lester, David. 1987 "Availability of guns and the likelihood of suicide." Sociology and Sociological Research (July): 287-288.

————. 1988 "Effect of changes in handgun control laws on suicide rates." Psychological Reports 62: 298.

Mercer, John and Michael A. Goldberg. 1986 Value differences and their meaning for urban development in Canada and the U.S. In Gilbert A. Stelter and Alan F.J. Artibise (eds.), Power and Place in Canadian Urban Development: The North American Context. Vancouver: U.B.C. Press.

Scarff, Elisabeth. 1983 Evaluation of the Canadian Gun Control Legislation. Ottawa: Minister of Supply and Services.

Sproule, Catherine F. and Deborah J. Kennett. 1988 The use of firearms in Canadian homicides 1972-1982: The need for gun control. Canadian Journal of Criminology 30: 31-37.

Stenning, Philip C. and Sharon Moyer. 1981 Firearms Ownership and Use in Canada: A Report of Survey Findings, 1976. Toronto: Centre of Criminology, University of Toronto.

United States Department of Health and Human Services, National Center for Health Statistics. 1986 Vital Statistics of the United States. Vol. II. Washington: U. S. Government Printing Office.

United States Department of Justice, Bureau of Justice Statistics. 1980 Intimate Victims: A Study of Violence Among Friends and Relatives. Washington: U.S. Government Printing Office.

Wright, James D. 1981 Public opinion and gun control: A comparison of results from two recent national surveys. Annals 451: 24-39.

Wright, James D. and Peter H. Rossi. 1986 Armed and Considered Dangerous: A Survey of Felons and Their Firearms. New York: Aldine de Gruyter.

Wright, James D., Peter H. Rossi and Kathleen Daly. 1983 Under the Gun: Weapons, Crime, and Violence in America. New York: Aldine.

Zimring, Franklin E. and Gordon Hawkins. 1987 The Citizen's Guide to Gun Control. New York: Macmillan.

■ POSTSCRIPT

Sproule and Kennett counter the arguments of anti-control forces by arguing that gun control legislation has not resulted in potential killers seeking out alternative ways to kill. The rate of nonshooting killings is lower in Canada than in the United States. Further evidence of the reduction in killings resulting from gun control is found in the observation that killers without guns are less likely to have multiple victims than killers with guns.

Mundt argues that any decrease in the criminal use of guns resulting from the Criminal Law Amendment Act of 1977 may be more apparent than real. He notes that both the United States and Canada experienced a drop in the criminal use of guns from 1977 onward. The fact that the drop in gun use was higher in Canada than in the United States does not, Mundt contends, mean that the 1977 legislation was effective in reducing the criminal use of guns. He hints that other factors may be influencing the use of guns but, other than to say that the decline may be attributed to a secular trend similar to that in the United States, he does not specify what these other factors might be. More convincing is Mundt's finding that Canadian suicide rates, deaths from accidents, and the number of privately owned guns have all increased since the legislation came into effect. If gun control legislation were effective, these rates should have declined.

The above studies raise several concerns. First, is Sproule and Kennett's use of the killing rate, calculated from U.S. murder rates and Canadian homicide rates, justified? Sproule and Kennett note that the U.S. murder rate is not as inclusive as the Canadian homicide rate. The Canadian rate includes first- and second-degree murder, as well as manslaughter and infanticide. This has undoubtedly influenced their results.

Second, Mundt's data includes homicide rates from 1974 to 1988, whereas Sproule and Kennett examine data from only 1977 to 1983. Mundt has the advantage, then, of examining the impact of the legislation over a longer term; observing trends over a longer period generally increases the reliability of the findings. Less constructively, while Mundt admits that the mean rate for homicide in Canada was lower after 1978 than it was from 1974 to 1978, he dismisses the drop as insignificant. But if the intent of the legislation was to reduce the murder rate attributable to the use of guns, does the drop have to be dramatic in order for the legislation to be called effective? How big a drop is needed?

■ QUESTIONS

1. Which of these articles presents the most convincing argument? How has your own view on gun control influenced your decision?

2. Is there a compromise position between the "Yes" and "No" sides of this debate?
3. What role should sociologists play in the debate?
4. How would you improve upon the research of either Sproule and Kennett or Mundt?
5. How would you attempt to document public support for or against gun control?
6. Which social groups are more likely to support gun control?
7. Which social groups are more likely to reject gun control?

■ FURTHER READING

In Support of Sproule and Kennett

Scarff, Elizabeth. *Evaluation of the Canadian Gun Control Legislation.* Ottawa: Minister of Supply and Services, 1983.
Sproule, Catherine F. and Deborah J. Kennett. "The Use of Firearms in Canadian Homicides 1972-1982: The Need for Gun Control." *Canadian Journal of Criminology* 30 (1988): 31-37.

In Support of Mundt

Gates, Don B. "Why a Civil Libertarian Opposes Gun Control." *Civil Liberties* 3 (1976): 24.
Kaplan, John. "The Wisdom of Gun Prohibition." In *Exploring Crime: Readings in Criminology and Criminal Justice.* Edited by Joseph F. Sheley. Belmont, Calif.: Wadsworth, 1987.

Other Voices

Kennett, Lee and James LaVerne Anderson. *The Gun in America: The Origins of a National Dilemma.* Westport, Conn.: Greenwood Press.
Wright, James D. "Public Opinion and Gun Control: A Comparison of Results from Two Recent National Surveys." *The Annals of the American Academy of Political and Social Science* 455, (May 1981): 24-39.

SHOULD RETRIBUTION BE

THE OBJECTIVE OF

CRIMINAL SANCTIONS?

YES   **Andrew von Hirsch,** "The Politics of 'Just Deserts,' " *Canadian Journal of Criminology* 32, no. 3 (July 1990): 397-413

NO   **Thomas Gabor,** "Looking Back or Moving Forward: Retributivism and the Canadian Sentencing Commission's Proposals," *Canadian Journal of Criminology* 32, no. 3 (July 1990): 537-546

The previous debates in this section have centred on mechanisms for controlling specific behaviours. In Debate Fifteen, the focus shifts to a more general concern, the role of punishment in the control and prevention of crime. From its beginnings in the 1700s, modern criminology has debated the purpose of punishment. According to early criminologists like Cesare Beccaria, writing in Italy in 1764, punishment should be proportional to the interests violated by the crime. It should not be excessive, and should be used only to deter crime. It should never be used for the purpose of rehabilitation (Taylor et al., 1973). Beccaria claimed that the threat of punishment should be sufficient to deter a rational man from committing crime. To the extent that irrational men commit crimes, they should be punished for the crimes they commit but no action other than imprisonment should be undertaken to reform them. In other words, punishment should be administered only for the purpose of retribution, making the criminal pay for his/her crime.

Other criminologists of the time, like Jean Villan of Belgium and John Howard of England, agreed that excessive punishment was immoral, but disagreed on the need for rehabilitation. They said that punishment must be used to reform offenders, to transform them into law-abiding citizens and wage earners capable of making positive contributions to society (Gosselin, 1982).

More than two hundred years after the emergence of modern criminology, heated debate on the purpose of punishment in society continues among contemporary criminologists. For example, advocates of the "just deserts" model of criminal justice have adopted a variation of the proportionality doctrine of the early criminologists. According to von Hirsch (1985) and other just deserts theorists, punishment must be proportionate to the offence committed. They claim that contemporary criminal justice policies have swung too far in the direction of rehabilitation, and have neglected the retributive role of punishment. They also say that judges are ill-equipped to assess the rehabilitative needs of individual criminals. Advocates of this perspective say that judges must be given more precise sentencing guidelines and fewer discretionary powers in sentencing.

Critics of the just deserts model have argued that its claims to being able to measure how much punishment should be administered for specific crimes are unrealistic. In addition, the just deserts model leads to overcrowded prisons, and to abolition of parole, which the critics see as an essential part of the rehabilitation process (Grygier, 1988). They note that inmates released directly from prison without parole have higher recidivism rates (repeat offences) than inmates released on parole. Thus, whereas just deserts theorists say the punishment should fit the crime, advocates of rehabilitation say that the punishment should fit the offender. Other critics say that sentencing tends to be more severe under the just deserts model than under other sentencing models, and that members of lower socioeconomic groups are likely to receive harsher sentences under the just deserts model (Hudson, 1987).

In Debate Fifteen, von Hirsch argues in favour of a just deserts, or retribution, model of criminal justice, while Gabor takes an opposing viewpoint.

References

Gosselin, Luc (1982) *Prisons In Canada* (Montreal: Black Rose Books).

Grygier, Tadeusz (1988) "A Canadian Approach or an American Band-Wagon?" *Canadian Journal of Criminology* 30, no. 2: 165-172.

Hudson, Barbara (1987) *Justice Through Punishment: A Critique of the "Justice" Model of Corrections* (New York: St. Martins Press).

Taylor, Ian, Paul Walton, and Jock Young (1973) *The New Criminology* (London: Routledge and Kegan Paul).

von Hirsch, Andrew (1985) *Past or Future Crimes: Deservedness and Dangerousness in the Sentencing of Criminals* (New Brunswick, N.J.: Rutgers University Press).

THE POLITICS OF "JUST DESERTS"[1]

Andrew von Hirsch

■ I. INTRODUCTION

The Canadian Sentencing Commission's (1987) report has helped stimulate thinking and debate over sentencing policy in this country. One of the report's best features is a clear articulation of rationale. The Commission made the principle of proportionality—that penalties should be justly commensurate with the gravity of crimes—its central guiding principle. That principle shapes the proposed guideline structure: penalties are graded according to the gravity of offenses; the seriousness of the crime of conviction is to carry more weight than the criminal record; and predictive judgments are to be restricted in the choice of sanction. Having a guiding rationale not only provides the guidelines with an intelligible form; it also would aid the courts in interpreting the guidelines. Under the Commission's proposals, the courts are authorized to depart from the prescribed ranges on account of circumstances of aggravation and mitigation—and to invoke grounds for departure other than those specifically listed. An express rationale helps the courts decide which departure grounds are and are not appropriate (von Hirsch 1989).

Stating an explicit rationale raises the question of whether it is the right one. *Should* proportionality and desert be the guiding ideas? Proportionality reflects people's intuitive sense of fairness. When penalizing someone for a wrong in everyday contexts, we naturally tend to look to the gravity of the offense, and suspect there is something unfair about doing otherwise. Desert theorists, including myself, have argued that this intuitive is correct: that punishment, by its very nature, conveys blame, and therefore should be distributed according to the degree of blameworthiness of the criminal conduct. The rationale underlying proportionalist sentencing doctrine has been described at length elsewhere (von Hirsch 1985: chs. 3-8, 11-12) and does not have to be rehearsed here. . .

I wish, in this article, to address another set of questions: political ones. What general political viewpoint, if any, is presupposed by a proportionality-oriented sentencing theory? Are proportionality and desert useful or dangerous conceptions for reformers who seek a fairer and more human sentencing policy? What implications does a desert rationale hold for overall levels of penalties?

While I think the Canadian Sentencing Commission crafted its proposed scheme well, I shall not go into the scheme's particulars (von Hirsch

1989). My theme, here, is a wider one: the political presuppositions and consequences of emphasizing proportionality and desert in sentencing reform. I shall try to be broadly thematic: my interest is in how one might think about reform politics. . . .

■ II. DO PROPORTIONATE SANCTIONS TEND TO BE MORE SEVERE?

Another theme of critics has been that proportionate sanctions will, in practice, be more severe. Barbara Hudson (1987: ch. 3) emphasizes this theme, citing evidence about increases in punishment levels in California and elsewhere since the justice model was first proposed in the mid-70's. The arguments, unfortunately, fall prey to the *post hoc ergo propter hoc* fallacy: since A has been followed by B, A must be the cause of B. No attempt is made to consider whether the increases occurred *because* of the influence of proportionalist sentencing theory, or despite that theory and due to other influences.

The use of imprisonment in California has doubtless increased, substantially, since adoption of the state's Determinate Sentencing Law in 1976 (von Hirsch and Mueller 1984: 293-294). Citing such increases proves little, however, unless other critical questions are examined. Are the increases associated with features of the law which are proportionalist, or with ulterior features? Have increases of comparable magnitudes occurred in jurisdictions using a different technique of implementing proportionality—e.g., sentencing-commission guidelines? Have states which eschewed the justice model succeeded better in avoiding penalty increases? When such questions are addressed, the desert-severity link becomes far from apparent.

California's increase in prison populations has been attributable, in considerable part, to a sharp rise in prison commitments (von Hirsch and Mueller 1984: 293-294). A desert-based model should supply standards for the decision whether to commit to prison—viz., ones that would limit incarceration to more serious (e.g., violent) crimes. The California Determinate Sentencing Law has never had such standards. The law only specifies the duration of confinement *if* the judge commits the defendant to prison, but (from the law's original enactment) left to the judge the decision to commit.[2] California's judges became less reluctant to send offenders to prison, once they knew those individuals would no longer serve indeterminate, possibly lengthy terms. There has been a sharp increase in commitments for intermediate-level crimes such as burglary which, on desert-based standards (and indeed, under Minnesota's guidelines), would not ordinarily be candidates for commitment (von Hirsch, Knapp and Tonry 1987: ch. 5). So one wonders what California's increase in commitment-rates shows: is it that desert leads to severity, or rather that *failure* to adopt a desert-based standard for commitment[3] leads to more people going to prison?

Were desert, indeed, responsible for more severity, one would expect those states which rejected the idea to be less draconian. But have they been? The case of New York comes to mind. New York is comparable to California in demographics (both states have large cities with substantial low-income minority populations), and in the politics of law and order (crime is a big political issue in both states). New York, however, has never adopted any desert-based sentence-reform scheme, and has instead made extensive use of mandatory minimum sentences having a marked incapacitative flavor (von Hirsch, Knapp and Tonry 1987: 79-83). Contrary to Hudson's thesis, the absence of a justice model has in no way led to less punitiveness in New York: the state has experienced well over a doubling of its prison population in a decade and a half.

In 1985, New York had the opportunity to move toward more proportionate sanctions. A sentencing commission was established, and it proposed guidelines that (albeit in somewhat crude fashion) would have given the seriousness of the offense increased weight in deciding sentence (New York State Committee on Sentencing Guidelines 1985). The proposal—although it did not call for penalty reductions—was roundly denounced as too lenient, and rejected. Leading the calls for rejection was the Manhatten district attorney, a former member of the commission. Prosecutors, he asserted, already had extensive powers to imprison under existing mandatory minima. The guidelines could only dilute the power to get tougher, by eliminating the ability to imprison for lesser second felonies, and by limited discretion to go above the guideline ranges. If proportionalism is likely to lead to greater harshness as Hudson contends, the point was apparently lost on the real get-tough advocates in New York (von Hirsch, Knapp and Tonry 1987: 76-83).

California's standards were statutory, and thus vulnerable to law-and-order pressures within the legislature. Dissatisfaction with statutory standards led, beginning in the late 70's, to the movement in other states for sentencing-commission guidelines. A commission, it was believed, would be less exposed to such pressures, and would have more time and expertise to devote to writing the guidelines (von Hirsch, Knapp and Tonry 1987: ch. 1).

What has been the experience with sentencing guidelines? Some, most notably the U.S. federal guidelines which took effect in November 1987, have been unashamedly draconian. The federal guidelines call for halving of the use of probation and for a vast increase in prison commitments (U.S. Sentencing Commission 1987: 60-64). The guidelines, however, do not purport to be based on desert: a desert-based scheme was jettisoned early in the commission's deliberations, and the final product expressly disavows adoption of a desert orientation (U.S. Sentencing Commission 1987: 15-16; von Hirsch 1989). The most conservative (and now seemingly most influential) member of the commission has recently written that extensive reliance on desert rationale would have been inconsistent with the statutory mandate that multiple penal aims be relied upon, and would give insufficient scope to deterrence and incapacitation of criminals (Nagel 1990: 916-925).

What of guidelines schemes developed with proportionality concerns expressly in mind? The most notable instance is Minnesota's scheme, which has been in operation since 1980 (Minnesota Sentencing Guidelines Commission 1990). Minnesota's guidelines scale sentences according to the gravity of offenses; and generally limit prison terms to crimes of violence and other serious offenses—except in cases where the defendant has a substantial criminal record. During the first decade of their operation, the guidelines had considerable success in restraining the escalation of sanctions. The guidelines were designed to keep prison populations within prisons' capacity when the guidelines were written—and, during this period, largely succeeded in doing so (von Hirsch, Knapp and Tonry 1987: chs. 5 and 8). (While Hudson (1987: ch. 3) feels obliged to mention the Minnesota guidelines, she remains curiously silent about this result, seemingly so inconsistent with her thesis on the severity-enhancing effects of desert.) The Minnesota experience has also sometimes been dismissed by American commentators on grounds that the state has an atypically "liberal" political environment. That contention, however, scarcely is sustainable for present purposes—since Canada's politics seem more comparable with Minnesota's than with such law-and-order states as New York or California.

Even Minnesota is not exempt from panics over criminality, and one occurred in 1989 following a series of grisly sexual homicides in Minneapolis. Faced with heavy pressures from the legislature, the state's sentencing commission significantly increased the prescribed prison terms for violent crimes. However, the commission was able to exact its *quid pro quo*: the guidelines' criminal-history score was recalculated, so as to make it substantially more difficult to incarcerate property offenders with long records.[4] The change was made to help maintain proportionality in the whole system, and to limit the increase in prison populations that otherwise would have occurred. Had there been no guidelines, I suspect that prison terms for violent crimes would still have risen comparably or still more; but there would have been no compensating reduction for property offenders. Indeed, without the guidelines, there would have been no vehicle to help ensure that judges would make more sparing use of the prison for repeat property offenders.

In assessing the link between sentencing rationale and penal severity, a certain realism is needed. A sentencing theory cannot, Canute-like,[5] stop the waters from rising: where the law-and-order pressures in a particular jurisdiction are sufficiently strong, punishments will rise, and no penal theory can stop that. Increases in sanction levels are best understood with reference to the underlying political dynamics, and those have been apparent enough in the U.S. in the last decade-and-a-half: increased public resentment over high crime rates, identification of crime in the public mind with unpopular minority and lower-class groups, and an environment of political opportunism that has fostered official posturing about "law 'n order." All a penal theory can do is offer reasons for limiting penalty increases. The question—to which I turn next—is whether desert, or utilitarian conceptions, can best supply such reasons.

■ **III. GROUNDS FOR LIMITING PENAL INTRUSION: DESERT VS. UTILITARIANISM**

An adequate penal theory, in a society that values personal liberty, is one that supports constraints on how much offenders are punished. As a constraining rationale, desert remains superior to its major alternative, penal utilitarianism.

In the first six decades or so of this century, it was utilitarianism that was the dominant idea. The sentence, it was widely assumed, should be designed to reduce levels of criminality. Indeed, an attempt was made to embody the idea in Canadian penal legislation, by a declaration that "the fundamental purpose underlying imposition of a sentence is . . . the protection of the public" (Canadian Sentencing Commission 1987: 481)

Traditionally, the leading version of penal utilitarianism was the treatment model: criminal justice policy (including sentencing) was supposed to foster the rehabilitation of the offender. Faith in rehabilitationism—at least, as the primary sentencing aim—has declined in the last decades, not only in Canada and the U.S. but in other countries (including Sweden) that once embraced it enthusiastically (Allen 1981; von Hirsch 1983). Doubts about the treatment ethic have sometimes been overstated, in assertions that "Nothing Works" (attributed, not quite accurately, to Martinson 1974). The latter claims can backfire—by implying that if *any* programs can be shown to succeed, then the treatment model could be revived.[6] Even when programs succeed, however, they typically work only for selected subgroups of offenders, carefully screened for their amenability (Palmer 1984; Sechrest 1987: 293-322). Treatments do not (and are not likely to) exist that can be relied upon to decide sentences routinely—that can inform the judge, when faced with the run-of-the-mill burglary or car theft, what the appropriate sanction should be, and that provide even a modicum of assurance that the sanction will contribute to the offender's ceasing to offend. Unless treatment had such routine, predictable applicability, it is difficult to see how it could serve as the primary sentencing rationale.

With the decline of rehabilitation, penal utilitarianism has not disappeared, but merely shifted emphasis to other preventive strategies, notably, deterrence and incapacitation. If punishment cannot cure criminals, the thinking has run, other, more realistic ways of reducing crime exist: namely, intimidating potential offenders and restraining actual ones. In the late 70's, it was deterrence that became fashionable. Mandatory minimum sentences, making it more certain that felony convicts go to prison, would enhance deterrence and also (by confining persons who might otherwise reoffend) enhance "general" incapacitation. Wilson (1975: ch. 8) predicted that such a strategy could reduce robberies by 20%. Unhappily, the strategy did not live up to its promises; although prison populations rose sharply as many states beefed up their mandatory-minimum laws, rates of serious crime did not diminish.[7] As a result, the fashion shifted in the 80's to incapacitation. Prisoner self-reports seemed to suggest that a small and identifiable group of felons commit a disproportionate share of serious felonies. By targeting these individuals for substantially increased prison terms, a marked incapacitative effect could supposedly be achieved, without any major further increase in prison population. Peter W. Greenwood (1982) developed a "selective incapacitation" index that, supposedly, would identify the high risks among convicted robbers. He asserted that if these individuals were given lengthy prison terms while lower-risk robbers had their prison sentences reduced, a 15% reduction in the robbery rate could be achieved simultaneously with some reduction in prison populations.

These deterrent and incapacitative strategies entail a particular risk of sanction escalation. There exists not only a danger of overall penalty increases (if a moderate dose of punishment fails to reduce crime, why not try a bigger dose?); but especially, a danger of disproportionate escalation in sanctions for offenders targeted for special attention. Illustrative of this tendency are recent measures that sharply increase penalties for drug offenses.[8] Likewise illustrative are the lengthy prison sentences proposed for "high risk" offenders under selective-incapacitation strategies. What makes such strategies so worrisome is their plausibility. While it is hard to imagine widely effective treatments, why cannot dangerous felons be separated from the community? Doubts have by now been cast on the reliability of Greenwood's estimates of how much his selective-incapacitation scheme would reduce crime (Panel on Research on Criminal Careers 1986: ch. 5; von Hirsch 1988). However, utilitarians might argue, what would prevent us from doing better if we continue to hone our forecasting skills?

One of the main ideas behind the desert model has been to provide a constraint against these harsher varieties of penal utilitarianism. (Indeed, my most recent book on sentencing theory (1985) deals, as its title suggests, with the issue of "past or future crimes"—of penal desert vs. selective incapacitation.) Desert theory provides such constraints in the following ways:

1. Desert theory's guiding principle, of proportionality, is grounded in notions of equity, not prevention efficacy. Preventive success—the impact of sentencing reform on crime rates—is not the theory's criterion for success. If a desert model is implemented and does not lead to reduction of

the incidence of crime, this is not a mark of the scheme's failure (von Hirsch 1985: ch. 15). Indeed, most desert advocates are (as is the Canadian Sentencing Commission) rather pessimistic about our ability to achieve significant crime reduction through changes in sentencing criteria and practice (Ashworth 1989). Sentencing reforms are to be evaluated, instead, in terms of their success in scaling the penal response to crime gravity in human fashion. Because crime rates are not the criterion, there will be less temptation, if moderate penalties fail to reduce crime, to escalate punishments in the hope of achieving preventive impact. Indeed, the Minnesota sentencing commission opted for desert over incapacitation in writing its standards, in part because it did not wish to present its scheme to the public as a crime-control device—and then, if crime rates did not fall, face pressure to resort to tougher preventive medicine (von Hirsch, Knapp and Tonry 1987: 88-89).

2. The criteria for desert also serve to restrict reliance on the more scary crime-control strategies. Consider selective incapacitation. That technique calls for imposition of substantially extended sentences on "high risk" felons; and relies upon indicia of risk which have little bearing on crime gravity—such as prior arrests, drug abuse, schooling, and unemployment. A proportionalist conception of sentencing—as I have argued elsewhere at length (von Hirsch 1985: ch. 11)—*must* reject such an approach, because it relies on factors so ulterior to the blameworthiness of the criminal conduct, and also because (to achieve any significant preventive impact) it calls for such large disparity in the severity of sentence of those deemed dangerous, as compared with other persons convicted of similar crimes.[9]

Could one argue against these troubling forms of penal utilitarianism, without relying on desert? One can try, but the arguments do not carry much moral authority. Take selective incapacitation, again: Elliott Currie (1985: 81-101) devotes much of his book to criticizing this strategy but is unwilling to invoke desert for the purpose. Instead, he offers a number of technical arguments about why selective incapacitation is unlikely to work. (The ready answer to those arguments could be: provided selective incapacitation is not going to cost too much, why not try anyway and see if it does work?) Missing from his discussion is the critical moral dimension: that there is something *wrong*, not just possibly ineffectual or counterproductive, in singling out some armed robbers for eight years' confinement while other robbers, whose criminal acts were no less reprehensible, get a year (Greenwood 1982).

One substitute response sometimes advocated today is the reaffirmation of rehabilitation. Treatment, it is said, is a more humane notion than deterrence or incapacitation; and it is now widely understood that the prison is no cure for offenders' criminal tendencies. A return to rehabilitation, supposedly, would pave the way for less harsh penal policies (Cullen and Gilbert 1982).

Ideologies cannot be revived at will, however. The rehabilitative ethic seemed so attractive in past decades, because people really believed that offenders routinely could be cured. That claim scarcely rings true today: even the proponents of the new rehabilitationism put more emphasis on the idea's positive policy consequences than on the widespread potential effectiveness of treatment (Cullen and Gilbert 1982: ch. 7). Certain treatments may, indeed, succeed on selected subgroups of offenders. But it remains unlikely, as I have said already, that most offenders regularly coming before the courts can be treated with reasonable prospects of success. (Even such treatment advocates as Gendreau and Ross (1987: 345) concede that we are still "... absolutely amateurish at implementing ... experimentally demonstrated programs within ... systems provided *routinely* by government.") I thus do not see rehabilitation replacing the newer forms of penal utilitarianism, especially incarceration.

The supposed intrinsic humaneness of treatment may also be doubted. The rehabilitative ethic offers few, if any, limits on how severe penal therapies may be. Rehabilitationism has had worrisome embodiments in the past, such as long, indeterminate terms of confinement for the sake of treatment. Nor are the new rehabilitative techniques always reassuring. Drug treatments, especially, may be quite intrusive: compulsory residence in community-based facilities; strict and sometimes humiliating treatment routines; repeated searches and urine tests to detect continued abuse (Anglin and Hser 1990). The drug user or small-time seller may, on a rehabilitative sentencing ethic, face such burdensome interventions as these instead of the more modest sanction he would receive under a desert-based scheme.

A good test of the comparative merits of desert and utilitarian schemes is their applicability to intermediate community sanctions. Interest has newly been developing in various sorts of such sanctions; day fines, intensive supervision, community service, house arrest, etc. There have been two major difficulties, however. First, the sanctions often are employed on lesser offenders—those who otherwise would have received probation but are seen as cooperative recruits into the new programs. Second, imprisonment may be invoked as the penalty for those who breach the terms of their community penalty, thereby ultimately increasing rather than reducing reliance on the prison sanction (Tonry 1990: 177-180). Utilitarian theories offer no principled response to these problems: is not breach, for example, a significant indicator of increased risk that could justify incapacitation?[10]

Desert theory does offer such a principled response. Imprisonment, because of its severity, would be appropriate only for serious crimes; other offenses would have to receive non-custodial community sanctions (von Hirsch, Wasik, and Greene 1989: 599-600). The more onerous of these community sanctions—e.g., substantial financial penalties, house arrest, etc.—would, moreover, be appropriate only for crimes of middle seriousness; so that it would be wrong in principle to impose these substantial penalties on lesser offenses (von Hirsch *et al.*, 1989: 600-606). The theory also puts limits on breach sanctions: these, too, must be proportionate to the gravity of the conduct involved. Imprisonment may not be invoked for breach, unless the act of breach involves criminal conduct of a fairly serious criminal nature (von Hirsch *et al.*, 1989: 609-610). A strong feature of the Canadian Sentencing Commission report (1987: ch. 12) is its emphasis on scaled community sanctions.

■ IV. ARGUMENTS ABOUT "UNDERLYING ILLS"

Another cluster of criticisms of desert theory concerns its supposed failure to address certain fundamental ills, such as the underlying causes of crime or possible discrimination at earlier stages of the criminal process. Let me examine these objections.

1. Proportionalist sentencing doctrine sometimes is said to involve "blaming the victim." Bad social conditions, assertedly, are actually responsible for crime (or at least a high incidence of crime). The desert rationale diverts attention from these conditions, by focusing on the culpability of convicted offenders whose crimes may in large part stem from their own economic victimization (Hudson 1987: 164-169).

Here, we need to distinguish the view of conservative utilitarian theorists such as Wilson. In a much-quoted passage, he argues that government is not in a position to remedy fundamental social ills; and moreover, that it need not try to do so, because crime can more efficiently be dealt with through rigorous crime-prevention and punitive measures (Wilson 1975: 52-57). Thus his prescriptions for preserving public order truly do come at the expense of efforts to alleviate social injustice.

That is *not* the position of desert theorists. I do not think a modern state incapable of alleviating poverty or social disorganization. The European states which have made real (albeit admittedly costly) efforts in this direction have had considerable measure of success; and the United States is not so much incapable of reducing want as unwilling to undergo the necessary effort and expense. Nor do I concur with Wilson's view that we can—without trying to alleviate social misery in our cities—reduce crime through this or that prevention technique. It is no accident that Stockholm or Munich are safer than Newark or New York, and the reasons why relate more to living conditions in those places than to criminal-justice efficiency.

Unlike Wilson, desert theorists do not offer their conception of sentences as a solution to the crime problem. Graded, proportionate sentencing (as the Canadian Sentencing Commission was careful to note) can produce a fairer sanctioning system, not necessarily safer cities. Sentencing policy is simply not a very good tool either for reducing criminality or promoting wider social justice. (Rehabilitative programs, notwithstanding their proponents' rhetoric, also did not rectify fundamental social injustices.) If one wants a more decent society, one will need to establish and pay for the requisite programs of social assistance. That *may* also help— although one cannot be certain how much or when—shrink criminogenic conditions in the community.

The sentencing of convicted persons, however, cannot wait until underlying social ills are addressed, nor can it be abandoned once they are addressed. Some crime (including crime of serious nature) will occur in any event and cannot be overlooked. So the question is unavoidable: when convicted offenders face sentence (as fewer or more inevitably will) what guiding rationale will help assure that these decisions are made with the minimum feasible injustice? Addressing fundamental social ills (desirable and, indeed, essential as this is) cannot constitute a substitute for trying to make sentencing policy more coherent or fair.

The Swedish experience illustrates this point. Sweden has for decades had a wide network of state-financed welfare supports, ranging from unemployment insurance through health care to child support. These programs have doubtless helped eradicate want; and the country's wide sharing of prosperity may have contributed to the relative absence of violence and disorder. Crime has not disappeared in Sweden, however, nor with it the need for an intelligible sentencing policy. Sweden switched in 1988 to a desert-oriented sentencing framework because that was felt to provide better guidance for judges, and more just norms. The adoption of the new law did not, however, constitute an implicit abandonment of the larger social welfare supports—which continue despite the more difficult economic climate which Sweden is now experiencing. If one asked the drafters of the new sentencing statute whether it "addressed" the country's remaining social ills, they would answer certainly not and it is not supposed to— because that is the proper task of social-welfare not criminal-justice legislation.

2. Desert theorists assert that—even if their scheme cannot cure social disadvantage—it at least does not leave disadvantaged offenders *worse* off. The factors determining crime-seriousness (and hence the severity of the penalty) concern the conduct's harm and the actor's degree of criminal intent; social factors (such as employment status, education, age) generally carry no weight. (Indeed, the Minnesota guidelines expressly rule out the use of these factors.[11]) Desert is preferable in this respect to utilitarian strategies, for the latter allow consideration of social factors in a manner that put badly off defendants in a still worse position when they face sentence: unemployment, lack of skills, unstable residence and so forth can increase the penalty as indicia of risk (von Hirsch 1976: 147-148).

Barbara Hudson (1987: ch. 4) has replied that such claims are misleading. Indigent defendants are at a disadvantage at all the stages of the criminal process preceding the sentence. These disadvantages—ranging from greater likelihood of pretrial confinement to assignment to less qualified counsel—make them likely to be convicted on more serious charges than their more privileged fellows who engaged in comparable actual behaviour. Those more serious charges would, under an offense-based scheme, mean severer penalties. The supposed neutrality of desert is thus a sham. To offset their burdens at earlier stages, indigent offenders would have to have their social status expressly considered as grounds for extenuation. Hudson thus urges less reliance on desert, and more on a variety of "non-legal" factors she lists.

One wonders, however, about the consistency of Hudson's viewpoint. If her critical account of the dynamics of criminal justice is correct—that it mostly serves majoritarian or class interests and ignores the concerns of the disadvantaged—then what makes her think that, were desert rejected, the "non-legal" factors introduced would be ones to her liking? Would not the preferred non-legal factors be precisely those targeted against the so-called "dangerous classes": viz., incapacitative concerns that treat social deprivation as a sign of increased risk?

A consistent perspective is essential here. One might begin with something approaching an ideal perspective: what sentencing policy should look like in a reasonably just (or at least not manifestly unjust) society. In such an environment, much can be said for desert theorists' view that punishment ought to reflect the blameworthiness of the conduct, and not ulterior social-status factors. There might be some exceptions, for those social factors that seem to bear directly on the blameworthiness of the criminal conduct. Martin Gardner (1976: 804-805) has suggested that extreme want reduces the culpability of the actor in committing a criminal act, and thus should be treated as an extenuating circumstance. Assuming the society had only small pockets of deprivation, such departures would be rather rare. Next, one could shift one's focus to the grimmer realities of the real world, in which deprivation is more extensive and the deprived are at a real disadvantage in the legal process. There, however, it may be hazardous to urge heavy reliance on "non-legal" factors. If crime rates are high, it will practically become impossible to get poverty-based mitigating factors approved that diminish punishments for significant numbers of low-income convicted criminals. Increased use of social-status factors is likely to produce just the opposite result: the entry of risk-considerations in sentencing that make poor defendants worse off still. What one cannot do, however, is try to have it both ways: criticize the use of desert factors from a "realistic" perspective, and at the same time urge use of other, "non-legal" ones for immediate use, from a utopian viewpoint.

■ V. "JUST DESERTS IN AN UNJUST SOCIETY"

The foregoing questions about social ills raise a larger philosophical issue: that of "just deserts in an unjust society." A desert rationale differs from utilitarian ones precisely in that it purports to be fair, not merely to prevent undesired conduct. How can punishment be fair in a society that is not itself equitable?

I addressed this issue fifteen years ago, in the last chapter of *Doing Justice* (1976), but find myself dissatisfied with my answers. The topic deserves a full separate essay, which I hope to undertake soon. Let me make a few tentative observations, however.

My theory of desert in *Doing Justice* made the question even harder than it has to be. There, I espoused the so-called "benefits and burdens" view of desert (1976: ch. 6). That view sees the law as a jointly beneficial enterprise: each person is required to desist from certain conduct that harms others; but benefits by their reciprocal self-restraint. The offender obtains an unjust advantage when he or she victimizes, while benefiting from other citizens' self-restraint. Punishment's role is to impose an offsetting disadvantage (Murphy 1973).

This view of penal desert is, of course, particularly vulnerable to "unjust society" objections. Unless it is in fact true that a country's political and social system succeeds in providing mutual benefits to all citizens, the lawbreaker has not necessarily gained from others' law-abiding behaviour (Murphy 1973).

However, I have become convinced that the "benefits and burdens" view is philosophically unsound (von Hirsch 1985: ch. 5), and also fails to provide any meaningful guidance on how much punishment is deserved (von Hirsch 1990).[12] More persuasive, I believe, is an "expressive" theory of desert, which focuses on punishment's role in censuring or conveying disapproval of criminal conduct (von Hirsch 1987: ch. 5; von Hirsch 1990).

A censure view of penal desert, unlike the "benefits and burdens" view, does not depend directly on how much the actor supposedly benefits from others' compliance with the law. Instead, it focuses on how much harm the conduct does, and how culpable the actor is for the harm. The unfairly-treated actor might well be to blame if he knowingly injures others who are not themselves responsible for his ill-treatment. (The underpaid worker, for example, would still be doing something reprehensible if he vents his frustrations on his spouse, children, or neighbors who are in no better position than he.) Moving to a censure theory of desert by no means resolves the "unjust society" issue, but it does make it a bit more complicated. It is no longer enough to point to social injustices; one needs to explain how the fact of social injustice undercuts claims about the harmfulness of culpability of criminal conduct.

There was a period (indeed, as I was writing *Doing Justice*) when many critical criminologists took the "left idealist" view of crime: that criminal conduct is not so much intrinsically harmful as it is a social construct whose definition chiefly serves certain class interests. By recognizing the skewedness of existing social arrangements, the argument ran, the actual injuriousness of the conduct could legitimately be called into question (Sparks 1980: 159-210).

If this somewhat roseate view of criminal behaviour ever had any plausibility, it has lost it today—thanks in part to the criticisms of so-called "left realists." These criminologists have pointed to the grim realities of crime in poor neighborhoods: to the injury done not only to individual victims but to social bonds within the community. Whatever social injustice might otherwise do, it does not diminish (and indeed may increase) the harmfulness of common victimizing crime (Lea and Young 1984).

The other issue is culpability: to what extent does social injustice diminish criminal actors' responsibility for their conduct? Space (and the still-fragmentary character of my own thinking) does not permit any full answer, but let me make a few observations.

First, there is the question of how much culpability is diminished. Restricted economic and social opportunities doubtless make it harder to remain law-abiding. When the difficulty of compliance is great enough, Gardner's view—that culpability is reduced—is at least arguable (albeit subject to the caveats mentioned in Part V, above). But is culpability actually *eliminated?* And for *whom* would it be eliminated? Only the most deprived? Lower-class criminals generally? All offenders? I have difficulty believing that social deprivation—especially in the measure it is found in Canada—renders all lawbreakers beyond fault, whether they be petty thieves, burglars, drug importers or tax cheaters.

Second, it may be worth worrying about the implications of denying fault for the deprived. Persons deemed incapable of responsibility for their actions tend to be seen as less than fully adult, and can become the target of proactive forms of state intervention that may be still more intrusive than the criminal law—witness the history of involuntary civil commitment. (That is why some feminists object to the use of "premenstrual syndrome" and other defenses that seem to call women's capacity for responsible choice into question.)

I do not wish to overstate the doubts I have just raised. The "unjust society" query about deserved punishment is a tough philosophical issue, and it cannot be resolved by a few pages' commentary. All I wish to point out here is that it is not straightforwardly obvious that social injustice, in any degree, subverts the justice of deserved punishment. One would need to address hard questions about harm, culpability, the state's moral standing to censure, etc. If I need to give such questions more thought, so do my critics.

■ VI. TAKING REFORM POLITICS SERIOUSLY: THE NEED TO EXAMINE THE CANADIAN CONTEXT

Sweeping factual generalizations have become suspect these days. Nowhere is such skepticism more warranted than in the politics of criminal justice reform. The institutional and political substructure of criminal justice varies greatly from place to place—and with it, the impact of reforms will vary also. Proportionalist sentencing schemes do not have an intrinsic, inevitable political dynamic, as Hudson and other critics seem to assume. Instead, the sponsorship, and the settings, of the reforms can vary strikingly. Thus:

• The political sponsors of the measures differ greatly from place to place. The 1988 Swedish sentencing-reform act, mentioned above, was steered through Parliament by the ruling Social Democratic government. In England, legislation with a comparable philosophy, and a somewhat analogous structure, is being proposed in a White Paper by the Thatcher government (Great Britain 1990). Does that mean that such proposals are intrinsically Social Democratic or intrinsically Thatcherite? Life is not so simple. One may dislike (as I happen do) the Thatcher government's basic policies on education, welfare, union rights, and local government, and still have more sympathy for a sentencing blueprint that emphasizes proportionate sanctions and calls for limiting the use of imprisonment to serious offenses. It is essential to look at the small print—at the specifics of the proposal (Wasik and von Hirsch 1990).

• Severity trends following enactment of proportionalist sentencing law or regulation have also varied greatly from place to place. In Finland, the enactment of its 1976 sentencing-reform statute was followed by significant reductions in prison populations over the ensuing decade-and-a-half (Lang 1989). In Minnesota, the story was more complicated, as we have seen. In California, a flawed determinate-sentencing statute had little success in restraining the rise of prison populations, in a political atmosphere in which crime issues had become increasingly visible and contentious.

To assess the politics of proportionalist sentencing reform in Canada, therefore, we need to look at the *particulars* of the Canadian setting. First, to what extent has crime and its repression become a political issue, or is likely to become so? The more visible and the more strident "law-and-order" politics becomes, the less chance sentencing reforms have of succeeding—as the experience of states such as California and New York all to painfully suggests (von Hirsch, Knapp and Tonry 1987: 79-82). One thus needs to consider such questions as: How much has punishment policy typically become an issue in Canadian political campaigns? Have many politicians in Canada made "getting tough" a focus of their campaigns or of their public posture in office? How successful have such strategies been? It would also be helpful to consider whether there are deeper factors present which might "ignite" crime as a political issue in future. Are rates of crime, especially violent crime, rising substantially? How much is criminality associated in the public mind with otherwise-unpopular ethnic or national groups? How much are styles of campaigning or political utterance shifting away from programmatic and substantive concerns toward more posturing stances?

Second, what interests would be affected by the reform, and how? The most obvious interest is a financial one, of restraining the growth of spending on prison construction. Sentencing guidelines can assist in such spending restraint, by limiting the use of confinement to the more serious offenses. These fiscal concerns were an important reason for the Minnesota legislature's support of Minnesota's guidelines (Martin 1984: 34-61). Such concerns did not, however, act as much of a restraint in the writing of the U.S. federal guidelines—as prisons constitute so small a share of the U.S. federal budget. Are there significant budgetary constraints in Canada on prison expenditure, and how much incentive might these provide for creating guidelines that would limit reliance on imprisonment?

There are other questions of this nature worth asking. The Canadian Sentencing Commission's proposals rely on the provincial Courts of Appeal to develop a jurisprudence interpreting the guidelines. Is it likely, given these Courts' tradition, that they will cooperate?

With more reflection, one might elaborate such questions more fully, or with more sophistication. My point is simply that if we are to talk about the politics of sentencing reform, we need to take politics seriously: that is, look at the political environment of Canada's criminal justice system. Generalities will not help.

Where then, will the Canadian Sentencing Commission's proposals lead, if adopted? I wish I could be as sure of the answer as some of the scheme's critics seem to be. In a reasonably propitious environment, the proposals could lead to more predictable and fair penalties; in an unpropitious one, they will fail, Canadians—not an outsider such as myself—need to reflect on the institutional and political realities within which sentencing takes place in Canada and think about what those realities might portend for sentencing reform. But remember: complete success is not the aim. If adoption of the Canadian Sentencing Commission's proposals were to make sentencing somewhat fairer or more predictable (or even somewhat less unfair than it otherwise would be) that is all that can reasonably be expected.

Notes

1. I am indebted to Jean-Paul Brodeur, Ronald Clarke, Anthony Doob, Judith Greene, Lisa Maher, Julian Roberts, and Martha Jane Smith for their helpful comments on this paper.

2. For fuller discussion, see von Hirsch and Mueller, 1984, pp. 267-270. California has enacted some mandatory minima *requiring* commitment in certain cases, but no systematic guidelines limiting prison commitments to more serious crimes.

3. Another major contributor to rising population has been a sharply increased rate of parole and probation revocations (Messinger and Berecochea 1990). On a desert rationale, however, reimprisonment for probation or parole violation would be sharply restricted (von Hirsch and Hanrahan 1979: chs. 6-7).

4. The changes were made at the end of 1989, and are set forth in Minnesota Sentencing Guidelines Annotated (1990), Parts IIB and IV.

5. Actually, the charge is unfair to King Canute, for reasons the reader should recall.

6. In *Doing Justice*, I was thus careful to note that—despite failures of most treatment efforts up to that time—some programs could well succeed in future on selected subjects; and hence that the real issue was how just and commensurable is reliance on treatment in the determination of sentence (von Hirsch 1976: 127-130).

7. Among academics, a skeptical view of the effectiveness of such deterrence strategies has prevailed, since the publication of the National Academy of Sciences' report on deterrence (Panel on Research on Deterrent and Incapacitative Effects 1978: 3-90).

8. See, e.g., the sharp penalty increases for drug offenses provided in the U.S. federal guidelines (U.S. Sentencing Commission 1987: 62-64).

9. Some American penologists, most notably Norval Morris (1982: ch. 5), has argued that—to constrain the less attractive forms of penal utilitarianism—primary reliance on a desert model is not needed. Instead, Morris advocates a hybrid scheme, in which desert sets the permissible outer bounds on punishment within which preventive concerns may operate. I shall not address what I consider to be this approach's conceptual difficulties, having attempted that elsewhere (von Hirsch 1985: chs. 4, 12; von Hirsch 1988: 21-31). The practical difficulty should be apparent enough, however: Morris neither delineates (nor offers a theory on how to delineate) the supposed desert limits—so that we have no idea about where or how these limits can be located (von Hirsch 1985: ch. 12). The narrower those limits, the more desert concerns will determine the scaling of punishments and the more modest will be the scope for preventive considerations (which seemingly is why Morris wishes to avoid narrow limits). The wider the desert limits, however, the less impact they will have in constraining the more troublesome varieties of penal utilitarianism, such as selective incapacitation.

10. It is thus not surprising that intermediate sanction schemes of a strongly utilitarian thrust, such as Morris and Tonry's recent work (1990) offer no principled limits on the use of breach sanctions.

11. The guidelines ($ II.D.1) bar consideration in sentencing of race, employment factors, or social factors (including educational attainment, living arrangements, length of residence, or marital status).

12. *Doing Justice* (von Hirsch 1976: chs. 6, 8) used the "benefits and burdens" theory only to help justify the existence of punishment; and relied on expressive (i.e., censure-based) arguments to support the principle of proportionality. My present thinking is to extend the expressive arguments to the justification of punishment's existence.

References

Allen, Francis A. 1981 The Decline of the Rehabilitative Ideal: Penal Policy and Social Purpose. New Haven: Yale University Press.

Anglin, Douglas M. and Yih-Ing Hser. 1990 The treatment of drug abuse. In

Michael Tonry and James Q. Wilson (eds.), Drugs and Crime. Vol. 13 of Michael Tonry and Norval Morris (eds.), Crime and Justice: An Annual Review of Research. Chicago: University of Chicago Press.

Canadian Sentencing Commission. 1987 Sentencing Reform: A Canadian Approach. Ottawa: Ministry of Supply and Services.

Cullen, Francis T. and Karen Gilbert. 1982 Reaffirming Rehabilitation. Cincinnati: Anderson.

Currie, Elliott. 1985 Confronting Crime: An American Challenge. New York: Pantheon.

Duff, R.A. 1986 Trials and Punishments. Cambridge: Cambridge University Press.

Gabor, Thomas. 1990 Looking back or looking forward: Retributivism and the Canadian Sentencing Commission's proposals. Canadian Journal of Criminology 32: 537-546.

Gardner, Martin. 1976 The renaissance of retribution: An examination of "Doing Justice." Wisconsin Law Review [1976]: 781-815.

Gendreau, Paul and Robert R. Ross. 1987 Revivification of rehabilitation: Evidence from the 1980's. Justice Quarterly 4: 394-407.

Great Britain—H.M. Government. 1990 Crime, Justice and Protecting the Public (White Paper) London: H.M. Stationery Office.

Greenberg, David F. and Drew Humphries. 1982 Economic crisis and the justice model: A skeptical view. Crime and Delinquency 28: 601-617.

Greenwood, Peter W. 1982 Selective Incapacitation. Santa Moncia, Cal.: RAND Corporation.

Hudson, Barbara. 1987 Justice Through Punishment: A Critique of the "Justice" Model of Corrections. New York: St. Martin's Press.

Jareborg, Nils. 1988 Essays in Penal Law. Uppsala, Sweden: Iustus Förlag.

Kleinig, John. 1973 Punishment and Desert. The Hague: Martinus Nijhoff.

Lang, K.G. 1989 Upplever Fängelsesfraffen Renässans? Nordisk Tidsskrift for Kriminalvienskab 76: 83-94.

Lea, John and Jock Young. 1984 What is to be Done about Law and Order? Harmondsworth: Penguin.

Martin, Susan E. 1984 Interests and politics in sentencing reform: The development of sentencing guidelines in Minnesota and Pennsylvania. Villanova Law Review 29: 21-113.

Martinson, Robert. 1974 What works?—Questions and answers about prison reform. Public Interest 35: 22-54.

Messinger, Sheldon and John Berecochea. 1990 The prison population and the corrections process. California Bureau of Criminal Statistics. Crime and Delinquency in California. Forthcoming.

Minnesota Sentencing Guidelines Commission. 1990 Minnesota Sentencing Guidelines Annotated. St. Paul, Minn.: Minnesota CLE Press.

Morris, Norval. 1982 Madness and the Criminal Law. Chicago: University of Chicago Press.

Morris, Norval and Michael Tonry. 1990 Between Prison and Probation: Intermediate Punishments in a Rational Sanctioning System. New York: Oxford University Press.

Murphy, Jeffrey G. 1973 Marxism and rebribution. Philosophy and Public Affairs 2: 217-243.

Nagel, Ilene H. 1990 Structuring sentencing discretion: The new federal sentencing guidelines. Journal of Criminal Law and Criminology 80: 883-943.

New York State Committee on Sentencing Guidelines. 1985 Determinate Sentencing: Report and Recommendations. New York State Committee on Sentencing Guidelines.

Palmer, Ted. 1984 Treatment and the role of classification: A review of the basics. Crime and Delinquency 30: 245-67.

Panel on Research on Criminal Careers. 1986 Report. In A. Blumstein, J. Cohen, J. Roth and C. Visher (eds.), Criminal Careers and "Career Criminals." Washington, D.C.: National Academy Press. Vol. 1.

Panel on Research on Deterrent and Incapacitative Effects. 1978 Report. In A. Blumstein, J. Cohen and D. Nagin (eds.), Deterrence and Incapacitation: Estimating the Effects of Criminal Sanctions on Crime Rates. Washington, D.C.: National Academy of Sciences.

Sechrest, Lee. 1987 Classification for treatment. In D.M. Gottfredson and M. Tonry (eds.) Prediction and Classification: Criminal Justice Decision Making. Chicago: University of Chicago Press.

Singer, Richard G. 1979 Just Deserts: Sentencing Based on Equality and Desert. Cambridge, Mass.: Ballinger.

Sparks, Richard F. 1980 A critique of Marxist criminology. In N. Morris and M. Tonry, Crime and Justice: An Annual Review of Research. Chicago: University of Chicago Press. Vol. 2.

Tonry, Michael. 1990 Stated and latent functions of ISP. Crime and Delinquency 36: 174-191.

U.S. Sentencing Commission. 1987 Supplementary Report on the Initial Sentencing Guidelines and Policy Statements. Washington, D.C.: U.S. Sentencing Commission.

von Hirsch, Andrew. 1976 Doing Justice: The Choice of Punishments. New York: Hill and Wang. Reprinted, 1986, Boston: Northeastern University Press.

_____. 1983 "Neoclassicism," proportionality, and the rationale for punishment: Thoughts on the Scandinavian Debate. Crime and Delinquency 29: 52-70.

_____. 1985 Past or Future Crimes: Deservedness and Dangerousness in the Sentencing of Criminals. New Brunswick, N.J.: Rutgers University Press.

_____. 1988 Selective incapacitation: The National Academy of Sciences' Report on Criminal Careers and "Career Criminals." Criminal Justice Ethics 7: 18-35.

_____. 1989 Federal sentencing guidelines: Do they provide principled guidance? American Criminal Law Review 27: #2.

_____. 1990 Proportionality in the philosophy of punishment: From "Why Punish?" to "How Much?" Criminal Law Forum 1: #2.

von Hirsch, Andrew, Kay A. Knapp and Michael Tonry. 1987 The Sentencing Commission and Its Guidelines. Boston: Northeastern University Press.

von Hirsch, Andrew and Julia M. Mueller. 1984 California's determinate sentencing law: An Analysis of its structure. New England Journal on Criminal and Civil Confinement 10: 253-300.

von Hirsch, Andrew, Martin Wasik and Judith Greene. 1989 Punishments in the community and the principles of desert. Rutgers Law Journal 20: 595-618.

Wasik, Martin. 1987 Guidance, guidelines and criminal record. In M. Wasik and K. Pease (eds.), Sentencing Reform: Guidance or Guidelines? Manchester: Manchester University Press.

Wasik, Martin and Andrew von Hirsch. 1990 Statutory sentencing principles: The 1990 White Paper. Modern Law Review. Forthcoming.

Wilson, James Q. 1975 Thinking About Crime. New York: Basic Books.

THE FALLACY OF "JUST DESERTS"[1]

Thomas Gabor

In this paper, I will comment on the rationale underlying the proposals of the Canadian Sentencing Commission, as well as some other matters. In commenting on the rationale, I recognize that some scholars, including those on the Commission, distinguish between justifications for legal sanctions in general and justifications relating to the allocation of sanctions. I believe that such a distinction is somewhat artificial as these rationales are not independent. According to the Commission's sentencing guidelines, "the sentence should be proportionate to the gravity of the offence and the degree of responsibility of the offender for the offence" (Canadian Sentencing Commission 1987: 154). Thus, in the Commission's view, the allocation of sanctions rests on the notion that offenders are to blame for their conduct and hence deserve to be punished. Thus, proportionality in allocating sentences is clearly tied to a legal system founded on the principle of desert. Despite the interdependence of these rationales, where appropriate, I will indicate whether I am referring to the Commission's general rationale for penal interventions or to the sentencing guidelines they have proposed.

My remarks must also be qualified by the fact that, at this point, any discussion of the Commission's proposals is purely hypothetical. Even assuming that these proposals are accepted by Parliament and incorporated in the *Criminal Code*, the manner in which the sentencing guidelines would be implemented in practice is difficult to foresee. Judges would be empowered to override the presumptive sentences in any case provided they give reasons for so doing. It is unknown whether such departures from the guidelines would occur in very exceptional cases only or whether judges would use this authority as a means of reclaiming their pre-eminent role in sentencing.

The effects on prison populations of changing sentencing practices also cannot be foreseen, although the experience of some American states with presumptive sentencing systems indicates that overpopulation may be the result. While such an outcome is highly speculative, if it does materialize, sentencing practices may be affected as a consequence. Furthermore, where sanctions become more circumscribed, as they would be with the institution of the Commission's sentencing guidelines, it is possible that prosecutors may compensate for some of their lost leverage when exercising their discretion about the charges to proceed with and those to dismiss. As an example, a woman who killed her abusive husband while being battered might ordinarily be charged with manslaughter. In their guideline prototypes, the Canadian Sentencing Commission (1987: 519) suggests that manslaughter should generally carry a prison term of between four and six years. The Crown counsel might believe that this is an exceptional case warranting a far lighter sentence. If judges in that jurisdiction tend to show a reluctance to deviate from the prescribed sentences, the Crown may not want to risk proceeding against the woman and drop charges altogether.

All the aforementioned forms of adjustment, whether initiated by judges, Crown attorneys, or even the police, can undermine the objectives of sentencing reform pursued by the Commission. They all constitute what Singer (1979: 123) has referred to as "hydraulic discretion":

> A particularly depressing criticism against any proposal for sentencing reform is that it is irrelevant, since it tinkers with only one part of an entire system, blindly ignoring the effect that such reform will have on the other parts. Specifically, the argument is that to opt for judicial sentencing rather than parole decisions is to opt for sentencing by plea bargain . . . the presence of plea bargaining is especially anathema to the desert model of sentencing, since the model seeks consistent sentencing not only because equality is basically a desirable goal, but because all persons who commit the same offence should receive both the sanction and social stigma of having committed that offence. If plea bargaining allows some offenders to incur reduced stigma, the goal of equality of desert will have been seriously undermined.

Having made these preliminary remarks, let us examine the rationale for sentencing of the Canadian Sentencing Commission (1987: 151):

> It is recognized and declared that in a free and democratic society peace and security can only be enjoyed through the due application of the principles of fundamental justice. In furtherance of the overall purpose of the criminal law of maintaining a just, peaceful, and safe society, the fundamental purpose of sentencing is to preserve the authority of and promote respect for the law through the imposition of just sanctions.

> The proposed purpose is not to be confused with deterrence. It rests on the premise that the majority of the population need to be spared more from the outrage and demoralizing effect of witnessing impunity for criminal acts than to be deterred from indulging in them . . . the fundamental purpose of sentencing is to impose just sanctions to impede behaviour denounced by the criminal law. Promoting respect for the values embodied in the law would then strengthen the conviction in citizens that they can be made to account for unlawful behaviour, and that the costs of such behaviour out-weigh the anticipated benefits.

I believe that the eclecticism of the Commission's statement of purpose is laudable. Rather than recommending that sanctions be based on one rationale, an attempt is made to blend retributive (the Commission prefers the less pejorative term "justice") and utilitarian goals. The system of sentencing guidelines proposed is also a compromise between mandatory or fixed sentences on one hand and indeterminate or highly variable sentences on the other.

The utilitarian objectives of rehabilitation and selective incapacitation are discarded as primary objectives of legal sanctions. Only very few people consider offender reform as justifying legal interventions. Andrews, in this issue, argues that rehabilitation ought to be the cornerstone of corrections and that parole be maintained. Although I agree with his point that the Commission's treatment of rehabilitation was perfunctory, I disagree with his overly optimistic view of the potential of treatment and a "human science" perspective. The *imposition* of rehabilitative programs, whether psychotherapeutic, educational, vocational, or social, is practically unfeasible and ethically objectionable. The re-emergence of neoclassical thinking in criminology in the 1970s was a response, in part at least, to the sentencing disparities produced by a system with a greater emphasis on treatment.

The Commission laudably dismisses selective incapacitation as a goal of sentences. The nascent state of risk assessment and prediction technologies, as well as what I consider to be the inherent indeterminacy of human behaviour (Gabor 1986), would seem to preclude the ascendance of this approach to the level of a primary sentencing objective. Even if risk assessments could be shown to be fairly accurate, sentences based on them would create such disparity that the credibility of such a legal system would be rapidly undermined in the eyes of victims and the general public. This is so because many of those committing the most serious crimes (e.g., murder or manslaughter) might be assessed as unlikely to re-offend and, hence, may receive light sentences whereas chronic property offenders, for example, might receive stiff sentences. The Commission has recognized that vigilantism may arise in response to such perceived "injustices."

Also sensible, in my view, is the Commission's emphasis on the need to impose sanctions to promote respect for the law (Canadian Sentencing Commission 1987: 151). The failure to impose sanctions, according to the Commission, has a demoralizing effect on the public. Witnessing repeated violations of the law committed with impunity may weaken the inhibitions that keep members of society from breaking the law. While I believe that such a position constitutes more of a justification for sanctions in general than for the Commission's specific proposals, it is firmly grounded in empirical research.

The social learning theorist's concept of disinhibition can be useful here. Bandura (1977), in explaining the effects of media violence on the behaviour of the viewer, contends that witnessing others behave aggressively lowers the inhibitions of the viewer in relation to such behaviour. Seeing others commit transgressions without being held accountable may, therefore, legitimize such actions.

Studies of progressive vandalism show that property destruction is more likely to occur where property is already in a state of disrepair or has been defiled (Zimbardo 1973; Wilson and Kelling 1983; Samdahl and Christensen 1985). Wilson and Kelling (1983: 31) have shown, for example, that buildings in which windows are broken and left unrepaired are more likely to have other windows broken. Signs of incivility, disorder, and decay have a demoralizing effect on people and lead to the release of otherwise inhibited aggressive behaviour. Thus, while one may question the dissuasive effect of legal sanctions on those already contemplating crimes, it may be more difficult to argue that repeated assaults upon society's legal norms, with the absence of enforcement, cannot unleash a widespread pursuit of self-interest with all its socially harmful ramifications. It can be argued, however, that promoting conformity can be done more effectively by rewarding virtue than by punishing the violation of norms (Walker 1980: 35). Even if this argument were correct, establishing a system of such reinforcements would be a bureaucratic nightmare.

The Commission's sentencing guidelines are likely to be perceived as less capricious by the public than current practices as they involve more realistic sentences. The abolition of parole, while controversial and having some liabilities, ensures that the length of a prison sentence can be reduced by only 25 percent for good behaviour. The current situation, in which an inmate can receive a full parole after one-third of his sentence is served and day parole after only one-sixth is served, creates a sham of the entire sentencing process, seriously undermining the authority of the courts. Since members of the public seem to overestimate the proportion of inmates being paroled (Hann and Harman 1986) and the damage they do (Roberts and Doob 1989), their loss of confidence in the judicial system comes as little surprise. One wonders whether offenders, too, lose respect for a system in which one part imposes one penalty only to see another part, the Parole Board, roll back a substantial part of it. This "schizoid" characteristic of the justice system lends itself to disrepute, as decisions are neither irrevocable nor comprehensible.

Some have argued that abolishing parole will increase the prison sentences actually served (Dozois, Fréchette, Lemire, Normandeau and Carrière 1989)—such an outcome would not necessarily occur. For one thing, the Commission's emphasis on exercising restraint in sentencing is supported by its proposals to reduce the maximum penalties for a number of offences. Secondly, it would be naive to believe that judges today are unaware, when passing sentence, of the possibility that the offender will be paroled. It is well known that they tend to compensate for early release by passing harsher sentences. When an offender fails to gain early release, he may actually serve more time than under the system proposed by the Commission.

■ SOME DIFFICULTIES WITH THE PROPOSALS

The reader may infer, at this juncture, that my intention is not to bury the Commission but to praise it. The Commission's proposals have been carefully formulated and their limitations acknowledged. There is an attempt to take into account different principles of punishment, as well as recent empirical research. It would be erroneous to either condemn or embrace, in their totality, the multitudinous proposals that have been advanced. Having mentioned some of the areas in which I believe the proposals are well-founded, I wish now to tackle matters which cause me some concern. Foremost among these is the role of the desert principle and the manner in which it would be applied.

The Proposals: Retributive or Utilitarian?

Although I have commended the Commission for its attempt to blend retributive and utilitarian goals, there are many ways to do this and the Commission tries to achieve this objective in a curious way. Its sentencing scheme is purely retributive, as it is based on the offender's past conduct—the offence under consideration—as well as his/her degree of culpability. So as not to be perceived as endorsing the intrinsic merits of punishment or pure retribution, however, the Commission justifies this retributive system of sanctions by its utilitarian features. Thus, we are told that "just" sentences will promote respect and, hence, compliance with the law. The Commission clearly wants to have its cake and eat it too. Although, as I have mentioned, such a utilitarian goal has an empirical foundation, the fact remains that the sentencing system being proposed is a retributive one and I shall critique it on that basis. Any retributive system of sanctions will undoubtedly carry some utilitarian benefits through deterrence, incapacitation, and the reinforcement of social norms; however, they are incidental by-products of such a system. On the basis of these by-products, the Commission casts its system as largely utilitarian. Presumably, they do not wish to be branded retributive. In fact, they cite von Hirsch when making the point that "the pursuit of penal justice for its own sake appears purposeless" (Canadian Sentencing Commission 1987: 131). Since it is hard to conceive of any retributive system that is without some utilitarian benefits, do they mean to say that any ancillary crime preventive effects qualify the system as other than strictly retributive? To be considered as other than strictly retributive, shouldn't the proposed guidelines have to expressly incorporate utilitarian considerations? Rhetoric underscoring the utilitarian benefits of justice-oriented sentences is not sufficient. The model the Commission has advanced tries to make sentences proportional to the harm done and the perceived responsibility of the offender.

Even the list of aggravating and mitigating factors that is to serve as the basis for departures from the guidelines contains no references to the risk the offender poses to the community nor any other preventive objectives. The Commission considers youth a mitigating factor, whereas most predictive studies show that a young person, other things being equal, poses a greater threat to the community than an older one (Gabor 1986). The sentencing guidelines do not, in any way, explicitly consider preventive goals.

Despite the retributive sentencing model it proposes, the Commission repeatedly asserts that utilitarian goals are worth pursuing. At several junctures, the point is made that legal sanctions have at least some deterrent effect. While this statement is undoubtedly true, it provides no justification for the particular system of sentencing proposed by the Commission.

The Focus on the External Effects of Sentencing

As for the assertion that "the fundamental purpose of sentencing is to impose just sanctions to impede behaviour denounced by the criminal law" (Canadian Sentencing Commission, 1987: 151), the Commission turns on its head the idea that "justice must not only be done but must be seen to be done." Despite the cursory attention paid to the denunciative role of sentences, the Commission is suggesting that the paramount objective in sentencing lies in its effect on society in general. The communication of society's vigilance in relation to lawbreaking seems to have a considerable denunciative component to it.

The perception by the public that justice is done is accorded primary importance by the Commission. The effects of the sentence on the offender receive less attention. It might be argued that distributive justice entails an individualization of sentencing—this point will be discussed more fully below. The reform and deterrence of the offender, too, has been given short shrift. The role given to the effects of sentencing on the *external* audience rather than on those implicated in a criminal case is curious in light of the Commission's position that "there is a wide discrepancy between the public's knowledge of criminal sanctions and their actual features" (Canadian Sentencing Commission, 1987: 142). If the public's perception of actual sentences is so distorted, is it justified to place such a pre-eminent emphasis on the impact of sentencing on the public? Does the Commission feel that its reforms would suddenly enlighten the public about the sentencing process? The Commission cannot regulate the media's coverage of criminal justice issues. Nor can much be done about the tendency of the public to develop stereotypic images of criminals and over-simplified views of sanctions.

The excessive focus on the external effects of the system leaves the offender out in the cold. Although Commissioners stress that their sentencing model does not preclude rehabilitative efforts within the correctional system (Doob and Brodeur 1989), both the sentencing guidelines and the formal Declaration of Purpose and Principles of Sentencing (Canadian Sentencing Commission 1987: 153) make no specific reference to the welfare of offenders. The point is well taken that the philosophy of sentencing to which the Commission subscribes can foster a brutal and vindictive system (Grygier 1988). Sentences that pinpoint blame for past deeds, while ignoring compassion in the present and both offender risk and reform in the future, signal to correctional personnel that their efforts are futile. I am not arguing for a treatment or risk-based system, merely that the Commission's proposals cannot easily accommodate such considerations.

The Fallacy of "Just Deserts"

A sentencing system based on desert might not be so objectionable were commensurate or proportional sentences as readily quantifiable as justice-oriented sentencing guidelines suggest. These highly systematized schemes promote the illusion that there is a fairly precise penalty fitting each type of offence. In this context, Monahan (1984: 12) has asserted that while "the prediction of recidivism is a Herculean task, the assessment of culpability is a divine one." Indeed, there are many shortcomings of sentencing based on the desert principle.

For one thing, most legal systems, when allocating blame do consider the offender's state of mind (*mens rea*), so, one might ask, why not consider other characteristics of the offender, such as a disadvantaged background, personal stresses prior to the offence, and his motives for the offence (Singer 1979: 21). The proposed presumptive sentences may be able to accommodate such considerations but only within the narrow range allowed by the guidelines. The argument for the individualization of sentences can be made on retributive rather than merely utilitarian grounds as very unequal offenders may be sentenced equally due to similarities in the offence itself. In his dissenting opinion regarding the proposed presumptive guidelines, Commissioner Pateras indicated that "the actual restraint imposed by presumptive guidelines is the restriction of a sentencing judge's discretion to impose the sentence (type, range, etc.) which he or she believes is the just and appropriate one for that offence and that offender" (Canadian Sentencing Commission 1987: 339).

Another problem in establishing a sentencing system based on desert is whether the sentence should reflect the offender's intent or merely the outcome of an offence. Whether the victim of an assault dies, suffers serious injuries, or escapes injury altogether is partly beyond the offender's's control. The physical condition and attributes of the victim, the intervention of third parties, the response of emergency medical services, and many other extraneous factors can affect the outcome of an offence. A fortuitous element can also enter into property crimes such as, for example, the crime of theft. The proposed sentences are different for theft over and under $1000 although chance may determine the amount of money an offender finds in, say, a wallet he has stolen.

Any rating of offences on the basis of seriousness must take into account the psychological harm to the victim (Singer 1979). In sexual assaults and robberies, for example, the emotional effects tend to be more acute and enduring than the physical injuries incurred. The sentencing guidelines are silent about this factor, which is also relevant to some property crimes (e.g., break and enter). Here again, the difficulties in measuring harm and in using it as a criterion in sentencing are evident.

What of the so-called victimless crimes, such as drug trafficking and the sale of pornography? If there is no definable harm, should these be offences at all if desert is based on harm? If so, how do we measure the amorphous injuries inflicted on society by these offences?

Another issue that proponents of sentencing on the basis of desert must wrestle with is that of foreseeable harms (Singer 1979: 26-27). Suppose A rapes B who then commits suicide as a result of the disgrace she feels; or, A robs B who shoots at A, but instead kills C, a bystander. Should offenders be responsible for these additional consequences of their crimes? Should offenders be held accountable for still other effects on third parties such as the disintegration of a family after a mother is sexually assaulted or after the breadwinner has been disabled following an assault or a robbery?

The desert philosophy also assumes that what appears to be the same punishment will be objectively the same and will be perceived in the same way. Suppose two robbers receive five-year prison terms. The first, a gang leader, has many contacts in the institution and, upon entering, is greeted as though the event was some form of homecoming. The other robber, serving his first penitentiary sentence, is carefully sized up when he enters the prison. The objective experiences of these two individuals in prison will be very different, as the neophyte is far more likely to be attacked and intimidated by both fellow prisoners and guards. Even if one could hold these objective experiences constant, the impact of incarceration would differ from one person to the next depending on such things as one's social status, one's habituation to institutional life, marital status, the proximity of one's family to the institution, and many other factors. The sentencing guidelines offered by the Canadian Sentencing Commission camouflage the fact that neither legislators nor the courts have any control over the application of sanctions and what these sanctions mean to different offenders.

Yet the Commission speaks of fundamental justice. With all the intangibles involved in both crime and punishment, the most "equitable" and proportional system of sanctions constitutes an extremely crude representation of what is "deserved." My greatest objection to the type of guidelines formulated by the Commission is the pretense that one can somehow quantify what is a "just" sentence in a given type of case. Or, is the Commission prepared to reverse Oliver Wendell Holmes' famous aphorism by asserting that the perception of justice is more important than that justice is actually done?

The fact is there is no rational method of determining the exact sentence that is proportional to a particular crime. Decisions based on desert will be more subjective than those based on utilitarian aims as they cannot be validated by agreed upon criteria. One can at least attempt to ascertain whether sentences based on some utilitarian consideration (e.g., deterrence) are achieving their objectives.

Hydraulic Discretion

Furthermore, a system of sentencing guidelines can be undermined by adjustments at earlier phases of the criminal justice system. The police and the Crown can decide not to lay charges or to drop charges where they feel the prospective sentence would be too harsh. The Crown would have more leverage in extracting plea bargains as this would be the final point at which considerable discretion would remain. Alschuler (1978: 577) writes:

> Eliminating or restricting the discretionary powers of parole boards and trial judges is likely to increase the powers of prosecutors, and these powers are likely to be exercised without effective limits through the practice of plea bargaining. The substitution of fixed or presumptive sentences for the discretion of judges and parole boards tends to concentrate sentencing power in the hands of officials who are likely to allow their decisions to be governed by factors irrelevant to the proper goals of sentencing—officials, moreover, who typically lack the information, objectivity and experience of trial judges.

Even members of the public, if they were as informed about the sentencing guidelines as the Commission hopes they would be, may be reluctant to report offences carrying a presumption of a prison sentence where they may for some reason wish to protect the offender. Aggravated assault, for example, may be perpetrated by a spouse. The victim, under the current system, may report the offence and testify against her husband in order to "shock" him. If she is aware that a serious assault can result in a certain and fairly lengthy prison term, she may be more reluctant to come forward.

The Selective Use of Punishment

Case attrition in the criminal justice system also seriously undermines the desert principle. According to the Commission's own figures, at best, only three percent of all offenders committing a criminal offence during any given year end up before a sentencing court in that same year (Canadian Sentencing Commission 1987: 119). Chance, skill in crime, economic clout, and other factors having little to do with justice play a major role in whether one is punished for one's transgressions. Such a state of affairs, which is largely beyond the control of the justice system, renders more credible the common refrain of convicted offenders that their plight is due to simple bad luck or harassment by the authorities.

A related issue concerns the type of people who come before the courts and populate our prisons. Since they derive disproportionately from the lowest economic strata of society, from the ranks of aboriginal Canadians, and "street" criminals, the argument can easily be made that the filtering of criminal cases through the criminal justice system is not based exclusively on objective behaviour. That the rich and the powerful, those polluting the environment, marketing dangerous products, or abusing the public's trust are subject to preferential treatment is a truism requiring little documentation here. As long as different standards exist for members of different social groups and for different types of offenders, any system based on the desert principle will have limited credibility.

How many of the Mulroney cabinet officials violating conflict of interest guidelines are serving time in our prisons? Until such large-scale injustices are rectified, measures designed to promote respect for the criminal law, such as those proposed by the Sentencing Commission, will have limited value. Nowhere in its 600 page report does the Commission address the fundamental inequities in our justice system. Its goal, it would appear, is to promote equity in sentencing among the highly selective group of Canadians who appear before a court, rather than among all citizens of this country. An illustration of this point is the rejection of the Swedish model of fines, whereby the amount of fines levied are proportional to the offender's income. Developing sanctions that have equal impact on all Canadians, regardless of their means, is long overdue.

Dangerousness of Offenders is not Considered

Through the retributive system it proposes, the Commission is remarkably silent about employing risk as a criterion in sentencing. Although, as mentioned, the danger posed to the community by the offender should not be the *primary* concern of sentencing, nor need it be completely ignored. While I agree that the prediction of future criminality is precarious, blanket dismissals of prediction grossly oversimplify the subject.

For one thing, the accuracy of prediction is contingent on the outcome one is trying to predict: crime of recidivism in general, violent crime, the rate of offending, or the timing or seriousness of future criminal behaviour. In general, the more precise or rare the outcome that is being predicted, the less accurate the prediction will be (Gabor 1986). Predictions can be made through clinical assessments of individuals, the application of statistical probabilities to groups, or through a combination of these two methods. An amalgamation of the two will tend to produce the best result. Also bearing on the prediction is the "base rate" issue. Where one is trying to predict unlikely events such as particularly heinous crimes, overpredictions of dangerousness may abound. On the other hand, predicting simply that *all* penitentiary inmates will be re-arrested at some point for some offence may be accurate in three-quarters or more of the cases. Applying predictions to an undifferentiated group will not yield predictions as accurate as those based on a more homogeneous subsample of offenders (Gabor 1986). Recidivism approaches certainty for those with an early onset of criminality and a long history of antisocial and criminal behaviour (Wolfgang, Figlio and Sellin 1972; Hamparian, Shuster, Dinitz and Conrad 1978).

The chronic offender, who may single-handedly be a significant menace to a community, would fall through the cracks of the system proposed by the Sentencing Commission. Both the aggravating conditions that could lead to a departure from the guidelines and the exceptional sentences proposed by the Commission are based primarily on the characteristics of the most recent offence rather than on the characteristics and record of the offender. While it is true that the Commission's guidelines and list of aggravating factors include the presence of a criminal record, this factor would be taken into account differently in retributive as opposed to utilitarian sentencing. As an example, a retribution would consider the length of time elapsing between a previous conviction and the most recent offence as a potential aggravating factor. Von Hirsch (1976: 87) writes that "The greater the time between the preceding offense and the current one, the harder it becomes to argue that the prior offense bears on the ascription of culpability for the current one." The utilitarian, on the other hand, would likely consider short intervals between offences as meriting a longer sentence due to the offender's high rate of criminal activity. Protection of the community from hardcore offenders who, in some cases, may be responsible for hundreds of crimes a year, again takes a back seat to retribution.

■ CONCLUSION

The establishment of sentencing guidelines is useful in structuring sentencing decisions. The issue is whether such guidelines should merely guide judicial decisions or be imposed on judges as is the case in the Commission's recommendations, where judges must state the reasons for departures from them. A principal goal of the Commission is to deal with sentencing disparity. Disparity can be defined in two ways. First, it can mean that people convicted of similar offences receive widely varying sentences. A second and tighter definition views disparities as variations in sentences for cases that are very similar, resulting from the different principles subscribed to by judges or personal prejudices. To consider all variation in sentencing as unjustified misses the idiosyncratic features of each criminal case and fails to take into account offender-related factors. Equity can mean similarity in the sentencing criteria used from case to case rather than identical sentences.

The Commission is of the view that there is considerable "unwarranted variation" in sentencing in this country (Canadian Sentencing Commission 1987: 77). Rather than establish guidelines that could be imposed optionally by the courts, their guidelines would limit the discretion of the sentencing judge. The Commission therefore has little faith in the fairness of Canadian judges even if sentencing guidelines were made available to them. The guidelines must therefore be more coercive than a mere nudge or prompt. The irony is that while placing such little faith in the judiciary, the Commission consolidates judicial authority over sentencing by abolishing parole and therefore reducing correctional input. Judicial discretion would presumably be reduced in absolute terms through the adoption of the sentencing guidelines but, in relative terms, would be expanded as judges would have more say in the *formal* discretion that would remain.

The desire of the Sentencing Commission to reduce disparities and enhance fairness in sentencing is to be commended. My fear is that the implementation of the Commission's proposals would engender an inertia in the criminal justice system, signalling to both convicted persons and criminal justice personnel that their efforts are fruitless. The implementation of these proposals would have a symbolic effect, marking the end of efforts to reform and show compassion towards offenders, many of whom have already been victimized by abuse, neglect, and economic privations. A system focusing exclusively on blame for past deeds would be morally and operationally bankrupt, fostering negativity and vindictiveness. Just as many current forms of psychotherapy advise clients not to dwell on the past but rather to face present realities, sentences that look only backwards will be unable to adapt to the ever-changing realities of a dynamic society.

Note

1. I am grateful to my colleague, Julian Roberts, for his comments and for engaging me in some animated discussions on various points made in this paper.

References

Alschuler, David. 1978 Sentencing reform and prosecutorial power: A critique of recent proposals for "fixed" and "presumptive" sentencing. University of Pennsylvania Law Review 126: 550-577.

Bandura, Albert. 1977 Mechanisms of aggression. In Hans Toch (ed.), Psychology of Crime and Criminal Justice. New York: Holt, Rinehart and Winston.

Canadian Sentencing Commission. 1987 Sentencing Reform: A Canadian Approach. Ottawa: Supply and Services.

Doob, Anthony N. and Jean-Paul Brodeur. 1989 Rehabilitating the debate on rehabilitation. Canadian Journal of Criminology 31: 179-192.

Dozois, Jean, Marcel Fréchette, Guy Lemire, André Normandeau and Pierre Carrière. 1989 La détermination de la peine au Canada: bilan critique de la Commission Archambault. Canadian Journal of Criminology 31: 63-80.

Gabor, Thomas. 1986 The Prediction of Criminal Behaviour: Statistical Approaches. Toronto: University of Toronto Press.

Grygier, Tadeusz. 1988 A Canadian approach or an American band-wagon? Canadian Journal of Criminology 30: 165-172.

Hamparian, Donna, Richard Schuster, Simon Dinitz and John Conrad. 1978 The Violent Few. Lexington, Mass.: Lexington Books.

Hann, Robert G. and William G. Harman. 1986 Full Parole Release: An Historical Descriptive Study. Ottawa: Solicitor General Canada.

Monahan, John. 1984 The prediction of violent behavior: Toward a second generation of theory and policy. American Journal of Psychiatry 141: 10-15.

Roberts, Julian V. and Anthony N. Doob. 1989 Sentencing and public opinion: Taking false shadows for true substances. Osgoode Hall Law Journal 27: 491-515.

Samdahl, D. and H. Christiansen. 1985 Environmental cues and vandalism. Environment and Behavior 17: 446.

Singer, Richard G. 1979 Just Deserts: Sentencing Based on Equality and Desert. Cambridge, Mass.: Ballinger.

Von Hirsch, Andrew. 1976 Doing Justice. New York: Hill and Wang.

Walker, Nigel. 1980 Punishment, Danger and Stigma: The Morality of Criminal Justice. Totowa, N.J.: Barnes and Noble.

Wilson, James Q. and George Kelling. 1983 Broken windows. The Atlantic Monthly.

Wolfgang, Marvin E., Robert F. Figlio, and Thorsten Sellin. 1972 Delinquency in a Birth Cohort. Chicago: University of Chicago Press.

Zimbardo, Phillip. 1973 A field experiment in auto shaping. In Colin Ward (ed.), Vandalism. London: Architectural Press.

■ POSTSCRIPT

Hirsch responds to critics of the just deserts model by claiming that the model will actually reduce the length of prison sentences. He criticizes critics of the model for falsely assuming that its adoption in California led to the lengthening of sentences in that state when actually other factors were instrumental in bringing about the increase. Hirsch also rejects the notion that introducing nonlegal variables into the sentencing process will reduce sentencing for disadvantaged groups in society. He argues that the introduction of nonlegal variables might actually have the opposite effect.

Gabor, on the other hand, argues that desert theorists cannot effectively measure how much punishment should be administered for particular crimes. In some cases, application of the same penalty to two criminals who have committed the same crime might cause more harm than good. Individual circumstances may make a five-year jail sentence appropriate for one offender, but either too harsh or too lenient for another. Criminals who believe they have been treated unfairly may commit more crimes in protest, while criminals who have received lenient penalties may commit further crimes because the deterrent was an insufficient one. Gabor adds that case attrition in the criminal justice system also undermines the deserts model, as cases are filtered out of the system before they are taken to court.

In this continuing debate, it is worth noting that some criminologists argue that both the retributive and rehabilitative ideals can be used to justify inhumane treatment of prison inmates. Gosselin (1982) and Culhane (1979), for example, point out that inhumane treatment of inmates has led to prison riots. According to these analysts, it matters little whether sentencing is called just deserts or rehabilitation. Prisons should be abolished.

■ QUESTIONS

1. Can the criminal justice system achieve both goals, retribution and rehabilitation, at the same time?
2. What other functions does the criminal justice system perform?
3. Should prisons be abolished?
4. Should parole and probation be abolished?

■ FURTHER READING

In Support of von Hirsch
Canadian Sentencing Commission. *Sentencing Reform: A Canadian Approach.* Ottawa: Ministry of Supply and Services, 1987.

van den Haag, Ernest. *Punishing Criminals: Concerning a Very Old and Painful Question.* New York: Basic Books, 1975.

von Hirsch, Andrew. "Why have Proportionate Sentences?: A Reply to Professor Gabor." *Canadian Journal of Criminology* 32, no. 3 (1990): 547-549.

In Support of Gabor

Grygier, Tadeusz. "A Canadian Approach or an American Band-Wagon?" *Canadian Journal of Criminology* 30, no. 2 (1988): 165-172.

Hudson, Barbara. *Justice Through Punishment: A Critique of the "Justice" Model of Corrections.* New York: St. Martin's Press, 1987.

Singer, Richard G. *Just Deserts: Sentencing Based on Equality and Desert.* Cambridge, Mass.: Ballinger, 1979.

Other Voices

Adelberg, Ellen and Claudia Currie. *Too Few To Count: Canadian Women in Conflict with the Law.* Vancouver: Press Gang, 1987.

Culhane, Claire. *Barred from Prison: A Personal Account.* Vancouver: Pulp Press, 1979.

Gosselin, Luc. *Prisons In Canada.* Montreal: Black Rose Books, 1982.

Scull, Andrew. *Decarceration.* Englewood Cliffs, N.J.: Prentice-Hall, 1977.

Is mandatory retirement justified?

Should access to abortion be restricted?

Does Canadian law protect human rights?

PART SIX

INTRODUCTION

The issues debated in this section deal with fundamental social issues and legal principles, with particular emphasis on the ability of the law to define and protect human rights (for previous discussion of various human rights issues, see Debates Four, Five, Thirteen, and Fourteen). Human rights issues are being debated in Canada because there is not yet a general consensus (an impossibility, some theorists would argue) on exactly which human rights should be protected in law. Similar disagreement exists on the extent to which the law can, or should, protect human rights. The first two debates in this section deal with issues of mandatory retirement and access to abortions. They focus on reasons for and against establishing specific human rights in the law. The third debate focuses on the ability of the law to protect human rights.

IS MANDATORY

RETIREMENT

JUSTIFIED?

In the fall of 1990, the Supreme Court of Canada ruled that mandatory retirement is justified. The majority of the Court ruled that, even though forcing someone to retire at a specific age was discrimination, it was legal under the Canadian Charter of Rights and Freedoms. A minority on the Court, however, took the dissenting opinion that age discrimination has no place in a democratic society.

Typical of social issues that are decided via court or legislative action, the debate does not stop with the Supreme Court decision. The Court declared that mandatory retirement is legal; it did not specify an age — 65 or any other — at which all workers must be forced to retire. Therefore, it is possible for individual organizations to devise retirement schemes that lower or raise the mandatory retirement age from age 65. Supreme Court judges, for example, are not required to retire until age 70, and there is no mandatory retirement age for members of the House of Commons.

Arguments in favour of mandatory retirement generally centre on the need to create jobs and promotion opportunities for younger workers; the need to avoid the establishment of stringent performance requirements for older workers; and the need to prevent the financial chaos that could result from having to fund pensions for large numbers of retired workers. The logic of the argument is quite simple. When older workers are forced to retire, job openings and opportunities for promotion are created within the organization. By forcing older, more senior workers to retire, the employer also avoids the messy task of having to dismiss employees whose work performance suffers as a result of aging. Some organizations would rather keep an older, less efficient worker on the payroll for a few years until retirement rather than risk potential backlash for appearing to act inhumanely toward its older workers.

The certainty of retirement at a specified age allows both the employer and the employee to make financial preparations for retirement. If this opportunity did not exist, and if workers were allowed to retire at whatever age they chose, company pension plans as they are currently arranged would be in disarray. Pensions depend on a uniform retirement age, with a general expectation that retired workers will draw pensions for a given number of years after retirement.

On the other side of the argument, opponents of mandatory retirement cite performance standards already in place through which older workers can lose their jobs for poor performance. They also note that, in an aging society, it is more costly to force retirement than it is to allow workers to continue working. There are more people over the age of 65 today than at any time in the past, and the percentage of the Canadian population over 65 is still growing. It is estimated that, by the year 2031 (approximately the time when most workers currently entering the labour force will retire), almost 27 percent of the population of Canada will be 65 or older (see Czerny and Swift, 1988). In contrast, only 11 percent of the population was 65 or older in 1986 (Devereaux, 1990). Clearly, more money will be needed to fund pension plans. Many pension plans, especially government-financed old age pensions and the Canada Pension Plan, are funded by using the pension contributions of current workers to pay the pensions of retired workers. Thus, forcing retirement at age 65 will oblige those who are still working to pay higher taxes and make higher pension contributions to pay the pensions of retired workers. Further, since 65 percent of Canadians have no pension income other than government pensions, or only minimal pensions of under $1,000 annually, forced retirement means forced poverty for the elderly (Czerny and Swift, 1988). Government pensions provide incomes well below the poverty line.

The following two articles are written by economists. Gunderson and Pesando, arguing in favour of mandatory retirement, say that "the mechanism of the market or the collective bargaining process" is the best way to create mandatory retirement schemes best suited to the needs of particular industries, employers, and employees. Krashinsky, arguing against mandatory retirement, says that mandatory retirement constrains few workers and provides little benefit to younger employees.

References

Czerny S.J., Michael and Jamie Swift (1988) *Getting Started on Social Analysis in Canada* (Toronto: Between the Lines), chap. 11, "Aging: Out of Sight."

Devereaux, Mary Sue (1990) "Aging in the Canadian Population," in *Canadian Social Trends*, edited by Craig McKie and Keith Thompson (Toronto: Thompson Educational Publishing).

THE CASE FOR
MANDATORY
RETIREMENT

YES

Morley Gunderson and James Pesando*

Mandatory retirement is controversial because of the extent to which it is intertwined with other controversial issues such as age discrimination, poverty among the aged, the job rights of the young, and the rights of employees and employers to enter into mutually binding arrangements. The purpose of this paper is to try to narrow the range of the controversy by outlining the case for *allowing* mandatory retirement. In our view, the word "allowing" is the key, and the relevant policy question ought not to be "are you for or against mandatory retirement?" but rather, "under what conditions should parties be prohibited from entering into contractual arrangements, like mandatory retirement, that may inhibit their flexibility at some time in the future, presumably in return for other benefits like pensions and promotion opportunities?"

In order to put the case for allowing mandatory retirement into its proper perspective, we first document its prevalence and forms, and the extent to which it constrains workers from continuing to work. We then discuss the coventional arguments for and against mandatory retirement. After outlining the case for mandatory retirement, we discuss the implications of a legislative ban on mandatory retirement and conclude with policy recommendations which we feel can maximize the benefits of allowing mandatory retirement while minimizing its adverse consequences.

■ PREVALENCE AND FORMS

Approximately half of the Canadian work force appears to be covered by some form of mandatory retirement provision, either as part of a collective agreement or a company personnel policy (Economic Council of Canada, 1979:68, based upon the 1975 Retirement Survey; Dunlop, 1980:7, based upon the Conference Board Survey; Herzog, 1980 and Taylor, 1980, based upon a British Columbia Survey of 2,200 firms). Roughly similar numbers have been documented in the United States prior to their legislative ban (Kittner, 1977; Lazear, 1979:14; Schultz, 1974; Stone, 1980:14; and Wall-fesh, 1978:14).

Data based upon major collective agreements (200 or more employees) in Ontario, as of 1979, indicated that there was considerable variability in the type of mandatory retirement and the age at which it applied (Gunderson, 1987). In fact *compulsory* retirement, whereby the existing contractual arrangement was terminated at age 65, but the employee could be retained under a new contractual arrangement until a later age such as 70, was much more common than *automatic* retirement with no possibility of renewal. Even under automatic retirement there was considerable variability in the age at which it applied, with age 65 being the required age in slightly less than half of the cases. Also, as indicated in Pesando and Gunderson (1987), most employees covered by an occupational pension plan and hence subject to some form of mandatory retirement, are also eligible for *early* retirement, typically after attaining age 55 and completing 10 years of service. Under early retirement, accrued pension benefits are reduced, either through an actuarial adjustment or a specified reduction formula. However, early retirees are often eligible for additional payments, such as bridging supplements, which continue through age 65, which is also the age at which the retired workers are eligible to receive (unreduced) Canada/Quebec Pension Plan Benefits and Old Age Security. Many employees, in addition, are eligible for *special retirement*, which allows them to retire before the normal retirement age set by the pension plan (typically age 65) with no reduction in their accrued pension benefits.

In short, there is considerable variability in the type of mandatory retirement, the age at which it applies, and the extent to which it is accompanied by early or special retirement provisions. In turn, this suggests that mandatory retirement is a component of the complex set of compensation arrangements that prevail around the time of retirement, and that it is affected by the varying circumstances of the different employment environments and work forces (Gunderson and Pesando, 1980). It is not simply a blunt instrument forcing everyone to retire at age 65.

Mandatory retirement is also associated with workers who are relatively advantaged in that they tend to have higher wages and pensions and a long-term employment relationship, often with the protection of a formal collective agreement or personnel policy (Dunlop, 1980; Lazear, 1979; Urban Institute, 1981:53). These workers tend to work in the primary or core labour market and not in the secondary or peripheral labour market. This is important because it reminds us that poverty amongst the aged, which is a real policy concern, is unlikely to be seriously exacerbated by mandatory retirement.

Nevertheless, *some* workers may not have the safety net of a satisfactory occupational pension plan if they are subject to mandatory retirement, even though mandatory retirement and occupational pension plans *tend* to go hand-in-hand. There is limited empirical evidence that suggests that about 10 per cent of workers subject to mandatory retirement may not have an occupational pension (Dunlop, 1980:7; Lazear, 1979:1281; Urban Institute, 1981:67). In addition, some short-service employees may enter the pension plan late in their careers and hence not accumulate substantial pension credits even if they are members of a generous plan. Also, there are obviously low benefit pension plans as well as low wage workers who would receive correspondingly low pension benefits. These are groups for which there may be legitimate policy concern to the extent that they are required to retire and yet have inadequate income from their occupational pension plan.

While not minimizing the potential importance of these groups, there are a number of observations suggesting that their actual importance is empirically not known and their effects are sometimes mitigated by other circumstances. First, the evidence that perhaps 10 per cent of workers subject to mandatory retirement age are not covered by an occupational pension plan is often anecdotal and not based upon hard evidence. Second, we do not know whether such workers are subject to automatic retirement (in which case they have to retire from that company) or compulsory retirement (in which case they can be rehired under a new contractual arrangement). Third, short-service employees, who may not have sufficient time to accumulate substantial credits, are likely to be entering the pension plan fairly close to the normal retirement age and hence are likely to be fully aware of the rules under which they are entering that contractual arrangement. In addition, they might not have been hired were their employer's obligations not limited somewhat by the existence of mandatory retirement. Fourth, low wage employees rationally may be reluctant to give up any compensating wages to obtain more generous pension benefits in view of the fact that income replacement rates under public pension programs (the CPP/QPP, Old Age Security) are highest for low-income workers. In addition, such workers may rationally prefer high cash wages because any private pension income may simply reduce their entitlements to income-tested benefits such as the Guaranteed Income Supplement.

The "twinning" of mandatory retirement and occupational pension plans also may give the impression that, if mandatory retirement is banned, the features of occupational pension plans can readily be adapted to serve as a substitute for mandatory retirement. For example, benefit accruals and actuarial adjustments could be changed to create a monetary disincentive to delay retirement beyond the normal retirement age. In theory, this is the case. In practice, however, as shown in the simulations in Pesando and Gunderson (forthcoming), those postponed retirement provisions that have the greatest potential to discourage work beyond age 65 (no further benefit accruals and no actuarial adjustments after attainment of the normal retirement age) have also been banned in jurisdictions (Quebec, Manitoba, federal) which have banned mandatory retirement.

■ CONSTRAINING EFFECT

While about half of the work force appears to be subject to some form of mandatory retirement, the evidence is less conclusive about the numbers who are involuntarily constrained by mandatory retirement (i.e., those who would like to continue working if mandatory retirement were banned). The general consensus is that the numbers are small: 18 per cent of men and 3 per cent of women are subject to compulsory retirement according to the Department of Health and Welfare (1973:9, 23); about 6 per cent of those who planned to retire at the mandatory retirement age according to the Economic Council of Canada (1979:68); at most half of those who are compelled to retire at age 65 according to Dunlop (1980: 12). The downward trend in the labour force participation rate of older workers also indicates that the trend is towards earlier and not delayed retirement.

If mandatory retirement were banned, however, this trend toward earlier retirement could change in the future for a number of reasons. For example, workers would have more time to change their retirement plans, and they might be more likely to do so if substantial numbers of their peers also began to retire later. Further, the proportion of the work force that is white-collar and professional will continue to increase, and this group tends to retire at a later age. If pensions, public or private, were redesigned to become available at a later effective age as the result of a ban on mandatory retirement, the trend towards early retirement also could be reversed.

In addition, the empirical evidence of the impact of the ban on mandatory retirement in the United States is likely to be of limited relevance for Canada because of the differences in the public pension schemes in the two countries. In the United States, after a modest level of earned income, there is a high implicit tax on earnings for those who continue working past 65, in that such workers forgo some Social Security benefits if they earn income in the labour market. This "tax-back" feature can be a powerful incentive to retire, and may have significantly reduced the number of employees who chose to continue working after mandatory retirement was banned in the United States. The Canada/Quebec Pension Plan, in contrast, does not have this "tax-back" feature; recipients do not forgo any public pension if they continue to work. For this reason, the number of employees who would continue working, if mandatory retirement were banned, could be larger in Canada than in the United States. This also means that the adjustment consequences could be more prominent in Canada than they have been in the United States.

Whatever the numbers who, *at the time of retirement*, indicate that they would like to continue working, our contention is that that is not a meaningful measure of the numbers who are involuntarily constrained by mandatory retirement. If, as we contend, mandatory retirement is typically a component of a long-term contractual arrangement which enables the wages of older workers to be higher than they would be in the absence of mandatory retirement, it should not be surprising that employees may prefer to continue working at the time that the mandatory retirement constraint becomes binding. Employees may well prefer the removal of the one element of the contractual arrangement that is no longer favourable to them, once they have received other benefits associated with that constraint. Our contention is that the evidence of whether people are involuntarily constrained by mandatory retirement is better examined when they make such long-term contractual arrangements, not when the constraining point of the arrangement becomes binding.

■ CONVENTIONAL ARGUMENTS AGAINST MANDATORY RETIREMENT

The main argument against mandatory retirement is that it appears to violate the human rights of some older workers, and that it thus represents age-based discrimination. This argument is given credence by the fact that all Canadian jurisdictions prohibit discrimination on the basis of age. However, those jurisdictions that allow mandatory retirement do so by specifying that their legislation does not apply to persons 65 years of age and older. These exemptions may give the appearance that it is acceptable to discriminate against individuals aged 65 or older. Since the Canadian *Charter of Rights and Freedoms* contains no age limit on its prohibition of discrimination on the basis of age, these age exemptions are in violation of the Charter unless they are deemed to be "reasonable limits prescribed by law as can be demonstrably justified in a free and democratic society." Hence, the debate over mandatory retirement is essentially a debate over whether it is a reasonable restriction or one that constitutes age-based discrimination. Our contention is that the restriction is a reasonable one, and the analysis that follows makes this case.

■ CONVENTIONAL ARGUMENTS FOR MANDATORY RETIREMENT

The arguments in favour of allowing mandatory retirement can be grouped into four main categories: (1) it promotes work sharing, (2) it facilitates planning, (3) it minimizes monitoring and evaluation, and (4) it facilitates deferred compensation systems.

Work Sharing

Mandatory retirement is often justified on the grounds of opening up job and promotion opportunities for younger workers. In essence, it may be thought of as a form of life cycle work sharing, whereby older workers vacate jobs that create promotion opportunities for middle-aged workers. Their promotion, in turn, creates new job opportunities for younger workers which may also lead to infusion of new ideas and talents into the organization. This can be especially important for particular sectors, like universities, where new openings are often predicated upon retirements in particular departments. In times of sustained high unemployment, especially youth unemployment, policies to share the available jobs have taken on particular appeal. Alternative forms of work sharing include delayed school leaving, unpaid leaves, reduced workweeks, restrictions on overtime, unemployment-insurance-assisted work sharing plans, and early retirement. European countries, for example, are emphasizing many of these forms of work sharing. The emphasis is on the promotion of early retirement, not the removal of mandatory retirement, in part because of a chronic problem of youth unemployment (Cuvillier, 1984).

While it may be true that a particular worker who does not retire may occupy a job that cannot be filled by another worker, this need not be true for the economy as a whole. Economists tend to emphasize that it is a fallacy (termed the "lump-of-labour" fallacy) to assume that there are a fixed number of jobs in the economy, so that one person occupying a job means that another person does not have a job (Pesando, 1979). Rather, the economy is more accurately characterized as dynamic and continuously in a state of flux, as workers with jobs help create jobs elsewhere through their spending patterns. Nonetheless, the absorption of new entrants into the labour force may require adjustments, perhaps in real wages, and may thus take time. This may explain why the discussion in the media gives a great deal of attention to this rationale for mandatory retirement, while economists would assign it a somewhat lower level of importance.

Facilitate Planning

Mandatory retirement may facilitate planning on the part of both employers and employees. For employers, having a known termination date to a particular contractual arrangement facilitates planning for replacements, pension payouts, training and upgrading, as well as for medical and disability payments. The latter may be particularly important for older workers (Billings, 1986).

For employees, a fixed retirement date pressures them to plan for their retirement and this, in turn, is likely to leave them better prepared for the eventuality of retirement (Burke, 1984; Wall and Shatshat, 1981). If they know their likely retirement date, employees are more likely to participate in retirement planning programs, to save for retirement, perhaps even to search for alternative employment or to prepare for a geographic move.

Minimize Monitoring and Evaluation of Older Workers

A fixed retirement date minimizes the need to monitor and evaluate the performance of older workers. If the performance of older workers declines, employers are likely to carry them through to retirement, when this date is known in advance. This is also true of co-workers in work groups.

Conversely, if mandatory retirement is banned, employers will have to monitor and evaluate the performance of their older workers more carefully. The pay of older workers will have to be linked more closely to their performance, given the indefinite term of their employment relationship. In addition, employers will be faced with the inevitability of having to dismiss some older workers. Documentation of performance will be important to avoid wrongful dismissal charges through the courts, or unjust dismissal charges through employment standards provisions (in some jurisdictions). Documentation of performance will also be important to avoid possible age discrimination charges; a likelihood that will increase if older workers receive deferred wages (discussed subsequently) and wages are realigned to reflect more closely productivity subsequent to a ban on mandatory retirement.

In short, one should not presume that a ban on mandatory retirement means that older workers will be able to retain their jobs. In fact, some older workers may be dismissed prior to what would have been their mandatory retirement age, and others will be subject to more scrutiny and evaluation. This in turn may jeopardize their human rights and affect the notion of their retiring with dignity (Gunderson, 1983).

Facilitate Deferred Compensation

Mandatory retirement may also facilitate a system of deferred compensation in which workers are paid more than their productivity when they are older, and less than their productivity when they are younger. (In competitive markets, equilibrium requires that the expected present value of the compensation and productivity streams be equal.) Mandatory retirement facilitates a deferred compensation system by providing a finite termination date to the contractual arrangement. Without such a termination date, compensation could exceed productivity indefinitely and hence the contractual arrangement could not exist. Lazear (1979) has argued that such a deferred compensation system ensures honesty and work effort on the part of employees because they want to be retained in order to receive the deferred compensation. The situation is analogous to that of posting a performance bond, with the reputation of the firm ensuring that the employer will be fair in repaying the bond.

Deferred compensation may prevail for reasons other than those advanced by Lazear. It may reduce unwanted turnover, as employees have an incentive to stay with the company to receive their deferred compensation. This in turn may encourage employers to provide training since they will have a longer period over which to amortize their training costs. Deferred compensation may also provide workers with an interest in the financial solvency of their employer, since that solvency is necessary for employers to pay the deferred compensation. Deferred compensation may also reduce the need for the constant monitoring and evaluation of workers. All that is necessary is periodic, retrospective appraisals (i.e., based on past performance), with continuation with the firm and hence the right to receive the deferred compensation contingent upon satisfactory performance.

Employees may prefer, or at least willingly accept, a system of deferred compensation. To the extent that this system promotes honesty, work effort, training, and reduces monitoring and evaluation costs, the gains in productivity and the reduction in costs may be shared with employees. Deferred compensation can also constitute a form of forced savings, as it ensures a steady increase in wages even if productivity does not increase commensurately. Employees may also prefer periodic, retrospective monitoring to a system of more constant monitoring. Employees may also be guaranteed a degree of certainty in receiving their deferred wage, through such procedures as seniority-based wage increases, pension guarantees and the protection of a collective agreement. All of these characterize the longer-term, contractual employment relationship of which deferred compensation and mandatory retirement are likely to be a part.

Empirically, there is evidence that deferred compensation arrangements are prevalent. Abraham and Medoff (1982:308-18) summarize their own research and the results of 21 other studies. They conclude that productivity is roughly constant by age and seniority, while wages rise sharply with seniority. As a result, younger workers are paid less than their productivity and older workers are paid more than their productivity. Abraham and Farber (1987) and Altonji and Shatatko (1987) provide empirical evidence indicating that the effect of seniority on earnings is reduced considerably when one controls for the effect of conventionally unobserved variables such as the quality of the worker or of the worker-employer match. Nevertheless, they do find evidence of some independent effect of seniority. In addition, neither of these studies included pension benefit accruals which are an important vehicle through which the deferral of compensation can take place, especially as workers approach the normal retirement age (Pesando and Gunderson, forthcoming).

■ CASE FOR ALLOWING MANDATORY RETIREMENT

It is important to recognize that our argument is not for or against mandatory retirement *per se*. Rather, our argument is for *allowing* mandatory retirement to be negotiated by employers and their employees, either as part of a collective agreement or as a personnel policy.

The economic case for allowing mandatory retirement favours allowing the bargaining parties to weigh the pros and cons of mandatory retirement in their particular employment relationship. If mandatory retirement is beneficial to a particular employer, but undesirable to many of the employees, the employer will have to provide a quid pro quo (e.g., a generous pension plan or a compensating wage) to offset this 'unattractive' element in the package of work rules and pay policy. This could take place in formal collective bargaining or the informal bargaining that underlies the formation of a personnel policy. If employees found mandatory retirement to be attractive, no compensating quid pro quo would be required or it would be minimal.

In essence, through the mechanism of the market or the collective bargaining process, the cost considerations of employers will confront the preferences of employees. One would expect this interaction to result in a diversity of mandatory retirement (and other) arrangements. If employers begin to view mandatory retirement as unnecessary, or if employees begin to find it increasingly unattractive, then mandatory retirement should become less prevalent over time.

This perspective views the role of government as mainly one of requiring that the parties are informed of their rights and responsibilities, and that the parties carry out their contractual arrangements such as pension commitments. Governments may even want to set examples in their own employment relationship in hope that such practices will be emulated elsewhere.

Clearly, there are cases when society overrides the preferences of the market, because it deems the outcomes to be socially unacceptable. Such is the case, for example, for transactions as varied as prostitution, the sale of drugs, indentured service and the hiring of labour below the minimum wage. The payment of discriminatory wages for women or racial minorities is not allowed, even if the parties are willing to accept such arrangements.

There are other times when society sanctions contractual arrangements that may inhibit flexibility and freedom at some time in the future, presumably because of the benefits of such contractual arrangement over a longer period of time. Such may be the case with marriage contracts or contracts to repay a loan.

There may also be times when internal union trade-offs are deemed to be socially unacceptable, for example, if they ignore minority rights, including the rights of older workers. However, union preferences generally reflect their median voter, who is likely to be older and interested in pensions and retirement related issues. Presumably, most union members expect ultimately to be affected by their decisions with respect to retirement issues, and hence are unlikely to bargain for mandatory retirement if they expect to find it to be unduly constraining. In essence, there is little reason to believe that internal union trade-offs inadequately reflect the legitimate preferences of their members with respect to mandatory retirement. Hence, unions should be allowed to bargain for its existence, and they should be allowed to bargain for its removal or a change in its form.

■ CONCLUDING OBSERVATIONS

Given that there is a legitimate trade-off between the rights of parties to enter into contractual arrangements, and the rights of employees to be protected against age discrimination, a possible solution is to remove the age limit in anti-discrimination legislation but to exempt bona fide collective agreements and pension plans from the resultant ban on mandatory retirement. This practice, which exists in New Brunswick, effectively would allow mandatory retirement to prevail in most circumstances since it is usually associated with a pension plan or collective agreement. However, it would ensure that mandatory retirement existed only in situations of reasonable employee bargaining power or where it was accompanied by an explicit quid pro quo in the form of an occupational pension plan that would, typically, provide a degree of income security to the retiring employee. Allowing the normal age discrimination provisions to apply would ensure the protection of anti-discrimination legislation to persons of all ages, including that small portion who are subject to mandatory retirement but who may not be covered by an occupational pension plan.

This is simply meant to be illustrative of one possible compromise in balancing the right to be protected against age discrimination against the right to enter into mutually beneficial contractual arrangements. It also illustrates that the economic case is not for mandatory retirement per se, but for the right of employers and employees to enter into mutually beneficial contractual arrangements that might include provisions like mandatory retirement. This is important, since it highlights the fact that the relevant policy question for the legislatures and the courts is not "are you for or against mandatory retirement?" but rather "are you for or against prohibiting private parties from entering into contractual arrangements like mandatory retirement?"

Note

* The authors are indebted to the Social Sciences and Humanities Research Council of Canada for financial support, and to two anonymous referees for comments.

References

Abraham, K. and H. Farber (1987) "Job Duration, Seniority, and Earnings," *American Economic Review*, 77:278-97.

Abraham, K. and J. Medoff (1982) "Length of Service and the Operation of Internal Labour Markets." *Industrial and Labour Relations Research Association Proceedings*, 35:308-18.

Altonji, J. and R. Shakotko (1987) "Do Wages Rise with Job Seniority?" *Review of Economic Studies*, 54:437-59.

Billings, A.E. (1986) "Age-Related Employment Costs at the Travelers Companies in 1981," *Aging and Work*, 6:7-14.

Burke, Ronald J. (1984) "Disengagement from Organizations: Termination, Permanent Layoff, and Retirement," in K. Srinivas (ed.), *Human Resources Management: Contemporary Perspectives in Canada* (Toronto: McGraw-Hill).

Canada. Department of Health and Welfare (1973) *Early Retirement: A Preliminary Analysis* (Ottawa: Health and Welfare).

Cuvillier, R. (1984) *The Reduction of Working Time* (Geneva: International Labour Organization).

Dunlop, Donald (1980) *Mandatory Retirement Policy: A Human Rights Dilemma?* (Ottawa: Conference Board).

Economic Council of Canada (1979) *One in Three: Pensions for Canadians to 2030* (Ottawa: Ministry of Supply and Services).

Gunderson, M. (1983) "Mandatory Retirement and Personnel Policies," *Columbia Journal of World Business*, 28:2:8-15.

_____ (1987) *Effect of Banning Mandatory Retirement on Industrial Relations Functions* (Toronto: Report to the Ontario Task Force on Mandatory Retirement).

_____ and J. Pesando (1980) "Eliminating Mandatory Retirement: Economics and Human Rights," *Canadian Public Policy—Analyse de Politiques*, VI:352-60.

Herzog, J. (1980) *Mandatory Retirement in British Columbia* (Victoria: The Human Rights Commission of British Columbia).

Kittner, D. (1977) "Forced Retirement: How Common Is It?" *Monthly Labor Review*, 160:60-6.

Lazear, E. (1979) "Why is There Mandatory Retirement?" *Journal of Political Economy*, 87:1261-84.

Pesando, J. (1979) *The Elimination of Mandatory Retirement: An Economic Perspective* (Toronto: Ontario Economic Council).

_____ (1985) "The Usefulness of the Wind-Up Measure of Pension Liabilities: A Labor Market Perspective," *Journal of Finance*, 40:927-40.

_____ and M. Gunderson (forthcoming) "Retirement Incentives Contained In Occupational Pension Plans and Their Implications for the Mandatory Retirement Debate," *Canadian Journal of Economics*.

Schultz, J. (1974) "The Economics of Mandatory Retirement," *Industrial Gerontology*, 1:1-10.

Stone, J. (1980) "Age Discrimination in Employment, A Review of the Findings," *Monthly Labor Review*, 103:32-6.

Taylor, L. (1980) "Almost Everyone Leaves Before Age 65," *Benefits Canada*, 4:7-11.

Urban Institute (1981) *Mandatory Retirement Study: Final Report* (Washington: Urban Institute).

Wall, Jerry L. and M.M. Shatshat (1981) "Controversy Over the Issue of Mandatory Retirement," *Personnel Administrator*, 26:25-45.

Wallfesh, H. (1978) *The Effects of Extending the Mandatory Retirement Age* (New York: AMACOM).

THE CASE AGAINST MANDATORY RETIREMENT

Michael Krashinsky*

■ I INTRODUCTION

Mandatory retirement has emerged as a policy issue in North America over the last decade. The United States in 1978 eliminated mandatory retirement in the federal public sector and, before age 70, in most of the private sector. In Canada, Quebec abolished mandatory retirement in 1982 (Bill 15), while it was effectively eliminated in Manitoba in 1981 by judicial interpretations of that province's *Human Rights Act.*[1] More generally, the new Canadian Constitution forbids discrimination under the law on the basis of, among other things, age. Section 15(1) of the *Charter of Rights* states:

> Every individual is equal before and under the law and has the right to equal protection and equal benefit of the law without discrimination and, in particular, without discrimination based on race, national or ethnic origin, colour, religion, sex, age or mental or physical disability.

Under section 32, the Charter applies to all matters under the authority of Parliament and the provincial legislatures.

The exact interpretation of these equality rights rests with the courts. Because implementation of section 15 was delayed for three years—until 1985—its implications are just emerging. Early in 1986, the federal government announced that it would be eliminating mandatory retirement in the federal civil service, and law suits on the issue are now in progress in some of the provinces. In particular, a number of Ontario university faculty due to be retired in 1985 have sued their respective universities and the Ontario Attorney General. The Supreme Court of Ontario ruled against those faculty members, and the case is now under appeal to the Supreme Court of Canada.

Some members of the general public and many employers are concerned that the abolition of mandatory retirement will permit older workers to block access to jobs for young people already facing high rates of unemployment. Most economists dismiss such fears, at least in the long run, but they are more concerned about the effects of prohibiting specific clauses in freely-bargained collective agreements. Economic theory suggests that such clauses are efficient and that outlawing them would generate losses that would be shared by both labour and management. Eliminating mandatory retirement would thus make workers in general worse off and might result in a number of changes in the collective agreements that are far more threatening to older workers (including more careful monitoring, lower wages, more termination for cause, and so on). It would seem then that protecting the human rights of older workers might involve significant losses in efficiency, losses that in the long run would affect all workers and reduce the average worker's lifetime income.

These concerns are more than just academic. The Charter in section 1 states that the rights and freedoms set out in it are "subject only to such reasonable limits prescribed by law as can be demonstrably justified in a free and democratic society." If it can be shown that mandatory retirement benefits both workers and employers, then it might well be such a reasonable limit. In his judgment in the Ontario case, Justice Gray made such a ruling, reasoning that mandatory retirement achieved the dual objectives of ensuring the integrity of pension plans and improving the prospects of unemployed youth with minimal impairment of the rights of older workers (Gray, 1986).

This article will argue that mandatory retirement provisions in labour contracts are not necessarily efficient and that, in any case, any benefits of such provisions can be provided at relatively low cost by other arrangements that do not discriminate on the basis of age. Recent economic theorizing suggests that mandatory retirement is an efficient part of a system of deferred compensation that reduces the incentives for workers to shirk. I will argue that this efficiency depends upon the doubtful assumption that young workers can rationally assess the expected costs of mandatory retirement many years in advance. Furthermore, mandatory retirement constrains few workers and hence generates relatively few benefits. Those benefits can be provided by other provisions—for example, modifications in pension arrangements—that do not violate the human rights provisions of the Charter.

This article is therefore both positive and normative. It makes the positive prediction that eliminating mandatory retirement will impose relatively few costs on society and involve relatively little disruption of the industrial relations system. It makes the normative argument that mandatory retirement therefore is hardly a reasonable limit on the human rights of older workers.

The next section discusses the role of mandatory retirement in collective agreements and suggests why the normal conclusions of contract theory—that all such agreements must be efficient—may well not hold. Section III argues that even if mandatory retirement is efficient, it is of relative minor importance and can be replaced at relatively low cost by other provisions. Section IV considers briefly the issue of youth employment. Section V applies all these arguments to the university faculty case, both because of the pivotal role of this case in the courts, and because it serves to focus on the issues surrounding mandatory retirement.

■ II MANDATORY RETIREMENT AND CONTRACT THEORY

The fundamental economic defence of mandatory retirement involves contract theory. If two well-informed parties enter into a contract, it must be because the contract (including any related side payments) makes both of them better off, and any clause included in that contract will be efficient. A specific clause of course may harm one party. But that harm will be outweighed by the benefits received by the other party, and the party that suffers harm will be compensated elsewhere in the contract.

Consider for example a clause which causes $100 in harm to party A but benefits party B. A will agree to its inclusion if the price specified in the contract is altered to transfer to A at least an additional $100. But B will agree to this only if the clause provides him with more than $100 in benefits. Thus the clause is included only if the benefits to B exceed the harm to A.

This result is independent of the bargaining power of the two parties. If B is strong enough to extract an additional $100 from A, then B will do so using the clause in question only if he derives more than $100 in benefits from it. If B derives less than $100 from the clause, he is clearly better off to apply his power to force another change in the contract, for example a change in price which shifts $100 directly from A to B.

The economic argument for mandatory retirement fits into this analysis. Mandatory retirement is negotiated as part of free collective bargaining between employee and employer and hence must be efficient. Labour will suffer if mandatory retirement is removed by fiat because management will bargain for other more harmful changes in the contract to compensate for this removal. Put another way, management will withdraw concessions made to compensate labour for including mandatory retirement in the contract, concessions whose benefit to labour exceeds the harm caused by mandatory retirement.

Variations on this theme can be found in Gunderson and Pesando (1980), Pesando (1979), Gunderson (1983), Dunlop (1980:42-3), and Labour Canada (1985:4-5). For example, Gunderson and Pesando (1980:356-7) suggest that eliminating mandatory retirement will result in older workers facing more monitoring, more formal dismissal procedures (and involuntary dismissals), and, potentially, lower wages. These responses compensate for the loss of retirement provisions in the employment contract. Because contracts are efficient, these changes must leave workers on average worse off.

But why is mandatory retirement valuable to management? Lazear (1979) argues that mandatory retirement exists as part of a system of deferred compensation which attempts to deal with unsupervised employees' incentive to shirk (that is, to avoid working as hard as is anticipated in the employment agreement). Firms find it costly to monitor performance systematically, but shirking can be deterred by increasing the losses when workers are caught and fired. Deferred compensation involves paying workers less than they are worth (in terms of productivity) when they are younger and more when they are older. Since these deferred wages are forfeited if workers are fired, the cost of job loss increases and the incentive to shirk is reduced.[2]

Lazear argues that mandatory retirement is a critical part of deferred compensation because paying older workers more than the value of their marginal product gives them an incentive to delay retirement beyond the optimal point in time. This delay in retirement can be taken into account in designing the time-profile for wages in the deferred compensation scheme, but such arrangements are inefficient and can be eliminated by requiring workers to retire at what is, for most workers, the optimal age. Mandatory retirement thus benefits workers because it "allows the worker's present value of marginal product to be higher than it would be in the absence of such a contract, and these 'rents' will spill over to the worker" (Lazear, 1979:1265).[3] Eliminating mandatory retirement hurts workers because it increases the costs associated with shirking: monitoring increases; efficiency is reduced; productivity net of enforcement costs falls; and firms must therefore reduce the amounts that workers are paid over their lifetimes.

There is evidence that older workers are paid more than productivity alone might explain. Abraham and Medoff cite a number of studies that show that older workers are neither more nor less productive than younger workers, and therefore "more (less) senior employees are generally paid more (less) than the value of their marginal product." They conclude that there are a variety of explanations for this phenomenon, all suffering from the lack of an empirical basis (Abraham and Medoff, 1982:312-7). However, the existence of deferred compensation means that employees will have an incentive to retire at later than the optimal time. Permitting labour retirement imposes costs on the employer which he in turn will seek to pass on to workers. Recent work, however, casts doubt on the prevalence of deferred compensation (Abraham and Farber, 1987).

Supporters of mandatory retirement also argue that it allows firms to carry unproductive older workers soon due to retire. Without it, firms would be less willing to tolerate older workers' inadequacies, and both monitoring and involuntary termination would increase (see Gunderson, 1983:12-3; Pesando, 1979:3; and Dunlop, 1980:38-40). Mandatory retirement can be seen as part of an arrangement between workers and management that implicitly includes decreased monitoring after a certain age. Management is protected from the loss of critical employees because it can rehire highly productive workers after the retirement age.[4] Employees have decreased risk by reducing the probability of involuntary termination, and have paid for that benefit by giving up the right to continued employment at a certain age.

All these arguments are variations on the theme introduced earlier. Mandatory retirement is efficient because it is voluntarily included in employment contracts. Explanations for why it is efficient vary in their ingenuity.[5] But the bottom line is that abolishing mandatory retirement will impose costs on employers. When these costs are passed on to workers (either through lower wages or through changes in other explicit and implicit clauses in the contract), the average worker will be left worse off than before.

The logical structure of the contract theory argument is unassailable. It rests however on key assumptions about rationality and information. It can be shown that contracts are always efficient, but only if we assume that both parties to the agreement act rationally and have good information about the size and the likelihood of the various costs and benefits of the clauses being discussed.[6] This assumption seems particularly inappropriate when thinking about retirement issues.

The problem is that if workers systematically underestimate the cost of facing a mandatory retirement clause when they are older, then they will not demand sufficient compensation for including such a clause in the contract. Thus, even if mandatory retirement were inefficient—if the benefits to management were less than the costs to workers—such a clause might end up in the freely-negotiated contract.

The assumption of good information and rationality is made by economists in analysing most issues. But it remains an assumption.[7] It works reasonably well in predicting behaviour in most markets because those markets involve repetition. Consumers and producers acquire experience over time and use it to make reasonable choices and decisions. But the same need not be true about life cycle type decisions where experience by definition cannot apply. Even though people can observe what happens to others, they seem reluctant to believe that this evidence is relevant to their own situations.

The notion that individuals do not adequately appreciate the risks that they face is not new. In examining product liability, Calabresi and Bass (1970:88-9) conclude that inadequate risk awareness is a form of "externalization" that explains why market mechanisms often fail to deal with risk. They suggest that good information is costly and hard to comprehend, in part because experience is not a useful guide. Even where information is available, individuals systematically underevaluate the probability of their own involvement in a serious accident, whatever the statistics.[8]

Irrationality is rather hard to prove—but then so is rationality. One technique is to build models of how rational individuals would act in certain situations, making reasonable assumptions about tastes. If we find that a significant part of the population behaves differently, then rationality can be questioned in those cases.[9] One would then not be surprised to find that government often intervenes in normal contracting procedures in those areas.

Consider several examples. Objective evidence about the fragile nature of modern marriages abounds, and young people should take this into account when they marry. Specifically, young women should not compromise their own careers to assist their husbands or to care for children without firm contractual arrangements about compensation were the marriage to fail. Yet few young people really believe that the risks apply to them. Feminist warnings notwithstanding, women make choices that prove very costly when marriages fail, and few bother with prenuptial agreements. Because society believes that those entering marriage cannot rationally assess all future possibilities, laws are passed protecting those whose marriages break up, even though in theory all such problems could be covered in individually-negotiated marriage contracts.

Objective evidence also abounds about the increased risks of serious injury or death in traffic accidents to those not wearing seat belts. Yet few consumers were willing to pay for these restraints before they were required equipment, and a significant number do not use them even when they are present (although the cost of buckling up is far less than the expected benefit of doing so). Again, laws are passed requiring certain behaviour because we do not trust the rationality of all consumers in this case. Similar arguments can be made about safety requirements on a variety of consumer products.

Finally, young people are notoriously unwilling to accept the fact that they will ever age, become infirm, become unable to work, die. Many of them find it difficult therefore to plan rationally for their old ages. Diamond has examined savings behaviour by Americans during periods in which expectations of Social Security entitlements were relatively low, and has compared that behaviour with what would be predicted by models of rational lifetime planning under reasonable assumptions about lifetime consumption goals. He concluded that "a sizable fraction of American workers would not follow sensible savings plans in the absence of Social Security" (Diamond, 1977:292).

This provides the rationale for the forced savings involved in compulsory government pension plans (the Canada Pension Plan, for example), as well as the legislation setting minimum standards for private pension plans. Similarly, if younger workers are not able to assess correctly risks involving old age, then they are unlikely to weigh correctly the expected costs of clauses in contracts that specify an age of mandatory retirement.

Generally, most workers are quite happy to retire at that age. But some will arrive at it and find that they have not correctly anticipated such things as rates of inflation, the adequacy of their pension, their physical condition, their personal financial resources and the requirements of their families, and the satisfaction they will derive from continuing to work. For these workers, mandatory retirement is more costly than they had ever contemplated.

Of course workers are often represented by union leaders whose job it is to negotiate contracts in the interests of their members. But if workers systematically underestimate the cost of mandatory retirement provisions, there is little reason to believe that union leaders are better informed. And an enlightened union leader might well find little popular support for assigning the "correct" weight to mandatory retirement in contract negotiations.

Furthermore, employers themselves may also have bad information about older workers. If employers as a group act on stereotypes and underestimate the productivity of older workers, then they may put too much weight on the mandatory retirement clause in the contract.

The point of this section is not to assert that mandatory retirement is *necessarily* inefficient. Rather it is to raise serious questions about the contract theory approach that asserts that because mandatory retirement occurs in contracts affecting about half the work force, it is necessarily efficient.

This debate is not merely academic. The contract theory approach weighed heavily in the judgment handed down in the Ontario case. Justice Gray made much of the testimony of economists that outlawing mandatory retirement would have serious repercussions in all dimensions of the personnel function, and this was a central part of his finding that mandatory retirement was a "reasonable" limit on rights as defined by the Charter (Gray, 1986). If the efficiency of mandatory retirement rests on arbitrary assumptions about human behaviour, then a key support for its constitutionality is removed.

Of course, the arguments in this section might be applied to provisions within many contracts. I am not arguing for wholesale public intervention into contracts whenever doubt exists about complete rationality and information. Rather the issue is that when contracts violate human rights guaranteed by the Charter, the burden of proof must surely rest on those who argue that such contract provisions are clearly efficient and of great value.

Interestingly, Justice Gray felt that mandatory retirement was essential to maintain the integrity of pension arrangements. Although this issue will be addressed below, it should be pointed out that if those who do not retire at the "normal" age cease contributions and have their pensions actuarially adjusted when they do retire, abolishing mandatory retirement need not have any effect on pension obligations. The issue becomes somewhat more complicated in defined benefit pension arrangements that set pensions based on the employee's highest earnings, since these plans are often weighted towards older employees and contain a significant component of deferred compensation. If deferred compensation decreases, then pension plans will have to be renegotiated, but defining plans so as to protect the interests of contributors is not an insurmountable administrative problem.

But if mandatory retirement is not efficient, why does it persist? The above discussion suggests one explanation: it is a way for management to extract benefits from labour that workers do not regard as costly and hence do not resist. Another possibility is of course the power of custom. If both labour and management believe that retirement at age 65 is both natural and proper, it seems obvious to include it in labour contracts, especially since it makes pension calculations much easier (pension plans and mandatory retirement usually go hand-in-hand). The fact that the age of retirement persists in many contracts at age 65 over a period of time which has seen both longer lifespans and an increasing trend to early retirement (so that it would be unusual for the "efficient" age of retirement to be stable) suggests that custom plays a far more important role in this matter than occurs in economists' models.

■ III THE COST OF ABOLISHING MANDATORY RETIREMENT

The previous section emphasized the fragility of the "proof" under contract theory that mandatory retirement is efficient. But even were one to accept the assumptions of rationality and good information, contract theory states only that eliminating a freely negotiated clause in a contract will be inefficient, not how large that inefficiency might be. It is reasonable to restrict constitutionally-guaranteed human rights only if such restrictions significantly benefit society. The data suggest that mandatory retirement is at best a relatively unimportant part of the employment contract, one that can be replaced at relatively little cost to both sides.

Under contract theory, the cost of abolishing mandatory retirement should depend on two factors. First, in the absence of any other mechanism that might substitute for mandatory retirement, how many workers would continue to work beyond the age of retirement previously specified in the contract and how long would they stay on? Second, what would be the cost of the alternative mechanisms that would be inserted in contracts to replace mandatory retirement?

On the first question, the data suggest that relatively few workers are seriously constrained by mandatory retirement provisions. For example, Pesando (1979: 8) suggests that "current econometric studies in general do not demonstrate that a demand for work is now being thwarted by compulsory retirement provisions." Labour Canada (1985:5) suggests that, in other jurisdictions, "the negative implications of terminating mandatory retirement have been minimal."[10] Kapsalis (1979) estimates that only about 7 per cent of those bound by mandatory retirement are in fact constrained by that provision. Finally, the Special Senate Committee on Retirement Age Policies (1979:48-9) concluded "that the elimination of mandatory retirement would not increase significantly the labour force participation rates of the older population for the next few years." This was based in part on the general trend to earlier retirement (a point also made by Pesando, 1979:5).[11] If most workers retire anyway at or before the age of mandatory retirement, then it is hard to argue that the provision is a critical ingredient in labour-management relations.

Furthermore, the loss in efficiency is not the entire wage bill for those workers who would not retire. The firm loses at most the excess of salaries over productivity (the excess occurs either because of some deferred wage scheme or because productivity declines[12] while wages do not), and society may well lose even less. If firms did nothing, then the social loss would be less because of the gain to older workers.[13] If firms attempt to reduce their own losses through measures whose cost is relatively large, then the loss to society may be close to the initial loss to the firm.[14] On the other hand, if the firm is able to find other relatively inexpensive ways to reduce these losses, then social losses are also cut.

This is the second issue raised above — are there low cost alternatives to mandatory retirement? Those who support mandatory retirement suggest that no such alternatives exist: firms will increase monitoring and involuntary terminations, and reduce wages, all of which will harm workers far more than does mandatory retirement. But there is a significant limit on how harmful these alternatives can be to workers — under contract theory, the harm cannot exceed the excess of wages over productivity for all unretired workers.[15] Because most workers retire before the previously specified age of retirement, and because those that do not are relatively productive (unproductive employees are unhappy and tend to retire early — see Labour Canada, 1985:A5), the maximum cost of eliminating mandatory retirement is quite low.

Furthermore, it seems unreasonable to suggest that substitutes involving even lower costs will not be found for mandatory retirement. If economics teaches us anything, it is that markets are ingenious in their ability to develop substitutes when conditions change. Thus if one believes that mandatory retirement emerged within markets as a useful part of a system of deferred compensation, then it is natural to suspect that reasonable alternatives will emerge when society judges mandatory retirement to be a violation of the rights of older workers. Just what those substitutes would be is hard to predict, since they will be determined within the collective bargaining system and will likely vary among workplaces. I will however suggest two relatively low cost and not unreasonable alternatives.

First, changes in pension plan arrangements can compensate for the removal of mandatory retirement. One obvious way would be to deny pension benefits to late retirees while they continue to work for the firm. Assuming that later benefits are not actuarially adjusted, the saving to the pension plan is a substantial fraction of the worker's wage and the incentive to continue working is significantly reduced. Since this reduces or even reverses the excess of wages over productivity once the worker passes the normal age of retirement,[16] deferred wage systems may be retained. These changes in pension plans are unlikely, since legislation in Manitoba and Quebec—where mandatory retirement has been eliminated—severely limits the extent to which pension entitlements of older workers can be reduced if they do not retire, and the other provinces might be expected to do the same.

What is more likely is that firms will simply improve pensions. Since financial security is the most critical consideration in the decision to retire (see Dunlop, 1980:7-23), it is employees who are not adequately covered by pensions (because they joined the firm later in life, for example) who are likely to resist retirement. If pensions are a significant fraction of earnings and are properly indexed, the major financial barrier to retirement is removed. Improved portability will address the needs of workers who change firms frequently (alternatively, firms might require employees who join later in life to make larger contributions so as to ensure adequate pensions).

If pension plans are generous enough, they may come up against maximum limits imposed by Revenue Canada on pension benefits. These rules could prevent the pension adjustments foreseen in the Manitoba and Quebec legislation and hence increase retirement incentives. Those who continue to work would enjoy increased pension benefits (because of a higher earnings base), but these would not be of much value if pensions were also adjusted for inflation.[17]

It is also reasonable to expect changes in public pension plans that will reinforce retirement incentives. The increasing pressure on public expenditures inherent in an aging population is likely to lead to some sort of income testing of public pension payments, with the probable result being that those who continue to work full-time will not collect public pensions. Such a change would cause a significant reduction in the incentive to work past the age of 65—as Gunderson and Pesando (1980:355-6) suggest has happened unambiguously in the United States.

A second alternative to mandatory retirement is increased monitoring of performance. This would be necessary in industries where performance fell off noticeably with age and employees continued to work in significant numbers beyond the previous age of retirement. Supporters of mandatory retirement have focused on the high cost that such changes would impose on employees. However, I expect that increased monitoring would likely be accompanied by significant safeguards to protect employees and reduce that cost. For example, grievance procedures could protect employees from arbitrary action, while contracts might restrict salary reductions and specify compensation for long-term employees terminated before a certain age.[18]

Changes in pensions and in monitoring will of course cost money. The appeal of mandatory retirement is its administrative convenience. The point of this section is that the adjustments that will take place need not be "unreasonable," at least in terms of what is implied in the Charter.

Finally, it must be emphasized that arrangements to compensate for the loss of mandatory retirement will vary significantly by industry. Where the cost of this is low, most industries will do nothing. Those that do act will design their responses to minimize the cost to employees.

■ IV MANDATORY RETIREMENT AND YOUTH UNEMPLOYMENT

In public discussions of mandatory retirement, the issue of jobs for young Canadians often emerges.[19] In the Ontario faculty case, youth unemployment was one of the two issues that, in Justice Gray's opinion, made mandatory retirement a "reasonable" limit under the Charter (Gray, 1986). However economists, even those who strongly support mandatory retirement, argue that mandatory retirement has little to do with youth unemployment (see, for example, Gunderson and Pesando, 1980:358, and Pesando, 1979:21-2).

The fundamental reason for this is that unemployment rates, at least in the long run, are not generally dependent on the size of the labour force. The economy can absorb an increase in the labour force (for example, workers who stay in the labour force instead of being forced to retire) because such an increase itself increases demand. To believe that the economy consists of only a fixed number of jobs is to accept the "lump-of-labour" fallacy. In the short run, there may be some impact on youth unemployment, but that impact will fade relatively quickly. Moreover, the abolition of mandatory retirement would occur during a period in which the economy has to absorb relatively few young people, relative to the past two decades, ameliorating any short-run problems.

Justice Gray seems to have emphasized the short-run problems, assuming that no adjustments will take place in the macro-economy. He quotes extensively from an affidavit submitted by the universities which estimates the number of additional persons there would be in the labour force if mandatory retirement is eliminated and then projects the impact on youth unemployment "*if this results in an equivalent increase in the number of unemployed*" (D. Foot, quoted in Gray, 1986:64, emphasis mine). Since this simply assumes that the increase in the labour force will result in no new jobs, even in the long run (estimates are made for the year 2000), it in effects assumes away the adjustment that virtually all economists believe will take place.

■ V MANDATORY RETIREMENT IN THE UNIVERSITY

If the case for mandatory retirement is anywhere valid, it is probably so in Canadian universities. Because salaries rise over the lifetime of the faculty member (salaries at age 65 are generally about 2.5 times those paid to new assistant professors[20]), while academic work is pleasant and not physically taxing, universities expect to be more affected than other employers if mandatory retirement is removed. Furthermore, universities find productivity relatively hard to monitor.

In the case before the Ontario Supreme Court, the universities asserted that productivity dropped as professors aged. Although this was not proven, deferred compensation is still probably present, since it is hard to argue that faculty near retirement are as much as 2.5 times as productive as their young colleagues. Therefore, if mandatory retirement is eliminated and no other adjustments occur, some faculty members are likely to retire at later than the optimal date, probably in numbers somewhat above those projected for the economy as a whole. Hansen and Holden (no date) suggested that eliminating mandatory retirement in universities in the United States would increase the average age of retirement by about one year, while the Bovey Commission in Ontario, using the experience of the University of Manitoba after mandatory retirement was abolished, projected that the impact in Ontario would be to increase the average retirement age by just under two years (Commission on the Future Development of the Universities of Ontario, 1984:49).

The universities have also argued that the impact on them of abolishing mandatory retirement will be exaggerated in the next decade. The age distribution of faculty (with most faculty now over 35 but not yet near retirement) along with cutbacks in government funding make universities critically dependent on retirements as a source of funds for faculty renewal. All this would seem to make universities an extreme example of the potential harm that can result from eliminating mandatory retirement.

I believe instead that the harm done to universities if mandatory retirement is held to violate the Charter will be both minor and transitory. Consider first the issue of faculty renewal. Even accepting the Bovey projections, the effect on renewal is simply to delay it. In the steady state, there is little change in the number of retirements each year. During the transition between steady states, there will be some dislocations. These were foreseen by the framers of the Charter, who delayed implementation of the relevant portion of the Charter by three years to allow those affected to adjust. That the universities did nothing to prepare for the elimination of mandatory retirement is hardly an argument against it.

Moreover, the issue of faculty renewal is something of a red herring. There has been precious little renewal in recent years, despite mandatory retirement, due largely to government policy that has cut real allocations to the universities, and exacerbated by the skewed age distribution of faculty. Furthermore, the Bovey Commission itself suggested that short-term government funding be provided to reduce the transitional impact of eliminating mandatory retirement, financing new appointments until expected retirements materialized. Faculty renewal, therefore, has little to do with mandatory retirement and everything to do with public policy, and blaming older faculty members who do not wish to retire for the problem is unreasonable.[21]

However, all this presumes that eliminating mandatory retirement will have a dramatic impact on university finances. As I suggested above, it is unlikely. All universities run quite generous pension plans. If pensions begin at age 65 and arrangements are made to pay those who continue to work only the difference between the pension and the salary entitlement, then the cost to the university is significantly reduced. This might be permitted by enriching pension plans up to the Revenue Canada limits and ensuring portability, moves that would in any case improve retirement incentives.

Furthermore, it is not that difficult to monitor the productivity of faculty members. Research productivity is already monitored, both regularly to determine merit increases, and more intensely to determine tenure and promotion. Some fear that eliminating mandatory retirement would lead to more monitoring in order to permit involuntary terminations. Since this process would affect faculty members, it would both be expensive and hurt faculty directly by reducing security. But, as contract theory tells us, since the cost of those who do not retire is minimal, an expensive system of monitoring is unlikely.

If there is a concern about unretired faculty members who have ceased to be productive as researchers, then I would envision a much less draconian use of monitoring. For example, the "standard" teaching load might be increased to four courses, with automatic reductions to today's loads for faculty members prior to tenure and for ten years after the tenure decision. At that point, the reduction could be extended for five year periods for all faculty members who had met certain standards for research productivity. Unproductive faculty members of any age would find their loads rising substantially, a change that might in any case be valuable to the university. Unproductive older faculty members would find even less reason to postpone retirement past the usual date (the point at which pension eligibility began), and the net cost to the university of those who did not retire would decline even further.

The purpose of this discussion is not to predict what will happen in universities if mandatory retirement is eliminated. This will depend on the universities' experience with the change and on collective bargaining. Rather, I mean to suggest that the changes are likely to be minor and relatively inexpensive to both the institutions and their faculty.

■ VI CONCLUSION

This article has argued that the costs of eliminating mandatory retirement are relatively minor and somewhat transitory, and that this is true even in institutions—like universities—where the impact is likely to be largest.

This is because relatively few workers will choose to work much past the currently-specified age of retirement, and because the changes that will ameliorate any harm are themselves likely to be relatively inexpensive. Thus there is little argument for further delays in implementing the Charter, and little reason to expect dramatic changes in society when that occurs.

Why then are universities so resistant to eliminating mandatory retirement? Partially, this reflects the desperate financial situation of most universities in the 1980s where any cost increase has a dramatic effect on the institution. This of course is a problem for the provincial governments which will have to deal with the impact of the Charter throughout the civil service. But I suspect that the resistance stems more from the unwillingness of most bureaucracies to deal with change, especially imposed from without. On that point, London's (1983) comment is an appropriate way to conclude this paper:

> Historically, all advances in human rights have been opposed by those with vested interests, who inevitably have predicted all manner of resulting evil and destruction. My own view is that the benefits of eliminating "ageism" from our employment systems far out-weigh the costs. Stereotypical victimization cannot be tolerated. Administrative inconvenience can.

Notes

* Earlier drafts of this article were written while the author held a Leave Fellowship from the Social Sciences and Humanities Research Council of Canada. The author would like to thank J. Buttrick and M. Gunderson and Referees of this journal for their useful comments.

1. For a discussion of the recent experience in North America, see Labour Canada, (1985:Annex I).

2. Deferred wages can be thought of as a performance bond posted by workers. As Lazear (1979:1270) points out, Becker and Stigler (1974) explicitly suggest such a bond. Of course, workers would have to make sure that employers do not "cheat" by firing high-wage older workers who have not shirked. Lazear suggests that this explains the limits on the size of the bond that workers are prepared to post, and that the value of the firm's reputation for honest treatment of employees limits the incentive to cheat. However, because the bond is limited, mandatory retirement will not be entirely efficient, and retirement need not occur at the efficient date.

3. That present value is maximized by having workers work until they die. The point here is somewhat different. First, work beyond the optimal age of retirement is inefficient because those workers value leisure more than wages equal to their marginal product. Second, mandatory retirement permits an optimal deferred wage scheme that minimizes shirking. In both cases, there are efficiency gains to be shared by management and labour.

4. Mandatory retirement does not generally preclude rehiring the employee, it simply terminates the existing employment contract.

5. The work of Lazear and others who have written about mandatory retirement generally does not *prove* that it is efficient; rather it begins with the assumption that mandatory retirement must be efficient because of contract theory and then looks for explanations for why this might occur.

6. Furthermore, all this ignores the theory of the second best. Arrangements that would be part of a completely efficient economy are not necessarily desirable when other inefficiencies are present.

7. The assumption of rationality also is not accepted in all disciplines—see, for example, Kahneman, Slovic, and Tversky (1982) for psychological research on non-rational behaviour.

8. This is a phenomenon that Tom Wolfe calls "the right stuff." Calabresi and Bass, in their cited article, were commenting on an economic analysis of product liability that suggests that the implicit contract between buyer and seller could handle the policy issues surrounding product liability.

9. The key to this approach lies in making reasonable assumptions about tastes, since utility theory can explain virtually any behaviour over time by assuming the appropriate utility function and discount rate.

10. After examining the evidence from other jurisdictions that have eliminated or limited mandatory retirement, the article concludes that this experience "shows that the tendency of a vast proportion of the working population is to retire at or before the age of 65." The legislation does permit workers to continue beyond normal retirement age, but "the number of those employees is small compared to their age group or the size of the labour force."

11. The labour force participation rates for males age 65 and above fell consistently between 1953 and 1977, from 34.8 to 15.5%. The participation rates for males ages 55-64 fell from 86.5 to 76.6% over the same period (Special Senate Committee on Retirement Age Policies, 1979:49).

12. It should be noted that there is no particular evidence to suggest that productivity declines with age, at least in the age range around the current age of mandatory retirement. For example, Abraham and Medoff (1982:312) suggest that productivity is not related to length of service, while the Special Committee on Aging of the United States Senate (1984:58-67) found substantial evidence that productivity does not decline with age.

13. The entire loss to the firm is not an efficiency loss to society, since some of that loss is a transfer to older workers. Technically, the loss in efficiency by having those workers continue to work is the amount by which their productivity in the labour force is less than their productivity in generating utility for themselves through leisure time activity.

14. Under contract theory, firms will only undertake actions whose total cost (to workers and the firm) does not exceed the excess of unretired workers' salaries over productivity. Since those actions may not transfer resources to workers, the entire cost may represent a loss in efficiency.

15. For example, if that excess is $10,000, then firms will not impose measures which cause harm to workers totalling $15,000. The reason is that workers would prefer to avoid those measures and instead transfer $10,000 to the firm through wage reductions.

16. The key of course is both the lack of actuarial adjustment and permitting the employer to enjoy any savings to the pension plan.

17. Since Justice Gray was concerned in his decision about the integrity of pension plans, it is interesting that one result of eliminating mandatory retirement might be a general improvement in pension provisions.

18. Of course, it remains to be seen whether such a clause would not itself violate the Charter. I suspect not, since it would be similar to the pension plan itself which defines eligibility for benefits in terms of age.

19. For example, Cliff Pilkey, president of the Ontario Federation of Labour, argued that mandatory retirement "provides job opportunities for young people coming into the workplace" (Haliechuk, 1986).

20. The University of Toronto (1984:Table 4) shows the standard salary for a faculty member at age 30 and age 65 to be $30,000 and $73,804, respectively, using the University's formula for PTR (Progress Through the Ranks).

21. A measure of the peculiar way many view the elderly is to insert any other group into the discussion. It would be considered intolerable to ask women or Asians or Roman Catholics or humanities instructors to step aside to provide the financial resources for faculty renewal!

References

Abraham, K.G. and H.S. Farber (1987) "Job Duration, Seniority, and Earnings," *American Economic Review*, 77:3:278-97.

Abraham, K.G. and J.L. Medoff (1982) "Length of Service and the Operation of Internal Labour Markets," *Proceedings of the 35th Annual Industrial Relations Research Association*, pp. 308-18.

Becker, G. and G. Stigler (1974) "Law Enforcement, Malfeasance, and Compensation of Enforcers," *Journal of Legal Studies*, 3:1:1-18.

Calabresi, G. and K.C. Bass (1970) "Right Approach, Wrong Implications: A Critique of McKean on Products Liability," *The University of Chicago Law Review*, 38:74-91.

Commission on the Future Development of the Universities of Ontario (1984) "Ontario Universities 1984: Options and Futures," pamphlet, Ottawa.

Diamond, P.A. (1977) "A Framework for Social Security Analysis," *Journal of Public Economics*, 8:275-98.

Dunlop, D. (1980) *Mandatory Retirement Policy: A Human Rights Dilemma* (Ottawa: Conference Board).

Gray, W.G. (1986) "Reasons for Judgment" (in the case of various Ontario faculty members and librarians against their respective universities and the Attorney General of Ontario). Supreme Court of Ontario. Released October 15, 1986.

Gunderson, M. (1983) "Mandatory Retirement and Personnel Policies," *Columbia Journal of World Business*, 28:2:8-15.

_____ and J.E. Pesando (1980) "Eliminating Mandatory Retirement: Economics and Human Rights," *Canadian Public Policy—Analyse de Politiques*, VI:2:352-60.

Haliechuk, R. (1986) "Professors head to court over mandatory retirement," *The Toronto Star*, Tuesday, April 26, 1986, p. A18.

Hansen, W.L. and K.C. Holden (undated, *circa* 1983) "Major Results of the

Wisconsin Study for the Department of Labor," report, xeroxed, University of Wisconsin-Madison.

Kahneman, D., P. Slovic and A. Tversky (eds.) (1982) *Judgment Under Uncertainty: Heuristics and Biases* (New York: Cambridge University Press).

Kapsalis, C. (1979) "Pensions and the Work Decision," Economic Council of Canada, Ottawa.

Labour Canada (1985) *An Industrial Relations Perspective on Mandatory Retirement* (Ottawa: Policy and Strategic Analysis).

Lazear, E.P. (1979) "Why Is There Mandatory Retirement?" *Journal of Political Economy*, 87:6:1261-84.

London, J.R. (1983) "Universities Should Prepare for Abolition of Mandatory Retirement," *University of Toronto Bulletin*, June 6, 1983, p. 10.

Pesando, J.E. (1979) *The Elimination of Mandatory Retirement: An Economic Perspective*, Discussion Paper (Toronto: Ontario Economic Council).

Special Committee on Aging, United States Senate (1984) *The Costs of Employing Older Workers* (Washington: U.S. Government Printing Office).

Special Senate Committee on Retirement Age Policies (1979) *Retirement Without Tears* (Ottawa: Supply and Services Canada).

University of Toronto (1984) *Excellence and Diversity: The University of Toronto's Submission to the Commission on the Future Development of the Universities of Ontario*. Toronto.

■ POSTSCRIPT

Gunderson and Pesando discuss several conventional arguments for allowing mandatory retirement. These include work sharing, the facilitation of planning, the minimization of monitoring of older workers, and the opportunity to create deferred compensation plans. Gunderson and Pesando argue that establishing a government-sponsored, uniform mandatory retirement plan for all workers results in inflexible retirement schemes that do not meet the needs of employers or employees. They favour flexible retirement schemes whereby employers and employees are free to bargain for the mandatory retirement age that best suits their individual and collective needs.

Krashinsky concludes that supporters of mandatory retirement have vested interests. Employers, such as universities, defend mandatory retirement because they believe its elimination would mean added costs. Krashinsky disputes this, saying that costs could be reduced by using the workers' pension benefits to pay a portion of his/her wages after normal retirement age. Further, he suggests that allowing workers to continue to work beyond normal retirement age would cause only a short-term disruption in job openings for younger workers, as older workers would eventually need to be replaced.

The social planning consequences of accepting either argument are significant. Both sides of the debate recognize a need to revise and update current funding formulas for pension plans. Further, both sides acknowledge that there are fundamental issues of human rights that must be decided. The debate is between those who agree with the Supreme Court ruling that it is legal to discriminate on the basis of age in the case of mandatory retirement, and those who regard mandatory retirement as a violation of the fundamental principles enshrined in the Charter of Rights and Freedoms. It is a debate that is far from over.

■ QUESTIONS

1. Which side presents the strongest case for its position? Is your decision affected by your previous beliefs about mandatory retirement?

2. What evidence would you require in order for you to favour the opposed position?

3. Which social groups are most likely to favour mandatory retirement?

4. Which social groups are least likely to favour mandatory retirement?

5. Are there other solutions to the mandatory retirement debate that are not discussed in these two articles?

■ FURTHER READING

In Support of Gunderson and Pesando

Burke, Ronald J. "Disengagement from Organizations: Termination, Permanent Layoff, and Retirement." In *Human Resources Management: Contemporary Perspectives in Canada*. Edited by K. Srinivas. Toronto: McGraw-Hill, 1984.

Gunderson, M. "Mandatory Retirement and Personnel Policies." *Columbia Journal of World Business* 28, no. 2 (1983): 8-15.

In Support of Krashinsky

Czerny S.J., Michael and Jamie Swift. *Getting Started on Social Analysis in Canada*. Toronto: Between the Lines, chap. 11, "Aging: Out of Sight," 1988.

London, J.R. "Universities Should Prepare for Abolition of Mandatory Retirement." *University of Toronto Bulletin*, June 6 (1983).

Other Voices

Cohen, Leah. *Small Expectations: Society's Betrayal of Older Women*. Toronto: McClelland and Stewart, 1984.

Dunlop, D. *Mandatory Retirement: A Human Rights Dilemma*. Ottawa: Conference Board of Canada, 1980.

SHOULD ACCESS

TO ABORTION

BE RESTRICTED?

YES **Iain T. Benson,** "An Examination of Certain 'Pro-Choice' Abortion Arguments: Permanent Concerns About a 'Temporary' Problem," *Canadian Journal of Family Law* 7 no. 1 (1988): 146-165

NO **Ontario Coalition for Abortion Clinics,** "State Power and the Struggle for Reproductive Freedom: The Campaign for Free-standing Abortion Clinics in Ontario," *Resources for Feminist Research* 17, no. 3 (1988): 109-114

On January 28, 1988, the Supreme Court of Canada struck down the existing abortion law on the grounds that it unduly restricted women's access to abortion. With that move, the Court removed abortion from the Criminal Code of Canada and opened the door to an unprecedented use of Canadian courts by men seeking injunctions to prevent their former lovers from having abortions. The tangled lives of Chantal Daigle and Jean-Guy Tremblay, and Barbara Dodd and Gregory Murphy made front-page news across Canada (see *Maclean's,* July 31, 1989).

In response to the Supreme Court decision and the subsequent push for court injunctions, the federal government proposed a new law to recriminalize abortion. The proposed legislation would have made it illegal for anyone to perform an abortion unless continuation of the pregnancy threatened the mother's health. The legislation was passed by the House of Commons, but defeated in the Senate on January 31, 1991. Curiously, this result pleased extremists from both sides of the abortion debate. Pro-life advocates opposed to abortion in any circumstances were concerned that the legislation would have permitted abortions in special circumstances. Pro-choice advocates who favoured abortion on demand objected to the recriminalization of abortion and argued that the defeated law would have restricted women's access to abortion at a time when the

Supreme Court of Canada had ruled that Canadian women had a right to an abortion.

Other positions in the abortion debate lie somewhere between these two extremes. Not all of those who call themselves pro-life are opposed to abortions in all circumstances; nor do all pro-choice advocates defend abortion on demand. The federal government had hoped its proposed legislation would appeal to Canadians occupying this middle ground. However, the combined opposition from the improbable alliance of pro-life and pro-choice camps was strong enough to bring about its demise.

Abortion debates, however, seldom end with the defeat or passage of legal statutes. As Francome (1984) has shown, after passage or defeat of a statute, both sides attempt to use whatever other means they have at their disposal to promote their views. Following the defeat of the government abortion bill in the Senate, both sides in the debate began to lobby provincial governments, who control health care expenditures, to either restrict or provide greater access to abortion. Pro-life forces seek to have provincial health care plans stop paying for abortions, while pro-choice forces seek to increase access to abortion by establishing provincially funded abortion clinics. The struggle over abortion in Canada mirrors that in the United States, with both sides in the debate trying to gain the attention of the lawmakers.

The sociological debate focuses on a number of issues. Some sociologists seek to understand the social processes by which people become identified as either pro-life or pro-choice, or any of the variants between the two extremes. For example, Francome (1984) offers a painstaking historical account of the worldwide abortion movement, with special emphasis on the movements in Britain and the United States. It is worth noting, too, that pro-choice advocates have opposed abortion on occasion. For example, upon discovering that women in India were seeking abortions after amniocentesis tests revealed the foetus to be female, women's groups, appalled that the medical profession was profiting from femicide—the destruction of women—fought to prevent testing for this purpose (Mies, 1986, 151-153).

Other sociologists have sought to identify the social context within which supporters of either pro-life or pro-choice positions function. How do they recruit members? How do they sustain their memberships and their enthusiasm for the struggle in the face of determined opposition? Who are the most likely people to defend or oppose abortion? How does each group defend its own position while attacking its opponent's? Under what social conditions will either group achieve its objectives? The answers to these questions are profoundly different for sociologists than they are for active participants in the abortion debate. Sociologists seek to locate the debate and the debaters in a social context. They also seek to identify the conditions that give rise to the debate, and to the major players in the debate, at any moment in history.

The two articles that follow are not written by sociologists. Arguing the "No" side of the debate is a lawyer, Iain T. Benson. The "Yes" side of the debate is argued by the Ontario Coalition for Abortion Clinics. Examine each article carefully. To what extent do their arguments match the kinds of concerns that sociologists would have in studying the issues? What do they reveal about the process and tactics used by both sides of the debate to get their message across to the public?

References

Francome, Colin (1984) *Abortion: A Worldwide Movement* (London: George Allen and Unwin).

Mies, Maria (1986) *Patriarchy and Accumulation on a World Wide Scale: Women in the International Division of Labour* (London: Zed Books).

A CRITIQUE OF "PRO-CHOICE" ARGUMENTS

Iain T. Benson

YES

... In this paper, I propose to examine certain of the arguments used by proponents of the "pro-choice" position in the abortion debate. Since, in the debate, we are concerned even arguably, with when our society chooses to protect life by law, anyone concerned with human rights must be concerned with the arguments that allow the taking of life. Some will immediately disagree with the statement that the abortion debate involves the taking of developing human life; to these people, and those who say that human life and animal life are morally the same, I have nothing to say. For others, this paper will suggest that certain arguments often used by those advocating the "freedom of choice" side of the debate are insufficient to allow the taking of foetal life. It is not the place of this paper to describe the limited circumstances in which abortion may be morally acceptable.

I will examine the use of "freedom of choice," "some terms regarding the nature of the foetus," "pluralism," "the life or health of the woman," "compromise" and "the woman's right to 'control her own body.'" I will argue that "choice" itself should not be determinative in moral debates and that several other terms frequently relied upon by "pro-choice" advocates are unacceptable. We must make no mistake; when philosophers such as Canada's George Grant say that "this is one of the crucial issues of our time," it is incumbent on all fair-minded members of society to examine their own arguments and their presuppositions.

■ THE PLACE OF "CHOICE" IN MORAL DEBATES

What is meant by the phrase "pro-choice"? It is my view that due to its central position in the abortion debate (it seems to have assumed, for some, the status of a self-evident, self-contained justification) this phrase must be examined; once examined, it is evident that it is not a valid position to take in a moral debate at all and that because it is unsound, arguments can easily be developed to show that the term itself is of no use in moral debates.

To those who have followed the abortion debate from its inception, it is clear that this phrase is the one preferred by its adherents to the earlier term "pro-abortion." The latter phrase was dropped as indicating approval of abortion when, it is argued, the proponents of "freedom of choice" are not, really, in favour of abortion itself but favour "the right to choose"; those who oppose abortion are, then, said to be "anti-choice." What is behind all this terminology?

I argue that to approach the abortion issue on the basis of choice is, simply put, poor philosophy, and that those who say they are pro-choice are using an argument which they themselves would not allow in other areas of moral debate.

Choice itself is morally neutral, and can only be evaluated as right or wrong in terms of the framework of rights in which it is exercised. Thus, to ask "should I have the freedom of choice to fire my pistol?" can only be evaluated *morally* in terms of what you intend to shoot and in what setting. Another example which will strike a chord with many of those in the "pro-choice" camp in the abortion issue is the issue of pornography.

Is one who wishes to restrict the pornography producer's right to produce pornography "anti-choice"? In one sense, of course he is, yet many of those who are "pro-choice" in the abortion debate are also "anti-pornography" in the sense that they recognize the fact that there are "moral" factors which are a part of the issue of the pornography debate that would be completely ignored if "choice" alone was the focus. There is another aspect of the "choice" debate that is used where abortion is at issue but would scarcely be permitted in other areas.

It is sometimes said that those who are against abortion are "seeking to enforce *their* moral views on other people." It is important to note what this statement implies. It implies that moral views may be held personally but have no applicability between individuals. This in turn suggests that morals are purely subjective, and that no person should attempt to force his view of what is right or wrong on other people. I am not going to discuss here the relationship between morals and law except to say that there is a difference between saying that law and morality are not co-extensive (a proposition which I accept), and that law is not concerned with morality (a proposition which I deny).

Most of our criminal law is based on moral notions of what is "right" and "wrong" and that such rules should apply regardless of the views of individual citizens. Furthermore, it is worth asking whether people who say that "no one should attempt to force his view of what is 'right' or 'wrong' on others" really function in accordance with this themselves? I would say that they do not.

Over a whole host of issues, advocates of particular moral positions expect the law to restrict behaviour of certain types; one here might list sexual abuse, discrimination of various sorts, as well as matters such as restrictions on the production of pornography. In so doing, they are seeking to enforce through law their notions of what should or should not be in society. . . . In all areas of moral debate, one must evaluate what the rights are that are at issue and in the abortion debate this necessarily involves an evaluation of what the foetus is and whether it has an interest to be taken into account. Since human rights are the property of those who are alive and being a member of the human species undeniably begins at conception (as a matter of scientific fact), whether the foetus is deemed to have moral and legal rights is a matter of critical concern which ought not to be avoided by a philosophical unsound use of "choice."

The real issue in the abortion debate (and all debates involving when we should protect life by law) is "when and on what basis do we recognize the right to have rights?" The onus is on those who would seek to remove rights to indicate why the right should be removed. This leads to the question (regarding the rights of the foetus) "what is the morally relevant distinction between the foetus before birth and a child after birth such that we say one has a right to life and the other doesn't?" Various attempts, some of them exceedingly ingenious, have been made to devise a morally significant distinction.[1] I have never heard a satisfactory answer to this question, and until one is given must support the "presumption in favour of life" referred to by the Law Reform Commission of Canada in another setting.[2] To conclude on this point, therefore, we have seen that "choice" itself is incapable of providing a satisfactory resolution in the abortion debate. Since the debate involves, even arguably, the most central of "rights" issues, we must proceed carefully and with an honest philosophical approach: "choice" itself will not do in this or in any other area of moral debate.

■ SOME "PRO-CHOICE" ARGUMENTS REGARDING THE NATURE OF THE FOETUS

Apart from avoiding the issue altogether, one of the most common techniques to avoid dealing with an issue is to say that what is at issue is not an aspect of the problematic category. Thus, in the abortion debate where the "pro-life" side is continually talking about the "right to life"[3] of the foetus and the fact that abortion pits the life of the foetus against the life or will of the woman, one of the techniques used by the "pro-choice" side is not to mention the foetus at all.[4] This failure to address the developing foetus becomes even more striking in the "foetal intervention" cases in which certain feminists have argued that intervention to save the life of the late-term foetus is never justified over the will of the woman no matter how unreasonable the position taken by the woman. Thus, no matter how great the risk to the foetus or how minimal the risk to the woman, nothing should interfere with the decision of the woman. Such an approach, though it does not address the issue, would seem to suggest that birth is the relevant point at which to attribute rights. This approach effectively denies any rights in the foetus despite the fact that, when a late-term case is concerned, the "foetus" is in all respects except location identical to a newborn child.[5] Given that determination of the moral status of the foetus in the abortion issue is bound to affect the way in which the foetus is treated within the whole gambit of advancing medical technology, the denial of status until birth is ominous.

A second method used by "pro-choice" advocates is to deny that the foetus has rights because it lacks some quality necessary to the holding of rights. The most common manner in which this is done is to say that the foetus does not have standing in the matter of "life-rights" because it is not yet a person and does not have moral personhood. Another similar argument says that the foetus is not "human," while yet another, referred to by one of the Judges of the Supreme Court of Canada, says that the foetus is "potential life" merely and therefore has a lesser interest or no interest at all, its "right" to protection accruing, somehow, at a later stage of its development.[6]

Attempts have been made to suggest that the foetus's rights should exist only from a certain point, whether it be development of the central nervous system, viability, birth itself or some version of the trimesteral approach taken by the U.S. Supreme Court.[7]

All of these arguments turn on two conceptual errors; these are first, ignoring or confusing the "potential" of the foetus and second, ignoring that its genetic individuality remains unchanged from the moment of conception through to death (whenever this occurs).

A good example of the way in which commentators confuse the "potentiality argument" may be seen in Jane Fortin's article.[8] In discussing the argument, which she says "has great popular appeal," Fortin suggests that the fact that sperm and eggs equally have "the potential for life" is "persuasive criticism" of the potentiality argument. Fortin and others have failed to recognize that it is not "the potential *for* human life" that "pro-lifers" argue for protecting; it is *the unique developing human life itself* (and it is *already*, after conception, unique, needing only time and nutrition to be fully developed).

Some commentators, like certain judges in both the Supreme Courts of Canada and the United States, have failed to note an ambiguity in the use of the term "potential." The error is a failure to distinguish between a thing that has the present capability for something (needing only time for it to occur) and the possible future achievement of a thing, in which the thing itself will never become anything else. It is not true of the sperm or the egg to say that it is potentially a unique individual in the same way that it is true of the foetus to say that it is potentially a fully developed adult.

A failure to recognize this improper use of "potential" is what leads some writers into a failure to differentiate between contraception (about which it is possible to speak of a particular sperm and egg as containing the constituent elements of life and therefore being "potential life" in the "possible future achievement" sense, above) and that particular unique genetic entity that exists after conception (about which we can only speak correctly as "life," "developing life," or "life with potential" in the "present capability" sense). Thus, for Fortin to speak of the Warnock Committee's minority opinion as opposing the use of human embryos for research purposes, "since this would obviously deprive them *of their potential for life*"[9] highlights the absurdity of the confusion. An embryo that is only potential life cannot be deprived in a way that is morally offensive of what it only has potentially. If the minority of the Committee objected to research on human embryos, it must have been because they, "having accepted the potentiality argument," recognized that research on a human embryo would deprive that embryo of its developing life, not its "potential life."[10]

Another common example of this failure to distinguish the two senses of "potential" is when it is said of the foetus that it is merely "potential life," meaning that because it does not have some factor considered relevant (life), it is not wrong to terminate it. But this means that the foetus must not yet be alive and therefore, logically, it cannot be terminated because it cannot be deprived of life that it does not already have. If termination in the sense of ending something is the issue, "something" must have begun. If nothing is alive, there is nothing that can be, properly speaking, aborted.

The developing foetus is not "potential life"; it is, much more significantly, life with potential (in the present capability sense). It is, without argument, "a developing life." The absence of life has generally been considered to be death. If one wants to say that it is "a potential rights holder" and that, prior to a certain point, the foetus has no rights, then this, as far as it goes, make some kind of sense; but to say that the foetus is "potential life" is, literally, nonsense.

All the changes after conception are changes of degree, not of kind; the foetus is merely the beginning stage of all of us at the start of the continuum of life; as unique individuals we are the same from conception onwards. To hold otherwise is bad science.[11] The fact that criminal law has said that life begins, as far as murder is concerned, only after the child has proceeded in a living form outside the mother does not mean that it is unworthy of consideration prior to this point. This is precisely why the law has historically criminalized abortion,[12] due to the realization that the foetus prior to birth was in need of protection.

■ THE "LIFE OR HEALTH" OF THE WOMAN

It is important to recognize that the Supreme Court, in the *Morgentaler* decision, has not defined either what it means by the life and health of the pregnant woman or the context or extent of foetal rights. This is central due to the fact that the Court has said that it is likely that Parliament will want to recognize a balancing between the rights of the foetus and the rights of the woman. This means a definition of the rights involved and this in turn requires a delineation of the interests of the respective "parties." The interest of the foetus will be to be left to develop.[13] The interest of the woman will vary along a whole spectrum from emotional trauma (over a wide range of severity) through physical risks and dangers up to actual threat to her continued existence itself.

The Supreme Court has recognized that the foetus has some interests and that the protection of the foetus would be a valid legislative objective. One cannot say much more than that the foetus has "some interests" because the Court expressly did not address the extent of these rights; it addressed itself, rather, to evaluating then striking down section 251 of the *Criminal Code*, largely on grounds relating to the manner in which the section was operating procedurally. Parliament must therefore decide the extent of any limitation on the foetus's right to life, taking into account, one hopes, principled reasons setting out clearly what circumstances will allow the termination of life of the foetus; it is critical that the interests of the foetus to the continuance of its *life* be weighed against well-defined and strictly delineated criteria before abortion is allowed. The current vagueness surrounding the term "health" and the grounds on which abortion is allowed are unacceptable and were, in fact, part of the procedural unfairness which the Supreme Court ruled had infringed the *Charter of Rights*.

The term "health" contained in the section of the *Criminal Code* that was recently struck down by the Supreme Court was not defined in the *Code*. Obviously, if abortions are going to be allowable in certain "life and health" situations, it is necessary to give some substance to these terms. The definitions of "health" that were used by therapeutic abortion committees functioning under s. 251 of the *Criminal Code* varied considerably. Where abortions were liberally available, the working "definition"[14] of "health" was often the World Health Organization's statement of health. That statement says health is "a state of complete physical, mental, emotional and social well-being, not simply the absence of illness and disease." This, it need scarcely be observed, is a definition of almost complete elasticity and impracticality. While it may be a positive statement of objectives in the area of health, it is useless as a working definition for purposes of abortion. Daniel Callahan has commented as follows:

> Its attractiveness as an ideal is vitiated by its practical impossibility of realization. Worse than that, it positively misleads, for health becomes a goal of such all-consuming importance that it simply begs to be thwarted in its realization. The demands which the word "complete" entail set the stage for the worst false consciousness of all: the demand that life deliver perfection.[15]

In one of its Working Papers, the Law Reform Commission of Canada itself voiced concern over the W.H.O. "definition" in the following terms:

> Those general terms of wide public use have ethical, social and political implications and their reach extends to every element of human happiness. The concept of "social well-being" far exceeds the meaning presently contemplated in Canadian criminal law for it includes political injustice, economic scarcity, food shortages and unfavourable physical environments. *All human*

misfortunes and disorders are not forms of illness from which one must be saved under the rubric of health in criminal law. . . . [A] state of well-being, in law, ought first to be notionally sufficient to cope with the ordinary living in modern society, but does not carry a guarantee of stress-free, non-responsible life-style, because stress as well as responsibility for one's behaviour are incidents of living in society.[16]

If, in the future, Parliament makes any attempt to draft a law "taking into account the interests of the foetus," it will be necessary to ensure that pivotal definitions are clearly expressed. At the least, the danger to life of health must be grave and potentially permanent and should expressly *exclude* social health reasons such as familial, social or economic well-being, all of which were used under the World Health Organization's statement of health. Particular care should be taken to avoid the use of definitions which would allow abortions for "psychiatric" reasons where the "threat" is not related to some meaningful criterion of health. Quite apart from the lack of meaningful definition of health is the fact that evidence exists which suggests that most of the vast medical literature available on abortion is seriously deficient in various areas, making it impossible to speak without doubt about *any* situations in which abortion is psychiatrically indicated: in a study prepared at the behest of the scientific council of the Canadian Psychiatric Association, B. K. Doane and B. G. Quigley, after reviewing approximately two hundred and fifty journal articles and books on the psychiatric and related aspects of therapeutic abortion, had the following comments:

. . . both the antagonists and the protagonists of therapeutic abortion should be aware that no scientific evidence exists to show that emotional risks vary in accordance with legislative restrictions on abortion . . . [and that] despite the large number of articles and studies in the literature, there are insufficient data on which to base planning of medical and social programs for the management of undesired pregnancies.[17]

In a more recent article in the same Journal, following a review of all the available literature on the incidence of complications of pregnancy in women who had been denied abortion, an editorial writer raised several important points as follows:

Few interventions are accepted without systematic evaluation. Drugs shown to be effective in the laboratory are evaluated in clinical trials, and surgical procedures are constantly criticized and revised. Even diagnostic tests must be shown to be safe, to cause only minor side effects and to have adequate test validity. Therapeutic abortions appear to be a major exception; they apparently have been "privileged" to bypass evaluation. *Why are they being done without clinical validation, even in the face of mounting evidence that they are not necessary for the prevention of maternal disease or the birth of unwanted children?* . . . Physicians must take a more scientific approach to unwanted pregnancies and realize that abortion is not the answer to social ills. *Legislators should base their decisions on clinical reviews rather than succumb to public pressures.*[18]

Finally, given that the initial response of some provincial governments to the striking down of the *Criminal Code* provisions appears to involve issues related to the funding of abortions, etc., it is essential to distinguish between the primary issue (the morality of abortion itself) and those which are secondary (funding and access to abortion). A failure to distinguish between these two types of questions can result in an ongoing failure to address the primary issue and a disproportionate expenditure of time and energy on secondary aspects. This was clearly seen under the old law in the emphasis placed by some upon the "problems of access to the procedure" between one area of Canada and the next. The Supreme Court of Canada decision requires that governments address the primary issue of *when and in what circumstances should abortion be permitted.* The *manner* of the provision of abortion services is clearly a secondary issue which can only be answered once the primary issue has been addressed. . . .

■ THE IDEA OF COMPROMISE

. . . One occasionally hears people argue that in a country which has such divided views on a moral issue, "compromise" is the only way to "solve" the social debate. What is missed in such an approach is that it assumes both approaches to be morally acceptable prior to the compromise. Thus, where fundamental presuppositions are not shared, the attempt at resolution may be morally impossible because what one side deems moral is to the other side immoral. In such a situation, "compromise" is meaningless and, potentially, dangerous. If one opposes the murder of people and is told by others that due to debate on the issue, they have decided to make a law which allows the killing of small people, one could be excused for concluding that the law fails to make moral sense; to those who view abortion as the killing of the innocent allowing abortions until some arbitrary point is arrived at cannot be an acceptable "compromise." To allow wife-beating on Saturdays but not on other days would be similarly unacceptable to those who think it is wrong in all circumstances; to allow some people to be slaves over the objections of those who believe there should be no slavery at all would not be a satisfactory "compromise." A gestational approach is not a "compromise" in the abortion issue. As with arguments using notions of "choice," there is often a failure to note that "compromise" is only useful once one has established whether or not the subject is one that admits of "compromise" at all. A failure to recognize that there are various forms of compromise, some of which vitiate one of the positions at issue, like a failure to see the limitations of "choice" in moral debates, is another example of poor thought.

■ THE WOMAN'S RIGHT TO "CONTROL HER OWN BODY"

It is sometimes asserted that the fact that the foetus is inside a woman means that it cannot have any rights separate from the wishes of the woman. These arguments all turn on notions of "power" or "control" and it is suggested are unacceptable for several reasons. In the first place, to ignore the foetus for the sake of power seems to me eerily like arguments used to deny the personhood of women (the husband's right to control his own wife, the two, perhaps, being "one flesh"), though, even this control did not allow a right to terminate life. There is something counter-intuitive about attempts to square this kind of control over life with notions of "life-nurturingness."

Secondly, such arguments amount to weighing *any* reason (or no reason at all) against what is, undeniably, a life right. The emphasis on control rather than life is more clearly seen as the foetus develops and will be most difficult to justify in late-term abortions or situations such as the *Baby R* case.[19] Where power or control is seen as the significant issue, predictably, concern for the foetus is not expressed. This is seen very clearly in the approach taken by those who view abortion merely as another means of contraception.[20] Power trumping life becomes no more moral because it is being done by the historically disadvantaged. Such approaches raise uncomfortable questions.

If the foetus is merely "tissue," as some would have it, then why should we have any scruples about using, not to say farming, such "tissue" for the good of society? What reasons can there be for restricting such research on the unborn? The Medical Research Council in recently re-leased guidelines states that it is unwise and unjustified to ban embryo research, but that such research should not be allowed on embryos older than seventeen days; one must ask "why the hesitation *after seventeen days?*" Surely if foeti are going to be disposed of, they should be used if possible "for the good of society" and, given that viability is somewhere between five and six months of gestation, seventeen days seems rather frugal, not to say arbitrary.[21]

Lest anyone think that he can dispose of such arguments by simply stating that they are of the "slippery-slope" variety, it should be pointed out that categorizing a concern is not the same thing as answering one. In life areas where medical technology is increasingly allowing us to do what we have never done before, the realization that technology is not its own moral guide must inform all our steps where life issues are concerned.

■ CONCLUSION

Where life is concerned, or even arguably concerned, all who claim to be civilized and interested in human rights or civil liberties must make principled arguments to support their positions. I have shown that certain prevalent arguments often used in an attempt to justify the "pro-choice" position are unacceptable. Those vested with the responsibility of making laws for the social good must formulate laws based on correct moral approaches that are not based on erroneous philosophy. Those who have torn down the philosophical walls which historically protected the unborn and seek now to protect that life at some other point with walls of sentiment can have no moral basis for complaint when sentiment changes.

Given developments over past decades, it is likely that technology will sooner or later provide a way in which the whole human generational process can be accomplished "artificially." Once this occurs and the issue of foetal development is separated, on one level, from issues of "control by the woman over her own body," what is and has been said about the nature of the foetus and how and why we do (or do not) respect it, will inevitably colour future developments (and the way to those developments). However, if arguments based on "control" have so denuded the values historically considered to be innately worth protecting, it remains a matter of speculation on what basis any future protection can be non-arbitrarily erected. If "control" has, as suggested, a limited time-frame given the advances of technology and does not provide a consistent ethic of protection of life, then it is foolhardy to embrace "control" arguments until such an ethic is (if it ever could be) established. If there is any doubt, we must err on the side of life and presume, if at all, in favour of it.

Notes

1. For a review of the various approaches see, for example, L.W. Sumner *Abortion and Moral Theory* (Princeton: Princeton Univ. Press, 1981). Sumner himself advocates a "third way" between the liberal and conservative positions which focusses on "sentience" (or consciousness). This approach itself has been criticized as focussing on a *philosophical* preference rather than a scientific one in that it shows a preference for *qualitative* conceptions of personal identity; see Oliver O'Donovan *Begotten or Made?* (Oxford: Clarendon, 1984) at 57 ff. Another approach that should be considered is that discussed by the Spanish Constitutional Court in its recent abortion decision. R. Stith states that in this approach:

   ... the Spanish Court considers the fetus neither a person possessing rights, as U.S. pro-life people argue, nor subject to a person possessing rights, as pro-choicers argue. *Instead, unborn life is treated as a distinct constitutionally protected legal good. Infra*, note 9 at 514.

2. "The Commission believes that *any reform having to do with human life* must begin by admitting a firm presumption in favour of life" (at 36, emphasis added) Law Reform Commission of Canada, (Working Paper No. 28) *Euthanasia, Aiding Suicide and Cessation of Treatment.*

3. Though it is outside the direct scope of this paper, it must be stated that any approach to the issue of abortion that purports to be moral must perceive and attempt to provide solutions for the very real difficulties faced by women with unwanted pregnancies. The principles upon which a "pro-life" position ought to be based are well set out by S. Callahan in *Abortion: Understanding Differences* (New York: Plenum, 1984) at 329. Another more recently published essay sets out, from a "pro-life" perspective, a holistic framework within which to approach the problems for which abortion is sometimes seen as the solution. After setting out three underlying concerns (the brokenness of male-female partnership, the abdication of men from fatherhood and the dilemma of single mothers), the author sets out the need for twelve positive measures for enhancing the "free choice of women to bear children." Some of these measures

include education, housing, transportation, welfare, child support payments, childcare and the need for "just labour laws"; Dianne Marshall "The Decision to Bear a Child" in Denys O'Leary ed., *The Issue is Life* (Burlington: Welch, 1988) 28 at 37-43.

4. Sumner, *supra* at 57 notes that "in feminist treatments of abortion few meaningful steps have been taken toward clarifying the status of the fetus, locating the threshold of moral standing, developing a general criterion, or deploying a theory that can support such a criterion. By and large the fetus has simply been ignored or forgotten."

5. Apart from the abortion issue, it is apparent that courts, legislators, or both, are going to be faced with the necessity of specifying at what point prior to birth the foetus/child is to be protected. The law relating to the status of the unborn is in disarray. It will be interesting to see how the higher courts deal with Re "*Baby R*," unreported decision, B.C. Prov. Ct. No. 876215 (Davis J.) Sept. 3, 1987 in which the Court recognized an interest in a foetus (by making it a ward of Court) when its mother refused to have a caesarean section in circumstances in which both the mother and child were in peril. The case is under appeal.

In *D. v. Berkshire* C.C. [1987] 1 All E.R. 20, the English House of Lords, in a unanimous decision, recently ruled that when considering the need to make a care order in respect of a baby girl born with drug withdrawal symptoms, the juvenile court had quite properly considered events occurring and circumstances existing prior to the child's birth. Both sets of reasons in the decision of the Lords stated that the justices should be entitled to have regard to events which occurred before the child was born and that broad and liberal construction must be given to the language of the *Children and Young Persons Act 1969* lest its purpose be thwarted. That Act defined a "child" as ". . . a person under the age of fourteen. . . ." A useful comment on the *Berkshire* decision, and current inconsistencies with regard to the manner in which the foetus is viewed at law and by moral philosophy, may be found in Jane E. S. Fortin "Legal Protection for the Unborn Child" (1988) 51 Mod. L. Rev. at 54. I shall argue below, however, that in certain key respects, Fortin's support of certain philosophical positions is somewhat questionable.

6. The approaches taken by the Constitutional Courts of West Germany and Spain provide a different manner of evaluating the abortion issue. Both should be considered more fully by Canadian Courts in the future. For the West German approach, see the Decision of 25 February 1975, [1975] 39 BVerfGE 1. Translated into English by Jonas & Gorby, "West German Abortion Decision: a Contrast to *Roe v. Wade*—with Commentaries" 9 John Marshall J. of Prac. and Proc. 551 (1976). For the Spanish approach (and useful comments on the West German decision), see R. Stith "New Constitutional and Penal Theory in Spanish Abortion Law" (1987) 35 Am. J. of Comp. Law 513. This latter article points out, for example, that the Spanish Court, in evaluating the constitutional word "everyone," specifically held that the term ". . . includes 'everyone living' and that no distinction can be made, with regard to the right to life, between unborn and born life" (at 527).

7. *Roe v. Wade*, 410 U.S. 113 (1973). To describe this decision as heavily criticized is an understatement. Two notable criticisms from what may loosely be described as "non-pro-life" positions are John Hart Ely "The Wages of

Crying Wolf: A Comment on *Roe v. Wade*" (1973) 82 Yale L.J. 920 and Mark Tushnet "The Supreme Court on Abortion" in J. D. Butler and D. F. Walbert *Abortion, Medicine and the Law* (New York: Facts on File, 1986, 3rd ed.) at 161-71. Tushnet makes the following statement by way of conclusion: "In short, philosophers have provided some strong secular arguments against restrictions on abortion, but even the strongest seem open to question" (at 171).

8. *Supra*, note 5 at 59.

9. *Id.* at 59, emphasis added.

10. The various ways and metaphors with which writers have attempted to debunk the potentiality argument would make a fine basis for a humourous, if sardonic, essay. A future writer may use, as a starting point, the following: "a brick is not a house" in Henry Morgentaler (*Abortion and Contraception*, 1981); "a potential president of the United States is not Commander-in-Chief [of the U.S. Army and Navy]," Stanley Ben, quoted by Joel Feinbert (T. Regan ed. *Matters of Life and Death*, 1980); "Prince Charles is a potential King of England, but he does not now have the rights of a king . . ." Peter Singer (*Practical Ethics*, 1979); "if it is a cake you are interested in, it is equally a pity if the ingredients were thrown away before being mixed or afterwards" J. Glover (*Causing Death and Saving Lives*, 1977); "a woman [who believes moral relevance begins at conception] should pray over her menstrual fluids because there will be fertilized eggs discharged in the toilet quite often" Arthur Schafer (C.B.C. Television News Forum "Abortion: the Fight for Rights" Sat. March 5, 1988); "an acorn is not an oak-tree" (ubiquitous).

11. A review of the language of the abortion and euthanasia debates and how terminology is manipulated in questionable ways is to be found in two essays by George and Sheila Grant, "Abortion and Rights" and "The Language of Euthanasia" in George Grant, *Technology and Justice* (Toronto: Anansi, 1986) at 103 and 117. Given the way in which the term "person" has been used historically to deny the rights of women and blacks, we should be more than a little sceptical about denials of foetal rights based on a lack of "personhood" in the foetus. On use of the term "person" in the abortion debate, see Oliver O'Donovan "And Who Is a Person?" in *Begotten or Made?* (Oxford: Clarendon, 1984) at 49-66; and "Again: Who is a Person" in *Abortion and the Sanctity of Life*, ed. J.H. Channer, (Exeter: Paternoster Press, 1985) at 125-37. Finally, a quotation from J. Glover is apposite here: "There is often an immense resistance to killing [which must be overcome] by attempts to make the enemy seem less than human" *Causing Death and Saving Lives* (London: Penguin, 1977) at 115.

12. There have been recent attempts (to little effect in terms of historical accuracy, but of rather greater effect on the Supreme Court of the United States) to suggest that, historically, other reasons for prohibiting abortions were more important than the concern for the foetus; for a critique of the methodology of historical reviews in the area of abortion and, particularly, how many discussions of the history of abortion laws have failed to consider the impact of technology on law, see: Joseph Dellapenna's "The History Of Abortion: Technology, Morality, and Law" (1979) 40 University of Pittsburgh Law Review 359.

13. Here one must point out what many have considered obvious: that there is a difference between "things that happen naturally," and "doing things." Thus, there is a moral distinction between spontaneous abortions (which happen "in nature") and abortions that are the result of the interposition of human action. People do die occasionally (or even often) as a result of having heart attacks; this is not a sufficient reason to allow a person to induce a heart attack in another with impunity.

14. I thank Bernard Dickens of Toronto for bringing to my attention the fact that use of the W.H.O. statement of health by therapeutic abortion committees was largely a matter of "default" due to the fact that Canada had not got a working definition of "health" to use. It scarcely needs stating that it is high time a sound, workable, definition of "health" is available for the guidance of physicians in Canada, particularly since the Canadian Medical Association, as early as 1978, petitioned the Federal Government about ". . . the need for a definition of the term 'health' as used in the *Criminal Code* relative to the legal grounds for therapeutic abortion" ("The Canadian Medical Association and Abortion," July, 1978).

15. Daniel Callahan, "The W.H.O. Definition of Health" (1973) 1 Hastings Centre Studies 90 at 95.

16. Law Reform Commission of Canada, Working Paper No. 26 "Medical Treatment and Criminal Law" 1980 at 7 (emphasis added). I am indebted to lawyer Colleen M. Kovacs of Victoria, B.C., for bringing this to my attention; her "A Response to *Options for Abortion Policy Reform: A Consultation Document*," April 1987, unpublished, contains many perceptive criticisms of the Federal Law Reform Commission's consultation document which, itself, contains no definition of "health."

17. "Psychiatric Aspects of Therapeutic Abortion" (1981) 125 Canadian Medical Association Journal 427 at 431.

18. Carlos Del Campo, "Abortion denied—Outcome of Mothers and Babies" (1984) 139 Canadian Medical Association Journal 361 at 362, emphasis added.

19. *Supra*, note 5.

20. See, for example, A. and A.T. McLaren, *The Bedroom and the State* (McClelland and Stewart: Toronto, 1986).

21. See "New Guidelines Control Research on Human Embryos" *Globe and Mail*, (Saturday, March 5, 1988) A3. The English Warnock Committee decided that the period beyond which embryo research should not extend ought to be 14 days. The difference between the two recommendations supports suggestions that such a period is arbitrary and not based on any sound philosophical approach. Whatever the reasons, a point made by Fortin (*supra*, note 5) is equally applicable to the Canadian setting. Discussing the 14 day period chosen by the Warnock Committee, Fortin notes:

> The Report implied that since it had a greater potential, [a more developed foetus] had a greater right to protection than a younger one, but ironically, the form of protection envisaged is the embryo's destruction (at 60).

It is a strange kind of concern that insists on destruction for those it wishes to protect.

THE CAMPAIGN FOR FREE-STANDING ABORTION CLINICS*

NO

Ontario Coalition for Abortion Clinics

Abortion has been one of the most hotly contested points of conflict between the contemporary women's movement and the state.[1] Its latest stage, the January 28, 1988 Supreme Court decision that the existing abortion law was unconstitutional, was a tremendous victory for the women of Canada.

The Court essentially ruled that the law unfairly interfered with women's right to control our bodies and lives. What the Chief Justice referred to as "state interference with bodily integrity" will no longer be tolerated. This decision was, in part, the culmination of a campaign begun in 1982 for free-standing abortion clinics. It was the result of the work of thousands of reproductive rights activists and supporters in the women's movement, lesbian and gay groups, unions, immigrant organizations, churches and many other community groups. In a very fundamental sense this was a victory for all who are fighting against state regulation of our reproductive and sexual lives.

However, the limits of even the most dramatic legal victory quickly became clear as reactionary provincial governments moved to restrict public funding and eligibility, and the federal government began to draft a new abortion law. How we in OCAC think the pro-choice movement can capitalize on the opportunities presented by the Supreme Court ruling to move on to win full and equal access to free abortion for all women will be discussed later, but first, the paper will look at the strategy and campaign that got us to this point.

This article examines the history of the Ontario Coalition for Abortion Clinics (OCAC) and the clinic campaign that contributed to the Supreme Court decision.[2] The analysis here is posed at a strategic rather than theoretical level. The focus is not so much on what the abortion struggle reveals of the nature and dynamics of the capitalist patriarchal state, but more prosaically and concretely, on the following questions: What were the guiding principles of our strategy? What dilemmas and complex questions have we confronted in trying to put them into practice? What have been the key lessons we have learned which would be of interest to other struggles? And finally, what are some of the implications of our experience for socialist feminist engagement with state power?

■ ORIGINS OF THE CLINIC MOVEMENT

OCAC was established in 1982 by activists from the women's health movement appalled by increasingly limited and unequal access to abortion and the demeaning treatment women were receiving. Our goal was the establishment of free-standing clinics as the best way to provide women-centred abortion and other reproductive care, and to force the repeal of the federal law. Feminists had been lobbying the government with briefs detailing the crisis of access and models for women's clinics, and pressuring hospitals to increase access for years. We had looked to the experience of Quebec where feminists and their supporters had been able to win far better abortion services through clinics.

The strategy of opening clinics in direct defiance of the law had a number of goals. The clinics would first of all provide women with desparately needed services. In so doing they would highlight the crisis of access to abortion and the oppressive nature of the existing law. Even more fundamentally, we believed that setting up and defending clinics would provide a vital spark to galvanize and build the choice movement. By so directly challenging the state, the clinics would be a living symbol of our determination and a rallying point for political mobilization. OCAC's political perspective integrated the demand for clinics, which arose initially out of the women's health movement, with socialist feminist principles of mass action, movement building and putting the maximum pressure on the state.[3]

The Morgentaler Clinic opened in Toronto in the summer of 1983 and was quickly raided by the police. Dr. Morgentaler and the other physicians were acquitted in November 1984—the fourth jury acquittal in two provinces. The clinic reopened in December 1984 and, in spite of further charges, has been open continuously ever since, joined in June 1985 by the Scott Clinic.

It was this strategy which brought us to the Supreme Court. The ruling accomplished one of our major goals: the repeal of a law that we had long emphasized, and the Court echoed, was profoundly inequitable and dangerous to women's health. It also made the clinics we had been fighting to defend legal.

Before the discussing the dangers as well as the opportunities we are now facing, the article will address some of the more revealing facets of our particular struggle with state power.

■ STRATEGY INTO PRACTICE

The struggle to win abortion clinics and repeal the law has brought the pro-choice movement into one of the most sustained conflicts with state power in the recent history of Canadian feminism. This section briefly highlights some of the more interesting facets of this engagement.

OCAC has organized a campaign with a very specific focus. But this has not meant that it is a single-issue group. It has never seen the demand for abortion in isolation, but rather as one of a number of interdependent struggles—from autonomous midwifery to universal daycare, from employment equity to the capacity to define and live independent sexualities—which must be fought and won for women to control their bodies and their lives. This reproductive and sexual freedom in its widest sense is its ultimate goal. OCAC has found this broader reproductive rights perspective to be vital, not simply because it reflects the reality of women's lives, but because linking up these various struggles strengthens us all.[4]

Such a perspective also allows us to take account of the diversity of women. Different groups of women have very different access to abortion and abortion can have a very different meaning in their lives. Although reproduction affects all women as women and in this sense transcends differences of class, race or sexuality, reproductive control means very different things to different women. To some, the vital struggle is to win the basic conditions within which to raise children decently, or to prevent coerced sterilization.[5] We have tried to engage in movement building that reaches out to different constituencies and takes such differences into account. For example, we have had forums bringing together disabled women, lesbians and native women to speak of their particular struggles for sexual and reproductive control and consider how we can support each other. We have begun, like others in the women's movement, the ongoing task and struggle of incorporating an anti-racist perspective into all elements of our politics.[6]

We knew the struggle for abortion rights would be long and complex, involving many different stages and difficult political decisions to be made. For example, the Morgentaler Clinic was crucial to the whole campaign, not simply for the services it provided, but as a focal point for political organizing. This first clinic was not—and could not be in the circumstances—our ultimate goal of comprehensive women-centred reproductive care. But it was an essential political challenge to existing state and medical regulation of abortion. We could not be defeated at this initial stage or we would never get to our long-term goals.

Some would have preferred to have a woman physician from the start or to have the first clinic owned and controlled by the women's community. But these possibilities and resources simply were not available. Others remembered the experiences of Quebec, where the clinic campaign had the tremendous advantage of being part of a broad upsurge of feminist and left political movements, and doubted that we could succeed without such favourable conditions. Dilemmas such as these point to the simple fact that we cannot choose the overall political and ideological environment under which we fight. So what should we have done—wait for conditions to become perfect or begin the fight to transform the political constraints and obstacles we faced? We believed that seizing the initiative through establishing and defending a clinic was the vital starting point upon which to build a strong movement.

From the start we knew that once a clinic was established our movement would face an immediate counter-attack from the state. We never let an attack on us go unchallenged: from the arson at the clinic that destroyed the Toronto Women's Bookstore next door to anti-choice harassment. But in responding to this constant pressure, how could we avoid being forced onto the defensive? Even when under attack we tried to reset the political agenda to our advantage; so when clinic doctors were charged, we used the court cases to "put the state on trial" by demonstrating the crisis of abortion care.

We always believed that no jury would convict physicians performing safe abortions in clinics and we have been proven right so far. We felt that this would put the state in an extremely contradictory position: if it continued to prosecute doctors through acquittal after acquittal then the basic fairness and legitimacy of the legal system itself could be called into question. Sooner or later, clinics would have to be recognized regardless of the federal law, as had been the case in Quebec for years, or the law itself would have to be changed.

This does not mean that we saw the legal system to be the way to win abortion rights. We fought in the courts because we had to—we could hardly not, when clinic staff were charged. But we always saw the basis of our strength to be in building the broadest possible movement and in developing alliances with other progressive struggles. We worked to maintain a visible presence on the streets, in actions ranging from demonstrations of thousands to guerilla theatre. Our goal in all of this was to put the maximum pressure on the state.

In any movement there is both the struggle for immediate goals and long-term objectives. How are these different levels of strategy reconciled? How do we ensure that we don't get stuck in the immediate and pressing issues of the day? OCAC tried to develop strategy that works at two levels simultaneously: both to radically address immediate conditions and to build a consciousness and movement that could transform the existing oppressive relations of reproduction. We have tried to pose the argument for clinics in this double way. The existing free-standing clinics have been indispensable in dramatizing daily how unfair and unworkable the existing law was and in showing the solution in the most concrete and immediate fashion possible. At the same time, clinics can be posed as a model for the future: centres providing care for the full spectrum of women's reproductive lives, from birthing through abortion, from alternative insemination through sexuality counselling. Having clear and attractive vision of ultimate goals is very important, not so much as a blueprint of what will be in the future, but for the present, as an understandable and realizable alternative that can seize people's imagination and enthusiasm.[7]

A clear vision of ultimate goals is also important in helping to avoid co-optation, and in helping to identify those reforms that will not move us towards those long-term goals but will diffuse and divert the movement. For example, we had successfully been able to define the limited and inequitable access as a major health care crisis and to use this framework to condemn the law as inherently unworkable and unequal. However, access is the problem that is most easily addressed by the government through reforms of the hospital delivery system. What if they really could improve—or at least be seen to improve—access in hospitals? Would it seem that there no longer was any "crisis"? that there was no urgent need to repeal the present law and legalize clinics?

As the clinics were so firmly established and public support for them and women's need for abortion remained firm, the provincial government attempted to use reforms in just such a way. In late 1986, it commissioned Dr. Marion Powell, the director of a Toronto birth control clinic, to find a way to improve access to abortion in hospitals,[8] and in late 1987 a series of women's health centres in hospitals were announced to streamline the referral process. We used the Powell Report documentation of the poor quality of care in the hospitals to contrast the advantages of clinics as the safest and most sympathetic environment for abortion care and to argue that these hospital-based centres simply could not solve the access problem. Just as fundamentally, improvements in access—as significant as this could be in improving many individual women's immediate situations—would still leave control over the decision to have an abortion in the hands of doctors rather than women themselves.[9]

We also learned to avoid being caught in our own rhetoric. For example the slogan of *choice* has tremendous polemical value and real resonance in a democratic political culture. It allows us to define ourselves as supporting the right of women to make a complex and at times difficult decision themselves, and to define the opposition as anti-democratic, attempting to impose the views of a small minority on all. It also allows those who would choose not to have an abortion to support the right of others to make their own decisions. But at the same time, we also tried to be aware of the limits of the notion of choice. Even full and free access to abortion, as significant a change as that would be, would not guarantee that all women would have real "choices" over their lives or over having and raising children. We tried to show these limits concretely by stressing that the choice to have a child can never be free in a society in which women earn so much less than men and in which quality daycare and affordable housing are not available for so many.

The notions of abortion or reproductive rights more generally also have important limitations. The concept of *rights* has its origin in highly individualistic liberal philosophy. Rights are held within a given social order, and this can ignore the wider social organization of reproduction and the overall subordinate position of women in contemporary society. Individual rights can be purely legal or formal; we have seen from the experience of other countries that even when women have a legal right to abortion, access can remain horribly unequal and this certainly remains a danger in the post-Supreme Court period. Our response is to demand not simply the legal right to abortion but the wide range of public resources and services—from birthing centres to multilingual contraceptive and sexuality counselling—with which women really can exercise the right to control their reproduction. Most fundamentally, we fight to win not merely the right to choose, but to transform the social and material conditions under which choices are made. That is why we see the fight for abortion as part of other struggles for equal pay, universal daycare, and an end to sexual harassment and violence.

In these ways we have learned to recognize the contradictions and tensions of demands based in the conventional liberal discourse of choice and rights and not to minimize the limits of our slogans. But the political content of slogans and demands is not inherent in their philosophical origin or their place in conventional discourse. We have tried to inject radical political content into our demands, whatever their origins. So we don't simply talk about the right to choice on abortion in the abstract, but as essential to women's bodily self-determination and overall well-being. We stress control of one's body as a fundamental individual and social need: "Control of one's body—including for women, control over whether, when and in what circumstances they shall bear children—is not just a "libertarian" right . . . it is, rather, a positive and enabling condition for full human participation in social and communal life."[10] The right to control one's body is both a demand for individual empowerment and very much a direct challenge to a system in which women's ability to control our reproduction underpins our overall subordination. So we try to capitalize on the political salience of notions of choice and individual rights while at the same time pushing these ideas to their radical limits by showing that the real issue—and the real struggle—is to transcend a social structure in which women must make choices within such narrow constraints.

To keep up the movement's momentum through the inevitable ebbs and flows of a long campaign we have had to develop considerable strategic and tactical flexibility. Some important limitations of the clinic strategy only became clear after its initial success. For example, this strategy is based at the provincial level and its strength lies in locally-based coalitions.[11] But how does this help women in other areas not able to establish and sustain clinics? We knew that repeal of the federal law, which was the fundamental basis of unequal access to abortion and the demeaning treatment women receive, was crucial, but years of feminist lobbying had been unsuccessful. We believed that the political challenge posed by establishing free-standing clinics was our most powerful lever to force repeal. The Supreme Court ruling provided us right so far.

But we also saw the need to build a strong movement across the country and we solidified our links with groups in other regions. One reflection of these links has been joint actions, such as the 1986 tribunals held in many cities in which women spoke out about the impact of restrictive abortion laws on their lives. OCAC activists have gone to BC, Alberta, Manitoba and Quebec to share our experience, especially valuable to those coalitions working to establish clinics. Such links have never been more vital than in laying the groundwork for concerted action in the coming post-Supreme Court stage of the struggle.

It is very difficult to get the best balance between short and long-term objectives, between the polemical value of the choice slogan and the constraints of such arguments, and between abortion and the broader struggle for reproductive freedom. Such strategic complexities and dilemmas are made no easier in a movement that is constantly under attack from the state and conservative right. Nonetheless, it is clear that these complex questions cannot be left until after we have won our short-term objectives. How we organize to win and the very terms upon which we win our demands are very much shaped by how we address these vital questions. We will never get to the long-term if we don't integrate a clear analysis of issues such as these into our immediate politics as well.[12]

■ THE WAY FORWARD FOR ABORTION RIGHTS

How can we capitalize on the opportunities presented by the Supreme Court ruling to continue the struggle for full and equal access to free abortion for women in every community in Canada? How can we beat back the harsh counter-attack from state and anti-choice forces?

In the aftermath of the ruling, especially as reactionary provincial governments moved to restrict public funding and access, it became clear that the struggle would still have to be fought province by province as well as at the federal level. We are working closely with our counterpart reproductive rights groups from other regions and national feminist organizations on how to support each other in this critical period. We are also pressuring the federal government to act on its responsibility to ensure universal and equal access to health care, including abortion, across the country. We are demanding that the federal government must penalize provinces refusing to provide universal access by holding back cost-shared funding, as they did to prevent extra-billing.

In Ontario, the province has already been forced to drop the hospital committees formerly required to approve abortions and to provide OHIP funding to the existing clinics. We will now be pressing the province to fund any community health centre that wants to provide abortions and to quickly establish a new network of community clinics providing abortion and related services. What we will be demanding is publicly funded clinics in every community, working in every language and providing all the care women need: from safe and effective contraception to abortion; from birthing and midwifery to well-woman and well-baby care; and from sexuality counselling to reproductive technology developed according to women's needs and priorities. We will settle for nothing less.

■ FINAL REFLECTIONS

Having promised earlier that this was a strategic rather than theoretical discussion, it is time to sketch out a number of general reflections relevant to a socialist feminist analysis of state power, the social organization and regulation of reproduction and women's resistance. First of all, the abortion struggle confirms a fundamental tenet of socialist feminist political theory. State regulation of women's reproduction through abortion has always been contested. Women are *never* merely victims of state (or medical, or church, etc.) control, but are active agents in resisting this regulation and struggling to control our own reproduction and the way reproduction is socially organized. This resistance occurs constantly in individual women's reproductive lives[13] and collectively as women come together to organize for change or to establish alternatives.

One of the guiding premises of socialist feminist politics is the preeminent importance of the state, both as vital to maintaining the overall structure of male domination and class and racial oppression, and as a key site of struggle against these oppressions in all their interconnected forms. State regulation of reproduction and sexuality is pervasive; from taxation and welfare policy that reinforces women's dependence within families through judicial structures that enforce heterosexual norms. Within this, abortion has been one of the most visible and immediate mechanisms for regulating gender relations, and probably the most contested. This underlies why the state has resisted so strongly and consistently, not only in Canada but in all other advanced capital countries, feminist demands for full and free access to abortion.[14]

A crucial premise of our strategy was that establishing clinics in open defiance of the law and winning jury acquittals would face the state with a contradiction between its regulation of women's bodies through abortion and its broader imperatives to maintain the overall legitimacy of the legal and justice systems. However, the state is a complex system of institutions, agencies, and structural imperatives; where and how this contradiction would be manifested was very much an open question. In Quebec, the provincial government had decided not to prosecute clinics, in effect legalizing them. At the federal level it was the Supreme Court that provided the first major breakthrough. Both illustrate the relative autonomy of different spheres within the state. At first glance, the Supreme Court made a decision that went against government policy and overturned a major means of state regulation of fertility. A more sophisticated reading might see the Supreme Court as providing a potential "solution" to the unworkability of the existing abortion law and an opening for reform that the government for electoral and ideological reasons could never openly propose. To whatever extent this is true and whether or not the federal government would have hoped to take up this opening, that it could not illustrates the importance of immediate party and electoral factors. The Conservative government faced an open revolt from its more right wing backbenchers who would not countenance any liberalizing of the abortion law.

The abortion struggle also shows that pressure tactics and mass action can make an immediate difference. We understand that when a further series of charges was laid in 1986 after the Scott Clinic opened in Toronto some within the provincial cabinet wanted to close the clinics. The government was deterred by the potential widespread opposition this would engender, not least because we had organized an immediate highly spirited protest demonstration. From the other side, anti-choice harassment has very much intimidated the current Minister of Health and has been an important factor in the government's caution.

This article, and the politics of the abortion rights movement, has focused upon state power. The strategy of the choice movement has largely been to mobilize against the state: to force the repeal of the criminal law restricting abortion and to press for public provision of reproductive health care, highlighted in the campaign for free-standing abortion clinics. This may have been politically wise, but it certainly does not capture the complexity of all the ways in which abortion, and reproduction and sexuality more generally, are regulated and socially organized. This regulation involves a diverse range of institutions, practices and discourses: including the administration and funding of health care, family planning counselling and the organization of sex education, in addition to criminal law, within the state system[15]; and the medical profession, birth control research, social work and other service provision, religion and the media outside the state. This regulation is resisted and challenged across equally diverse sites and terrains.[16]

This emphasis has been a strategic and pragmatic choice (to the extent that such complex considerations are ever explicitly articulated in the hurly-burly world of political organizing). We decided that the state was the best site to fight for free and equal access to abortion. Organizing to remove an oppressive law has a far sharper focus, and is therefore much easier to mobilize around, than organizing around equally oppressive but far less visible medical practices. Demands on the state put issues of women's rights and the conditions of reproductive freedom squarely on the public agenda. Although this certainly does challenge traditional discourses of femininity, motherhood, sexuality, etc., we would never have been able to organize a broad-based movement solely around familial or ideological facets of abortion and reproductive control. Having said all this, it can't be maintained that the state has any absolute theoretical primacy over other sites/mechanisms or regulation/resistance around abortion. Strategic openings and theoretical analysis are very different things.

There is a dialectic interplay between state regulation and women's resistance. Is a further reason that the conflict over abortion has become so important to the state simply that we have made it so? simply because the women's movement has focused so much of its energy on winning abortion rights and reproductive and sexual freedom? Confronted with this—and with all of the implications for women's autonomy that such reproductive freedom would entail—the state inevitably counterattacks. It cannot let a popular movement win on an issue that the movement itself defines as central. Put most crudely, what would be next?

Mariana Valverde and Lorna Weir have discussed the complexity of "moral regulation" elsewhere in this issue. Abortion law has certainly come to be a crucial component of contemporary moral regulation at several levels. It is one of the major means through which state, and in a more or less mediated fashion, medical regulation of women's sexuality operates. In the context of unsafe and ineffective contraception and male irresponsibility, abortion is an absolutely essential back-up for sexually active heterosexual women and restricted and unequal access to abortion denies the possibility of sexual autonomy. Categorization of "therapeutic" or "medically necessary" abortions—as opposed to unnecessary and frivolous—is one of the major means through which women's sexual autonomy is defined as selfish and dangerous. The moral and legal discourses around "illegitimate" births—as opposed to legitimate and moral—is central to defining and constraining young women's sexuality ("bad girls" must pay the price of shame and despair).

More generally, the conflict over abortion has become critical to the moral climate of our time. Abortion has become a cental rallying point for the conservative right, a "condensed symbol" of all the far right hates and fears from feminism.[17] The supposed increasing availability of abortion has become for them one of the dominant metaphors for the decline of traditional "family values." If the preceding speculations are at all correct, then abortion has a similar symbolic importance for the state, as an issue that the women's movement must not be allowed to win. It is these ways in which abortion has become so central to the overall moral regulation of gender and sexual relations that underpin the heated nature of this conflict. This is especially so now because free-standing clinics, particularly were they to be run by feminists, make the politics of abortion much more visible.

This struggle has also taken place at the level of moral discourse. In one sense we have been quite successful. One of the most significant lasting effects of our movement may be our popularizing of the idea of choice. For example, although the Supreme Court worked within the discourse of rights to personal security and liberty and legal jurisprudence, its language does show how firmly embedded notions of women's choice and autonomy and the right of equal access to abortion have become in the political culture. Such feminist ideas and values are of course in constant danger of being incorporated and distorted in the dominant culture. But the salience of choice and the widespread recognition that our sexual and reproductive lives are an important part of individual autonomy must be seen as significant changes.

On the other hand, it has been far more difficult to define the overall terms of public debate around abortion. The anti-choice groups' deployment of the fetus and the way in which this graphic imagery has become such an important presence in contemporary debate serves to shift attention from women's conditions and lives.[18] More specifically, in the post-Supreme Court period there has been much media and public concern with late abortion. While the spectre of irresponsible and feckless women having abortions up to the moment of birth has been seized upon by the more lurid anti-choice commentators, many liberal and some pro-choice supporters worry about an increase of late abortions without legislation. Our response has been to try to turn this question around: the answer lies in preventive measures—most fundamentally in equal access to comprehensive care and counselling and in changing those circumstances that bring women to the dilemma of late abortions—not criminalizing women and their health care providers. We try to put the onus back on the state to take up its public responsibility for such preventive reproductive care. And we try to put the focus back on women and the necessary conditions for our autonomy.[19]

■ FINAL WORDS

Because of the many problems and quandaries that have been discussed, this might read as a gloom-ridden account. That was not the intention nor would it accurately reflect the prognosis of the reproductive rights movement or our accomplishments. So the article will end on an optimistic note with the simplest point of all.

Abortion has been one of the most decisive points of struggle between the women's movement and state power. When we worry about the fine print of the Supreme Court decision or think about all the work still to do across the country, it is easy to forget what a major victory we have won. For the first time, the highest court has had to recognize women's right to control our bodies. Whatever the next stages of this struggle bring, this recognition of women's basic rights gives governments far less freedom of action in their attempts to regulate reproduction. If we are able to use this initial victory to push on to win free and equal access to abortion for all women then it will be a highly significant advance for the women's movement.

More than this, this victory for abortion rights is a victory for us all. Our particular success has only been possible through the broadest alliances and support and we are all strengthened when a progressive movement is able to force a significant advance from the state. What this shows above all else is that progressive movements can fight against consistent state and conservative opposition and win.

Postscript

This article was written in April 1988. OCAC's view that the Supreme Court decision was not the end of the struggle for full access to free abortion has certainly been confirmed. Access has gone from bad to worse in some areas, especially the Atlantic provinces; several reactionary provincial governments, with B.C. taking the lead here as it does on so many "moral" issues, have attempted to reimpose cumbersome requirements for medical approval and funding; and there has been a determined counter-attack from "moral majority" right-wing forces, conservative churches and anti-choice organizations whose goal is nothing less than the prohibition of virtually all abortions. The spectacle of male MPs endlessly parading their consciences and exercising their "free vote" on the federal government's ill-conceived resolution on abortion while the women of Canada were ignored has finally ended. However, the really important point is that the government still plans to introduce criminal legislation designed to restrict abortion past a certain stage of pregnancy.

What all this means is that women's reproductive autonomy is very much under threat. OCAC and other activists see the key task to be preventing any recriminalization of abortion. And what is needed to ensure this is a major mobilization of pro-choice support. Get in touch with your local reproductive rights group on events in your area and plans for coordinated actions across the country.

Notes

1. There is nothing particularly new about this. The struggle for sexual and reproductive self-determination has long been a central goal of feminism as a social movement. And throughout the last hundred years this has brought feminists up against the state, organized medicine and conservative forces that would deny women's reproductive autonomy. See Linda Gordon, *Women's Body, Women's Right: A Social History of Birth Control in America* (New York: Penguin, 1977); Rosalind Pollack Petchesky, *Abortion and Women's Choice: The State, Sexuality, and Reproductive Freedom* (New York: Longman, 1984); and Angus McLaren and Arlene Tigar McLaren, *The Bedroom and the State: The Changing Practices and Politics of Contraception and Abortion in Canada, 1880-1980* (Toronto: McClelland and Stewart, 1986).

2. For a fuller analysis see Patricia Antonyshyn, B. Lee and Alex Merrill, " 'Marching for Women's Lives': The Campaign for Free-standing Abortion Clinics in Ontario" in Frank Cunningham, Sue Findlay, Marlene Kadar, Alan Lennon and Ed Silva, eds. *Social Movements/Social Change: The Politics and Practice of Organizing* (Toronto: Between The Lines, 1988).

3. A key role in the formation of OCAC's politic (and our practice ever since) was played by women from the International Women's Day Committee, the major socialist feminist group in Toronto, now celebrating its tenth year of existence (and resistance). See Carolyn Egan, "Toronto's International Women's Day Committee: Socialist Feminist Politics" in Heather Jon Maroney and Meg

Luxton, eds. *Feminism and Political Economy: Women's Work, Women's Struggle* (Toronto: Methuen, 1987).

4. See Petchesky, *Abortion and Woman's Choice*; Adele Clark and Alice Wofson, "Socialist-Feminism and Reproductive Rights" *Socialist Review* 78 (1984), pp. 110-120.

5. Adele Clarke, "Subtle Forms of Sterilization Abuse: A Reproductive Rights Analysis" in Rita Ardetti, Renate Duelli Klein and Shelley Minden, eds. *Test-Tube Women* (London: Pandora, 1984), pp. 188-212; Rosalind Pollack Petchesky, " 'Reproductive Choice' in the United States: A Social Analysis of Female Sterilization" in Karen L. Michaelson, ed. *And the Poor Get Children: Radical Perspectives on Population Dynamics* (New York: Monthly Review Press, 1981).

6. Carolyn Egan, Linda Gardner and Judy Vashti Persad, "The Politics of Transformation" in Cunningham et al., *Social Movements*.

7. For a discussion of such long-term goals of reproductive care see the interview with two activists from OCAC and the Midwives Collective of Toronto, "Visions for Reproductive Care" *Healthsharing* (Spring 1988), pp. 30-32.

8. Dr. Powell apparently had a recommendation to this effect removed from her report by the Ministry of Health.

9. See "Visions" for a pre-Supreme Court critique of the proposed government centres as an explicit attempt to diffuse support for free-standing abortion clinics and autonomous midwifery. We illustrate this by contrasting them to the fundamental principle of feminist reproductive care.

10. Rosalind Pollack Petchesky, "Abortion in the 1980s: Feminist Morality and Women's Health" in Lewin and Olesen, eds. *Women, Health and Healing*, (1985).

11. To an important degree this reflects the fragmented structure of the Canadian state, where abortion and so many other "women's issues" are regulated, and therefore also fought, at both federal and provincial levels.

12. See Brenda Cossman, "The Precarious Unity of Feminist Theory and Practice: The Praxis of Abortion" *University of Toronto Faculty of Law Review* 44:1 (Spring 1986), pp. 85-108.

13. In this regard we may wish to remember those thousands of women who went to Toronto abortion clinics officially deemed to be illegal; perhaps almost never as an explicitly political act, but almost always in some measure of defiance.

14. Petchesky, *Abortion and Woman's Choice*; Joni Lovenduski and Joyce Outshoorn, eds. *The New Politics of Abortion* (London: Sage, 1986).

15. See Carole Joffe, *The Regulation of Sexuality: Experience of Family Planning Workers* (Philadelphia: Temple University Press, 1986) for a most interesting analysis of the bureaucratization of state regulation of sexuality and the key role of family planning clinics in this process.

16. On this complexity, see Mariana Valverde and Lorna Weir "The Struggles of the Immoral: Preliminary Remarks on Moral Regulation" in this issue.

17. Allen Hunter, "In the Wings: New Right Ideology and Organization" *Radical*

America 15:1 & 2 (Spring 1981), p. 132; and Petchesky, *Abortion and Women's Choice*, Ch. 7.

18. Rosalind Pollack Petchesky notes, "The strategy of anti-abortionists to make foetal personhood a self-fulfilling prophesy by making the foetus a *public presence* addresses a visually oriented culture. Meanwhile, finding 'positive' images and symbols of abortion hard to imagine, feminists and other pro-choice advocates have all too readily ceded the visual terrain." "Foetal Images: The Power of Visual Culture in the Politics of Reproduction" in Michelle Stanworth, ed. *Reproductive Technologies: Gender, Motherhood and Medicine* (London: Polity Press, 1987), p. 58. Petchesky goes on to discuss insightfully the ways in which we can put women back into the imagery and discourse of pregnancy and abortion and reassert a feminist ethic of reproduction.

19. Vicki Van Wagner and B. Lee, "Take the State Out of Gestation" *Broadside* vol. 9, no. 6 (April 1988), p. 4.

*   The author of this article is a member of the Ontario Coalition for Abortion Clinics.

■ POSTSCRIPT

Benson attacks pro-choice supporters for having a narrow conception of choice, and for assuming that morality and decisions of what is right and wrong have no place in lawmaking. He also criticizes the notion that a compromise solution is possible. A compromise is only possible, Benson says, if both positions are morally acceptable, a notion he rejects. Compromise is impossible when both sides argue the immorality of their opponents' positions.

The Ontario Coalition for Abortion Clinics sees the 1988 Supreme Court decision to strike down the existing abortion law as a recognition that the old law "unfairly interfered with women's right to control" their bodies and their lives. The Coalition says that the decision was the culmination of a six-year campaign by abortion rights activists to establish free-standing abortion clinics. The heart of the article deals with the process by which the Coalition fought to achieve its goals, and with the extent to which those goals have been achieved.

Given that the federal government has no current plans to reintroduce criminal legislation, the debate now shifts to the provincial sphere. Provincial governments, responsible for licencing medical facilities and funding health-care plans, will now be lobbied by both sides. It is unlikely that either side will change its tactics. It is also uncertain that the forces occupying the middle ground between the two extremes will be able to marshall sufficient strength to arrive at a compromise solution, if one is possible.

In sociological terms, both authors are acting as moral entrepreneurs, i.e., people who campaign to have their moral values adopted as the values of their group or the wider society (Becker, 1963), attempting to persuade their audiences that their own positions on the legitimacy or illegitimacy of abortion are morally superior to those of their opponents.

■ QUESTIONS

1. Which article did you find most convincing? Is your answer to this question affected by your own beliefs concerning the morality or immorality of abortion?

2. Is Benson right in arguing that a compromise solution is impossible?

3. Do you agree or disagree with the Coalition's conclusion that "abortion has been one of the most decisive points of struggle between the women's movement and state power"?

4. Which issues were absent from this debate? Why do you suppose they were left out?

5. Are there any points of agreement between the opposed viewpoints in this debate?

■ FURTHER READING

In Support of Benson

Nolen, W.L. *The Baby in the Bottle.* New York: Coward, McCann and Georghegan, 1978.
Viguerie, Richard. *The New Right.* New York: Caroline House, 1981.

In Support of the Ontario Coalition for Abortion Clinics

Morgentaler, Dr. Henry. "The Case for Safe Abortion on Request." *Canadian Speeches* 4, no. 3 (1990): 9-14.
Oakley, Ann. "Wisewoman and Medicine Man." In *The Rights and Wrongs of Women.* Edited by Juliet Mitchell and Ann Oakley. Middlesex: Penguin Books, 1976.
Tateishi, Susan Alter. "Apprehending the Fetus En Ventre Sa Mere: A Judicial Sleight of Hand." *Saskatchewan Law Review* 53 (1989): 113-141.

Other Voices

Collins, Ann. *The Big Evasion: Abortion—This Issue that Won't Go Away.* Toronto: Lester and Orpen Dennys, 1985.
Gavigan, Shelley A.M. "Women, Law and Patriarchal Relations: Perspectives within the Sociology of Law." In *The Social Dimensions of Law.* Edited by Neil Boyd. Scarborough, Ont.: Prentice-Hall, 1986.
Roberts, Helen, ed. *Women, Health and Reproduction.* London: Routledge and Kegan Paul, 1981.
Rubin, Eva. *Abortion, Politics, and the Courts: Roe v. Wade and its Aftermath.* Westport, Conn.: Greenwood Press, 1982.

DOES CANADIAN

LAW PROTECT

HUMAN RIGHTS?

YES   Mr. Justice John Sopinka, "How the Charter Helps Secure Women's Rights," *Canadian Speeches* 3, no. 3 (May 1989): 34-39

NO   James S. Frideres and William J. Reeves, "The Ability to Implement Human Rights Legislation in Canada," *Canadian Review of Sociology and Anthropology* 26, no. 2 (1989): 311-332

Debates Sixteen and Seventeen focused on the extent to which the law should be used to define specific human rights. The focus in Debate Eighteen is on the ability to implement human rights legislation. Human rights in Canada are protected by a variety of legal codes. The federal government and the individual provinces each have their own human rights codes defining which rights are protected in each jurisdiction.

As the provincial and federal governments debated human rights legislation, concerns were expressed that the proposed laws would grant either too much or too little protection, and that some groups and some forms of discrimination did not need to be protected by anti-discrimination laws. Consequently, there emerged a variety of prohibited grounds of discrimination in Canada. As Knopff (1989) points out, every jurisdiction in Canada prohibits discrimination on the basis of race, colour, ethnicity, religion, sex, age, and physical handicap. Other prohibited grounds of discrimination may include language, mental handicap, political belief, religious belief, family status, pregnancy, place of residence, place of origin, social origin, social condition, sexual orientation, nationality, national and ethnic origin, citizenship, creed, ancestry, pardoned offence, criminal record, source of income, public assistance, attachment of pay, and drug and alcohol dependency.

Complicating the situation is the fact that most of these rights are not given unrestricted protection. Some are extended only to people working for federal or provincial governments. Most of the human rights codes also contain some qualifying clause that the right is protected within "reasonable" limits. For example, section 15 of the Canadian Charter of Rights and Freedoms imposes limits according to what is "demonstrably justified in a free and democratic society." The Supreme Court of Canada used this section of the Charter to rule that age discrimination is legal under some circumstances. Decisions such as this one strike at the heart of the issue to be debated in the following debate.

Given the observations made in Debates Four, Five, Thirteen, Fifteen, and Sixteen, it is possible to argue either for or against the need for human rights legislation. But Debate Eighteen concentrates on what happens after the law has been enacted. Determining the ability of the law to protect human rights is a different task from assessing the need for such a law. Frequently, the law does not work as intended. This has profound implications for lawmakers and law enforcers, who must decide why the law is not working. Does it have some inherent flaw? Is the enforcement apparatus ineffective? Or is the law not working because of a combination of legal flaws and ineffective enforcement practices? Whatever the lawmakers and law enforcers conclude will have an impact on the people whose lives are affected by either the legislation or the enforcement practices.

In Debate Eighteen, Justice Sopinka, arguing for the "Yes" side of the debate, illustrates how the Charter of Rights and Freedoms protects women's rights, while Frideres and Reeves, arguing for the "No" side of the debate, say that enforcement of these rights is subject to differences in enforcement procedures.

Reference

Knopff, Rainer (1989) *Human Rights and Social Technology: The New War on Discrimination* (Ottawa: Carleton University Press).

HOW THE CHARTER
HELPS SECURE
WOMEN'S RIGHTS

YES

Mr. Justice John Sopinka

The *Canadian Charter of Rights and Freedoms* has been with us for close to seven years. It is a document which has affected the lives of all Canadians—both men and women. While issues raised under the Charter are of interest to everyone—such as mandatory retirement, soon to be argued before our Court—there are issues which are of particular interest to women. Issues such as abortion and employment equity have a specific and profound impact on the lives of Canadian women. And there are sections of the Charter which are looked to to address some of these issues. This evening, I would like to talk about some of these sections; touch on a few of the judicial decisions which they have produced and perhaps give you a sense of what issues may arise in the future.

Our Charter arose in the liberal tradition of documents such as the *Declaration of Rights* of the French Revolution, and the Constitution of the United States: documents which assert the dignity and humanity of the individual in the face of the state. As such, the Charter has been viewed by some as a guarantee of the rights for those who are traditionally dispossessed in society.

On the other hand, some commentators have been less optimistic. Perhaps their concerns about the protection of the rights of women under a Charter are best introduced by noting that the "charter" of the French Revolution was entitled the *Declaration of the Rights of Man and Citizen.* These commentators argue that a document whose aim is to protect individuals from the power of the state may block real change for women since it is state action which has, in recent years, ameliorated some of the inequities faced by women—through, for example, "equal pay" legislation.

I think it may be said that neither the optimists nor the pessimists have been proved entirely correct. The decisions on issues of particular interest to women have produced mixed results: results which are not unexpected from a Charter in which the interests of all Canadians must be considered.

Noted activist Dr. Helen Caldicott is reported to have made the following observation: "Women are 53% of the earth's population, do two-thirds of the world's work, own 1% of the property, have all the babies and no power" (*Globe & Mail*, January 7, 1989, p. D-6).

While I may not agree with the absolutist tone of her statement, the observation does identify some of the issues on which women have looked to the Charter for assistance: issues such as poverty, reproductive rights, and inequality. I would now like to talk about some of the provisions of our Charter which are relevant to these, and other, issues.

Section seven is the "basket clause" of the legal rights which are protected under the Charter. Section seven states:

"Everyone has the right of life, liberty and security of the person, and the right not to be deprived thereof, except in accordance with principles of fundamental justice."

As you can hear, the words of the section are broad; it is the breadth of the language that allows arguments on topics as diverse as economic rights and abortion, all to be made under section seven.

As you may know, there exists in Canada and other nations a trend which has been labelled "the feminization of poverty." This label simply means that more of the people on the low end of the economic scale are women. It was recently reported, for example, that 73% of the elderly poor in Canada are women (*Globe & Mail*, January 7, 1989, p. D-6). It has been argued by some that section seven of the Charter can be used to establish that a certain minimum level of economic well-being is part of the right to "life, liberty and security of the person" (Stalker, "Remarks on the Use of the Charter in Alleviating Welfare Discrimination," in *Women, the Law, and the Economy*, p. 157). Recently, it was argued before our Court that the "security of the person" of a single mother on welfare was infringed when her lease of subsidized housing was terminated on less than the three month's notice which other tenants in her province receive (*Bernard v. Dartmouth Housing Authority*, Application for Leave to Appeal, List of November 28, 1988).

The obstacle faced by those who hope to use the Charter to attack economic inequity is that the courts will not use section seven to protect those rights which are "purely economic." In this area, the courts are, quite properly, deferring to our legislators, since the framers of the Charter specifically rejected the inclusion of a right to enjoy property in the "basket clause." I am sure, however, that the issue of economic rights will arise again, as the courts are asked to decide which interests are "purely economic" and which involve a liberty or security of the person interest protected under section seven. It is often difficult to divorce economic interests from the interest of individuals in freedom and security. For example, deprivation of the right to earn a livelihood impinges on freedom and security yet economic interests are certainly involved.

One of the most well-known decisions to be made by the Supreme Court in recent years involved section seven; I am speaking of the *Morgentaler* case, decided just over one year ago. In that case, a majority of our Court found that the procedure set down in the *Criminal Code* by which a woman could obtain a therapeutic abortion infringed the guarantee of "security of the person," and could not be justified as a "reasonable limit." One member of the majority—Madame Justice Wilson—went further, and found that a woman's "liberty" was also infringed since the procedure affected her right to make a fundamental personal decision.

As you know, the *Morgentaler* decision did not settle the abortion issue. However, it has been left to the legislators to decide what, if any, rules should govern the obtaining of an abortion; it is the political realm that the efforts of those on all sides of the debate must now be concentrated. This is especially so since our decision in *Borowski* which refused to rule on the rights of the fetus in the abstract.

While the issue of abortion was argued under section seven, another issue related to pregnancy could well arise under section 15—the equality provision of the Charter. In 1979, prior to the Charter, the Supreme Court of Canada decided that the denial of unemployment insurance benefits to pregnant women did not violate the right to equality before the law under the Canadian Bill of Rights (*Bliss v. A.G. Canada*, [1979] 1 SCR 183). The Court decided that the challenged provision of the *Unemployment Insurance Act* did not impose a penalty, but rather conferred a benefit; choosing not to confer that benefit on women who were pregnant, while conferring it on other women and men, did not offend the Bill of Rights.

A case such as this one might be decided differently under the Charter. Section 15(1) of the Charter states:

"Every individual is equal before and under the law and has the right to the equal protection and equal benefit of the law without discrimination and, in particular, without discrimination based on race, national or ethnic origin, color, religion, sex, age, or mental or physical disability."

What I hope you picked up on in that rather large mouthful of rights which I just read out, is that a right to "equal benefit of the law" has been specifically included. The language of the section, it will be argued, was deliberately chosen to overcome decisions such as the one I described to you.

The language of section 15 has also been influenced by the 14th Amendment of the Constitution of the United States which reads: "No state . . . shall deny to any person within its jurisdiction the equal protection of the laws." On the other hand, one part of section 15 was specifically included to avoid some of the problems which have arisen out of this equality guarantee in the United States. Section 15(2) of our Charter permits "inequality" if the object behind the activity is the amelioration of the conditions of disadvantaged individuals or groups. In other words, affirmative action programs are specifically protected from the legal controversy which has hindered them in the United States.

Section 15 is the newest provision of the Charter; it came into effect on April 17, 1985. As such, it is likely to be a "growth" area in Charter litigation.

Of the cases considering inequality on the basis of sex that have been decided, it is interesting to note that many of these early decisions have been launched by men, challenging a particular benefit that only women receive. In Nova Scotia, for example, it was successfully argued that the section of that province's *Family Benefits Act* which extended more limited social assistance benefits to men than to women violated section 15 (*Reference Re Family Benefits Act (N.S.) Section 5* (1986), 75 N.S.R. (2d) 338 (C.A.)). The argument that there were more females than males requiring long-term assistance was not accepted. In the end, the section was struck down. This type of decision seems to lend credence to those who view the Charter as an obstacle to improving the lot of women in Canada.

However, the optimists can also find support in some judicial decisions on challenges brought by men. A section of the *Unemployment Insurance Act* which provided for benefits for time taken off work to look after a new-born infant was recently challenged. These benefits were paid to natural mothers and to adoptive parents of either sex, but not to natural fathers. The Federal Court found that this distinction was inequality on the basis of sex, and therefore was a violation of section 15. But rather than striking down the legislation—which would have eliminated these benefits for *everyone*—the Court declared that natural parents are entitled to the same benefits as adoptive parents (*Schachter v. Canada*, June 7, 1988, 88 CLLC 14:021, Fed. Ct. T.D.).

Just recently, our Court released its first decision under section 15, in a case called *Law Society of British Columbia v. Andrews.* The case concerned inequality based on a citizenship requirement in the *Barristers and Solicitors Act* of British Columbia. However, in its decision, the Court considered what the words of section 15 mean and how they should be applied. It was decided that equality means more than treating similar groups similarly; the essence of true equality is the accommodation of differences (*Andrews p. 13*). In so deciding, the Court rejected the legal test which had been applied by some lower courts—such as the Nova Scotia court in the case about social assistance benefits which I described to you earlier (*Andrews p. 10*). Generally, those representing traditionally disadvantaged groups—such as the disabled and women—have reacted positively to the *Andrews* decision. While I cannot—and in fact may not— tell you the outcome of future challenges involving inequality on the basis of sex, I can say that the decision in *Andrews* will now affect all challenges launched under section15.

Clearly, the range of issues on which women might look to section 15 in the future is very broad—wage inequity and hiring practices are just two topics that spring to mind. Before the substance of any of these issues can be decided, however, those seeking to use the Charter to challenge inequality must climb a barrier that confronts all who seek to use the Charter: that is, the decision that the Charter does not apply to the acts of private individuals and corporations devoid of any connection with government (*Retail, Wholesale and Dept. Store Union Local 580 et al. v. Dolphin Delivery*, [1986] 1 SCR 573). This decision reflects the Charter's roots in the liberal tradition of protecting the individual from the power of the state.

What this decision means is that if, for example, you worked for a retail store which pays female cashiers less than male cashiers, you could not directly challenge this inequity using section 15 of the Charter. However, remedies other than the Charter do exist. You could take action under the human rights legislation enacted by the province.

But what if the human rights legislation does not cover your particular situation? That was a question faced by young Alison Blainey when she was denied the opportunity to play hockey on a boy's team. The Ontario Human Rights Commission was powerless to intervene because the Human Rights Code specifically exempted amateur athletics from the provision that prohibits discrimination on the basis of sex. So Blainey used section 15 of the Charter to challenge the exemption in the Human Rights Code. And she won. The Blainey case illustrates that, although the Charter does not apply to "private" relationships, it can in some circumstances be used indirectly to affect those relationships.

This is quite a change from the days before the Charter. In my previous incarnation as a lawyer, I argued a similar case before the Ontario Court of Appeal. In *Bazo v. The Ontario Softball League* the Court held that the Human Rights Code as it then stood simply did not cover athletes. And that was the end of it. While Bertha Wilson, then on the Court of Appeal, dissented, the Supreme Court of Canada did not consider the issue of sufficient national importance to hear the appeal.

Section 15 and most other sections of the Charter are subject to the "reasonable limits" clause which is section one. If it has been established that a right protected under the Charter has been violated, a court may decide that the violation has been "demonstrably justified" under section one and is not, therefore, rendered invalid. As with most aspects of the Charter, this section can have either positive or negative effects, depending on your perspective. One decision in which the use of section one had a positive impact on the interests of women is the case of *Canadian Newspapers*, decided by the Supreme Court of Canada last year ([1988] 2 SCR 122). A section of the Criminal Code enables a judge to place a ban on publication of the identity of a victim of sexual assault. A newspaper chain challenged this section, claiming that it infringed the Charter guarantee of freedom of the press. Our court agreed that freedom of the press was infringed; however, it held that the publication ban was a "reasonable limit" and could therefore be "saved" under section one. The Court was sensitive to the need to protect victims of sexual assault from further trauma, and to encourage other victims to come forward.

The final section of the Charter of particular relevance to women, which I will discuss this evening, is a section which was included in the Charter because of the concerted efforts of women. Section 28 reads: "Notwithstanding anything in this Charter, the rights and freedoms referred to in it are guaranteed equally to male and female persons."

While the exact meaning and effect of this section have not yet been determined, women's organizations across the country considered its inclusion in the Charter important—so important that they lobbied vigorously to ensure that the section could not be overridden by legislation passed "notwithstanding" the rights guaranteed in the Charter. The full reach of this provision has not yet been explored.

The efforts of women's organizations have not ceased since the enactment of the Charter. Groups such as the Legal Education and Action Fund (LEAF) use the courts to further the interests of women, both by launching new actions and by intervening in existing cases. Our Court has generally been open to requests for interventions by interest groups—for example, organizations concerned about violence against women took part in arguments in the *Canadian Newspapers* case which I told you about earlier. In important cases—particularly ones dealing with a document as fundamental to Canadian society as the *Charter of Rights and Freedoms*—it is important that the many differing interests are represented before the Court.

More frequently than ever those interests are represented by women barristers—top counsel who take a back seat to no one. There are opportunities for women in the law, and in particular in the field of litigation. In increasing numbers, experienced women barristers are moving from the bar to the bench. And their places at the bar are filled by the many women who graduate each year from our law schools. The influence of this trend can be seen not only in the counsel who appear before us, but also in the judges who sit on our highest court. Two excellent women jurists are my colleagues at the Supreme Court of Canada. They have had a tremendous impact. I am certain that they will be joined by equally eminent women in the years to come.

The legal profession has come a long way since Myra Bradwell was denied admission to the Illinois Bar in 1879 on the ground that "the natural and proper timidity and delicacy which belongs to the female sex evidently unfits it" for law and practice; or since Clara Brett Martin's application to the Law Society of Upper Canada in 1894 was initially defeated because she was not considered a "person." Such obvious barriers have been removed. But women in the legal profession—along with women in all walks of life— continue to face many less obvious obstacles to equality.

However, the building of new structures to protect and enhance the rights of women cannot be completed using only one tool. As the optimists contend, the Charter may prove to be important in safeguarding these rights; however, it is not and cannot be a panacea for all inequity in society. The Charter does not, for example, guarantee that women receive equal representation in our Parliament or in our courts—that is a goal to be reached through political effort. There are many tools which may be used to right the imbalance of which Dr. Caldicott spoke; the Charter is but one of them.

THE ENFORCEMENT OF HUMAN RIGHTS IN CANADA

James S. Frideres and William J. Reeves

■ INTRODUCTION

It was not until after World War II that a sustained interest in anti-discriminatory legislation developed in Canada (Hill, 1977). At that time, it was assumed that discrimination was not a pervasive phenomenon in Canadian society and that ending discrimination would be a simple matter. Passage of the Bill of Rights in the early 1960s was viewed as filling the necessary gap since many of the provinces had already enacted anti-discrimination statutes. It was also believed that discriminatory acts were easily recognized and penalties to punish such acts would be easy to implement. As such, mechanisms for the implementation and enforcement of human rights legislation could be put in place (Tarnopolsky and Pentney, 1985).

This study comments on how successful Canada has been in achieving its goal of reducing discrimination directed toward a variety of minority groups (Canada, 1984). It addresses the effectiveness of the *Canadian Human Rights Act* as currently implemented. A comparison of the resolution of complaints based on different grounds such as race, colour or origin compared to sex or disability was undertaken. An investigation of the role and importance of documentation and the existence of formal records in an organization with regard to the processing of evidence is also dealt with (Zimmerman, 1969). . . .

■ CONCEPTUAL FRAMEWORK

The theoretical framework employed in the present study provides an explanation as to why some state agencies are unsuccessful in carrying out their mandate. Utilizing a structural perspective, we argue that the operation of an agency is partially determined by the structure of the formal organization, the existence of documents and the efforts of status groups in society.

There are many areas of life that are not governed by institutional or organizational prescriptions. In fact, most interpersonal behaviors under normal circumstances are not regulated by formal documented rules. In cases where there is a lack of formal, documented rules, an external investigative agency, such as the CHRC, finds it difficult to take action against an organization. In these cases, the social norms are invisible to outsiders such as the investigators for CHRC and thus not subject to external scrutiny. For example, in most circumstances, people believe that behavior has a logical, causal and moral texture that is shared by all of the participants, i.e., definition of the situation. If this belief is not shared or a person violates the contextual ethos, the other person must decide what is the proper or appropriate behavior. Certain behavior may result in charges of discrimination by individuals. However, because of the informal nature of the situation, a formal investigation will be most unlikely to lead to any definite conclusion.

In cases where organizations have formally stated rules, a record of such rules and violations and a formal grievance procedure, external agencies can assess the validity of claims that the rules have been violated. The question as to whether or not the internal operating procedures of the organization and requirements are in compliance with the law can then be asked and investigated through the use of documents. In these cases, the investigative process deals only with the formal organizational prescriptions and the pre-existent rules within the organization provide a trustworthy and legitimate basis for taking action.

Some interest groups, such as women and the disabled, have pressured organizations to modify existing regulations and create new rules that formally acknowledge their rights. Once formalized, these rights become more enforceable. Within the context of legitimate and formalized institutions, it is easier to get agreement on the "facts" and thus substantiate complaints of human rights violations. Other groups, notably immigrant and visible racial groups, have had much less success in vesting their interests as formally recognized rights. As a consequence, it has been much more difficult to get agreement on the "facts" and thus substantiate complaints of discrimination on the basis of race, colour or origin.

■ METHODOLOGY

On the basis of the summary statistics presented in its Annual Report, the CHRC had noted that the resolution of investigated complaints varied according to the type of complaint. To its credit the CHRC took the initiative and sponsored a series of investigations by the authors. An exploratory study carried out by Reeves and Frideres (1985) developed an inventory for coding the contents of CHRC case files. This inventory registered the types of evidence and style of argumentation reported by CHRC investigators. A test of this inventory, using a small unrepresentative sample of case files, found that factors taken into account when resolving race, colour, and origin complaints appeared to differ systematically from the factors reported involving complaints or discrimination on the basis of sex or disability. Furthermore, these differences in content appeared to have some bearing on the ultimate resolution of the complaint, e.g., whether the complaint was substantiated or dismissed.

Sample

A total of 184 files were selected for the present survey; 40 per cent of the cases closed in a one year period (1982-83).[1] For each ground of complaint, these files constitute a representative sample of the 1982-83 CHRC caseload across all regions of Canada. To avoid problems associated with the statistical analysis of small numbers of cases, the sample included a disproportionately large number of race, colour, national and ethnic origin files. This paper compares the resolution of 61 files involving complaints of discrimination on the basis of race, colour or national/ethnic origin with CHRC decisions on 95 cases involving complaints of discrimination on the basis of sex or disability. Twenty-eight cases involving grounds such as age, marital status and religion have not been included in the present analysis (see Table I). . . .

TABLE I Decision of CHRC by Ground of Complaint (Percentage)[a]

DECISION OF CHRC	SEX	PHYSICAL DISABILITY	RACE	ETHNIC	OTHER[c]	ALL CASES SAMPLED
Complaint(s) substantiated	43%	36%	12%	7%	22%	25%
Dismissed with notation	13%	13%	7%	2%	7%	9%
Case dismissed without notation	35%	47%	31%	38%	70%	47%
Other findings (case terminated)	5%	0%	2%	0%	0%	2%
Dismissed as unfounded	5%	4%	49%	53%	0%	17%
	100%	100%	100%	100%	100%	100%
N =	(45)	(50)	(61)[b]	(58)[b]	(28)	(184)

GROUND OF COMPLAINT

a Rounding may result in percentages that do not sum to 100%
b The cases in these columns are not mutually exclusive because more than one complaint may be registered
c These cases include complaints based on grounds such as religion, marital status, and age

■ RESULTS

Indicators measuring the investigative procedures and reasoning of CHRC investigators were found to be correlated with resolution of complaints. Indicators of the nature of the content and circumstances surrounding the complaint, and the status of the complainant and respondent were not related to either the grounds of complaint listed or the ultimate resolution of those complaints. For example, indicators of the character of the organizational context—work versus nonwork, public versus private, larger corporations versus smaller organizations—were found to be uncorrelated. Most indicators of file contents were not correlated with either the grounds or the resolution of the complaint.

Virtually all complaints were made against individuals who were powerful by virtue of their position in an organization. Complaints were registered against individuals with the authority to hire and fire, to promote and demote, to supervise and discipline employees; to select and reject applicants; to approve or deny credit, social assistance, housing benefits or to assess immigration status. Subordination in an unequal power relationship was constant and therefore could not account for differences in the resolution of different types of complaint. Two general patterns emerged from the analysis of the data. One pattern involved complaints of discrimination on the basis of sex and disability. Approximately 40 per cent of these cases were substantiated.[2] A second pattern involved complaints of discrimination on the basis of race, colour, national origin, and ethnic origin.[3] Only about one in ten of these cases were substantiated (see Table I).

Complaints on the Ground of Sex

For the 45 files involving complaints on the ground of sex, the most strongly correlated factor was the existence of written documentation. Among files which contained written documentation in support of the complainant, 57 per cent of the complaints were substantiated and 29 per cent were dismissed with notation, that is, the respondent was cited for unacceptable conduct or practices that were unrelated to the complaint. In cases lacking such written documentation, 50 per cent were dismissed, 35 per cent had been substantiated, and only 4 per cent dismissed with notation (see Table II). Written documentation in support of the respondent was also strongly correlated with the resolution of the case. Where absent, 73 per cent of the complaints were substantiated or otherwise dealt with; only 13 per cent were dismissed. In contrast, if the file included written documentation favoring the respondent, only 24 per cent were substantiated or otherwise dealt with, and 48 per cent of the cases were dismissed.

These two factors—documents supporting the complainant and documents supporting the respondent—were independent variables and uncorrelated. Some files contained references to documents of both types, some contained references either to one or to the other, and some files contained neither. This accounts for the less than perfect correlation between the presence of documents favoring the complainant and substantiation of the complaint.

The more global thematic review of the files revealed a pattern of investigation and reasoning that validated this correlational evidence.

TABLE II Relationship between the Use of Written Documents to Support the Complainant and the Disposition of Sex Cases

DECISION OF CHRC	DOCUMENTS SUPPORT COMPLAINANT		ALL SEX CASES SAMPLED
	NO	YES	
Complaint(s) substantianted	34.6%	57.1%	42%
Dismissed with notation	3.8%	28.6%	13%
Case dismissed without notation	50.0%	7.1%	35%
Other findings (case terminated)	3.8%	7.1%	5%
Dismissed as unfounded	7.7%	0.0%	5%
	100%[a]	100%[a]	100%[a]
	(28)	(17)	(45)

[a] Rounding may result in percentages that do not sum to 100%

Typically, in both confirmed and dismissed cases, investigators sought out written records that might identify others in the setting with a status or in a position similar to the complainants. Validation of the complaint hinged on being able to show that others of similar status and position had experiences that paralleled those of the complainant. We have used the phrase, "comparative style," when referring to this pattern of investigation and verification.

In addition to the identification of others of similar status, the comparative style of investigation involved a search for written documentation that might justify the actions of the respondent. Documented bona fide occupational requirements allowed employers to ignore proscriptions against discrimination when making appointments to particular jobs.[4]

If the documented regulation did not bear scrutiny or if the regulation looked acceptable but was not implemented in regular, formal and consistent fashion, the investigator continued his/her investigation. The investigator gathered information from others in the setting regarding accepted organizational practices wherever incomplete documentation lent creditability to the complainants' allegations.[5] The CHRC substantiated the complaint if the investigation was able to demonstrate that other people like the complainant had been systematically discriminated against by the actions of the respondent and could trace this discrimination to informal behavior that subverted otherwise legitimate formal regulations.

There was a depersonalizing of the complainant, especially in substantiated cases. Particulars that were idiosyncratic to the complainant's individual case received scant attention. The investigators did not concern themselves with issues such as whether or not the complainant related the alleged events in a logical or even truthful manner. Once the larger picture was discovered and documented, the credibility of the details of the complainant's particular story became somewhat beside the point.

Complaints on the Ground of Disability

Both correlational analysis and the more global review of the files in which disability was a ground of complaint revealed a pattern of results similar to that found for sex cases. Written documentation was the factor most strongly correlated with the resolution of complaints.

Testimony from professional experts such as physicians was a second factor correlated with the resolution of disability complaints, an element unique to disability cases. Most documentation in these cases had been produced by these professional experts, and this evidence provided a comparative basis for evaluating the merits of the complaint. Given this unquestioned reliance on documented testimony from experts, a comparative style of investigation and verification had been followed in almost all cases. Sixty-two per cent of the cases which included written documentation supporting the complainant were confirmed as opposed to only 13 per cent where such documentation was not in the file.

There was a tendency to treat sex and disability cases as a "class action" against the respondent's organization. The investigation in substantiated cases uncovered a history of complaints against the respondent. This accumulation of "other" complaints against the respondent was a central component of the document-based comparative style of investigation.

Complaints on the Ground of Race

The research strategy outlined above was repeated for cases involving complaints on the grounds of race, colour, national origin, and ethnic origin. For each ground, the results of a correlational analysis were reassessed in terms of a more global review of file contents. However, the low rate of confirmation of these complaints required a shift in the focus of the correlational analysis. The most frequent resolution of cases involving complaints of racial discrimination was dismissal without notation or dismissal as unfounded; only 12 per cent of race complaints were substantiated.[6]

The coding for the resolution of the complaint was taken from the cover sheet the accompanied each file. The format of the cover sheet provided boxes that could be check marked to indicate whether the complaint(s) had been substantiated, dismissed with notation, or dismissed (without notation). However, our initial inspection of the files revealed the fact that no check mark had been put on some dismissed cases. While this anomaly appeared trivial, it was coded as a distinct category. Analysis found that this "clerical" omission was strongly correlated with the grounds of complaint. Approximately half of the race, colour, national and ethnic origin cases had been dismissed, but not check marked. This occurred in fewer than five per cent of the cases involving other grounds of complaint.

The files were reviewed to assess the significance of being dismissed without the appropriate box on the cover sheet being check marked. Files for which the resolution had been check marked showed that the evidence and reasoning was clear, favoring either substantiation or dismissal. In files that were not check marked, evidence and argumentation were inconclusive. Typically, the complaint centred on an incident of personal harassment alleged to be discriminatory. The evidence confirmed that the incident had occurred.

The investigator frequently suggested that the complainant had been placed at a disadvantage. However, when people involved in the events that prompted the complaint were interviewed, no consensus of opinion emerged vis-à-vis discrimination. Investigators were unable to recommend in favor of the complainant in the face of dissensus. These cases had been dismissed, but the resolution was not check marked. We labelled this outcome "Dismissed as unfounded."

For the 61 cases involving complaints of racial discrimination, the factor most strongly correlated with the resolution of the case was the number of additional grounds of complaint—colour, national origin, and/or ethnic origin—in addition to race. No other factor coded in the content analysis of case files was found to be correlated with the resolution of these complaints. Sixteen per cent of the 19 race cases that did not also register colour as a ground of complaint were substantiated and 58 per cent were dismissed. Only 16 per cent were dismissed as unfounded. Of the 42 cases that registered both race and colour as grounds of complaint, 10 per cent were substantiated or otherwise dealt with, and 19 per cent dismissed. Almost two-thirds—64 per cent—were dismissed as unfounded (see Table III).

The statistical results for national origin and ethnic origin are virtually the same as those for colour. Indeed, many cases combined all four grounds of complaint—race, colour, national origin and ethnic origin—with the above pattern of results becoming more pronounced the greater the number of grounds registered. Cases registering two or more grounds of complaint were much more likely to be dismissed as unfounded, and much less likely to be dismissed or substantiated.

A review of the files confirmed that these statistical results represented a distinct pattern of investigation and validation. The test for discrimination appeared to centre on evidence of the respondent's motivation to discriminate and on indications that the respondent's actions and intentions were officially condoned. In practice, substantiation seemed to require: 1/ that the complainant be able to point to at least one specific

TABLE III   Resolution of Complaints in Sixty-One Race Cases as a Function of Registering Additional Grounds of Complaint

			ADDITIONAL GROUNDS OF COMPLAINT			
DECISION OF			NATIONAL		ETHNIC	
CHRC	COLOUR:		ORIGIN:		ORIGIN:	
	NO	YES	NO	YES	NO	YES
Complaint(s) substantiated	16%	10%	24%	3%	18%	8%
Dismissed with notation	11%	5%	16%	0%	18%	0%
Case dismissed without notation	58%	19%	52%	17%	59%	15%
Other findings (case terminated)	0%	2%	4%	0%	5%	0%
Dismissed as unfounded	16%	64%	4%	81%	0%	77%
	100%	100%	100%	100%	100%	100%
N =	(19)	(42)	(25)	(36)	(22)	(39)

incident in which the respondent's behavior explicitly demonstrated an intention to discriminate on the basis of race; 2/ that the complainant's allegations be corroborated by at least two witnesses to the incident; 3/ that some record existed showing that the respondent's superiors had been formally notified of the incident; and 4/ that no corrective action had been taken. In virtually all race cases, inconsistencies in testimony made it impossible to complete this test and most cases were dismissed as unfounded in the face of inconsistent testimony. Complaints of racial discrimination were substantiated only if all four of the components identified above were present. (See Figure 1.)

File contents of cases involving complaints of racial discrimination gained coherence and form to the extent that the investigation yielded evidence of relevance to all four of the above criteria. Where the complainant did allege that an explicit incident of racial discrimination had occurred, the investigation focussed on reconstructing the circumstances and the events leading up to and following the alleged incident. The reports of these investigations display a distinctive chronological ordering of the evidence, prompting the authors to use the phrase, "sequential style," to describe this pattern of investigation and verification.

The sequential style of investigation was fully developed in the few cases that were substantiated or otherwise dealt with. These cases involved allegations of at least one incident of personal harassment. Some complainants also claimed that they had been implicitly discriminated against,

FIGURE 1   Factors Associated with the Investigation and Resolution of Race, Colour, Ethnic and National Origin Complaints

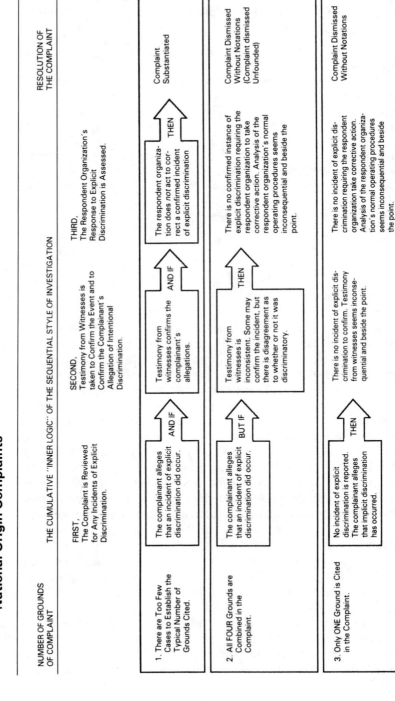

reporting an explicit incident of discrimination as additional evidence in support of their contention that they were victims of systematic discrimination. However, the subsequent investigation of race complaints invariably centred on the incident involving explicit discrimination.

Testimony was sought from potential witnesses to confirm that the incident had indeed occurred and that the complainant was essentially correct in interpreting it as discrimination motivated by considerations of race. In cases in which complaints of racial discrimination were substantiated, investigation had yielded at least two witnesses who agreed with the complainant's interpretation of the incident. Attention then shifted to an analysis of the respondent's organization's response to a confirmed incident of explicit discrimination. Further investigation established the fact that, although the complainant had lodged a formal complaint with the respondent's superiors, no action had been taken to repudiate the respondent's behavior or to remedy the situation. If the investigation discovered the discriminatory situation had not been rectified, the Canadian Human Rights Commission found in favor of the complainant.

All cases in which four grounds of complaint were listed—colour, national origin, and ethnic origin in addition to race—involved allegations of an explicit incident of racial discrimination. Most cases that listed four grounds of complaint were dismissed as unfounded. Two factors appeared to be crucial to the CHRC decision to dismiss these cases: the absence of consensus among witnesses and the absence of documentation.

First, witnesses did not corroborate the complainant's interpretation of events. In the cases that were dismissed as unfounded, witnesses did testify that the incident had occurred and often suggested that the complainant had been disadvantaged. However, they were unwilling to agree that the complainant had been singled out on the basis of race. Witnesses often claimed that many individuals in the setting (including the complainant) had initiated and had been the butt of racial slurs. Members of various minority groups were unwilling to find common cause with the complainant. Typically, the social settings were described as racially and ethnically mixed. Although the investigator's reports were vague on the precise racial and ethnic identities of the individuals involved, it appeared that no one else shared the complainant's particular combination of race, colour, national origin, and ethnic origin. While the complainant's account of the incident indicated that he or she felt that he/she had been singled out, the investigator concluded that members of the other minority groups were present and reportedly able to persevere. Investigators appeared to conclude that the very existence of a racial mixture belied the complainant's allegation of racial discrimination.

Lack of documentation appeared to be a second factor that contributed to the ultimate dismissal of these cases. In contrast to the cases in which complaints were substantiated, the complainants in the cases that were dismissed as unfounded had not launched an appeal prior to seeking the assistance of the CHRC. In some cases, the absence of any channels for formal appeal or grievances made this difficult. In any event, the complainant in cases that were dismissed as unfounded had gone directly to the CHRC without making a prior formal complaint to the respondent's organizational superiors.

Unlike cases that were either confirmed or dismissed as unfounded, cases that were "merely" dismissed did not involve explicit incidents of alleged racial discrimination. Rather, complainants claimed that they were victims of systemic or institutional discrimination. On the face of it, one might expect that investigators would have implemented a comparative investigation of such complaints, seeking out others like the complainant whose experiences might validate the complainant's allegations. This did not occur in any of the race cases in the sample.

The investigations of complaints of institutional racial discrimination attempted to follow a sequential style of investigation and verification. Testimony from others in the setting was sought in an attempt to corroborate the complainant's interpretation of the situation. Where "witnesses" could be found, they proved to be unaware of specific facts regarding the alleged racial imbalance and unable to give an authoritative assessment. The investigators did not attempt to review the respondent's formal records or initiate a survey to generate relevant evidence. The research strategy for analyzing complaints of racial discrimination was repeated for colour, national and ethnic origin. The pattern of the results for these cases virtually duplicated the results for racial discrimination. Cases registering two or more grounds of complaint were much more likely to be dismissed as unfounded, much less likely to be dismissed, and less likely to be substantiated or otherwise dealt with.

Race and Sex Compared

While launching a prior formal appeal appeared to be essential for CHRC substantiation of race/origin complaints, its absence did not appear to hamper CHRC investigation or substantiation of sex or disability complaints. Complainants in sex and disability cases often went directly to the CHRC without first registering a formal complaint to the respondent's organizational superiors. Our reading of cases involving complaints of institutional discrimination on the basis of race, colour and origin indicated that, in contrast to substantial sex or disability cases, suspicions or inferences of institutional discrimination in the absence of an explicit and witnessed racial incident simply would not do. The respondent had to refer explicitly to the complainant's race, and witnesses had to confirm this as a fact as well as validate "racial discrimination" as a plausible interpretation of the incident. Without evidence regarding the motivational disposition of the respondent and the respondent's organizational superiors, complaints of institutional racial discrimination were dismissed.

The more basic problem appeared to be that there was no public indication that the respondent intended to discriminate on the basis of race. Interestingly, in none of the sex/disability cases did the complainant have to produce an explicit and witnessed instance of discrimination. The CHRC investigator proceeded on the suspicions of the complainant. Few of the substantiated sex-disability cases involved any incident in which the respondent explicitly made reference to the complainant's sex or disability. In sex/disability cases, witnesses were treated as informants. Testimony from informants was not regarded as problematic and was used to obtain descriptions of normal operating arrangements that may be a source of implicit discrimination. An explicit discriminatory incident was not a prerequisite for launching the investigation and was not needed to substantiate the complaint. An explicit incident, however, appeared to be the most important element for the resolution of race cases.

It appears that initial decisions by investigators predetermined the file contents, with evidence and argumentation addressing issues of either indirect institutional discrimination or individual harassment, not both. The investigation and verification of sex and disability complaints revolved around issues of institutional discrimination in which the intention to discriminate was not at issue. On the other hand, race, colour and origin complaints were always regarded as allegations of intentional discrimination, with the investigation and verification focusing on incidents in which the alleged institution is displayed. Given this predeliction of CHRC investigators to transform the case into one style of report or the other, it was difficult to ascertain on the basis of file contents alone the proportion of cases that included individual and institutional forms of discrimination.

■ INDIVIDUAL VERSUS INSTITUTIONAL DISCRIMINATION

Over the past decade it has become clear that the concept of discrimination ha0 two general meanings: 1/ individual discrimination; and 2/ institutional or systemic discrimination. Individual discrimination refers to harmful actions taken deliberately by an individual against members of a subordinate group, actions that compromise individual rights to human dignity. Sexual harassment and racial slurs are examples of individual discrimination. Persons who discriminate in this fashion may do so with social support from others in the setting (Marger, 1985; Baron 1967). This type of discrimination involves actions taken by individuals to injure or deny something to members of minority groups. These intentional acts are carried out to harm or restrict in some way minority group members, such as management practices that exclude women for promotion.

Complaints of discrimination on the basis of race, colour and origin were interpreted by the CHRC as allegations of individual or deliberate discrimination. Confirmation of such allegations required evidence establishing the intent to injure or deny because of *race, colour or origin*. The CHRC has found it difficult to substantiate *intent* to discriminate and, as a result, had had difficulty enforcing the right to human dignity in these cases.

Institutional or systemic discrimination refers to the direct or indirect effects of accepted organizational or community practices. Direct institutional discrimination occurs when laws or legally endorsed customs intentionally discriminate between various categories of people. Systems of custom and law are interwoven which legitimize discriminatory behavior. The intent may be to bestow certain rights and privileges upon members of specific groups or to deny members of subordinate groups rights and privileges more generally enjoyed by others in society. These actions are not episodic or sporadic but are routinely carried out by a large number of people who are being guided by the norm of the large scale organizations or community. Examples would include mandatory retirement age, *Lord's Day Act*, and gender differences vis-à-vis rights regarding children.

Indirect as opposed to direct institutional discrimination occurs when conformity to previously unchallenged institutional norms produces discriminatory effects. Unlike institutional discrimination, indirect institutional discrimination does not necessarily imply an intention to discriminate. Indirect discrimination refers to often unintended consequences of normal operating procedures of existing societal institutions. In conforming to existing norms, there may be no intent to harm members of the subordinate group (Feagin and Feagin, 1978). However decisions are made, agendas set, and resources allocated under conditions of indirect systemic discrimination, certain groups will be systematically deprived or exploited. For example, there may be systematic underrepresentation of women and members of certain minority groups in senior management and professions or members of these groups may be systematically denied credit.

It is where individual and institutional discrimination overlap that we often have difficulty in determining the character of discrimination. From the complainant's perspective, individuals exercising authority within an organization may be regarded as having discriminatory intent. The complainant may point out instances which reveal, at least to the complainant's satisfaction, the discriminatory attitudes of such individuals. However, the accused individuals may or may not harbor discriminatory attitudes and, even if they do, they may not be required to make their personal attitude public. The ambiguity of such situations often makes it difficult for everyone (the investigator, the complainant and the accused) to agree on some interpretation of events, let alone agree on the guise that discrimination may have assumed—implicit or explicit.

What constitutes evidence of an intent to discriminate? Social scientists attempting to measure power may give us some insight into the problems involved. According to Max Weber's classic definition, power is the ability to impose one's "will" on another during a contest of wills in which the contrary intentions of the parties involved are made public. A demonstrated capacity to enlist the support of third parties to reward those who obey and/or penalize those who resist is an important power resource, and an essential ingredient of authority. Authority rests on precedents and formal arrangements that express a "general will" to provide collective support for the enforcement of certain orders or demands by those in power (Hirsch, 1975). Racial discrimination involves the exercise of power or authority in ways that publicly demonstrate racial inferiority.

When conceived in this fashion, certain behaviors become unequivocal indicators of power and authority, and racial discrimination. Evidence of power superiority-inferiority requires that both parties publicly acknowledge that they are at cross-purposes and engaged in a "contest of wills," with the outcome of the contest indicating power superiority and inferiority (Laswell and Kaplan, 1950). Active co-operation with one party in a public contest of wills and/or active rejection of requests for assistance by the other party delimit the resources of both parties. Tangible actions that express the "general will"—active support during similar contests in the past or public consent to formal arrangements designed to handle such contests of wills—provide evidence that those in power have authority to enforce their demands.

By analogy, evidence of racial discrimination would require that the respondent exercise power or authority with the publicly declared intention of demonstrating the racial inferiority of the complainant. The complainant must indicate that he/she does not agree with the respondent's values and sentiments by publicly objecting to the intent of the respondent, entering into a "contest of wills" and/or by publicly appealing to others for assistance when resisting the respondent's demands. Racial discrimination becomes a fait accompli if others refuse the complainant's appeal for justice. File contents also show that the CHRC's ability to verify the existence of racial discrimination was frustrated in almost every case by refusal of others in the setting to corroborate the complainant's allegations.

Passive acts of omission (versus active acts of commission) create problems for verification of intentional discrimination. The intent of the respondent may not become apparent and subject to investigation unless the complainant has forced a public confrontation. Launching a formal appeal addressed to those in authority creates documented evidence that can be accessed by a subsequent CHRC investigation but may not succeed in forcing the issue into the open if those in authority fail to respond publicly and positively. If others, especially those in authority, condone the respondent's conduct, the complainant may not be able to force either the respondent or others in the setting to declare the real purpose behind their actions. . . .

■ CONCLUSION

A comparison of the sequential and comparative style of substantiating complaints reveals important differences in the way each tests the respondent organization's standards and procedures. The sequential style considers only the particulars of the individual complaint and not the general experience of others similar to the complainant. It questions the treatment accorded the complainant during and particularly after the occurrence of an explicit incident of discrimination. In contrast, the comparative style examines the treatment accorded the complainant and others like the complainant in the recent past to detect a general pattern of systemic discrimination. This latter style of investigation tested normal operating procedures by: 1/ using documents to assess the legitimacy of official rules and regulations; 2/ employing records to discover others like the complainant who were subjected to these rules and regulations in the recent past; and 3/ comparing the treatment accorded the complainant and others vis-à-vis these official requirements to assess consistency and legitimacy of application. Where the sequential style assesses the adequacy of the respondent organization's grievance or appeal procedures, the comparative style considers the legitimacy of the respondent organization's normal operating procedures.

The comparative style of investigation in typical substantiated sex/disability cases appeared to test for systemic forms of discrimination. What is puzzling is the fact that CHRS files on race/origin cases typically did not include this detailed and comparative style of investigation. An inability to substantiate explicit discrimination does not preclude the possibility that institutional systemic discrimination has occurred (Tarnopolsky, 1979).

There is much that recommends the comparative style of investigation: 1/ The procedures involved are well understood and can be implemented by agencies like the Canadian Human Rights Commission; 2/ the criteria for resolving complaints are well understood by the investigators and administrators; 3/ the criteria for substantiating or dismissing complaints are legally defensible; and 4/ based upon our analysis of case files, this test for implicit or institutional discrimination probably would substantiate a greater proportion of the complaints of discrimination on the basis of race/origin.

The difficulties of substantiating a complaint do not seem to be a result of the investigation per se but rather with the style of the CHRC investigation. The problem may be that the Canadian Human Rights Commission is unable to adopt a uniform set of criteria or style of investigation for all grounds of complaints. The essential problem facing the Canadian Human Rights Commission is to arrive at a legitimate and widely accepted style of investigation. At present, The Canadian Human Rights Commission is designed to combat violations of formalized, institutionalized behavior. In these cases, it is able to adjudicate such behavior. However, in cases of informal forms of discrimination, e.g., status degradation, informal behavior, modes of behavior that are not governed by written documents, the Canadian Human Rights Commission is generally unable to substantiate the existence of discrimination.

Notes

1. The time period 1982-83 was chosen because it represented the most recent year for which CHRC had complete data in their active files. In addition the data were accessible in raw form before being placed in archival form.

2. They were resolved: 1/ through the appointment of a conciliator, 2/ by having the investigative officer monitor the organization or 3/ by the imposition of an immediate negative sanction, e.g., fine, rule change. In all instances, the agent of the Canadian Human Rights Commission stayed with the case until it was resolved to the satisfaction of the Commission.

3. For the sake of brevity, we will refer to cases involving race, colour, ethnicity and/or national origin as race/origin.

4. The comparative style of investigation followed the legal test for assessing bona fide occupational requirements. Investigators used documented practices of the organization as their point of departure. The investigator had to show (in a documented fashion) that the requirements were: 1/ nonjustifiable; 2/ inconsistent; or 3/ applied differentially. For all three conditions, it had to be shown that others in the organization suffered the same fate.

5. The authors were not permitted to interview any of the individuals involved in the cases nor observe the standard operating procedures for processing the files. We know that multiple grounds of complaint were listed in the vast majority of cases involving an explicit incident of racial discrimination. We do not know the circumstances surrounding the registration of complaints nor those who might have pressed for the registration of several grounds of complaint in response to complaints of racial harassment: the officials who initially screen complaints, and/or the investigators. We do not know why the boxes on the cover sheet for indicating the resolution of these cases were left blank.

6. Our evidence indicates that only one ground of complaint—race—tended to be registered in the cases that were confirmed. However, there were so few cases in the sample that were confirmed that this finding may not be a reliable result. The fact that complainants in these cases had not lodged a formal complaint with the respondent's superiors (or were not able to do so because no formal mechanism existed for appeal) appeared to be almost a moot point. The absence of agreement between witnesses and the complainant meant that racial discrimination was not an acknowledged social fact. There was no racial discrimination to be repudiated or remedied.

References

Baron, H. 1967 "Black Powerlessness in Chicago." Transaction 6 (November): 27-33.

Canada, Government of. 1984 Equality Now. Report of the Special Committee on Visible Minorities in Canadian Society, Ottawa.

Feagin, J., and C. Feagin. 1978 Discrimination American Style: Institutional Racism and Sexism. Englewood Cliffs, N.J.: Prentice Hall.

Hill, D. 1977 Human Rights in Canada: A Focus on Racism. Ottawa: Canadian Labour Congress.

Hirsch, P.M. 1975 "Organizational Effectiveness and the Institutional Environment." Administrative Science Quarterly 20: 327-44.

Lasswell, H., and A. Kaplan. 1950 Power and Society: A Framework for Political Enquiry. New Haven: Yale University Press.

Marger, M. 1985 Race and Ethnic Relations. Belmont, California: Wadsworth Publishing Co.

Reeves, W.J., and J. Frideres. 1985 "The Resolution of Complaints Based on Race and Origin: The Canadian Human Rights Commission." In N. Nevitte and A. Kornberg (eds.), Minorities and the Canadian State, Chapter 8. New York: Mosaic Press.

Tarnopolsky, W. 1979 "The Control of Racial Discrimination." In R. Macdonald and J. Humphrey (eds.), The Practice of Freedom. Toronto: Butterworths.

Tarnopolsky, W., and W. Pentney. 1985 Discrimination and the Law. Toronto: R. DeBoo Publishers.

Zimmerman, D. 1969 "Record-Keeping and the Intake Process in a Public Welfare Agency." In S. Wheeler (ed.), On Record. New York: Russell Sage.

■ POSTSCRIPT

It is important to note that Justice Sopinka is not offering an unqualified defence of The Charter of Rights and Freedoms. He clearly says that the Charter cannot be expected to protect all human rights, and that other mechanisms of protection, including "political effort," are also needed. For example, the Charter does not protect economic rights, nor does it ensure that women will have equal representation in the House of Commons or in the courts (as members of the judiciary). But Sopinka points out that, while rulings under the Charter might not always favour the positions adopted by women's groups such as LEAF (Legal Education and Action Fund), the Charter can still do a better job of protecting women's rights than previous legislation. Both the Blainey and Morgentaler cases are examples of how the Supreme Court of Canada used the Charter to reverse previous court decisions based on prior legislation. It is this capacity that enables the Charter to protect women's rights.

From a sociological viewpoint, Sopinka offers an analysis similar to the theory of law, which says that the law can be used for the purpose of generating social change (for a more complete discussion of this issue, see Cotterrell, 1984). Advocates of law reform as a means of social change believe that the law can be used to alter not only the way people interact with each other, but also mores or basic values. In the case of protecting women's rights, law reform advocates like Justice Sopinka argue that the Charter of Rights and Freedoms was needed to change the way men and women interact, and to change the value structures by which women and women's place in society are devalued.

Greschner (1985) agrees with Sopinka that the Charter has the potential to protect women's rights, and that women must engage in political as well as legal struggles to secure the protection it offers. In addition, Tarnopolsky and Beaudoin (1982) have suggested that federal and provincial governments will look to the Charter when either creating new laws or amending old laws. Other defenders of human rights legislation argue that creation and enforcement of these laws permits the reconstruction of society. According to this view, human societies can be improved by using the coercive powers of the state (for a review and critique of this position, see Knopff, 1989).

Not everyone, however, is confident about the ability of the law to promote social change, and about the ability of the Canadian Charter of Rights and Freedoms to protect human rights. Some sociologists have argued that the success of the law in changing behaviour often depends on the willingness of people to initiate legal procedures (for a discussion of this issue, see Cotterrell, 1984). In the absence of such initiation, it is impossible for the law to produce social change.

Others who are sceptical of the ability of human rights law to produce social change say that the concept of human rights has been overextended to the point where it has lost any real meaning (Knopff, 1989). Knopff argues that so many alleged acts of discrimination are being included under such legislation that human rights laws are actually limiting human rights. Frideres and Reeves, as well as Martin (1986), argue that enforcement practices frequently undermine the intent of the law. Frideres and Reeves cite the methods used by the Canadian Human Rights Commission (CHRC) to enforce the Canadian Human Rights Act. They point out that the style of investigation used in sex/disability cases differs significantly from the style of investigation used in race/origin cases. In the former, investigators typically look for systemic discrimination, using a comparative method. In the latter, investigators typically look for evidence of discrimination in specific cases, using a sequential method. As a result, cases in which systemic discrimination can be demonstrated are more likely to be determined as valid cases of discrimination than are cases in which the sequential method was used. One implication of Frideres and Reeves' analysis is that the difference in investigative techniques and enforcement procedures undermines the credibility of the CHRC, the Canadian Human Rights Act, and the enforcement of human rights law in Canada.

Martin (1986) adds that, in order for human rights legislation to effectively protect human rights, the judiciary must play a far more activist role in transforming society than it has in the past. According to Martin, however, the activism of the judiciary in the past has tended to limit rather than extend human rights. Another critic suggests that it is unlikely that human rights law will protect women's rights because the lawmaking and law enforcement processes are controlled by men acting in accordance with male biases (King, 1986).

■ QUESTIONS

1. Upon what issues do both sides of this debate agree?
2. Is it possible for lawmakers and law enforcers, including the judiciary, to eliminate their biases when making or interpreting the law?
3. Does the exclusion of some groups (such as women, blacks, and other racial or ethnic minorities, etc.) from the lawmaking, interpreting, and enforcement process mean that their interests are necessarily ineffectively protected by human rights law?
4. Is there an alternative method to protecting human rights?

■ FURTHER READING

In Support of Sopinka

Greschner, Donna. "Affirmative Action and the Charter of Rights and Freedoms." *Canadian Woman Studies* 6, no. 4 (1985): 34-36.

McKercher, W.R. "The U.S. Bill of Rights: Implications for Canada." In *The U.S. Bill of Rights and the Canadian Charter of Rights and Freedoms*. Edited by W.R. McKercher. Toronto: Ontario Economic Council, 1983.

Tarnopolsky, W.S. and G.A. Beaudoin, eds. *The Charter of Rights and Freedoms: Commentary*. Toronto: Carswell, 1982.

In Support of Frideres and Reeves

King, Lynn. "Censorship and Law Reform: Will Changing the Laws Mean a Change for the Better?" In *The Social Basis of Law*. Edited by Stephen Brickey and Elizabeth Comack. Toronto: Garamond Press, 1986.

Knopff, Rainer. *Human Rights and Social Technology: The New War on Discrimination*. Ottawa: Carleton University Press, 1989.

Martin, Robert. "The Judges and the Charter." In *The Social Basis of Law*. Edited by Stephen Brickey and Elizabeth Comack. Toronto: Garamond Press, 1986.

Other Voices

Cotterrell, Roger. *The Sociology of Law: An Introduction*. London: Butterworths, 1984.

McKercher, W.R. *The U.S. Bill of Rights and the Canadian Charter of Rights and Freedoms*. Toronto: Ontario Economic Council, 1983.

■ CONTRIBUTOR ACKNOWLEDGMENTS

Permission to reprint copyrighted material is gratefully acknowledged. Information that will enable the publisher to rectify any error or omission will be welcomed.

Debate 1

Reprinted with the permission of The Free Press, a Division of Macmillan, Inc. from Max Weber, *The Methodology of the Social Sciences*, translated and edited by Edward A. Shils and Henry A. Finch. Copyright © 1949 by The Free Press; copyright renewed 1977 by Edward A. Shils.

© 1967 by the Society for the Study of Social Problems. Reprinted from Howard Becker, *Social Problems*, Vol. 14, No. 3, Winter '67, pp. 239-247, by permission.

Debate 2

A.W. Djao, "The State and Social Welfare," reprinted from A.W. Djao, *Inequality and Social Policy: The Sociology of Welfare*, John Wiley and Sons, Toronto, 1983, by permission of the author.

R. Ogmundson, "Good News and Canadian Sociology," reprinted by permission from *Canadian Journal of Sociology*, Vol. 7(1): 1982, pp. 73-78.

Debate 3

E. Hugh Lautard and Donald J. Loree, "Ethnic Stratification in Canada," reprinted by permission from *Canadian Journal of Sociology*, Vol. 9(3): 1984, pp. 334-344.

Gordon Darroch, "Another Look at Ethnicity, Stratification and Social Mobility in Canada," reprinted by permission from *Canadian Journal of Sociology*, Vol. 4(1): 1979, pp. 1-25.

Debate 4

Walter Block and Michael A. Walker, "The Plight of the Minority," reprinted from W.E. Block and M.A. Walker, eds., *Discrimination, Affirmative Action and Equal Opportunity*, 1982, pp. 5-11, by permission of The Fraser Institute, Vancouver.

Mona Kornberg, "Employment Equity: The Quiet Revolution?", reprinted from *Canadian Women Studies*/les cahiers de la femme, "Affirmative Action/Action Positive," Vol. 6(4): 1985, pp. 17-19, by permission of the author and the publisher.

Debate 5

Roberta Edgecombe Robb, "Equal Pay for Work of Equal Value: Issues and Policies," reprinted from *Canadian Public Policy* XIII, 4: 1987, pp. 445-61, by permission of *Canadian Public Policy-Analyse de Politiques*.

Thomas Flanagan, "Equal Pay for Work of Equal Value: Some Theoretical Criticisms," reprinted from *Canadian Public Policy* XIII, 4: 1987, pp. 435-44, by permission of *Canadian Public Policy-Analyse de Politiques*.

Debate 6

R.A. Young, "Political Scientists, Economists, and Canada-U.S. Free Trade," reprinted from *Canadian Public Policy* XV, 1: 1989, pp. 57-71, by permission of *Canadian Public Policy-Analyse de Politiques*.

Michael R. Smith, "A Sociological Appraisal of the Free Trade Agreement," reprinted from *Canadian Public Policy* XV, 1: 1989, pp. 49-56, by permission of *Canadian Public Policy-Analyse de Politiques*.

Debate 7

Tom Waterland, "Integrated Land Use Key to Economic and Environmental Goals," reprinted from *Canadian Speeches*, Vol. 2: #8, December 1988, pp. 27-34, by permission of the author and *Canadian Speeches: Issues of the Day*.

Fazley K. Siddiq and M. Paul Brown, "Economic Impact of Environmental Production," reprinted by permission from *Canadian Journal of Regional Science* XIII, 3: 1989, pp. 355-365.

Debate 8

Thomas J. Courchene, "A Market Perspective on Regional Disparities," reprinted from *Canadian Public Policy* VII, 4: Autumn 1981, pp. 506-518, by permission of *Canadian Public Policy-Analyse de Politiques*.

Ralph Matthews, "Two Alternative Explanations of the Problem of Regional Dependency in Canada," reprinted from *Canadian Public Policy*

VII, 2: Spring 1981, pp. 268-283, by permission of *Canadian Public Policy-Analyse de Politiques.*

Debate 9

T.R. Balakrishnan, K. Vaninadha Rao, Evelyne Lapierre-Adamcyk and Karol J. Krotki, "A Hazard Analysis of the Covariates of Marriage Dissolution in Canada," reprinted from *Demography* 24, 3: Autumn 1987, pp. 395-406.

Jay D. Teachman and Karen A. Polonko, "Cohabitation and Marital Stability in the United States," reprinted with omissions from *Social Forces* 69, 1: September 1990, pp. 207-220. Copyright © University of North Carolina Press.

Debate 10

M.B. Brinkerhoff and Eugen Lupri, "Interspousal Violence," reprinted by permission from *Canadian Journal of Sociology* 13, 4: 1988, pp. 407-434.

Walter S. DeKeseredy, "In Defense of Self Defense: Demystifying Female Violence Against Male Intimates," reprinted by permission of the author.

Debate 11

Gary Natriello, Aaron M. Pallas, and Karl Alexander, "On the Right Track? Curriculum and Academic Achievement," reprinted from *Sociology of Education* 62, April 1989, pp. 209-218.

George Martell, "Labelling, Streaming, and Programming of Working Class Kids in School," reprinted from *Our Schools/Our Selves: A Magazine for Canadian Education Activists*, Vol. 1, #8, 1989, pp. 19-30, reprinted by permission of the author.

Debate 12

Yonatan Reshef, "Union Decline: A View from Canada," reprinted by permission from *Journal of Labour Research* XI, 1: Winter 1990, pp. 25-39.

Graham S. Lowe and Harvey Krahn, "Recent Trends in Public Support for Unions of Canada," reprinted from *Journal of Labour Research* X, 4: Fall 1989, pp. 391-410.

Debate 13

Neil Boyd, "Sexuality, Gender Relations and the Law: The Limits of Free Expression," reprinted from J. Lowman, et al., eds., *Regulating Sex: An Anthology of Commentaries on the Findings and Recommendations of the Badgely and Foch Reports*, Burnaby, B.C.: School of Criminology, Simon Fraser University, 1986, pp. 127-41, by permission of the author.

Jane Rhodes, "Silencing Ourselves? Pornography, Censorship and Feminism in Canada," reprinted from *Resources for Feminist Research* 17, 3: 1988, pp. 133-35, by permission of *Resources for Feminist Research* and the author.

Debate 14

Catherine F. Spoule and Deborah J. Kennett, "Killing With Guns In the USA and Canada: 1977-1983, Further Evidence for the Effectiveness of Gun Control," reprinted by permission from *Canadian Journal of Criminology* 31, 3: July 1989, pp. 245-251. Copyright by the Canadian Criminal Justice Association.

Robert J. Mundt, "Gun Control and Rates of Firearms Violence in Canada and the United States," reprinted by permission from *Canadian Journal of Criminology* 32, 1: January 1990, pp. 137-154. Copyright by the Canadian Criminal Justice Association.

Debate 15

Andrew von Hirsch, "The Politics of 'Just Deserts' ", reprinted by permission from *Canadian Journal of Criminology* 32, 3: July 1990, pp. 397-413. Copyright by the Canadian Criminal Justice Association.

Thomas Gabor, "Looking Back or Moving Forward: Retributivism and the Canadian Sentencing Commission's Proposals," reprinted by permission from *Canadian Journal of Criminology* 32, 3: July 1990, pp. 537-546. Copyright by the Canadian Criminal Justice Association.

Debate 16

Morley Gunderson and James Pesando, "The Case for Allowing Mandatory Retirement," reprinted from *Canadian Public Policy* 14, 1: 1988, pp. 32-39, by permission of *Canadian Public Policy-Analyse de Politiques*.

Michael Krashinsky, "The Case for Eliminating Mandatory Retirement: Why Economics and Human Rights Need Not Conflict," reprinted from

Canadian Public Policy XIV, 1: 1988, pp. 40-51, by permission of *Canadian Public Policy-Analyse de Politiques.*

Debate 17

Iain T. Benson, "An Examination of Certain 'Pro-Choice' Abortion Arguments: Permanent Concerns About a 'Temporary' Problem," reprinted by permission from *Canadian Journal of Family Law* 7, 1: 1988, pp. 146-165.

Ontario Coalition for Abortion Clinics, "State Power and the Struggle for Reproductive Freedom: The Campaign for Free-Standing Abortion Clinics in Ontario," reprinted from *Resources for Feminist Research* 17, 3: 1989, pp. 109-114, by permission of *Resources for Feminist Research* and the Ontario Coalition for Abortion Clinics.

Debate 18

Mr. Justice John Sopinka, "How the Charter Helps Secure Women's Rights," reprinted from *Canadian Speeches* 3, 3: May 1989, pp. 34-39, by permission of the author and *Canadian Speeches: Issues of the Day.*

James S. Frideres and William J. Reeves, "The Ability to Implement Human Rights Legislations in Canada," reprinted from *Canadian Review of Sociology and Anthropology* 26, 2: 1989, pp. 311-332, by permission of *The Canadian Review of Sociology and Anthropology* and the authors.